W9-BEX-508

THE COMPLETE ENCYCLOPEDIA OF

BATTLESHIPS

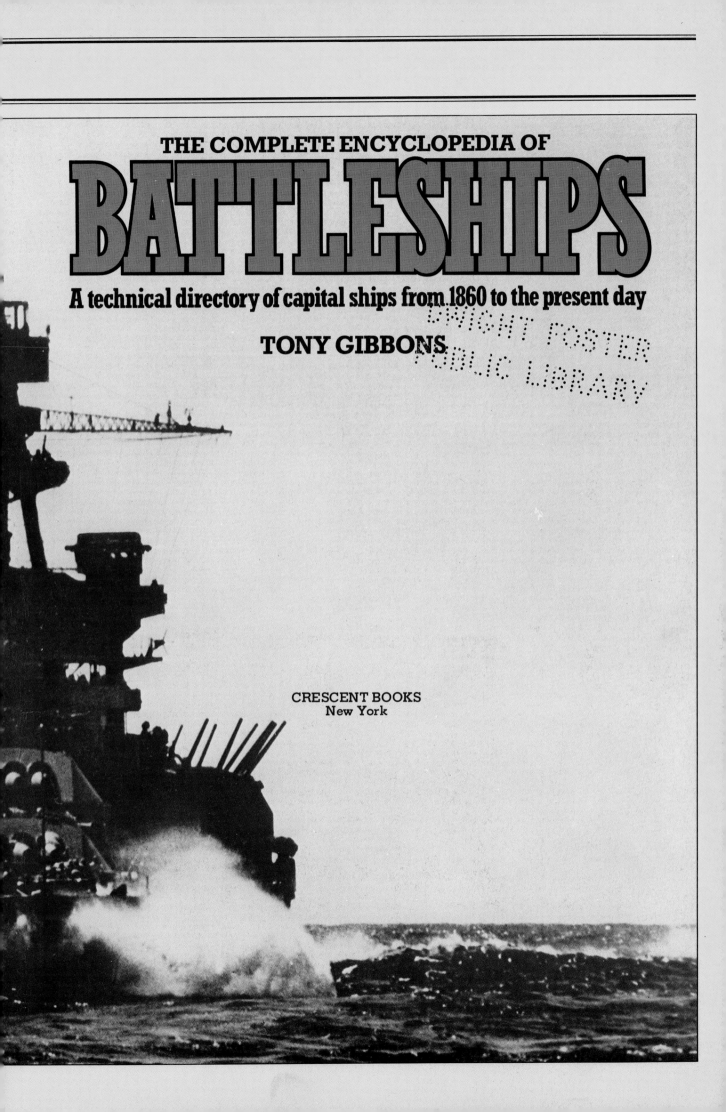

THE COMPLETE ENCYCLOPEDIA OF

BATTLESHIPS

A technical directory of capital ships from 1860 to the present day

TONY GIBBONS

CRESCENT BOOKS
New York

A Salamander Book

Credits

First English edition published by
Salamander Books Ltd.

This edition is published by
Crescent Books,
distributed by
Crown Publishers, Inc.,
One Park Avenue,
New York,
New York 10016,
United States of America.

h g f e d c b a

Library of Congress Cataloging in Publication Data

Gibbons, Tony.
Complete Encyclopedia of Battleships

  1. Battleships.   2. Battle cruisers.   I. Title.
V815.G5 1982   623.8'252   82-17204
ISBN 0-517-378108

All correspondence concerning the
content of this volume should be
addressed to Salamander Books Ltd.,
Salamander House,
27 Old Gloucester Street,
London WC1N 3AF,
United Kingdom.

Editor: Philip de Ste. Croix
Editorial consultant: Roger Chesneau
Contributing authors: Chris Chant and Richard O'Neill

Designer: Nick Buzzard
Line diagrams: John Roberts © Salamander Books Ltd.

Filmset: Modern Text Typesetting Ltd., England
Color and monochrome reproduction: Bantam Litho Ltd., England
Printed in Belgium: Henri Proost et Cie, Turnhout

Contents

Author's Foreword	6
Introduction	8
1860-1869	24
1870-1879	68
1880-1889	96
1890-1899	116
1900s Pre-Dreadnoughts	146
1900s Dreadnoughts	166
1910-1919	176
1920-1929	224
1930-1939	238
1940 onwards	250
Index	270

Author's Foreword

In 1860 the French ironclad *Gloire* was completed and this event ushered in a new era of warship construction. Gone were the once proud wooden walls with their tiers of smoothbore guns that once dictated the course of world history. Now they were to be pushed into the wings to fade quietly away, as the *Gloire*, with her single row of guns shielded behind protective armour, stalked into the limelight. She was an epoch-making vessel and her appearance initiated an 'arms race' in which naval architects continually introduced improvements and refinements into their designs in an effort to remain in front of the opposition.

This is the first time that any attempt has been made to produce a book that describes and illustrates all the first-class battleships and battlecruisers, plus a substantial number of armoured coast defence vessels, constructed from 1860 to the present day. The book has been divided into ten-year periods, with the completion dates of the vessels dictating where they appear. This system has been employed because clearly only upon completion can a vessel be considered an effective addition to its nation's naval power. It allows unusual and fascinating comparisons to be made between vessels that may have been launched in widely varying years, as was often the case with the United Kingdom and France in the 1880s and 1890s when the rate of construction in French yards tended to be slower.

Each section is introduced by an essay which describes the major advances in gunnery, armour, machinery etc. during the period. These introductions allow the reader plot the evolving principles governing naval architectu and equipment as they came to prominence. In the boc text of the book a standard approach to the presentation ship data has been adopted so that comparisons may easi be made between displacements, dimensions, armov schemes, armament and so on. Data is given in imperi and metric units except in the case of some smaller gur and the later AA armament which are conventional identified by a single unit of measurement. Armour pr tection is listed for the vital parts of the ship, rangir (where applicable) from the thickest to the thinnest pa of the armour scheme. Length is usually overall. Rang is generally given in nautical miles/kilometres; it mu be remembered that the condition of the boilers ar machinery, as well as the quality of the coal carried, wou have made the figures vary in practice.

Displacement is usually standard; any variations ar fully noted. A word of explanation about the differer ways of expressing displacement may help avoid confusic in some readers' minds.

Standard: The displacement specified by the 1922 Was ington Naval Treaty, which included the weight of hu armour, all machinery, all guns and ammunition, and crev but no fuel or boiler feed water.

Full load: As standard, but with all stores and fuel carrie

ABBREVIATIONS

AA: anti-aircraft
AP: armour-piercing
BHP: brake horsepower
BL: breechloader
BLR: breechloading rifle
cal:: calibre i.e. the internal diameter of a gun barrel; often used to express the length of a barrel as a multiple of its diameter
CT: conning tower
DP: dual purpose
HA: high-angle
IHP: indicated horsepower
KC: Krupp cemented
kt: knot
LA: low-angle
LP: low pressure
MG: machine gun
MLR: muzzle-loading rifle
NC: non-cemented
NHP: nominal horsepower
nm: nautical mile
oa: overall
pdr: pounder
pp: between perpendiculars
QF: quick-firing i.e. having propellant in a cartridge with the projectile rather than a bag charge, so speeding up loading
RML: rifled muzzle-loader
SAM: surface-to-air missile
SB: smoothbore
SHP: shaft horsepower
SSM: surface-to-surface missile
TE: triple expansion
TL: torpedo launcher
TT: torpedo tubes
VTE: vertical triple expansion
wl: waterline
WT: wireless telegraphy

oad: Similar to standard but with a small proportion of
el and stores.

ctual: As standard, but with a given amount of fuel and
ores; usually between half and two-thirds supply.

eep load: Refers to a vessel with all fuel and stores on
ard, plus an additional margin not usually carried, plus
y additional armament and ammunition.

ormal: As standard, but with varying quantities of fuel
d stores according to the requirements of the navy in
estion.

Speed refers to full speed achieved on trials, and
e indicated horsepower is that of the main machinery
easured on the same trials. Fuel capacity is for normal
ading, although some figures are given for normal and
aximum loading where they are available.

The figure for the number of crew carried refers to the
mplement on completion. Major variations are also listed,
articularly in the case of early ironclads which underwent
bstantial modernisation.

The vessel classes are named after the first unit to be
mpleted. The other vessels in the class are listed below
e name ship.

The illustrations generally depict the warships upon
mpletion, and any later views are specifically dated in
e captions. In many cases paintings of the same battleship
different times in her career are included to highlight

changes in her appearance. Thirty-nine significant ships
have been allocated a double-page spread each so that
they may be described in greater detail. These spreads
feature plan and bow views of the vessel plus underwater
configuration, so that a complete picture of her overall
appearance is given. Additional drawings are included,
as well as photographs—many of them published for the
first time—to illustrate the appearance of sister-ships, conversions, camouflage patterns etc.

The small scale drawings that accompany each entry
show the ship in question compared in size to the epoch-
making *Dreadnought* of 1906, from which sprang the long
line of battleshps and battlecruisers that fought in World
War I and World War II. These drawings immediately highlight the enormous increase in the size of battleships that
occurred during the late 19th and 20th Centuries.

Blue drawings show preliminary designs before construction began, or designs that never got past the drawing
board stage. Otherwise, final designs or projects that were
cancelled or redefined (e.g. *Lexington*, completed as an
aircraft carrier) are shown as they would have appeared if
made ready for sea.

Tony Gibbons

Tony Gibbons, 1983

Introduction

The big naval gun—and the warship that carried it—was the final arbiter in struggles for sea power, both local and national, for four centuries. It was the foundation upon which European supremacy was built, and it was the dominant factor in shaping a political world map the legacies of which are a prime ingredient of current global problems. We are concerned here with the evolution of this weapon over the last one hundred and twenty-five years and, more particularly, with the type of ship that took it to sea, but first it is necessary to consider, briefly, the background to its development.

Once the practicability of extended sea voyages had been demonstrated, from the exploratory cruises of the late 15th and early 16th centuries, through the establishment of regular trade routes and the opening up of colonies by the European powers, the sea became, as it were, a vast highway, along which vehicles carrying great quantities of wealth would ply, ripe for attack by profit-conscious parties, and along which armies might efficiently be carried in order to prosecute national interests, together with the supply vessels necessary to maintain them. Concurrent with the expansion of seaborne transport came the organisation of fleets of ships to attack or defend it, and, moreover, a gradual revolution in the means of waging war at sea. For centuries, the principal fighting ship had been the oar-propelled galley, built for speed with fine lines and armed with a projecting ram then considered the most likely means of stopping an enemy vessel. Tactics generally relied on the head-on attack, the enemy being despatched by direct contact, perhaps by sinking his ship but more commonly by immobilising it and then boarding it with the aim of rendering its crew *hors de combat.* Stand-off tactics—with the objective of causing maximum damage to the enemy before actually closing with him—were certainly practised: since Roman times the value of on-board artillery had been appreciated, but the slow, cumbersome launchers were space-consuming and inaccurate, and more faith was placed in the massed arrows and bolts of the fighting men who might be embarked. Attack ranges were, then, opened, but for the purposes of deploying anti-personnel rather than anti-ship weapons.

The growing reliability of the gun, however, meant that, around the turn of the 14th century, it gradually began to assume some importance in sea fights, and pieces were mounted in galley bows. Tactics, not to speak of on-board accommodation, dictated their siting, but as the weapons increased in efficiency they began to grow in size, and neither the established methods of fighting a naval engagement nor the design of the galleys themselves were conducive to the carriage of a large number of heavy guns. Nor was the galley suited to the sort of blue-water confrontations that inevitably accompanied the promotion and dispute of ocean-going trade. The merchant sailing ship, broad of beam to accommodate the optimum amounts of cargo and high of freeboard to give the vessel the necessary seaworthiness, proved readily adaptable to the carriage of guns on the high seas; moreover, it was of sufficiently robust construction to be able to offer some sort of effective barrier to any enemy's shot.

Meanwhile, the specialised, purpose-built warship was evolving, first as a hybrid, with an armament of heavy guns complemented by lighter pieces in high 'castles' fore and aft from which rapid fire could be poured down on to the decks of an enemy prior to the still-dominant tactic of hand-to-hand combat as soldiers disembarked when the enemy was

Below: End of an era: the passing of the 'wooden-walled' line-of-battle ship is captured dramatically in J.M.W. Turner's immortal *The* *Fighting Temeraire*, painted in 1838. Within a generation the pure sailing man o' war would have disappeared completely

alongside. Through the 16th century, however, as the early culverins gave way to cast, larger-bore cannon, the prospect of inflicting conclusive damage on an enemy purely by means of stand-off tactics emerged, and sailing warships reflected this by being designed to accommodate larger numbers of heavy guns. Ships grew in size, openings ('gun ports') were cut in the hull to deploy the weapons, and decks were extended and added in order to get more guns on board.

THE LINE-OF-BATTLE SHIP

The advent of the heavy shipboard gun brought about a change in naval warfare that, while not sudden, was, viewed in the perspective of history, at least dramatic. It was accompanied by an equally radical change in battle tactics, a change occasioned by the nature of ships and the guns they carried, and the seemingly insoluble problem of the rigid relationships between the two in terms of disposition — a problem that would contribute signally to the lack of advance in basic warship design throughout the 17th, 18th and early 19th centuries and would only then be tackled effectively as a result of technological progress in territory as yet unexplored. The requirement that a ship be capable of movement through water defines, in general terms, a particular shape of hull, most obviously one that is considerably longer than it is broad; the desire for speed — and, clearly, a speedy vessel possesses certain advantages in battle over a slower adversary — further determines the form of hull, one factor being the fineness of the lines forward. The installation of numerous heavy guns, on the other hand, dictates that the latter be arranged along the length of the hull, and the need for stability requires that they be positioned where that stability is least compromised, in other words as close to the waterline as practicable and towards amidships. Hence the end-on attack practised by the war galleys was replaced by ships opposing each other broadside on, where the guns could be employed to maximum effect. Training angles were limited first by the disposition of the weapons and further by the need to keep gun ports as small as possible in order to preserve the ship's structural integrity and afford protection to the guns and their crews. Forward fire was possible, but only by light guns sited high in the bows, and only by a very limited number of individual pieces.

The advantages of sailing ships, as against oar-propelled ships, for employment as gun-carrying men-of-war were thus unanswerable, but their one drawback was their dependence on the elements for movement through the water, aggravated by their lack of manoeuvrability when compared to galleys. Hence battle tactics came to be dependent on the state and direction of the wind, opposing fleets struggling for the 'weather gage': ships to windward would have indisputable command of the action since they could manoeuvre themselves relative to the enemy much more easily and moreover would not be encumbered by drifting smoke on firing. Once a fleet had the weather gage, the greatest volume of fire could be brought upon an enemy by arranging the individual ships in a line formation.

However, it was quickly appreciated, especially by English commanders after their experiences in the Dutch Wars of the mid-17th century, that the frantic manoeuvres frequently required to gain the weather gage could result in groups of ships becoming detached from the main fleet and 'doubled' (overwhelmed by superior forces), particularly if vessels had been damaged in early exchanges or if the fleet comprised units of differing characteristics. As a result, the doctrine of the battle line became the essence of naval tactics: consisting of ships of comparable capabilities, the line would manoeuvre according to strict battle instruc-

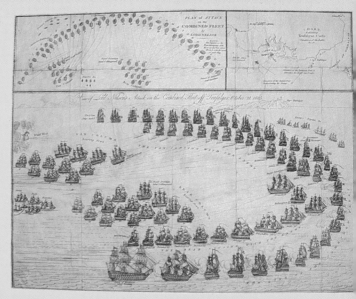

Above: With the advent of the broadside, the standard fleet battle tactic became the line, thus enabling the maximum number of guns to be brought to bear upon an enemy vessel.

Below: At Trafalgar, 1805, Nelson first broke the French line and then sought close engagement, in which small-arms fire played an important part. Nelson himself, as shown here, fell to a French musket ball.

tions, each vessel being allocated an opposing ship or ships in the enemy line, whose manoeuvres would be countered according to a specific code of conduct designed to ensure that the enemy would be denied all opportunity of breaking the formation. Numbers, then, would determine the outcome.

Nevertheless, rigid doctrine, when broken, might bring about spectacular results, and the tactics adopted by Rodney at the battle of the Saintes in 1782, when the French fleet, commanded by de Grasse, was broken by the British line driving through it and then pounded to defeat by superior gunnery in the ensuing *mêlée,* proved to be the forerunner of a number of victories against the French, including, of course, Trafalgar. British naval supremacy, which would remain unchallenged—and untested— through the 19th century, was firmly established, and the British line-of-battle ship was the undisputed mistress of the seas.

CAUSE AND EFFECT

The afterglow of Trafalgar was to persist for many decades, its psychological effects on the Royal Navy and on its potential adversaries reinforced by the growing capacity of British industry to ensure that any foreign threats to maritime supremacy could be dealt with swiftly and firmly. This was the essence of *Pax Britannica:* ideas and innovations spawned by others could be assessed, acted upon if necessary, and rendered impotent by the British ability to build faster, bigger and in greater quantity. It was not in the British Admiralty's interests to set the pace; neither did it. However, even as Trafalgar was being fought, three important technological moves were under consideration, all of which would be accommodated in ship design within half a century, so marking the birth of the battleship as a distinctive and unique type of vessel.

The symbol of the Industrial Revolution of the late 18th century was the steam engine. It did not take long for the potential of this form of propulsion to be demonstrated on water, as in 1801 William Symington, a Scot, towed two barges along the Forth & Clyde Canal in his diminutive *Charlotte Dundas.* Ocean-going steamships, and steam-powered warships, took somewhat longer to emerge, but in 1812 the American engineer Robert Fulton designed and began construction of *Demologos,* a 156ft (47·5m) vessel similar in its broad characteristics to a conventional frigate, mounting 24 x 32pdr guns and with a centre-line paddle wheel amidships.

Both the British and French navies adopted steam engines for use in sea-going vessels, but at first only in unarmed or lightly armed auxiliaries. The problem was self-evident: with the paddle wheel being the only practicable propulsion system in prospect, large warships so fitted either would be extremely vulnerable to disabling enemy fire or could incorporate the wheel(s) only at the expense of vital amidships space—or both. The breakthrough, and the impetus for change forced on an Admiralty desperately anxious to avoid encouraging any move that might threaten the superiority of the Royal Navy, came with the introduction of the screw propeller. In 1825 a Commander Brown had installed a tractor-type propeller aboard a small boat and successfully demonstrated it, but the two leading exponents of the system were Francis Pettit-Smith, whose applications convinced the Admiralty of the effectiveness of the screw and culminated in the famous *Rattler* versus *Alecto* public relations tug-of-war in 1845, and Captain John Ericsson, whose patent for screw propulsion failed to impress the Admiralty but who received support in the US Navy, resulting in the construction of the screwship *Princeton*. In France, meanwhile, the sailing frigate *Pomone* was completed with an auxiliary engine and Ericsson-type screw in 1845.

The application of screw propulsion to line-of-battle ships was not long delayed, the British *Agamemnon* and the French two-decker *Napoléon* being converted while on the stocks in the early 1850s and further ships of the line being undocked as screwships over that decade. Although by 1860 the sailing ship *per se* had been rendered obsolete in the line of battle, the steam engine was generally viewed askance in the Royal Navy: undeniably useful for manoeuvring in harbour, it was nevertheless disliked for the filth it created and was rarely employed at sea, at least initially.

While argument and counter-argument about the merits of steam propulsion continued during the 1850s, different technologies, each feeding off the other, were being set in train, and the foundations were being laid for the struggle for ascendancy that would characterise battleship development through the second half of the 19th century. For centuries the desirability of inflicting fire devastation upon an enemy vessel had been very well appreciated; the problem had always been the method of conveyance. 'Greek fire', the terrifying weapon of the pre-medieval era, had been rendered ineffective with the opening ranges brought about by the introduction of the shipboard gun, and the principal fire weapon had evolved into the fire ship, used with such success by Drake. However, the fire ship was generally limited to deployment against an immobilised fleet, or one in a confined environment, such as a harbour. The explosive nature of gun firing mechanisms made cannon-launched fire bombs an extremely hazardous option, to say the least, and their use was generally eschewed throughout the era of the sailing line-of-battle ship. Championed by the French artillery expert Colonel Paixhans, however, and aided by the development of rifled guns, which made long-range, high-velocity shell-fire a viable proposition since elongated (as against spherical) projectiles could thereby be stabilised in flight, the explosive shell gradually gained favour—and with its introduction in numbers came the impetus towards devising effective means of stopping it.

The best counter to the explosive shell would be some means of preventing its penetration, and the most obvious method by which this might be achieved was protecting ships by iron plating. Early experiments, in the 1830s, were not encouraging, for it was shown that armour, both solid and laminated, could be pierced provided the projectile was heavy enough and possessed sufficient velocity. Further, the devastating effect of iron splinters on impact

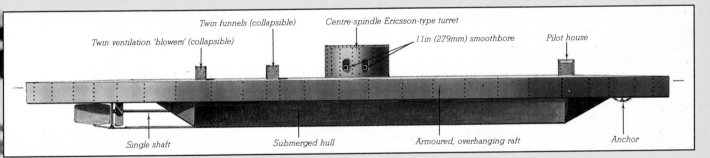

Above: The 1850s saw considerable numbers of sailing ships converted on the stocks for auxiliary screw propulsion. This is HMS *London* (completed 1860): note the funnel abaft the foremast.

Left: HMS *Warrior*, the world's first all-iron armour-clad capital ship. Shown here in 1876, she survives to this day in remarkable condition—a tribute to her designers and builders.

Above: On board *Monitor*, four months after Hampton Roads. The turret housed a pair of 11in (279mm) smoothbores and trained by steam; rate of fire was one round every six or seven minutes.

Below: Ericsson's impregnable *Monitor*, essentially an armoured raft with a freeboard of only some 15in (0·38m), was in no sense a sea-going vessel; her concept was, however, widely imitated.

Twin ventilation 'blowers' (collapsible) — Twin funnels (collapsible) — Centre-spindle Ericsson-type turret — 11in (279mm) smoothbore — Pilot house

Single shaft — Submerged hull — Armoured, overhanging raft — Anchor

discouraged its adoption, certainly in the Royal Navy. The French, however, were not deterred, and during the Crimean War in the early 1850s opportunities presented themselves for theories and experimentation to be tested in action. Such innovations were spurred on by the appointment of Dupuy de Lôme as *Directeur du Material* in 1857.

The war proved to be a turning point in battleship development, and was directly responsible for the large-scale introduction of both armour plate and explosive shells to naval fleets. First, in 1853, a Turkish squadron of frigates and corvettes were completely destroyed by shell-firing Russian line-of-battle ships at Sinope; secondly, in 1855, a small group of specially constructed shallow-draught French artillery batteries, *Dévastation, Lave* and *Tonnant,* armoured with 3·9in (100mm) iron plate, forced the capitulation of the Russian fort at Kinburn and although repeatedly hit by both shells and solid shot suffered negligible damage. Encouraged, the French proceeded with the design of the *Gloire,* an ocean-going frigate whose wooden hull was protected by wrought iron plates. The British reply was *Warrior,* superior to *Gloire* in being constructed of iron, larger and faster, and carrying a more formidable battery of guns. The true capital ironclad—the true battleship, in fact—had been born.

THE IRONCLADS MEET

As the first European ironclads were entering service, events across the Atlantic were ushering in further developments in warship construction. As in Europe, technological progress was stimulated by the necessities of war, in this case a direct product of the conflict that erupted in 1861 between the Confederate forces of the southern states of the USA and the Federals to the north.

The Confederates had found in their possession the scuttled remains of the screw frigate *Merrimack* and, with a view to inflicting severe damage on the numerically superior Federal Navy, set about converting her into an armoured, self-propelled floating battery. The result was a bizarre, low-freeboard raft with a casemated armament of assorted heavy-calibre weapons and, devoid of masts and sails, a top speed of about 3 knots (5·5km/h). The Federals, in some panic, commissioned John Ericsson, the Swedish engineer who had helped to pioneer screw propulsion, for the purposes of providing a reply, and in early 1862 the *Monitor,* a vessel which, like the *Dreadnought* of the next century, lent her name to a complete family of warships, left New York under tow to Hampton Roads. *Monitor,* like her adversary, was a low-freeboard vessel powered ex-

clusively by steam, but her design was chiefly remarkable for its turret-mounted guns and armoured conning tower, features which would figure significantly in capital ship lay-out in succeeding years. The combat that took place between these two strange craft on 9 March 1862 was inconclusive, each vessel pounding the other, but only superficial damage being caused and fighting ability remaining unaffected. The invulnerability of the armoured warship was amply demonstrated to the world; the answer must lie, clearly in projectiles and guns of increased potency.

But there was a further move which, it seemed, might effectively defeat the ironclad fighting ship: it entailed a temporary swing away from stand-off tactics and a return to the ancient concept of the ram. With the apparent stalemate reached in the development of guns versus armour, even at point blank range, considerable faith began to be placed once more in this form of attack. Its proponents gathered supporting evidence on 20 July 1866.

The Seven Weeks' War in the summer of 1866 between Prussia and Austria had presented the newly united king-dom of Italy, Prussia's ally, with the opportunity for terri-torial gain at the expense of the Austrians, and on 16 July, after considerable hesitation, the commander of the Italian fleet, Admiral Count Carlo di Persano, was per-suaded to sally forth and attempt to take the Adriatic island of Lissa. The Austrian commander, Rear Admiral Tegethoff, sailed for battle, and for the first time since Trafalgar—and for the last time, as it happened, for a further forty years—two sizeable fleets of capital ships were about to engage one another.

The two fleets were not evenly balanced, there being six Austrian ironclads mounting a total of 140 guns but nine Italian ships with well over 200 guns; moreover, the over-whelming majority of the Italian guns were modern, rifled pieces, while only about half their opponent's weapons were such. The Italian fleet, led by the flagship *Re d'Italia*, was formed up in the accepted line of battle, the new turret ram *Affondatore* being employed as an independent unit on the lee side; the Austrian fleet, with *Erzherzog Ferdinand Max* in the van, was disposed in three arrowhead forma-tions of nine vessels each, those at the rear being composed principally of unarmoured ships. Tegethoff's tactics were clear: outgunned, in terms of numbers, range and accuracy, he decided to present the smallest possible target to his opponent and drive straight for the Italian line.

Tegethoff's attack sliced through a gap in Persano's fleet, but as his leading formation turned and split to tackle the van and centre of the Italian line the second squadron fell upon the enemy and a confused *mêlée* erupted, broad-sides smashing into ships at close range while each, acting independently, twisted and turned in desperate efforts to ram. As the battle wore on, *Re d'Italia,* disabled, was chanced upon by Tegethoff, who drove *Ferdinand Max* at full speed into the hapless Italian flagship, which rolled to starboard and disappeared from view. Smoke and con-fusion continued throughout the rest of the battle, but by the time Persano withdrew the only other loss had been the Italian iron-hulled coast defence ship *Palestro*, destroyed by a magazine explosion. Other than in the two ships sunk, casualties had been amazingly light on both sides.

As at Hampton Roads, Lissa had apparently proven the general ineffectiveness of guns against armoured battle-ships; the spectacular achievement in the Adriatic had been that of the ram. Naval tacticians hastily recast their ideas: the battle line was condemned and the ram was obviously the weapon *par excellence.* It was conveniently overlooked that *Re d'Italia* had posed a virtually stationary target, and while the gun was not abandoned, it was soon consigned by some to a subordinate role. This extreme view did not persist for long, but battleships continued to be designed with ram bows for the next forty years or so.

NEW DIMENSIONS—NEW THREATS

The effects of the Crimean War, the US Civil War and, most recently, Lissa were far-reaching, and with numerous pointers as to the various avenues along which capital ship evolution might proceed, it is hardly surprising that battle-ship design was thrown into some confusion for the next two or three decades. All the engagements of the 1850s and 1860s had shown decisively the absolute necessity of armouring ships against enemy attack. The Russians at Sinope and the Austrians at Lissa had proven that the explosive shell was capable of inflicting devastation, given the right circumstances; Lissa had, further, demonstrated the value of the ram and the consequent desirability of end-on (in particular ahead) fire. The ability of screw-propelled vessels both to manoeuvre in action and to present the pros-pect of low-profile warships had been demonstrated. The superiority of the rifled gun had now been established. Ships embodying these features now proliferated.

Guns grew in size in an attempt to render armour penetrable, and the breech-loader finally triumphed over the muzzle-loader; armour in turn thickened in order to stop heavier shells. Ships were built to larger dimensions, and of iron, in order to support increased weights. Even so, broadsides shrank in length in order to save weight, both in terms of the weapons themselves and of the armour required to protect them, and the 'central battery' ship evolved as a distinctive type. Some degree of end-on fire was achieved by angling the gun ports, particularly at the corners of the battery, but the only viable alternative seemed to be the revolving turret ,as pioneered by *Monitor.* However, its prodigious weight dictated that the turret

Left: An artist's engraving of the inconclusive duel between *Merrimack* (right) and *Monitor* at Hampton Roads, March 1862. Both vessels received superficial damage during a four-hour engagement.

Below left: The ironclad frigate *San Martino*, part of Persano's line at Lissa. Ram bows would be accorded an exaggerated importance as a result of the battle—which would later be regretted.

Right: Low freeboard was at first a penalty accepted in the design of turret ships, but combined with a towering top hamper, which created instability, it was fatal. This is the tragic *Captain*, 1870.

Below: A fictitious battleship, showing the major design characteristics that evolved from 1860 to 1900. Other than the means of propulsion, the significant point is, perhaps, the wide range of possibilities concerning the mounting of the main armament.

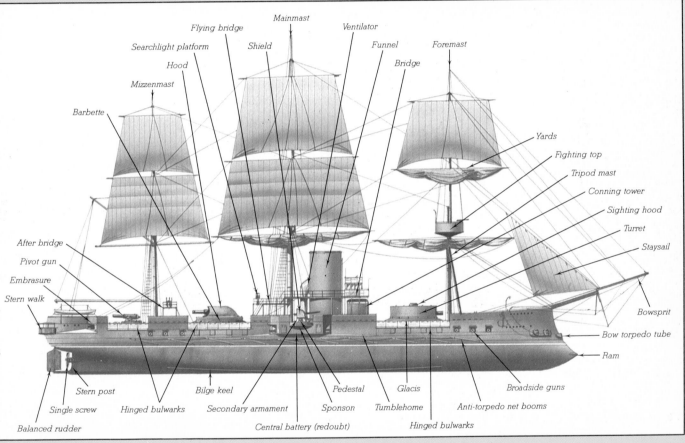

be sited close to the waterline, with all the problems of low freeboard that entailed (as demonstrated tragically in the loss of HMS *Captain* in the Bay of Biscay in September 1870), and also a restriction to very few individual barrels; moreover, the problem of mounting turrets on board sailing ships, albeit powered ones, and ensuring that arcs of fire were kept clear of masts and rigging proved virtually insurmountable. Low-freeboard, mastless turret ships were, nevertheless, of value in sheltered waters, and the development of the *Monitor* principle was pursued vigorously, particularly in the United States during the Civil War years but also elsewhere as a coast defence vessel, a sort of off-shore mobile fort whose hull would not have to contend with ocean swells. In a further effort to save weight, the barbette principal, whereby heavy guns were mounted on armoured, revolving platforms, gained favour, and all the while steam engines increased in power and efficiency, hastening the inevitable disappearance of sail.

The American Civil War foreshadowed further developments, new threats which, as they matured towards the close of the nineteenth century, would add worrying factors to the calculations of battleship designers. One was the problem of the mine, epitomised by the Federal Admiral Farragut's celebrated 'Damn the torpedoes' sortie into Mobile Bay, when his monitor *Tecumseh* was lost through striking a 'torpedo' (actually a mine). The 'spar' torpedo, in the form of a gunpowder keg on the end of a boom detonated by the occupant of the 'torpedo boat' carrying it, appeared to pose a threat, as demonstrated so daringly by Lieutenant Cushing when he sank the Confederate battery *Albemarle* and, twenty years later, by the French Admiral Courbet against the Chinese in the Min River.

The true locomotive torpedo, too, was born about this time. Pioneered by an Austrian, Captain Luppis, and developed by the expatriate Englishman Robert White-

head, manager of an engineering works at Fiume, the self-propelled, compressed-air-driven torpedo became a standard warship weapon, launched from specially designed carriages on deck or, subsequently, from submerged bow or beam tubes. Rather more sinister was the submarine. The idea of a submersible craft was nothing new, the first recorded experiments having taken place in Elizabethan times and far-seeing projects having been promoted by, in particular, the Americans Bushnell and Fulton. However, it was the American Civil War, again, that would witness the first effective use of an underwater craft, albeit in somewhat desperate circumstances. The plans for the vessel were drawn up by one H.L. Hunley, whose name the craft would bear, and utilised by the Confederates to construct what amounted to little more than a converted boiler casing. Driven by eight men working a hand-cranked propeller, it achieved fame, after several abortive forays, by sinking the Federal *Housatonic* in early 1864 with a spar torpedo, unfortunately destroying itself in the explosion. Submarine designers were first afflicted by the twin problems of propulsion unit and suitable armament, but with the perfection of electric batteries and the success of the locomotive torpedo, development of the craft, culminating in the French *Gustave Zédé*, an early 1890s design based on the earlier *Gymnote* which had been produced by Dupuy de Lôme and Zédé himself, was such that by the turn of the century the threat it posed was regarded as severe if, in some quarters, 'unfair'.

SCARES AND SKIRMISHES

The Battle of Lissa in 1866 proved to be the only significant fleet action of the ironclad era, but there occurred further events which would be seized on by naval strategists and tacticians. One of the first took place in South America, where in 1877 the crew of the Peruvian armoured turret ship *Huascar* was involved in supporting an attempted *coup* and threatened British interests in the area. The unarmoured frigate *Shah* and the screw corvette *Amethyst* were despatched to deal with the offending vessel. In the action which ensued, the Peruvian monitor was struck by about sixty 9in (229mm), 7in (178mm) and 64pdr rounds, only one of which managed to penetrate her armour. In 1879 *Huascar*, now the sole Peruvian ironclad, was again in combat, involved in the war against Chile. In a battle with the Chilean central battery ironclads *Almirante Coch-*

rane and *Blanco Encalada*, she was badly damaged by more than two dozen 9in (229mm) shells fired at very short range seven of which penetrated, causing horrific casualties. Two years earlier. *Huascar*'s British opponents had been loath to close owing to the ships' unarmoured hulls, but here was a decisive victory that demonstrated a superiority o: guns over armour. Conclusions were drawn.

The 1877 incident was also remarkable for being the first time a genuine locomotive torpedo was fired in action *Shah* managing to launch a Whitehead from one of he: two carriages. However, despatched from a range of about 400 yards (365m), there was very little chance of it reaching its target, and the first successful hit by such a torpedo did not take place until January 1878, when a Russiar torpedo boat sank a Turkish guard ship outside Batum harbour.

The late 1870s and early 1880s were marked, as far as Britain was concerned, by a growing anxiety about conflict with Russia owing to the latter's adventures in Eastern Europe and, more importantly, against the Turkish Empire, which was seen as a bulwark against expansionism in the Middle East and southern Asia and was thus actively backed. A major feature of the British concern was the perceived threat to the Suez Canal, and in 1882, after the Russians and Turks had settled their differences, Egypt was brought under British administration, a move resisted by factions in Egypt led by Colonel Arabi, who organised the setting up of forts at Alexandria, the naval base where British and French warships were on hand as an insurance against recriminatory action. The French withdrew, fearing German involvement, but following rioting in Alexandria the battleships *Inflexible, Alexandra, Superb, Sultan, Monarch* and *Temeraire*, plus many smaller units, were ordered to take action. A day-long bombardment on 11 July 1882 caused the Egyptians to retreat with over 500 casualties, although it was subsequently discovered that only about 150 out of some 3,000 shells fired had actually

Right: British ironclads first took the offensive in 1882, putting down a revolt in Alexandria. This is *Inflexible*, one of the battleships that took part.

Below: The massive Italian battleship *Dandolo*, just prior to launch in 1878. The armour belt is not yet installed. Note the bow-mounted submerged torpedo tube.

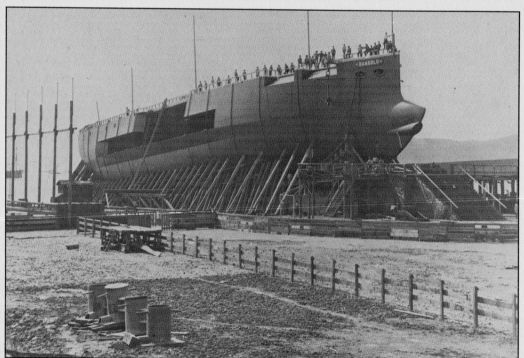

Above: The protected cruiser *Matsushima*, Japanese flagship at the Yalu River. Designed by Bertin, she carried a single 12·6in (320mm) gun aft and a dozen 4·7in (119mm) weapons forward.

Below: Inadvertent victor: the battleship *Camperdown*, which rammed and sank *Victoria* during a series of fleet manoeuvres in the summer of 1893 that went disastrously wrong.

hit their target. The poor quality of the shooting, attributable probably to the unwieldy nature of the giant guns and to the complete absence of any fire control facilities, was overshadowed by the result, which reinforced the supreme position of the Royal Navy but goaded other European powers into attempting to establish some sort of realistic challenge to Britain's maritime might.

The Russian 'war scare' of 1878, when the prospect of conflict had resulted in the purchase by the Admiralty of two battleships originally destined for service in South America and two armoured rams ordered by Turkey, was heightened after Alexandria by signs that France and Russia were growing more friendly towards each other, and this trend was primarily responsible for the introduction, via the 1889 Naval Defence Act, of the famous 'Two-Power Standard', which deemed that the Royal Navy should be of a size equal to the combined strength of the next two most powerful navies in the world.

The next naval action of any significance, however, took place across the other side of the globe when, in 1894, Japanese expansionism brought about direct conflict with China. Troops were landed in the Korean peninsula, and Chinese reinforcements were rushed to the area by sea, with warships providing cover. Off the mouth of the Yalu River, the Japanese fleet closed. The Japanese force, comprising heavily armoured British- and French-designed protected cruisers, advanced in line ahead formation towards the right wing of the Chinese fleet, where the enemy's weakest ships were disposed, her two principal vessels, the battleships *Chen Yuen* and *Ting Yuen*, being located in the centre of the Chinese line abreast formation. The right wing was crushed as the Japanese held their fire until within about 3,000 yards (2,750m), and the Chinese capital ships were then circled and heavily pounded. At the end of the action three Japanese ships, including the flagship *Matsushima*, had been severely mauled, but the Chinese had lost five of their number.

The Japanese victory, for such it indisputably was, provided the raw material for fresh analysis and argument, not only about the characteristics of fighting ships and of gunnery requirements but also about battle tactics in fleet actions, which had been in a state of flux since Lissa and the presumed efficacy of the ram. There were several possibilities, the line ahead formation still finding favour because of the influence of broadside fire, but the ascendancy of turret and barbette ships, which by now, because of the final abandonment of sail in capital ships, were the major element in battle fleets by 1890, meant that heavy end-on fire was at last a practical proposition. Thus the line abreast formation was propounded by other schools: ships could present themselves as minimum targets, would be enabled to close the range quickly and, moreover, would be virtually immune from torpedo attack, which was a very real, if overstated, hazard. Variations on these classic dispositions included 'indented line ahead', with two parallel formations, that on the lee covering the gaps between the individual vessels in the battle line, and 'double indented line ahead'; and there were modifications of standard cruising formations ('divisions'), and 'group' tactics. Pamphlets published by Sir John Colomb, an ex-Royal Marine, and a book, *The Influence of Sea Power on History*, by the American naval officer Alfred Mahan, established themselves as 'bibles' of strategical naval doctrine, but tactical doctrine did not settle, and the problems were highlighted in June 1893 when precision fleet manoeuvres off North Africa by the British Mediterranean Squadron resulted, through an error of judgement on the part of the commander, Admiral Sir George Tryon, in the accidental ramming and sinking of his flagship, *Victoria*, by HMS *Camperdown*. Admiral Tryon and 358 officers and men died in this disaster; 284 survivors were recovered.

One other capital ship engagement took place in the closing years of the 19th century, although the opposing fleets were ill-matched. The destruction by internal explosion of the US armoured vessel *Maine* in Havana harbour in 1898 provided the United States with the excuse for declaring war on Spain. After the Spanish cruiser squadron at Manila Bay, Philippines, was destroyed by US cruisers under Commodore Dewey on 1 May 1898, on 3 July a force of four US battleships and one armoured cruiser, led by Commodore Schley in *Iowa*, was presented with the opportunity for action when the Spanish squadron at Santiago di Cuba was ordered to break out of the blockaded harbour. The Spanish force, which included three modern Infanta Maria Teresa class vessels, was annihilated, although poor gunnery resulted in only some 120 hits being achieved from some 6,000 rounds fired by the US squadron. Following the Spanish-American War, the United States took over a number of ex-Spanish possessions and her standing as a world power, fed by massive industrial expansion from the 'New Navy' establishment in 1883 onwards, rose dramatically.

THE GREAT RACE

The rise of the US Navy was mirrored in Europe by the emergence of a united Germany as an aspiring naval power. Driven by the Kaiser, an ambitious arch-devotee of the 'big navy' concept, and steered through by Admiral Tirpitz, a massive German rearmament plan was put in train, made possible by staggering advances in industrial capacity and promoted by the Naval Laws of 1898 and 1905 and by the retreating threat of the French Navy as the *jeune école* 'small ship' theorists sowed confusion as to what kinds of vessels constituted an effective fleet. The German objectives were clearly anti-British, a point which Tirpitz did not refute and which the British Admiralty took note of. By 1904 the position was regarded so seriously that the *Entente Cordiale* between Britian and France had been agreed, quite against the trends of recent decades and only a few years after the French had been unceremoniously ejected from the Sudan.

For the next ten years argument and counter-argument bounced to and fro across the North Sea, Wilhelm II protesting that that a fully fledged battle fleet was a necessary contingency in view of Germany's world-wide trade and colonial interests, Britain replying that as a land power such a navy was unnecessary and, even if it was, long-range cruisers were preferable to heavy-gun battleships. The whole issue was punctuated by rapid technological (in particular gunnery) advances during the first few years of the 20th century and by the startling arrival on the scene of the epoch-making *Dreadnought*, which rendered all existing capital ships obsolete at a stroke, including, of course, those of the Royal Navy.

Dreadnought's appearance rocked the navies of the world and gave Britain a two-or three-year lead as designers hastily recast plans and strategists, especially the latter, reassessed their views. The German hierarchy was spurred into action, for here was the chance to match the British fleet, and massive building programmes for Dreadnought-type ships were sanctioned. The worrying feature from the British Admiralty's point of view was not so much that such a programme was obviously being embarked upon, but rather that Germany now had the industrial muscle to endanger the hitherto unchallenged British capacity to out-build any other nation. Projections about the strength of the German Navy by such-and-such a date wrinkled Admiralty foreheads; each was denied with professed amazement by the Germans. The building race gathered momentum, and other navies followed: 'Dreadnought fever' spread across the globe, and guns grew in calibre

and number, leapfrog fashion, and ships in dimensions power and speed.

Meanwhile a significant naval action had been fough out, again in the Far East and again involving the Japanes Navy. The outbreak of the Russo-Japanese War in Februar 1904 had been signalled by a largely unsuccessful pre emptive torpedo boat attack on the Russian fleet lying at anchor at Port Arthur, and followed up by an indecisiv engagement between the two main fleets at the same loca tion the next day, when several hits were scored but n serious damage inflicted or sustained. In August the sam year the two fleets met again, this time at sea. Makarov the Russian commander, had perished when his flagship *Petropavlovsk* had struck a mine during exercises off Por Arthur, and it was a new commander, Vitgeft, that led hi fleet in a run to Vladivostok to avoid encirclement b advancing Japanese land forces. The Japanese, unde Admiral Togo, were waiting, and, in line formation but a long range, fire began to be exchanged. Honours wer even throughout much of the action, but late in the after

noon of the battle a Japanese shell fired by the *Asahi* hit the conning tower of the Russian flagship *Tsessarevitch*, killing Vitgeft, while a second heavy shell jammed the ship's steering. The Russian line was reduced to chaos and Togo closed, pounding the enemy with his secondary batteries at short range. The effects were indecisive, and the scattered Russian fleet was able to reorganise and escape under cover of darkness.

In October 1904 the Russian Baltic Fleet set sail on the long haul to the Far East in an attempt to stem the tide of Japanese successes. By December, with Rozhdestvenski the commander in the Indian Ocean, the Port Arthur fleet had been eliminated by Japanese land artillery. By late March Rozhdestvenski was off Indo-China and on 27 May he was approaching the Straits of Tsushima, en route for Vladivostok. Togo was there, too.

Within six hours the Russian Navy had been all but eradicated. The Japanese ships, led by *Mikasa*, keeping immaculate station and unhindered by the prescence in their formation of defective vessels which limited the Russians' speed to about 8 knots (15km/h), chose both their range and their bearing. The Russian flagship *Suvarov* was reduced to a blazing wreck; the *Osliaba* was then hit twice close to the waterline, flooded and sank; *Alexander II*, shattered and leaking from prolonged bombardment, capsized; *Borodino* disappeared in a magazine explosion; and the now limping *Suvarov* was finally torpedoed by destroyers at point blank range. More ships were lost that night; the Russians surrendered the next day.

BATTLESHIPS AT WAR, 1914-18

The staggering achievement of Togo at Tsushima, by far the most important and most decisive naval engagement since Trafalgar, was naturally seized upon as an object lesson in battle procedure, but careful analysts were able to point out that, complete though the Japanese victory had been, it was in many ways achieved with old-fashioned methods. For example, there was no co-ordinated fire control, each gun crew acting independently in time-honoured tradition. One of the difficulties was the varying calibres of guns carried by each ship, it being at times impossible to differentiate the origins of the fall of shot. Nevertheless, Tsushima had demonstrated the advantages of speed and gunnery training and had totally vindicated the claims of experts like Captain Percy Scott and Lieutenant William Sims, under whose guidance the scientific use of battleship weapons was bringing quite startling results in the Royal and US Navies.

On 4 August 1914, with the Dreadnought 'race' in full flight, came the outbreak of World War I. It was fully expected that the British Grand Fleet and the German High Seas Fleet would steam out to confront each other, a massive battle would ensue, and the struggle would be decided. In fact, caution dictated that this would not be so: neither side could afford to risk defeat, and it would be almost two years before a major clash occurred, and then in fortuitous circumstances. Admiral Sir John Jellicoe, the British Commander-in-Chief, had no intention of being drawn over protective minefields to seek out the German dreadnoughts in harbour: in exercising distant blockade by keeping the Grand Fleet back, yet ready to meet its foe should the latter threaten to seek battle, he ensured that stalemate persisted. There was no reason to do otherwise: an alliance with Japan took care of German shipping in the Far East, the Austrians were bottled up by the French in the Mediterranean, and such German vessels as roamed the oceans were, step by step, being mopped up.

The actions involving capital ships that did take place were peripheral affairs, and most involved battlecruisers rather than battleships. Fast and heavily armed, but lightly protected, these derivatives were introduced to the navies of the world by *Invincible*, which commissioned in 1908 as the first of a line of hybrid vessels which could function in the traditional commerce protection role but also operate as fast squadrons of battle fleets, able to deliver heavy fire at long range. Two German cruisers were caught and annihilated by British battlecruisers off the Heligoland

Above left: By the close of the 19th century, Britain's traditional European rival, France, was fast being displaced by a unified, invigorated Germany. The forerunners of a large programme of modern pre-dreadnoughts were the eight Siegfried class coast defence battleships. This is *Beowulf*: note the unusual disposition of the forward 9·4in (240mm) barbettes.

Left: The coast defence battleship *General Admiral Graf Apraksin* was one of the units of the Russian Baltic Fleet to voyage to Japan to avenge Vitgeft's defeat, but she surrendered to Togo's devastating fire at Tsushima. Captured by the Japanese along with other Russian survivors, she was renamed *Okinoshima* and served for some years in the training role.

Right: Although armed on the scale of the battleship, the battlecruiser had an entirely separate ancestry. It evolved from the armoured cruiser (and was still referred to as such some time after the first of the type appeared), and hence was lightly armoured in comparison to ships built for the battle line. The requirement for high speed led to its quickly overtaking the battleship in size, but employment in big-gun actions (especially Jutland) demonstrated flaws. Ultimately the two types merged, to become the 'fast battleship'. This is *Inflexible*, in dock at Gibraltar in 1915.

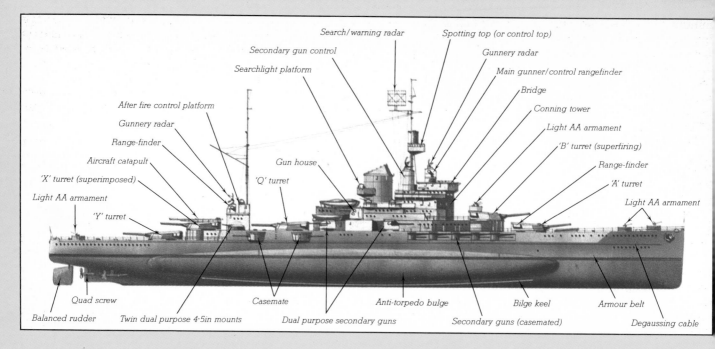

Search/warning radar
Spotting top (or control top)
Secondary gun control
Gunnery radar
Searchlight platform
Main gunner/control rangefinder
After fire control platform
Bridge
Gunnery radar
Conning tower
Range-finder
Light AA armament
Aircraft catapult
Gun house
'B' turret (superfiring)
'X' turret (superimposed)
'Q' turret
Range-finder
Light AA armament
'A' turret
'Y' turret
Light AA armament
Quad screw
Balanced rudder
Twin dual purpose 4·5in mounts
Casemate
Dual purpose secondary guns
Anti-torpedo bulge
Bilge keel
Secondary guns (casemated)
Armour belt
Degaussing cable

Bight shortly after the outbreak of war, and when, in December that year, the armoured cruisers *Scharnhorst* and *Gneisenau* were, after a hard fight, defeated by *Invincible* and *Inflexible* off the Falkland Islands, the concept appeared to be fully justified.

Hints that all might not be well with the design of British battlecruisers became apparent the next month when Sir David Beatty's Battle Cruiser Force became involved in chasing a smaller German squadron in the North Sea. Vice Admiral Hipper, in *Seydlitz,* was engaged in a reconnaissance sortie with two other battlecruisers and the armoured cruiser *Blücher,* when he was caught by the British ships and turned tail. The superior speed of the Royal Navy units enabled them to open long-range fire, which was exchanged, and both sides suffered severely. *Blücher,* at the rear, was disabled and, owing to a mishap in signal interpretation, became the centre of attraction for the British forces while the major vessels in Hipper's force made their escape. However, both *Lion*, Beatty's flagship, and *Seydlitz* were badly mauled, the latter experiencing an ammunition explosion which almost sank the ship. The dangers of 'flash' were highlighted, foreshadowing future calamities.

The appointment of Vice Admiral Reinhardt Scheer early in 1916 as the German C-in-C brought with it a more positive approach to the problem of raising German morale, which following the disappointing performance at Dogger Bank and twelve months of inactivity was becoming extremely low. Hit-and-run raids against English coastal towns were organised, and plans were laid for enticing out a squadron of British capital ships, dispersed as the latter now were in response to the raids. On 31 May 1916 Admiral Hipper swept out into the North Sea with five battle-cruisers, his flag in *Lützow;* he was followed by Scheer some 40 miles (65km) astern with sixteen dreadnoughts and half a dozen pre-dreadnoughts. The British fleet had already left harbour, forewarned by increasing German radio traffic: Beatty from Rosyth with six battlecruisers and also the 5th Battle Squadron, comprising four fast Queen Elizabeth class battleships, and Jellicoe from Scapa, with sixteen battleships and the three Invincibles, later joined by a further eight dreadnoughts based at Cromarty.

There is not space here to do other than outline the main features of the Battle of Jutland. The opposing battle-cruisers were brought together by the chance sighting and subsequent investigation of a neutral merchantman. Beatty closed and Hipper turned towards Scheer, drawing the British ships on to the guns of the High Seas Fleet. Fire was exchanged at 15,000 yards (13,700m), and within fifteen

Above: Features of 20th century capital ship design. Note the growth of the superstructure and the standardisation in main armament mounting type.

Below: *Prinz Regent Luitpold* typified German World War I dreadnought design and was a sister-ship to Scheer's flagship *Friedrich der Grosse* at Jutland.

minutes *Indefatigable* was hit by 11in (280mm) shells from *Von der Tann* and disappeared in a ball of flame. *Lion* almost met the same fate, her life saved by the prompt action of a mortally wounded Royal Marines officer who somehow managed to arrange for the flooding of 'Q' turret magazine and shell room. As the 5th Battle Squadron came into action the battlecruiser *Queen Mary* was hit by 12in (305mm) shells from *Derfflinger* and exploded.

The German capital ships were not unscathed, *Von der Tann* suffering from the 15in (381mm) shells of the 5th Battle Squadron in particular and *Seydlitz* being struck by a destroyer-launched torpedo. Beatty sighted the dreadnoughts of the High Seas Fleet and, as Hipper had done before him, turned towards his commander-in-chief, who was steering south at 20 knots (37km/h). Hipper and Scheer, unaware of the Grand Fleet bearing down, took the bait.

The three scouting battlecruisers attached to the Grand Fleet were the first to make contact, and a fierce exchange with *Derfflinger* left *Invincible* broken in two by the third magazine explosion of the afternoon. On being briefly engaged by Jellicoe, however, Scheer executed the now-famous *Gefechtskehrtwendung,* or 'battle turnaway' and disappeared from view, his retreat facilitated by a destroyer torpedo attack which forced Jellicoe to turn to evade, thereby opening the range, and by the 'death ride' of the German battlecruisers. Caution overruled all thought of a decisive action: Jellicoe would not chase too far, fearing being led over mines: Scheer would not fight, fearing defeat at the hands of the numerically superior Grand Fleet. As darkness fell the skirmishes died away, and although brief, sporadic contact was made as the fleets steamed almost parallel courses, by the morning of 1 June Scheer had slipped astern of Jellicoe and escaped.

Claims of victory were advanced by both sides: the Germans pointed to the loss of three British capital ships against one (*Lützow*), plus a pre-dreadnought, of their own, the British to the fact that the much-vaunted High Seas Fleet had run away from the battlefield. The result was inconclusive, since neither navy was much impaired by the damage it had suffered, and the strategic situation had not changed. There were, to be sure, lessons to be learned, mostly for the Royal Navy and especially with regard to their battlecruisers, which, so brilliantly employed in the South Atlantic, had revealed serious design deficiencies in fleet action. Anti-flash precautions were heightened, horizontal armour increased in thickness and shells improved, but tactical and strategical doctrine was little affected. The Germans intensified their submarine offensive and new problems were raised for the Royal Navy, but the great gun was still the final arbiter, even if it did not actually fire.

INTERLUDE

The High Seas Fleet met an ignominious end. Inactive for the remainder of World War I, it was turned over to Royal Navy guardianship after the Armistice and interned at Scapa Flow. There, in May 1919, it was scuttled in its entirety. However, although the 'war to end all wars' had come to a close, the dreadnought building programmes which had, no doubt, contributed in part to its outbreak in the first place proceeded apace once more, the excuse of defending 'national interests' being championed this time by the United States and Japan. Ships of unprecedented dimensions and gun power were being laid down and contemplated in these countries, and Britain, whose navy had so recently preserved the state of her empire, could not ignore the challenge and prepared designs accordingly. However, the crippling costs of such programmes and the memory of what just such a similar rivalry had brought about just a decade earlier, led President Harding to propose a meeting of the great powers with a view to limiting naval rearmament.

The Washington Conference opened in November 1921. After much argument and controversy, agreement was reached concerning the quantitative and the qualitative composition of the world's major battle fleets. Among the terms, all capital ships under construction were to be scrapped, with the exception of the 16in (406mm) gunned Japanese *Mutsu* and three US Marylands, to balance which Britain would be permitted to lay down two new vessels with a main armament of the same calibre. No further construction was to be initiated for ten years, and then only to replace units which were twenty years old. Future battleships would be limited in displacement to 35,000 tons (35,560 tonnes) and in maximum gun calibre to 16in (406mm), and the total size of dreadnought fleets would be restricted to 580,450 tons (589,737 tonnes) for the Royal Navy, 500,650 tons (508,660 tonnes) for the US Navy, 301,320 tons (306,141 tonnes) for Japan, 221,170 tons (224,709 tonnes) for France and 182,000 tons (184,912 tonnes) for Italy, the approximate strengths thus being in the ratios 11·5:10:6:4·5:3·5 with numbers of individual ships set at 22, 28, 10, 10 and 10 respectively. Further terms in the agreement, concluded in February 1922, ordained the dissolution of the Anglo-Japanese alliance, the banning of further military bases in the Pacific, and the permitting of 3,000 tons (3,048 tonnes) of displacement to be added to existing capital ships so that defence against aircraft and submarines might be improved.

Left: Despite the advent of bomb- and torpedo-carrying aircraft and the threat of the submarine and the mine, the battleship was still held to be the mistress of the seas during the post-World War I years, and the line was still the standard fleet tactic. Here *Royal Oak* leads other British units on manoeuvres.

Below: The Washington Treaty did not forbid the renovation of existing battleships, and many were upgraded. *Nevada,* for example, received new machinery, on-board scoutplanes and tripod masts, her secondary battery was relocated and her main guns had their elevation increased; not evident is her enhanced deck armour.

Below: Big-gun actions during World War II were confined to small groups of vessels, or even individuals, rather than battle fleets. Here *Bismarck* fires on *Hood*, 24 May 1941.

Right: *West Virginia* succumbs to Japanese bombs and torpedoes at Pearl Harbor, 7 December 1941. Naval air power was proven in dramatic and conclusive fashion on that day.

Although Washington stopped the development of a new battleship race it had the effect of encouraging the progress of aircraft and submarine design: even so, throughout the interlude between Washington and the outbreak of World War II battleship design continued apace, and battle fleet exercises were the major peacetime manoeuvres. The expiry of the building 'holiday' in the early 1930s brought about the London Naval Conference of 1930; under the terms of the agreement reached, new battleship construction was denied for a further five years, although France and Italy refused to be bound. Japan would not countenance agreement at the second London Conference of 1935-6, when main calibres were maximised at 14in (356mm), provided all other countries kept to this limit. The building ban was not, however, renewed, and hence the dreadnought race was rekindled.

WORLD WAR II

It can reasonably be argued that the rearmament programmes of the late 1930s were the effect of a growing trend towards international hostilities rather than the cause of them. Whichever the case may be, the conflict which engulfed the world from 1939 to 1945 involved battleships of a size hitherto unseen, but it also laid bare their vulnerabilities: after centuries of evolution, the big gun would be seen to be discredited, at least in its traditional role.

The huge fleets, the guarantors of national integrity in the past, had of course disappeared, banished by Washington and economics. Instead, a new type of capital ship was emerging, one whose potency would very soon be proven. The early months of World War II followed very much the pattern, at least in naval terms, of the global conflict a quarter of a century earlier, with probes and thrusts by German heavy units like *Graf Spee*, *Scharnhorst* and *Gneisenau* and counter-sorties, and distant blockade, by capital ships of the Royal Navy. There was even a parallel, in a sense, to the Battle of the Falklands, when *Graf Spee* was run to ground off Montevideo after an engagement with three British cruisers. However, when the German Army overran Norway, the Low Countries and France in the first half of 1940 the picture changed dramatically and the Royal Navy was dispersed to fill the vacuum created in the Mediterranean by the neutralising of the French fleet as an allied force. A brief action in July 1940 between *Warspite*, veteran of Jutland, and the Italian battleship *Giulio Cesare* involved few hits but caused an enemy withdrawal, and in mid-November a classic strike by the Fleet Air Arm disabled the Italian battle fleet.

The torpedo-bomber, in fact, was to play a decisive role in two actions in the spring of 1941. First, at Matapan in the Mediterranean, a single hit stopped the Italian heavy cruiser *Pola* and enabled three British battleships, *Warspite*, *Barham* and *Valiant*, to close and destroy both her and two sister-ships which had come to her rescue. Second, in the North Atlantic, an aerial torpedo slowed and a subsequent torpedo crippled the German battleship *Bismarck*, which had ventured out to strike at British merchant shipping. *Bismarck* had some days earlier accounted for the famous old battlecruiser *Hood*, largest and most handsome warship in the world during the interwar years, when one of her salvoes triggered a magazine explosion and caused a catastrophe unnervingly reminiscent of the events of 31 May 1916. The air attacks on the German battleship, however, brought her within range of the guns of *King George V* and *Rodney*, which reduced her to a blazing wreck.

The potency of air power was further emphasized in dramatic fashion in December 1941 when Japanese carrier-based torpedo- and dive-bombers disabled the bulk of the US Pacific Fleet at Pearl Harbor in a pre-emptive raid, and again three days later when the British *Repulse* and *Prince of Wales* were summarily sunk by land-based aircraft off the Malay peninsula. With the British battleship *Barham* having succumbed to a torpedo which detonated her magazines in the previous month, 1941 was indeed a gloomy year in the history of the capital ship. The giant Japanese battleships *Yamato* and *Musashi*, the largest ever constructed, and the Italian battleship *Roma* would also be sunk at sea as a direct result of air attack, the latter by an air-launched guided missile, and further capital units would be victims of air attack while in harbour. However, there were to be three more surface actions involving battlefleets.

The first was a night action off Guadalcanal in November 1942: the new US battleships *Washington* and *South Dakota* engaged the Japanese *Kirishima*, opened devastating fire and finished her with nine 16in (406mm) and forty

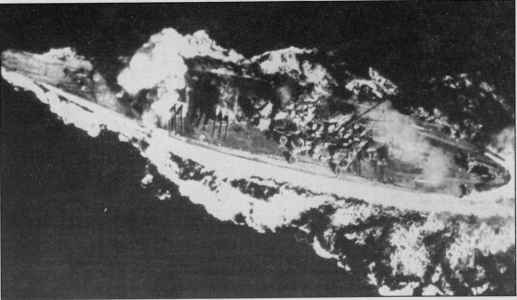

Above: The giant among them all: the 70,000-ton (71,000 tonne) *Yamato*, under attack by US aircraft at Leyte Gulf, October 1944. While they could absorb tremendous punishment, even vessels such as these could be overwhelmed.

Below: The US battleship *New Jersey*, completed during World War II, is now in service once again, her big guns augmented by Harpoon and Tomahawk anti-ship missiles. She is shown here prior to her 1982 conversion.

5in (127mm) shells in just over four minutes. Off Norway, in the last week of 1943, the German raider *Scharnhorst* was intercepted by units of the British Home Fleet headed by *Duke of York* and pounded to a blazing hulk, torpedoes finally sending her to the bottom. In both these contests the important factor had been radar, with the US and British ships possessing high-quality search and gunnery systems which enabled them both to achieve surprise and to maintain accurate ranging.

In October 1944 came the last big-gun action in history. In an attempt to stem the tide of the US advance towards Japan, the Combined Fleet was despatched to oppose the American landings in the Philippines. One component of a pincer movement endeavouring to trap US forces in the Surigao Straits included the elderly battleship sisters *Fuso* and *Yamashiro*. Supporting the landings was a force of six US battleships, together with cruisers and destroyers, commanded by Rear Admiral Oldendorf. Vice Admiral Nishimura steamed on, into the US line which stretched across the Straits, waiting. Destroyer attacks were launched, as a result of which both Japanese capital ships were hit, *Fuso* fatally. Finally only *Yamashiro* and the cruiser *Mogami*, both severely damaged, were left. Two of Oldendorf's battleships, the 16in (406mm) gunned *West Virginia* and the 14in (356mm) gunned *Mississippi* delivered the final shells. Never again would battleships join combat.

EPILOGUE

The battleship proved to be a naval weapon of immense durability, and though fleets of big-gun warships have vanished from the inventories of the world's navies, some examples still remain. A few are preserved in the USA, silent memorials to a bygone age. Togo's flagship from Tsushima can be inspected by visitors to Japan, and as these words are written the progenitor of the armour-clad line-of-battle ship, HMS *Warrior*, is being restored to her former beauty in the United Kingdom. A handful of veterans, the American Iowas, are in the process of being recommissioned as hybrid gun/missile carriers and will no doubt remain in service for some years to come. But just as explosive shells and advances in gunnery technology doomed the wooden ship of the line, so have a combination of aircraft, radar and missiles provided the ultimate answer to the armoured big-gun battleship. The Soviet rocket cruiser *Kirov*, however, shows a possible way forward. No doubt the current mistresses of the seas, the aircraft carrier on the surface and the submarine below, will in turn be rendered obsolete in some as yet unexplored future.

1860-1869

The early 1860s marked the acceptance of several innovations in capital ship development whose introduction had been foreshadowed for some time: the efficacy of steam propulsion, first as an auxiliary and then as the primary means of motive power, was recognised; the fact that naval gunnery was poised for great changes, both in the weapons themselves and in the projectiles that would be fired from them, was appreciated and acted upon; the wisdom of protecting ships' hulls by covering vital areas with iron plates was readily grasped; and, in large part a result of these ideas and the consequent increased weight they brought about, iron was adopted for construction rather than wood. At the same time, this was a period of great uncertainty in ship design, with no recognisable themes developing, simply because of the varying approaches to accommodating these novel features.

ARMOUR

European armour plate was made by hammering or rolling several thin plates of wrought iron into a greater thickness. Any blow on these plates was localised: the shock was not transmitted to the bolts or to adjacent parts of the structure. Wrought iron armour was extensively used in the 1860s, but as it increased in thickness—to 14in (356mm) by the early 1870s—to counter the growing power of guns, difficulties arose in achieving the necessary homogeneity of the material.

In America the armour plate industry was not sufficiently advanced to permit the production of solid plates. Although laminated armour had only two-thirds the resisting power of solid plate of the same thickness, it was used even on the largest sea-going monitors; in the Kalamazoo class, several 1in (25mm) plates were bolted together to achieve the desired thickness. All the smaller Union monitors employed in the attack on Charleston in 1863 had laminated armour, and when shot struck their turrets the bolts securing the plates were forced out and sent hurtling around in the confined space of turret and pilot house. Some monitors had a sheet iron screen fitted internally to counter this hazard.

One measure to strengthen the monitors' armour, used on the huge turret of the *Dictator*, was to have an inner layer of 4 x 1in (25mm) plates separated from an outer layer of 6 x 1in (25mm) plates by curved segments of iron, 5in (127mm) wide, which fitted into the gap.

On its riverine ironclads, the Confederate States Navy employed armour made up of rolled railroad irons, usually laid on at an angle to increase resisting power. This armour was not of high quality—and the South's railroad system was soon reduced to chaos as the authorities commandeered every available piece of track for conversion into armour.

GUNS

Before the 1850s, all naval guns were muzzle-loading smoothbores, but in the decade preceding the completion of the *Warrior* rifled guns firing elongated projectiles with ogival heads began to make their appearance. Since the smoothbores in service at the beginning of the period were unable to pierce the armour protecting the first ironclads, efforts were soon made to produce more powerful weapons with greater penetrative qualities.

In America the smoothbore was preferred. It was argued that the racking effect—crushing and breaking up

861499

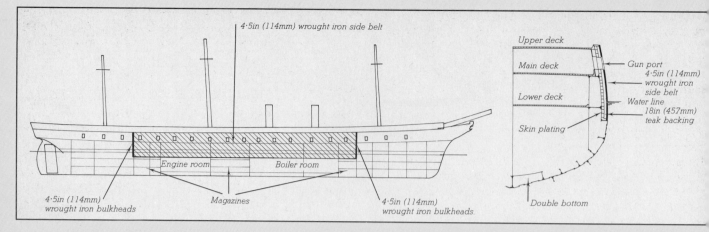

4·5in (114mm) wrought iron side belt

Upper deck
Main deck
Gun port
4·5in (114mm) wrought iron side belt
Lower deck
Water line
18in (457mm) teak backing
Skin plating
Engine room
Boiler room
4·5in (114mm) wrought iron bulkheads
Magazines
4·5in (114mm) wrought iron bulkheads
Double bottom

the armour—of large smoothbores was more damaging than the effect of rifled guns, the early examples of the latter being poorly made and thus able to employ only small charges. However, when better materials were used for rifled guns, higher gas pressures were possible, giving higher velocities and greater penetration. Tests made in 1867 would show that against moderate armour the heavy smoothbore inflicted far more damage than the smaller rifled gun, which simply punched holes in the armour. Against thicker armour, however, the smoothbore was less successful and the rifled gun proved to be very much more effective.

Dahlgren's cast iron smoothbores, in which the thickness of the metal was in proportion to the gas pressure, giving them a characteristically swollen appearance at the vent, were extensively used in the American Civil War and for long afterwards, guns of up to 20in (508mm) calibre being cast. Cast iron rifled guns on the Parrott system were also tried, but were not considered to be successful. The Confederacy produced large numbers of Brooke cast iron rifled guns with wrought iron reinforcing bands.

The 8in (203mm) cast iron smoothbores of the *Warrior*, each weighing 4·75 tons (4·83 tonnes), were the most powerful guns afloat in the Royal Navy in 1860. Armstrong then introduced a rifled breechloader that promised greater range, accuracy and penetration. However, these breechloaders were found to be too complex and to be subject to bore flaws, and thus prone to accidents: during the attack on Japanese forces at Kagoshima in August 1863, there were 28 accidents out of 365 rounds fired.

Although Armstrong felt that the problems could be solved in time, the rifled breechloaders were withdrawn from service. To replace them, Armstrong developed a rifled muzzle-loader made up of wrought iron coils shrunk over a steel inner tube. This was adopted by the Royal Navy and, in principle, by other naval powers.

The world's leading ordnance works—including Krupp in Germany; the newly-formed Obukov company in Russia; and Whitworth, developer of the 'all steel' gun, in the UK—made considerable progress. They were matched by the British Army's ordnance works at Woolwich, headed by Fraser, which produced a gun similar to the Armstrong but constructed of fewer components and thus cheaper to manufacture.

Unlike the Royal Navy, which relied upon the Woolwich works, the French Navy was responsible for either ordering its equipment from private contractors or manufacturing its own guns. It experienced many problems with its guns, which were reinforced with layers of steel hoops. France made good initial progress with rifled breechloaders, but the enormous cost of replacing the great number of smoothbores in service was so daunting that the French Navy was forced to persist with cast iron weapons until the mid-1870s.

Above: The armour scheme of HMS *Warrior*. The hull was protected amidships by wrought iron plating; not shown in these drawings is the advanced system of subdivision incorporated in the unarmoured ends, which helped reduce the level of flooding if damaged in action.

Below: A British 12in, 35-ton (305mm 35·6-tonne) muzzle-loading rifled gun, shown in cross-section. In essence, it comprised a steel lining over which were shrunk wrought iron coils or barrels. Muzzle-loaders were retained in Royal Navy service until well into the 1880s.

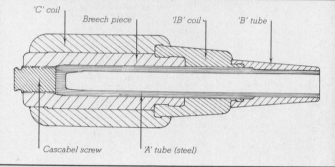

'C' coil
Breech piece
'IB' coil
'B' tube
Cascabel screw
'A' tube (steel)

During the 1860s, when 1,000 yards (914m) was accepted as the typical battle range, there was a constant race for supremacy between guns and armour. By 1865, a 9in (229mm) gun weighing 12 tons (12·2 tonnes) and firing a 250lb (113kg) projectile was capable of piercing 10in (254mm) of armour. Even this creditable performance was soon to be outclassed.

MINES AND TORPEDOES

Mines (then called torpedoes) came into prominence during the American Civil War, when they played a major role in protecting the harbours and estuaries of the South. As well as stationary mines of both the remotely-detonated and contact types, spar torpedoes were used: launches and

primitive submersibles were rigged with pole-mounted explosive charges that detonated on contact. A total of 28 vessels was destroyed in the Civil War by mines and spar torpedoes.

MACHINERY

Early steam-driven warships were propelled by paddles and had exposed side lever beam engines virtually identical to those originally designed by Watt. The vacuum was maintained by injecting water into the steam after exhausting it from an unjacketed cylinder into a jet condenser. The use of salt feed water quickly degraded boiler performance; nor were paddles suitable for warships, because of their vulnerability.

The introduction of the screw propeller gave greater safety from enemy fire. Now faster-running machinery could be made lighter and the engine—in 1860, the simple horizontal type—could be protected. A single propeller was fitted on the centre line, dictating a short piston stroke and connecting rod. The introduction of return connecting rod engines and trunk engines allowed a longer stroke and longer connecting rods in a restricted area. Compound engines improved considerably; their introduction was at first opposed, but as their superior economy became evident they were more readily accepted.

Boilers were of the box type, with a pressure of 20 psi. Tubes were used to increase the heating surface and higher steam pressures were achieved. Surface condensers found favour: they enabled purer water to be used, reducing fouling and increasing the vacuum, and thus permitting yet higher steam pressures. Superheating, in which 'dry' steam was used in the cylinders to produce greater economy, was briefly tried.

Left: *Catskill* was one of a large class of US low freeboard monitors completed in the early 1860s; the single turret, which dominates this 1865 photograph, carried one 11in (279mm) Dahlgren (visible) and one 15in (381mm) Dahlgren, which latter fired from behind the gun port rather than through it. The weapons either side are probably 12pdr smoothbore howitzers. Note the pilot-house atop the turret.

Above left: One of USS *Kearsarge's* two 11in (279mm) smoothbores, seen here in June 1864, showing clearly the slide along which it was run out—a refinement of the time-honoured carriage truck system. Also visible, on deck, is part of the track that facilitated gun training. Many 11in (279mm) Dahlgrens were relined down to 8in (203mm) rifles in the 1870s, at the instigation of Captain Jeffers.

Above: The US-built French ironclad *Rochambeau*, formerly the USS *Dunderberg*, reflected Civil War experience and was broadly similar in concept to the famous *Merrimack*. As with many US designs of the period, freeboard and sea-going qualities were sacrificed in favour of structural strength, a heavy armament and thick armour. The funnel dominates the upperworks, but the ship is brigantine-rigged.

GLOIRE

1860 France
Other ships in class: *Invincible, Normandie*

Laid down: March 1858.
Launched: 24 November 1859.
Builder: Toulon Dockyard.
Displacement: 5,630 tons (5,720 tonnes).
Dimensions: 255ft 6in (77·88m) wl x 55ft 9in (16·99m) x 27ft 10in (8·48m) max.
Machinery: Horizontal Return Connecting Rod engines; 8 oval boilers; 1 shaft; 2500 IHP.
Armour: Iron 4·75 (121mm) belt; 26in (660mm) backing; 4·5in (114mm) battery; 4in (102mm) conning tower.
Armament: 36 x 6.4in (163mm) RML.

Performance: 13kt (24km/h); coal 665 tons (676 tonnes).
Crew: 570.

Dupuy de Lôme, designer of the *Gloire*, submitted proposals for an armoured frigate as early as 1845. He planned to use iron rather than wood for the hull, achieving a saving in weight of *c*20 per cent which would be devoted to an armoured belt 6·5in (165mm) thick at the waterline and 8ft (2·44m) in depth. The project was rejected; notably, because a 6·5in (165mm) belt of laminated or single plates would not be shot proof, and because the battery would be unprotected. However, tests on armoured floating batteries proved that the elasticity of wood backing, which also served for framing, aided armour in its resistance to shot.

The success of the French floating

Above: *Gloire* photographed in the 1860s. The life span of France's early wooden-hulled ironclads was relatively short: *Gloire*'s two sisters lasted only about 10 years.

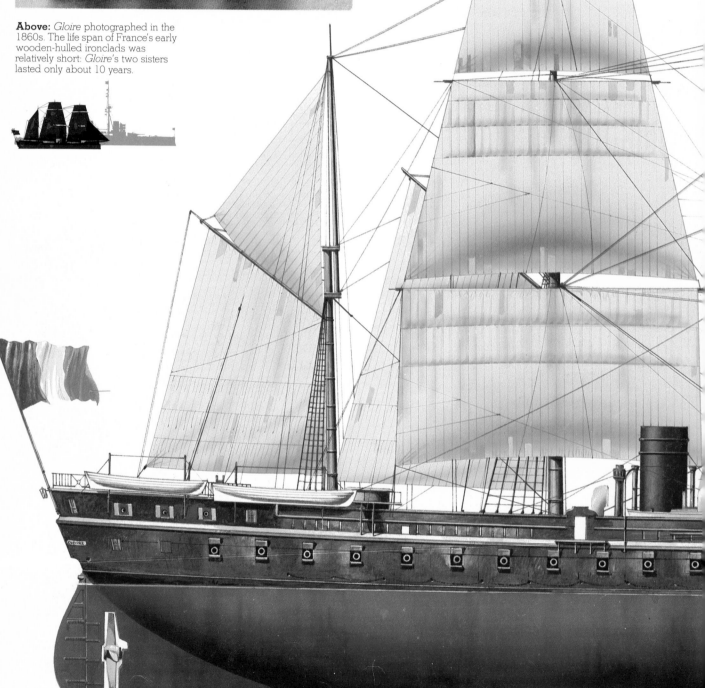

atteries in the bombardment of nburn on the Black Sea, 17 ctober 1855, during the Crimean ar, decided the *Conseil des avaux de la Marine* to sanction a ea-going ironclad. Dupuy de Lôme's ans, submitted in November 1857, ere quickly approved and the onstruction of *Gloire* began at oulon in March 1858.

Dupuy de Lôme was convinced at in an action between two ships ith equal armament, protection, eed and sea-keeping qualities, the naller vessel would have the dvantage. He therefore fixed the splacement of *Gloire* at 5,620 tons ,710 tonnes). This was 500 tons 08 tonnes) more than his earlier nasterpiece, the 92-gun, wooden, crew line-of-battle ship *Napoleon*, hich made 13·86kt (25·64km/h), ut he planned to achieve a similar

speed on the same horsepower in *Gloire* by lengthening the hull by 19ft 6in (5·94m) while retaining the same beam and draught. The finer lines of *Gloire* also contributed to speed by reducing her immersed midship section.

The great increase in weight of the ship's side and the elimination of one deck raised problems over the transverse strength of the vessel. These were solved by fitting a 0·375in (10mm) layer of sheet metal beneath the wooden upper deck, securely fixed to the hull sides.

In February 1859 several companies submitted 4·75in (121mm) armour plate for trials, among them Schneider, who had furnished the armour for the floating batteries, and Petit et Gaudet. Tests with 68pdr smoothbores showed Petit et Gaudet's armour to be

superior, no plates being pierced—and also proved that it was possible to manufacture armour of a consistently high quality, which had not always been the case. Another result was the replacement of the smoothbores originally planned for *Gloire* by rifled 68pdrs.

Gloire had a complete belt extending from 6ft (1·83m) below the waterline to the upper deck. It was 4·75in (121mm) thick with 26in (660mm) oak backing at the waterline, and 4·5in (114mm) backed by 24in (610mm) of wood in wake of the battery. The backing formed the skin, framework and backing proper. The armour plates were screwed into place rather than bolted, since tests showed that bolts flew off when the plates were struck by shot. The original plans called for the armour to be fitted in three layers, but instead

solid plates were used, with eight strakes over the battery and five in the waterline area.

Thirty-four 6·4in (163mm) RML were carried in the battery, 6ft 2in (1·88m) above water, and two more were mounted on the upper deck. All were soon replaced by breechloaders of the same calibre. Later a lesser number of more powerful 6·4in (163mm) were mounted, along with 12 x 55pdr and, on the upper deck, four shell guns converted to 8·8in (224mm) howitzers.

Gloire was removed from the Navy list in 1879, her two sister ships having been stricken in the early 1870s when their hulls were found to be unsound. *Normandie,* however, had achieved the distinction of being the first armoured ship to cross the Atlantic in July 1862.

Below: With the broadside frigate *Gloire,* the great naval architect Dupuy de Lôme laid the foundation of a French ironclad fleet that only Britain could rival.

WARRIOR

1861 *UK*
Other ships in class: *Black Prince*

Laid down: 25 May 1859.
Launched: 29 December 1860.
Builder: Ditchburn and Mare, Blackwall, London.
Displacement: 9,137 tons (9,283 tonnes).
Dimensions: 420ft (128m) oa x 58ft 4in (17·78m) x 26ft (7·92m).
Machinery: Penn Horizontal Single Expansion Trunk engines; 10 rectangular boilers; 1 shaft; 5267 IHP.
Armour: Iron 4·5in (114mm) belt; 18in (457mm) wood backing; 4·5in (114mm) bulkheads.
Armament: 10 x 110pdr BL; 4 x 70pdr BL; 26 x 68pdr SB.
Performance: 14·08kt (26km/h); coal 850 tons (864 tonnes).
Crew: 707.

France and Britain, allies during the Crimean War, soon began to show mutual distrust. In Britain, there were fears of a Franco-Russian alliance; in France, revelations that the Orsini assassination conspiracy against Napoleon III had been planned in Britain raised Anglophobia to a frightening level. Against this unhappy background, Britain realized that France had gained parity in the production of fast, steam-driven ships-of-the-line. British superiority was soon reasserted — the number of wooden, screw line-of-battle ships completed rose from 29 in early 1859 to 40 in mid-1860 — but France was not idle meanwhile. The laying down of *Gloire* and her consorts opened a new era of warship construction and increased Britain's fear of her rival. Thus, *Warrior,* ordered in May 1859, and her sister ship ordered in October of the same year, were designed to overtake and destroy any warship then in service.

The size of *Warrior's* battery was dictated by the intention to mount 40 guns at 15ft (4·57m) intervals, and the requirement for great speed also influenced her design. She emerged with a length 6·5 times greater than her beam; almost the same proportion as in the large, fast wooden frigates of the Mersey class.

Right: *Black Prince* in the early 1870s, showing the graceful lines of the ship-rigged vessel. She and *Warrior* were the last British capital ships to carry figureheads.

But unlike those ships, whose proportions were limited by the size of the timbers that could be used, the iron-hulled *Warrior's* size was limited only by the capacity of the docks available.

To ensure that she attained the high speed specified, the forward part of the vessel had a V-shaped transverse section and, to ensure buoyancy, wa[s] left unarmoured. Amidships, *Warrio[r]* was protected by a belt of 4·5in (114mm) armour, 213ft (64·92m) long and 22ft (6·7m) in depth, with 18in (457mm) teak backing. The potential danger of battle damage t[o] the unarmoured ends was offset by the provision of 92 watertight

compartments, although the fact that the steering gear was left unprotected by the unarmoured stern caused some concern.

Outside the battery, the hull was made up of thin plating without backing, resembling the plating of the Simoon class frigates which had been downgraded to troopships.

Even though *Warrior* was to prove a success, doubts were expressed at the Admiralty over the next batch of ironclads, and a study was requested to determine whether they could be used as transports, with their armour removed.

On completion, *Warrior* received four new 110pdr Armstrong BLR

and 13 x 68pdr on each side, with two more 110pdrs on the upper deck. It was planned that she should later be armed entirely with 110pdrs — such an armament making it possible to mount fewer guns and thus reduce the number carried outside the armoured area — but the Armstrong BLRs

proved unsatisfactory. Her 1867 armament of 28 x 7in (178mm) MLR, 4 x 8in (203mm) MLR and 4 x 20pdr BL marked the beginning of the Royal Navy's 20-year period of return to the muzzle-loader.

Warrior's generous bunkerage was dictated by the needs of her uneconomical boilers and engines. It had been suggested that four or five iron masts should be shipped, but she was given a full rig similar to that of an 80-gun ship. She could make 13kt (24km/h) under sail and on one occasion, under both sail and steam, made 17·5kt (32·4km/h)

Warrior served with the Channel Fleet, and in 1868 was involved in a collision with *Royal Oak*. She had become a coastguard ship by 1875 and in the 1880s was classified as an armoured cruiser. She was a torpedo depot and training ship until she was hulked in 1923, becoming an oil pipeline pontoon at Milford Haven. In 1979 she was taken to Hartlepool for restoration.

Left: *Black Prince* seen with funnels raised (compare with the photograph opposite). The two funnels were telescopic, and were lowered when the ship was moving under sail only, as opposed to using sail and steam.

Below: Flying the Red Ensign, *Warrior,* designed by Isaac Watts, is shown soon after completion in 1861.

Below: *Defence* as completed, with the white painted strake formerly carried by wooden frigates.

DEFENCE

1861 *UK*
Other ships in class: *Resistance*

Laid down: December 1859.
Launched: 24 April 1861.
Builder: Palmers, Jarrow.
Displacement: 6,150 tons (6,248 tonnes) load.
Dimensions: 302ft (92·04m) x 54ft (16·46m) x 25ft (7·62m).
Machinery: Penn Trunk engines; 4 rectangular boilers; 1 shaft; 2540 IHP.
Armour: Wrought iron 4·5in (114mm) with 18in (457mm) wood backing belt; 4·5in (114mm) bulkheads.
Armament: 8 x 7in (178mm) BL; 10 x 68pdr; 4 x 5in (127mm) BL.
Performance: 11·6kt (21·5km/h); coal 460 tons (467 tonnes).
Crew: 460.

When the first ironclads for the Royal Navy were under consideration, doubts were expressed concerning the high cost of repeating the type. Together with the fact that only two docks were available to take such long vessels, this prompted the Board to order plans for a smaller ship, with the same protection and still carrying the heaviest guns available.

Plans were submitted in November 1859 by Sir Baldwin Walker, the Controller, who explained that in such a design, with the available engine power, only 10·5kts (19·4km/h) could be achieved: slower than the French *Gloire*. Because fears were now being expressed at the growth of the French fleet, Walker proposed building six of these units: although earlier, when the *Black Prince* contract was being considered, he had persuaded the Board not to build smaller vessels.

Only two ships were authorized. Some felt that the day of wooden line-of-battle ships was not yet over; so while the Royal Dockyards continued to build wooden vessels, private yards constructed the second pair of ironclads. Although they exceeded designed speed by more than 1kt (1·85km/h), they proved inferior to their French rivals in speed, armament, protection and sea keeping qualities. The armoured belt was 140ft (42·7m) long and the ends of the vessels and the steering gear

were left unprotected. Instead of the clipper bow of *Warrior*, a ram bow was fitted. Original armament was to have been 18 x 68pdr, but on completion they shipped 8 x 7in (178mm), 10 x 68pdr and 4 x 5in (127mm). They were rearmed in 1867 with 2 x 8in (203mm) MLR and 14 x 7in (178mm) MLR.

Slowness in answering the helm nearly led to *Defence's* loss in a gale: in 1864 she was modified to ship rig, reverting to barque during the 1866-68 refit. *Defence* decommissioned in 1885, was renamed *Indus* in 1898, and hulked in 1922.

MAGENTA

1862 *France*
Other ships in class: *Solferino*

Laid down: 22 June 1859.
Launched: 22 June 1861.
Builder: Brest.
Displacement: 6,715 tons (6,822 tonnes).
Dimensions: 282ft (85·95m) wl x 56ft 8in (172·27m) x 27ft 8in (8·43m) max.
Machinery: Horizontal Return Connecting Rod engine; 9 oval boilers; 3450 IHP.
Armour: Wrought iron 4·7in (119mm) belt; 4·7in (119mm) battery.
Armament: 16 x 55pdr SB; 34 x 6·4in (163mm) BL; 2 x 8·8in (224mm) RML howitzers.
Performance: 13kt (24·05km/h).
Crew: 674.

Magenta and *Solferino*, the final element of France's ambitious initial programme, were the only two-decked broadside ironclads built, although four more were originally planned for 1859 and plans were submitted by eight naval constructors.

De Moras proposed a ship of 7,967 tons (8,094 tonnes), making 13·5kt (25km/h), with 56 guns on two decks, the lower armoured along its entire length but the upper covered only amidships. Also suggested was a wooden vessel with 38 guns on two levels, behind armour amidships; its ends would be of iron to reduce fire risk. Another plan, judged unstable, resembled *Gloire* with a greatly reduced beam. Neither these plans nor suggestions for armouring wooden ships-of-the-line found favour; although the latter, as permitting utilization of existing

ships, was seriously considered.

Dupuy de Lôme suggested that one ship should be an adaptation of de Moras's design. For the other three, he himself submitted plans based upon confidential details, in French possession, of the British *Warrior*. Determined that French ships should be faster and at least as well armed as their English rivals, de Lôme planned for more guns and greater speed and range than in the vessels already building. Displacing 6,724 tons (6,832 tonnes) and making 14kt (25·9km/h), his ships carried 52 rifled 30-pounders. Armour ran the length of the waterline, although the wooden ends above the shallow belt were unprotected, and was concentrated amidships where the guns were housed on main and upper decks. Shotproof transverse bulkheads protected the battery from raking fire. The two-tier placing gave the upper guns increased elevation and lightened the ends of the vessel. The lower battery was 6ft 3in (1·9m) above water; the height of the upper tier was 14ft (4·27m).

On completion (at a cost of some 6 million francs each), the lower deck housed 16 x 55pdr and 10 x 6·4in (163mm), with 24 x 6·4in (163mm) above. Howitzers were on the upper deck. Later rearmament updated the 6·4in (163mm) guns and replaced the main deck guns with 4 x 9·4in

(239mm) and 4 x 7·6in (193mm), plus 4 x 7·6in (193mm) on the upper deck. In 1867-68, the main deck was rearmed with 10 x 9·4in (239mm).

On 31 October 1875, a fire took hold in *Magenta's* wardroom galley and the ship exploded and sank.

SALAMANDER

1862 *Austria-Hungary*
Other ships in class: *Drache*

Laid down: February 1861.
Launched: August 1861.
Builder: Stabilimento Tecnico Triestino (STT).
Displacement: 3,027 tons (3,075 tonnes).
Dimensions: 206ft (62·8m) pp x 45ft 8in (13·9m) x 20ft 7in (6·3m).
Machinery: 2-cylinder Horizontal LP engine, 1 shaft; 2,060 IHP.
Armour: 119mm belt amidships.
Armament: 14 x 48pdr; 14 x 15cm.
Performance: 11·36kt (21km/h).
Crew: 343.

Under the far-sighted command of the ill-fated Archduke (Ferdinand) Maximilian, the Austrian Navy soon

Below: *Magenta*, originally
barquentine rigged, as barque (1864)
with 21,000ft² (1,951m²) of canvas.
Her long ram bow, cutaway stern
and two gun tiers look impressive.

entered the ironclad race with two
small, wooden, broadside armoured
rigates, *Salamander* and *Drache*,
designed by Joseph von Romako.

The Styrian iron armour belt ran
the full length of the vessel's waterline
and rose in height forward of the
foremast to protect the battery. But
although the armour was of high
quality, Austria's industrial resources
were limited: the guns were of an old
pattern, and at the Battle of Lissa
1866) proved inferior to the Italian
rifled guns. *Salamander*, serving in
the First Division at Lissa, was struck
35 times without receiving serious
damage.

Salamander was refitted in
1867-68, when her sail area was
increased to 11,733ft² (1,090m²).
Stricken in 1883, she served
thereafter as a mine store ship and
was scrapped in 1895-96.

Above: The first iron-hulled capital
ship laid down, *Couronne* remained
afloat for 70 years.

Below: *Salamander* as built. She
and *Drache* were the first ships in a
fast-growing Austrian ironclad fleet.

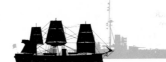

COURONNE

1862 France

Laid down: 14 February 1859.
Launched: 28 March 1861.
Builder: Lorient.
Displacement: 6,076 tons
(6,173 tonnes).
Dimensions: 262ft 5in (79·98m)
wl x 54ft 9in (16·69m) x 26ft
11in (8·2m) max.
Machinery: Horizontal Return
Connecting Rod engines; 8 oval
boilers; 2900 IHP.

Armour: Wrought iron 4in (102mm)
to 3·2in (81mm) belt.
Armament: 30 x 6·4in (163mm);
10 x 55pdr.
Performance: 13kt (24·05km/h);
coal 650/1,000 tons (660/1,016
tonnes).
Crew: 570.

Satisfactory tests with a target
representing the armoured sides of
an iron-hulled ironclad designed by
Audenet led to the acceptance of his
plans for *Couronne*. She was the
first iron-hulled capital ship laid down
and the longest-lasting; proving, at a
cost of some 6 million francs, both a
better investment and a better sea
boat than her wooden-hulled
contemporaries.

A full-length belt protected the
36-gun battery, 7ft (2·1m) above
water, with 4 x 6·4in (163mm) guns
on the upper deck. An armoured
deck of 0·5in (12mm) sheet iron
supported by wood and iron beams
protected against plunging fire, but
did not extend over engines and
boilers.

Several armament changes ended
in 8 x 9·4in (239mm) and 4 x 7·6in
(193mm) in the battery, plus smaller
on the upper deck. Conversion to a
gunnery training ship in 1881-85
involved removal of armour and an
added poop and light iron spar deck.
Hulked in 1910, *Couronne* was still
afloat in 1932.

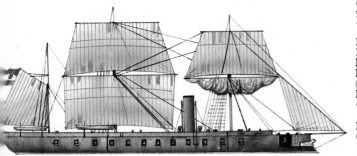

NEW IRONSIDES

1862 USA

Laid down: 1862.
Launched: May 1862.
Builder: Cramp's Shipyard, Philadelphia.
Displacement: 3,486 tons (3,523 tonnes).
Dimensions: 230ft (70m) x 57ft 6in (17·6m) x 15ft 8in (4·78m).
Machinery: 2 Horizontal Direct Acting; 1 screw; 700hp.
Armour: Iron 4in (102mm) sides; 1in (25·4mm) deck.
Armament: 2 x 150pdr; 2 x 50pdr 14 x 11in (279mm) smoothbore.
Performance: 8kt (14·8km/h) planned; 6kt (11·1km/h) actual.
Crew: 449 (460).

On 3 August 1861 Congress voted $1,500,000 for the construction of ironclads to combat the growing number of Confederate armoured vessels then building. Three designs were selected of which *New Ironsides* was the most conventional.

The contract was awarded to Merrick and Sons who furnished the engines and armour while the hull was built by Cramp's Shipyard from designs produced by B. Bartol and Charles Cramp. Supplying the heavy timber proved a problem and the surrounding country was denuded of suitable trees. The battery was 170 feet (51·8m) long and was originally intended to carry 8 inch (203mm) weapons but 11 inch (279mm) guns were substituted. These had no axial fire, and the narrow ports only allowed 4·5° of turn.

Although Turner, her captain, considered the vessel a good sea boat the engines were not powerful enough and her best speed was only 6·5kt (12km/h). Further, the coal consumption was 40 tons (40·6 tonnes) per day—not the estimated 25 tons—which restricted her range considerably.

She served as the flagship of Rear Admiral Du Pont during the abortive attack upon Charleston in April 1863 and was struck hundreds of times, including torpedo attack, without sustaining major damage. The rig was reduced to pole masts, and sandbags were packed onto the upper deck and at the ends of the vessel to improve protection. *New Ironsides* was destroyed by fire in December 1866.

PERVENETZ

1862 Russia
Other ships in class: *Netron Menya*

Laid down: 1861.
Launched: 1862.
Builder: Thames Ironworks.
Displacement: 3,277 tons (3,330 tonnes).
Dimensions: 221ft 9in (67·6m) x 53ft (16·1m) x 14ft 9in (4·5m).
Machinery: Rectangular boilers; 1 screw; 1600 IHP.
Armour: Wrought iron 4·5in (114mm) sides; 4·5in (114mm) CC.
Armament: 34 x 8in (203mm) 9 ton smoothbore plus smaller. Later 6 x 8in (203mm); 9 x 6in (152mm) plus smaller.
Performance: 9kt (16·6km/h); 250/500 tons (254/508 tonnes) coal.
Crew: 395 (later 260).

A broadside, iron-hulled, schooner-rigged ironclad, *Pervenetz* was designed with a pronounced tumblehome of 15 per cent which greatly increased the resisting power of the armour. The hull was

Below: *New Ironsides* in March 1863 prior to the attack on Charleston.

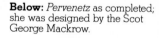

Below: *Pervenetz* as completed; she was designed by the Scot George Mackrow.

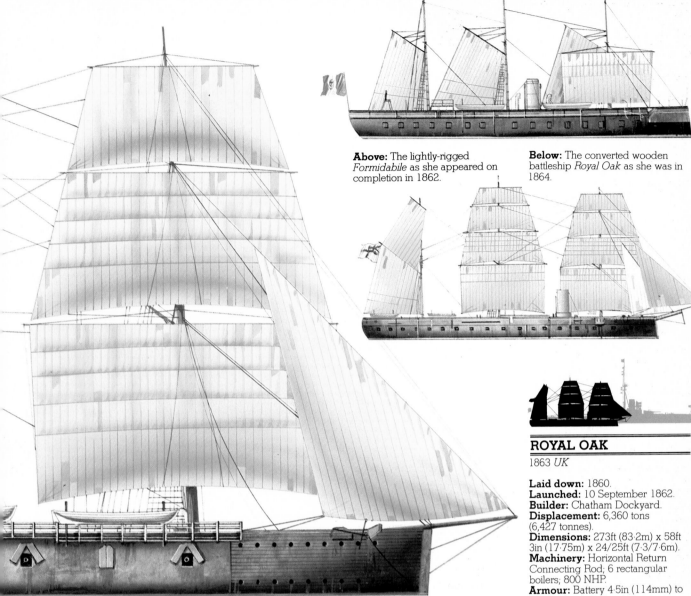

Above: The lightly-rigged *Formidabile* as she appeared on completion in 1862.

Below: The converted wooden battleship *Royal Oak* as she was in 1864.

ROYAL OAK

1863 *UK*

Laid down: 1860.
Launched: 10 September 1862.
Builder: Chatham Dockyard.
Displacement: 6,360 tons (6,427 tonnes).
Dimensions: 273ft (83·2m) x 58ft 3in (17·75m) x 24/25ft (7·3/7·6m).
Machinery: Horizontal Return Connecting Rod; 6 rectangular boilers; 800 NHP.
Armour: Battery 4·5in (114mm) to 3in (76·2mm); belt 4in-3in (102mm/76·2mm).
Armament: 8 x 7in (178mm) BLR. 24 x 68pdr.
Performance: 12·5kt (23km/h); range 2,200nm (4,074km) at 5kt (9·25km/h); coal 550 tons (559 tonnes).
Crew: 585.

Britain's reaction to the large French naval programme of 1860 was swift, yet still overlain with caution with regard to the different types to be developed. It had even been suggested that Britain should come to an agreement with France in 1861 over limiting the number of ironclads but still leaving Britain with a clear superiority.

In view of the progress being made in France, and while awaiting the results of the *Warrior*, it was decided in May 1861 to convert some of the wooden battleships then on the stocks into ironclads. *Royal Oak* was the first to be chosen and lengthened by 21 feet (6·4m) to carry its battery on one deck. As this was a wooden vessel, there could be no watertight subdivision nor bulkhead between the engine and boiler-room. She was handy under steam and sail although a heavy roller, but was considered an unsteady gun platform. *Royal Oak* was rearmed in 1867. She was in collision with *Warrior* in fog and ran aground at the opening of the Suez Canal on an uncharted bank. She was laid up in 1871 as an economy measure, and sold in 1885.

completely armoured above the waterline and had a projecting bow and stern. All the guns were carried in the main battery except for three 6in (152mm) in the *Pervenetz* and two 8in (203mm) in *Netron Menya* which were mounted on deck.

The engines of the *Netron Menya* were taken from the wooden screw ship *Konstantin*. Both ships of this class eventually served in the Gunnery Training Squadron where each carried a wide variety of guns. *Pervenetz* was stricken in 1905.

FORMIDABILE

1862 *Italy*
Other ships in class: *Terribile*

Laid down: December 1860.
Launched: 1861.
Builder: La Seyne.
Displacement: 2,725 tons (2,754 tonnes).
Dimensions: 215ft 10in (65·8m) x 47ft 3in (14·4m) x 17ft 10in (5·4m).
Machinery: 6 rectangular boilers; 1 screw; 1080 HP.
Armour: Iron belt 4·3in (109mm); citadel 4in (102mm).
Armament: 16 x 6·5in (165mm) ML; 4 x 8in (203mm) guns.
Performance: 10kt (18·52km/h). Range c1,300nm (2,410km) at 10kt (18·52km/h).
Crew: 371.

As early as 1856 the leading Italian artillerist, Cavalli, proposed three ironclad designs and these influenced the far-sighted Minister of Marine, Cavour, to order in 1860 the first Italian ironclads from France.

Originally intended as armoured coast defence floating batteries carrying 30 guns, these ships underwent a dramatic change before completion and emerged as 20 gun ocean-going corvettes with their sides completely armoured.

Both ships took part in the attack on the defences of the island of Lissa on 18/19 July 1866 when *Formidabile*, almost alone, fought several batteries at a range of only 300 yards (274m). After a fierce action *Formidabile* was forced to retire with severe damage, at one stage closing all the ports to stop the entry of shot. As a result of her damage this vessel did not take part in the naval battle of Lissa.

She was reboilered in 1872-3 and her armament was altered to eight 8in (203mm) guns. This was changed again in 1887 to six 4·7in (119mm) guns when *Formidabile* became a gunnery training ship. She was discarded in 1904.

Below: *Roanoke* in 1864, when in deep-draught use in coastal waters.

ROANOKE

1863 *USA*

Laid down: 1853.
Launched: 1855, converted 1862.
Builder: Novelty Iron Works, NY.
Displacement: 6,300 tons (6,401 tonnes).
Dimensions: 265ft (80·77m) x 52ft 6in (16m) x 24ft 3in (7·4m).
Machinery: Two Horizontal Direct. Acting engines; 4 Martin boilers; 1 shaft; 997 HP.
Armour: Iron 11in (279mm) turrets; 4·5in (114mm) sides; 1·5in (38mm) deck; 9in (29mm) pilot house.
Armament: 2 x 15in (381mm) SB; 2 x 11in (279mm) SB; 2 x 150pdr Parrott RML.
Performance: 6kt (11·1km/h); coal 550 tons (559 tonnes).
Crew: 350.

Roanoke, a wooden 40-gun frigate, came near loss at Hampton Roads, 8 March 1862, when the ironclad CSS *Merrimack (Virginia)* attacked the Federal blockading squadron. From May 1862, *Roanoke* was converted to a monitor, her hull being cut down to the battery deck. Three Ericsson turrets were fitted: the fore turret mounted 1 x 15in (381mm) Dahlgren SB and 1 x 150pdr Parrott rifle; the second, 1 x 15in (381mm) and 1 x 11in (279mm) Dahlgren SB; the aft turret 1 x 11in (279mm) and 1 x 150pdr.

Roanoke was not a success, rolling heavily even in a moderate sea. Her hull could not adequately support the great weight of the turrets which, when jacked up for . use, threatened to force out her bottom. She was decommissioned in June 1865 and was sold in 1883.

ROLF KRAKE

1864 *Denmark*

Laid down: 1 December 1862.
Launched: 1863.
Builder: Napier, Glasgow.
Displacement: 1,320 tons (1,341 tonnes).
Dimensions: 183ft 9in (56m) pp x 38ft 2in (11·63m) x 10ft 6in (3·2m) max.
Machinery: 1 screw; 750 IHP.
Armour: Iron 4·5in (114mm) sides; 3in (76mm) ends; 4·5in (114mm) turret; 9in (229mm) backing.
Armament: 4 x 68pdr SB.
Performance: 9·5 kt (17·6km/h); coal 135 tons (137·2 tonnes).
Crew: 150.

Denmark was the first Scandinavian country to build an ironclad fleet of any size, beginning in the 1860s with large, deep-draught, broadside frigates. Because of increasing contention with Prussia over Schleswig-Holstein, the Danes in

1862 decided to build an armoured vessel of monitor type for coastal service. Rough seas were often experienced, so the vessel needed sufficient freeboard to work its guns in a seaway.

Napier received a contract for a small vessel, *Rolf Krake*, carrying two Coles turrets. Similar ships were soon demanded by other navies; notably Russia, which first ordered *Smerch* (1,460 tons; 1,483 tonnes), completed 1865. Four more twin turreted units, from 2,100 to 3,900 tons (2,134 tonnes to 3,962 tonnes), and two triple-turreted ships of 3,800 tons (3,861 tonnes) were completed by 1870. Although powerful, their low freeboard limited them to coastal defence: they would not have been able to cope with the larger, high-sided, ocean-going ironclads of Britian or France.

Completed for £74,000, *Rolf Krake* had a continuous armoured belt extending from 3ft (0·91m) below the waterline to the height of the main deck (itself with 1·5in, 38mm, plate) 3ft (0·91m) above it. There was an armoured conning tower aft, and hinged bulwarks were lowered in action. Four 68pdrs were carried, two in each turret. In 1867, the two forward guns were replaced by 1 x 8in (203mm) MLR; the after turret was similarly converted in 1878. In 1885, 2 x 3·4in (86mm) Krupp guns and 4 x 1pdr revolving cannon were added. The original three-masted schooner rig was reduced to two pole masts in 1878.

When war with Prussia and Austria broke out, the Danes established a partial blockade of Prussia—but on land the Prussians soon drove back the Danish Army. On 9 June 1864, *Rolf Krake* engaged enemy artillery during an unsuccessful attempt to prevent Prussian troops crossing the channel between Schleswig and Alsen (Als). She became a gunnery training ship in 1893 and was sold in 1907.

Below: *Rolf Krake*, 1864. The first warship to carry Coles turrets, she was ideal for inshore operations.

KAISER MAX

1863 *Austria-Hungary*
Other ships in class: *Prinz Eugen, Juan de Austria.*

Laid down: October 1861.
Launched: 14 March 1862.
Builder: Stabilimento Tecnico Triestino.
Displacement: 3,588 tons (3,645 tonnes).
Dimensions: 230ft 7in (70·28m) x 42ft 2in (12·85m) x 20ft 9in (6·32m) mean.
Machinery: Two cylinder Horizontal engine; 1 shaft, 1926 IHP.
Armour: 4·3in (110mm) belt.
Armament: 16 x 48pdr SB; 14 x 24pdr rifles; 2 x 4pdr.
Performance: 11·4kt (21·1km/h).
Crew: 386.

Below: *Kaiser Max*, 1863; open bow.

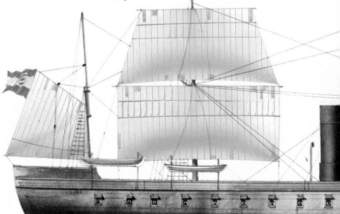

The wooden-hulled *Kaiser Max* and her two sisters were enlarged ships of the Salamander class, with uprated engines, more guns and a sternchase casemate. The bow section, at first open, was later plated over in an attempt to improve sea-keeping qualities: the ships pitched alarmingly and were very wet.

At the time they were built, Austria suffered from both poor industrial capacity and conflict with Hungarian interests: the latter nation opposing all plans for a powerful fleet. Not until about 1910 did the Austro-Hungarian Monarchy seriously attempt to build a fleet to match those of other European powers of the time.

In the First Division at Lissa, *Kaiser Max* was hit 28 times as ships passed within pistol shot of each other in the general melee. The class was rearmed in 1867, with 12 x 7in (178mm), plus smaller.

Within a few years the wooden hulls were badly rotted, and since it was easier to obtain funds for repairs rather than for new construction, *Kaiser Max* and *Juan de Austria* were sent to Stabilimento Tecnico Triestino in December 1873, while *Prinz Eugen* went to Pola Navy Yard. Under the guise of "repairs" the trio reappeared in 1876-78 as entirely new vessels: powerful central battery ships, utilizing the original machinery and armour, the wooden hulls having been scrapped.

DANNEBROG

1864 *Denmark*

Laid down: 1850.
Launched (converted): 1863.
Builder: Copenhagen Dockyard.
Displacement: 3,057 tons
(3,106 tonnes).
Dimensions: 214ft 8in (65·43m) x
50ft 10in (15·49m) x 23ft 4in
(7·1m) max.
Machinery: 1 shaft; 1150 IHP.
Armour: Iron 4·5in (114mm).
Armament: 16 x 60pdr.
Performance: 8·7kt (16·1km/h).
Crew: 330.

Dannebrog's conversion from a
wooden, two-decker, sail, 72-gun
line-of-battle ship to a screw
propelled broadside ironclad began
in 1861 and was completed on 30
March 1864. Such conversions were
economically justifiable in the short
term, although wooden hulls had a
limited life-span: *Dannebrog* left
first-line service in 1870.
    Barque-rigged, with a ram bow,
Dannebrog had a final armament of 6
x 8in (203mm) Armstrong rifled guns
and 10 x 6in (152mm) rifles. She was
stricken in 1898-99.

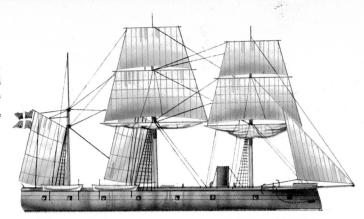

Above: The wooden-hulled
Dannebrog, converted in 1861-64,
had a very short service career as an
ironclad.

Below: *Brasil* on completion in
Europe. She was built by the private
French yard: F.C. de la Méditerranée
at La Seyne.

BRASIL

1864 *Brazil*

Laid down: 1864.
Launched: 1864.
Builder: La Seyne.
Displacement: 1,518 tons
(1,542 tonnes).
Dimensions: 179ft 8in (54·76m) x
35ft (10·67m) x 12ft 5in (3.78m).
Machinery: Single Expansion
engine; 1 shaft; 975 IHP.
Armour: Iron 4·5-3in (114-76mm)
belt and battery, 8·5in (216mm) wood
backing.
Armament: 4 x 7in (178mm)
Whitworth MLR; 4 x 68pdr.
Performance: 11·3kt (21km/h).
Crew: 210.

Brasil was an iron-hulled central
battery ship with a ram bow. A belt
encircled her waterline to the height
of the main deck and the upper deck
casemate had ports allowing the end
guns to be trained for axial fire. The
only direct access below decks
between the ends was by the
casemate ports. She saw extensive
action in the War of the Triple Alliance
(1864-70) and became a floating
battery in 1887.

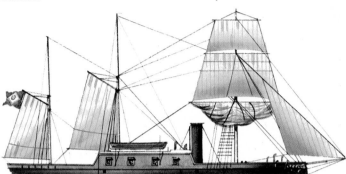

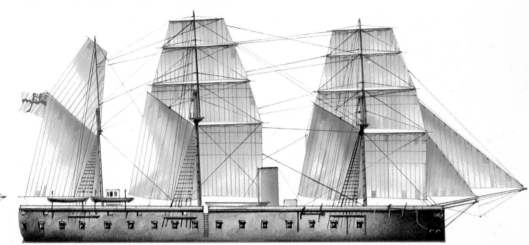

Above: *Hector* during service with
the Channel Squadron in 1864 when
she had double topsails.

HECTOR

1864 *UK*
Other ships in class: *Valiant*

Laid down: March 1861.
Launched: 29 September 1862.
Builder: Napier, Glasgow.
Displacement: 6,710 tons (6,817
tonnes) load; 7,000 tons (7,112
tonnes) actual.
Dimensions: 280ft (85·34m) pp x
56ft 3in (17·14m) x 25ft (7·62m).
Machinery: Return Connecting
Rod engines; 6 boilers; 1 shaft; 3260
IHP.
Armour: 4·5in-2·5in (114-64mm)
main deck battery; 4·5in
(114mm) belt; 4·5in (114mm)
bulkhead.
Armament: 4 x 7in (178mm) BL;
20 x 68pdr.
Performance: 12·65kt (23·4km/h);
coal 450 tons (457 tonnes).
Crew: 530.

British caution over building more
ironclads until trials were made of
Warrior, then still under
construction, led to a further group
with wooden hulls. The ambitious
French programme and the success
of *Gloire* forced the Admiralty to
respond in January 1861 with

contracts for two units similar to
Defence.
    In order to carry an added 300
tons (305 tonnes) of armour and
heavier engines, *Hector* and
Valiant had 2ft (0·6m) more beam.
On completion, however, it was
found that they were 1ft (0·3m)
deeper than planned. The coal
supply had to be reduced,
precluding service overseas. The
designed armament of 32 x 68pdr
was to have been modified to 24 x
68pdr and 8 x 110pdr, but was
reduced to the figures tabulated
above. In 1867-68 the ships were
again rearmed with 2 x 8in (203mm)
and 16 x 7in (178mm).
    Armour ran the full length of the
vessels at battery level, with waterline
protection stopping short of bows
and stern to conserve buoyancy.
Although bulkheads were fitted
across the end of the waterline
protection, the steering remained
exposed.
    Both *Hector* and *Valiant*
exceeded the contract price: Napier
received an added £35,000 from the
Admiralty; Westwood & Baillie, who
went bankrupt while building
Valiant, received £50,000. After some
delay, *Valiant* was completed by
Thames Ironworks in 1868.

Left: *Regina Maria Pia* as coast defence vessel in 1895, rearmed and with military masts.
Below: As completed; schooner rig.

REGINA MARIA PIA

1864. Italy.
Other ships in class: *San Martino, Castelfidardo, Ancona.*

Laid down: 22 July 1862.
Launched: 28 April 1863.
Builder: La Seyne.
Displacement: 4,201 tons (4,268 tonnes) normal; 4,527 tons (4,600 tonnes) full load.
Dimensions: 265ft 9½in (81·2m) oa x 50ft (15·24m) x 20ft 10in (6·35m).
Machinery: Reciprocating; 6 rectangular boilers; 1 screw; 2924 IHP.
Armour: Iron 4·75in (121mm) belt; 4·3in (109mm) battery.
Armament: 4 x 72pdr; 22 x 164mm.
Performance: 13kt (24km/h); range 2,600mm (4,810km) at 10kt (18·5km/h).
Crew: 484.

Lacking resources for iron-hulled warships, Italy ordered four broadside ironclads from France. *Regina Maria Pia* and *San Martino* were slightly the larger.

At Lissa, *Maria Pia* bombarded Porto San Giorgio from as close as 200yds (183m). Engaging the Austro-Hungarian fleet, she was set afire and collided with *San Martino.*

Modified so that guns could fire ahead and astern, *Maria Pia* was rearmed with 2 x 220mm and 9 x 8in (203mm), and later 8 x 6in (152mm) and 5 x 4·7in (120mm), plus smaller. The class served well for 40 years.

Below: *Royal Sovereign* undergoing gunnery trials to test the strength of the Coles turrets. She had a length to beam ratio of 4:1, the smallest in a British armoured ship. The rounded stern shielded the rudder.

ROYAL SOVEREIGN

1864 UK

Laid down: 17 December 1849.
Launched: 25 April 1857.
Builder: Portsmouth Dockyard.
Displacement: 5,080 tons (5,161 tonnes).
Dimensions: 240ft 6in (73·3m) pp x 62ft (18·9m) x 25ft (7·62m) max.
Machinery: Maudslay 2 cylinder Return Connecting Rod; 2460 IHP.
Armour: Iron 5·5in (140mm) belt;

4·5in (114mm) ends; 36in (914mm) ship's side; 10in-5·5in (254-140mm) turrets; 5·5in (140mm) conning tower; 1in (25mm) upper deck.
Armament: 5 x 10·5in (267mm) ML.
Performance: 11kt (20·35km/h); coal c350 tons (356 tonnes).
Crew: 300.

With the advent of the ironclad, Britain was left with many newly obsolescent, steam, wooden line-of-battle-ships, valued at about £10 million. In 1862, work began on the conversion of one such vessel, the wooden, 131-gun *Royal Sovereign,* into Britain's first turret ship.

An increase in Britain's ironclad fleet was desired, but it was assumed that France would counter with a like increase. Thus, it was decided to convert *Royal Sovereign* and other

suitable vessels into turret ships, as suggested by Captain Cowper Coles, RN. These would be good for coastal defence and yet not too expensive.

Although the Construction Department feared that wooden hulls designed for sail power might be unable to cope with heavy turrets, it was agreed that one conversion be made for comparison with a purpose-built iron hull.

The first plan was for 10 x 68pdr or 110pdr guns in five Coles turrets, which were tall, conical and weighed 80 tons (81·3 tonnes). As bigger guns appeared, so 5 x 10·5in (267mm) firing 150lb (68kg) shot were mounted in four turrets: two guns in the fore turret, weight 163 tons (165·6 tonnes); three single turrets aft, each weighing 151 tons (153·4 tonnes).

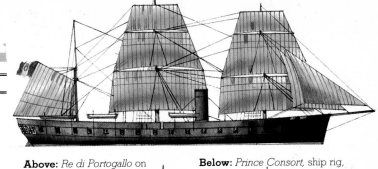

RE DI PORTOGALLO

1864 Italy
Other ships in class: *Re d'Italia*

Laid down: August 1861.
Launched: 29 August 1863.
Builder: Webb, New York.
Displacement: 5,700 tons
(5,791 tonnes) normal.
Dimensions: 326ft 9in (99·6m) x
55ft (16·76m) x 23ft 6in (7·16m).
Machinery: 6 rectangular boilers;
1 shaft; 1812 IHP.
Armour: Iron 4·75in (120mm) sides.
Armament: 2 x 10in (254mm);
26 x 164mm.
Performance: 12kt (22·2km/h)
designed; 10·6kt (19·6km/h) actual;
range *c*1,800nm (3,330km)
at 10·5kt (19·4km/h).
Crew: 552.

Italy ordered her second pair of
ironclads from Webb, New York,
early in theAmerican Civil War, when
the Federal Navy was embarking on
a limited ironclad programme, which
included the similar *New Ironsides*,
to counter the Confederate ironclads.

These were the heaviest warships
completed for the Italian Navy for five
years. Being wooden, they had no
internal subdivision, and although
the sides were armoured from end to
end the steering gear was exposed.
At Lissa (20 July 1866) this doomed
Re d'Italia: with her steering
disabled, she was rammed and sunk
by the Austrian flagship. *Re di
Portogallo* was rammed by the
Austrian wooden two-decker *Kaiser*
(itself severely damaged) and had
60ft (18·3m) of armour displaced,
port lids scraped away and a field
gun swept overboard.

Re di Portogallo was rearmed in
1870 and again in 1871 as a gunnery
training ship, with 20 x 8in (203mm),
2 x 4·7in (120mm), plus smaller. She
was broken up in 1877.

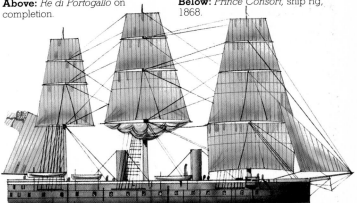

Above: *Re di Portogallo* on
completion.

Below: *Prince Consort*, ship rig,
1868.

PRINCE CONSORT

1864 UK
Other ships in class: *Caledonia,
Ocean*

Laid down: 1860.
Launched: 26 June 1862.
Builder: Pembroke Dockyard.
Displacement: (Original) 3,715
tons (3,774 tonnes) burden;
(Conversion) 6,830 tons (6,939
tonnes).
Dimensions: 273ft (83·21m) pp x

58ft 6in (17·83m) x 24ft (7·31m).
Machinery: Maudslay Horizontal
Reciprocating engine; 8
rectangular boilers; 1 shaft;
1000 NHP.
Armour: 4·5in (114mm) belt and
battery amidships; 3in (76mm) ends.
Armament: 7 x 7in (178mm) BLR;
8 x 100pdr SB; 16 x 68pdr SB.
Performance: 12·5kt (23km/h);
range 2,000nm (3,700km) at 5kt
(9·25km/h).
Crew: 605.

Closely related to the *Royal Oak* but
intended to be faster, these vessels
were built as an emergency measure,
temporarily to maintain the strength
of the Royal Navy.

Provision of greater engine power
and more boilers failed in that it led to
increased draught and a consequent
reduction in coal capacity, greatly
reducing range. Hull distortion by the
added weight amounted, in
Caledonia, to 3in (76mm) within two
years service, necessitating frequent
alterations in shafting. The two
funnels, widely spaced because the
engines were concentrated amidships with the boiler rooms at either
end, gave the vessels an unusual
appearance. Their hulls were
completely cased in armour from the
upper deck level to 6ft (1·8m) below
the waterline. A barque rig was first
fitted.

Since the French programme
failed to progress quickly, these
vessels were completed at yearly
intervals. It was thus possible to
incorporate the latest advances in
gunnery: with a displacement much
less than that of *Warrior*, they
carried a broadside only a little
inferior. During their first
commission, they formed the backbone of the Mediterranean
Squadron. Nevertheless, although
handy, they were poor gun platforms:
a low centre of gravity made them
deep rollers; *Ocean* rolled 45° on
one occasion in 1872.

First rearmed along with her
sisters in 1867, *Prince Consort* was
again rearmed in 1871 with 7 x 9in
(229mm) MLR and 8 x 8in (203mm)
MLR. She was sold for breaking up
in 1882. *Ocean*, having spent much of
her service career in the Far East,
was sold for breaking up in 1882, as
was *Caledonia* in September 1886.

The "success" of USS *Monitor* at
Hampton Roads in 1862 may have
been encouraging, but the failure of
US monitors at Charleston one year
later persuaded the Admiralty to
await trials of *Royal Sovereign* and
the iron-hulled *Prince Albert*
before fully endorsing Coles' ideal of
the sea-going turret ship.

Royal Sovereign was armoured
over her entire hull, which had timber
sides 3ft (0·9m) thick, and hull and
decks were strengthened to cope
with turret weight and firing stresses.
Her freeboard was 7ft (2·13m)
amidships, with hinged bulwarks
3·5ft (1·06m) high. No changes were
made to the engine room. She had
made 12·25kts as a two-decker, but
with increased draught speed fell to
11kts (20·35 km/h). *Royal Sovereign*
was sold for breaking up in 1885.

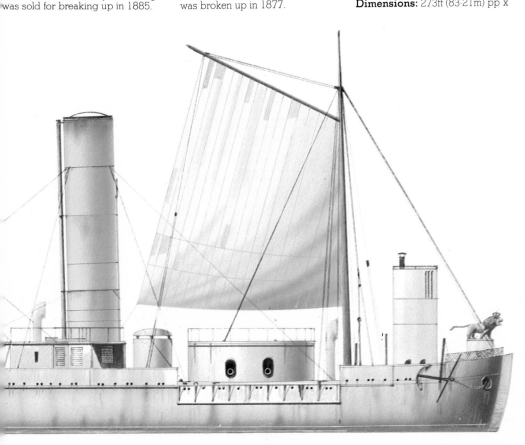

RESEARCH

1864 *UK*
Other ships in class: *Enterprise*

Laid down: 3 September 1861.
Launched: 15 August 1863.
Builder: Pembroke Dockyard.
Displacement: 1,743 tons (1,771 tonnes) load; 1,900 tons (1,930 tonnes) full load.
Dimensions: 195ft (59·44m) pp x 38ft 7in (11·76m) x 14ft 6in (4·42m) mean.
Machinery: Watt Horizontal Direct Acting; 2 tubular boilers; 1 shaft; 1040 IHP.
Armour: Iron 4·5in (114mm) belt; 4·5in (114mm) battery; 19·5in (459mm) timber backing; 4·5in (114mm) bulkheads.
Armament: 4 x 100pdr SB.
Performance: 10·3kt (19km/h); coal 130 tons (132 tonnes).
Crew: 150.

In the early 1860s Edward Reed suggested that some smaller wooden sloops should be converted to ironclads. The Board had been told by the Constructor's Department that it was not possible to produce a satisfactory sea-going ironclad on less than 4,000 tons (4,064 tonnes), with protection of no less than 4·5in (114mm), guns no smaller than 68pdr, high speed and good range. Only small low-freeboard turret ships with limited sea-going capability could be produced on lesser tonnage. Reed disagreed, and was supported by the Board. *Research* thus became the first lightweight battleship (although Reed's account suggests that her near-sister *Enterprise* may have been designed first).

Ordered in November 1860 as the *Trent*, a Perseus class sloop of 950 tons (965 tonnes) and 17 guns, she was laid down in September 1861. One year later, when Reed was given the task of redesigning her, she was renamed *Research*. She had then progressed no further than being up in frame, so it was comparatively easy to lengthen her by 10ft (3·05m) and to increase her beam from its original 33ft 2in (10·1m) to achieve a beam:length ratio of 1:5. Draught at the stern was increased by 3ft 6in (1·07m). A full oval stern replaced the conventional sloop stern and a ram bow was fitted, the hull profile remaining otherwise unchanged, with a forecastle, poop and open waist. (A spar deck was fitted, giving a clean run, in the 1869-70 refit.)

Some flexibility in distribution of weight was possible, since the original design had heavy armament in proportion to displacement. Armour thickness was the same as on *Research*'s larger consorts, but it was more generously applied, with a continuous 10ft (3·05m) deep and 4·5in (114mm) thick belt half above and half below water. The 34ft (10·36m) long box battery was protected by 4·5in (114mm) armour, with 4·5in (114mm) bulkheads to guard against raking fire. (In *Enterprise* the unprotected wooden hull—comprising around 80 per cent of the total length—was married with iron upperworks, reducing fire risk. The lower hull remained wooden, for this fouled less).

Research's battery housed four formidable guns, 100pdr 'Somersets', and to permit end-on fire the hull sides before and abaft the battery were recessed so that the guns could fire through end ports, almost along the sides of the ship. But to do this the guns, set some 6ft 6in (1·98m) above water, had first to be worked round from the side ports—a hazardous procedure with a sea running. Nevertheless the system was retained in later box battery ships until replaced by fixed guns firing along side embrasures. In 1869-70, 4 x 7in (178mm) MLR replaced the 100pdrs, this change having been ordered in June 1866.

The funnel originally ran up through the box battery close before the main mast, thus gaining some protection for the funnel base. This was usual in the spacious batteries of big broadside ironclads, but *Research*'s short battery — accommodating 80 men, 4 guns, steering wheel and ammunition hatch—was badly crowded. To

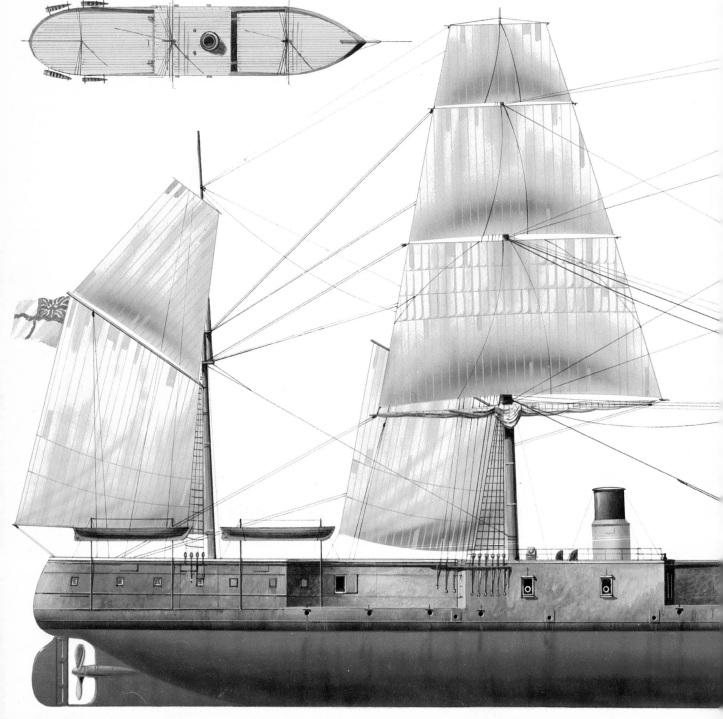

...ermit the guns to be worked ...fficiently, the funnel was moved ...orward of the battery in 1869-70.

With a barque rig of 18,250ft² ...,695m²), *Research* made 6kt ...1·1km/h) under sail and 9-10kt ...6·6-18·5km/h) under steam and ...ail—reaching 11·6kt (21·5km/h) in ...865. A poor sea boat with a deep ...oll, she was customarily confined to ...arbour during the winter. She was ...ith the Channel Fleet in 1864-66, ...he Mediterranean Fleet in 1871-78, ...nd then in Reserve until her sale in ...887.

Enterprise (originally *Circassian*) was ordered from ...eptford Dockyard in 1861. Smaller ...han *Research*—1,350 tons (1,372 ...onnes) load—she carried less ...mour. Her armament was similar: 2 ... 100pdr SB and 2 x 110pdr BL.

Right: Displacement increased by ...ore than 500 tons (508 tonnes) ...hen *Research* underwent con-...ersion to an ironclad. There were ...ide angles on which guns could not ...ear.

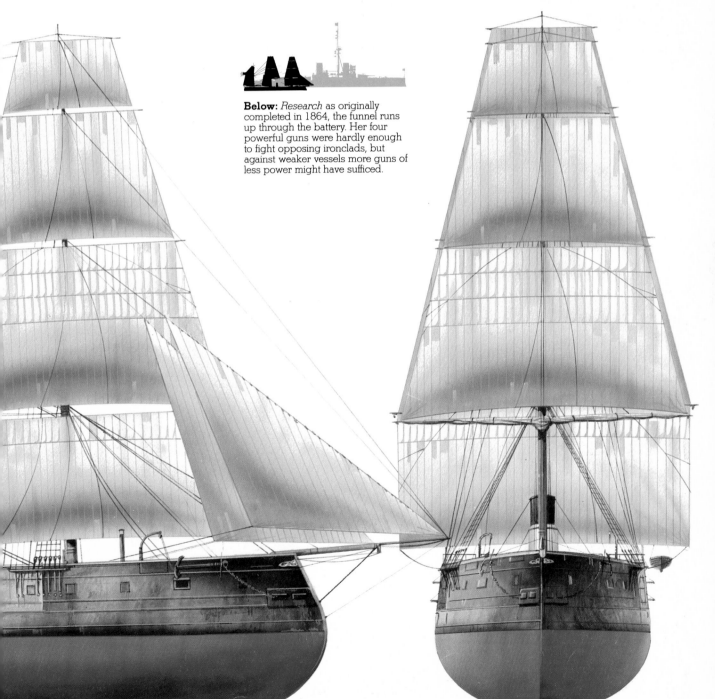

Below: *Research* as originally completed in 1864, the funnel runs up through the battery. Her four powerful guns were hardly enough to fight opposing ironclads, but against weaker vessels more guns of less power might have sufficed.

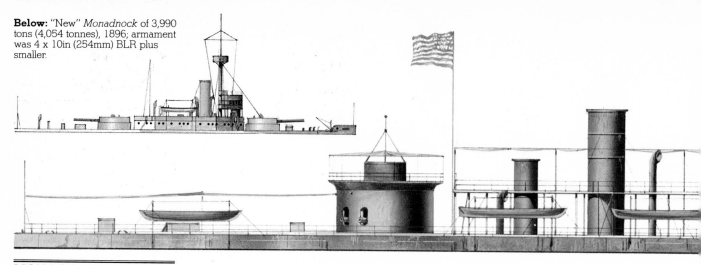

Below: "New" *Monadnock* of 3,990 tons (4,054 tonnes), 1896; armament was 4 x 10in (254mm) BLR plus smaller.

MONADNOCK

1864 USA
Other ships in class:
Agamenticus, Miantonomoh, Tonawanda

Laid down: 1862.
Launched: 23 March 1864.
Builder: Boston Navy Yard.
Displacement: 3,295 tons (3,348 tonnes).
Dimensions: 250ft (76·2m) x 53ft 8in (16·36m) x 12ft 3in (3·73m).
Machinery: 2 Vibrating Lever engines; 4 Martin boilers; 2 shafts; 1426 IHP.
Armour: Iron 5in (127mm) sides; 1·5in (38mm) deck; 10in (254mm) turrets; 8in (203mm) pilot house.
Armament: 4 x 15in (381mm) Dahlgren SB.
Performance: 9kt (16·65km/h); coal 300 tons (305 tonnes).
Crew: 167.

This class is generally accepted to be the most successful group of monitors built for the US Navy in the Civil War. Designed by John Lenthall, they were a logical development from Ericsson's original *Monitor*, the Passaic and Canonicus classes, and the double-turreted *Onondaga* designed by Quintard. An earlier design of November 1861, by Lenthall and Engineer-in-Chief Isherwood, featured a double-turreted ironclad with Coles turrets. A plan for a fleet of vessels of this superior design was approved, but the influence of Ericsson's political associates resulted in its cancellation.

The larger, wooden-hulled, double-turreted Monadnocks differed slightly in dimensions. They had no overhang and freeboard was only 2ft 7in (0·79m): water washed freely over their decks in adverse seas and *Monadnock* rolled considerably. Nevertheless, they had a reputation for reliability, and two made long ocean voyages: between 5 October 1865 and 21 June 1866, *Monadnock* went from the east coast to San Francisco via Cape Horn; in 1866 *Miantonomoh* crossed the Atlantic (being towed part of the way) and returned from Europe in 1867 after covering nearly 18,000 miles (29,000km).

Lenthall's 1861 design had specified solid plates, but the USA could not then manufacture plates of the required thickness, and single 1in (25mm) plates were bolted together to produce laminated armour. Although this lacked the resistance of solid armour, all the US Navy's monitors were thus armoured. *Puritan* and *Dictator* had, in addition, curved segments of iron fitted into the space between the inner and outer

layers of turret armour.

Monadnock took part in the attacks on Fort Fisher, N.C., in December 1864—January 1865, and later in the final assault on Richmond up the James River. In April 1865 she was sent to Havana to watch for the Confederate raider *Stonewall*. She decommissioned five days after her arrival in San Francisco in June 1866.

By the 1870s the wooden hulls of the Monadnocks had rotted; in June 1874, it was decided to use "repair" funds to build replacements. The "new" *Monadnock* was built by the Continental Iron Works. Launched in 1883, she was not completed until 1896, by which time she was a poor match for the latest battleships. She spent most of her later service career in the Philippines and Far East, having crossed the Pacific in under eight weeks in 1898.

DICTATOR

1864 USA

Laid down: 16 August 1862.
Launched: 26 December 1863.
Builder: Delameter Iron Works, N.Y.
Displacement: 4,438 tons (4,509 tonnes)
Dimensions: 312ft (95·1m) x 50ft (15·24m) x 20ft 6in (6·25m).
Machinery: 2 Ericsson Vibrating Lever engines; 6 Martin boilers; 1 shaft; 1000 HP.
Armour: Iron 6in (152mm) side;

Below: Ericsson's iron-hulled *Dictator*, 1864. The huge turret weighed 500 tons (508 tonnes).

42in (1·07m) wood backing; 15in (381mm) turret; 1·5in (38mm) deck; 12in (305mm) pilot house.
Armament: 2 x 15in (381mm) SB.
Performance: 9kt (16·65km/h); coal 300 tons (305 tonnes).
Crew: 174.

In *Dictator*, following complaints from monitor officers, Ericsson greatly reduced the overhang of the raft and gave it finer lines. Excess draught resulted in only 16in (0·4m) freeboard. Coal supply was also reduced and a designed speed of 15kt (27·75km/h) was not achieved. Laminated armour covered the sides to a depth of 6ft (1·83m) and both funnel and ventilator were armoured.

Worn bearings caused *Dictator* to break down en route to the attacks on Fort Fisher, N.C., December 1864. She was sold in 1883.

Below: *Monadnock,* 1886. A light bridge connects the two turrets, each with an armoured conning tower on top. The funnel and huge ventilator have armoured bases.

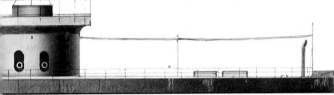

ACHILLES
864 UK

Laid down: 1 August 1861.
Launched: 23 December 1863.
Builder: Chatham Dockyard.
Displacement: 9,820 tons (9,977 tonnes).
Dimensions: 380ft (115·82m) pp x 58ft 3in (17·75m) x 27ft 3in (8·31m).
Machinery: Penn Trunk engines; 10 rectangular boilers; 1 shaft; 5720 IHP.
Armour: Iron 4·5in (114mm) battery; 4·5in (114mm) belt; 18in (457mm) wood backing; 4·5in (114mm) bulkheads.
Armament: 4 x 110pdr SB; 16 x 100pdr SB.
Performance: 14·3kt (26·5km/h); coal 1,000 tons (1,016 tonnes) max; radius 1,800 miles (2,896km) at 6·5kt (12km/h).
Crew: 709.

Achilles was one of Isaac Watts' outstanding designs. She was to have resembled *Warrior*, but in January 1861 it was decided to redesign her with a complete waterline belt. No iron ship had previously been built in the Royal Dockyards and building at Chatham was somewhat delayed by the need for special equipment and the training of workers in new methods. *Achilles* emerged as the steadiest platform in the battle fleet, once carrying the largest spread of canvas of any warship.

Achilles was completed with an armament of 4 x 110pdr BL on the upper deck and 16 x 100pdr in the battery. All were on wooden carriages, as were the 6 x 68pdr added at the battery end in 1865. In 1868 she was rearmed with 4 x 7in (178mm) MLR on the upper deck and 18 x 7in (178mm) MLR on the main deck, plus 4 x 8in (203mm) MLR, all on iron carriages. She was again rearmed in 1874 with 2 x 7in (178mm) MLR and 14 x 9in (229mm) MLR. She ended her sea-going career in 1885, serving as a depot ship under various names until her sale in 1925.

Below: *Achilles* in 1864 with four-masted rig, the only one ever carried in a British warship. The foremast and bowsprit were removed in 1865.

PEDER SKRAM
1864 Denmark

Laid down: 1861.
Launched: 29 April 1862.
Builder: Copenhagen Dockyard.
Displacement: 3,379 tons (3,433 tonnes).
Dimensions: 226ft 4in (68·99m) x 49ft 6in (15·1) x 21ft 7in (6·58m).
Machinery: 1 shaft; 1650 IHP.
Armour: Iron 4·5in (114mm) belt and battery; 2·875in (73mm) ends.
Armament: 6 x 8in (203mm); 8 x 6in (152mm); 2 x 18pdr.
Performance: 11kt (20·35km/h).
Crew: 450.

The effect of shellfire on wooden ships was demonstrated off Schleswig-Holstein on 5 April 1849, when the Danish line-of-battle ship *Christian VIII* and frigate *Gefion* were destroyed by German coastal batteries at Eckenforde. Subsequently, tests on ironclads showed that 4·5in (114mm) wrought iron plates with wood backing could withstand the fire of existing smoothbores and new rifled guns.

Peder Skram was one of three ironclads added to Denmark's fleet in the early 1860s. Ship-rigged and ram-bowed, she was completely armoured to 4ft 3in (1·3m) below the waterline. As originally armed, the 6in (152mm) guns were carried between the 8in (203mm) weapons on the same deck, the hull sides aft at battery deck level being recessed to allow 2 x 6in (152mm) to fire astern. She was later rearmed with 8 x 8in (203mm) and 8 x 6in (152mm) rifles, plus two smaller. She was relegated to harbour duties by the 1880s.

Above: *Peder Skram,* 1886. Finding such deep-draught ships unsuited to inshore work, Denmark turned to smaller vessels of monitor type.

DANMARK
1864 Denmark

Laid down: 1862.
Launched: 24 February 1864.
Builder: Thompson, Clydebank.
Displacement: 4,747 tons (4,823 tonnes).
Dimensions: 270ft (82·29m) pp x 50ft (15·24m) x 19ft 6in (5·94m) max.
Machinery: 2 engines; 1000 IHP.
Armour: Iron 4·5in (114mm) amidships; 3in (76mm) ends; 18in (457mm) teak backing.
Armament: 12 x 8in (203mm) RML; 12 x 6in (152mm) RML; 2 x 18pdr carronades; 8 x 4pdr howitzers.
Performance: 8·5kt (15·7km/h); coal 700 tons (711 tonnes); radius 20 days steaming.
Crew: 530.

Lieutenant North of the Confederate States Navy, sent to Europe for the purpose, contracted with Thompson of Glasgow for a completely armoured, iron-hulled broadside frigate. She would have been the most powerful vessel in Confederate service, but both bad weather and the poor state of the Confederacy's finances forbade her completion for the Southern cause. Denmark, then at war with Prussia and anxious to expand her fleet, purchased the almost completed vessel, which had been launched with her armour in position.

Danmark's ram was later removed and a conning tower was added. She was rearmed in 1867-68 with more powerful 8in (203mm) guns and her stern was altered to permit end fire. Hulked in 1893, she was broken up in 1907.

Below: *Danmark* in 1864. Deep draught would have restricted her use by the Confederacy, as would the manning requirement.

TETUAN

1864 *Spain*

Laid down: 1861.
Launched: 1863.
Builder: Ferrol.
Displacement: 6,200 tons (6,300 tonnes).
Dimensions: 279ft 1in (85m) wl.
Machinery: Horizontal Trunk engines; 1 shaft; 1000 IHP.
Armour: Iron 5·1in (130mm) belt and battery.
Armament: 30 x 68pdr and 32pdr.
Performance: 10kt (18·5km/h); coal 1,200 tons (1,220 tonnes).
Crew: 500.

A building programme for nine ironclad frigates to place Spain ahead of the USA began in 1861 with *Tetuan*, a wooden-hulled vessel plated entirely with 5·1in (130mm) armour and originally intended to mount 40 guns. Six more units were built or converted in the next eight years, but there was then a sixteen-year gap before work began on the next battleship, *Pelayo*.

In mid-July 1873, *Tetuan* and other vessels were seized by Republican insurgents at Cartagena. Badly damaged in an action with the loyalist ironclad *Vitoria* on 10 October, and then suffering more damage from field artillery, *Tetuan* was left behind when the rebels evacuated the port. She was blown up on 31 December to prevent capture by Government forces; the hulk was later scrapped.

BARROZO

1864 *Brazil*

Launched: 1864.
Displacement: 1,354 tons (1,376 tonnes).
Dimensions: 186ft (56·69m) x 37ft (11·28m) x 8ft 10in (2·69m).
Machinery: Single Expansion; 1 shaft; 420 IHP.
Armour: Iron 3·8-2·5in (97-63mm) belt and battery; 25in (635mm) wood backing.
Armament: 2 x 7in (178mm); 2 x 68pdr; 3 x 32pdr.
Performance: 9kt (16·65km/h).
Crew: *c*230.

Barrozo was a wooden-hulled coast defence ship with a raised battery amidships housing 2 x 7in (178mm) Whitworth MLR and 2 x 68pdr. These guns could not fire directly ahead or astern. Armour covered the battery and machinery amidships to the height of the main deck.

Barrozo's shallow draught was an advantage in the largely riverine War of the Triple Alliance (1864-70) fought by Brazil, Argentina and Uruguay against Paraguay. In September 1866 she narrowly escaped mine damage before the repulse of the Allied fleet from Curupaity; at Humaitá in July 1868 she ran past the river forts with a monitor lashed alongside to attack the town from the rear. She was discarded in the mid-1880s.

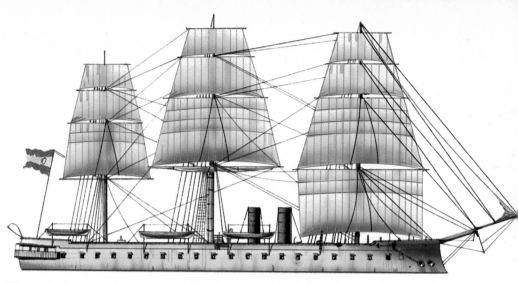

Above: The Spanish ironclad *Tetuan* on completion in 1864; note the comparatively small gunports.

Below: *Barrozo* with light rig; the raised battery housing the MLRs is prominent.

STONEWALL

1864 *Confederate States of America*
Other ships in class: *Cheops*

Laid down: 1863.
Launched: 21 June 1864.
Builder: Arman, Bordeaux.
Displacement: 1,560 tons (1,585 tonnes) full load.
Dimensions: 194ft (59·13m) oa x 31ft 6in (9·6m) x 15ft 8in (4·77m).
Machinery: Horizontal Direct Acting Mazeline engines; 2 Mazeline rectangular boilers; 2 shafts; 1300 IHP.
Armour: Iron 4·5in (114mm) belt/side; 3·5in (89mm) ends; 4in (102mm) aft turret; 5·5in (140mm) bow gun; 24in (610mm) max backing.
Armament: 1 x 9in (229mm) 300pdr; 2 x 70pdr.
Performance: 10·8kt (20km/h); coal 100/280 tons (102/284 tonnes)
Crew: 135.

Stonewall was a composite-hulled vessel with a complete belt. Armoured bulwarks on the upper deck protected the forward 9in (229mm) 300pdr Armstrong gun; the 2 x 70pdr were housed aft in a fixed armoured turret, with limited arcs of fire. Unusual twin rudders and screws allowed great manoeuvrability.

In 1863 the Confederate Navy had accepted the offer of Arman of Bordeaux to build four sloops and two armoured rams of shallow draught, suitable for service in Southern waters. Delivery was planned for summer 1864, when the rams, *Sphinx* and *Cheops*, could cross the Atlantic unaided. But before completion the French Government forbade their sale to the Confederacy. Prussia and Denmark being at war, *Cheops* was purchased by Prussia as *Prinz Adalbert* and *Sphinx* was sold to Denmark as *Staerkodder*—but the war then ended and she was returned to Arman.

Surreptitiously repurchased by the Confederacy, she sailed for America as *Stonewall* under Captain Page. She was shadowed in Spanish waters by the Union wooden warships *Niagara* and *Sacramento*, which avoided battle with so formidable an opponent. But Page was never happy with the ship and, arriving in Havana in May 1865 to learn that the Civil War had ended, he sold her to the Captain General, who handed her over to the United States.

She was now bought by the Shogun of Japan, but on arrival at Yokohama in April 1868 was claimed by the Emperor. Renamed *Koketsu*, she led the attack on the Shogun's stronghold at Hakodate in July 1869. Renamed *Adzuma* in 1881, she was stricken in January 1888 and then served for many years as an accommodation ship.

PURITAN

1864 USA

Laid down: 1863.
Launched: 2 July 1864.
Builder: Continental Iron Works, New York.
Displacement: 4,912 tons (4,990 tonnes).
Dimensions: 340ft (103·6m) x 50ft (15·24m) x 21ft (6·4m).
Machinery: 2 Ericsson Vibrating Lever engines; 6 Martin boilers; 2 shafts; c1000 HP.
Armour: Iron 6in (152mm) sides; 15in (381mm) turret; 12in (305mm) pilot house.
Armament: 2 x 20in (508mm) SB.
Performance: Unknown.
Crew: Unknown.

Designed by John Ericsson, the huge monitor *Puritan* was a near-sister to the *Dictator*. With these craft, the US Navy Department sought to develop true ocean-going warships with high speed (15kt, 28km/h) and a large cruising radius (with a bunker capacity of 1,000 tons, 1,016 tonnes). Displacing nearly 5,000 tons, *Puritan* was among the largest vessels contracted for at this time: only *Dunderberg* and the four units of the Kalamazoo class, which were not completed, were larger.

Unlike *Dictator*, which had a single shaft and an enormous screw, *Puritan* was

provided—against her designer's wishes—with twin shafts. The Navy Department also specified twin turrets, but Ericsson protested strongly, claiming that on the given displacement the weight that would be expended in a second turret could be better used to mount heavier guns and thicker armour. Ericsson prevailed: *Puritan* was to have had a single huge turret with an inside diameter of 26ft (7·92m), carrying 2 x 20in (508mm) smoothbores. (It should be noted that a ship of this configuration would have been rendered defenceless by any accident or damage to the turret machinery.)

Problems in casting *Puritan's* massive guns delayed her completion beyond the end of the Civil War, and in 1865 all work stopped. The delays also caused

acute financial problems to her consortium of builders. The combined cost of *Puritan* and *Dictator* was estimated at $2,300,000 but the figure should be seen in comparison with $62,000,000 expended during the Civil War on 121 ships that were to be rated as useless within a few years.

In 1867, a 20in (508mm) Rodman smoothbore was at last test-fired, revealing daunting mechanical problems in loading the 1,080lb (490kg) ball. The best time achieved was only one shot in 8·5 minutes.

Lack of funds for new construction led at last to the decision to "repair" *Puritan*. Under this guise she was sold, with other vessels, as scrap to John Roach. The proceeds of the sale were supposedly intended to help finance the building of her replacement.

Left: The "new" *Puritan* of 1896. Note the low freeboard of this 6,060 ton (6,157 tonne), 297ft (90·5m) long vessel, which carried 4 x 12in (305mm) plus smaller. She served in the Spanish-American War.

Below: The uncompleted *Puritan*. In a heavy sea, only the turret and funnel would have been above water.

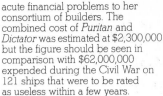

Left: *Stonewall* under the Confederate flag, 1865. The forward 9in (229mm) gun fired ahead or on the beam through large ports. The ram projected 17ft (5·18m) below water.

Below: *Arminius*, laid down at Samuda Bros yard as a private venture, was hastily bought by Prussia to bolster her navy during strained diplomatic relations with Denmark.

Below: *Surveillante* in 1867. The barque rig had an area of about 21,000ft² (1,950m²). *Héroine* was the only iron-hulled Provence class ship

Below: *Arminius* with reduced rig in the 1890s.

ARMINIUS

1865 Germany

Laid down: 1863.
Launched: 20 August 1864.
Builder: Samuda Bros, London.
Displacement: 1,887tons (1,917 tonnes).
Dimensions: 207ft 4½in (63·21m) oa x 35ft 9in (10·9m) x14ft 11in (4·55m).
Machinery: Single Horizontal 2-cylinder engines; 1 shaft; 1440 IHP.
Armour: Iron 4·5in (114mm) belt; 3in (76mm) ends; 4·5in (114mm) turret; 9in (229mm) conning tower.
Armament: 4 x 8·2in (208mm).
Performance: 11·2kt (20·7km/h); coal 171 tons (174 tonnes); range 2,000nm (3,700km) at 8kt (14·8km/h).
Crew: 131.

Anxious to build a small but effective navy, but lacking funds and home facilities, Prussia went to Britain and France for craft to defend her Baltic coast against the Danes. The iron-hulled *Arminius* was the first ironclad to join what would become the German Navy.

Laid down speculatively by her builders, she was a twin-turreted vessel of Coles type, with moderate freeboard. Hastily completed after purchase by public subscription while on the stocks, she was not in time to join the Prussian forces fighting Denmark in the Baltic.

Originally to have carried 4 x 72pdr bronze guns, she was fitted with 4 x 8·2in (208mm). In 1881, 4 x 37mm revolving cannon were added, with a torpedo tube in the bows. Her armour extended 2ft 9in (0·83m) below the waterline and was 4·5in (114mm) thick amidships , reducing to 3in (76mm) at the ends, with 9in (229mm) teak backing. She was refitted in 1868-69, with a light superstructure and bridge running from funnel to stern, an extra fireroom, and a rig reduced to a single pole mast.

Because the Prussian fleet was too small to face the powerful French Navy , *Arminius* spent much of the Franco-Prussian War (1870-71) in the Elbe. She was a coast defence vessel until 1872 and then became a machine school ship. In 1882 she became a tender to the training ship *Blücher* and was later an icebreaker at Kiel. Discarded in 1901, she was broken up the next year.

PROVENCE

1865 France
Other ships in class: *Flandre, Gauloise, Guyenne, Magnanime, Revanche, Savoie, Surveillante, Valeureuse, Héroine*

Laid down: March 1861.
Launched: 29 October 1863.
Builder: Toulon.
Displacement: 5,700 tons (5,791 tonnes).
Dimensions: 262ft 5in (79·98m) wl x 55ft 9in (16·99m) x 26ft 10in (8·18m).
Machinery: Horizontal Return Connecting Rod, Compound; 9 boilers; 1 shaft; 3600 IHP.
Armour: Iron 6in (152 mm) waterline; 4·3in (109mm) battery
Armament: 10 x 55pdr SB; 22 x 6·4in (163mm); 2 x 8·8in (224mm) howitzers.
Performance: 13·9 kt (25·7km/h); coal c600 tons (610 tonnes).
Crew: 579.

In the late 1850s France planned a new ironclad programme, initially for 30 sea-going vessels and 11 armoured floating batteries. This was beyond French capabilities, financial and constructional , and Dupuy de Lôme therefore suggested that ten ironclads should be built within 18 months; nine with wooden hulls and one with iron. All iron vessels would have been preferable, but the French iron industry had expended much of its resources on a large group of floating batteries.

Authorized in November 1860, this was the largest single group of French ironclads. The British were still building ironclads only in small groups, but France seemed unable to match British finance and skill, even sending naval constructors to England to study her rival's methods.

The Provence ironclads were closely modelled on *Gloire*, but were larger, carried thicker armour, and had gun ports set 6ft (1·82m) above the waterline and a 4·3in (109mm) strake above it. *Héroine* was iron

hulled, but her compartmentation was not thorough.

Two howitzers and two of the 6·4in (163mm) guns were carried on the upper deck. Some of the class were later given a 7·6in (193mm) gun which fired ahead from under the forecastle. Rearmament in 1868 resulted in 8 x 9·4in (239mm) in the battery and 4 x 7·6in (193mm) on the upper deck.

Provence served with the Mediterranean Fleet at the start of the Franco-Prussian War and then formed part of the blockading force in the North Sea. She was stricken in 1884.

PRINCIPE DI CARIGNANO

1865 Italy
Other ships in class: *Messina, Conte Verde*

Laid down: January 1861.
Launched: 15 September 1863.
Builder: La Foce, Genoa.
Displacement: 3,446 tons (3,501 tonnes) normal; 4,021 tons (4,086 tonnes) full load.
Dimensions: 249ft 3in (75·97m) x 49ft 10in (15·2m) x 23ft 6in (7·16m).
Machinery: Single Expansion; 4 rectangular boilers; 1 shaft; 1968 IHP.
Armour: Iron 4·75in (121mm) sides.
Armament: 10 x 8in (203mm); 12 x 164mm.
Performance: 12kt (22·2km/h) designed.
Crew: 572.

Designed by Insp Eng Mattei, this vessel was converted to an ironclad while on the stocks; a sister ship, *Principe Umberto*, being left as a screw frigate. *Messina* was similarly converted. *Conte Verde* was designed by Insp Eng De Luca as an ironclad, but only bow and stern were armoured. All three ships differed slightly in size.

Principe di Carignano took part in the Lissa campaign, bombarding Comisa on 18 July 1866, supporting the attack on Porto San Giorgio on the next day, and participating in the major naval action, where she sustained little damage.

She was rearmed in 1870: the 8in (203mm) guns were reduced to four and the 64pdrs increased to sixteen. Discarded in 1875, she was broken up in 1877-79.

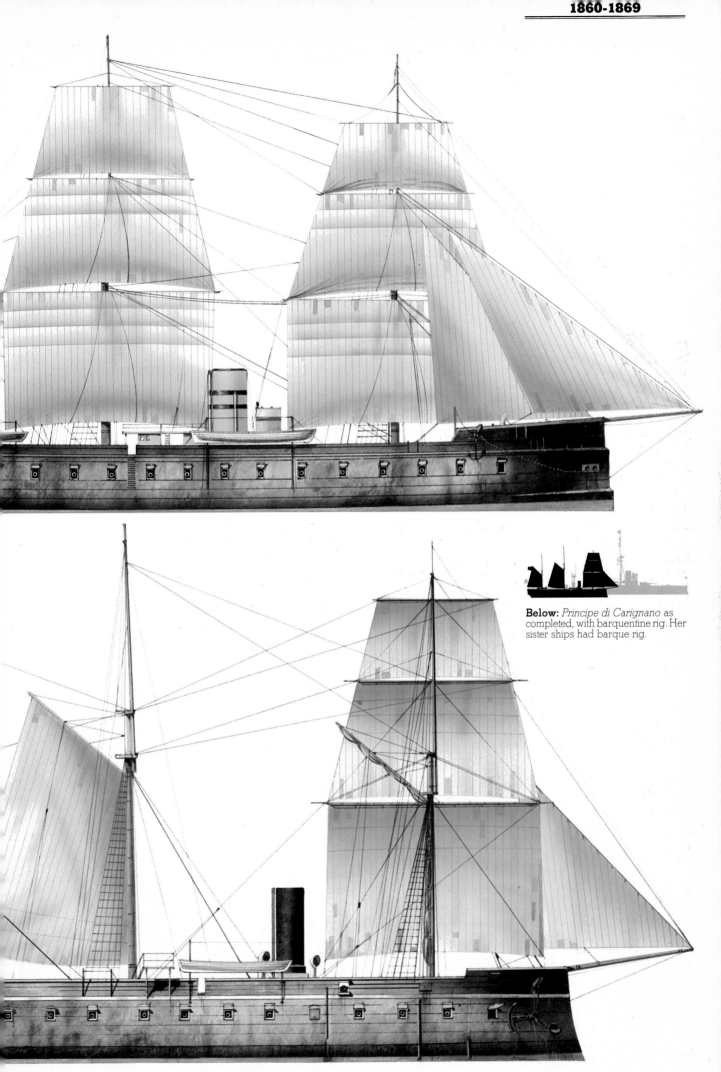

Below: *Principe di Carignano* as completed, with barquentine rig. Her sister ships had barque rig.

INDEPENDENCIA

1865 Peru

Launched: 8 August 1865.
Builder: Samuda Bros. London.
Displacement: 3,500 tons (3,556 tonnes).
Dimensions: 215ft (65·53m) x 44ft 9in (13·64m) x 22ft (6·7m).
Machinery: Penn engine; 1 shaft; 2200 IHP.
Armour: Iron 4·5in (114mm) belt; 4·5 in (114mm) battery.
Armament: 2 x 7in (178mm) MLR 12 x 70pdr; 4 x 32pdr; 4 x 9pdr.
Performance: 12kt (22·2km/h).
Crew: 250.

Above: The broadside ironclad frigate *Independencia* in 1866. Note the ram bow. The largest armoured vessel built for Peru, she was lost early in the war with Chile, 1879.

Right: Named after a Peruvian emperor, *Huascar* was ordered to combat Spain, then fighting her former colonies on the western Pacific coast. The turret was hand-turned.

Below: *Wivern* with tripod masts.

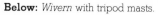

SCORPION

1865 UK
Other ships in class: *Wivern*

Laid down: April 1862.
Launched: 4 July 1863.
Builder: Laird Bros, Birkenhead.
Displacement: 2,750 tons (2,794 tonnes).
Dimensions: 224ft 6in (68·43m) x 42ft 6in (12·95m) x 16ft 3in (4·95m).
Machinery: Lairds 2-cylinder Horizontal Direct Acting engines; 1 shaft ; 1450 IHP.
Armour: Iron 4·5in (114mm) sides

dependencia and the turret ship *Huascar* were the only major armoured vessels built for Peru; their loss in 1879 during the war with Chile was disastrous.

Built at Samuda Bros yard, London, where some of the world's major warships were then produced, *dependencia* was an iron-hulled broadside ironclad with three watertight compartments. Her armour belt extended to 4ft (1·22m) below the waterline, with 10in (254mm) teak backing. The battery was 12 x 70pdr guns, with two 7in (178mm) Armstrong MLRs on pivot-mountings on the spar deck. The latter were replaced around 1878 (when she was also reboilered) by an 8in (203mm) 250pdr Lavasseur MLR in the bows and a 7in (178mm) Parrot MLR in the stern.

On the outbreak of war with Chile, *Independencia* (Captain Moore) safely escorted President Prado from Callao to the new capital of Arica. With *Huascar*, she went on to Iquique, which was blockaded by two small Chilean gunboats. Arriving on 21 May 1879, *Independencia* engaged the 400-ton (406-tonne) *Covadonga*, which ran south along the shore, often among the breakers, with the untrained Peruvian gunners making poor practice in pursuit. On Moore's third ramming attempt the Chilean gunboat was within 100yds (91m) of the beach and had just scraped a reef. Aiming at her starboard quarter, Moore missed his helmsman being killed at a critical moment—and *Independencia* piled up on the rocks. Falling off to starboard, *Covadonga* set the ironclad afire aft and she became a total loss.

HUASCAR

1865 Peru

Launched: 6 October 1865.
Builder: Laird Bros , Birkenhead.
Displacement: 2,030 tons (2,062 tonnes) max.
Dimensions: 200ft (60·96m) x 35ft (10·67m) x 18ft (5·5m) max.
Machinery: Single Expansion; 1 shaft; 1650 IHP
Armour: Iron 4·5in (114mm) belt; 2·5in (63mm) ends; 6in (152mm) turret sides ; 8in (203mm) face.
Armament: 2 x 10in (254mm) ; 2 x 40pdr.
Performance: 12·3kt (22·75km/h); coal 200-300 tons (203-305 tonnes).
Crew: 170-200.

This diminutive iron-hulled vessel had an eventful life, at one time doing most of the fighting at sea in Peru's desperate and unsuccessful struggle against Chile and Bolivia in the War of the Pacific.

Huascar was a low-freeboard turret ship with a 4·5in (114mm) armour belt amidships, tapering to 2·5in (63mm) at the ends. The belt ran from 5ft (1·52m) above water, the maximum freeboard amidships, to 3ft (0·91m) below, backed by 13in (330mm) of wood. An armoured transverse bulkhead, 4·5in (114mm) thick, protected the magazines, turret mechanism and boilers against raking fire. The deck plating was 2in (51mm) thick over the hatches, with 3in (76mm) armour on the hexagonal-shaped conning tower.

The Coles turrets housed 2 x 10in (254mm), 12·5 ton (12·7 tonne), Armstrong MLR, firing a 300lb (136kg) projectile. Two 40pdr guns were carried on the quarterdeck and one 12pdr in the stern. The hull had a double bottom beneath the turrets, machinery and boilers. At the bows

Below: The powerful *Osmanieh* in 1866.

the sides were carried up an added 6ft (1·82m) above the main deck to form a small forecastle, housing the anchors. Amidships were hinged iron bulwarks which were lowered when the ship was in action. *Huascar* was extremely handy, able to turn through 180° in little more than two minutes.

On 29 May 1877, after *Huascar*'s crew had mutinied and committed several acts of piracy, the turret ship fought an inconclusive action with the British unarmoured iron frigate *Shah* (6,250 tons, 6,350 tonnes) and corvette *Amethyst*. In this engagement *Shah* fired a Whitehead torpedo, the first time this weapon was tried in action, which *Huascar* evaded.

When war with Chile began in 1879, *Huascar* (Captain Miguel Grau) was sent with *Independencia* to raise the blockade of Iquique by two old Chilean gunboats. In action on 21 May, *Huascar* rammed and sank the *Esmeralda* after four hours' fighting, but *Independencia* was lost after going aground.

Over the next months *Huascar* raided Chilean commerce, evading pursuit by her superior speed. In an action against the corvette *Abtao* she launched a wire-guided torpedo. The missile turned and headed back towards the turret ship , which was saved only by the prompt action of an officer.

Huascar was soon badly in need of an overhaul, but President Prado ordered Grau to keep her at sea. On 8 October 1879, now capable of only about 8 kts (15km/h),she met the Chilean ironclads *Almirante Cochrane* and *Blanco Encalada*. After several hours' hard fighting, badly damaged and with nearly half her crew dead or wounded, *Huascar* surrendered.

Rebuilt and rearmed, with 2 x 8in (203mm) BLR plus smaller, by the Chileans, *Huascar* saw some action in the Chilean Civil War of 1891. After serving for gunnery training, she is now preserved as a museum ship.

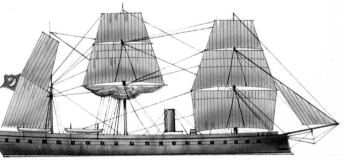

in (76mm) bows; 2in (51mm) stern ; in (127mm) turret; 10in (254mm) ace; 0·75in (19mm) skin.
Armament: 4 x 9in (229mm) MLR.
Performance: 10·5kt (19·5km/h); coal 336 tons (341 tonnes); range ,052nm (1,947km) at 10kt (18·5km/h).
Crew: 153.

The Confederate States Navy wished to obtain ironclads from Europe to counter the Federal blockade. In July 1861, the Confederate agent James D. Bulloch contracted with Lairds for two ironclad rams—*North Carolina* and *Mississippi*—for delivery early in 1863. The ships were to be sold to Egypt to avoid Britain's neutrality law and then transferred to the Confederacy. But they were seized by Britain and sold to the Royal Navy. They were small ships of long

range and shallow draught (suited for operation off and up the Mississippi). Freeboard of only 6ft (1·83m) amidships was increased by hinged bulwarks 5ft (1·52m) high; seaworthiness was improved by adding a forecastle and poop, with guns for ahead and astern fire. The polygonal turrets had 22in (559mm) wood backing and the hull was fully armoured from the upper deck to 3ft 3¼in (1m) below the waterline. An armament of 4 x 300pdr was allotted in 1965, but they received instead 4 x 9in (229mm) MLR, then the heaviest guns afloat in the RN.

Wivern had tripod masts to reduce the amount of rigging, which was further reduced in 1868. Both ships rolled heavily and steered badly before the wind because of small rudders and flat bottoms. *Scorpion* was sold in 1903.

OSMANIEH

1865 Turkey
Other ships in class: *Mahmudieh*, *Abdul Aziz*, *Orkanieh*

Laid down: 1863.
Launched: 2 September 1864.
Builder: Napier, Glasgow.
Displacement: 6,400 tons (6,502 tonnes) normal.
Dimensions: 293ft (89·31m) pp x 55ft 9in (16·99m) x 25ft 7in (7·8m).
Machinery: Horizontal Compound; 6 boilers; 1 shaft; 3735 IHP.
Armour: Iron 5·5in (140 mm) belt;

3in (76mm) ends; 5in (127mm) battery; 4·5in (114mm) ends; 9in (229mm) wood backing.
Armament: 1 x 9in (229mm) MLR; 14 x 8in (203mm) MLR; 10 x 36pdr
Performance: 12kt (22·2km/h); coal 750 tons (762 tonnes).
Crew: 600.

These iron-hulled broadside ironclads had telescopic funnels and ram bows. A 4in (102mm) armoured breastwork protected the forward 9in (229mm) gun, remaining armament being divided between upper and main decks. Two 5·9in (150mm) later replaced the forward 9in (229mm) and 1 x 9·2in (234mm) was added aft. The belt extended 2·5ft (0·76m) above the load waterline and 6ft (1·82m) below the waterline.

Osmanieh was modernised as a central battery ship in 1890-91.

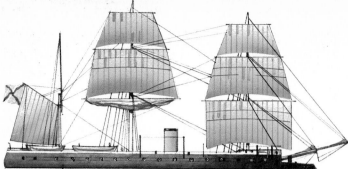

Above: *Sevastopol* as completed, showing pronounced ram bow.

Below: 2nd class cruising ironclad *Belliqueuse* in the late 1860s.

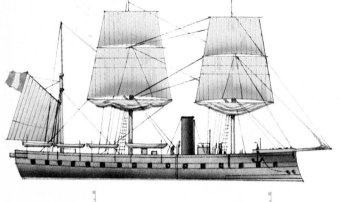

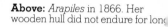

Above: *Arapiles* in 1866. Her wooden hull did not endure for long

SEVASTOPOL

1865 *Russia*
Other ships in class: *Petropavlovsk*

Laid down: 1860.
Launched: 24 August 1864.
Builder: Kronstadt.
Displacement: 6,130 tons (6,228 tonnes).
Dimensions: 295ft (89.9m) wl x 52ft (15.85m) x 26ft (7.92m) max.
Machinery: Horizontal Return Connecting Rod engines; 1 shaft, 3090 IHP.
Armour: Iron 4.5in (114mm) belt; 3in (76mm) ends; 4.5 (114mm) battery; 24in (610mm) backing.
Armament: 16 x 8in (203mm); 1 x 6in (152mm); 8 x 3.4in (86mm).
Performance: 12kt (22.2km/h).
Crew: 607.

Conversion to a broadside ironclad of the 5,212-ton (5,295 tonne) wooden unarmoured frigate *Sevastopol*, orginally intended to mount 28 x 60pdr SB guns, began in 1862. The rebuilding gave her a complete waterline belt extending from 5ft 2in (1.57m) below water to the main deck beams. An armoured battery some 195ft (59.44m) long, with armoured bulkheads fore and aft, was situated amidships. Two of her 16 x 8in (203mm) guns were carried outside the battery.
    At the same time, her sister ship *Petropavlovsk*, laid down in 1861 and launched in 1865, was converted into a broadside ironclad of 6,040 tons (6,137 tonnes), with a blunt ram bow projecting some 8ft (2.44m). She was armed with 24 x 8in (203mm) guns—20 of them carried in the battery—4 x 6in (152mm) and 10 x 3.4in (86mm). She was converted at the New Admiralty yard.
    Sevastopol was fitted with a light three-masted schooner rig; *Petropavlovsk* was ship-rigged, less topgallant sails. Both ships were stricken from the Navy list in the middle to late 1880s.

BELLIQUEUSE

1866 *France*
Other ships in class: *Alma, Armide, Atalante, Jeanne D'Arc, Montcalm* (ex-*Indienne*), *Reine Blanche, Thetis*

Laid down: September 1863
Launched: 6 September 1865.
Builder: Toulon.
Displacement: 3,717 tons (3,776 tonnes).
Dimensions: 229ft 8in (70m) wl x 46ft (14.02m) x 22ft 10in (6.96m) max.
Machinery: Horizontal Return Connecting Rod; 4 oval boilers; 1 shaft; 1200 IHP.
Armour: Iron 6in (152mm) belt; 4.7in (119mm) battery; 8.5in (216mm) backing.
Armament: 4 x 7.6in (193mm); 6 x 6.4in (163mm).
Performance: 11kt (20.35km/h); coal 259 tons (254 tonnes).
Crew: 300.

Belliqueuse had a ram bow and a complete waterline belt running from 4ft 11in (1.5m) below water to the battery deck, where the 7.6in (193mm) guns and four of the 6.4in (163mm) were housed 6ft (1.8m) above water. Two 6.4in (163mm) were carried on the upper deck. The battery bulkheads were of thin plating only and there was no metal skinning on the hull sides outside the armoured area.
    Her barque rig of 15,600ft² (1,449m²) was later increased to 19,000ft² (1,765m²) and she was rearmed with Model 1870 7.6in (193mm), 5 x 5.5in (140mm) and smaller, two 6.4in (163mm) being landed. She was condemned in 1886 and expended as a target.
    An improved class of wooden-hulled vessels was laid down in 1865. These carried 6 x 7.6in (193mm): four mounted amidships behind 4.7in (119mm) armour and two on the upper deck in overhanging barbettes with 4in (102mm) armour. Plating covered unarmoured areas.

ARAPILES

1865 *Spain*

Launched: 1864.
Builder: Green, Blackwall.
Displacement: 5,700 tons (5,791 tonnes).
Dimensions: 280ft 11in (85.37m) x 54ft (16.45m).
Machinery: 1000 NHP.
Armour: Iron 4.75in (121mm) belt; 4.25in (108mm) ends.
Performance: 12kt (22.2km/h).
Crew:

Arapiles was planned as a wooden screw frigate but modified while still on the stocks to carry a midships armoured belt, adding 2ft (0.6m) to her beam and c200 tons (203.2 tonnes) to her displacement.
    In 1870 she carried 2 x 10in (254mm) RML, 5 x 8in (203mm) RML and 10 x 7.9in (201mm)BL. By 1878 this had become 2 x 8in (203mm) and 12 x 6.3in (160mm) Hontoria BL.
    Arapiles grounded off Venezuela in 1873 and was sent to New York for repairs. This coincided with Spanish-American tension over the *Virginius*, an American steamer illegally stopped by a Spanish ship. The repairs were not made.

NUMANCIA

1865 Spain.

Laid down: 1861.
Launched: 19 November 1863.
Builder: La Seyne.
Displacement: 7,189 tons (7,304 tonnes).
Dimensions: 315ft (96·01m) p x 57ft (17·37m) x 27ft (8·22m) max.
Machinery: Non-compound engines; 1 shaft; 3700 IHP.

Armour: Iron 5·5in (140mm) belt; 4in (102mm) ends; 17·5in (444·5mm) max wood backing.
Armament: 40 x 68pdr.
Performance: 13kt (24km/h); coal 1,000 tons (1,016 tonnes); range 2,610nm (4,826km) at economical speed.
Crew: 590.

The iron-hulled Numancia was the second element in an ambitious ironclad programme. First armed with 40 x 68 pdr, by 1880 she

mounted 4 x 10in (254mm), 3 x 8in (203mm) and 16 x 6·5in (165mm). In 1890 her armament was 8 x 10in (254mm) and 4 x 8in (203mm),main deck; 3 x 8in (203mm), upper deck; and 3 x 7·8in Hontoria guns, forecastle.
Numancia was with Admiral Nuñez' squadron during the Spanish-Peruvian War, bombarding Valparaiso on 31 March 1866 and suffering damage in Nuñez' abortive attack on Callao on 2 May. Seized by insurgents in the Carlist conflict,

1873, she was badly damaged while attacking Alicante and, on 10 October, saw action against Spanish warships.
In 1897-98 Numancia was completely rebuilt by La Seyne , with new engines (13kt, 24km/h) and an armament of 4 x 6·4in(163mm) QF, 6 x 5·5in (140mm) QF and 3 x 4·7in (119mm) QF, plus smaller. By 1914 she was a gunnery training ship. Numancia sank on 17 December 1916 off the Portuguese coast while under tow to the breakers.

Left: Numancia in 1866. During Spain's war against Peru and Chile in the 1860s, this powerful vessel formed the backbone of the Spanish fleet in the Pacific.

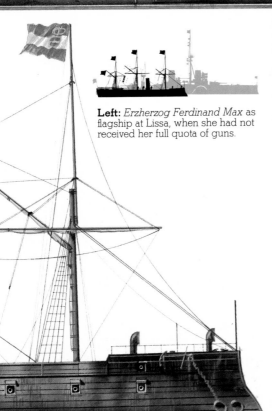

Left: Erzherzog Ferdinand Max as flagship at Lissa, when she had not received her full quota of guns.

ERZHERZOG FERDINAND MAX

1866 Austria-Hungary
Other ships in class: Habsburg

Laid down: 6 May 1863.
Launched: 24 May 1865.
Builder: Stabilimento Tecnico Triestino
Displacement: 5,140 tons (5,222 tonnes).
Dimensions: 274ft 9in (83·74m) oa x 52ft 4in (15·96m) x 23ft 3in (7·1m).
Machinery: 2-cylinder Horizontal engine; 1 shaft; 3150 IHP.
Armour: Iron 5·25in (133mm) belt; 3·5in (89mm) ends; 5in (127mm) battery.
Armament: 16 x 48pdr SB; 2 x 4pdr.
Performance: 12kt (22·2km/h).
Crew: 489.

Erzherzog Ferdinand Max and Habsburg were designed by Joseph von Romako, Director of Naval Construction, and after launching were hurried to completion in order to participate in the war of 1866, when Italy attempted to reclaim Italian-speaking territories then under Austrian rule.
Somewhat resembling Gloire, but with a more pronounced ram, they were completely armoured from below the waterline to the spar deck, with armour stepped down to the

ram. The side armour varied in thickness from 5·25in (133mm) to 5in (127mm) at the extremities, with wood backing of nearly 28in (711mm). At first intended to mount 32 x 48pdr SB, they were first commissioned with 16 SB, firing a 55lb (25kg) steel ball, and 2 x 4pdr. In 1867 the armament became 14 x 7in (178mm), 4 x 9cm and 2 x 7cm. The rig was also reduced from that planned and was not increased until after 1866.
Ferdinand Max was Admiral Tegethoff's flagship on 20 July 1866, when, having been defeated on land at Custozza, the Italians made a naval attack on Lissa island. Engaging the larger Italian fleet,the Austrian force broke through a gap in the Italian ironclad squadron and Ferdinand Max rammed Palestro and Re d'Italia, but without doing major damage. In the ensuing melee, Ferdinand Max once more encountered Re d'Italia, this time striking her squarely on the port side as the Italian ship lay immobile. Re d'Italia sank within two minutes. During the battle Ferdinand Max had fired 156 shots and taken 42 hits.
In 1882, 2 x 47mm and 3 x 25mm were added to her armament, with further changes in 1886 and 1887, by which time she had been hulked. After serving as tender to a gunnery training ship, Erzherzog Ferdinand Max was scrapped in 1916.

PRINCE ALBERT
1866 *UK*

Laid down: 29 April 1862.
Launched: 23 May 1864.
Builder: Samuda Bros, London.
Displacement: 3,880 tons (3,942 tonnes).
Dimensions: 240ft (73·15m) pp x 48ft (14·63m) x 20ft 6in (6·25m) max.
Machinery: Humphreys & Tennant 2-cylinder Horizontal Direct Acting engine; 4 rectangular boilers; 1 shaft; 2130 IHP.
Armour: Iron 4·5in (114mm) belt; 3·375in (86mm) ends; 18in (457mm) backing; 5·5in (140mm) turrets; 10in (254mm) faces; 1·125in-0·75in (29-19mm) deck.
Armament: 4 x 9in (229mm) MLR.
Performance: 11·26kt (21km/h); coal 229 tons (233 tonnes); range 930 miles (1,496km) at 10-11kt (18·5-20·35km/h) in 3·5 days; 7 days economical steaming.
Crew: 201.

Cowper Coles put forward several ideas for turret ships to the Admiralty. One, a vessel of 5,660 tons (5,690 tonnes), was considered too costly; another, for two smaller ships, each with two turrets, was not liked because of poor protection. But to provide adequate armour and reasonable speed necessitated increased displacement and a cost per gun far higher than that of any ironclad yet built.

On 13 January 1862 it was decided to build on Coles' system a mastless vessel carrying twelve breechloading rifled guns in six turrets, each weighing 80 tons (81·3 tonnes). Estimated displacement was 4,020 tons (4,084 tonnes), and provision was made for temporary masts in the event of long ocean voyages. Because of delayed materials, and armament problems, *Prince Albert* was not completed until 1866.

Coles wished to install the 12-ton (12·19 tonne), 10·5in (267mm), 300pdr gun, maintaining that this weapon could be worked in his turrets but not on the broadside. Early in 1864, Captain Cooper Key of the gunnery establishment *Excellent* stated that, because of inadequate mountings, the 6·5-ton (6·6 tonne), 9·2in (234mm), 100pdr was the heaviest gun that could be properly manhandled aboard ship. In February 1865, the number of turrets was reduced to four, with 1 x 300pdr MLR in each.

Since *Prince Albert* was planned originally to mount six turrets, it was necessary to armour the entire 7ft (2·13m) side to ensure stability and to position the guns at the same level as on a broadside ironclad. The turrets were given end-on fire, but to promote dry sailing in a seaway, hinged bulwarks, 5ft (1·52m) high, were fitted. The turrets, each weighing 111 tons (112·78 tonne) were carried two before and two aft of the funnel, all on the centre line. The upper deck, sloping up to the centre line, was plated with 0·75in (19mm) iron; the turret bases were not protected below this deck.

In 1866-67, a flying bridge was fitted over the two forward turrets; this later carried six machine guns. Reboiled in 1878, *Prince Albert* — in deference to Queen Victoria — was on the effective list for 33 years.

Below: *Prince Albert* as completed. Shallow draught and length/beam ratio of 5:1 gave better speed lines than the largest wooden 3-deckers.

Below: *Palestro*, destroyed at Lissa, existed for only eight months.

Below: *Pallas*, 1867, ship-rigged. Stiff and deep-rolling, she nevertheless handled well.

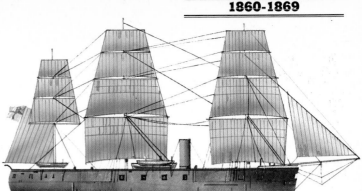

Above: *Favorite* as seen in 1869.   **Below:** *Lord Clyde* in 1866.

PALESTRO

866 *Italy*
Other ships in class: *Varese*

Laid down August 1864.
Launched: 5 September 1865.
Builder: La Seyne.
Displacement: 2,600 tons (2,642 tonnes) full load.
Dimensions: 212ft 6in (64.8m) x 2ft 8in (13m) x 18ft 3in (5.6m) max.
Machinery: Reciprocating engines; boilers; twin screw; 930 IHP.
Armour: Iron 4.75in (121mm) side nd battery.
Armament: 4 x 8in (203mm); 1 x 5in (165mm).
Performance: 8kt (15km/h); coal 80 tons (183 tonnes); range 800nm ,480km) at 8kt (15km/h).
Crew: 250.

Palestro and *Varese* were iron-hulled, arque-rigged, ironclad corvettes, esigned by Eng Insp Giuseppe de uca.

Eight months after completion, *alestro* (Captain Capellini) fought at issa, 20 July 1866. With *Re d'Italia* nd *San Martino*, she faced seven ustrian ironclads in a melee in ense smoke. Attempting to aid *Re 'Italia*, on which Austrian fire was oncentrated, *Palestro* took several roadsides astern, some of heated hot. On fire, *Palestro* retired and two alian vessels came to her aid, one king her in tow. Capellini was ffered boats to take off his crew, ut he himself refused to leave and his en volunteered to stay and fight the re. The magazines were flooded, but ready store of loaded shells xploded, destroying the ship. Only 9 men survived.

Varese was rearmed in 1870 and om 1886 to 1891, the year in which ne was discarded, served first as a ospital ship and subsequently as a aining ship, and then as a depot essel.

PALLAS

1866 *UK*

Laid down: 19 October 1863.
Launched: 14 March 1865.
Builder: Woolwich Dockyard.
Displacement: 3,794 tons (3,855 tonnes) full load.
Dimensions: 225ft (68.58m) pp x 50ft (15.24m) x 21ft 8in (6.6m) mean.
Machinery: Humphreys & Tennant Compound Horizontal engines; 4 boilers; 1 shaft; 3580 IHP.
Armour: 4.5in (114mm) belt, battery and bulkheads; 22in (559mm) wood backing.
Armament: 2 x 7in (178mm) Armstrong BL; 4 x 7in (178mm) MLR.
Performance: 13kt (24km/h); coal 260 tons (264 tonnes).
Crew: 253.

Designed by E.J. Reed as a private venture, *Pallas* had the high speed of 14kt (26km/h), although she made 12.5kt (23km/h) on trials and 13kt (24km/h) after modifications. She was the first vessel fitted with compound engines and, designed primarily as a ram, had a length to beam ratio of 4.5:1, making her extremely handy. Reed planned an iron hull, but Woolwich Dockyard could not construct iron hulls and there was a surplus of wood, so wood was used.

Originally, 2 x 7in (178mm) MLR were carried on each broadside, some axial fire being made possible by deeply recessed embrasures. Bow and stern fire were provided by single 7in (178mm) guns; the fore gun, however, was only 9ft (2.74m) above water, limiting its use as water piled up over the ram. Reed planned to mount 300pdrs, but such a crowded battery could not have been successfully worked with the means then available. Rearmed in 1866 and 1871, *Pallas* was sold in 1886.

FAVORITE

1866 *UK*

Laid down 23 August 1860.
Launched: 5 July 1864.
Builder: Deptford Dockyard.
Displacement: 3,230 tons (3,282 tonnes).
Dimensions: 225ft (68.58m) pp x 46ft 9in (14.25m) x 21ft 6in (6.55m) mean.
Machinery: Humphreys & Tennant Direct Acting engines; 4 boilers; 1 shaft; 1770 IHP.
Armour: Iron 4.5in (114mm) belt and bulkheads; 26in (660mm) wood backing; 4.5in (114mm) battery; 19in (483mm) wood backing.
Armament: 8 x 100pdr SB.
Performance: 11.8kt (21.8km/h); coal 350 tons (356 tonnes).
Crew: 250.

Begun in 1860 as a 22-gun wooden corvette, *Favorite* was converted to an ironclad in 1862 while still on the stocks. Her protection equalled that of the larger, iron-hulled ironclads, with a continuous belt from below the waterline to the upper deck. However, the height of the upper deck permitted only 3ft (0.91m) of armour below water: even a slight roll revealed the vessel's unarmoured hull.

The box battery housing eight 100pdr guns was 66ft (20.12m) long and rested in a central position on the upper deck, with 20ft (6.1m) long bulwarks hinging inboard to permit limited ahead and astern fire. In 1869 the 100pdrs were replaced by 7in (178mm) MLR, and 64pdrs were added at bow and stern for end fire.

Favorite was a good sea boat, but rolled heavily even in a moderate sea, once recording a 30° roll. Although she had more coal stowage than was usual, she made long voyages under sail alone. She was sold in 1886 for £3,500.

LORD CLYDE

1866 *UK*
Other ships in class: *Lord Warden*

Laid down: 29 September 1863.
Launched: 13 October 1864.
Builder: Pembroke Dockyard.
Displacement: 7,750 tons (7,874 tonnes).
Dimensions: 280ft (85.34m) pp x 59ft (17.98m) x 26ft (7.92m) mean.
Machinery: Ravenhill Trunk engines; 9 boilers; 1 shaft; 6100 IHP.
Armour: Iron 5.5in (140mm) belt and battery; 4.5in (114mm) belt and battery ends; 4.5in (114mm) conning tower.
Armament: 24 x 7in (178mm) MLR.
Performance: 13.5kt (25km/h); coal 630 tons (640 tonnes); range 1,360 miles (2,188km) at 10kt (18.5km/h).
Crew: 605.

Lord Clyde and *Lord Warden* were the last broadside ironclads. Reed adapted the design of the iron-hulled *Bellerophon* to a wooden hull, with some iron worked in for stiffening and a hold divided into five compartments by thin iron bulkheads. The hull was a "sandwich" of 24in (610mm) oak with 1.5in (38mm) iron skin. The 5.5in (140mm) armour had 6in (152mm) backing and an oak strip, 4in (102mm) thick and 8ft (2.44m) deep, at the waterline. Armour covered the battery and ran the length of the ship, rising in the bows to cover the chase guns. This protection helped make the class the heaviest wooden ships built.

Because of poor ventilation, the ships were not over-healthy: they always had longer sick lists than their iron-hulled contemporaries. *Lord Clyde* was rearmed in 1870 — 2 x 9in (229mm) MLR, 14 x 8in (203mm), 2 x 7in (178mm), plus smaller — but in 1872, discovered to have rotten timbers, she was sold.

AFFONDATORE

1866 Italy

Laid down: 11 April 1863.
Launched: 3 November 1865.
Builder: Harrison, London.
Displacement: 4,307 tons (4,376 tonnes) full load; later 4,540 tons (4,613 tonnes) full load.
Dimensions: 307ft 9in (93·8m) oa x 40ft (12·2m) x 20ft 10in (6·35m).
Machinery: Single Expansion engines; 1 shaft; 2717 IHP.
Armour: Iron 5in (127mm) max side; 9in (229mm) backing; 5in (127mm) turrets; 2in (51mm) deck.
Armament: 2 x 10in (254mm) MLR.
Performance: 12kt (22·2km/h); coal 475 tons (483 tonnes) max; range 1,647nm (3,047km) at 10kt (18·5km/h).
Crew: 309; later 356.

Because of deteriorating relations with Austria, Italy decided to acquire a 'turret ship': a type felt to be superior to the ironclads already in service. A contract signed with Mare of Millwall, London, on 11 October 1862 stipulated completion in nine months. Mare's bankruptcy led to a new contract with Harrison of Millwall on

11 April 1863. The plans were modified and the ship was to be completed within 18 months — but delivery was again delayed.

Affondatore was an iron-hulled schooner-rigged vessel with a pronounced wrought-iron ram. Her full-length armoured belt extended from 7ft 3in (2·2m) above water to 4ft (1·22m) below. Her two turrets were of the Coles type, resting upon rollers positioned a short distance inside the line of the turret walls. Each housed a single 10in (254mm) 300pdr Armstrong MLR. They were placed at the ends, giving fields of fire of 130° for the fore turret and 105° for the aft. The guns' elevation was poor.

Delivered, still incomplete, on 6 June 1866, *Affondatore* was hurried out to Italy to escape detention in Britain on the outbreak of the Austro-Italian War, 20 June 1866. Soon after her arrival she joined the fleet commanded by Admiral Count Persano in the attack on the island of Lissa. On 19 July she supported the ironclad *Formidabile* in an attack on Fort George at Port San Giorgio. Withdrawing in the afternoon, Persano planned to renew the attack early next morning but, delayed by poor visibility, he learned of the rapid

approach of the Austrian fleet.

At this critical time, Persano decided to transfer his flag from *Re d'Italia* to *Affondatore,* but when *Re d'Italia* hove to for the transfer a gap was created in the battle line through which the Austrian ships steamed, cutting the Italian fleet in two. The Italian ships' confusion was increased because they were not aware of the transfer of Persano's flag.

Meanwhile *Affondatore* cut in between *Re d'Italia* and *Palestro,* her next astern, and steamed across the rear of the Austrian armoured vessels before heading for the Austrian unarmoured division, led by the 92-gun line-of-battle ship *Kaiser. Affondatore* engaged *Kaiser,* attempting to ram and firing as she came. One of her 300pdrs badly damaged *Kaiser,* but the wooden two-decker replied with two broadsides into *Affondatore.* More damage was caused to both ships as they scraped alongside on the second ramming attempt.

After steaming in a wide circle through the smoke of battle, *Affondatore* again encountered *Kaiser,* which had meanwhile been severely damaged by other Italian ironclads. *Affondatore* charged the wooden ship but sheered away at

Right: *Affondatore* as completed, 1866, showing her relatively clear decks and low freeboard. Her enormous ram projected 26ft (7·92m). She was considered a poor sea boat and was not particularly handy: at Lissa, where she was Admiral Count Persano's flagship, she took 8·5 minutes to complete a full circle at 11kt (20·35km/h).

e last moment. After engaging
e ironclad *Don Juan d'Austria,*
ffondatore retired with damaged
nnels and upperworks and a fire
elow decks.

Following hurried repairs at
ncona, *Affondatore* sank at her
oorings in a severe storm on 6
ugust 1866. Salvaged on 25
ctober 1866, she was repaired at
enoa in 1867-68 and rebuilt in
873, with larger bridges and a
ngle military mast. In 1882-85 she
as rebuilt once more, receiving new
achinery (3240 IHP), two military
asts and a 5in (127mm) armoured
onning tower. She was built up
midships and rearmed with 2 x
)in (254mm) 30-cal Armstrongs, 6 x
7 (119mm), 1 x 75mm QF, 8 x
7mm QF, 4 x 37mm and four
rpedo tubes.

Affondatore was placed in reserve
La Spezia in 1899 and was used as
torpedo training ship until
ovember 1907 when, having been
moved from the Navy list, she was
onverted to a barracks ship.

ight: *Affondatore* towards the end
her long career. Like many early
onclads she underwent extensive
construction, including the fitting
new machinery and armament.

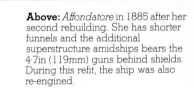

Above: *Affondatore* in 1885 after her
second rebuilding. She has shorter
funnels and the additional
superstructure amidships bears the
4·7in (119mm) guns behind shields.
During this refit, the ship was also
re-engined.

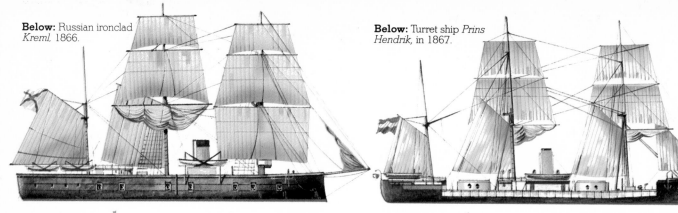

Below: Russian ironclad *Kreml*, 1866.

Below: Turret ship *Prins Hendrik*, in 1867.

KREML

1866 Russia

Laid down: 1 December 1864.
Launched: 1865.
Builder: Baltic Works, St Petersburg.
Displacement: 3,412 tons (3,467 tonnes) standard; 3,664 tons (3,723 tonnes) full load.
Dimensions: 220ft 9in (67·3m) x 53ft (16·2m) x 15ft (4·6m).
Machinery: Single Horizontal Direct Acting engine; 1 shaft; 1121 IHP.
Armour: Iron 5in (127mm) belt;

4·5in (114mm) stern; 5in (127mm) bow; 4·5in (114mm) battery.
Armament: 16 x 8in (203mm).
Performance: 9·5kt (17·5km/h).
Crew: 260.

Considered to be an improvement on *Pervenetz*, *Kreml* had a less pronounced ram, a flatter stern, and was barque-rigged. Her machinery came from the wooden *Ilya Mourometz*. Her armour, 5in (127mm) at the waterline, thinned to 4·5in (114mm) over the battery, and had a maximum backing of 17·5in (445mm).

Kreml's broadside battery of 16 x 8in (203mm) Obukov guns, plus smaller, was later changed to 8 x 8in (203mm), 6 x 6in (152mm), 8 x 4pdr and five machineguns. A gunnery training ship in the 1890s, she was stricken in 1905.

PRINS HENDRIK DER NEDERLANDEN

1867 Netherlands

Laid down: 1865.
Launched: 9 October 1866.
Builder: Laird Bros, Birkenhead.
Displacement: 3,376 tons (3,430 tonnes).
Dimensions: 240ft (73·15m) oa x 44ft (13·41m) x 18ft (5·49m) max.
Machinery: 2 Twin Cylinder Horizontal engines; 4 boilers; 2 shafts; 2400 IHP.
Armour: Iron 4·5in (114mm)

amidships; 3in-2·5in (76-63mm) ends; 4·5in (114mm) sides; 9·25in (235mm) backing; 4·5in (114mm) conning tower; 5·5in (140mm) turret; 11in (279mm) face.
Armament: 4 x 9in (229mm) MLF
Performance: 12·9kt (24km/h); coal 380 tons (386 tonnes); range *c*550 miles (885km) at 7kt (13km/h)
Crew: 230-267.

This turret ship was originally three-masted but was found to be a poor sailer. She was given two pole masts and then schooner-rigged in 1875 for a colonial voyage.

The full-length armour belt was 4 8in (1·42m) deep, extending 3ft 5in (1·04m) below the waterline. Above to the upper deck level amidships, was an armour strip 109ft 9in (33·45m) long to protect turret base and engines.

Below: *Zealous* 1867.

Below: *Royal Alfred* in 1867.

ZEALOUS

1866 *UK*

Laid down: 24 October 1859.
Launched: 7 March 1864.
Builder: Pembroke Dockyard.
Displacement: 6,100 tons (6,198 tonnes).
Dimensions: 252ft (76·81m) pp x 58ft 6in (17·83m) x 25ft 5in (7·75m) mean.
Machinery: Maudslay Return Connecting Rod engines; 6 boilers; 1 shaft; 3623 IHP.
Armour: Iron 4·5in (114mm) belt;

2·5in (63mm) ends; 4·5in (114mm) battery; 3in (76mm) bulkheads; 30in (762mm) backing.
Armament: 20 x 7in (178mm) MLR.
Performance: 11·7kt (21·6km/h).
Crew: 510.

In 1861, seven wooden two-deckers were selected for conversion into ironclads as an answer to France's ambitious building programme. French progress being slower than anticipated, only four of the conversions — one Royal Oak class and four Prince Consorts — were completed in 1863-66. The experience gained was applied to *Zealous* and the remaining two conversions. The earlier group, which had been lengthened by about 20ft (6·09m), lacked longitudinal strength; so the remaining conversions were not lengthened,

Left: *Bellerophon* as completed in 1866. The ram bow made the ship wet forward, so a light overhanging knee was added. The 91ft (27·73m) long battery was concentrated amidships.

and *Zealous* was altered only above the waterline.

A wooden hull could not support the same weights as an iron hull, so *Zealous* carried fewer guns and less armour. Since she was intended to served in remote areas where she would be the only ironclad, this was acceptable. In *Zealous*, the full-length battery armour of *Prince Consort* was reduced to a 103ft (31·4m) long area on the main deck amidships. A full-length belt along the waterline ran from the main deck to 6ft (1·82m) below water.

Armstrong breechloaders had been withdrawn, so *Zealous* carried 7in (178mm) MLRs. Except for two at each end, all were concentrated in the battery. The weapons were on wooden mounts and slides worked by ropes; sent to the Pacific before the advantages of mechanical working were fully appreciated, *Zealous* could not work her guns efficiently in a seaway.

Engines and boilers were in a single compartment amidships. The hull was bulky, with a length/beam ratio of 4·3:1; and with more than 3500 IHP, *Zealous* could make only about 11·5kt (21·3km/h). However, she carried 29,200ft² (2,713m²) of canvas and covered more miles under sail alone than any of her contemporaries; once making 30,000 miles (48,270km) on only 1,500 tons (1,526 tonnes) of coal. She was sold in 1886.

BELLEROPHON

1866 *UK*

Laid down: 28 December 1863.
Launched: 26 April 1865.
Builder: Chatham Dockyard.
Displacement: 7,551 tons (7,672 tonnes).
Dimensions: 300ft (91·44m) pp x 56ft 1in (17·09m) x 24ft 8in (7·52m) mean.
Machinery: Penn Horizontal Trunk engines; 8 boilers; 1 shaft; 6521 IHP.
Armour: Iron 6in (152mm) belt; 4·5in (114mm) ends; 10in (254mm) backing; 5in (127mm) bulkhead; 8in (203mm) conning tower (fitted later); 0·5in (13mm) upper deck; 1in (25mm) main deck below battery.
Armament: 10 x 9in (229mm) MLR; 5 x 7in (178mm) MLR; 4 saluting.
Performance: 14·7kt (27km/h); coal 640 tons (650 tonnes); radius 1,500 miles (2,413km) at 8kt (14·8km/h).
Crew: 650.

Bellerophon was a major advance in ironclad development, with an improved hull form (on the bracket frame system; the use of some steel

imparting strength and saving weight), more powerful engines, better protection and heavier guns — all on a shorter hull with greater manoeuvrability and seaworthiness. A double bottom raised the centre of gravity, increasing steadiness.

Adoption of the 12-ton (12·19 tonne), 9in (229mm) gun meant that fewer guns would be needed for the same weight of fire, with concentration amidships providing a steadier gun platform. The 9in (229mm) guns were in a box battery, with 2 x 7in (178mm) in the bows and 3 x 7in (178mm) in the stern. Armour was full-length, from the main deck to 6ft (1·82m) below water.

In 1885 the main armament was changed to 10 x 8in (203mm) BL, but the longer weapons proved difficult to work in the battery. *Bellerophon* was sold in 1922.

ROYAL ALFRED

1867 *UK*

Laid down: 1 December 1859.
Launched: 15 October 1864.
Builder: Portsmouth Dockyard.
Displacement: 6,707 tons (6,814 tonnes).
Dimensions: 273ft (83·21m) pp x 58ft 6in (17·83m) x 25ft 5in (7·75m) mean.
Machinery: Maudslay Horizontal Return Connecting Rod engines; 6 boilers; 1 shaft; 3230 IHP.
Armour: Iron 6in (152mm) belt; 4in (102mm) ends; 4·5in (114mm) bulkheads.
Armament: 10 x 9in (229mm) MLR; 8 x 7in (178mm) MLR; 6 saluting.
Performance: 12·36kt (23km/h); coal 550 tons (559 tonnes); range 2,200 miles (3,540km) at 5kt (9·25km/h).
Crew: 605.

Conversion of *Royal Alfred*, laid down as a 90-gun wooden two-decker, was ordered in 1861. She was lengthened in the same way as the Prince Consort class. Work halted to await their trials; when it resumed, the extra 600 tons (610 tonnes) displacement was used to install 10 x 9in (229mm) guns in a box battery amidships, with 6in (152mm) armour, as on *Bellerophon*.

A full-length belt ran from the main deck to 5ft 6in (1·7m) below the waterline. The 7in (178mm) guns at bow and stern were protected by 4in (102mm) armour, and armour also covered the funnel uptake.

Royal Alfred handled well, as fast under sail — carrying 29,200ft (2,713m²) of canvas, ship-rigged — as under steam, but rolled heavily. She was sold in 1885.

KRONPRINZ

1867 Germany

Laid down: 1866.
Launched: 6 May 1867
Builder: Samuda Bros. London.
Displacement: 6,297 tons (6,398 tonnes).
Dimensions: 293ft 5in (89·44m) x 50ft (15·2m) x 25ft 9in (7·85m).
Machinery: Horizontal Single Expansion engines; 8 boilers; 1 shaft; 4870 IHP.
Armour: 5in (127mm) max belt; 3in (76mm) battery; 16in (406mm) backing.
Armament: 16 x 8·25in (210mm).
Performance: 14·3kt (26·5km/h); coal 646 tons (656 tonnes); range 3,220nm (5,957m) at 10kt (18·5km/h), 1,730nm (3,200km) at 14kt (26km/h).
Crew: 541.

Designed by Reed, *Kronprinz* was not unlike the French-built *Friedrich Carl*, but had two funnels and a less pronounced ram. An iron-hulled central battery ship, she was first intended to carry 32 x 72pdr; most would have been outside the central armoured battery. Six revolving cannon and five torpedo tubes were later added to her armament.
    Kronprinz was in the Channel when war with France began in 1870: she steamed immediately to Wilhelmshaven and spent most of the war in the Jade Estuary.

FRIEDRICH CARL

1867 Germany

Laid down: 1866.
Launched: 16 January 1867.
Builder: Cie des Forges et Chantiers, Toulon.
Displacement: 6,932 tons (7,043 tonnes).
Dimensions: 308ft 10in (94·14m) x 54ft 6in (16·6m) x 26ft 5in (8·05m).
Machinery: Horizontal Single Expansion; 6 boilers; 1 shaft; 3550 IHP.
Armour: 5in-4·5in (127-114mm) belt; 4·5in (114mm) battery.
Armament: 16 x 8·25in (210mm).
Performance: 13·5kt (25km/h); range 2,210nm (4,088km) at 10kt (18·5km/h).
Crew: 531.

Germany's first ironclads were being ordered from foreign yards by the mid-1860s, and even after work began on a home-built fleet, heavy forgings and machinery were still ordered from the United Kingdom.
    Built in France, *Friedrich Carl* was a ship-rigged central battery ship, originally intended to carry 26 x 72pdr. Six revolving cannon and five 14in (356mm) torpedo tubes were later added. Her wrought iron armour had 15in (381mm) teak backing. She was considered a good sea boat.
    During the Franco-Prussian War, *Friedrich Carl* was stationed in the Jade Estuary. A torpedo school ship from 1892, she was renamed *Neptun* in 1902 and was sold in 1905.

ZARAGOSA

1867 Spain

Laid down: 1865.
Launched: 1867.
Builder: Cartagena.
Displacement: 5,530 tons (5,618 tonnes).
Dimensions: 280ft (85·34m) wl x 54ft 6in (16·64m) x 26ft 6in (8·1m) max.
Machinery: 1 shaft; 2500 IHP.
Armour: Iron 5·25in (133mm) belt; 4in (102mm) ends; 5·25in (133mm) battery; 26in (660mm) wood backing.
Armament: 21 x 68pdr.
Performance: 10·9kt (20km/h); coal 690 tons (701 tonnes).
Crew: 500.

Zaragosa was a wooden-hulled ironclad of the broadside type, armed with 21 x 68pdr smoothbores. The belt was 5·25in (133mm) thick amidships, tapering to 4in (102mm) at the ends, with 5·25in (133mm) over the battery. By 1885, her armament had been changed to 4 x 9in (229mm) Armstrongs on the main deck, 1 x 7·1in (180mm) Hontoria under the forecastle and 2 x 7·1in (180mm) Hontoria on slightly sponsoned broadside mounts. Also carried were 4 x 6·4in (163mm) Hontoria, 1 x 4·7in (119mm) and 6 x 12pdr.
    In 1873, during Spanish-American tension over the *Virginius* affair, *Zaragosa* was part of a strong Spanish force in Cuban waters. She was recalled to Spain, however, when civil war broke out there. Refitted in 1889, she became a torpedo training ship in the mid-1890s and was stricken about 1899.

Right: The imposing profile of *Agincourt* in 1867. These were the longest single-screw warships built. They were re-rigged as three-masted barques in 1893-94.

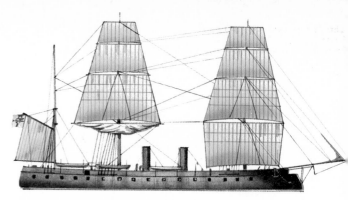

Above: *Kronprinz* in 1868.

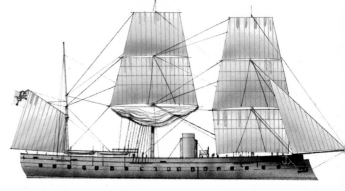

Below: *Friedrich Carl* in 1890.

Below: *Zaragosa* during the 1880s.

...GINCOURT

...367 UK

...ther ships in class: Minotaur, ...orthumberland

...aid down: 30 October 1861.
...aunched: 27 March 1865.
...uilder: Laird Bros, Birkenhead.
...isplacement: 10,600 tons (10,770 ...nnes).
...imensions: 407ft (124m) x 59ft 6in ...8·14m) x 27ft 9in (8·46m).
...achinery: Maudslay Return ...onnecting Rod engines; 10 boilers; ... shaft, 6870 IHP.
...rmour: Iron 5·5in (140mm) belt; ...5in (114mm) ends; 5·5in (140mm) ...ulkhead; 10in (254mm) teak ...acking.
...rmament: 4 x 9in (229mm) MLR;

24 x 7in (178mm) MLR; 8 x 24pdr saluting howitzers.
Performance: 14·8kt (27·4km/h); coal 750-1,400 tons (762-1,422 tonnes); radius 1,500 miles (2,413km) at 7·5kt (13·9km/h) on 6 boilers, 1,000 miles (1,609km) at 10kt (18·5km/h) on 10 boilers.
Crew: 800.

With an original specification for a 50-gun frigate with all its guns behind armour, Isaac Watts, designer of the Minotaur class, gave *Agincourt* and her sisters a greater length than *Achilles* and achieved a high speed, relative to engine power, without unduly increasing beam or draught.

An armament of 40 x 100pdr Armstrong BL in the battery and 10 more on pivots on the upper deck was envisaged, but by the time of *Agincourt*'s completion these guns had been withdrawn. They were replaced by 4 x 9in (229mm) MLR and 24 x 7in (178mm) MLR. Two 7in (178mm) were carried as chase guns firing through embrasures under the

forecastle; another fired astern from a port under the poop. The 9in (229mm) guns were mounted on metal carriages, with a rammer in the port lid, which remained closed until the gun was ready to fire; the 7in (178mm), on rope-worked carriages, could not be worked safely even in a moderate sea.

Armour extended from the upper deck to 5ft 9in (1·75m) below the waterline, covering the entire side except for a small area in the bows above the main deck, where a 5·5in (140mm) bulkhead running up to the bulwarks protected battery and chase guns. The battery deck ran almost the full length of the ship. A double bottom was fitted under the engine and boiler rooms.

Although five masts were fitted, all the class were poor sailers, making only 10kt (18·5km/h). But they steamed well and were steady. *Agincourt* was rearmed in 1875 with 17 x 9in (229mm). She served as a training ship in 1889-1909 and was then a coal hulk until sold in 1960.

DUNDERBERG

1867 USA

Laid down: 4 October 1862.
Launched: 22 July 1865.
Builder: Webb, New York.
Displacement: 7,060 tons (7,173 tonnes).
Dimensions: 377ft 4in (115·01m) x 72ft 10in (22·19m) x 21ft (6·4m).
Machinery: 2 Horizontal Back-Acting engines; 6 'return flame' boilers; 1 shaft; 4500 IHP.
Armour: Iron 3·5in (89mm) sides; 4·5in (114mm) casemate.
Armament: 4 x 15in (381mm) SB; 12 x 11in (279mm) SB.
Performance: 11·5kt (21·3km/h).
Crew: 590.

Dunderberg was designed by Lenthall as a 7,000-ton (7,112 tonne) casemate vessel with two turrets (later eliminated) and a speed of 15kt (27·75km/h).

The low freeboard hull was surmounted by a casemate with sides sloping back at 35°. There were six gun ports along each side, only 4ft 8in (1·4m) above water; two on each corner; two ahead and two astern. She first mounted 2 x 15in (381mm) and 8 x 11in (279mm) Dahlgren SB; later, one 15in (381mm) and one 11in (279mm) were added to each broadside and one 11in (279mm) at each end. The 15in (381mm) guns were at the foremost broadside ports; four of the 11in (279mm) could traverse at the end ports.

Dunderberg's hull was built up of heavy timbers with a thickness of 7ft 6in (2·3m) at the knuckle. Much green timber was used, leading to speedy deterioration. She had a double bottom, a collision bulkhead, longitudinal and transverse water-tight bulkheads, and a 50ft (15·24m) long ram of solid oak. The funnel, 13ft (3·96m) in diameter, had armoured gratings within to keep out debris.

Construction was slow because of material shortages and eventually, being no longer needed, *Dunderberg* was taken back by her builder and sold to France. Renamed *Rochambeau*, she was rearmed with 4 x 10·8in (274mm) and 10 x 9·4in (239mm). She was briefly in commission during the Franco-Prussian War as one of Bouet's squadron attacking Kolberg. She was stricken in 1872.

VITORIA

1867 *Spain*

Launched: 4 November 1865.
Builder: Thames Iron Works.
Displacement: 7,135tons (7,249 tonnes).
Dimensions: 316ft 2in (96·37m) pp x 57ft (17·37m) x 26ft 5in (8·05m) max.
Machinery: Penn engines; 1 shaft; 4500 IHP.
Armour: 5·5in (140mm) belt; 3·9in (98mm) ends; 5in (127mm) battery; 14in (356mm) backing.
Armament: 30 x 68pdr.
Performance: 12·5kt (23·1km/h).
Crew: 500.

Vitoria was a ship-rigged, iron-hulled, broadside ironclad frigate with a ram bow. A full-length belt extended from 13ft (3·96m) above the waterline, covering the main battery, to 7ft (2·13m) below. By 1886 her main armament was 8 x 9in (229mm) MLR mounted on the broadside. Amidships, above the battery, was an armoured redoubt housing 2 x 8in (203mm) Armstrong RML and also giving added protection to the conning tower. One 7·9in (201mm) Hontoria was carried in the bows beneath the topgallant forecastle.

Reconstructed and reboilered at La Seyne in 1897-98, she received 6 x 6·4in (163mm) QF, 6 x 5·5in (140mm) QF, 6 x 6pdr plus smaller, and two torpedo tubes. Her rig was reduced to two military masts. Plans for new hull armour were abandoned, but she was later again rearmed with 4 x 8in (203mm) Hontoria QF, 12 x 5·9in (150mm) Skoda QF, 8 x 57mm MG and 10 light guns.

In 1873 *Vitoria* was seized by insurgents at Cartagena. Recovered by Government forces within a few weeks, she was in action on 10 October against an insurgent force of three ironclads. In 1898 she was relegated to coast defence, with a crew reduced to 420. Her speed was by then 11kt (20·35km/h) with a range of about 2,500 miles (4,022km) at economical steaming. A gunnery training ship after 1900, she was disarmed in 1908, stricken in 1912.

Below: When completed, *Vitoria* helped put Spain fifth among naval powers.

Below: *Hercules* in 1869. The 9in (229mm) armour amidships had 40in (1·02m) of teak backing.

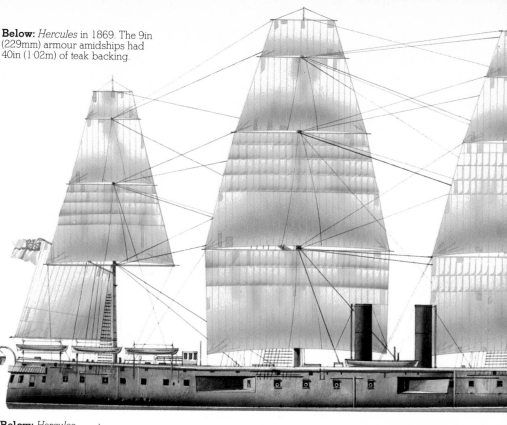

Below: *Hercules,* 1894 reduced rig.

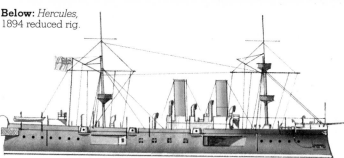

HERCULES

1868 *UK*

Laid down: 1 February 1866.
Launched: 10 February 1868.
Builder: Chatham Dockyard.
Displacement: 8,677 tons (8,816 tonnes); 8,830 tons (8,971 tonnes) full load.
Dimensions: 325ft (99·06m) pp x 59ft 0½in (18m) x 25ft (7·62m) mean.
Machinery: Penn 2-cylinder Horizontal Trunk; 9 boilers; 1 shaft; 7178 IHP.
Armour: Iron 9in (229mm) belt; 6in (152mm) ends; 10in-20in (254-508mm) wood backing; 6in-5in (152-127mm) bulkheads; 8in (203mm) battery.

Below: *Vitoria* after 1897-98 refit.

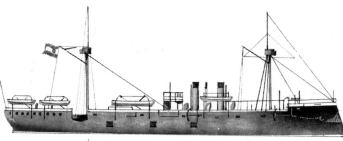

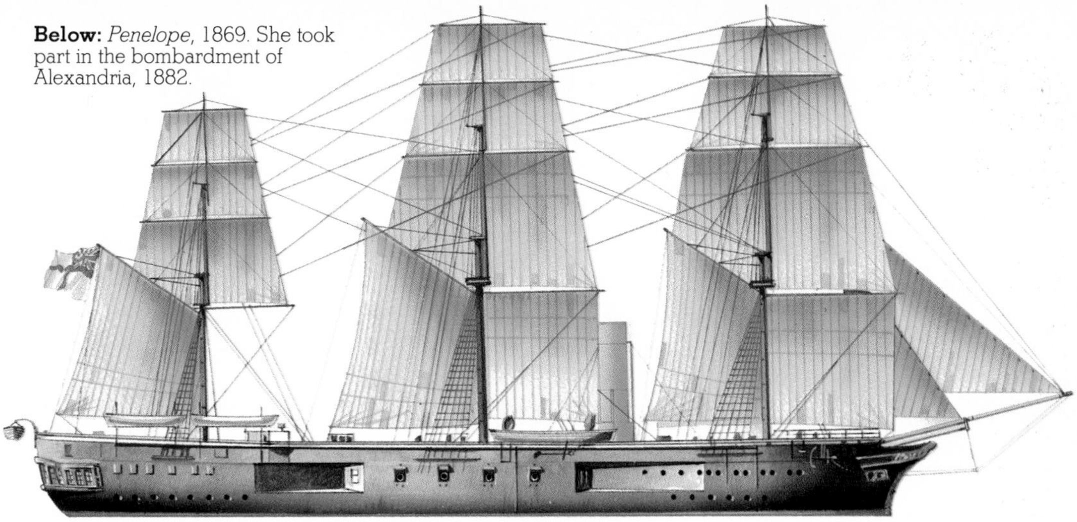

Below: *Penelope*, 1869. She took part in the bombardment of Alexandria, 1882.

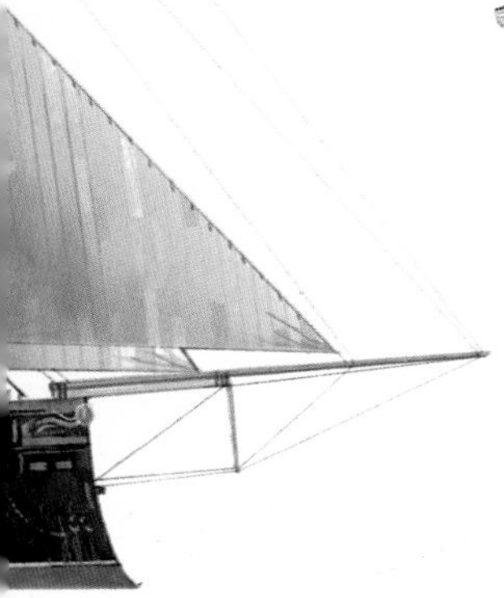

rmament: 8 x 10in (254mm) MLR; x 9in (229mm) MLR; 4 x 7in 78mm) MLR; 8 saluting.
rformance: 14·69kt (27·2km/h); al 610 tons (620 tonnes); range 600 miles (2,574km) at 8kt 4·8km/h).
ew: 638.

a report in June 1866, Captain ooper Key of the gunnery tablishment *Excellent* stressed the ed for all-round fire in ironclads. A od reason for adopting turrets, this so encouraged Reed in the policy providing end-on fire. In *Hercules*, improved *Bellerophon*, he added ıbrasures at each end of the battery nidships.

The new and more powerful 10in 54mm) gun was specified for *ercules*, all these weapons being ncentrated in the main battery. Two ı (178mm) were mounted at each d of the upper deck, with 1 x 9in 29mm) immediately below.

A waterline belt, 9in (229mm) ck, ran for 73ft 9in (22·48m) nidships, reducing to 8in (203mm) d then 6in (152mm) at the ends d rising at each end of the upper ck to screen the chase guns. The les of the battery were protected 8in (203mm) armour, with a 6in 52mm) thick bulkhead forward d a 5in (127mm) bulkhead aft. Improved hull lines, more efficient gines and increased boiler essure of up to 30 psi gave a speed 14·69kt (27·2km/h). The initial rig s increased to 49,400ft² (4,589m²), cluding stunsails, but *Hercules* uld only make 11kt (20·35km/h) der sail. She was a steady gun atform and, although difficult to ndle in a storm, a good sea boat.

In 1878 two torpedo carriages ere added and, in 1886, a net fence. She was re-engined in 92-93 with vertical triple pansion and boilers of 140 psi, ving 15·9kt (29·4km/h). Six 4·7in 19mm) QF were added to the per deck; 2 x 6in (152mm) QF placed the 7in (178mm) at the bow; d 9 x 6pdr and 13 x 3pdr were ded to the upper works. Placed in serve after her refit, *Hercules* was raining ship at Portsmouth until she s sold in 1932.

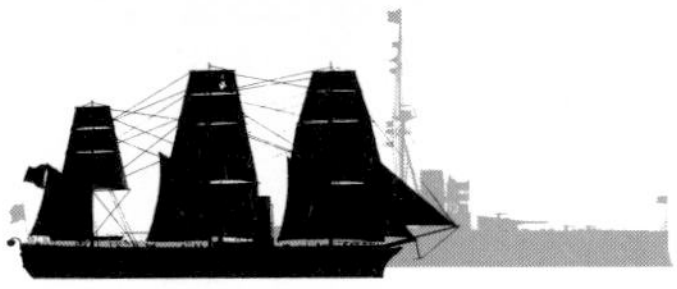

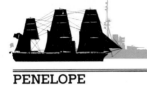

PENELOPE

1868 *UK*

Laid down: 4 September 1865.
Launched: 18 June 1867.
Builder: Pembroke Dockyard.
Displacement: 4,470 tons (4,542 tonnes).
Dimensions: 265ft (80·77m) pp x 50ft (15·24m) x 16ft 9in (5·1m) mean.
Machinery: Maudslay Horizontal Reciprocating 3-cylinder; 4 boilers; 2 screws; 4763 IHP.
Armour: Iron 6in (152mm) belt; 5in (127mm) ends; 10in-11in (254-279mm) wood backing; 6in (152mm) battery; 4·5in (114mm) bulkheads.
Armament: 8 x 8in (203mm) MLR; 3 x 5in (127mm) BLR; 2 x 20pdr BLR.
Performance: 12·76kt (23·6km/h); coal 500 tons (508 tonnes); range 1,360 miles (2,188km) at 10kt (18·5km/h).
Crew: 350.

Designed by Barnaby, *Penelope* had an unusually shallow draught—only 17·5ft (5·33m)—because of the provision of a square and full hull for buoyancy. A single screw could not operate efficiently at such a depth, so two screws were fitted; the space in the hull between them was hollowed out to allow water to flow up from the keel. Twin rudders were also fitted.

The last of the small ironclads, *Penelope* had limited protection: the belt, 5ft 6in (1·7m) deep, did not reach the main deck. The 68ft (20·7m) long battery amidships was covered by 6in (152mm) armour, with a 96ft (29·3m) strake of 6in (152mm) armour running between battery and belt. The battery housed the 8in (203mm) MLR, with embrasures permitting near ahead and astern fire by the corner guns. One 5in (127mm) BLR was mounted aft on the upper deck, with two more forward.

Two large sets of engines were laid in a width of 50ft (15·24m), each with three small cylinders. This demanded a huge coal supply, restricting range in spite of the large bunkerage. She was ship rigged with 18,250ft² (1,695m²) of canvas, but made only 8·5kt (15·7km/h): her shallow draught gave no grip and allowed drift to leeward.

A prison hulk at Cape Town from 1897, *Penelope* was sold in 1912.

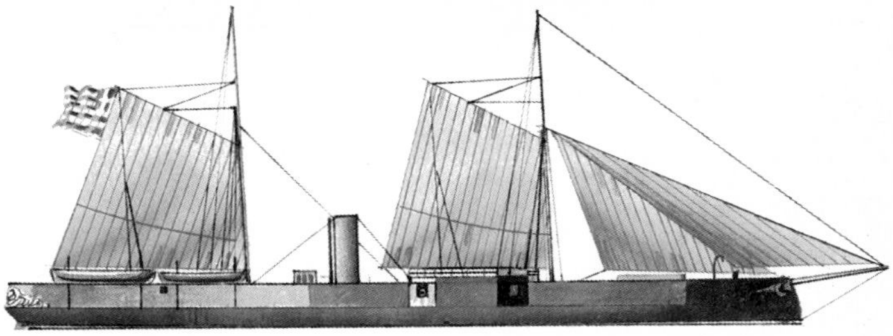

Above: *Basileos Georgios* in 1868.

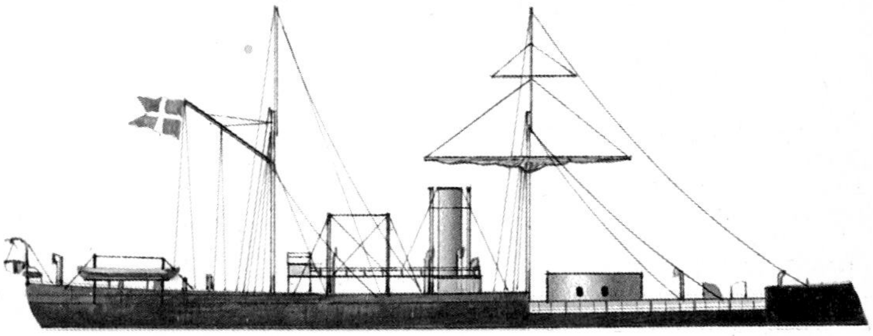

Below: *Lindormen* in 1869.

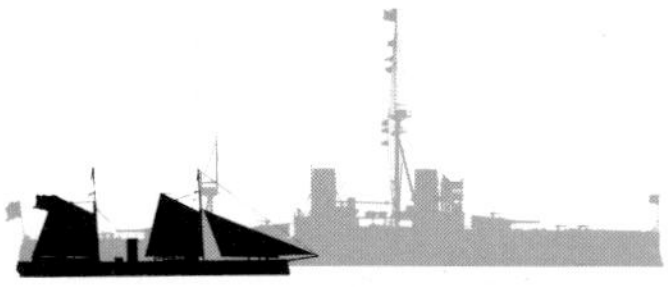

BASILEOS GEORGIOS

1868 *Greece*

Laid down: 1866.
Launched: 28 December 1867.
Builder: Thames Iron Works.
Displacement: 1,774 tons (1,802 tonnes).
Dimensions: 200ft (60·96m) pp x 33ft (10·06m) x 16ft (4·88m) max.
Machinery: Two engines; 2 screws; 2400 IHP.
Armour: Iron 7in (178mm) belt; 6in (152mm) ends; 6in (152mm) battery; 9in (229mm) backing.
Armament: 2 x 9in (229mm) RML; 2 x 20pdr.
Performance: 13kt (24km/h); coal 210 tons (213 tonnes); range 1,200 miles (1,931km) at 10kt (18·5km/h).
Crew: 152.

Designed by George Mackrow, *Basileos Georgios* was a small central battery ship with a full-length belt extending 3ft 6in (1·07m) below the waterline and 6ft 6in (1·98m) above. Armour accounted for 330 tons (335 tonnes) of the displacement.

The battery, forward of centre and ahead of the funnel, had end ports enabling the 9in (229mm) guns—later replaced by 2 x 8·2in (208mm)—to fire almost ahead and astern. Mackrow claimed that, for her size, she had greater offensive/defensive powers than any other ironclad.

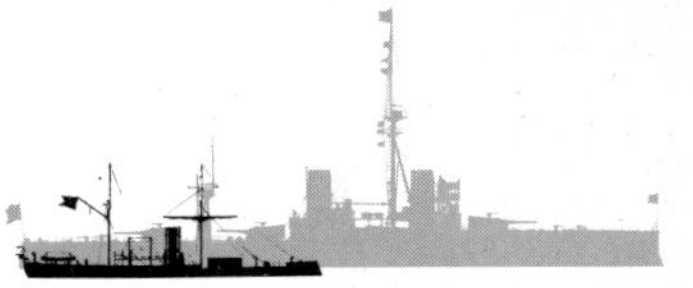

LINDORMEN

1868 *Denmark*

Laid down 1867.
Launched: 1868.
Builder: Copenhagen Dockyard.
Displacement: 2,048 tons (2,081 tonnes).
Dimensions: 217ft 11in (66·42m) x 39ft 4in (11·99m) x 14ft 7in (4·44m) max.
Machinery: 2 shafts; 1560 IHP.
Armour: Iron 5in (127mm) belt; 3in (76mm) ends; 5in (127mm) conning tower; 5·5in (140mm) turret; 10in (254mm) backing.
Armament: 2 x 9in (229mm) RML; 2 light machine guns.
Performance: 12kt (22·2km/h); coal 120 tons (122 tonnes).
Crew: 150.

Denmark continued to strengthen her Navy in 1864-70, when *Lindormen*, like the majority of Danish warships, was built at Copenhagen Dockyard. She had a low freeboard and a single turret. The bridge was aft, with the conning tower beneath it. In 1875, 2 x 3in (76mm) ML were added, and in 1879 a further 2 x 3·4in (86mm) BL and 4 x 1pdr. In 1885, the 3in (76mm) ML were replaced by 3·4in (86mm) BL and the 9in (229mm) in the turret by 2 x 5·9in (150mm). She was discarded around 1907.

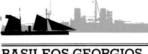

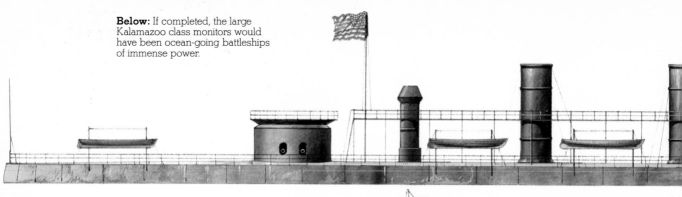

Below: If completed, the large Kalamazoo class monitors would have been ocean-going battleships of immense power.

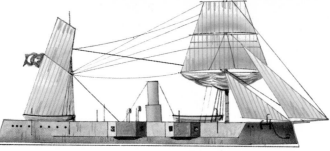

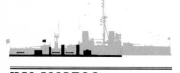

KALAMAZOO

1869 *USA*
Other ships in class: *Passaconaway, Quinsigamond, Shackamaxon*

Laid down: 1863.
Launched: Never launched.
Builder: New York Navy Yard.
Displacement: 5,660 tons (5,751 tonnes).
Dimensions: 345ft (105·15m) x 56ft 8in (17·27m) x 17ft 6in (5·33m).
Machinery: 2 sets of 2 Horizontal Direct Acting engines; 8 Martin boilers; 2 shafts.
Armour: Iron 6in (152mm) side; 15in (381mm) turret; 3in (76mm) deck.
Armament: 4 x 15in (381mm).
Performance: 10·5kt (19·4km/h).
Crew: Not known.

In 1863, at the height of the Civil War, the US Navy increased by 130 ships but lost 32. A total of 58 new ships was ordered. Among these were the four Kalamazoo class, designed by Delano. Apart from the *Dunderberg*, these were the largest warships of any type ordered during the Civil War; the original specification was for 10,000-ton (10,160 tonne) casemate ships, but the Kalamazoos emerged as huge monitors, able to fight their guns in a seaway. They were, along with (possibly) the four Monadnocks, the only monitors that would have been able to confront European ironclads.

They had wooden hulls with finer lines than previous monitors. The freeboard was 3ft 9in (1·14m) and the turret weights were to be supported by iron truss girders. The side armour comprised 2 x 3in (76mm) plates, reducing to 1 x 3in (76mm) at the lower edge, with 8in (203mm) square iron stringers at the waterline for greater strength. Six boilers were originally specified, but by 1865 this had increased to eight, with coal consumption estimated at about 84 tons (85·34 tonnes) per day.

All four were laid down in US Navy Yards, but progress was slow; late in 1865, all work stopped. The ships lay exposed to the elements and, being built largely of unseasoned timber, their hulls rotted. *Shackamaxon*, renamed *Hecla* and then *Nebraska*, was broken up on the stocks in 1874. The remaining three—*Kalamazoo*, renamed *Colossus*; *Quinsigamond*, renamed *Hercules* and then *Oregon*; *Passaconaway*, renamed *Thunderer* and then *Massachusetts*—suffered the same fate in 1884. The United States Navy had to wait thirty years to receive another such class of ocean-going battleships.

Above: *Avni Illah*, 1869. She was sunk in the Turco-Italian War, 1912.

Below: *Assari Shevket* with brig rig, 1869. Battery shields funnel base.

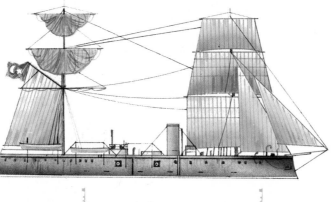

Below: *Lufti Djelil* in 1869. The freeboard of this Turkish ironclad was only 4ft 3in (1·3m) amidships.

AVNI ILLAH

1869 *Turkey*
Other ships in class: *Muin-i-Zaffer*

Launched: 1869.
Builder: Thames Iron Works.
Displacement: 2,362 tons (2,400 tonnes).
Dimensions: 238ft 6in (72·7m) x 36ft (10·97m) x 16ft 5in (5m) max.
Machinery: Horizontal Compound; 1 shaft; 2200 IHP.
Armour: Iron 6in (152mm) belt; 5in (127mm) ends; 5in (127mm) battery.
Armament: 4 x 9in (229mm).
Performance: 12·5kt (23km/h); coal 220 tons (223·5 tonnes).
Crew: 140.

The iron-hulled *Avni Illah* had two octagonal batteries amidships, with gun ports 6ft 6in (1·98m) above the waterline. The belt extended from 3ft 9in (1·14m) below water to 3ft (0·91m) above. A partial double bottom was fitted.

Reconstructed by Ansaldo in 1903-07, she was rearmed with 4 x 5·9in (150mm) QF plus 18 smaller. She was reboilered and a conning tower and a single military mast amidships were added. She was sunk by Italian cruisers at Beirut on 23 February 1912. *Muin-i-Zaffer* was also reconstructed by Ansaldo; she was discarded in the early 1920s.

ASSARI SHEVKET

1869 *Turkey*
Other ships in class: *Nijmi Shevket*

Launched: 1868.
Builder: La Seyne.
Displacement: 2,046 tons (2,079 tonnes).
Dimensions: 203ft 5in (62m) pp x 42ft 7in (12·98m) x 16ft 5in (5m) max.
Machinery: 1 shaft; 1750 IHP.
Armour: Iron 6in-4·5in (152-114mm) belt; 4·5in (114mm) battery; 9in (229mm) wood backing; 4·5in (114mm) barbette.
Armament: 1 x 9in (229mm); 4 x 7in (178mm).
Performance: 12kt (22·2km/h); coal 250 tons (254 tonnes).
Crew: 170.

These were small, iron-hulled ironclads with ram bows and double bottoms. The complete waterline belt was 6in (152mm) thick, reducing to 4·5in (114mm) below the waterline, and 10ft 3in (3·12m) deep, with 6ft (1·83m) below water. The battery housed 4 x 7in (178mm) ML; above and to the rear was mounted a centreline barbette housing 1 x 9in (229mm) ML with 100° training to port or starboard.

By 1891, six small guns had been added. The ships were reboilered in 1892 and were discarded in 1900.

LUFTI DJELIL

1869 *Turkey*
Other ships in class: *Hifzi Rahman*

Launched: 1868.
Builder: Bordeaux.
Displacement: 2,540 tons (2,581 tonnes).
Dimensions: 204ft 6in (62·18m) pp x 45ft 11in (14m) x 14ft 6in (4·42m) max.
Machinery: 2 shafts; 2000 IHP.
Armour: Iron 5·5in (140mm) belt; 4·6in (117mm) ends; 5·5in (140mm) turrets.
Armament: 2 x 8in (203mm); 2 x (178mm).
Performance: 12kt (22·2km/h); coal 300 tons (305 tonnes).
Crew: 130.

By the time of the outbreak of the Russo-Turkish War of 1877-78 Turkey had built up an ironclad fleet of reasonable size. But during the 14-month conflict, because her ships had been neglected, Turkey seemed unable to make adequate use of her overwhelming strength in the Black Sea, where she had 15 ironclads and many smaller craft.

Among the Black Sea force was *Lufti Djelil* ("Divine Grace"). She and her sister ship, *Hifzi Rahman*, had been ordered by Egypt after that country had achieved almost total

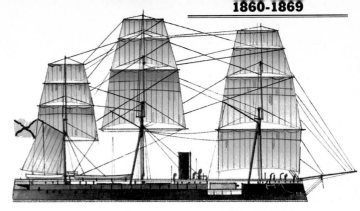

Above: Author's impression of *Minin* as planned as a full-rigged turret ship with tripod masts.

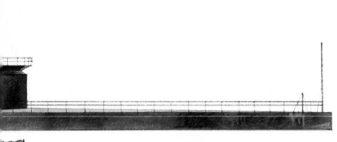

MININ

1869 (1878 as cruiser) *Russia*

Laid down: 12 November 1866.
Launched: 22 October 1869.
Builder: Baltic Works, St Petersburg.
Displacement: 5,740 tons (5,832 tonnes).
Dimensions: 309ft 4in (94·28m) x 49ft (14·9m) x 23ft 7in (7·19m) max.
Machinery: Single Horizontal Direct Acting engines; 8 boilers; 1 shaft; 4000 IHP.
Armour: Iron 6in (152mm) belt; 15in (381mm) wood backing; 4·5in (114mm) bulkheads; 2in (51mm) main deck; 1in (25mm) upper deck.
Armament: 4 x 11in (279mm); 4 x 6in (152mm).
Performance: 14kt (25·9km/h); coal c700 tons (711 tonnes); range 3,000nm (5,550km) at c14kt (25·9km/h).
Crew: c500.

dependence of Turkey. Fearing the ossibility of later hostilities with Egypt, however, Turkey took over the essels in 1869 while they were still in ench hands—both vessels were ilt by the Bordeaux yard.

Lufti Djelil had a raised forecastle d poop, a ram bow, and carried o turrets on the centre line. The rger fore turret housed 2 x 8in 03mm) guns; the 7in (178mm) uns were housed in the aft turret. orked by hand, the turrets needed 4 men to rotate them. Turret bases, agazines and machinery had 3in 6mm) side armour and were vered by a 1·5in (38mm) protective ck. Hinged bulwarks amidships uld be lowered during action. rmour on the belt amidships was 5in (140mm) thick, tapering to 4·6in 17mm) at the ends and extending t 6in (0·76m) above and below the aterline. The forecastle was moured: later, in *Hifzi Rahman*, it used a 4·7in (119mm) gun.

A light barque rig was fitted. To duce the shrouds, which interfered th the working of the turret guns, pod masts were shipped.

Early in the Russo-Turkish War, fti Djelil formed part of the Danube tilla. On 10 May 1877, while acking Russian land positions at aila, she was struck by a shell nich exploded in a magazine and estroyed her. *Hifzi Rahman* was re-med, and was not taken out of rvice until the turn of the century.

ght: *Ryujo* in 1869. She became a nnery training ship in 1894 when her guns were removed and 1 x 7in (170mm) and 5 x 64pdr added place of them.

RYUJO

1869 *Japan*

Laid down: 1864.
Launched: 1864.
Builder: Hall, Aberdeen.
Displacement: 1,864 tons (1,894 tonnes).
Dimensions: 213ft 3in (65m) x 38ft 10½in (11·85m) x 17ft 6in (5·3m).
Machinery: 2-cylinder Compound engines; 1 shaft; 800 IHP.

Armour: Iron 4·5in (114mm) belt; 4in (102mm) battery.
Armament: 2 x 6·5in (165mm); 10 x 5·5in (140mm).
Performance: 9kt (16·65km/h); coal 350 tons (356 tonnes).
Crew: 275.

Speculatively built, possibly for the Confederate States, this composite-hulled broadside corvette was bought by a Japanese prince as *Ihosho Maru* and presented to the Emperor late in 1870 as *Ryujo*.

Her hull was divided into several large compartments. Armour extended from the spar deck, where the 6·5in (165mm) were pivot-mounted, to 3ft (0·91m) below the waterline. She was hulked in 1902 and broken up in 1904.

Originally planned as a sister to the armoured corvette *Kniaz Pojarski*, *Minin* was altered to a turret ship and was to have mounted 2 x 11in (279mm) in each of two turrets and 4 x 6in (152mm) in armoured positions, two on the forecastle and two on the poop.

Work halted after launching, following the loss of the British turret ship *Captain*, and she was completed in 1878 as an armoured cruiser, with 4 x 8in (203mm), 12 x 6in (152mm), plus smaller. The belt extended to 5ft (1·5m) below water.

Minin served in the Pacific in the 1880s and in 1909 was converted to a minelayer and renamed *Ladoga*. On 15 August 1915, she sank on a mine laid by the German U-boat *UC 4*.

KÖNIG WILHELM

1869 Germany

Laid down: 1865.
Launched: 25 April 1868.
Builder: Thames Iron Works.
Displacement: 10,761 tons (10,933 tonnes).
Dimensions: 368ft 1in (112·2m) x 60ft (18·3m) x 28ft (8·56m).
Machinery: Horizontal Single Expansion engine; 8 boilers; 1 shaft; 8345 IHP.
Armour: Wrought iron 12in (305mm) belt; 6in (152mm) ends; 8in (203mm) battery; 6in (152mm) ends; 2in (51mm) deck; 10in (254mm) backing.
Armament: 18 x 9·4in (240mm); 5 x 8·3in (210mm).
Performance: 14·7kt (27·2km/h);

coal 750 tons (762 tonnes); range 1,300nm (2,405km) at 10kt (18·5km/h).
Crew: 730.

As part of the British Government's policy of strengthening the Turkish Navy developed by Sultan Abdul Aziz, Chief Constructor Edward Reed was instructed to design a large central battery ship named *Fatikh*. Reed had nothing to do with her construction after January 1867 when, work having already begun, she was purchased by the Prussian Government and renamed *Wilhelm I*. She was renamed *König Wilhelm* on launch.

The hull was built up on the bracket frame system and had a deep double bottom. A ram bow was fitted. A full-length belt covered the sides up to the main deck: it was 12in

(305mm) thick, reducing to 6in (152mm) at the ends, and was reduced in depth in front of the casemate, this section being covered by a thin steel deck. The battery ends were protected by a bulkhead rising to the spar deck. At each end of the battery, standing up clear of the upper deck, was a narrow structure running across the deck. Each housed two guns, firing ahead or on the beam in the forward structure and to the rear and abeam in the after structure, which overlapped the hull by several feet.

During the Franco-Prussian War *König Wilhelm* spent most of her time in the Jade with defective engines. On 31 May 1878, while serving as flagship of Rear-Admiral von Batsch, she collided with and sank the 7,718-ton (7,841 tonne)

turret ship *Grosser Kurfürst* off Folkestone. She was thoroughly overhauled at Wilhelmshaven in 1878-82: her ram was replaced and she was given new boilers. By the 1890s, 7 x 5·9in (150mm), 4 x 3·1in (80mm), 6 x 37mm automatic cannon and 5 x 13·8in (350mm) torpedo tubes had been added and 1 x 8·3in (210mm) removed.

She was reclassified as a heavy cruiser after a major conversion by Blohm und Voss in 1895-96: the 9·4in (240mm) guns were retained, but the smaller guns now numbered 1 x 5·9in (150mm) and 16 x 3·5in (88mm). The rig was reduced to two military masts with fighting tops and a small mizzen. A harbour ship in 1904-07, she was extensively altered to become a school ship. She was sold in 1921.

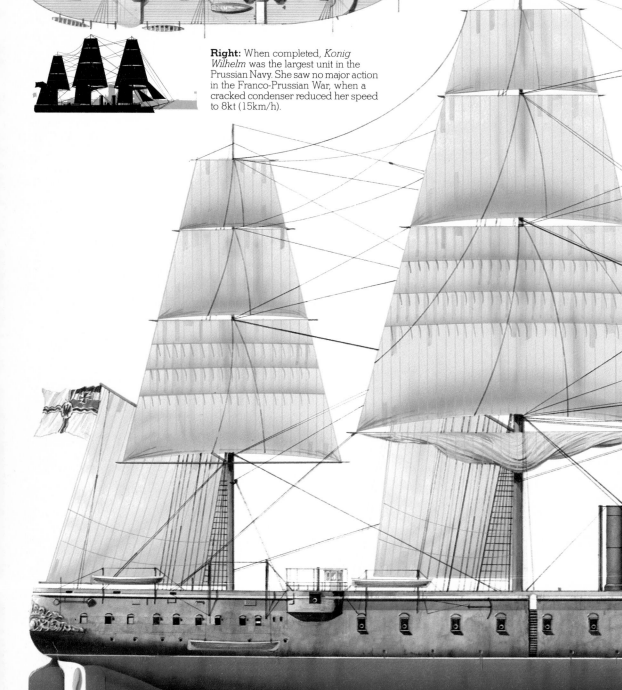

Right: When completed, *König Wilhelm* was the largest unit in the Prussian Navy. She saw no major action in the Franco-Prussian War, when a cracked condenser reduced her speed to 8kt (15km/h).

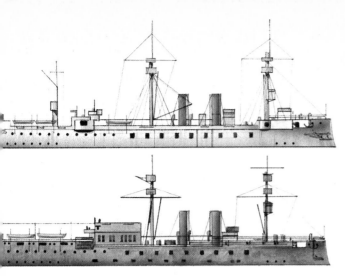

Top: *König Wilhelm* as a heavy cruiser after her extensive refit in 1895-96, when many light guns were added and coal supply was raised to 1,030 tons (1,046 tonnes).

Above: *König Wilhelm* as school ship to the Naval Academy after 1907, following another refit.

Above right: *König Wilhelm* in the early part of her career. On 31 May 1878, turning to avoid two sailing ships crossing her bows, she rammed the large turret ship *Grosser Kurfürst*, which sank within five minutes with great loss of life.

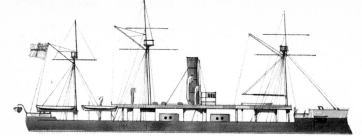

MONARCH

1869 *UK*

Laid down: 1 June 1866.
Launched: 25 May 1868.
Builder: Chatham Dockyard.
Displacement: 8,322 tons (8,455 tonnes).
Dimensions: 330ft (100·58m) pp x 57ft 6in (17·53m) x 24ft 3in (7·39m) mean.
Machinery: Humphreys & Tennant 2-cylinder Return Connecting Rod; 9 boilers; 1 shaft; 7842 IHP.
Armour: Iron 7in-6in-4·5in (178-152-114mm) sides; 4·5in-4in (114-102mm) bulkheads; 5in (127mm) bow screen; 8in (203mm) turrets; 10in (254mm) face; 8in (203mm) conning tower.
Armament: 4 x 12in (305mm) MLR; 3 x 7in (178mm) MLR.
Performance: 14·94kt (27·6km/h); coal 600 tons (610 tonnes); range 2,310 miles (3,717km) at 11kt (20·35km/h).
Crew: 575.

Monarch was the first large sea-going turret ship, departing from the monitor type in having high freeboard and a full spread of canvas. Designed by Reed, she was to have had both a forecastle and poop. A full rig was considered essential, since unreliable and uneconomic engines gave a poor radius of action.

The Admiralty first asked for 15-ton (15·24 tonne) guns and 6in (152mm) armour, but Reed demanded more tonnage to allow for the carriage of 25-ton (25·4 tonne) guns and 7in (178mm) armour. As completed *Monarch* had the hull form of a central battery ship but with finer lines, three decks, and a forecastle but no poop. Freeboard amidships was 14ft (4·27m), with guns carried 17ft (5·18m) above the waterline—7ft (2·13m) higher than the batteries in the rest of the fleet. Unfortunately, the forecastle and rig prevented axial fire.

The two closely grouped turrets were surrounded by a flying bridge running from foremast to aft of the mainmast and supported by casings for ladders, mainmast and funnel base. Forward of the funnel was a small conning tower with limited side vision.

The short forecastle housed 2 x 7in (178mm) MLR, with another aft, 8ft (2·4m) above water, to give some end-on fire. Hinged bulwarks of light iron could be lowered in action. A continuous belt extended from the main deck to 5ft (1·5m) below the waterline; atop this rested a 100ft (30·5m) long box citadel, protecting the turret bases and, in part, the magazines. Forward, a deep curved screen 5in (127mm) thick protected against raking fire and shielded the

chase guns, which fired through embrasures.

Monarch was the fastest battleship of her day, making 14·94kt (27·6km/h) on trial; during a six-hour full-power trial she averaged only 0·25kt (0·46km/h) less. Her range under steam with full bunkers was 1,560 miles (2,510km) at 12·5kt (23km/h) in 5 days 5 hours. She had a first class rig with 27,700ft² (2,573m²) of canvas, giving a speed under sail in favourable conditions of 13kt (24km/h). Auxiliary equipment was comprehensive, with steam engines, steam steering and steam capstan. Although a good sea boat and steady gun platform, she was difficult to handle; steam power was necessary when staying or wearing. Handling improved when the balanced rudder was altered.

Although *Monarch* satisfied all the Admiralty's requirements, Reed did not regard her as his ideal fighting ship: he would have preferred to have had no forecastle or poop on a freeboard of 12ft (3·66m), with turrets farther apart and lightly rigged masts nearer the ends, thus permitting axial fire.

Monarch was altered to barque rig in 1872. Between 1890-97, the rig was removed and numerous small guns were added, with speed increasing to 15·75kt (29km/h). A guard ship at Simonstown until 1905, she was sold in 1906.

Left: *Monarch*, 1897, after refit: rig removed; funnel heightened; a charthouse, military tops and many small weapons added. Torpedo launchers added 1878; 2 x 9in (229mm) in 1871.

ROMA

1869 *Italy*
Other ships in class: *Venezia*

Laid down: February 1863.
Launched: 18 December 1865.
Builder: La Foce, Genoa.
Displacement: 6,250 tons (6,350 tonnes) full load.
Dimensions: 261ft 4½in (79·67m) pp x 57ft (17·37m) x 24ft 10in (7·57m).
Machinery: Single Expansion; 6

cylindrical boilers; 1 shaft; 3670 IHP.
Armour: Iron 6in (152mm) belt; 26in (660mm) backing.
Armament: 5 x 10in (254mm); 12 x 8in (203mm).
Performance: 13kt (24km/h); coal 580 tons (589 tonnes); range 1,940nm (3589km) at 10kt (18·5km/h).
Crew: 550.

Roma took six years to build and wa[s] completed as a wooden broadside ironclad. Her sister *Venezia* took ten years, but had a central battery.

Roma was rearmed in 1875 and 1886 and from 1890, as main defence ship at La Spezia, carried 5 x 8in (203mm). In 1895 she became a floating ammunition ship. She was set afire by lightning and scuttled in 1896.

Below: *Roma* in 1870.

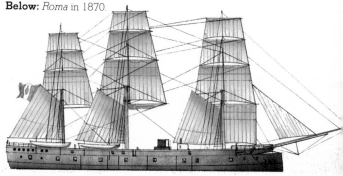

Left: *Monarch* as completed in 1869, when she was the first British battleship to mount 12in (305mm) guns. The shell weight was 600lb (272kg) and a double round could be fired within two minutes.

SAGUNTO

1869 *Spain*

Launched: 1869
Builder: Ferrol.
Displacement: 7,352 tons (7,470 tonnes).
Dimensions: 294ft (89·61m) x 57ft (17·37m) x 29ft (8·83m) mean/31ft (9·44m) max.
Machinery: Horizontal Trunk engines; 1 shaft; 3700IHP.
Armour: Iron 6in (152mm) belt; 5·5in (140mm) battery; 5in (127mm) barbette; 4in (102mm) bulkheads; 24in (610mm) backing.
Armament: 10 x 8·625in (219mm); 3 x 7·06in (179mm).
Performance: 12kt (22·2km/h); coal 900 tons (914 tonnes).

Sagunto, planned as a 100-gun ship-of-the-line, was completed as a 30-gun armoured frigate with a ram bow and a complete waterline belt. There was a box battery amidships, with a small barbette above it. One 7·06in (179mm) gun was positioned in the bows under the forecastle.

By 1885, *Sagunto* carried 6 x 9in (229mm) RML, 2 x 8in (203mm) RML and 3 x 7·1in (180mm), plus smaller. By then her hull was rotten and speed reduced to 8kt (14·8km/h).

MENDEZ NUNEZ

1869 *Spain*

Laid down: Not known.
Launched: 1869.
Builder: Not known.
Displacement: 3,382 tons (3,436 tonnes).
Dimensions: 236ft 3in (72·02m) x 49ft 4in (15·05m) x 21ft 11in (6·43m) mean.
Machinery: 1 shaft; 500 NHP.
Armour: 5in (127mm) belt; 5in (127mm) battery; 3in (76mm) ends; 20·375in (518mm) backing.
Armament: Not known.
Performance: 8kt (14·8km/h); coal 400 tons (406 tonnes).
Crew: Not known.

During Spain's war against Peru and Chile, the 38-gun wooden screw frigate *Resolucion*, launched in 1861, was severely damaged, along with several other Spanish ships, while taking part in the bombardment of Callao, 2 May 1866. While docked for repair, she was rebuilt as an armoured corvette with a ram bow and renamed *Mendez Nunez*.

During the 1880s she was rearmed with 4 x 9in (229mm) MLR and 2 x 8in (203mm) RML, all of Armstrong design.

Below: *Mendez Nunez*, 1870.

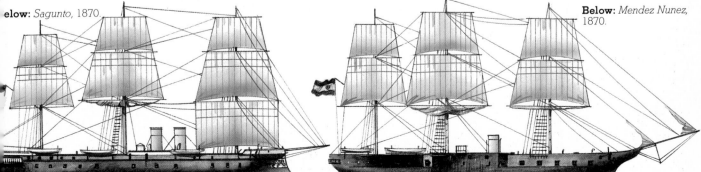

Below: *Sagunto*, 1870.

1870-1879

The production of ever-larger guns and ever-thicker armour continued at a hectic pace through the 1870s, and the navies of most nations were still characterised by new ships of widely differing configurations. Central battery ships, rather than broadside ironclads were the dominant type in many navies, but the turret ship was also pressed forward, despite the weight penalties (shown up in low freeboard and hence poor seakeeping), it imposed. The introduction of steel in place of iron in battleship construction heralded an important development. The effects of the Civil War in the United States led to that country's navy declining in importance, but the decade witnessed the emergence of a German Navy that would within a generation be one of Europe's most potent forces.

ARMOUR

During the 1860s steady progress had been made in increasing the thickness of armour. At first, the entire hull side down to 5ft-6ft (1·5-1·8m) below water was armoured, with ports cut between the upper and main decks for numerous guns mounted on the broadside. As guns increased in size, their number diminished; thus, the area that needed to be protected was smaller and could carry thicker armour. The hull outside the main battery was left unarmoured save for a narrow belt at its extremities. Solid plate was generally considered superior to laminated armour of the kind used on many vessels in the US Civil War: 4in (102mm) solid plate was preferred to 6in (152mm) laminated.

The 1870s saw massive improvements in the development of both armour and guns. Until early in the decade, wrought iron armour was in general use, but as the thickness of the plates increased, so did the difficulty of maintaining the necessary homogeneity of the material. Armour in excess of 14in (356mm) thickness presented the major problem, and experiments were made with 'sandwich' armour, using one 8in (203mm) and one 6in (152mm) plate as the elements of the protective 'sandwich'.

Trials against solid 14in (356mm) plate showed that sandwich armour was superior in resistance and had other advantages. By overlapping the plates rather than placing one directly over the other, any weakness caused by the gaps, however small, between the plates was decreased. The size of individual plates was limited by weight rather than area; thus, fewer sandwich plates covered a larger area than solid plates, reducing still further the weakness inherent in the edges and butts of joints. Wrought iron was still used, but if it was applied in any great thickness, the sandwich system was adopted.

Armour development was hastened by the appearance of such powerful guns as the French Marine Artillery Model 1870, the Woolwich 38-ton (38·61 tonne) gun and heavy weapons from Krupp of Germany. There was soon another rapid increase in the size of guns, to 76 tons (77·22 tonnes), 80 tons (81·28 tonnes) and more than 100 tons (101·6 tonnes)—and even the thickest armour was shown to offer insufficient protection against the projectiles delivered by these monster weapons.

In 1876, in tests at Muggiano, Italy, steel plates proved to be superior to wrought iron. The steel plates tested were manufactured by Schneider using an open hearth process: this produced a uniform material which was then forged. In 1877, Creusot used the process to cast a 110-ton (111·76 tonne) ingot.

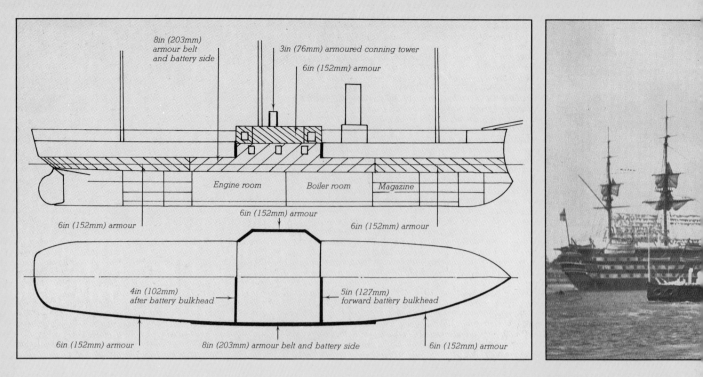

8in (203mm)
armour belt
and battery side

3in (76mm) armoured conning tower

6in (152mm) armour

Engine room   Boiler room   Magazine

6in (152mm) armour

6in (152mm) armour

6in (152mm) armour

4in (102mm)
after battery bulkhead

5in (127mm)
forward battery bulkhead

6in (152mm) armour

8in (203mm) armour belt and battery side

6in (152mm) armour

Above: The armour layout of a typical central battery ship, in this case the British *Audacious*. The main armament was concentrated in an armoured redoubt amidships, with upper-deck weapons firing through angled corner ports, and those on the main deck below, on the broadside. Hull protection was achieved via a narrow, full-length waterline belt.

Below: The development of the turret—which might provide battleships with all-round fire and, if mounted on the centre-line, would halve the number of individual guns required in comparison with a broadside ship of similar firepower—was a continuing theme during the 1870s. This drawing shows an early example, that fitted to the British *Monarch*.

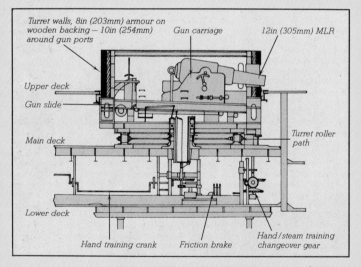

Turret walls, 8in (203mm) armour on wooden backing—10in (254mm) around gun ports

Gun carriage   12in (305mm) MLR

Upper deck

Gun slide

Main deck

Turret roller path

Lower deck

Hand training crank   Friction brake   Hand/steam training changeover gear

Above: The German armoured corvette *Sachsen* characterised the many uncertainties surrounding capital ship design during the 1870s: two of her main 10·25in (260mm) guns were mounted in an open barbette forward, and the other four in a central citadel amidships.

Although steel armour was better able to resist the heavy blows of large ordnance than iron, its crystalline structure caused it to crack if it was struck repeatedly. Schneider steel, although superior to all its contemporaries, was not exempt from this fault, and although Italy fitted steel armour on its Duilio class turret ships, other countries did not follow suit.

In compound armour, developed in Britain simultaneously by A. Wilson of Cammell and J. D. Ellis of John Brown, there appeared a material that was to be in fierce competition with steel for some years. Compound plates combining strength and resilience to a degree not previously achieved were made by welding a steel front onto a tough but flexible iron rear plate, which prevented the steel from cracking under the stress imparted when it was struck by a large projectile.

GUNNERY

By the late 1860s, a 9in (229mm), 12-ton (12·19 tonne) gun firing a 250lb (113kg) projectile was able to pierce 10in (254mm) of iron at the then accepted battle range of 1,000yds (914m). A 12in (305mm), 25-ton (25·4 tonne) gun firing a 614lb (279kg) projectile appeared in 1870, to be followed one year later by a 12in (305mm), 35-ton (35·5 tonne) weapon firing an 820lb (372kg) projectile. In 1874 with a small increase in calibre to 12·5in (317mm), the gun was able to pierce 17·75in (451mm) of armour.

Even as these guns went afloat, more powerful weapons were being developed to counter a new phase in armour development. The Russian turret ship *Petr Velikiy* launched in 1872, was rumoured to have 20in (508mm) armour; the Italians were thought to be working on two ships with armour of at least the same thickness.

Britain had no guns capable of piercing such a mass of metal, so the Director of Naval Ordnance approached the War Office (which was then responsible for naval ordnance) with a request for a gun able to penetrate 20in (508mm) of iron at 1,000yds (914m) range. At a cost of £8,000, an experimental gun of 75 tons (76·2 tonnes)—the final weight being 80 tons (81·28 tonnes)—was constructed on the Fraser system, with a steel tube surrounded by a small number of heavy interlocking coils.

Completed in 1875, the gun was of 14·5in (368mm) calibre—increased to 16in (406mm)—and used a 370lb (168kg) charge of hexagonal powder to a fire a 1,700lb

771kg) projectile capable of piercing 21in (533mm) of iron at 1,000 yards (914m). When a number of rounds were fired at a range of c4,700yds (4,300m), the mean error in direction was less than 2yds (1·83m) and in range less than 15yds (13·72m).

When the chamber was later bored out to 18in (457mm), the gun used 445lb (202kg) of powder to fire a 1,760lb (798kg) projectile. It was three times as powerful as the 38-ton (38·6 tonne) weapons mounted in the turret ship *Dreadnought* earlier in the decade. Its projectile, instead of being fitted with studs to keep it seated in the grooves as it rotated on firing, was rotated by means of a copper disc, which also prevented erosion of the bore by propellant gases escaping over the shot.

In 1873, Italy, at the instigation of Admiral St Bon, the progressive Minister of Marine, and Commander Albini, Director of Ordnance, decided to make her battleships the most powerful afloat by arming them with 100-ton (101·6 tonne) muzzle-loading rifled guns (MLR). These were initially supplied by Armstrong.

The Armstrong gun consisted of an inner tube in two lengths, surrounded by successive layers of wrought-iron coiled cylinders, a larger number of coils being used than in the Fraser system. An improved 'progressive' powder, manufactured in Italy especially for these big guns, enabled larger charges to be used, increasing the velocity of the projectile and yet reducing the strain on the gun's fabric. Even more advanced weapons were supplied by Armstrong for Italy's *Duilio* and *Dandolo:* these 17·7in (450mm) guns used a charge of more than 500lb (227kg) to fire a projectile weighing in excess of 1,900lb (862kg).

In Germany, Krupp of Essen produced a 70-ton (71·12 tonne) gun of 15·75in (400mm) calibre, built up with four successive hoops over a central steel tube. It proved to be extremely accurate: eight shots were placed within a few feet of each other at 2,700yds (2,469m) range.

The French Navy, unlike the Royal Navy, manufactured its own weapons in the naval gun factory at Ruelle or purchased them directly from outside manufacturers. In the latter case, the weapons were delivered about 90 per cent complete and were sent to Ruelle for finishing. From 1870, French guns had a steel 'A' tube, or barrel, within a cast iron body, with two layers of steel hoops on larger weapons. After 1875 the guns were all-steel, with up to three layers of hoops for added strength. Unlike the British, the French were quick to develop successful breechloaders.

Towards the end of the 1870s, trials carried out by Krupp at Meppen proved that longer guns were more powerful than short weapons, especially when the newly-invented slow-burning powder was used. Britain was the last country to cling to the relatively short muzzle-loader, but steady progress in the development of propellants producing greater power and accuracy changed this preference. Another contribution to the Royal Navy's change of heart was an accident aboard the *Thunderer* in 1879: a 38-ton (38·6 tonne) muzzle-loader burst, killing 11 men, after being inadvertently double-loaded, an error that could not have occurred with a breechloader.

While rapid progress continued to be made with big guns, machine guns, notably the Gatling, Nordenfeld, Hotchkiss and Gardner, came into service with almost all the world's navies. Capable of rapid and sustained fire with bullets of small or moderate weight—the Gatling, for example, fired up to 1,000 rounds per minute, although 700 rounds per minute was more usual—they were intended to clear an enemy's decks and for use against the torpedo boats then entering service.

The locomotive torpedo developed at Fiume, Italy, by the British engineer Robert Whitehead, from an idea by the Austrian naval officer Giovanni de Luppis, was first used in action in the 1870s. The early torpedoes were cylindrical, about 14ft (4·27m) long and 14in (356mm) in diameter. A 14in (356mm) torpedo of 1876 carried a charge of 26lb (11·8kg) of guncotton; a 16in (406mm) model carried 67lb (30·4kg) of guncotton in its nose. Improved models continued to appear, including a 19ft (5·79m) long torpedo which achieved a speed of 25kt (46·25km/h) over a distance of 200yds (183m).

MACHINERY

Horizontal engines showed their limitations in the 1870s when, because of rising steam pressures, engine-room crews had to cope with extreme heat as well as mechanical defects. The introduction of the vertical engine in the middle of the decade gave both higher running speed and greater reliability. Vertical engines occupied less floor space than horizontal machinery, and although their greater height meant that they could not always be as well protected, they could still be housed beneath the protective decks of ironclads.

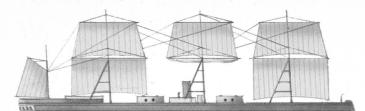

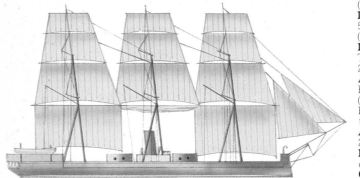

CAPTAIN

1870 UK

Laid down: 30 January 1867.
Launched (floated out): 27 March 1869.
Builder: Lairds, Birkenhead.
Displacement: 7,767 tons (7,891 tonnes) load.
Dimensions: 320ft (97·54m) pp x 53ft 3in (16·23m) x 25ft 6in (7·77m) max.
Machinery: 4-cylinder Horizontal Trunk engines; 8 rectangular boilers; 2 shafts; 5400 IHP.
Armour: Iron 8in-4in (203-102mm) belt; 9in (229mm) turrets; 10in (254mm) faces; 8in (203mm) turret bases; 7in (178mm) conning tower.
Armament: 4 x 12in (305mm) MLR; 2 x 7in (178mm) MLR.
Performance: 14·25kt (26·4km/h); coal 600 tons (610 tonnes).
Crew: 500.

Captain fulfilled Captain Cowper Coles' ideal of an ocean-going fully-rigged turret ship to rival the best of the more conventional broadside ironclads. Coles' concept stemmed from the *Lady Nancy*, a small raft with a single gun protected by a shield, which he built for inshore bombardment during the Crimean War. By 1859 he planned a vessel mounting no fewer than ten turrets, but the 1860s saw more modest proposals for fast, well-protected ironclads with one or two turrets housing 600pdr guns with near all-round fire. These ships had tripod masts to reduce the amount of rigging needed.

By the mid-1860s many ships carrying Coles turrets had entered service with foreign navies, while Britain had *Royal Sovereign* and *Prince Albert*. But Coles wished to see his turrets carried on a fully-rigged ocean-going ship and was not wholly satisfied when the

Top: Coles' proposal of 1862 introduced tripod masts which avoided masking the guns with rigging and shrouds.

Centre: A design of 1863, in which a full spread of nearly 34,000ft² (3,159m²) of canvas was carried.

Above and right: *Captain*, 1870. The turrets housed 25-ton guns which could be worked even with the decks awash. Unprotected 7in (178mm) MLRs on the forecastle and aft provided axial fire. *Captain* carried a full spread of canvas, equal to that usually fitted on high-freeboard ironclads. Coupled with her instability, this proved to be fatal.

admiralty agreed to build *Monarch.* At last, the Admiralty sanctioned a second turret ship, *Captain,* to be built along the lines Coles had persistently advocated. He was responsible only for the basic concept; the entire design was left to *Captain's* builder, Lairds who, much against Coles' wishes, added a forecastle and poop to improve her sea-keeping qualities.

Captain had two decks rather than *Monarch's* three and her turret guns were carried only 9ft (2·74m) above water as compared to 18ft 6in (5·6m) in *Monarch.* The designed freeboard was 8ft 6in (2·59m), but because overweight material was worked in during construction this meagre level fell to 6ft 6in (1·98m) while planned displacement rose from 6,950 tons (7,061 tonnes) to 7,837 tons (7,962 tonnes). A forecastle, poop and centre superstructure were fitted above the main deck—the main mast, funnel and ventilators running up

through the superstructure—and these were connected by a hurricane deck from which the sails were worked.

Although the amount of armour carried was less than on *Monarch,* it covered a smaller area and was thus generally thicker. The entire hull had 7in-4in (178-102mm) armour, with an 8in (203mm) section, 80ft (24·38m) long, amidships to protect the turret bases.

Initial trials were successful. *Captain* appeared to be all that Coles claimed—but on the night of 6-7 September 1870 she foundered in a storm in the Bay of Biscay. Among the 473 men lost was Coles himself. Only 17 men and the gunner managed to get ashore.

Right: *Captain* in dry dock, with her low freeboard apparent. In any kind of weather, seas would wash along the deck to break against the structure aft.

REPULSE

1870 *UK*

Laid down: 29 April 1859.
Launched: 25 April 1868.
Builder: Woolwich and Sheerness Dockyards.
Displacement: 6,190 tons (6,289 tonnes) load.
Dimensions: 252ft (76·8m) pp x 59ft (17·98m) x 26ft (7·9m) max.
Machinery: Penn Trunk engines; 6 rectangular boilers, 1 shaft; 3350 IHP.
Armour: Iron 6in-4·5in (152-114mm) belt; 6in (152mm) battery; 4·5in (114mm) bulkheads.
Armament: 12 x 8in (203mm) MLR.
Performance: 12·5kt (23km/h); coal 450 tons (457 tonnes).
Crew: 515.

Repulse's conversion from a 90-gun two-decker to the last wooden-hulled British battleship was prolonged by a five-year suspension of work while other conversions were evaluated. A 70ft (21·34m) box battery amidships housed 4 x 8in (203mm) MLR on each broadside; the remaining guns were in unarmoured positions, two at either end of the upper deck, for end-on fire. Armour was concentrated over the battery, leaving much of the main deck unprotected.

Repulse was ship-rigged with 29,200ft² (2,713m²) of canvas and made 10·5kt (19·4km/h) under sail. In 1877-80, 4 x 16in (406mm) torpedo carriages and a net defence were added. She was the only British armoured ship to round Cape Horn under canvas. She served as a guardship at Hull in 1881-85 and was sold in 1889.

Above: The handsome *Repulse* in 1880, after a three-year refit.

AUDACIOUS

1870 *UK*

Other ships in class: *Invincible, Iron Duke, Vanguard, Swiftsure, Triump*

Laid down: 26 June 1867.
Launched: 27 February 1869.
Builder: Napier, Glasgow.
Displacement: 6,010 tons (6,106 tonnes) load.
Dimensions: 280 ft (85·34m) pp x 54ft (16·46m) x 22ft 7in (6·88m).
Machinery: Two 2-cylinder Horizontal Return Connecting Rod engines; 6 rectangular boilers; 2 shafts; 4020 IHP.
Armour: Iron 8in-6in (203-152mm) belt; 10in-8in (254-203mm) teak

Below: *Audacious* in 1874, painted white in preparation for service as flagship on the China Station.

Above: A 'cut-price' Cerberus built for service at Bombay: the 2,900-ton *Abyssinia* in 1892. Although almost identical to the Cerberus class, she was never listed with them.

acking; 6in (152mm) battery;
n (127mm) bulkheads.
rmament: 10 x 9in (229mm) MLR;
x 6in (152mm) MLR; 6 x 20pdr
L saluting.
erformance: 13·2kt (24·4km/h);
al 460 tons (467 tonnes).
rew: 450.

he largest homogeneous battleship
roup until the five Admirals of
887-89, the Audacious class central
attery ships represented Reed's
rgely successful attempt at a design
uitable for service on overseas
ations where cruising ironclads of
e French and other navies were the
ost likely rivals. Adapting his
efence of 1861, with reduced
raught and improved layout, Reed
roduced ships that provided steady
un platforms with all-weather
nd-on fire from the main armament.
An 8in (203mm) belt tapering to
n (152mm) at the ends extended 5ft

(1·52m) below and 3ft (0·91m) above
the waterline at full load. In the 59ft
(17·98m) long main deck battery,
protected by 6in (152mm) armour
and 5in-4in (127-102mm) bulkheads,
3 x 9in (229mm) were mounted on
either broadside. The upper deck
battery was built out beyond the hull
sides, thus giving axial fire capability
to the 4 x 9in (229mm) mounted in
corner ports 16ft (4·88m) above
water. Two 6in (152mm) MLR were at
either end of the upper deck.
Although carrying the largest sail
area in proportion to displacement of
any capital ships—originally ship-
rigged, but from 1871 barque-
rigged with 23,700ft² (2,202m²) of
canvas—they were slow sailers,
largely because of the drag from their
twin screws. On 1 September 1875,
in thick fog off Kingstown, Ireland,
Vanguard was rammed below the
belt abaft the engine room by *Iron
Duke*. Because no wing
compartments were fitted, the engine
room flooded and she rapidly sank.
The remaining ships received 4 x
14in (356mm) torpedo carriages in
1878 and were refitted in the early
1880s. In *Audacious*, 8 x 4in
(102mm) BL replaced the 6in
(152mm) MLR and 4 x 6pdr QF and
6 x 3pdr were added.
Audacious was flagship on the
China station in 1874-78. Hulked in
1902, she was sold for breaking up
in the 1920s. The modified Audacious
class vessels *Swiftsure* and *Triumph*
were sold for breaking up in 1908
and 1921 respectively.

ASSARI TEWFIK

1870 *Turkey*

Launched: 1868.
Builder: La Seyne, Toulon.
Displacement: 4,687 tons
(4,762 tonnes) normal.
Dimensions: 272ft 4in (83m) pp
x 52ft 6in (16m) x 21ft 4in
(6·5m) max.
Machinery: Compound engines,
6 boilers; 1 shaft; 3560 IHP.
Armour: Iron 8in (203mm) belt;
3in (76mm) ends; 6in (152mm)
battery; 5in (127mm) barbettes.
Armament: 8 x 9in (229mm) ML.
Performance: 13kt (24km/h);
coal 400 tons (406 tonnes).
Crew: 320.

The iron-hulled *Assari Tewfik* had six
MLs in a central battery and two
more (replaced by 8·3in, 211mm, BLs
by 1891) single-mounted in barbettes
above it. Extensively modernised by
Krupp in 1903-06, she was
re-engined; given a 3in (76mm)
protective deck and a 6in (152mm)
armoured conning tower; and
rearmed with 3 x 5·9in (150mm) QF,
7 x 4·7in (119mm) QF, plus smaller.
On 11 February 1913, during the
First Balkan War, she was
abandoned after running aground.

IDJALIEH

1871 *Turkey*

Launched: 1870.
Builder: Trieste.
Displacement: 2,266 tons
(2,302 tonnes) normal.
Dimensions: 213ft 3in (65m) pp
x 42ft 7in (12·97m) x 17ft 4in (5·3m).
Machinery: 1 shaft; 1800 IHP.
Armour: Iron 6in-4·5in (152-
114mm) belt; 4in (102mm) ends;
4·5in (114mm) battery; 5in
(127mm) barbette.
Armament: 2 x 9in (229mm) ML;
3 x 7in (178mm) ML.
Performance: 12kt (22·2km/h);
coal 300 tons (305 tonnes).
Crew: 180.

Only three of the 21 Turkish
ironclads ordered in 1861-1876
were not laid down in France or
Britain. One was the Trieste-built
Idjalieh which, apart from a raised
forecastle, much resembled the
French-built Assari Shevket class. A
central battery housed four of her five
Armstrong MLs; one 7in (178mm)
ML—replaced by a 5·9 (150mm) BL
by 1891—was mounted in a
centreline barbette above and a little
aft. She served as a training and
barracks ship from c1897.

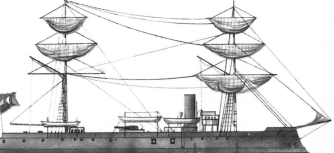

Above: *Assari Tewfik* as completed. **Below:** *Idjalieh* as seen in 1872.

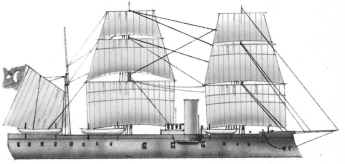

CERBERUS

1870 *UK*
Other ships in class: *Magdala*

Laid down: 1 September 1867.
Launched: 2 December 1868.
Builder: Palmers, Jarrow.
Displacement: 3,344 tons
(3,398 tonnes) load.
Dimensions: 225ft (68·58m) pp
x 45ft (13·72m) x 15ft 4in (4·67m).
Machinery: Maudslay; 2 shafts;
1370 IHP.
Armour: Iron 8in-6in (203-152mm)
belt; 11in-9in (279-229mm)
backing; 9in-8in (229-203mm)
breastwork; 10in-9in (254-229mm)
turrets; 1·5in-1in (38-25mm) decks.
Armament: 4 x 10in (254mm) MLR.
Performance: 9·75kt (18km/h);
coal 210 tons (213 tonnes) max.
Crew: 155.

elow: *Cerberus* as briefly
een after completion, with extended
ying bridge and pole masts.

The breastwork monitors *Cerberus*
and *Magdala* were designed by
Reed for coast defence duty at
Melbourne and Bombay
respectively. Because ocean-going
capability was not required, they
were low freeboard (3·5ft; 1·07m)
vessels with no permanent sailing rig.
Thus, with turrets carried fore and aft
on a central armoured breastwork,
and a superstructure bearing boats,
funnel and a single pole mast on the
shelter deck, the ships anticipated
the layout that was to characterise the
pre-dreadnought battleship.
The 8in (203mm) belt tapered to
6in (152mm) at the ends. Heavier
armour—9in (229mm) at the ends
and 8in (203mm) amidships—was
carried on the 7ft (2·13m) high
breastwork which extended for 112ft
6in (34·29m) amidships. At either
end of the breastwork, hand-worked

turrets of 26ft 3in (8m) diameter each
housed 2 x 10in (254mm), 18-ton
(18·29 tonne) MLR, protected by
10in (254mm) face armour and 9in
(229mm) walls. Being thus raised on
the breastwork, the guns could be
better worked in a seaway and,
unhindered by a rig, had very wide
arcs of bearing and full end-on fire.
Magdala's 10in (254mm) MLR
were replaced by 8in (203mm) BL in
1892 and both ships had MGs
added fore and aft on the shelter
deck. A full three-masted rig was
fitted to *Cerberus* for the voyage to
Melbourne, but thereafter she
shipped a single pole mast abaft the
funnel and, with twin screws and a
balanced rudder, proved handy
under steam. She spent almost all her
time in the port of Melbourne, finally
serving as a depot ship, renamed
Platypus II, until sunk in 1926.

OCÉAN

1870 *France*

Other ships in class: *Marengo, Suffren*

Laid down: July 1865.
Launched: 15 October 1868.
Builder: Brest Dockyard.
Displacement: 7,775 tons (7,899 tonnes) full load.
Dimensions: 287ft 10in (87·73m) x 57ft 6in (17·53m) x 29ft 9in (9·07m) max.
Machinery: Horizontal Return Connecting Rod Compound engines; 8 oval boilers; 1 shaft; 4180 IHP.
Armour: Wrought iron 8in-7in (203-178mm) belt; 6·3in (160mm) battery; 6in (152mm) barbettes.
Armament: 4 x 10·8in (274mm); 4 x 9·4in (239mm); 6 x 5·5in (140mm); 12 x 1pdr revolvers.
Performance: 14kt (25·9km/h); coal 650 tons (660 tonnes).
Crew: 778.

Britain's policy of building two warships for every one produced by France, her traditional rival, could not be maintained in the ironclad age. However, by 1868, when the central battery ship *Océan* was launched, the Royal Navy had gained numerical superiority in armoured ships, with 29 vessels launched in comparison with 26 in the French Navy. *Océan* was, moreover, less powerful than the British central battery ship *Hercules* or the turret ship *Monarch*, both launched in the same year.

The French fleet had greater homogeneity—its 26 armoured ships were of only 8 different types, compared to 21 different types in the British fleet—and the French 10·8in (274mm) BL was superior to the British 10in (254mm) RML. But the difficulty experienced by France in building iron hulls meant that most French armoured ships up to 1870 (31 out of 34 launched) were wooden-hulled and less well protected than their British equivalents.

Designed by Dupuy de Lôme, *Océan* and her two sisters had full-length waterline belts; with 0·6in (15mm) iron plating protecting the timber sides above. Three iron watertight bulkheads were fitted, b these were probably not of great utility in a wooden ship. Four 10·8i (274mm) were carried in the centra battery, c11·5ft (3·5m) above water. Above the battery, set on each of it corners, were 4 x 9·4in (239mm) guns for axial fire; they were in

Right: The imposing and graceful lines of *Océan* as first completed. Rig was later reduced and fighting tops were added to the main and mizzen masts. Torpedo nets were fitted in the 1880s.

BASILISSA OLGA

1870 *Greece*

Launched: 1869.
Builder: Stabilimento Tecnico Triestino.
Displacement: 2,030 tons (2,062 tonnes).
Dimensions: 249ft 4in (76m) pp x 39ft (11·89m) x 19ft 0in (5·79m) mean.
Machinery: 1 shaft; 1950 IHP.
Armour: Iron 7in-6in (178-152mm) belt; 4·75in (121mm) battery.
Armament: 2 x 9in (229mm) RML; 10 x 70pdr.
Performance: 11·5kt (21·3km/h); coal 240 tons (244 tonnes).
Crew: 400 (later 258).

During the 1870s Greece had the smallest navy in Europe: the two small ironclads *Basilissa Olga* and *Basileos Georgios*, six screw steamers and a few smaller craft.

Basilissa Olga was a wooden-hulled broadside corvette with a ram bow and a complete waterline belt. The battery occupied about one-third of her length amidships. The hull sides level with the battery, before and abaft the end ports, were slightly recessed so that the four end guns could fire almost axially: the forward pair trained almost in line with the keel; the after pair had less traverse.

She originally carried a large spread of canvas, but this was removed around 1896, when two military masts were shipped and new machinery installed. By 1886 she had been rearmed with 4 x 6·7in (170mm) 25-cal Krupp guns, 2 x 6·7in (170mm) 20-cal, 4 x 1pdr and 2 MGs. She was removed from the Navy List around 1905.

GORM

1870 *Denmark*

Launched: 1870.
Builder: Copenhagen Dockyard.
Displacement: 2,313 tons (2,350 tonnes)
Dimensions: 233ft 4in (71·12m) pp x 40ft (12·19m) x 14ft 4in (4·37m) max.
Machinery: 1600 IHP.
Armour: Iron 7in (178mm) side; 10in (254mm) max backing; 8in (203mm) turret; 17·5in (444mm) backing.
Armament: 2 x 10in (254mm) RML.
Performance: 12·5kt (23 km/h); coal 113 tons (115 tonnes) max.
Crew: 160.

The loss of Schleswig-Holstein in th war against Prussia and Austria in 1864 reduced Denmark's area by about one-third and, with the concomitant loss of population, removed any prospect of the countr maintaining a really powerful navy. Her main need in the 1870s was fo coast defence ironclads of low draught, like *Gorm*, rather than the larger broadside ironclad frigates built in the 1860s.

With an original cost of £104,000 *Gorm* was an iron-hulled vessel wit low freeboard, not unlike the earlie *Lindormen*. She carried a single turret in which were housed 2 x 10i (254mm) RML. Two light smoothbore guns were mounted or the upper deck. Her armament was altered several times: 4 x 3·4in (86mm) 24-cal guns—which were themselves later replaced by 6pdrs—and 4 x 1pdr revolvers wer added; 2 x 5·9in (150mm) 43-cal weapons replaced the 10in (254mm MLR. She was scrapped in 1912.

arbettes—originally with 6in
152mm) armour, later removed to
educe top-weight—that left both
uns and loading operations
nprotected. The ram, tipped with a
0-ton (20·32 tonne) bronze casting,
as close on 9ft (2·74m) long.
  Barquentine- or barque-rigged
ith some 22,000ft² (2,044m²) of
anvas, the Océans were deployed
ainly in the protection of French
verseas possessions: *Marengo* took
art in the suppression of Tunisian
surgency at Sfax and Gabes in
881. Four 14in (356mm) torpedo
ibes were added at some time
efore their disposal in 1894-97.

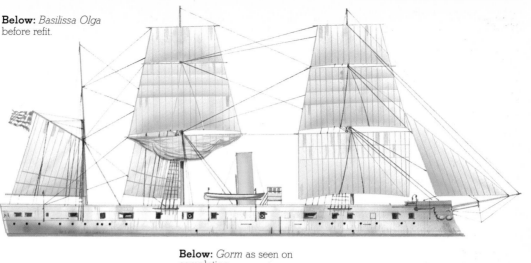

Below: *Basilissa Olga*
before refit.

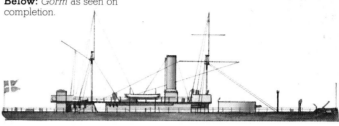

Below: *Gorm* as seen on
completion.

Below: *Fethi Bulend's* original rig.

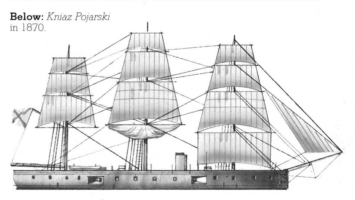

Below: *Kniaz Pojarski*
in 1870.

ETHI BULEND

70 Turkey
ther ships in class: *Mukaddami*
hair

aunched: 1870.
uilder: Thames Iron Works.
isplacement: 2,761 tons
,805 tonnes) normal.
imensions: 236ft 3in (72·01m) pp
39ft 4in (11·99m) x 18ft 1in
·51m) max.
achinery: Horizontal Compound
gines; 1 shaft; 3250 IHP.
rmour: Iron 9in-6in (229-152mm)
elt; 3in (76mm) ends; 9in-6in
29-152mm) casemates.
rmament: 4 x 9in (229mm).
erformance: 13kt (24km/h);

coal 300 tons (305 tonnes).
Crew: 180.

Fethi Bulend was an iron-hulled
vessel with high freeboard and a ram
bow. Four 9in (229mm) were carried
in amidships casemates with
maximum armour of 9in (229mm)
below the port sills. The sides of the
octagonal casemates were not cut
away between the ports: two guns
fired only on forward bearings and
two only on aft bearings. A full length
belt extended from 4ft (1·2m) below
the waterline to 2ft (0·6m) above.
  By 1891, 2 x 3·4in (87mm) and 2 x
2·5in (63·5mm) Krupp BL, plus two
smaller, were added. After
reconstruction by Ansaldo, Genoa,
in 1903-07, *Fethi Bulend's* casemates
housed 4 x 5·9in (150mm) Krupp QF.
Six 3in (76mm) QF were mounted at
upper deck level—one at each angle
of the casemates, one forward, one
aft—plus 10 x 6pdr and 2 x 3pdr.
Fethi Bulend was lost in the First
Balkan War (1912-13).

KNIAZ POJARSKI

1870 Russia

Laid down: November 1864.
Launched: September 1867.
Builder: Mitchell, St Petersburg.
Displacement: 5,138 tons
(5,220 tonnes) load.
Dimensions: 272ft 8in (83·1m) wl
x 49ft (14·94m) x 24ft 6in
(7·47m) max.
Machinery: Horizontal Direct
Acting engines; 8 cylindrical boilers,
1 shaft; 2835 IHP.
Armour: Wrought iron 4·5in
(114mm) belt; 18in (457mm) teak
backing; 4·5in (114mm) battery.
Armament: 8 x 9in (229mm) BLR.
Performance: 11·7kt (21·65km/h);

coal 600 tons (610 tonnes);
radius 3,000nm (5,550km).
Crew: 455.

A cruising ironclad, *Kniaz Pojarski*
was ship rigged with c27,000ft²
(2,508m²) of canvas and is said to
have been a steady gun platform and
a good sea boat. She was the first
Russian armoured ship to cruise in
the Pacific (c1874-75 and later).
  Eight 9in (229mm) Obukhov BLR
were mounted in an 80ft (24·38m)
long central battery, the end ports
being recessed to permit some
degree of axial fire. Her iron hull was
flat-bottomed and sheathed with
wood, and a complete waterline belt
extended from 5ft (1·52m) below
water to 6ft (1·83m) above.
  In 1884-85, during extensive
modernization, 2 x 6in (152mm)
guns mounted fore and aft on the
upper decks, plus smaller, were
added, and 8in (203mm) guns
replaced the 9in (229mm) weapons
in the battery.

SULTAN

1871 *UK*

Laid down: 29 February 1868.
Launched: 31 May 1870.
Builder: Chatham Dockyard.
Displacement: 9,540 tons
(9,693 tonnes) full load.
Dimensions: 325ft (99·06m) pp
x 59ft (17·98m) x 26ft 5in

Right: *Sultan* with full rig, 1872.
Fears for her stability led to its
reduction to barque rig in 1876.

(8·05m) mean.
Machinery: Penn 2-cylinder
Horizontal Trunk engines; 1 shaft;
7720 IHP.
Armour: Iron 9in-6in (229-152mm)
belt; 12in-10in (305-254mm) teak
backing; 9in (229mm) main battery;
8in (203mm) upper deck battery;
6in-4·5in (152-114mm) bulkheads.
Armament: 8 x 10in (254mm) MLR;
4 x 9in (229mm) MLR; 7 x 20pdr

BL saluting.
Performance: 14·13kt (26·1km/h);
coal 740 tons (752 tonnes).
Crew: 633.

Laid down before the early turret
ships *Monarch* and *Captain* had
been evaluated, *Sultan* was a central
battery ship based on the *Hercules* of
1868, with an improved armament
layout. A major difference lay in the

suppression of *Hercules'* bow and
stern gun-mountings at main deck
level in favour of an additional
armoured battery on the upper deck.
The full-length waterline belt was 9in
(229mm) thick amidships, where it
supported the 9in (229mm)
armoured main battery, tapering to
8in (203mm) and then to 6in
(152mm) at the ends.
  The main battery was 83ft (25·3m

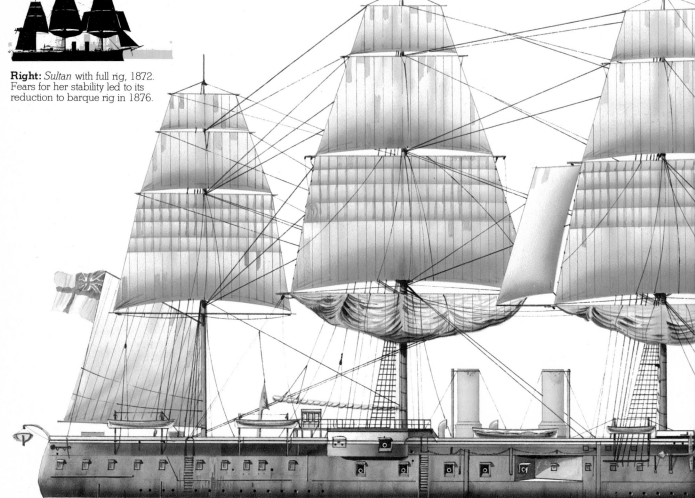

LISSA

1871 *Austria-Hungary*

Laid down: 27 June 1867.
Launched: 25 February 1869.
Builder: Stabilimento Tecnico
Triestino.
Displacement: 7,086 tons
(7,199 tonnes).
Dimensions: 293ft 3in (89·78m) oa
x 56ft 10in (17·73m) x 27ft 10in
(8·48m).
Machinery: 2-cylinder Horizontal
engines; 1 shaft; 3619 IHP.
Armour: Iron 6in (152mm) belt;
30in (770mm) max wood backing;
5in (127mm) battery; 28·5in
(724mm) backing; 4·5in (114mm)
bulkheads.
Armament: 12 x 9in (229mm) BL;
4 x 8pdr MLR; 2 x 3pdr MLR.
Performance: 12·83kt (23·7km/h);
coal 489 tons (497 tonnes);
range 1,420 miles (2,285km) at
10kt (18·5km/h).
Crew: 620.

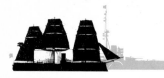

In the 1860s a separate Ministry of
Marine was established for the
Austro-Hungarian Navy. It was
short-lived: naval direction reverted
to the Ministry of War, where the head
of the naval section was Vice Admiral
Wilhelm von Tegetthoff. His
programme would have added eight
ironclads in ten years, but financial
problems forbade this: naval
development entered a period of
comparative inactivity and Tegetthoff
himself died in 1871.
  Lissa, completed in that year, was
the Austro-Hungarian Navy's first
armoured ship for five years. Her hull
was wooden beneath the armoured
area and the unarmoured upperworks were of iron. A complete belt
ran up to the main deck beams. Ten
9in (229mm) Krupp BL were
mounted in the battery with ports
only 6ft 5in (1·96m) above water.
Axial fire was provided by 2 x 9in
(229mm) in an upper deck redoubt
mounted on the forward end of the
battery and overhanging 5ft (1·52m).
  Lissa was refitted in 1875-77 and in
1881 her secondary armament was
changed to 4 x 3·5in (90mm) BL, 2 x
2·75in (70mm) BL, 3 x 47mm MG
and 2 x 25mm MG. In 1886 her first
rig of 33,497ft² (3,112m²) was
reduced to 15,113ft² (1,404m²). She
was scrapped in 1893-94.

Below: *Lissa* in the early 1870s. She
was the Austro-Hungarian Navy's
first central battery ship.

and housed 8 x 10in (254mm)
LR with port sills 11ft (3·35m)
ove water. Forward, where a 6in
52mm) bulkhead was fitted, the
ll sides were cut away to allow axial
e by the foremost pair of guns,
unted on turntables. No such
ovision was made aft, where a 5in
27mm) bulkhead protected the
ttery.
Fire aft was provided by 2 x 9in

(229mm) MLR, one mounted on
either side in a sponsoned upper
battery with 8in (203mm) sides and
4·5in (114mm) bulkheads. Two ports
were provided for each of the upper
battery guns: one on the broadside,
permitting fire 45° ahead of the
beam, and one aft for astern fire. The
two remaining 9in (229mm) MLR
were carried right forward, beneath
the topgallant forecastle.

Ship-rigged with 34,100ft²
(3,168m²) of canvas—or 49,400ft²
(4,589m²) with stunsails—*Sultan*
was a slow sailer, largely because of
the drag of her screw. Although very
steady, she required 600 tons (610
tonnes) of ballast for stability because
of the added topweight from the
upper battery. Reduction to barque
rig and the shortening of the fore and
main masts in 1876 helped improve
stability. Reboilered in her 1879 refit,
she subsequently made 15kt
(27·75km/h) at 7736 IHP.
Seven 4in (102mm) BL, 4 x 6pdr
QF and 4 x 14in (356mm) torpedo
carriages were added in 1879, and in
1882 *Sultan* took part in the
bombardment of Alexandria. In
March 1889 she grounded and sank
off Malta; raised in the same year, she
was temporarily repaired locally and
returned to Britain.
In 1893-96 *Sultan* was extensively
modernized. In a further effort to
improve stability, a 9in (229mm)
thick teak girdling was fitted at the
waterline. Four 4·7in (119m) QF
were added amidships, two military
masts and two taller funnels were
shipped, and new boilers and
engines gave 14·6kt (27km/h) at
6531 IHP.
From 1906 to 1931, renamed
Fisgard IV, she was a training hulk.
As *Sultan* once more, she was a repair
ship and then a minesweeper depot
ship in 1940-45, being sold for
breaking up soon afterwards.

Above: *Sultan* as she appeared in
1896, after the extensive refit that
followed her sinking in the Comino
Channel, off Malta, in 1889. The
original muzzle-loaders were retained
and numerous light guns were added.
She went to sea only once more after
the refit.

Below: *Hotspur* as completed. A
flying bridge was later added.

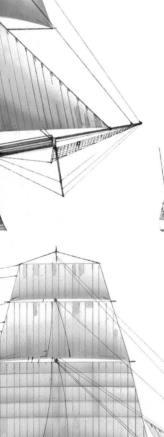

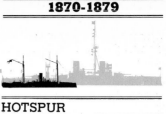

1870-1879

HOTSPUR
1871 *UK*

Laid down: 2 October 1868.
Launched: 19 March 1870.
Builder: Napier, Govan.
Displacement: 4,331 tons
(4,400 tonnes) load.
Dimensions: 235ft (71·63m) pp
x 50ft (15·24m) x 20ft 10in (6·35m).
Machinery: Napier engines;
2 shafts; 3500 IHP.
Armour: Iron 11in-8in (279-203mm)
belt; 8 in (203mm) breastwork;
10in-8·5in (254-216mm) turret;
10in-6in (254-152mm) conning tower.
Armament: 1 x 12in (305mm) MLR;
2 x 64 pdr MLR.
Performance: 12·65kt (23·4km/h);
coal 300 tons (305 tonnes).
Crew: 209.

Hotspur had a full-length belt which
extended to 5ft (1·52m) below water
and ran down to support the 10ft
(3·05m) ram, her primary armament.
A single 12in (305mm) MLR was
mounted on a turntable in a fixed
turret with four ports. In 1881-83 she
was totally reconstructed, with a
revolving turret housing 2 x 12in
(305mm) MLR, 2 x 6in (152mm) BL.

Below: *Glatton* in 1875. Note
the ventilators rising up through
the flying deck aft.

GLATTON
1872 *UK*

Laid down: 10 August 1868.
Launched: 8 March 1871.
Builder: Chatham Dockyard.
Displacement: 4,912 tons
(4,991 tonnes) load.
Dimensions: 245ft (74·68m) pp x
54ft (16·46m) x 19ft (5·79m) mean.
Machinery: Laird; 2 shafts;
2870 IHP.
Armour: Iron 12in-10in
(305-254mm) belt; 21in-15in

(533-381mm) backing; 12in (305mm)
breastwork; 14in-12in (356-305mm)
turret; 9in-6in (229-152mm) conning
tower; 3in-1·5in (76-38mm) decks.
Armament: 2 x 12in (305mm) MLR.
Performance: 12·11kt (22·4km/h);
coal 540 tons (549 tonnes) max.
Crew: 185.

Designed (unwillingly) by Reed to
combine harbour defence with a
sea-going offensive role, *Glatton* was
a low-freeboard (3ft; 0·91m),
deep-draught breastwork monitor
with very heavy armour, amounting
to 35 per cent of total displacement.
Two 12in (305mm) MLR were
housed in a turret forward of the
superstructure, which was narrowed
to allow fire aft. Only once risked on
sea service, in 1887, she served
mainly as a tender at Portsmouth.

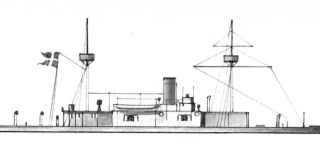

ODIN

1872 Denmark

Launched: 1872.
Builder: Copenhagen Dockyard.
Displacement: 3,170 tons
(3,221 tonnes).
Dimensions: 240ft 10in (73·4m) pp
x 48ft 6in (14·78m) x 16ft 5in (5m).
Machinery: 2300 IHP.
Armour: Iron 8in (203mm) side
and battery.
Armament: 4 x 10in (254mm) RML.
Performance: 12kt (22·2km/h);
coal 177 tons (180 tonnes).
Crew: 206.

The Danish Navy operated mainly in
coastal waters and its construction
programme concentrated on low
freeboard (3-4ft; 0·9-1·2m) vessels of
limited range and sea-going
capability. Such was *Odin,* which
had a retractable spur ram and
mounted 4 x 10in Armstrong RML
(later converted to BL by Krupp) in a
central battery protected, as was her
entire side above the waterline, by 8in
(203mm) armour. A refit added 4 x
3·4in (86mm), 4 x 1pdr revolvers and
2 x 1pdr QF.

DEVASTATION

1873 UK
Other ships in class: *Thunderer*

Laid down: 12 November 1869.
Launched: 12 July 1871.
Builder: Portsmouth Dockyard.
Displacement: 9,300 tons
(9,479 tonnes) load.
Dimensions: 285ft (86·87m) pp
x 62ft 3in (18·97m) x 26ft 8in
(8·13m) mean.
Machinery: Penn 2-cylinder Trunk
engines; 8 rectangular boilers;
2 shafts; 6650 IHP.
Armour: Iron 12in-8·5in
(305-216mm) belt; 18in-16in
(457-406mm) teak backing;
12in-10in (305-254mm) breastwork;
14in-10in (356-254mm) turrets;
6in-5in (152-127mm) bulkheads;
3in-2in (76-51mm) decks.
Armament: 4 x 12in (305mm) MLR.
Performance: 13·84kt (25·6km/h);
coal 1,600 tons (1,626 tonnes);
range 5,500 miles (8,850km) at
10kt (18·5km/h).
Crew: 358.

Reed's design of 1868 for
Devastation marked the major step in
the development of the monitor type
into the ocean-going battleship, with
good speed and range and heavy
and well-protected armament. Like
most revolutionary designs, it
aroused determined opposition.

Since no sailing rig was fitted,
Reed planned low freeboard all
round for maximum stability. But
even after modification by Barnaby,
who, against Reed's wishes, fitted a
light iron superstructure that
extended to the ship's sides and thus
raised her freeboard by one deck
over much of her length, many
believed that *Devastation* was
unseaworthy. Completion of her
sister-ship, *Thunderer,* was delayed

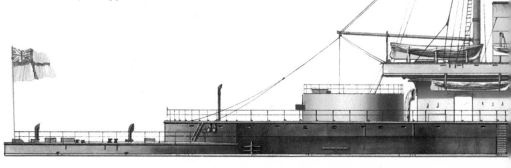

Above: *Odin* in 1885. She retained
her basic shape throughout her
career: only light guns were added.

Below: *Devastation* after her 1879
refit, with fighting top added. The
hull was cut back aft to form a
cul-de-sac. The temporary ladder aft
is for use in taking on supplies.

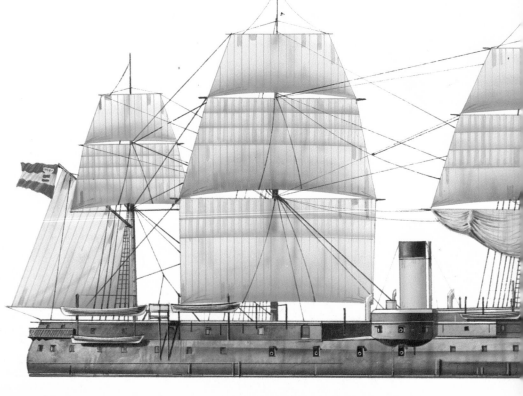

until after *Devastation*'s trials. In fact,
she proved to be both stable and
handy, although wet forward.

Generally low freeboard—a
maximum of 10·75ft (3·28m)
amidships and a minimum of 4ft
(1·22m) aft—and the absence of sails
permitted an armour weight
amounting to 27·2 per cent of total
displacement. A full-length belt ran
up from 5·5ft (1·68m) below the
waterline to the main deck, with a
maximum 12in (305mm) thickness
amidships. The two turrets, each of
30·5ft (9·3m) diameter, had 14in
(356mm) faces and 10in (254mm)
walls, the armour being fitted in two
layers with teak between them, and
were further protected by an internal
breastwork with a maximum

thickness of 12in (305mm) around
the turret bases. A 3in (76mm)
armoured deck rested on the belt
and a 2in (51mm) deck extended
over the breastwork.

Each steam-trained turret housed
2 x 12in (305mm), 35-ton (35·56
tonne) Armstrong MLR, with port
sills 13ft (3·96m) above water. The
superstructure aft was recessed to
allow the after guns to fire astern with
maximum depression. In *Thunderer,*
12in (305mm), 38-ton (38·6 tonne),
hydraulically-loaded Armstrongs
were mounted in the forward turret.
External hydraulic loading by way of
shafts leading up from the lower
deck permitted reduction of the
turret crew from 22 men to 10, and its
advantages might well have delayed

the re-introduction of breechloading
weapons beyond 1886. However, on
2 January 1879 one of *Thunderer*'s
guns burst, killing several men, after
both turret and loading crews had
failed to observe that the system had
resulted in double-loading.

Devastation was refitted in 1879
and *Thunderer* in 1881: machinery
was renovated, habitability improved
and 8 x MG and 2 x 14in (356mm)
torpedo carriages added. Modernised in 1891-92, they received triple-
expansion engines and cylindrical
boilers, giving 14·2kt (26·3km/h),
and were rearmed with 4 x 10in
(254mm) BL, 6 x 6pdr QF and 8 x
3pdr QF. Both ships were classified
non-effective in 1907 and were sold
for breaking up in 1908-09.

Above: *Gorgon* in 1875. *Cyclops*, *Hecate* and *Cerberus* carried a light pole mast stepped to port forward.

GORGON

1874 *UK*
Other ships in class: *Cyclops*, *Hecate*, *Hydra*

Laid down: 5 September 1870.
Launched: 14 October 1871.
Builder: Palmers, Jarrow.
Displacement: 3,480 tons (3,536 tonnes) load.
Dimensions: 225ft (68·58m) pp x 45ft (13·72m) x 16ft 3in (4·98m).
Machinery: Ravenhill Horizontal Direct Acting engines; 2 shafts; 1670 IHP.
Armour: 8in-6in (203-152mm) sides; 11in-9in (279-229mm) backing;

9in-8in (229-203mm) breastwork; 10in-9in (254-229mm) turrets; 9in-8in (229-203mm) conning tower; 1·5in (38mm) decks.
Armament: 4 x 10in (254mm) MLR.
Performance: 11·14kt (20·6km/h).
Crew: 150.

Fear of war with France in 1870 and a consequent threat to Britain's coasts led to hurried construction of the Cyclops class monitors, based on Reed's *Cerberus*—although their completion was long delayed when the emergency passed. They were low freeboard ships for harbour rather than coastal defence. Their poor stability and sea-keeping qualities were improved when the breastwork was extended out to the sides and plated over in 1886-89 (when 4 x 3pdr QF and 5 MG were added on the flying deck).

With a hull completely, if comparatively lightly, armoured above the waterline, *Gorgon* mounted 2 x 10in (254mm) MLR in each of two turrets atop her central armoured breastwork. The 18-ton (18·29 tonne) guns, on Scott carriages, were reckoned the most easily handled then afloat and she had the fine armament to tonnage ratio of 1:48. No sailing rig was fitted. *Gorgon* served mainly as a tender at Devonport. Classified non-effective in 1901, she was sold for breaking up in 1903.

Below: *La Galissonnière* painted white for tropical service, 1870s.

Above: *Kaiser* as originally completed: a wooden, two-decker line-of-battle ship.

Left: *Kaiser* after conversion into an ironclad, early 1870s, with a well-protected battery and ram bow.

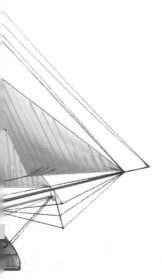

KAISER

1873 *Austria-Hungary*

Laid down: 25 March 1855.
Launched: (as ironclad) 1871.
Builder: Pola Navy Yard.
Displacement: 5,720 tons (5,812 tonnes).
Dimensions: 255ft (77·7m) wl x 58ft 3in (17·75m) x 24ft 2in (7·37m).
Machinery: 2-cylinder Horizontal engines; 1 shaft; 2786 IHP.
Armour: Iron 6in (152mm) belt; 4in (102mm) ends; 5in (127mm) battery.
Armament: 10 x 9in (229mm) ML; 6 x 8pdr RML.
Performance: 11·55kt (21·4km/h).
Crew: 471.

At the Battle of Lissa, 20 July 1866, the wooden two-decker ship-of-the-line *Kaiser* (90 x 30pdr ML; 2 x 24pdr BL) led the Second Division of the Austrian fleet against the Italian ironclads, herself ramming the *Re di Portogallo*. *Kaiser* suffered the greater damage: her bowsprit was lost, her stern wrecked by gunfire

and her foremast brought down across her funnel. Afire to port and with both steering and machinery damaged, she was swept by Italian fire, sustaining a total of 80 hits, before Commodore Anton von Petz was able to bring her out of action with 24 dead and 75 wounded.

In February 1869, found to be still structurally sound, *Kaiser* was taken in hand for conversion in to a central battery ship. Damaged and unsound timbers were made good and she was rebuilt in iron from the waterline up, with a reconstructed stern and a ram bow. Her 10 x 9in (229mm) 23pdr Armstrong MLs were mounted in casemates protected by 5in (127mm) armour; four guns were carried at the lower level on each side, with one each side on the upper deck, where the sides were cut away to permit some degree of axial fire. Her original machinery was supplemented by superheaters.

In 1882 she received new secondary armament of 6 x 3·5in (90mm) BL and 2 x 2·75in (70mm) BL; 4 x 47mm QF, 3 x 47mm revolving MG and 4 x 25mm MG were added. Three 13·8in (350mm) torpedo tubes, one in the bow and two on the beam, were added in 1885. From 1902 to 1918, renamed *Bellona*, she was a barracks hulk at Pola. She was broken up in 1920.

LA GALISSONNIERE

1874 *France*
Other ships in class: *Triomphante*, *Victorieuse*

Laid down: 22 June 1868.
Launched: 7 May 1872.
Builder: Brest Dockyard.
Displacement: 4,645 tons (4,719 tonnes).
Dimensions: 256ft (78·03m) wl x 49ft (14·94m) x 24ft 2in (7·4m) max.
Machinery: Vertical Compound; 4 oval boilers; 2 shafts; 2400 IHP.
Armour: Wrought iron 6in (152mm) belt; 4·7in (119mm) battery; 4·7in (119mm) barbettes.
Armament: 6 x 9·4in (239mm); 4 x 4·7in (119mm).
Performance: 12·7kt (23·5km/h); coal 500 tons (508 tonnes)
Crew: 352.

This wooden-hulled cruising ironclad carried 4 x 9·4in (239mm) on the broadside in a central battery and two more single-mounted in barbettes set upon the battery's forward angles.

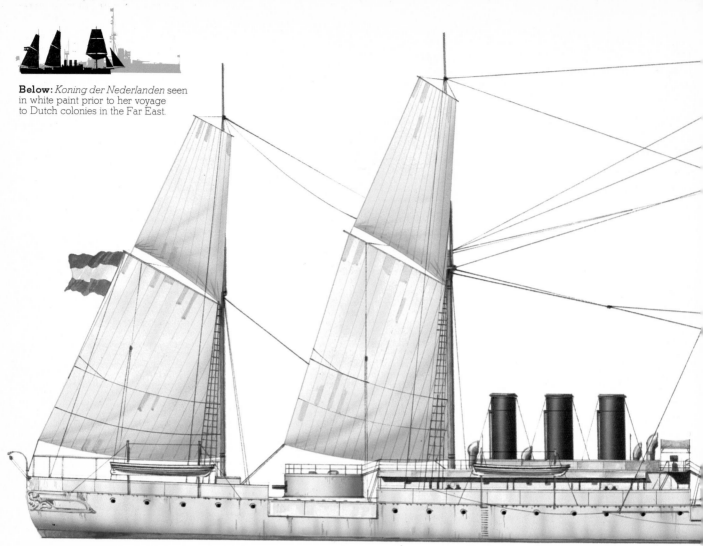

Below: *Koning der Nederlanden* seen in white paint prior to her voyage to Dutch colonies in the Far East.

KONING DER NEDERLANDEN

1874 Netherlands

Laid down: 1871.
Launched: 1874.
Builder: Amsterdam Navy Yard, Holland.
Displacement: 5,400 tons (5,486 tonnes).
Dimensions: 279ft (85m) oa x 49ft 8in (15·14m) x 19ft 6in (5·94m) max.
Machinery: 2 screws; 4630 IHP.
Armour: Iron 8in-6in (203-152mm) belt; 12in (305mm) teak backing; 12in-9in (305-229mm) turrets.
Armament: 4 x 11in (279mm) RML; 4 x 4·7in (119mm).
Performance: 12kt (22·2km/h); coal 620 tons (630 tonnes).
Crew: 250.

A sea-going vessel that could also navigate major waterways, *Koning der Nederlanden*, although over-long in building, was the Dutch Navy's most powerful warship for many years. Her two turrets each carried two 11in (279mm) Armstrong RML set almost 11ft (3·35m) above the waterline, and 4 x 4·7in (119mm) Krupp guns were set one at each angle of the superstructure at upper deck level. Spar torpedoes were also carried on this vessel.

Koning der Nederlanden served throughout in the Far East. In 1895-99 she was converted to a guardship at Surabaya, becoming a tender for destroyers and submarines in 1914. On 2 March 1942, when the Japanese invaded Java, she was set on fire and scuttled by her crew.

Below: *Javary* as seen in 1875.

JAVARY

1875 Brazil
Other ships in class: *Solimoes*

Laid down: 2 January 1874.
Launched: January 1875.
Builder: Le Havre.
Displacement: 3,641 tons (3,699 tonnes).
Dimensions: 240ft (73·15m) oa x 57ft (17·37m) x 11ft 5in (3·48m).
Machinery: Compound Double Cylinder; 2 shafts; 2200 IHP.
Armour: Iron 12in (305mm) belt; 7in (178mm) ends; 11in (279mm) turrets; 12in (203mm) faces; 3in (76mm) deck; 3·75in (95mm) conning tower.
Armament: 4 x 10in (254mm) MLR.
Performance: 11kt (20·35km/h); coal 200 tons (203 tonnes).
Crew: 112 (later 135).

At the time of their completion, *Javary* and *Solimoes* were the most powerful units of the Brazilian Navy—then comprising 18 ironclads and 52 unarmoured vessels of all types, mostly wooden.

Javary was a double-turretted, shallow-draught vessel with 3ft 3in (0·99m) freeboard. Her hull was completely armoured to 2ft 3in (0·69m) below the waterline, with 9·75in (248mm) teak backing. A 3in (76mm) deck of laminated armour rested on top of the belt. Above a double bottom, the hull was divided into six watertight compartments, four ventilated through hatches and two by way of the turrets.

A hurricane deck, 154ft (46·94m) long and 17ft (5·18m) wide, with a narrow section extending to the edge of the hull, stood above the turrets; aft the fore turret was a conning tower rising above the hurricane deck. A large centre trunk supplied light and extra ventilation to the engine room and stokehold.

Each of *Javary*'s 4 x 10in (254mm) Whitworth guns weighed 22 tons (22·35 tonnes) and fired a 400lb (181kg) shot or a slightly heavier shell. They were worked on the Armstrong system, which allowed MLs to be loaded outside the turret; this permitted a turret diameter of only 24ft (7·3m) and a corresponding reduction in the number of men needed to work the guns. No port stoppers were fitted.

Javary's rig was later reduced to pole masts, and by the early 1890s she had received 4 x 1in (25mm) Nordenfelts and two MG. In 1893, when Rear Admiral de Mello made an abortive attempt to depose President Peixoto, *Javary* formed part of the large insurgent fleet in Rio de Janeiro. On 22 November, engaged in the latest of a series of attacks on shore emplacements, she filled and sank: it was thought that the constant firing of her guns had started a leak in her hull.

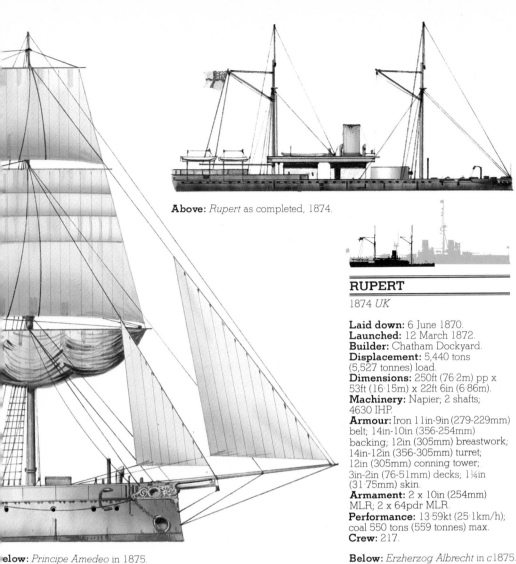

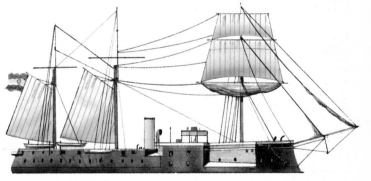

Above: *Rupert* as completed, 1874.

RUPERT

1874 *UK*

Laid down: 6 June 1870.
Launched: 12 March 1872.
Builder: Chatham Dockyard.
Displacement: 5,440 tons
(5,527 tonnes) load.
Dimensions: 250ft (76·2m) pp x
53ft (16·15m) x 22ft 6in (6·86m).
Machinery: Napier; 2 shafts;
4630 IHP.
Armour: Iron 11in-9in (279-229mm)
belt; 14in-10in (356-254mm)
backing; 12in (305mm) breastwork;
14in-12in (356-305mm) turret;
12in (305mm) conning tower;
3in-2in (76-51mm) decks; 1¼in
(31·75mm) skin.
Armament: 2 x 10in (254mm)
MLR; 2 x 64pdr MLR.
Performance: 13·59kt (25·1km/h);
coal 550 tons (559 tonnes) max.
Crew: 217.

The design of *Rupert* reflected
Reed's endorsement of the efficacy of
the ram—a belief fostered by the
Ferdinand Max's sinking of the
Italian ironclad *Re d'Italia* in
1866. *Rupert* was based on the
Hotspur of 1871, but a revolving
turret of the type fitted on the
breastwork monitor *Glatton*
replaced the fixed gun house of the
earlier, smaller ironclad ram.
 Unlike *Glatton*, however, *Rupert*
had no all-round fire capability with
her two turret-mounted 10in
(254mm), 18-ton (18·29 tonne) MLR,
which could be trained only from
ahead (the most important arc for a
ram) to c45° abaft the beam. Astern
fire was provided by 2 x 64pdr
MLR—the last guns of this type in a
British warship; replaced by 2 x 6in
(152mm) BLR in 1887—mounted in
the after breastwork. Armour
accounted for 27·6 per cent of
displacement: a full-length belt, 11in
(279mm) thick amidships and
tapering to 9in (229mm) at the ends,
ran forward to support the ram.
 Originally given fore-and-aft rig,
Rupert proved most unhandy under
sail. She was a heavy roller and, her
original machinery being
unsatisfactory, could not make more
than c12kt (22·2km/h) under
steam until she was reboiled and given
new triple expansion engines when
reconstructed in 1891-93. At that
time she shipped a single military
mast and was rearmed with 2 x 9·2in
(234mm) BL in the turret; 4 x 6pdr
QF and 6 x 3pdr QF on the upperworks were added to the four small
QF and four TT fitted in 1897.
 Rupert's poor sea-keeping
qualities limited her largely to
harbour defence duties, her last
station being Bermuda in 1904-07.
She was sold for breaking up in the
latter year.

Below: *Erzherzog Albrecht* in *c*1875.

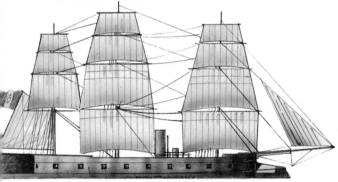

Below: *Principe Amedeo* in 1875.

PRINCIPE AMEDEO

1874 *Italy*
Other ships in class: *Palestro*

Laid down: August 1865.
Launched: September-October
1871.
Builder: La Spezia Navy Yard.
Displacement: 6,020 tons
6,116 tonnes) full load.
Dimensions: 261ft 7in (79·73m) pp
267ft 0½in (17·39m) x 25ft 11in (7·9m)
Machinery: Single Expansion
engines; 6 cylindrical boilers; 1 shaft;
8117 IHP.
Armour: Iron 8·7in (221mm) belt;
5in (140mm) battery; 2·4in
41mm) conning tower.
Armament: 1 x 11in (279mm);
6 x 10in (254mm).

Performance: 12·2kt (22·57km/h);
range 1,780nm (3,293km) at 10kt
(18·5km/h).
Crew: 548.

The first wholly native-built Italian
ironclads and the last to have wooden
(composite wood and iron) hulls and
to be rigged for sail. *Principe Amedeo*
and *Palestro* (the latter differing from
the former in armament layout) were
designed by Giuseppe de Luca.
Because of the stringent financial
limitations placed on Italian
construction after the Austro-Italian
War of 1866, they were some ten
years on the stocks.
 Principe Amedeo had a full-length
belt and a pronounced ram bow. She
carried 6 x 10in (254mm) guns in a
5·5in (140mm) armoured central
battery, with 1 x 11in (279mm)
mounted as a chase gun in the bows,
forward of a rudimentary conning
tower. She was barque rigged with
36,738ft² (3,413m²) of canvas.
Stricken in 1895, she was scrapped
in 1910.

ERZHERZOG ALBRECHT

1874 *Austria-Hungary*

Laid down: 1 June 1870.
Launched: 24 April 1872.
Builder: Stabilimento Tecnico
Triestino.
Displacement: 5,980 tons
(6,076 tonnes).
Dimensions: 294ft 3in (89·69m) oa
x 56ft 3in (17·15m) x 22ft (6·7m).
Machinery: 2-cylinder Horizontal
engines; 1 shaft; 3969 IHP.
Armour: Iron 8in (203mm) belt;
7in (177mm) casemates.
Armament: 8 x 9·5in (240mm) BL;
6 x 3·5in (90mm) BL; 2 x 2·75in
(70mm) BL.
Performance: 12·84kt (23·75km/h).
Crew: 540.

The Austro-Hungarian Navy's first
iron-hulled warship—the very similar
but somewhat larger *Custoza*,
completed in 1875, was the
second—*Erzherzog Albrecht* was
designed by von Romako. Since the
Battle of Lissa, 20 July 1866, had
appeared to confirm that the ram was
a potent weapon, the designer
sacrificed speed and weight of
armament in order to maximize
ramming potential. Well-protected,
she carried her main armament in a
two-deck central battery. Forward of
the battery, the hull sides were cut
away to allow ahead fire during a
ramming attack.
 Erzherzog Albrecht remained
active into the 1900s, 4 x 47mm QF, 5
x 47mm revolving MG, 2 x 25mm
MG and 4 x 13·8in (350mm) torpedo
tubes being added to her armament
in the 1880s. Renamed *Feuerspeier*
in 1908, she served as a tender and
barracks ship before being taken by
Italy in reparation after World War I
and renamed *Buttafuoco*. She was
not scrapped until 1946.

CUSTOZA

1875 Austria-Hungary

Laid down: 17 November 1869.
Launched: 20 August 1872.
Builder: Stabilimento Tecnico Triestino.
Displacement: 7,609 tons

Below: *Custoza* as seen in 1876.

(7,731 tonnes).
Dimensions: 311ft 9in (95·02m) oa x 58ft (17·68m) x 26ft (7·92m).
Machinery: 2-cylinder Horizontal engines; 1 shaft; 4158 IHP.
Armour: Iron 9in (229mm) belt; 7in-6in (178-152mm) casemate.
Armament: 8 x 10·2in (260mm) BL; 6 x 3·5in (90mm); 2 x 2·75in (70mm).
Performance: 13·75kt (25·4km/h).
Crew: 548.

Like *Erzherzog Albrecht,* completed eight months earlier, *Custoza* was designed by von Romako to maximize the effect of her ram. Her main armament was carried in a two-deck casemate, the hull sides forward being embrasured to permit ahead fire as the ship approached an enemy on a ramming course.

Custoza was reduced from full rig to schooner rig in 1877. In 1882, 4 x 47mm QF, 5 x 47mm revolving MG, 2 x 25mm MG and 4 x 13·8in (350mm) torpedo tubes were added to her armament. A barracks ship from 1914, she was taken by Italy as a war reparation in 1920 and was later scrapped.

PETR VELIKI

1875 Russia

Laid down: 1 June 1869.
Launched: 27 August 1872.
Builder: Koudryavtsev & Co, Galernii Island.
Displacement: 10,406 tons (10,572 tonnes).
Dimensions: 339ft 8in (103·53m) oa x 62ft 3in (18·97m) x 27ft 2in (8·28m) max.
Machinery: Horizontal Return

Above: *Petr Veliki* in 1910, following a complete rebuild.

Below: *Petr Veliki* as completed in 1876; the only Russian battleship completed in a 16-year period.

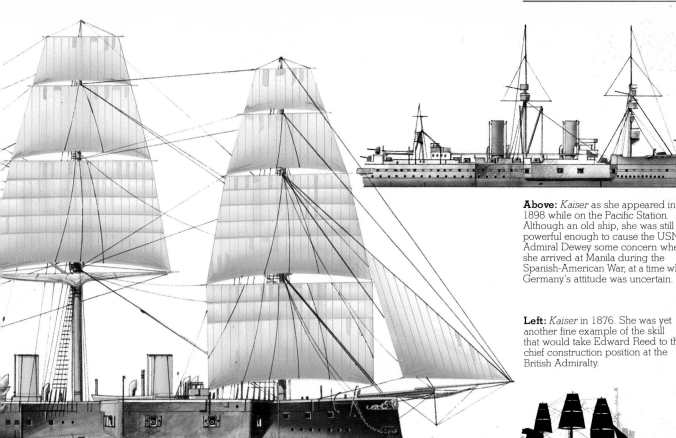

Above: *Kaiser* as she appeared in 1898 while on the Pacific Station. Although an old ship, she was still powerful enough to cause the USN's Admiral Dewey some concern when she arrived at Manila during the Spanish-American War, at a time when Germany's attitude was uncertain.

Left: *Kaiser* in 1876. She was yet another fine example of the skill that would take Edward Reed to the chief construction position at the British Admiralty.

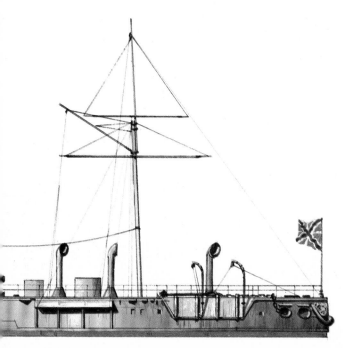

onnecting Rod; 2 shafts; 8000 IHP.
rmour: Iron 14in-11in
36-279mm) belt; 10in-8in
54-203mm) ends; 14in (356mm)
adel; 14in (356mm) turrets.
rmament: 4 x 12in (305mm);
x 3·4in (86mm); 13 smaller.
erformance: c10kt (18·5km/h).
rew: 374/432.

esigned by Vice-Admiral A.A.
opov, *Petr Veliki* was a large,
a-going breastwork turret ship,
ng the lines of the British
evastation. Following her
mewhat protracted completion, no
ajor Russian battleship was laid
own for eight years: the Ekaterina II
ass was begun in 1883, but the first
as not ready for sea until 1889.
Petr Veliki's iron hull had 8ft

(2·44m) freeboard and was recessed
abaft the second turret to form a
narrow platform over about half the
beam. The belt, made up of two 7in
(178mm) strips with 22in (559mm)
Hughes wooden backing
sandwiched between them, ran the
full length of the hull, but was almost
submerged at full load displacement.
Amidships was a 160ft (48·77m) long
citadel which supported a short
superstructure housing a single
funnel, ventilators, bridge and light
guns. There was a 1·5in (38mm) deck
over the citadel; the armoured deck
outside the citadel, resting on top of
the belt, was 3in (76mm) thick.

Petr Veliki was originally named
Kreiser but was renamed in May
1872, before launching. In 1876-77,
while she was ice-bound in Kronstadt

harbour, her main armament was
fired in temperatures as low as
−40°F (−40°C), damaging her
machinery and starting a leak in her
hull. In 1881 she was extensively
refitted by Elder of Glasgow: the
original unsatisfactory engines were
replaced by vertical compound
engines of 8250 IHP, giving 14kt
(25·9km/h).

In 1905-06 she was reconstructed
as a high-sided, twin-funnelled vessel
and rearmed with 4 x 8in (203mm)
guns on sponsons on the upper deck
and 12 x 6in (152mm) QF in the
battery below. She also received
cylindrical boilers. In World War I,
Petr Veliki (renamed *Respublikanets*
in 1917) was a gunnery training ship
with the Baltic Fleet. She was
scrapped in 1922.

KAISER

1875 *Germany*
Other ships in class: *Deutschland*

Laid down: 1872.
Launched: 19 March 1874.
Builder: Samuda Bros, London.
Displacement: 8,940 tons
(9,083 tonnes) load.
Dimensions: 293ft 1in (89·34m) oa
x 62ft 6in (19m) x 26ft (7·93m)
max.
Machinery: Penn Horizontal
Single Expansion engines; 8 box
boilers; 1 shaft; 5779 IHP.
Armour: Iron 10in-5in (254-127mm)
belt; 10in (254mm) teak backing;
8in-7in (203-178mm) battery; 2in
(51mm) deck.
Armament: 8 x 10·2in (260mm) BL;
1 x 8·25in (210mm).
Performance: 14·5kt (26·83km/h);
coal 684 tons (695 tonnes);
range 2,470nm (4,570km) at 10kt
(18·5km/h), 1,115nm (2,063km) at
14kt (25·9km/h).
Crew: 656.

Designed by Reed, the armoured
frigates *Kaiser* and *Deutschland*
were the German Navy's last foreign-
built ironclads. They reflected

Germany's need for powerful cruising
ships with which to maintain her
newly established empire

The belt had a maximum thickness
of 10in (254mm) at the waterline,
tapering through 8in (203mm) to 5in
(127mm) at the ends. Aft of the
battery, it extended from 5ft 6in
(1·68m) below the waterline to 6ft 6in
(1·98m) above. Forward of the
battery, extent above water was
reduced to 2ft 6in (0·76m), the height
of the 2in-1·5in (51-38mm) armoured
lower deck.

The central battery was protected
by 8in (203mm) side armour—with
10in (254mm) at the port sills—and
by 7in (178mm) bulkheads at each
end. The forward bulkhead ran
down to the lower deck to give
added protection to machinery and
boilers. A double bottom with
watertight compartmentation was
fitted and watertight compartments
also closed off the ram from the main
hull.

In the battery, 4 x 10·2in (260mm)
Krupp BL were mounted on either
side at main deck level, with port sills
11ft (3·35m) above water. The battery
overhung the hull sides by some 3ft
6in (1·07m) forward and 1ft 6in
(0·46m) aft; embrasured ports
permitted near-complete ahead fire
to the forward guns and good
all-round arcs. Astern fire was
provided by 1 x 8·25in (210mm)
Krupp gun in a protected position on
the main deck aft, with an arc of fire of
up to 15° on either side of the
centre-line.

Kaiser and *Deutschland* were said
to be good sea boats and were ship
rigged with some 36,000ft²
(3,344m²) of canvas. In 1882 the
8·25in (210mm) gun was removed
and 7 x 5·9in (150mm), 4 x 3·15in
(80mm) and six smaller were added.
Around 1895 both ships were rebuilt
as heavy cruisers. Two military masts
replaced the original rig and new
secondary armament was fitted: in
Kaiser, 1 x 5·9in (150mm), 6 x 4·1in
(105mm), 9 x 3·35in (85mm) and five
torpedo tubes.

HANSA

1875 *Germany*

Laid down: 1868.
Launched: 26 October 1872.
Builder: Danzig Dockyard.
Displacement: 4,334 tons
(4,403 tonnes).
Dimensions: 241ft 1in (73·48m) oa
x 46ft 3in (14·1m) x 22ft 3in (6·78m).
Machinery: Horizontal Single
Expansion; 1 shaft; 3275 IHP.
Armour: 6in-4·5in (152-114mm)
belt; 4·5in (114mm) battery.
Armament: 8 x 8·25in (210mm).
Performance: 12·5kt (23·1km/h).
Crew: 399.

Below: The armoured corvette
Hansa with full rig, 1876.

Having relied on French and British yards for the design and building of its first ironclads, the young German Navy wished to turn to home yards—for greater homogeneity in its fleet and for political and financial reasons. Thus, in 1868-70, the three Grosser Kurfürst class turret ships and the armoured corvette *Hansa* were ordered from German yards.

Because of the Danzig Dockyard's inexperience, *Hansa* was some seven years building and when completed her iron hull was badly corroded. She carried 8 x 8·25in (210mm) guns in a two-deck central casemate: at the lower level, two guns on either broadside; at the upper level, four guns in corner ports, with the hull sides embrasured to permit a certain amount of axial fire. She served mainly on harbour defence and was a training hulk from 1888 until she was scrapped in 1906.

LA PLATA

1875 *Argentina*
Other ships in class: *Los Andes*

Laid down: 1873.
Launched: 29 August 1874.
Builder: Laird, Birkenhead.
Displacement: 1,677 tons
(1,704 tonnes) full load.
Dimensions: 185ft 4in (56·49m)
x 51ft 7in (15·72m) x 10ft 6in
(3·2m) mean.
Machinery: Compound
(450 HP) engines; 2 shafts; 750 IHP.
Armour: Iron 6in (152mm) belt;
4·5in-4in (114-102mm) ends;
8in (203mm) breastwork; 9in-8in
(229-203mm) turret.
Armament: 2 x 9in (229mm);
4 x 11mm Nordenfeld.
Performance: 9·5kt (17·57km/h);
coal *c*120 tons (122 tonnes).
Crew: 200.

The low-freeboard turret ships *La Plata* and *Los Andes* were the first ironclads built for the Argentine Navy. A single turret was carried

Below: *La Plata* in Argentina, *c*1875.

forward of amidships, housing 2 x 9in (229mm), 12·5-ton (12·7 tonne) guns; 2 x 4in (102mm), plus smaller, were later added.

A light central superstructure carried a bridge fore and aft and was narrow enough to allow direct ahead fire from both turret guns, the guns ports being set widely apart. Aft, the superstructure was wider, allowing for accommodation; the arc of fire aft was thus reduced by about 6°. An 8in (203mm) breastwork protected the turret base.

The hull had a 2ft (0·6m) deep double bottom which terminated 4ft (1·2m) from the sides in a bulkhead running fore and aft. Abreast the magazines and machinery, the belt extended from 2ft (0·6m) below the waterline to 5ft (1·52m) above. The funnel, abaft the turret, had a 4·5in (114mm) casing.

Two light pole masts were fitted, but for the voyage out to Argentina only a single fore sail was spread. Rig was later reduced to a single military mast amidships, with two fighting tops. The ships had good range, burning 8 tons (8·13 tonnes) of coal per day at 6kt (11·1km/h).

On 29 September 1893, *Los Andes*, with an insurgent crew, was damaged in action with the 2,300-ton (2,337 tonne) coast defence ship *Independencia*. *La Plata* was discarded in November 1927.

Below: *Preussen* as completed, with
impressive spread of canvas.
bulwarks are partly lowered.

Below: *Preussen* in the 1890s,
after modernization that included
the removal of her rig.

MESSUDIEH

1876 *Turkey*

Laid down: 1872.
Launched: 28 October 1874.
Builder: Thames Iron Works.
Displacement: 9,710 tons
(9,865 tonnes) full load.
Dimensions: 331ft 5in (101·02m)
x 59ft (17·98m) x 25ft 11in
(7·9m) max.
Machinery: Horizontal Compound
engines; 8 rectangular boilers;
1 shaft; 7431 IHP.
Armour: Iron 12in-6in (305-152mm)
belt; 5in-3in (127-76mm) ends;
10in-7in (254-178mm) battery;
8in (203mm) conning tower.
Armament: 12 x 10in (254mm)
MLR; 3 x 7in (178mm) MLR;
6 x 20pdr.
Performance: 13·7kt (25·3km/h);
coal 600 tons (610 tonnes).
Crew: 700.

The Turkish Navy ranked high in
Europe in the 1870s, but lack of
finance prevented attempts to keep it
up to date. Three large armoured
ships building at the time of the
Russo-Turkish War (1877-78) were
sold to Britain when the immediate
need for them passed. One of these
was *Memdouhied*, a sister ship to
Messudieh, renamed *Superb*.
 Messudieh, designed by Reed,
was a fully-rigged, ram-bowed
central battery ship of the broadside
type then common in the world's
navies. She combined considerable
firepower with moderate armour
protection, great speed, good

Above: *Messudieh* (her name meant
Fortunate") as completed in 1876.
The most powerful vessel in the
urkish Navy, she was a good
xample of the skill in design of Sir
dward Reed.

elow: *Messudieh* shortly before
er loss in December 1914.
lthough obsolete, the soundness of
er construction had allowed her to
e modernized with some success.

endurance and excellent sea-
keeping qualities.
 Messudieh had a full-length belt
extending 5ft (1·52m) below and 4ft
(1·22m) above the waterline. Over
this, amidships, was a 153ft (46·63m)
long battery protected by three
armour strakes: 10in (254mm)
above; 12in (305mm) in the centre;
9in (229mm) thinning to 6in (152mm)
below. The conning tower was at the
forward end of the battery.
 The 10in (254mm) 18-ton (18·29
tonne) Armstrong MLR were on the
upper deck firing forward, with one
7in (178mm) aft. By the early 1890s
the 7in (178mm) guns had been
replaced by 5·9in (150mm) weapons.
 Between 1898 and 1903
Messudieh was totally reconstructed
by Ansaldo of Genoa. Her ends were
cut down and the superstructure
amidships built up. Her rig was by
now reduced to a single military mast.
Single 9·2in (234mm) guns were to
have been housed in 9in-6in
(229-152mm) steel armoured turrets
at either end, but the guns were never
mounted and wooden dummies
were carried. Twelve 6in (152mm)
Vickers guns were mounted in the
main battery and 14 x 3in (76mm)
QF in the upper battery; 10 x 57mm
and 2 x 47mm were also fitted. She
was given triple expansion engines
of 11,000 IHP, raising speed to 16kt
(29·6km/h).
 Messudieh was briefly in action
against Greek forces in 1912. Early in
World War I, she was in the
Dardanelles off Charnak, guarding a
minefield below the Narrows. On 13
December 1914, Lt N.D. Holbrook,
RN, commanding submarine *B 11*,
closed to within 800yd (732m) and
hit her with a single torpedo.
Messudieh sank within 10 minutes,
with 37 dead out of a crew of 673.
Most of her guns were salvaged and
were later mounted in shore
batteries.

PREUSSEN

1876 *Germany*
Other ships in class: *Grosser
Kurfürst, Friedrich der Grosse*

Laid down: 1870.
Launched: 22 November 1873.
Builder: Vulkan, Stettin.
Displacement: 7,596 tons
(7,718 tonnes).
Dimensions: 316ft 10in (96·57m)
oa x 53ft 0½in (16·17m) x
23ft 6in (7·16m).
Machinery: Horizontal Single
Expansion engines; 1 shaft;
5000 IHP.
Armour: Iron 9in-4in (229-102mm)
belt; 8in (203mm) citadel and
turrets.
Armament: 4 x 10·2in (260mm);
2 x 6·7in (170mm).
Performance: 14kt (25·9km/h).
Crew: 500.

The name ship of the Grosser
Kurfürst class, laid down as a central
battery ship, was changed to a turret
ship modelled on the British
Monarch of 1868. This partly
accounted for very long building
times: 10 years for *Grosser Kurfürst*;
8 years for *Friedrich der Grosse*; 6
years for *Preussen*, the only one built
in a private yard. Further delay was
due to the difficulty experienced in
ironclad construction by the
newly established Royal Dockyards
at Wilhelmshaven and Kiel.
 Although somewhat smaller than
their British model, the ships were
claimed to be equally as powerful
because of their main armament of
10·2in (260mm), 22-ton (22·35 tonne)
Krupp guns. But they cannot be
considered successful: only four big
guns were carried and the two
closely spaced turrets were
protected by only a short belt of
armour. The three masts were hollow,
giving added ventilation, and the
funnel collapsible, lessening wind
resistance when under sail. Even so
they were slow sailers, although good
responsive sea boats.
 The German Navy's advantage in
having three completely
homogeneous ships was quickly lost:
Grosser Kurfürst was sunk only 26
days after commissioning. On 31
May 1878 she was steaming off
Folkestone with the 10,700 ton
(10,871 tonne) broadside frigate
König Wilhelm and *Preussen*. The
former altered course to avoid two
sailing vessels and, through a
helmsman's error, rammed *Grosser
Kurfürst*, which filled and sank within
five minutes with the loss of 264 men.
 Preussen and *Friedrich der
Grosse* were modernized at
Wilhelmshaven in 1889-90. Both
ended fleet service in the 1890s and
then served as guard ships
(*Preussen* renamed *Saturn*) and later
as coal hulks. Both were sold for
breaking up in 1919.

FRIEDLAND

1876 France

Laid down: July 1865.
Launched: 25 October 1873.
Builder: Lorient Dockyard.
Displacement: 8,850 tons
(8,992 tonnes).
Dimensions: 317ft 2in (96·67m) wl
x 58ft (17·68m) x 29ft 6in
(8·99m) max.
Machinery: Horizontal Return
Connecting Rod Compound
engines; 8 oval boilers; 1 shaft;
4400 IHP.
Armour: Wrought iron 8in-7in
(203-178mm) belt; 6·3in (160mm)
battery.
Armament: 8 x 10·8in (274mm);
8 x 5·5in (140mm); 8 x 1pdr
revolving guns.
Performance: 13·3kt (24·6km/h);
coal 630 tons (640 tonnes).
Crew: 700.

Laid down as an Océan but much
modified during her long building
time, *Friedland* was iron-hulled and
had a less pronounced ram than the
Océans. She mounted 3 x 10·8in
(274mm) on either broadside in the
central battery, with two more
single-mounted for end-on fire in
unarmoured barbettes carried fore
and aft above it. Her rig was much
reduced, and 14 x 1pdr revolvers
and 4 x 14in (356mm) TT added
before she was stricken in 1902.

RICHELIEU

1876 France

Laid down: 1869.
Launched: 3 December 1873.
Builder: Toulon Dockyard.
Displacement: 8,984 tons
(9,128 tonnes).
Dimensions: 322ft (98·15m) wl
x 57ft 3in (17·45m) x 28ft 6in
(8·69m) max.

*Below: Don Juan d'Austria as
completed in 1876.*

Machinery: Horizontal Return
Connecting Rod Compound engines;
8 oval boilers; 2 shafts; 4200 IHP.
Armour: Wrought iron 8·7in-7in
(221-178mm) belt; 6·3in (160mm)
battery and barbettes.
Armament: 6 x 10·8in (274mm);
5 x 9·4in (239mm); 10 x 4·7in
(119mm); 8 x 1pdr revolving guns.
Performance: 13kt (24km/h);
coal 640 tons (650 tonnes).
Crew: 750.

Like *Friedland*, the wooden-hulled
Richelieu spent a lengthy period
undergoing alteration on the stocks.
Her wooden sides above a full-length
waterline belt—which ran down to
provide 4·5in (114mm) armour over
a 10ft (3·05m) spur ram—were
protected by 0·6in (15mm) iron plate.
   Three 10·8in (274mm) were
carried on each side in a central
battery and at each corner above it
were armoured barbettes, each
housing 1 x 9·4in (239mm), with a
fifth 9·4in (239mm) in the bow. Thus
she had axial fire from three heavy
guns forward and two astern, with
five firing on either beam.
   Richelieu was rebuilt in 1881,
following her capsize after a fire at
Toulon. Six 5·5in (140mm) guns
replaced the 4·7in (119mm) weapons
and ten more 1pdr revolvers and 4 x
14in (356mm) torpedo tubes were
added. Used in torpedo net trials in
1885, she was sold in 1901.

DON JUAN D'AUSTRIA

1876 Austria-Hungary
Other ships in class: *Kaiser Max,
Prinz Eugen*

Laid down: 14 February 1874.
Launched: 25 October 1875.
Builder: Stabilimento Tecnico
Triestino.
Displacement: 3,548 tons
(3,605 tonnes).
Dimensions: 249ft (75·9m) oa x
50ft (15·24m) x 20ft 2in (6·15m).
Machinery: 2-cylinder Horizontal

*Right: Alexandra as completed, with
barque rig. She is painted white for
service as Flagship, Mediterranean.*

Low Pressure engines; 1 shaft;
2755 IHP.
Armour: Iron 8in (203mm) belt;
4·5in (115mm) bulkheads; 5in
(125mm) battery.
Armament: 8 x 8·25in (210mm) B
4 x 3·5in (90mm) BL; 2 x 2·75in
(70mm); 6 x 47mm QF; 3 x 47mm
MG; 2 x 25mm MG; 4 x 13·8in
(350mm) torpedo tubes.
Performance: 13·28kt (24·57km/h)
Crew: 400.

A central battery ironclad with a
compete waterline belt, *Don Juan
d'Austria* was officially a rebuilt
armoured frigate of the Kaiser Max
class, although only parts of the old
wooden-hulled ship were
incorporated. She was stricken in
1904 and was a barracks ship until
she sank in 1919.

Below: Friedland as completed, 1876.

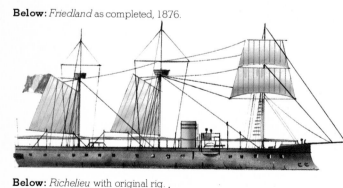

Below: Richelieu with original rig.

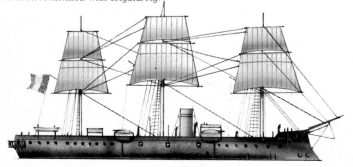

TEMERAIRE

_1877 UK_

Laid down: 18 August 1873.
Launched: 9 May 1876.
Builder: Chatham Dockyard.
Displacement: 8,540 tons
(8,677 tonnes) load.
Dimensions: 285ft (86·87m) pp
x 62ft (18·9m) x 27ft (8·23m).
Machinery: Humphreys & Tennant
2-cylinder Vertical Inverted
Compound engines; 12 cylindrical
boilers; 2 shafts; 7697 IHP.
Armour: 11in-5·5in (279-
140mm) belt; 12in-10in (305-
254mm) teak backing; 8in (203mm)
battery; 8in-5in (203-127mm)
bulkheads; 10in-8in (254-203mm)
barbettes; 1·5in-1in (38-25mm) decks.
Armament: 4 x 11in (279mm) MLR;
4 x 10in (254mm) MLR; 4 x 20pdr
BL; 2 torpedo carriages.
Performance: 14·65kt (27·1km/h);
coal 620 tons (630 tonnes).
Crew: 580.

Designed by Barnaby after a Design
Committee minority report in 1871
advocated provision of at least two
heavy guns in protected positions on
the centre line, _Temeraire_ was the
Royal Navy's first barbette ship. At
either end of the upper deck, a
pear-shaped barbette housed an
11in (279mm) MLR on a
disappearing mounting: on a
turntable, the gun was lowered and
reversed for loading, raised by
hydraulic arms to fire over the
barbette, and returned by recoil for
reloading. Although successful,
its excessive weight-for-space
demand prevented the system's
adoption. The 10in (254mm) MLR
were in a central battery.

With a low length-to-beam ratio of
4.6:1, _Temeraire_ was very handy. The
largest brig built, she carried
25,000ft² (2,322m²) of canvas but
was a slow sailer. By 1889 her rig was
reduced; 6 x 4in (102mm) BL
replaced her 20pdrs and 14 smaller
QF were mounted. A depot and
workshop ship from 1902 (renamed
Indus II, later _Akbar_) she was sold in
1921.

Below: Barbette ship
Temeraire, 1978.

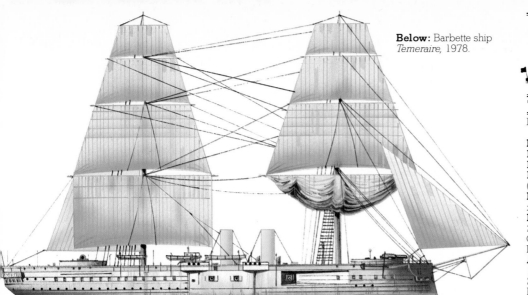

ALEXANDRA

_1877 UK_

Laid down: 5 March 1873.
Launched: 7 April 1875.
Builder: Chatham Dockyard.
Displacement: 9,492 tons
9,644 tonnes) load.
Dimensions: 325ft (99·06m) pp
x 63ft 10in (19·46m) x 26ft 3in (8m)
Machinery: Humphreys 2-cylinder
Vertical Inverted Compound engines;
12 cylindrical boilers; 2 shafts;
8498 IHP.

Armour: 12in-6in (305-152mm)
belt; 12in-10in (305-254mm) teak
backing; 12in (305mm) main battery;
8in (203mm) upper battery; 8in-5in
(203-127mm) bulkheads; 1·5in-1in
(38-25mm) decks.
Armament: 2 x 11in (279mm) MLR;
10 x 10in (254mm) MLR; 6 x 20pdr
BL; 4 torpedo carriages.
Performance: 15·09kt (27·9km/h);
coal 680 tons (691 tonnes);
range 3,800 miles (6,114km) at 7·5kt
(13·9km/h).
Crew: 674.

As a full-rigged central battery
ironclad, _Alexandra_ was obsolescent
when launched—but was
nevertheless successful. Influenced
by von Romako's 1869 design for
Custoza (p.84), Barnaby ensured
all-round firepower, especially bow

fire, by having a two-deck armoured
battery amidships. The lower battery
housed 8 x 10in (254mm) MLR: three
on each broadside in the main
section and, forward, two firing from
angle-ports in the forward corners.
In the upper battery, 2 x 11in (279mm)
fired from angle-ports forward and 2
x 10in (254mm) from angle-ports aft.
The ship's upperworks were set
back to give the corner ports an
angle of fire of _c_100°.

The fastest steaming battleship of
1877-87 and the first British warship
with vertical compound engines,
Alexandra was barque-rigged with
27,000ft² (2,508m²) of canvas but
was a slow sailer (_c_6kt; 11km/h). She
served as a flagship until
1889 and was a coastguard and
training ship until sold for breaking
up in 1908.

COLBERT

1877 *France*
Other ships in class: *Trident*

Laid down: 1870.
Launched: 16 September 1875.
Builder: Brest Dockyard.
Displacement: 8,750 tons
(8,890 tonnes).
Dimensions: 317ft 9in (96·85m) wl
x 57ft 3in (17·45m) x 28ft-29ft
(8·53-8·84m) max.

Below: *Colbert* as completed: a good
design but hampered by a wooden
hull and overlong in building.

Machinery: Horizontal Return
Connecting Rod Compound engines;
8 oval boilers; 1 shaft; 4600 IHP.
Armour: Wrought iron 8·7in-7in
(221-178mm) belt; 6·3in (160mm)
battery; 4·7in (119mm) bulkheads.
Armament: 8 x 10·8in (274mm);
1 x 9·4in (239mm); 8 x 5·5in
(140mm).
Performance: 14kt (25·9km/h);
coal 620 tons (630 tonnes) max.
Crew: 774.

Like many other French armoured
ships, *Colbert* and *Trident* were
overlong building, spending more
than seven years on the stocks at a
time when such British rivals as
Alexandra and *Temeraire* were

completed within four years. They
were the last French capital ships to
be wooden-hulled: iron plating
protected their timber sides above a
full-length belt and similar 0·6in
(15mm) protection was given to the
main deck.
 Six 10·8in (274mm) were in the
central battery, with two more set
above and forward in unarmoured
barbettes. Soon after completion, 2 x
5·5in (140mm) were removed to
make way for a single lightly shielded
9·4in (239mm) on the upper deck
aft—a similar weapon being already
mounted beneath the forecastle. Up
to 18 x 1pdr revolvers and 6 x 14in
(356mm) torpedo tubes were later
added.

ALMIRANTE COCHRANE

1875 *Chile*
Other ships in class: *Blanco
Encalada*

Laid down: 1873.
Launched: 25 January 1874.
Builder: Earle, Glasgow.
Displacement: 3,560 tons
(3,617 tonnes) full load.
Dimensions: 210ft (64·01m) pp

Above: *Shannon* as completed, with
full rig to increase range.

SHANNON

1877 *UK*

Laid down: 29 September 1873.
Launched: 11 November 1875.
Builder: Pembroke Dockyard.
Displacement: 5,670 tons
(5,761 tonnes) load.
Dimensions: 260ft (79·25m) pp
x 54ft (16·46m) x 22ft 3in
(6·78m) mean.
Machinery: Laird Compound
Horizontal Return Connecting
Rod engines; 8 cylindrical boilers;
1 shaft; 3370 IHP.
Armour: Iron 9in-6in (229-152mm)
belt; 13in-10in (330-254mm) teak
backing; 9in-8in (229-203mm)
bulkheads; 3in-1·5in (76-38mm)
decks; 9in (229mm) conning tower.
Armament: 2 x 10in (254mm) MLR;
7 x 9in (229mm) MLR; 6 x 20pdr BL.
Performance: 12·25kt (22·7km/h);
coal 560 tons (569 tonnes).
Crew: 452.

Often called an armoured cruiser, the
second class battleship *Shannon* was
too slow to justify that title, but lacked
true battleship armament and
protection. Two 10in (254mm) were
mounted for bows-on action, firing
through deep embrasures behind an
armour screen to the rear of the
forecastle. The 9in (229mm) guns
were in unprotected positions on the
upper deck. Her waterline belt
ended c60ft (18·3m) from the bows in
a 9in (229mm) bulkhead, forward of
which a 3in (76mm) armour deck
sloped down to the ram.
 Shannon was a good sea boat but
made only c12kt (22km/h) under
steam. In reserve by 1893, she was
sold in 1899.

45ft 9in (13·94m) x 21ft 10in
65m) max.
achinery: Compound Horizontal
unk engines; 6 cylindrical boilers,
shafts; 2920 IHP.
rmour: Iron 9in (229mm) belt;
n-4·5in (152-114mm) ends; 8in-
n (203-152mm) battery; 3in
6mm) conning tower; 14in-7·75in
56-197mm) backing.
rmament: 6 x 9in (229mm); 1 x
pdr; 1 x 9pdr; 1 x 7pdr;
MG (Nordenfeld or Gatling).
erformance: 12·8kt (23·7km/h);
al 300/500 tons (305/508 tonnes).
rew: 300.

esigned by Reed, *Almirante
ochrane* and *Blanco Encalada*.

(ex-*Valparaiso*) combined powerful
armament and good protection on a
relatively small displacement. They
were iron-hulled with a double
bottom beneath the engine room,
stokehold and magazines. Barque
rigged, they were very handy, with a
turning circle of 300yds (274m)
diameter in just over four minutes at
11kt (20·35km/h).

The main armament was
concentrated in a central battery
which overhung the sides to a
maximum of c5ft (1·52m). The
battery sides were recessed so that
four guns could fire ahead (two in line
with the keel) and two aft; all fired on
the broadside. The port sills were 7ft
6in (2·29m) above water.

The complete belt was 9in
(229mm) thick with a 6in (152mm)
strake tapering to 4·5in (114mm) at the
ends above and below it. The belt ran
from 4ft (1·22m) below water to the
height of the battery deck. The upper
deck, resting on the belt, was 0·75in
(19mm) thick outside the battery,
which was protected by an 8in-7in
(203-178mm) strake surmounted by
a 6in (152mm) strake.

When the ships were rebuilt by
Earle in 1889, the 9in (229mm)
Armstrong MLR were replaced by 6
x 8in (203mm) Armstrong BLR.
Three 6pdr Hotchkiss QF, 6 x 37mm
Hotchkiss and 3 x 14in (356mm)
torpedo tubes—one on either side of
the bow and one in the stern—were

added. New cylindrical boilers and
horizontal triple expansion engines of
4300 IHP allowed 13·6kt (25·2km/h).

Together, they captured the
Peruvian turret ship *Huascar* in
October 1879. Both fought with the
Congressionalists against President
Balmaceda in 1891, and on 23 April
Blanco Encalada was torpedoed and
sunk by the torpedo gunboats
Almirante Lynch and *Almirante
Condell*—the first successful
locomotive torpedo attack on an
ironclad. With her main armament
removed, *Almirante Cochrane* was a
gunnery training ship in 1897-1900.
Hulked by 1908, she was later armed
with 4 x 4·7in (119mm) plus smaller.
She was discarded around 1935.

Below: *Blanco Encalada* as
completed. She is shown here to
facilitate comparison with *Fuso*, a
fairly similar design by Reed in
the same period. Both ships
successfully combined great offensive
power with small displacement.

elow right: *Fuso* as she was during
e Sino-Japanese War of 1894-95.

eft: *Fuso* with full rig, 1978.

FUSO
1878 *Japan*

Laid down: September 1875.
Launched: 14 April 1877.
Builder: Samuda Bros, London.
Displacement: 3,717 tons
(3,776 tonnes) normal.
Dimensions: 220ft (67m) pp
x 48ft (14·63m) x 18ft 4in
(5·59m) mean.
Machinery: Penn Compound

Horizontal Surface Condensing
Trunk engines; 8 cylindrical
boilers; 2 shafts; 3932 IHP.
Armour: Iron 9in-4in (229-102mm)
belt; 8in (203mm) battery;
7in (178mm) bulkheads.
Armament: 4 x 9·4in (239mm) BLR;
2 x 6·7in (170mm) BLR; 6 x 3in
(76mm) BLR; 1-5 x 25mm four-
barrelled Nordenfeld MG.
Performance: 13kt (24km/h); coal
360 tons (366 tonnes); range
4,500nm (8,325km) at 10kt
(18·5km/h).
Crew: 386.

As part of the naval expansion
programme of 1875, Japan ordered
the central battery ironclad *Fuso* and
the armoured corvettes *Kongo* and

Hiei from British yards. All were
designed by Sir Edward Reed, the
iron-hulled *Fuso* resembling the
Almirante Cochrane class.

Barque-rigged with 11,700ft²
(1,087m²) of canvas, *Fuso* had a
length-to-beam ratio of c4·5:1,
making her very handy. The total
weight of armour was 776 tons (788
tonnes) and her belt was fitted on
continuous frames to avoid wasted
shelf space. Wing passages ran
alongside the engines, magazines
and stokehold. The 9·4in (239mm)
Krupp guns were carried 7ft 6in
(2·29m) above the waterline.

Rebuilt in 1894, she emerged with
two military masts and an armament
of 8 x 6in (152mm) QF, 7 MGs and 2
x 18in (457mm) torpedo tubes. A
refit in 1899-1900—following 11
months aground after a collision with
the cruiser *Matsushima* on 29
October 1897—gave her 2 x 6in
(152mm), 4 x 4·7in (119mm), 11 x
3pdr and 3 x 18in (457mm) TT.

Fuso sustained some damage and
14 casualties from Chinese fire at the
Battle of the Yalu River, 17
September 1894. She was
reclassified as a coast defence ship in
April 1900, serving as such during
the Russo-Japanese War. Stricken in
1908, *Fuso* was broken up in 1910.

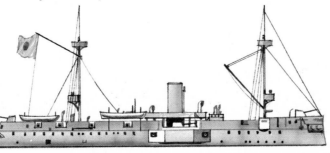

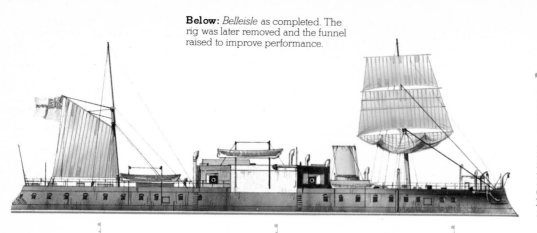

Below: *Belleisle* as completed. The rig was later removed and the funnel raised to improve performance.

REDOUTABLE

1878 *France*

Laid down: August 1873.
Launched: September 1876.
Builder: Lorient Dockyard.
Displacement: 9,224 tons
(9,372 tonnes).
Dimensions: 318ft 8in (97.13m) w
x 64ft 6in (19.66m) x 25ft 7in

BELLEISLE

1878 *UK*
Other ships in class: *Orion*

Laid down: 1874.
Launched: 12 February 1876.
Builder: Samuda Bros, London.
Displacement: 4,870 tons
(4,948 tonnes) load.
Dimensions: 245ft (74.68m) pp
x 52ft (15.85m) x 21ft (6.4m).
Machinery: Maudslay 2-cylinder
Horizontal Direct Acting engines;
4 boilers; 2 shafts; 4040 IHP.
Armour: Iron 12in-6in (305-152mm)
belt; 16in-10in (406-254mm)
backing; 10.5in-8in (267-203mm)
battery; 9in (229mm) conning
tower; 9in-5in (229-127mm)
bulkheads; 3in-2in (76-51mm)
main deck.
Armament: 4 x 12in (305mm) MLR;
4 x 20pdr; 2 x 14in (356mm)
torpedo carriages.
Performance: 12.99kt (24km/h);
coal 510 tons (518 tonnes);
radius 1,000 miles (1,609km)
at *c*12kt (22.2km/h).
Crew: 249.

Delivery to Turkey of the armoured
rams *Belleisle* (ex-*Peki-Shereef*) and
Orion (ex-*Boordhi-Zaffer*), designed
by Ahmed Pasha, was prevented by
Britain's neutrality during the
Russo-Turkish War of 1878.
Although their limited sea-keeping
qualities made them of little use to the
Royal Navy—in which they were the
last central battery ships—they were
purchased mainly to support their
British builder.
  Never meant to stand in the battle
line, the ships were well protected for
their intended coast-defence role. A
full-length belt extended from 5ft
(1.52m) below the waterline to 5ft
(1.52m) above: it was 12in (305mm)
thick amidships; 7in (178mm) at the
bow, where it supported the 8ft
(2.44m) solid-forged ram; and 6in
(152mm) aft. The two-deck octagonal
battery amidships housed 4 x 12in
(305mm) MLR on the broadside at
upper deck level, the corner ports
being sufficiently large to permit
limited end-on or quarter fire.
  In 1886, 6 x 3pdr and two
searchlights were mounted above
the battery and a torpedo net defence
added. *Belleisle* served mainly as a
coastguard ship and in 1900-03 was
used as a target for new lyddite shells
and for anti-torpedo defence
experiments. She was sold in 1904.
Orion saw service in the Far East and
was subsequently stationed at Malta.
In 1910 she became a store ship,
Orontes, and was sold in June 1913.

HELGOLAND

1879 *Denmark*

Laid down: 1876.
Launched: 1878.
Builder: Copenhagen Dockyard.
Displacement: 5,332 tons
(5,417 tonnes).
Dimensions: 259ft 7in (79.12m) x
59ft 2in (18.03m) x 19ft 4in
(5.89m) max.
Machinery: 2 shafts; 4000 IHP.
Armour: Iron 12in-8in (305-230mm)
belt; 10in (254mm) battery and
barbette.
Armament: 1 x 12in (305mm); 4 x
10.2in (259mm); 5 x 4.7in (119mm);
10 x 1pdr revolvers; 2 x 15in
(381mm) TT; 3 x 14in (356mm) TT.
Performance: 13.75kt (25.4km/h);
coal 224 tons (228 tonnes) max.
Crew: 331.

The casemate ship *Helogland* was
the Danish Navy's largest warship for
many years. She had the protection
and armament of a true battleship: a
full-length belt and a main deck
battery housing 4 x 10.2in (259mm)
Krupp guns, protected by 10in
(254mm) armour. Forward and
above the battery, armour extended
to form a barbette for a single 12in
(305mm) Krupp gun. In spite of a
high freeboard of *c*11ft (3.35m) she
was a successful coast defence ship
and was in service for some 30 years.

Below: *Helgoland* as seen in 1895;
note the forward barbette.

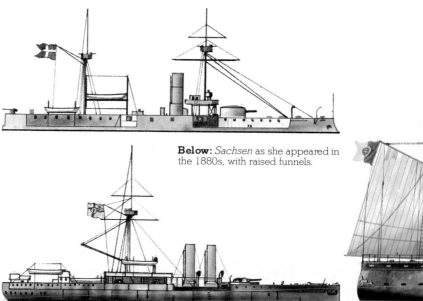

Below: *Sachsen* as she appeared in
the 1880s, with raised funnels.

SACHSEN

1878 *Germany*
Other ships in class: *Bayern,
Würtemberg, Baden*

Laid down: 1875.
Launched: 21 July 1877.
Builder: Vulkan, Stettin.
Displacement: 7,677 tons
(7,556 tonnes).
Dimensions: 322ft 2in (98.2m) oa
x 60ft 4in (18.39m) x 21ft 5in (6.53m).
Machinery: Horizontal Single
Expansion engines; 2 shafts;
5000 IHP.
Armour: Wrought iron 10in-8in
(254-203mm) citadel; 2in-2.5in
(51-63mm) deck.
Armament: 6 x 10.25in (260mm); 6
x 3.4in (87mm); 8 x 37mm revolvers.
Performance: 13.5kt (25km/h).
Crew: 317.

The Sachsen class armoured
corvettes carried two 10.25in
(260mm) in a pear-shaped barbette
on the forecastle and four in a
rectangular barbette abaft the four
funnels (also arranged in a
rectangle). Armour covered the central
citadel and an armoured deck extended
to the unprotected ends. A single
military mast was shipped: they had
no sail power. Three 13.8in (350mm)
torpedo tubes were fitted by 1886,
and before 1900 they received new
armour and engines.

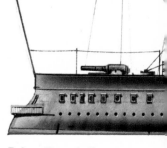

Below: *Vasco da Gama* seen prior t[o]
her voyage to Portugal in 1878.

8m) max.
Machinery: Horizontal Return
Connecting Rod Compound engines
oval boilers; 1 shaft; 6200 IHP
Armour: Wrought iron 14in-8.7in
(356-221mm) belt; 9.5in (241mm)
battery.
Armament: 8 x 10.8in (274mm);
x 5.5in (140mm); 12 x 1pdr
revolvers; 2 x 14in (356mm)
torpedo tubes.
Performance: 14.7kt (27.2km/h);
al 620 tons (630 tonnes).
Crew: 705.

aid down under the construction
ogramme of 1872, which called for
ironclads, 34 cruisers and more
an 100 lesser warships,

Redoutable was the first warship in
which steel was widely used. Her
designer, L. de Bussy, used mild steel
developed at the Creusot works and
some 25-30 per cent stronger than
iron for the greater part of her hull,
and although wrought iron armour
was retained it was heavier than in
earlier French ships. *Redoutable* was
of deeper draught and greater beam
than earlier central battery ships and
had a much improved armament
layout.

Her full-length belt had a
maximum thickness of 14in (356mm)
amidships, tapering to 8.7in
(221mm) forward and 9in (229mm)
aft. It extended from 4ft 10in (1.47m)
above the waterline to 5ft (1.52m)

below, reducing to 9in (229mm)
thickness at the bottom edge. A
double bottom—the inner bottom of
steel—and steel watertight transverse
bulkheads were fitted. Resting on the
upper edge of the belt, outside the
battery, was a 2.4in (61mm)
armoured deck. Above the belt the
hull sloped very sharply inwards: this
'tumblehome' allowed axial fire to
the battery guns.
   The 9.5in (241mm) armoured
battery was built out to the full beam
and housed 4 x 10.8in (274mm) BL
in angled ports at the four corners,
permitting end-on and quarter fire
but at the cost of restricted broadside
arcs. Of the remaining 10.8in
(274mm), one was mounted forward

beneath the forecastle, two in
semi-barbettes above the battery and
one aft, all in unarmoured positions.
The 5.5in (140mm) were in
unprotected positions on the upper
deck; they were later replaced by
3.9in (99mm). The battery guns later
gave way to 4 x 9.4in (239mm), and
the final light armament was 5 x 9pdr,
14 x 3pdr and 10 x 1pdr.
   At first fully rigged with 24,000ft²
(2,230m²) of canvas, *Redoutable* was
later barquentine rigged and finally
shipped two military masts. In 1894
she was reboiled and given vertical
triple expansion machinery. She
spent her final years on coast defence
duty in Indochina, being stricken in
1910.

Below: *Redoutable* in 1878: 2,500
tons (2,540 tonnes) of armour was
worked into the iron and steel hull.
The full rig was later reduced to two
military masts and a narrow platform
supporting light guns was added
round the large funnel.

Above: *Vasco da Gama* seen after
lengthening in a refit of 1901-03.

VASCO DA GAMA

1878 Portugal

Launched: 1 December 1875.
Builder: Thames Iron Works.
Displacement: 2,479 tons
(2,519 tonnes).
Dimensions: 216ft (65.84m) oa x
40ft (12.19m); 46ft 6in (14.17m)
over battery x 19ft (5.79m) max.
Machinery: Humphreys & Tennant
Compound engines; 2 screws;

3625 IHP.
Armour: Iron 9in (229mm) belt and
battery; 10in (254mm) backing.
Armament: 2 x 10.2in (259mm)
BLR; 1 x 6in (152mm); 2 x 40pdr.
Performance: 13.25kt (24.5km/h);
coal 300 tons (305 tonnes), later
468 tons (475 tonnes).
Crew: 218 (later 232).

Vasco da Gama was intended
primarily for the defence of Lisbon. A
full-length belt extended to the upper
deck and below the ram. The fixed
octagonal turret housing the two
heavy guns rose above the deck and
the casemate had a 3ft (0.91m)
overhang on each side. The single
6in (152mm) gun was positioned aft,
beneath the poop.
   In the 1890s her rig was reduced
to two masts, and in 1901-03 she was
given a major refit by Orlando,
Leghorn (Livorno). The casemate
was removed and she was
lengthened by 32ft (9.75m),
receiving steel armour of 10in-4in
(254-102mm) thickness. Her new
armament was 2 x 8in (203mm) on
sponsons, 1 x 5.9in (150mm), 1 x
12pdr, 4 x 9pdr and 6 x 3pdr.

DREADNOUGHT

1879 UK

Laid down: 10 September 1870.
Launched: 8 March 1875.
Builder: Pembroke Dockyard.
Displacement: 10,886 tons (11,060 tonnes) load.
Dimensions: 343ft (104·55m) oa x 63ft 10in (19·46m) x 26ft 6in (8·08m) mean.
Machinery: Humphreys & Tennant 2-cylinder Vertical Compound Expansion; 12 cylindrical boilers; 2 shafts; 8206 IHP.
Armour: Iron 14in-8in (356-203mm) belt; 18in-15in (457-381mm) wood backing; 14in-11in (356-279mm) citadel; 14in (356mm) turrets; 14in-6in (356-152mm) conning tower; 3in-2·5in (76-63mm) decks.
Armament: 4 x 12·5in (317mm) MLR.
Performance: 14·52kt (26·86km/h); coal 1,800 tons (1,829 tonnes); radius 5,700 miles (9,171km) at 10kt (18·5km/h).
Crew: 369.

Dreadnought was originally designed by Reed as a larger and faster unit of the Devastation class and was at first named *Fury*. She spent almost seven years on the stocks, work having been suspended in 1871 while the Committee on Designs considered measures for the improvement of stability, armament and protection. As a result of these deliberations, Reed's design was considerably modified, although he continued to claim the ship as his own and was, indeed, extremely proud of her.

As completed, the 12in-10in (305-254mm) breastwork envisaged by Reed was replaced by a 14in-11in (356-279mm) armoured central citadel, 184ft (56·1m) long and extending to the hull sides. It was protected at either end from raking fire by 13in (330mm) oval bulkheads and overhead by a 3in (76mm) weather deck. Outside the citadel, the unarmoured upper deck was built up fore and aft to make her flush-decked, thus raising her freeboard to 10ft 9in (3·28m) forward and 10ft (3m) aft and considerably improving sea-keeping qualities.

Armour accounted for almost

exactly one-third of *Dreadnought's* displacement. A complete belt—the thickest complete belt carried by any British warship—extended from 5ft 3in (1·6m) below water, where its lower edge tapered to 8in (203mm), to 3ft (0·91m) above. Its maximum thickness, amidships, was 14in (356mm) and it tapered to 8in (203mm) at the ends, running down. forward to support the ram. The 2·5in (63mm) armoured main deck outside the citadel rested on the belt and extended to bows and stern.

Behind the belt, amidships, coal bunkers were sited to provide added protection for the machinery and boilers. The engine and boiler rooms were divided by a longitudinal bulkhead—the first of its kind fitted—running for much of the length of the centre line, to within *c*40ft (12·2m) of either end. This allowed the boilers to be situated back to back along the length of the bulkhead, rather than face to face as had previously been the practice. This innovation greatly improved the working conditions for the firemen attending the boilers. Transverse bulkheads also divided the boiler rooms, creating two 42ft (12·8m) rooms forward and two 40ft (12·2m) rooms aft.

The turrets designed by Reed, protected by 14in (356mm) armour made up of two 7in (178mm) plates with wood backing, were retained, but instead of the 12in (305mm), 25-ton (25·4 tonne) guns originally specified each housed 2 x 12·5in (317mm), 38-ton (38·6 tonne) MLR, which remained unchanged throughout *Dreadnought's* long life. Set fore and aft above the citadel, the turrets had hydraulic training and steam traversing mechanisms that were protected only by the citadel itself. An anti-torpedo boat armament of 10 x Nordenfeld MG, added in 1884, was replaced by 6 x 6pdr QF and 10 x 3pdr QF in 1894.

Other than the much smaller *Pallas* of 1866, *Dreadnought* was the first British warship to be designed for

compound engines, although Reed had originally specified horizontal machinery. Yet another 'first' was the provision of artificial ventilation. With habitability thus improved, she was a well-liked ship as well as a successful one.

She was steady and did not roll excessively, although she was liable to pitch and was a wet ship when at speed in a seaway. In 1898 her funnels were raised, somewhat marring her impressively massive silhouette, and she was reboiled.

Dreadnought served in the Mediterranean in 1884-94 and was subsequently a coastguard ship at Bantry, Ireland. Rated a second class battleship in 1900, she was a tender and depot ship until 1905 and thereafter was placed in reserve until she was sold for breaking up in July 1908.

Right: Malta, 1879—*Dreadnought* is cleared for action. The boats are now lowered and towed aft, the topmast has been struck, the bulwarks in the bow lowered and the railings laid on the deck.

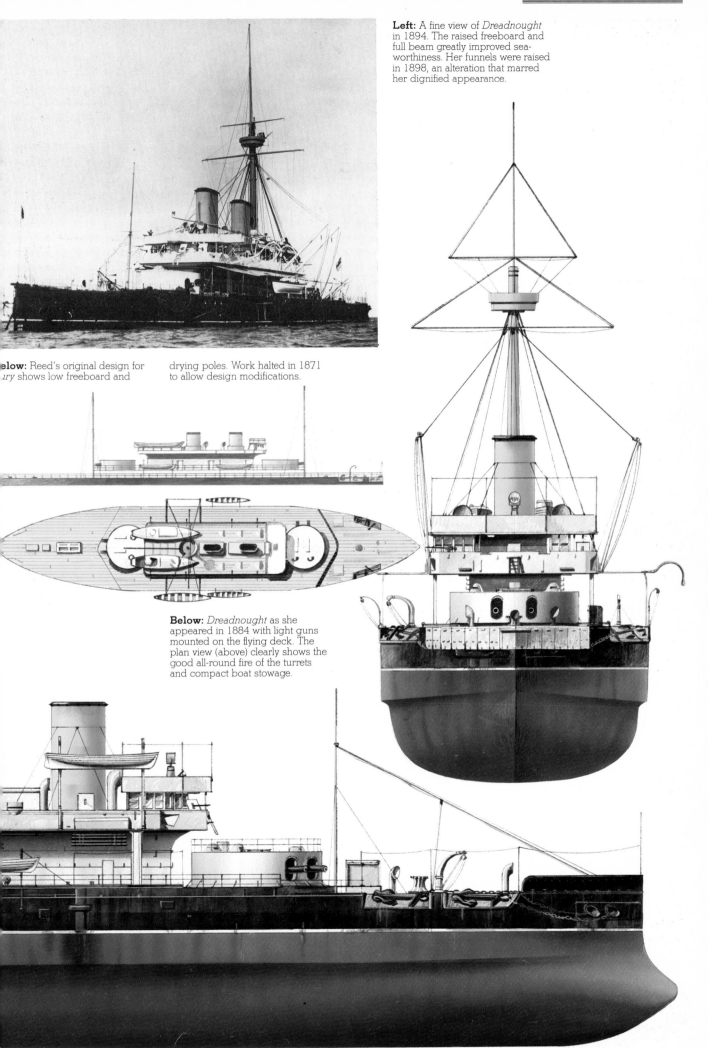

Left: A fine view of *Dreadnought* in 1894. The raised freeboard and full beam greatly improved seaworthiness. Her funnels were raised in 1898, an alteration that marred her dignified appearance.

Below: Reed's original design for *ury* shows low freeboard and drying poles. Work halted in 1871 to allow design modifications.

Below: *Dreadnought* as she appeared in 1884 with light guns mounted on the flying deck. The plan view (above) clearly shows the good all-round fire of the turrets and compact boat stowage.

1880-1889

The 1880s witnessed the last gasp of the heavy muzzle-loading gun as safe and efficient breech mechanisms were perfected, and also the final abandonment, in capital ships laid down in this decade, of sails as a means of propulsion. Gun calibres and weights increased dramatically, to a point where few individual pieces could be effectively mounted in any one ship. This trend accelerated the development of the barbette. At last the revolutionary advances initiated a quarter of a century earlier were bearing fruit, and the pattern for battleship construction that would remain virtually unchanged until the end of the big-gun era could be discerned.

ARMOUR

Although compound armour and steel armour were still in the experimental stage, they began gradually to replace wrought iron armour by the end of the 1870s. According to a leading authority of the period, Captain Orde Browne, wrought iron armour remained in use over a period of some 20 years because it did not transmit the shock of a blow to the bolts and contiguous areas, and, although sometimes penetrated with relative ease, it did not crack if supported by adequate backing. Wrought iron was still used by Britain in land fortifications in the 1880s, although some powers preferred chilled iron.

The Royal Navy adopted compound armour because it offered greater resistance than wrought iron; it was, for example, found possible to replace the 18in (457mm) thick wrought iron plates originally planned for the huge turrets of *Inflexible* with 16in (406mm) compound plates. And in spite of the success of British-manufactured steel plates in trials against compound armour in 1886 and 1888, compound armour was favoured for British warships throughout the decade. Although steel of limited thickness was used on some ships, it was not yet possible for Britain to produce steel armour to match its compound plates in both quantity and quality—and the Admiralty was, understandably, unwilling to purchase abroad.

Steel armour was perfected by Schneider and Creusot from 1880. In that year, trials between Schneider steel plates and rival compound armour had led to the French Navy's adoption of the latter. However, Creusot refused orders for compound armour in order to continue its development of steel, and the company's chief engineer, J. Barba, eventually developed the best steel then available. But in spite of steel's superiority, the French Navy continued to fit compound armour in conjunction with steel plates until well into 1880s, largely because Schneider could not supply steel in the necessary quantity.

In numerous trials made by Italy to determine which armour should be used on its huge battleships *Italia* and *Lepanto,* Creusot steel proved superior to Cammell Laird compound, which showed signs of scaling after being struck by only one round. The Terni Works began to manufacture high-quality steel armour in 1884. In the USA, the Creusot process was adopted by the Bethlehem Works in 1887—but in Russia compound armour would continue in favour for several years more.

ARTILLERY

In France the development of naval artillery continued apace, although not all guns were made of steel, since the production cost of a 9·4in (239mm) steel gun was then four

times that of an 18-ton (18·29 tonne) cast-iron hooped gun of the 1870 pattern. The Minister of Marine consequently advised that only guns of 10·6in (269mm) calibre and above should be made of steel.

French guns were reliable and generally cheaper than their British equivalents. The French breechloading mechanism resembled the Armstrong system, using an interrupted thread. Portions of the thread were cut away to leave three equal blank areas on the breechblock, and three identical blank areas were left in the breech of the gun. The blank areas on the block and in the breech were brought into opposition and the block was rammed almost home; a one-sixth turn then engaged the screw and firmly secured the breech. This system was adopted by the Royal Navy also in 1880.

Britain discarded the Woolwich system of construction in favour of the Vavasseur design, in which a thin steel inner tube encased in a long steel jacket gave longitudinal strength which was reinforced by shrinking on additional external hoops. As was to be expected, some difficulties were experienced with the new system—the early 12in (305mm) guns for *Collingwood* and her near-sisters caused particular concern—but these were soon overcome.

There then began a period of immense increase in size, culminating in the 16·25in (413mm), 110·5-ton (112·7 tonne) guns made for *Benbow, Sans Pareil* and the ill-fated *Victoria*. In the late 1880s, however, there was a reaction against such massive and expensive weapons. Because they were slow to manufacture, the ship intended to carry them was often completed before the guns were ready. Firing life was short: only an estimated 75 rounds per gun. Sometimes the hoops did not press tightly enough against each other, causing the gun to droop at the chase; this was treated by substituting one extra-long hoop for five smaller hoops. During trials on *Sans Pareil,* a new hoop split; it was replaced, but after six more rounds had been fired with full 960lb (435kg) charges the gun drooped and was bent over slightly from the centreline.

The rate of fire of these monsters was slow because of the weight of the ammunition, 1,800lb (816kg). Because of the great weight of the gun and its mounting, only two of the weapons could be carried in the largest battleship of the period if a powerful secondary battery was also required.

Elswick, the supplier of these huge breechloaders, also produced 100-ton (101·6 tonne) and 105-ton (106·68 tonne) guns for the Italian Navy, which at one time had 28 of these weapons at sea in seven warships. The Italian guns were slightly shorter than their British counterparts and had two-piece inner tubes, necessitating the fitting of larger outer hoops for longitudinal strength. They were generally satisfactory in service, although there was an early accident when the breech of one of *Dandolo's* 100-ton (101·6 tonne) weapons blew out.

Smaller guns, intended for protection against torpedo

boats, continued to improve. Maxim introduced th small-calibre gun in which the energy of the recoil wa harnessed to work the mechanism, eventually producin guns in 1in (25mm), 1·5in (38mm) and 2in (51mm) calibr However, the increasing size of torpedo boats called fo larger guns to deal with them, and the multi-barrelle machine guns of the 1870s could not be made in large calibres because of the problems of weight. A single-barr system known as the quick-firer (QF) was developed. In th smaller QF, powder charge and projectile were combine this speeded loading, and the cartridge case formed perfect gas seal, removing the need to clean the barrel afte each round.

The first successful QF was the 6pdr (57mm) weapon o 1883-84, developed by Hotchkiss and Nordenfeld. Soon 3in (76mm) and 4in (102mm) QF were in service, backe by 1pdr and 3pdr weapons. Krupp and Armstrong nex produced the 4·7in (119mm) QF; Armstrong also develope a more compact mount which allowed gun ports to b reduced in height, the gun recoiling on its direct axis.

Vavasseur produced the first successful mounting fo the high-powered breechloaders then rapidly becomin available. A pair of hydraulic cylinders, acting as a brake formed part of the carriage, and gearing enabled the gun t be trained up to the moment of firing. Smaller weapon dispensed with training gear, the gun being trained by shoulder piece.

One piece of ordnance that showed initial promise wa the pneumatic dynamite gun developed in 1884 by L Zalinski, USN. The first model was of 2in (51mm) calibre but by 1887 an 8in (203mm) model was being teste against an anchored target ship at 1,864yds (1,704m) range Accuracy was good, but the projectiles flight time of 10·5

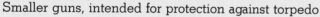

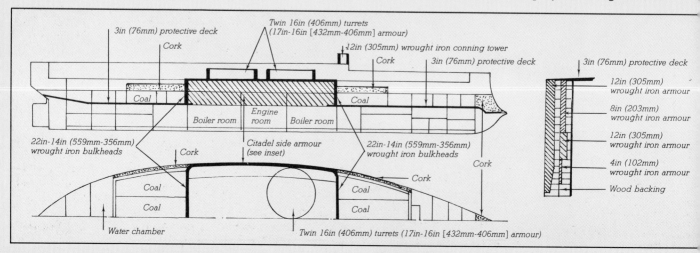

3in (76mm) protective deck

Twin 16in (406mm) turrets (17in-16in [432mm-406mm] armour)

Cork

12in (305mm) wrought iron conning tower

Cork

3in (76mm) protective deck

3in (76mm) protective deck

Coal

Coal

Boiler room

Engine room

Boiler room

12in (305mm) wrought iron armour

8in (203mm) wrought iron armour

12in (305mm) wrought iron armour

4in (102mm) wrought iron armour

Wood backing

22in-14in (559mm-356mm) wrought iron bulkheads

Citadel side armour (see inset)

22in-14in (559mm-356mm) wrought iron bulkheads

Cork

Cork

Coal

Coal

Coal

Cork

Coal

Coal

Water chamber

Twin 16in (406mm) turrets (17in-16in [432mm-406mm] armour)

:conds precluded its use against moving targets. Never-:heless, the dynamite-gun cruiser *Vesuvius* was built for :e US Navy in 1887-90, with 3 x 15in (381mm) pneumatic :uns. These had a 55ft (16·76m) long tube and fired a 966lb :·38kg) projectile containing 600lb (272kg) of dynamite by :eans of compressed air. The guns were mounted at a :xed angle: range was governed by the amount of com-:essed air used, and stability in flight was achieved by :cewed fins on a thin tube projecting from the rear of the :rojectile. During the Spanish-American War, 1898, *:esuvius* bombarded Santiago, with greater moral than :aterial effect.

Projectiles, like guns, improved in quality. Captain :nglish of the Royal Engineers first proposed that a coating :r cap of wrought iron be fitted on projectiles to enable :em to pierce amour without breaking up, and by 1882 Sir :Villiam Palliser had produced ribbed, steel-jacketed :rojectiles that cracked and opened up armour plate. :alliser's projectile was successful in trials against officially-:roduced chilled shot, but in 1883 further trials against :hilled shot of better quality reversed the outcome. As a :rivate indvidual with limited resources, Palliser could not :ompete with a government ordnance establishment.

In the early 1880s, common shells were of cast iron and :rmour-piercing (AP) shells were of chilled iron or steel. As :teel AP projectiles became available in quantity, cast iron :hells were withdrawn.

:ORPEDO CRAFT

: 1871, Thornycroft of Chiswick, London, had demon-:trated the viability of very small high-speed craft, :roducing a 7·5-ton (7·62 tonne), 57ft (17·37m) long vessel

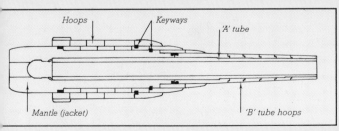

Hoops   Keyways   'A' tube

Mantle (jacket)   'B' tube hoops

capable of 16kt (29·6km/h) for Norway in 1873 and supplying similar craft to Austria, Denmark, France and Sweden. Britain did not launch the 27-ton (27·43 tonne), 18·5kt (34·2km/h) *Lightning* until 1877: by that time, torpedo craft had become so popular among the naval powers that more than 100 boats were building for the Russian Navy alone.

After *Lightning*'s successful trials more boats were ordered for the Royal Navy. There followed a period in which no more first-class boats were built for Britain, but in 1885 the Admiralty revived its torpedo boat programme and 54 first-class boats were ordered. By 1886 the speed of the British boats had risen to 21·5kt (39·77km/h), while the Spanish Navy's *Ariete* could make 26·18kt (48·4km/h).

Under the direction of Admiral Aube, Minister of Marine, France began to build a formidable force of torpedo boats. They were stationed along the French coast, presenting a potent threat to any fleet attempting a blockade. Meanwhile, many smaller navies, unable to afford expensive ironclads, equipped themselves with these comparatively cheap craft.

Swarms of fast torpedo boats constituted a very real threat to battleships, and a counter-measure was sought. One answer was the larger torpedo gunboat, but these vessels proved both costly and ineffective. The solution to this problem would not be found until the 1890s.

SUBMARINES

Increasingly, the submarine promised to be a threat to battleships and other surface craft. Early submarines were limited by the lack of a suitable underwater propulsion system. Although Plante invented the lead accumulator in 1859, it was not until 1880 that Faure applied to it a thick layer of red lead for speedy electrolyte reduction. The perfected accumulator was an ideal method of propulsion for submarines, since it needed no direct contact with the atmosphere.

Before 1880, also, there was no suitable underwater weapon for the submarine. Early submarines used the spar torpedo, which involved close proximity to the target, but by the end of the 1870s the Whitehead locomotive torpedo was sufficiently developed to provide a stand-off weapon.

Even so, the submarine would not be a serious threat for some years. A major problem, that of vision while submerged, would later be overcome by the development of the periscope: such a device was suggested by Major Clarke to Nordenfeld when one of the latter's steam-driven submarines was being tested in 1886, but the idea was not immediately taken up.

SUPERB

1880 UK

Laid down: 1873.
Launched: 16 November 1875.
Builder: Thames Iron Works.
Displacement: 9,710 tons
(9,865 tonnes) load.
Dimensions: 332ft 4in (101·3m)
pp x 59ft (17·98m) x 25ft 6in
(7·77m).
Machinery: Maudslay 2-cylinder
Horizontal Direct Acting;
9 rectangular boilers; 1 shaft.
Armour: Iron 12in-7in (305-178mm)
belt with 8in-12in (203-305mm)
backing; 12in (305mm) battery;
10in (254mm) bulkheads.
Armament: 16 x 10in (254mm)
MLR; 4 x 14in (356mm) TL.
Performance: 13·2kt (24·5km/h).
Crew: 654.

Designed by Reed as the *Hamidieh*
for Ottoman service, this ship was
completed 1877 but bought for the
Royal Navy in February 1878. The
design was a scaled-up version of
Hercules, and *Superb* had better
armour than any other contemporary
British ironclad. Barque-rigged,
Superb was virtually impossible to
sail, and later had her rig cut down.

Below: *Superb* shown as completed.

NEPTUNE

1881 UK

Laid down: 1873.
Launched: 10 September 1874.
Builder: Dudgeon, Millwall.
Displacement: 9,130 tons
(9,276 tonnes) load.
Dimensions: 300ft (91·44m)
pp x 63ft (19·20m) x 25ft (7·62m).
Machinery: Penn 2-cylinder
Horizontal Trunk engines;
8 rectangular boilers; 1 shaft;
7993 IHP.
Armour: Iron 12in-9in (305-229mm)
belt; citadel 10in (254mm) sides
and 8in (203mm) bulkheads;
13in-11in (330-279mm) turrets;
8in-6in (203-152mm) conning tower;
3in-2in (76-51mm) decks.
Armament: 4 x 12in (305mm) MLR;
2 x 9in (229mm) MLR; 6 x 20pdr BL;
2 x 14in (356mm) torpedo carriages.
Performance: 14·2kt (26·4km/h).
Crew: 541.

Designed by Reed as the Brazilian
Independencia in 1872, this vessel
was a masted turret ship and was
thus obsolete at the time of her
inception as an improved *Monarch.* If
anything, the machinery was even
more obsolete than the basic design.

It took three attempts before the
ship could be launched and taken for
completion to Samudas in Poplar.
After her trials she was bought for the
Royal Navy, as were other vessels
building for foreign navies, in view of

deteriorating Anglo-Russian
relations. *Neptune* was taken in hand
at Portsmouth for alteration to British
standards, the programme involving
the addition of electrical supplies and
the substitution of standard Royal
Navy guns for the original Whitworth
weapons.

The 12in (305mm) main guns were
placed in twin turrets, and the 9in
(229mm) guns were located under
the forecastle. Protection was
excellent, the full-length belt being 8ft
6in (2·59m) deep and extending 3ft
(0·91m) below the waterline.

Neptune proved a dismal sailer
except in conjunction with the
engines, and the location of the
main mast so close to the funnels
meant that its sails had to be replaced
frequently. The main yards were
removed, followed by the mast itself
in 1886, in which year the fore and
mizzen masts became military masts
with fighting tops.

Service with the Channel Fleet
soon revealed the *Neptune*'s poor
sea-keeping, wetness and tendency
to roll. After a spell in the
Mediterranean she was relegated to
coastguard and reserve service, and
broken up in 1903.

Below: *Neptune* as completed. Th
main yards were removed within
three years because of smoke rot.

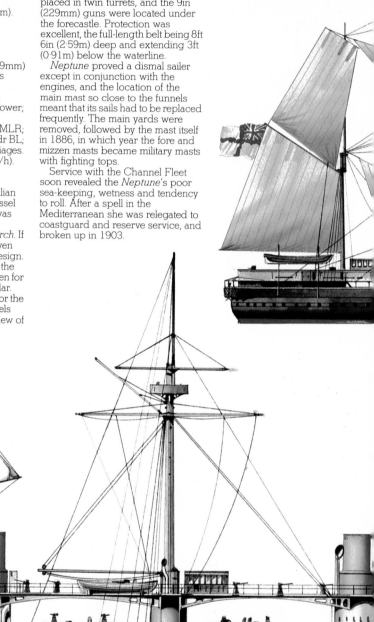

Below: The powerful *Duilio* in white
paintwork during the 1880s.

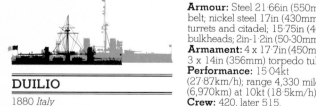

DUILIO

1880 Italy
Other ships in class: *Dandolo*

Laid down: 6 January 1873.
Launched: 8 May 1876.
Builder: Castellammare Navy Yard.
Displacement: 10,962 tons
(11,137 tonnes) normal; 12,071 tons
(12,264 tonnes) full load.
Dimensions: 358ft 1½in (109·16m)
x 64ft 9in (19·74m) x 27ft 3in (8·31m).
Machinery: Vertical; 8 rectangular
boilers; 2 shafts; 7711 IHP.

Armour: Steel 21·66in (550mm)
belt; nickel steel 17in (430mm)
turrets and citadel; 15·75in (400mm)
bulkheads; 2in-1·2in (50-30mm) deck.
Armament: 4 x 17·7in (450mm) ML;
3 x 14in (356mm) torpedo tubes.
Performance: 15·04kt
(27·87km/h); range 4,330 miles
(6,970km) at 10kt (18·5km/h).
Crew: 420, later 515.

Schemed by the fertile mind of
Benedetto Brin, the *Duilio* (and her
sister-ship *Dandolo*, built by La
Spezia Navy Yard and differing in a
slightly lower normal displacement
and altered machinery developing
higher power for a speed of
15·6kt/28·9km/h) remain of great
historical importance in the evolution
of the battleship. A turret ship (two
echeloned turrets each with two

guns), *Duilio* was the world's first
battleship with giant guns and no
provision for sailing. She was also the
first Italian two-shaft capital ship.

The progress of naval armament at
this time may be gauged from the fact
that *Duilio* was first envisaged with
35-ton (35·6 tonne) guns, then 60-ton
(61 tonne) weapons, and finally saw
light with 100-ton (101·6 tonne)
Armstrong guns, each capable of
firing one 1,905lb (846kg) shell
every 15 minutes. Protection was
equally powerful: Creusot steel plates
for the belt, nickel steel elsewhere,
and cellular compartmentation in
bow and stern rafts on the waterline.
An interesting offensive feature was
built into the *Duilio:* a stern
compartment able to house the 26·5-
ton (26·9 tonne) torpedo boat *Clio*,
which could sally forth with an

armament of 2 x 14in (356mm)
torpedo tubes.

The origins of the Duilio class ma
be traced to the Battle of Lissa in
1866, when a superior Italian fleet
had been defeated by the
Austro-Hungarian Navy. The moral
shock for the Italians was severe, and
an immediate result was a drastic
pruning of naval budgets, which
meant a further slowing down of
already lengthy building times.

But during the second ministry o
Augusto Riboty, matters began to ge
better as old ships were sold off and
assets concentrated on the
production of thoroughly modern,
even innovative designs. Riboty was
succeeded by the equally far-sighted
Saint Bon, and these two officers ga
Brin free rein to develop
heavily armed and fast capital ships

DÉVASTATION

1882 *France*
Other ships in class: *Courbet*

Laid down: January 1876.
Launched: April 1879.
Builder: Lorient Dockyard.
Displacement: 10,450 tons
(10,617 tonnes).
Dimensions: 311ft 6in (94·95m)
wl x 69ft 9in (21·26m) x 27ft (8·23m).
Machinery: Vertical Compound
engines; 12 cylindrical boilers;
2 shafts; 8300 IHP.
Armour: Wrought iron 15in-7in
(380-180mm) belt; 9·5in (240mm)
battery.
Armament: 4 x 13·4in (340mm)
M1875; 4 x 10·8in (275mm)
M1870M; 6 x 5·5in (140mm)
M1870; 8 x 1pdr revolvers;
5 x 14in (456mm) torpedo tubes.
Performance: 15·5kt (28·7km/h);
coal 1,100 tons (1,118 tonnes).
Crew: 689.

Dévastation (and her sister-ship
Courbet) were designed by de Bussy
on the pattern of the *Redoubtable,* and
the three units were the French
Navy's first capital ships built after the
disaster of the Franco-Prussian War.
The two Courbets were the largest
central battery ships ever built.

The four main guns were located at
the corners of the battery, the top of
whose armour was some 19ft 6in
(5·95m) above the waterline. The
guns were hydraulically worked, but
their efficiency was low as their
positions were limited in size and the
guns themselves possessed a low
rate of fire. The belt stretched from
the bow to within 28ft (8·53m) of the
stern, and ended in a 12in (305mm)
bulkhead.

The *Dévastation*'s main battery was
never satisfactory, and after the failure
of a gun of the same type in the
Amiral Duperré, the M1875s were
replaced by four 12·6in (320mm)
M1870-81 converted coast defence
weapons. Later revision led to the
M1870-81s' replacement by 10·8in
(275mm) M1875 guns. At the same
time the original 10·8in (275mm)
M1870Ms were replaced by two
9·4in (240mm) M1893/96 guns, and
the 5·5in (140mm) weapons by 3·9in
(100mm) guns. By 1895 a large
number of smaller guns had also
been added. In 1901 the machinery
was extensively revised to provide
vertical triple expansion engines and
12 Belleville boilers. *Dévastation* was
scrapped in 1922; *Courbet* had been
deleted in 1910.

TEGETTHOFF

1881 *Austria-Hungary*

Laid down: 1 April 1876.
Launched: 15 October 1878.
Builder: Stabilimento Tecnico
Triestino.
Displacement: 7,431 tons
(7,550 tonnes).
Right: *Tegetthoff* as seen in 1881.

Dimensions: 303ft 4in (92·46m) oa
x 71ft 5in (21·78m) x 24ft 10in
(7·57m).
Machinery: 2-cylinder Horizontal
Low Pressure engines; 1 shaft;
6706 IHP.
Armour: Iron 14in (356mm) belt
and casemates; 12in-10in
(305-254mm) bulkheads, 7in-5in
(178-127mm) conning tower.
Armament: 6 x 11in (280mm)
Krupp L/18 BL; 6 x 3·54in (90mm)
L/24 BL; 2 x 2·76in (70mm)
L/15 BL; 4 x 1·85in (47mm)
plus smaller.
Performance: 13·97kt (25·89km/h).
Crew: 525.

This was a central battery ship, with its
main battery disposed towards the
bow to allow it to remain in action
during the chase and ramming type
of action that had proved successful
at Lissa. To the same end there were
no sponsons jutting out from the
ship's sides, and the guns had
overlapping arcs of fire. During a refit
she was given Schichau triple
expansion engines and converted to
two shafts, and more modern
armament was fitted.

She became a floating battery at
Pola in 1897, and was renamed *Mars*
in 1912. Ceded to Italy in 1918, she
was scrapped in 1920.

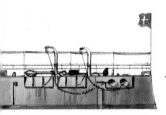

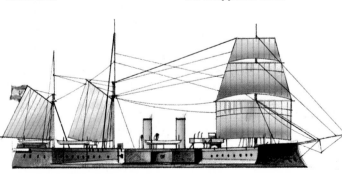

which the *Duilio* and *Dandolo*
were the first examples. Financial
and industrial restrictions were still
evident, however, in the ships'
lengthy building times.

Duilio was modernized in 1890
and 1900: in the former year she
received 3 x 4·7in (120mm) guns,
and in the latter year 2 x 2·95in
(75mm), 8 x 2·24in (57mm) QF and 4
1·46in (37mm) revolver guns. But in
1909 *Duilio* was stripped of
armament and converted into a
floating tank for coal and oil.

Dandolo had a more fortunate
career: she was rebuilt between 1895
and 1898 with an armament of 4 x
10in (254mm), 7 x 6in (152mm) and
9 smaller guns, plus 4 x 17·7in
(450mm) torpedo tubes. During
World War I she was used as a
floating defence battery.

Below: The central battery ship
Dévastation, 1888, with altered rig.

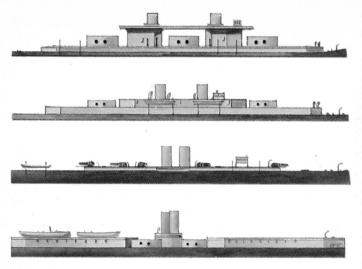

Above: Four of the preliminary designs for the *New Fury*, later to become the *Inflexible*, the only battleship in the British construction programme of 1873. Both top schemes envisaged the use of turrets coupled to a low freeboard, while the third design featured ten unprotected 35-ton (35·6- tonne) guns firing en barbette. The fourth plan allowed for a high hatchway freeboard the full length of the vessel with a gap amidships which necessitated siting the two turrets en echelon there. To avoid the possibility of blast damage the funnels were repositioned in the final design.

INFLEXIBLE

1881 UK

Laid down: 24 February 1874.
Launched: 27 April 1876.
Builder: Portsmouth Dockyard.
Displacement: 10,300 tons (10,465 tonnes) light; 11,880 tons (12,070 tonnes) load.
Dimensions: 344ft (104·85m) oa x 75ft (22·86m) x 25ft 6in (7·77m).
Machinery: Elder 3-cylinder Compound Expansion; 12 cylindrical boilers; 2 shafts; 8407 IHP.
Armour: Iron citadel 24in-16in (610-406mm) sides and 21in-14in (559-356mm) bulkheads; 17in-16in (432-406mm) turrets; 12in (305mm) conning tower; 3in (76mm) decks.
Armament: 4 x 16in (406mm) MLR; 6 x 20pdr BL; 2 x 14in (356mm) torpedo tubes.
Performance: 14·75kt (27·33km/h).
Crew: 440.

The *Inflexible* was designed by Nathaniel Barnaby in direct response to the Italian *Duilio* and *Dandolo*, and to French moves towards giant guns. The result was a ship notable for its extremes: it had the heaviest muzzle-loading battery of any Royal Navy ship, and also the thickest armour. The guns themselves were somewhat lighter than those fitted the Italian ships: they weighed 80 tons (81·3 tonnes) and each fired a 1,684lb (764kg) shell at the rate of one round per 2 minutes. The two hydraulically actuated turrets were disposed en échelon at opposite corners of the citadel to permit fore-and-aft fire. And as the guns were too long to be loaded from inside the turrets, they were designed to depress into an armoured glacis for reloading.

Inflexible was also the first ship to make use of compound armour which was designed on the 'all or nothing' principle: the citadel, some 110ft (33·53m) long, was massively protected against all possible shells while the ends were totally unprotected, it being reasoned that the buoyancy of the unbreached citadel section would allow the vessel to regain port even if the ends were so severely damaged that they were filled with water. The sides of the citadel reached 6·5ft (1·98m) below and 9·5ft (2·9m) above the load line on the outside was a layer of iron 12

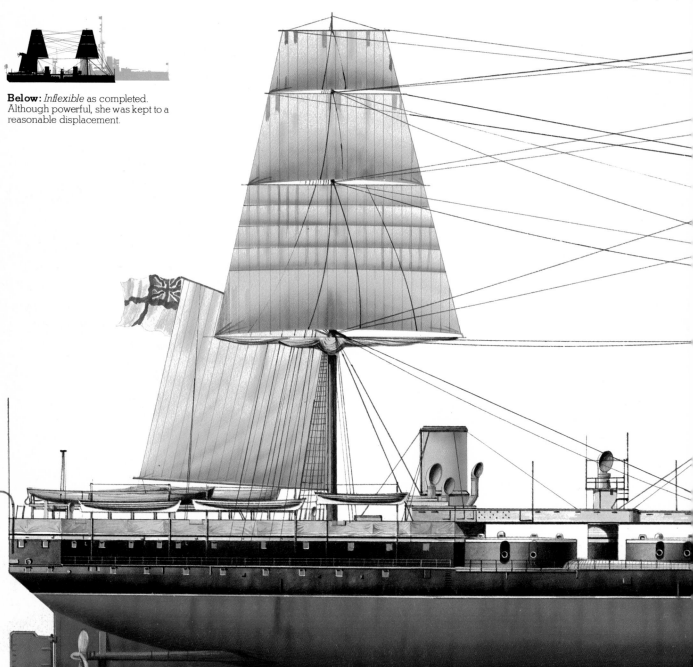

Below: *Inflexible* as completed. Although powerful, she was kept to a reasonable displacement.

05mm) thick with a wood backing, nd inside this was another wood-backed iron layer, the iron in this instance being 12in (305mm) thick on the load line, decreasing to in (102mm) below and 8in (203mm) above. This total thickness of the sides was 41in (1,041mm). The fore and aft ends of the citadel were closed off by bulkheads of similar construction, while the deck was 3in (76mm) iron. Like the citadel, the turrets were of sandwich construction: an outer face of 3·5in (89mm) steel and 4·5in (114mm) iron with an inner layer of 7in (178mm) of iron backed by 18in (457mm) of teak.

The two 14in (356mm) torpedo tubes were the first submerged units fitted. Armament alterations were minor: in 1885 the 20pdr BLs were supplanted by 4in (102mm) BLs, themselves replaced by 4·7in (119mm) BLs in 1897.

Inflexible was initially rigged as a brig, with 18,500ft² (1,719m²) of sail, but proved completely ineffective under sail. In 1885 she was thus converted to military masts with fighting tops. Under power Inflexible handled well, however, and was a first-class seaboat. Her one

drawback in this respect was connected with the water-filled anti-roll tanks, fitted to ensure stability if the ends should be flooded.

Inflexible took part in the bombardment of Alexandria in 1882, firing 88 16in (406mm) shells. She was damaged by several hits and

the blast of her own guns. An intermediate design produced in response to foreign developments, Inflexible was nevertheless a highlight in British naval construction, and was the ultimate masted turret ship. She was sold for breaking up in 1903.

Above: Inflexible late in her career, with military tops to her masts. This is how she appeared while serving out her time at Portsmouth prior to her sale for some £20,000 in 1903. She carried the thickest armour and largest muzzle-loading guns ever fitted on a British battleship.

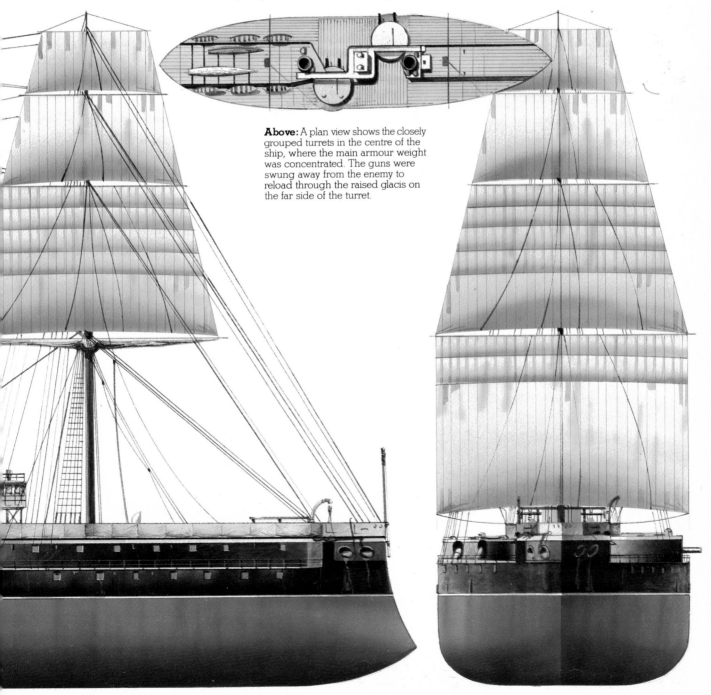

Above: A plan view shows the closely grouped turrets in the centre of the ship, where the main armour weight was concentrated. The guns were swung away from the enemy to reload through the raised glacis on the far side of the turret.

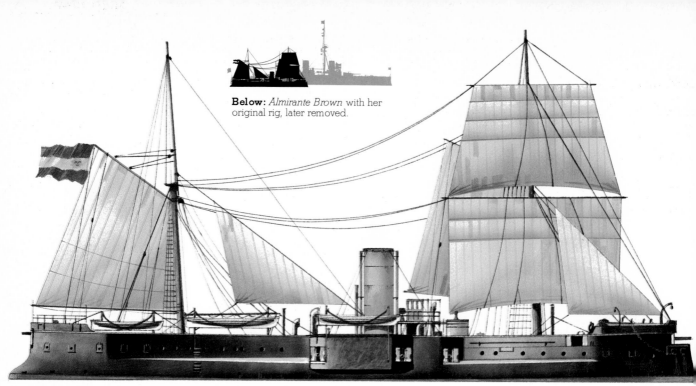

Below: *Almirante Brown* with her original rig, later removed.

ALMIRANTE BROWN

1880 *Argentina*

Launched: 1880.
Builder: Samuda Bros,London.
Displacement: 4,200 tons
(4,267 tonnes) full load.
Dimensions: 240ft (73·15m) x 50ft
(15·24m) x 20ft 6in (6·25m) max.
Machinery: Compound engines; 8
cylindrical boilers; 2 shafts; 5400 IHP.
Armour: Compound 9in-6in
(229-152mm) belt; 7·5in-1·5in
(190·5-37·5mm) ends; 8in-6in
(203-152mm) battery; 8in (203mm)
conning tower.
Armament: 8 x 8in (203mm) BLR;
6 x 4·7in (119mm); 2 x 9pdr;
2 x 7pdr.
Performance: 14kt (25·9km/h);
coal 650 tons (660·4 tonnes).
Crew: 520.

Almirante Brown was a central
battery corvette, and one of the first
fruits of Argentina's naval build-up of
the 1870s. Intended mainly for
coastal service, she had a ram bow,
and the two masts (10,000 ft², 929m²,
of sail) had military tops.
 The main battery consisted of six
Armstrong 11·5-ton (11·68 tonne)
8in (203mm) guns, disposed with
four firing ahead and two astern; the
two other 8in (203mm) guns were
located one each in the bow and
stern.
 The belt under the battery, which
overhung it, reached 4ft (1·22m)
below the load waterline to 3ft
(0·91m) above it, and was 6in
(152mm) and 9in (229mm) thick
respectively, decreasing at the ends
to a mere 1·5in (38mm). It was 120ft
(36·58m) long, and protected the
engines, boilers and magazines.
Horizontal protection was a maximum
1½in (38mm).
 Almirante Brown was refitted
between 1897 and 1898 in France: the
8in (203mm) guns were replaced by
10 x 5·9in (150mm) Canet QFs in the
same basic arrangement as before
except that two guns were fitted in
the bow and stern positions. The
secondary armament was also
renewed, the old 4·7in (119mm) guns
being replaced with more modern
4·7mm (120mm) QF's of French
manufacture. The crew was
reduced to 380. *Almirante Brown*
was scrapped in about 1930.

Below: *Bayard*
as completed.

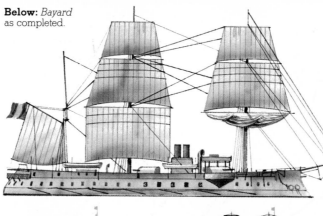

BAYARD

1882 *France*
Other ships in class: *Turenne*

Laid down: October 1876.
Launched: March 1880.
Builder: Brest Dockyard.
Displacement: 5,915 tons
(6,010 tonnes).
Dimensions: 265ft 9in (81m) wl
x 57ft 3in (17·45m) x 25ft 2in
(7·67m) max.
Machinery: Vertical Compound; 8
cylindrical boilers; 2 shafts;
4400 IHP.
Armour: Wrought iron 9·84in-5·9in
(250-150mm) belt; 7·87in (200mm)
barbettes.
Armament: 4 x 9·45in (240mm)
M1870; 2 x 7·5in (190mm);
6 x 5·5in (140mm); 4 x 3pdr;
12 x 1pdr revolvers..
Performance: 14·5kt (26·9km/h);
coal 450 tons (457 tonnes).
Crew: 451.

Bayard and her sister-ship *Turenne*,
were medium-size vessels that were
cheap and quick to build, but
nevertheless gave the French Navy
a useful long-range attack capability.
 The main armament was in two
sponsons forward of the funnels, and
in centreline turrets amidships and
aft; the secondary guns were forward
and aft under the forecastle.

AMIRAL DUPERRÉ

1883 *France*

Laid down: January 1877.
Launched: September 1879.
Builder: La Seyne.
Dimensions: 319ft 10in (97·48m) wl
x 66ft 11in (20·4m) x 27ft 8in
(8·43m) max.
Machinery: Vertical Compound
engines; 12 cylindrical boilers; 2
shafts;7300 IHP.
Armour: Wrought iron 22in-10in
(560-255mm) belt; 11·8in (300mm)
barbettes with 3·94in (100mm) tubes;
steel 2in (50mm) shields; 1·57in
(40mm) conning tower.
Armament: 4 x 13·4in (340mm)
M1875; 1 x 6·3in (160mm) M1881;
14 x 5·5in (140mm) M1870; 18 x 1pdr;
4 x 14in TT.
Performance: 14kt (25·9km/h);
coal 787 tons (780 tonnes).
Crew: 660.

Amiral Duperré had a very high
freeboard, a belt extending 6ft 7in
(2m) below the waterline to only
17·7in (0·45m) above it, and very
shallow barbettes. The main guns
were disposed in paired thwartships
barbettes forward and two centreline
barbettes, one amidships and the
other aft. Three of the M1875 guns
were later replaced by M1881
weapons of the same calibre.

Above: *Amiral Duperré* as she would
have appeared if completed, as
originally intended, with full rig.

AGAMEMNON

883 *UK*
Other ships in class: *Ajax*

Laid down: 9 May 1876.
Launched: 17 September 1879.
Builder: Chatham Dockyard.
Displacement: 8,510 tons
8,646 tonnes) full load.
Dimensions: 300ft 9in (91·67m) oa
66ft (20·12m) x 23ft 6in (7·16m).

Machinery: Penn 3-cylinder
Inverted Compound; 10 tubular
boilers; 2 shafts; 6000 IHP.
Armour: Iron citadel 18in-15in
(457-381mm) sides and 16·5in-13·5in
(419-343mm) bulkheads; 16in-14in
(406-356mm) turrets; 12in (305mm)
conning tower; 3in (76mm) decks.
Armament: 4 x 12·5in (317·5mm)
MLR; 2 x 6in (152mm) BL;
6 x 6pdr QF; 2 torpedo
carriages.
Performance: 13kt (24·1km/h).
Crew: 345.

Agamemnon and *Ajax* (completed
March 1883) were cut down versions
of the *Inflexible:* dimensions and

Below: *Agamemnon*
in 1885.

displacement were reduced to
provide a shallower draught,
deemed necessary for possible
deployment against the Russian
fleets in the Baltic and Black Seas. But
for economic reasons these two
unsatisfactory turret ships were not
provided with the same class of 'all or
nothing' protection as the *Inflexible*,
and the citadel had insufficient
buoyancy to support the ship with
flooded ends. The citadel was 104ft
(31·7m) long, and built in much the
same way as that of the *Inflexible:*
armour thickness on the waterline
was 18in (457mm) with a 19in
(483mm) wood backing, the side
thickness reducing to 15in (381mm)
armour above and below waterline.

Though they could only be
assessed as poor vessels, the two units
of the Agamemnon class mark a
significant turning point in British
naval design: they were the last Royal
Navy capital ships fitted with
muzzle-loading main armament, and
the first to have a secondary
armament, in the form of two 6in
(152mm) guns, one over the stern
and the other forward of the
foremast. In 1897 these guns were
replaced by 6in (152mm) QFs.

Neither ship was ever fitted for
sailing, and both proved most
unhandy. *Agamemnon* was broken up
in 1903, *Ajax* in 1904.

TING YUEN

1884 *China*
Other ships in class: *Chen Yuan*

Laid down: 1879.
Launched: 28 December 1881.
Builder: Vulkan, Stettin..
Displacement: 7,220 tons
(7,336 tonnes) normal;
7,670 tons (7,793 tonnes) full load..
Dimensions: 308ft (93·88m) oa x
59ft (17·98m) x 20ft (6·1m).
Machinery: Horizontal Compound
Reciprocating engines; 8 cylindrical
boilers; 2 shafts; 7500 IHP.
Armour: Compound 14in (355mm)
belt; 14in-12in (355-305mm)
barbettes; 8in (203mm) casemates
and conning tower; 3in (76mm) deck.
Armament: 4 x 12in (305mm)
Krupp BL; 2 x 5·9in (150mm)
Krupp BL; 3 x 13·8in (350mm)
torpedo tubes.
Performance: 15·7kt (29·1km/h);
coal 1,000 tons (1,016 tonnes);
radius 5,200 miles (8,370km).
Crew: 350.

Prolonged disputes with Western
nations attempting to secure major
footholds in Chinese economic
markets, often with the aid of armed
intervention against technologically
backward Chinese forces, had by the
end of the 1870s persuaded the
Chinese that their armed forces
needed restructuring along Western
lines. This was especially true of the
navy, which was structured in two
large (Northern and Southern, at
Peiyang and Nanking respectively)
and two small (Foochow and
Canton) fleets. The most important of
these was the Northern Fleet, and for
it were built the only two Chinese
capital ships.

These armoured turret ships were
the *Ting Yuen* and her sister *Chen
Yuan*, built in Germany by Vulkan,
though they were more akin to British
units such as the *Inflexible* and the
smaller Agamemnon and Colossus
class vessels than to German ships of
the period. The two Chinese ships
were steel-hulled, and featured a
central citadel 144ft (43·89m) long,
covering the engines, boilers and
magazines. The Ting Yuen class was
intended mostly for coastal
operations, so only a low hull was
provided, with the two twin barbettes
set en échelon on the narrow
superstructure running from bow to
stern. The 5·9in (150mm) guns were
mounted in the bow and stern of the
vessel.

Both vessels were delivered to
China in 1885, and were the main
units deployed against the Japanese
in the Battle of the Yalu on 17
September 1894. Both vessels
performed well, and would have
caused more damage to the
Japanese fleet had all their shells
been filled with high explosive! (It is
reported that coal dust and even
sawdust had been used to save
money). Both vessels pulled back
damaged to Wei-hai, and here the
Ting Yuen was sunk by a Japanese
torpedo boat on 6 February 1895.
Some evidence of her general
sturdiness is provided by the fact that
she had already survived very many
hits from Japanese shells during the
Battle of the Yalu. *Chen Yuan* was
sunk in shallow water by artillery fire
on 9 February 1895, but
subsequently was raised, refitted
and rearmed by the Japanese under
the name *Chin Yen*, as which she
served until 1910. She was scrapped
in 1914.

Below: *Ting Yuen* in July 1894, just
before the outbreak of the Sino-
Japanese War in which she was sunk.

ITALIA

1885 *Italy*
Other ships in class: *Lepanto*

Laid down: July 1876.
Launched: September 1880.
Builder: Castellammare Naval Dockyard.
Displacement: 13,898 tons (14,117 tonnes) normal; 15,654 (15,900) full load.
Dimensions: 409ft 1in (124·7m) oa x 73ft 11in (22·5m) x 28ft 8in (8·7m).
Machinery: Vertical Compound engines; 8 oval and 16 cylindrical boilers; 1 shaft; 12,000 IHP.
Armour: Steel 4in (102mm) deck; compound 19in (483mm) citadel; 16in (406mm) funnel base; 4in (102mm) conning tower.
Armament: 4 x 17in (432mm); 8 x 6in (152mm); 4 x 4·7in (119mm); 2 x 3in (76·2mm); 12 x 57mm (2·24in); 12 x 37mm (1·45in); 4 x 14in TT.
Performance: 17·8kt (*Lepanto* = 18·4kt); range c8,700nm (14,000km) at 10kt.
Crew: 756.

Until the early 1870s Italy's fleet had consisted of weak broadside vessels and a single turret ship. During the six years after Italy's defeat at Lissa only two small central battery ships were launched.

Money spent on the navy dwindled from 78 million lire in 1862, when a powerful fleet was being created, to a mere 25 million in 1870, making it difficult to finance the fleet during a quarrel with Civitavecchia, then still part of the Papal State. Not until 1883 did the budget exceed 60 million lire and although Italy later climbed to third position as a naval power behind England and France, she never overcame her financial difficulties — made worse by stagnant trade relations.

Grave concern was felt at the extent of Italy's long and vulnerable coastline, clearly at the mercy of any French attack by ships of slow speed and moderate fighting power. Italy had at this time built, or was building, a fleet of 10 ironclads including 5 huge vessels with no equal anywhere. The five large units were the results of the navy revival created in the early 1870s by Rear Admiral Riboty who started the process of selling outdated ships and building a few powerful ones which would outclass those of Italy's rivals. Rear Admiral Saint Bon took over in 1873 and pressed ahead energetically with an ambitious building programme, starting with the monster turret ships *Duilo* and *Dandolo* mounting four 100-ton (101·6 tonne) guns.

These vessels were seen as the answer to Italy's problem and were ordered from Benedetto Brin who must rank among the world's leading warship designers. Urged on by Saint Bon he created a series of battleships unique for their original concept and combination of fighting ability that would make them as outstanding as the first sea-going ironclad *Gloire* and the epoch-making British *Dreadnought* some thirty years later.

In spite of adverse comments levelled by some at the *Dandolo* and *Duilio*, Brin proceeded to follow these in 1875 by laying down two extraordinary ships — faster and more seaworthy than the two turret ships and able to fight anything afloat. At the same time they would carry a large number of troops.

These two ships were *Italia* and *Lepanto,* armed with four 103 ton guns plus eighteen 6in (152mm) guns with 3,000 tons (3,047 tonnes) of coal to increase the range, all on 13,850 tons (14,068 tonnes) displacement. Later displacement rose to 15,000 tons (15,237 tonnes) with 1,700 tons (1,727 tonnes) of coal and only eight 6in (152mm) weapons. 16,000 horsepower gave nearly 18kt which was 3kt faster than any ironclad at that time.

The race between the gun and armour now seemed to have swung in favour of the former and accordingly Brin cut out any waterline armour and relied solely upon a cellular raft made up of many small compartments between the armoured deck which reached the sides by sloping down 6ft (1·82m) above the waterline. Two bulkheads set back several feet from the side of the ship and running the full length were interspaced with more bulkheads to create small compartments, so that the effect of a hit would be minimised.

The four main guns were mounted on two turntables in one huge oval barbette running diagonally amidships across the deck and protected with 19in (483mm) compound armour. An armoured trunk carried the ammunition from below the armoured deck to the guns which fired one round every five minutes. Total armour amounted to 3,000 tons (3,047 tonnes) with backing, some 20 per cent of the normal displacement.

Unfortunately by the time these vessels entered service the rapid development of the quick firing gun and high explosive shells had rendered them useless as battleships but Brin could not be expected to foresee this.

Below: *Lepanto* in 1898 with added quick firing guns. By now, with no adequate side armour, they were little better than giant protected cruisers and were regarded as brilliant but unlucky concepts from the mind of a matchless naval architect: the Italian Benedetto Brin

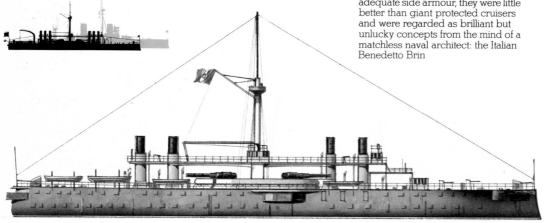

Below: *Italia* towards the end of her days when the central mast had been moved and two smaller masts added to the ends of the ship. By 1905/06 the six funnels had been reduced to four. She became a training ship in 1909, transferred to harbour defence duties in 1914 and converted in 1917 to carry cereal. She was stricken in 1921.

Below: This plan shows the angled armoured barbette spread across the ship providing a good field of fire for the main guns. However it was found necessary to reduce the number of planned smaller guns on the upper deck as they could not be used when the big guns were in action. The 25ft (7·62m) freeboard enabled the main guns to be carried 33ft (10m) above the waterline. Three of these guns were 26-cal 102·5-ton (104·1 tonne) weapons while the fourth was a 27-cal of 103·5 tons (105·1 tonnes) with a muzzle velocity of 1755fs.

VAUBAN

1885 *France*
Other ships in class: *Duguesclin*

Laid down: February 1879.
Launched: July 1882.
Builder: Cherbourg Dockyard.
Displacement: 6,112 tons
(6,210 tonnes).
Dimensions: 265ft 9in (81·00m) wl
x 57ft 3in (17·45m) x 25ft 3in
(7·7m) max.
Machinery: Vertical Compound
engines; 8 cylindrical boilers;
2 shafts; 4400 IHP.
Armour: Wrought iron 10in-5·9in
(255-150mm) belt, compound
7·8in (200mm) barbettes.
Armament: 4 x 9·45in (240mm)
M1870; 1 x 7·5in (190mm);
6 x 5·5in (140mm); 4 x 3pdr;
12 x 1pdr revolvers; 2 x 14in
(356mm) torpedo tubes.
Performance: 14·5kt (26·9km/h);
coal 450 tons (457 tonnes).
Crew: 440.

Designed by Lebelin de Diome, the
Vauban and her sister-ship
Duguesclin (built at Rochefort
Dockyard and completed in August
1886) were barbette ships, and the
epitome of the type of cruising
ironclad favoured by the French. The
class was based on the Bayard class,
but had steel rather than wooden
hulls, and a deeper belt. The original
brig rig with 23,200 ft² (2,155m²) of
sail was later cut down to two military
masts. *Vauban* was discarded in
1905, as *Duguesclin* had been the
previous year.

Below: *Vauban* with
brig rig, 1886.

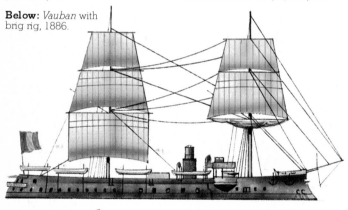

OLDENBURG

1886 *Germany*

Laid down: 1883.
Launched: 20 December 1884.
Builder: Vulkan, Stettin.
Displacement: 5,652 tons
(5,742 tonnes).
Dimensions: 261ft 2in (79·8m) oa
x 59ft (18m) x 20ft 8in (6·3m).
Machinery: Horizontal Compound
engines; 2 shafts; 3,942 IHP.
Armour: Iron 11·8in-7·9in
(300-200mm) belt; 7·9in (200mm)
battery; 5·9in (150mm) bulkheads.
Armament: 8 x 9·45in (240mm)
4 x 5·9in (150mm); 2 x 3·4in
(87mm); 4 x 13·78in (350mm)
torpedo tubes.
Performance: 13·5kt (25km/h).
Crew: 389.

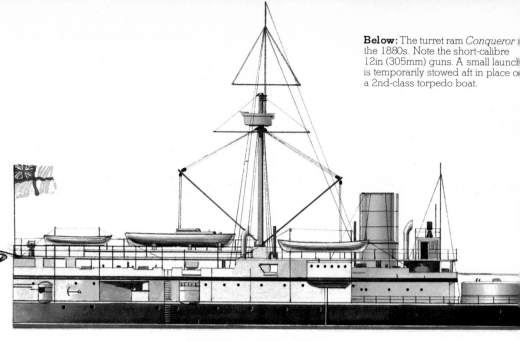

Below: The turret ram *Conqueror* in
the 1880s. Note the short-calibre
12in (305mm) guns. A small launch
is temporarily stowed aft in place of
a 2nd-class torpedo boat.

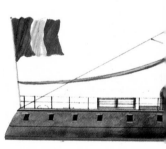

CONQUEROR

1886 *UK*
Other ships in class: *Hero*

Laid down: 28 April 1879.
Launched: 8 September 1881.
Builder: Chatham Dockyard.
Displacement: 6,200 tons
(6,299 tonnes) load.
Dimensions: 288ft (87·78m) oa x
58ft (17·68m) x 23ft 6in (7·16m).
Machinery: Humphreys 3-cylinder
Inverted Compound engines; 8
cylindrical boilers; 2 shafts; 4500 IHP.
Armour: Compound 12in-8in
(305-203mm) belt; 12in-10·5in
(305-267mm) citadel; 14in-12in
(356-305mm) turret; 11in (279mm)
bulkhead; 12in-6in (305-152mm)
conning tower; 2·5in-1·25in
(64-32mm) decks.
Armament: 2 x 12in (305mm) BL;
4 x 6in (152mm) BL; 7 x 6pdr QF;
5 x 3pdr QF; 6 x 14in (356mm)
torpedo tubes.
Performance: 14kt (25·9km/h).
Crew: 330.

A turret ram, the *Conqueror* was
evolved from the design of the
Rupert, the ironclad ram completed
in 1874, but was a larger vessel with
more modern machinery and
equipment, a steel hull and heavier
armament. The value of ramming
seemed to have been proved by the
Battle of Lissa in 1866, though few
had made the effort to assess how
Italian tactical ineptitude had allowed
the Austro-Hungarians to ram. But
Conqueror and her sister-ship *Hero*
(ordered four years later and
completed in May 1888, with a
displacement of 6,440 tons/6,543
tonnes and Rennie machinery) were
produced specifically for ramming,
with a fair turn of speed, great
manoeuvrability and the main

Designed between 1879 and 1881,
the *Oldenburg* was obsolescent at
this time and obsolete by the time she
was completed as a central battery
ironclad. The German Navy's original
intention had been that the
Oldenburg should be another unit of
the four-strong Sachsen class but
finances were not sufficient.
  The arrangement of the
Oldenburg's central battery was
decidedly odd: six 9·45in (240mm)
guns were placed in a main deck
battery (two on each broadside and
the remaining pair in a lateral
embrasure on each side to give a
modicum of fore and aft fire), while
the other two 9·45in (240mm) guns
were positioned as broadside
weapons on the upper deck, above
the main battery. Few gunnery
alterations were effected during the
Oldenburg's career, the most notable
being an increase in 3·4in (87mm)
guns to eight.
  In 1900 *Oldenburg* was relegated
to harbour guard duties, in 1912
becoming a target ship. She was sold
for breaking up in 1919.

armament concentrated to fire
forward. Trials soon showed that the
vessels were failures: they were too
small for ocean-going operations and
too large for coastal operations. So
both spent more of their careers in
the role of gunnery tender.
  The belt stretched between the
lower and main decks, and was
closed by a thick bulkhead some 27ft
(8·23m) short of the stern.
Operational efficiency was
hampered by the possibility of blast
damage to the forecastle when the
main turret was trained to fire
forwards. *Conqueror* was broken up
in 1907, while *Hero* was expended
as a gunnery target in 1908 before
being raised and broken up.

Below: *Oldenburg,* one of the last
central battery ships built for any
navy, soon after her completion.

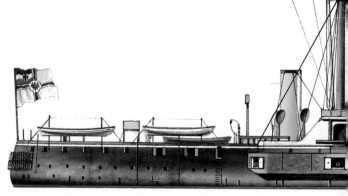

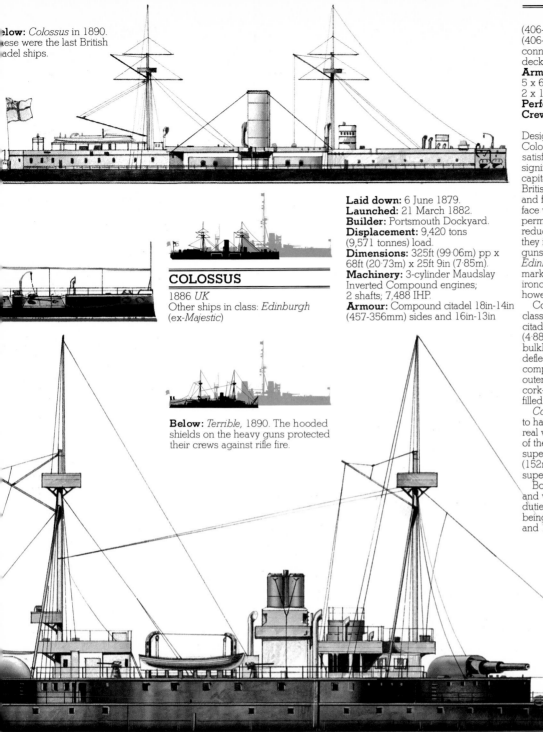

Below: Colossus in 1890.
These were the last British
...adel ships.

COLOSSUS

1886 *UK*
Other ships in class: *Edinburgh*
(ex-*Majestic*)

Below: *Terrible*, 1890. The hooded
shields on the heavy guns protected
their crews against rifle fire.

Laid down: 6 June 1879.
Launched: 21 March 1882.
Builder: Portsmouth Dockyard.
Displacement: 9,420 tons
(9,571 tonnes) load.
Dimensions: 325ft (99·06m) pp x
68ft (20·73m) x 25ft 9in (7·85m).
Machinery: 3-cylinder Maudslay
Inverted Compound engines;
2 shafts; 7,488 IHP.
Armour: Compound citadel 18in-14in
(457-356mm) sides and 16in-13in

(406-330mm) bulkheads; 16in-14in
(406-356mm) turrets; 14in (356mm)
conning tower; 3in-2·5in,(76-64mm)
decks.
Armament: 4 x 12in (305mm) BL;
5 x 6in (152mm) BL; 4 x 6pdr QF;
2 x 14in (356mm) torpedo tubes.
Performance: 16·5kt (30·6km/h).
Crew: 396.

Designed by Nathaniel Barnaby, the
Colossus class, while not wholly
satisfactory, are nonetheless.
significant as a watershed in British
capital ship design: they were the first
British battleships to be built of steel
and feature compound armour (steel
face with wrought iron backing),
permitting equal strength with
reduced weight; at the same time
they introduced breech-loading
guns of large calibre. *Colossus* and
Edinburgh may thus be regarded as
marking the turning point between
ironclad and battleship. As sea boats,
however, they handled poorly.

Compared with the Agamemnon
class, *Colossus* had an improved
citadel 123ft (37·49m) long and 16ft
(4·88m) deep, with semi-circular
bulkhead ends for enhanced shell
deflection. The ends of the ship were
compartmented for flotation, the
outer compartments being
cork-filled and the inner ones being
filled with coal.

Colossus was the first British ship
to have a secondary armament of any
real value, with two guns in each side
of the extreme forward and aft
superstructure, and the last 6in
(152mm) weapon on the rear of the
superstructure.

Both ships had short active lives,
and were relegated to secondary
duties in 1893 and 1894 respectively,
being sold for breaking up in 1908
and 1910.

TERRIBLE

1887 *France*
Other ships in class: *Caiman,
Indomptable, Requin*

Laid down: December 1877.
Launched: 1881.
Builder: Brest Dockyard.
Displacement: 7,530 tons
(7,650 tonnes).
Dimensions: 271ft 6in (82·75m) pp
x 59ft (17·98m) x 26ft 2in
(7·98m) max.
Machinery: Vertical Compound;
engines; 12 cylindrical boilers;
2 shafts; 6500 IHP.
Armour: Steel 19·7in-7·9in
(500-200mm) belt; 18·1in (460mm)
barbettes; 7·9in (200mm) tubes;
1·2in (30mm) shields and conning
tower.
Armament: 2 x 16·5in (420mm)
M1875; 4 x 3·9in (100mm)
M1881; 4 x 3pdr; 16 x 1pdr
revolvers.
Performance: 15kt (27·8km/h);
coal 500 tons (508 tonnes).
Crew: 373, later 332.

Terrible and her three sister-ships
Caiman, Indomptable and Requin,
were barbette ships typical of French
construction in the second half of the
1870s. Emphasis during this period
of reconstruction after France's
crushing defeat by Prussia in 1870
was on powerful offensive units with
only limited protection for the hull.
The key to French design was thus a
long but relatively shallow belt right
along the waterline, with an
armoured deck on top of the belt.
And whereas British ships of the
period had low-positioned turrets
that could not be used effectively in a
seaway, French practice was to place
the heavy guns on a high
superstructure, with shallow
barbettes to protect the guns'
turntables, and armoured tubes to
withstand the bursting of shells in the
sacrificial volume between the main
deck and the superstructure. The
secondary armament had no real
protection at all.

The Terrible class had lower
freeboard than other comparable
French units, and the belt was almost

completely under water even at
normal load. The belt, 19·7in
(500mm) thick at its upper edge and
15·75in (400mm) at its lower edge
amidships, thinned to 11·8in-7·9in
(300-200mm) aft. Compartmentation
was decidely inferior to that of British
ships of the era, and in the Terrible
class there were only 11 watertight
bulkheads.

Armament was also a problem, for
French guns were generally less
effective than British weapons,
having a slower rate of fire and less
penetration. Moreover, the two single
M1875 weapons of *Terrible* had to
be cut back to a length of 19·3
calibres from 22 calibres as a result of
failures near the muzzle during trials.
In 1898 *Terrible* was rearmed with
two 13·4in (340mm) M1893 guns,
while her sisters (which had
compound rather than steel armour)
were given a pair of 10·8in (275mm)
M1893/96s. After reboilering *Requin*
survived to see service in World
War I. *Terrible* was deleted in
1911, while the others survived to be
scrapped in the 1920s.

COLLINGWOOD

1887 UK

Laid down: 12 July 1880.
Launched: 22 November 1882.
Builder: Pembroke Dockyard.
Displacement: 9,500 tons
(9,652 tonnes) load.
Dimensions: 325ft (99·06m) pp x
68ft (20·73m) x 26ft 4in (8·03m)
Machinery: Humphreys 2-cylinder
Inverted Compound engines; 12
cylindrical boilers; 2 shafts; 9600 IHP.
Armour: Iron 18in-8in (457-203mm)
belt, 16in-7in (406-178mm)
bulkheads; 12in-2in (305-51mm)
conning tower; 3in-2in (76-51mm)
decks.
Armament: 4 x 12in (305mm) BL;
6 x 6in (152mm) BL; 12 x 6pdr;
8 x 3pdr; 4 x 14in (356mm)
torpedo tubes.
Performance: 16·8kt (31·km/h).
Crew: 498.

Collingwood was the first British
barbette ship, and undoubtedly the
best design produced by Nathaniel
Barnaby. The stimulus for the design
was the Terrible class of French
coastal defence battleships, but
Barnaby found his immediate pattern

Left: *Collingwood* in the early
1900s.

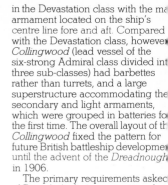

in the Devastation class with the ma[...]
armament located on the ship's
centre line fore and aft. Compared
with the Devastation class, however[...]
Collingwood (lead vessel of the
six-strong Admiral class divided int[...]
three sub-classes) had barbettes
rather than turrets, and a large
superstructure accommodating the
secondary and light armaments,
which were grouped in batteries fo[...]
the first time. The overall layout of th[...]
Collingwood fixed the pattern for
future British battleship developme[...]
until the advent of the *Dreadnough[...]*
in 1906.

The primary requirements asked
of Barnaby's design were speed,
range and armament. However, for
economic reasons the displaceme[...]
was fixed at a maximum of 10,000
tons (10,160 tonnes), which meant
that to a certain extent protection an[...]
freeboard had to be foregone in th[...]
interests of offensive capability.

The provision of barbettes rathe[...]
than turrets had several advantage[...]
the barbettes were in themselves
lighter, and the absence of the
vulnerable turret bases and trainin[...]
machinery meant that the citadel
could be reduced in size and weigh[...]
Thus the barbettes could be place[...]
higher up than turrets, with a
consequent improvement in the
ship's ability to fight in any kind of

Top: This drawing shows an early
design which is similar to the
French *Caiman* but with greater
freeboard, and mounting an 80- or
100-ton (81·2-or 101·6-tonne) breechloader at each end.

Above: This is an earlier design for
Collingwood based upon an improved *Dreadnought* of 1897 with
a central armoured citadel enclosing
the two turrets. The ends, however,
were to have been unarmoured.

a. The 12in (305mm) Mk III guns
re also significantly better
eapons than the earlier Mk I: shell
eight was about the same, at 714lb
24kg), but improved propellant
d greater barrel length (25·5
libres) raised muzzle velocity.
om 1,300ft (396m) per second to
914ft (583m) per second, and
netration from 15·9in (404mm) to
in (610mm) of wrought iron.
oreover, the Mk III was a
eechloading weapon, whereas the
ks I and II guns were
uzzle-loaders. The major drawback
the barbettes, however, was that
e guns could only be loaded when
ined fore and aft.
   The provision of concentrated
condary and light batteries in the
perstructure reflected the growing
preciation of the very real threat
w posed to capital ships by ever
ore effective torpedo boats. It was
so appreciated that a powerful
condary armament could prove
ost useful against the unarmoured
rtions of enemy ships'
perworks. The 6in (152mm) guns
re located three to a side on the
per deck, and had no protection
her than 6in (152mm) screens
ainst end-on fire. In 1896 the
ginal secondary battery was
placed by 6in (152mm) QF guns.
   Each of the twin-gun barbettes

measured 50ft (15·24m) in length
and 45ft (13·72m) in width, with
sloping sides of 11·5in (292mm)
thickness and backs of 10in
(254mm) thickness. The floors were
3in (76mm) thick, but the only
overhead protection was afforded by
thin bulletproof plates. Ammunition
was supplied through tubes of
12in-10in (305-254mm) armour
reaching down to the citadel, which
was 140ft (42·67m) long and 7ft 6in
(2·29m) deep, reaching 5ft (1·52m)
below the waterline. Extensive
compartmentation provided
protection against flooding, and was
used for coal and stores. Unlike
earlier ships *Collingwood* lacked
cork-filled buoyancy chambers, but
had the standard anti-roll tanks.
   Collingwood was the first capital
ship provided with forced-draught
boilers, but her engines were unable
to profit from the extra potential:
without forced draught she made
16·6kt (30·75km/h) on 8,369 IHP,
and with forced draught this rose to
only 16·84kt (31·21km/h) on 9,573
IHP. Though a first-class seaboat and
very handy, *Collingwood* suffered
from her low freeboard and was very
wet, and so spent most of her career
in the Mediterranean. She was
allocated to coastguard duties in
1887, put in reserve in 1903 and sold
for breaking up in 1909.

Below: *Collingwood* in 1902 with
an extended boat deck. Below this
are the 6pdrs while the 6in
(152mm) guns are concentrated
amidships (three per side) some
14ft (4·26m) above the water line.

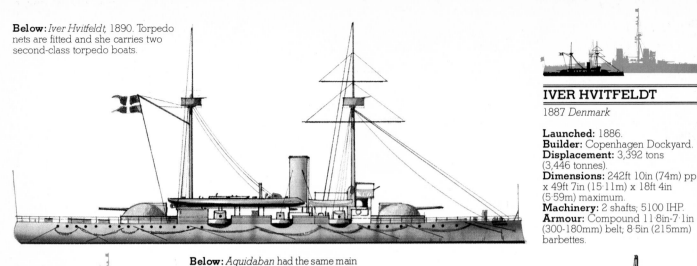

IVER HVITFELDT

1887 *Denmark*

Launched: 1886.
Builder: Copenhagen Dockyard.
Displacement: 3,392 tons (3,446 tonnes).
Dimensions: 242ft 10in (74m) pp x 49ft 7in (15·11m) x 18ft 4in (5·59m) maximum.
Machinery: 2 shafts; 5100 IHP.
Armour: Compound 11·8in-7·1in (300-180mm) belt; 8·5in (215mm) barbettes.

AQUIDABAN

1887 *Brazil*

Laid down: 18 June 1883.
Launched: 17 January 1885.
Builder: Samuda Bros, London.
Displacement: 4,921 tons (5,000 tonnes).
Dimensions: 280ft (85·34m) x 52ft (15·85m) x 18ft 4in (5·59m) mean.
Machinery: Inverted Compound; 8 cylindrical boilers; 2 shafts; 6500 IHP.
Armour: Compound 11in-7in (279-178mm) belt; 10in (254mm) wood backing; 10in (254mm) bulkheads; 10in (254mm) turrets and turret bases; 10in (254mm) conning tower; 2in (51mm) steel deck.
Armament: 4 x 9·2in (234mm); 4 x 5·5in (140mm); 13 x 1pdr; 5 x 14in (356mm) torpedo tubes (3 above water; 2 submerged).
Performance: 15·82kt (29·3km/h); coal 600 tons (610 tonnes).
Crew: 388.

Aquidaban was planned as a sister to *Riachuelo,* but her design was altered to give shallower draught and, consequently, a reduction in size, although with the same main armament and protection. A steel-hulled turret ship, she had a 7ft (2·13m) deep compound armour belt. A 2in (51mm) steel deck covered the central redoubt and curved down below water at either end.

The two hydraulically worked turrets, each housing 2 x 9·2in (234mm) Armstrong BLR, were set en échelon atop the redoubt. The narrow superstructure above permitted the turret guns to fire ahead and astern as well as on their broadsides, with gaps in the superstructure permitting 50° arcs on opposite broadsides. The 5·5in (140mm) 70pdrs were set at either end of the superstructure.

In the political turmoil following the establishment of Republican government in Brazil, the greatest threat to President Peixoto came when Admiral de Mello took over *Aquidaban* at Rio de Janeiro on 6 September 1893. The insurgents' strength ashore was small, so *Aquidaban* was almost daily in action against government shore batteries. She was hit several times but was not seriously damaged, escaping an attempt on 29 September to sink her with a torpedo from a launch commanded by an American mercenary. On 21 February 1894

Below: *Aquidaban* had the same main armament and protection as *Riachuelo* but was of shallower draught and thus somewhat smaller. Completed in 1887, she was then one of the most powerful ships in American waters.

she sailed to raise support in the south. The collapse of rebel forces in Rio on 11 March left her isolated, and on the night of 16 April, while anchored behind a mine barrier in Santa Catharina Strait, she was attacked by a flotilla of torpedo gunboats led by the *Gustavo Sampaio.* Struck in the bows by a 16in (406mm) torpedo, the turret ship settled in 24ft (7·3m) of water.

Aquidaban was refloated in June 1894, repaired at Rio and renamed *Vinte Quatro de Mayo.* In 1896-98 she was reconstructed at the Vulkan Works, Stettin. She was rearmed with 4 x 8in (203mm) and 4 x 4·7in (119mm), the forward guns being moved from the main deck to shielded positions above the superstructure. Two military masts (replaced in 1904 by a single military mast amidships) were shipped. In 1900 she was again named *Aquidaban.*

On 21 January 1906, *Aquidaban* exploded and sank while taking on ammunition.

RUGGIERO DI LAURIA

1888 *Italy*
Other ships in class: *Francesco Morosini, Andrea Doria*

Laid down: 3 August 1881.
Launched: 9 August 1884.
Builder: Castellammare Navy Yard.
Displacement: 9,886 tons (10,044 tonnes) normal; 10,997 tons (11,173 tonnes) full load.
Dimensions: 347ft 5in (105·9m) oa x 65ft 1in (19·84m) x 27ft 2in (8·29m).
Machinery: Compound engines; 8 cylindrical boilers; 2 shafts; 10,591 IHP.
Armour: Steel 17·75in (450mm) sides; 14·2in (360mm) citadel and

barbettes; 9·8in (250mm) conning tower; 2·95in (75mm) deck.
Armament: 4 x 17in (431mm); 2 x 6in (152mm); 4 x 4·7 (120mm); 2 x 14in (356mm) torpedo tubes.
Performance: 17kt (31·5km/h); endurance 3,225 miles (5,190km) at 10kt (18·5km/h).
Crew: 507, later 509.

Designed in 1880 by Giuseppe Micheli, the three ships of the Ruggiero di Lauria class were warships forced upon the Italian Navy by the Minister of the Navy, Ferdinando Acton, who regarded ships such as the previous 15,400-ton (15,646-tonne) Italia class wasteful of Italy's limited financial and industrial resources, and also a tactical disadvantages. Micheli's new design was thus in essence an improved version of the Duilio class with breech-loading guns, improved armour and better sea-keeping qualities. They took so long to build that these vessels were obsolete on completion.

Armament: 2 x 10·2in (260mm)
Krupp BL; 4 x 4·7in (120mm) Krupp
BL; 12 x 1pdr revolvers; 2 x 15in
(380mm) and 2 x 13·78in
(350mm) torpedo tubes.
Performance: 15·25kt (28·3km/h);
coal 290 tons (295 tonnes).
Crew: 277.

Iver Hvitfeldt was a barbette coast
defence battleship dating from the
second major period (1878-88) of
building following the loss of
Schlewsig-Holstein to Prussia in
1864. She had a midships belt, and
the main guns were carried in
centreline barbettes fore and aft of
the superstructure. She was rebuilt in
1904 with two 10·2in (260mm), 10 x
1pdrs, 6 x 1pdr revolvers and two 15in
(380mm) torpedo tubes.

Above: *Riachuelo* in early 1886. Her
influence on US thinking led to
the design of the ill-fated *Maine*
(1895). The close resemblance
between *Riachuelo* and *Aquidaban*,
which quickly followed her in the
rapidly-expanding Brazilian Navy,
is clearly apparent here.

RIACHUELO

1886 Brazil

Launched: 7 June 1883.
Builder: Samuda Bros, London.
Displacement: 5,610 tons
(5,700 tonnes) normal; 6,100 tons
(6,198 tonnes) full load.
Dimensions: 305ft (92·96m) pp x
52ft (15·85m) x 19ft 8in (5·99m).
Machinery: Vertical Compound
engines; 10 cylindrical boilers;
2 shafts; 7300 IHP.
Armour: Compound 11in-7in
(279-178mm) belt; 10in (254mm)
turrets and conning tower.
Armament: 4 x 9·2in (234mm)
Armstrong BLR; 6 x 5·5in (140mm)
Armstrong BLR; 15 x 1pdr; 5 x
14in (356mm) torpedo tubes.
Performance: 16·7kt (30·9km/h);
coal 800 tons (813 tonnes).
Crew: 367.

Riachuelo was a turret battleship,
and one of the few major warships
built for Brazil in the long period of
peace between 1870 and 1889.
Brazil's first effort to secure a vessel of
this type was *Independencia,* a
masted turret ship based on the
British Devastation class, but she was
bought for the Royal Navy as the
Neptune. Of South American rivals,
Argentina and Chile ordered central
battery ships, but Brazil opted for a
replacement turret vessel, the
Riachuelo built in the UK.

Armour and armament were
excellent. The belt was 250ft (76·2m)
long, and covered the machinery and
magazines to a thickness of 7in
(178mm) below the waterline, 11in
(279mm) above it in the area of the
machinery, and 10in (254mm)
elsewhere. The twin-gun turrets were
arranged en échelon to provide fore
and aft fire, and could be trained
through 180° on their own sides, and
through 50° on the inboard side to
fire through gaps in the
superstructure over the other beam.

Riachuelo missed the civil war of
1893-94 as she was being refitted at
La Seyne with four 9·45in (240mm),
six 4·7in (120mm) QF and six 1·85in
(47mm) QF guns. She was scrapped
in 1910. Her chief importance lies
perhaps in the impression she left
with the US Navy, which from 1886
began increasingly to devote its
efforts to stronger ships.

In 1900 the armament was
updated, and two 2·95in (75mm), ten
2·24in (57mm) QF, 12 1·46in (37mm)
and five 1·46in (37mm) revolver guns
were added. *Francesco Morosini*
and *Andrea Doria* were built at
Venice and La Spezia Naval
Dockyards respectively, had slightly
greater full load displacements and
were fractionally slower. *Morosini*
was sunk as a target in 1909, while
the other two survived World War I:
Doria was a floating battery at
Brindisi, and was broken up in 1929,
while *Lauria* was a floating oil tank
from 1909 to 1943.

Below: *Ruggiero di Lauria* shown as
completed, 1888. By the 1890s, the
after crane had been removed.

Below: *Formidable* in 1890. She was a follow-on to *Amiral Duperré*, but with three barbettes instead of four. The secondary battery was originally unprotected, but was removed to a redoubt replacing the central guns during the 1890s.

RODNEY

1888 *UK*
Other ships in class: *Anson, Camperdown, Howe, Benbow*

Laid down: 6 February 1882.
Launched: 8 October 1884.
Builder: Chatham Dockyard.
Displacement: 10,300 tons (10,465 tonnes) load.
Dimensions: 325ft (99·06m) pp x 68ft (20·73m) x 27ft 10in (8·48m).
Machinery: Humphreys 3-cylinder Inverted Compound; 12 cylindrical boilers; 2 shafts; 11500 IHP.
Armour: Iron 18in-8in (457-203mm) belt; 16in-7in (406-178mm) bulkheads; 11·5in-10in (292-254mm) barbettes; 12in-2in (305-51mm) conning tower; 3in-2·5in (76-64mm) decks.
Armament: 4 x 13·5in (343mm) BL; 6 x 6in (152mm) BL; 12 x 6pdr; 10 x 3pdr; 4 x 14in (356mm) torpedo tubes.
Performance: 17kt (31·5km/h).
Crew: 530.

Given the success of the *Collingwood* and the threat posed by the French Formidable class, it is hardly a matter for surprise that the Royal Navy decided to persevere with extra units of the Admiral class. This class was the first homogeneous class for some time, and comprised three sub-classes: *Collingwood; Rodney, Anson, Camperdown* and *Howe;* and *Benbow.* Gun developments and the Formidables were responsible for the introduction of the second sub-class, whose four

ships had 13·5in (343mm) 67-ton (68·1-tonne) guns in place of *Collingwood*'s 12in (305mm) 45-ton (45·7-tonne) weapons.

Rodney and *Howe* (the latter built at Pembroke Dockyard and completed in July 1889) were dimensionally identical with *Collingwood,* but displaced 800 tons (813 tonnes) more, so the belt was almost completely submerged. *Anson* and *Camperdown* (the former built at Pembroke Dockyard

Below: *Benbow* in 1889. Her 110-ton guns, although impressive, had a life limited to about 70 rounds.

and completed in May 1889, the latter at Portsmouth Dockyard with Maudslay machinery and completed in July 1889) were thus increased in size (330ft/100·58m pp x 68ft 6in/20·88m x 27ft 10in/8·48m) to keep their draught only 1ft 6in (0·46m) greater than that of the *Collingwood* despite an increase in the length of the belt by 10ft (3·05m) and of displacement to 10,600 tons (10,770 tonnes).

Forced-draught boilers were

fitted, but as in the *Collingwood* th[ ] improved speed only marginally. Th[ ] completion of the four ships was much delayed by problems with th[ ] main armament. Thereafter armament changes were small, consisting only of substitution of 6i[ ] (152mm) QF guns for the original 6i[ ] (152mm) weapons in 1896-97. The class served in home waters and in the Mediterranean; misfortunes included *Camperdown*'s accidental ramming and sinking of *Victoria* or

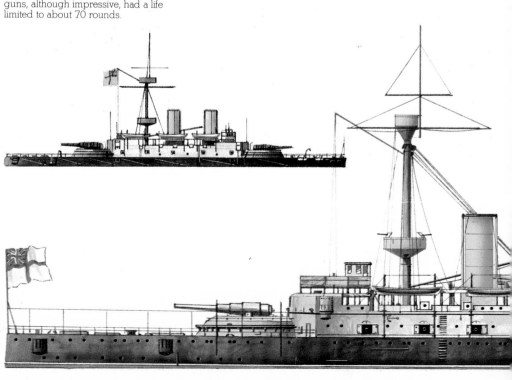

FORMIDABLE

1889 *France*
Other ships in class: *Amiral Baudin*

Laid down: September 1879.
Launched: April 1885.
Builder: Lorient Dockyard.
Displacement: 11,720 tons (11,908 tonnes).
Dimensions: 331ft 6in (101·04m)

wl x 70ft (21·34m) x 27ft 9in (8·46m) max.
Machinery: Vertical Compound; 12 cylindrical boilers; 2 shafts; 9700 IHP.
Armour: Steel and compound 22in-14in (560-355mm) belt; 15·95in (405mm) barbettes and tubes; 4·7-3·1in (120-80mm) conning tower; 1·2in (30mm) shields.
Armament: 3 x 14·6in (370mm) M1875/79; 4 x 6·3in (160mm) M1884; 10 x 5·5in (140mm); 1 x 3pdr; 12 x 3pdr revolvers; 18 x 1 pdr revolvers; 6 x 15in (380mm) torpedo tubes.
Performance: 16kt (29·6km/h); coal 790 tons (803 tonnes).
Crew: 650.

Typical of the barbette ships laid down by France between 1877 and 1879 (*Amiral Duperré*, four Terrible class and two Amiral Baudin class), the *Formidable* was the second unit of the Amiral Baudin class (the lead ship was built at Brest Dockyard and completed in December 1888). In comparison with the preceding Terrible class, the two Amiral Baudin units had higher freeboard, more tumblehome and a more projecting ram bow.

Amiral Baudin and *Formidable* both had three centre line barbettes (forward, midships and aft), but whereas *Amiral Baudin* had 71·4-ton (72·5-tonne) Creusot guns, *Formidable* had 75·1-ton

(76·3-tonne) St Chamond weapons of the same calibre, both types being about equal to the British 13·5in (343mm) Mk II gun, which was somewhat lighter. The secondary armament was sponsoned out on the main deck, and the 5·5in (140mm) guns were also located on this deck. In a refit between 1896 and 1898, the secondary armament was moved to a redoubt that replaced the midships barbette, and 5·5in (140mm) QF guns replaced the earlier weapons, while the light armament was improved. The belt was of steel and full length, with only 1ft (0·91m) of its 7ft 2·5in (2·2m) depth above water.

Amiral Baudin was hulked in 1909, and *Formidable* was deleted in 1911.

Below: Kronprinzessin Erzherzogin Stefani in 1895. Kuchinka's arrangement of the forward-facing main battery in barbettes meant the ship rapidly became obsolete.

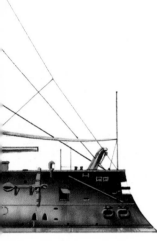

2 June 1893, and *Howe's* stranding on Ferrol Rock between 2 November 1892 and 1893. *Camperdown* was hulked in 1908, and all four units were sold for breaking up between 1909 and 1911.

The last of the Admiral class was *Benbow*, which was built at Thames Iron Works and completed in June 1888. She was almost identical with *Anson* and *Camperdown* except that her fore and aft barbettes each housed a single Armstrong 16·25in (413mm) 110-ton (111·8-tonne) gun, a change forced by lack of production capability for the chosen 13·5in (343mm) Woolwich guns. The weight saved was used to permit the installation of an extra four 6in (152mm) secondary guns. *Benbow's* active life was short, spanning the years 1888 to 1891, spent in the Mediterranean. She then became a coastguard ship, was put in reserve in 1904 and scrapped in 1909.

Below: Camperdown as completed; a taller foremast was later shipped. These graceful ships, designed by White, constituted the Royal Navy's last large group for many years.

KRONPRINZESSIN ERZHERZOGIN STEFANI

1889 *Austria-Hungary*

Laid down: 12 November 1884.
Launched: 14 April 1887.
Builder: Stabilimento Tecnico Triestino.
Displacement: 5,075 tons (5,156 tonnes).
Dimensions: 286ft 2in (87·24m) wl x 55ft 11in (17·06m) x 21ft 8in (6·6m).
Machinery: Compound Expansion; 2 shafts; 8000 IHP.
Armour: Iron 9in (229mm) belt; 11·1in (283mm) barbettes; 2in (50mm) conning tower.
Armament: 2 x 12in (305mm) Krupp L/35; 6 x 5·9in (150mm) Krupp L/35; 7 x 1·85in (47mm) Hotchkiss L/44 QF; 2 x 1·85in (47mm) Hotchkiss L/33 QF; 2 x 1·46in (37mm) QF; 2 x 2·76in (70mm) Uchatius; 4 x 15·75in (400mm) torpedo tubes.
Performance: 17kt (31·5km/h).
Crew: 430.

A barbette ship designed by Josef Kuchinka, the *Kronprinzessin*

Erzherzogin Stefani was well compartmented and fast, but was obsolete with her main armament arranged in two forward-firing barbettes abreast the conning tower. The ship was hulked in 1910 and scrapped in 1926 after being ceded to Italy in 1920.

KRONPRINZ ERZHERZOG RUDOLF

1889 *Austria-Hungary*

Laid down: 25 January 1884.
Launched: 6 July 1887.
Builder: Pola Navy Yard.
Displacement: 6,829 tons (6,938 tonnes).
Dimensions: 320ft 2in (97·6m) oa x 63ft 2in (19·27m) x 24ft 3in (7·39m).
Machinery: 2-cylinder Vertical

Triple Expansion engines; 2 shafts; 6000 IHP.
Armour: Iron 12in-2·4in (305-62mm) belt; 9·5in-8in (242-203mm) bulkheads; 10in (254mm) barbettes.
Armament: 3 x 12in (305mm) Krupp L/35; 6 x 4·7in (120mm) Krupp L/35; 5 x 1·85in (47mm) Hotchkiss L/44 QF; 2 x 1·85in (47mm) Hotchkiss L/33 QF; 2 x 2·76in (70mm) Uchatius; 4 x 15·75in (400mm) torpedo tubes.
Performance: 15·5kt (28·7km/h).
Crew: 447/450.

The *Kronprinz Erzherzog Rudolf* was also designed by Josef Kuchinka, and was a close relative of the *Kronzprinzessin Erzherzogin Stefani*, but was enlarged to allow the installation of a third large-calibre gun, in this instance firing astern.

Although only the vitals of the ship were protected by armour, it was anticipated that the excellent degree of compartmentation would go far towards ensuring salvation against heavy damage. *Kronprinz Erzherzog Rudolf* became the Yugoslav *Kumbor* in 1919, but was scrapped in 1922.

Below: The barbette ship *Kronprinz Erzherzog Rudolf*, a close relative of the *K.E. Stefani*, in 1890.

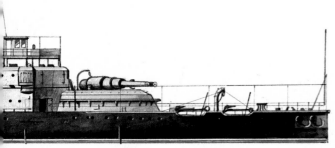

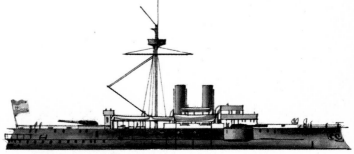

1890-1899

The last decade of the nineteenth century was a period of comparative stability in battleship design, of evolution and refinement rather than innovation, and one in which more attention was paid to the effectiveness of capital ships as fighting units rather than to pure sizes of guns and thicknesses of armour. As a result, battle efficiency improved, setting the scene for the momentous developments of the early 1900s. The British Naval Defence Act of 1889 had established the celebrated 'Two-Power Standard', decreeing the Royal Navy's superiority as a matter of political policy; the 'Tirpitz Era' had been ushered in in Germany, marking that country's ambitions in naval power; and perhaps most significantly, the decade saw the rise of the United States as the world's foremost industrial nation — which was to have far-reaching consequences in the next century.

ARMOUR

The French Schneider company continued to make progress in the development of armour plate, having discovered that by adding a small percentage of nickel to the steel used in the manufacturing process the plates could better resist cracking. However, the most important contribution to improved plate came from an American, H.A. Harvey, who in 1890 introduced 'face-hardened' steel: the outer surface of the armour could be toughened by carburising it — that is, by heating it in conjunction with charcoal over a period of several weeks and then cooling it rapidly by contact with water, a process which resulted in a resistance to penetration fifty per cent better than that of compound armour.

Developments in armour distribution were also taking place. The introduction of the barbette mounting required an armoured 'column' not only around the gun mountings proper but also carried down well into the ship's hull, protecting machinery, crew and ammunition supply. With the main armament thus disposed, the need for an armoured citadel protecting batteries of main-calibre weapons was obviated. Engine spaces and other vitals required adequate protection, however, and so the waterline belt was retained, but measures were also adopted to meet further developing threats.

One was the advent of the torpedo boat. It was seen that capital ships would be extremely vulnerable to torpedo attack while immobile, for example while at anchor. As a result, the fitting of defences in the form of nets, deployed by booms stowed along the hull when the ship was under way, became a characteristic feature of captial ships during this period. The second threat was the evolution of quick-firing guns of medium calibre, which, again, might be brought into action against a capital ship in mass attacks, before the latter could evade or otherwise deal effectively with them. To counter this, the main belt was topped by a thinner upper strake, which would not necessarily prevent penetration but would cause shells to explode on, rather than after, impact; concurrently, heavier anti-torpedo-boat batteries of quick-firing guns were placed aboard the capital ships themselves. The third threat, and one that would assume increasing significance (albeit in developed form) over the next fifty years, stemmed from the gradual recognition that, as gun ranges opened and elevation angles of guns increased, projectiles might plunge down on to a ship rather than impact against its side. Thus the armoured deck, laid across the belt and bulkheads, became an integral part of the protective system.

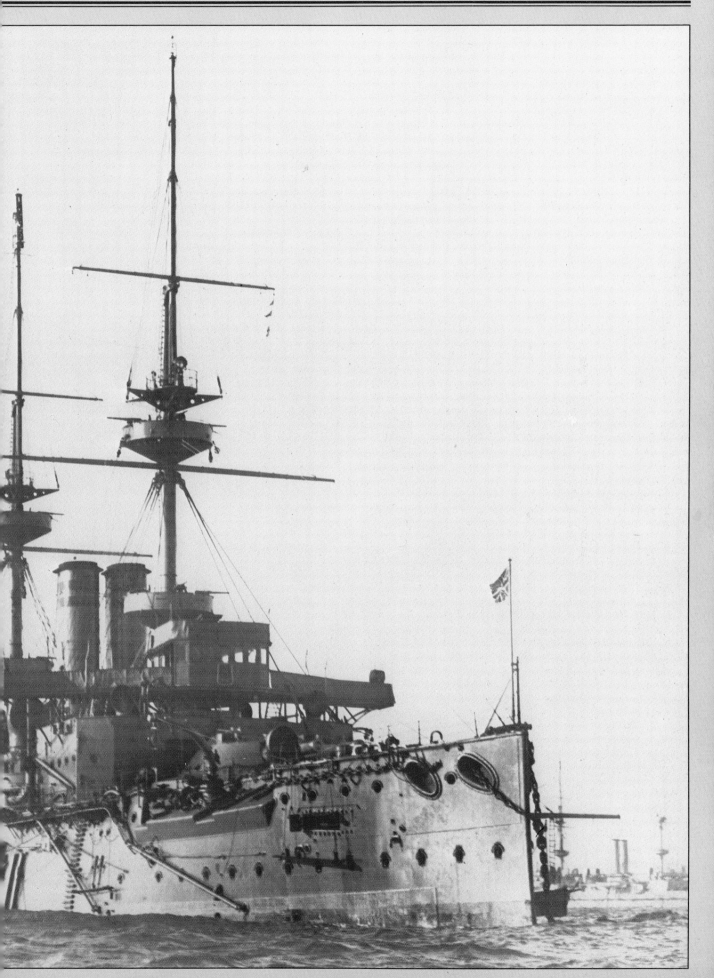

These emerging patterns in armour distribution had the effect of lowering centres of gravity, thereby permitting main armament positions—and hence freeboard—to be considerably higher than hitherto: for the first time, versatile, trainable heavy guns could be married to true ocean-going hulls, so creating a formidable combination.

GUNS

The turret system had by no means been abandoned by 1890: Britain (*Hood*), Russia (*Navarin, Tri Svititelia*) and France (*Brennus*) continued to build turret-battleships. However, its disadvantages—the prodigious weight of the necessary training machinery and the topweight brought about by the armouring of the turret itself—led to its rapid decline: it should be noted that 'turrets' carried by twentieth-century capital ships were quite different in concept from those of the 1870s and 1880s, and were a development of the barbette mounting, as will be seen later.

Gun mechanisms continued to be refined in the later Victorian period: the breech, elevation and training gear, recoil systems and ammunition hoists were by now hydraulically operated, permitting a smoothness and efficiency not seen before. Rates of fire of heavy guns were thereby increased to one round per minute or less, an improvement aided considerably by a general move away from 'monster' guns of 16in or 17in calibre to much more widely 11in, 12in and 13·5in pieces. All-round loading, available with the introduction of flexible chain rammers, gave capital ship fire-power a new dimension, while the British adoption of wire-wound barrels helped prevent droop and thus enhanced both accuracy and barrel life.

Shells, too, progressed. Concurrent with the introduction of carburised armour plate went strides to develop projectiles that could defeat it. A chrome-steel shell had been devised and produced by Holtzer in France in the late 1880s, and this encouraged the Russian Navy to introduce a developed, capped Holtzer shell over the next few years. Firth (Sheffield) successfully tested a similar projectile in England in 1894, and similar trials were carried out around the same time in the United States, where it was ordered into production immediately; it would be several

Above: A magnificent study of the after 13·5in (343mm) guns of HMS *Royal Sovereign*, mounted in open barbettes. Blast plates are fitted to the deck below the muzzles.

Below: A 12in (305mm) armour-piercing (AP) capped shell. An increase in penetrating power of anything up to 20 per cent was achieved by fitting projectiles with 'soft' steel caps which weakened face-hardened armour before the shell proper made impact on a target.

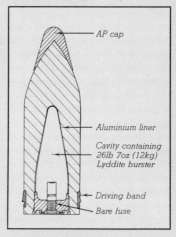

AP cap

Aluminium liner

Cavity containing 26lb 7oz (12kg) Lyddite burster

Driving band

Bare fuse

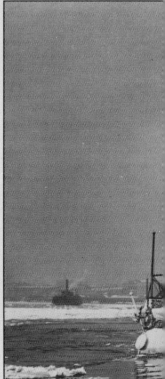

more years before the capped AP shell was accepted into Royal Navy service.

The invention of cordite, a propellant composed of nitroglycerine and nitrocellulose, with a small percentage of vaseline to keep down barrel wear, enabled the muzzle velocity imparted by guns to their shells to be much improved, thus enhancing the penetrating power of the projectiles themselves. It was a slower-burning powder, causing the shell to accelerate along the length of the bore of the gun instead of decelerate, which was the tendency after the initial massive explosion brought about by the ignition of guncotton or gunpowder. To take full advantage of this phenomenon, there was a general move towards barrels of increased length. One side-effect was to hasten the demise of the already-doomed muzzle-loader; a more important consideration was that cordite, and its foreign equivalents, produced far less smoke than existing propellants, thereby aiding the battle tactics of an attacking force.

MACHINERY

Significant advances in machinery installation were made in the 1890s, most particularly with the general introduction into service of the expansion engine. This plant, pioneered by the Frenchman Benjamin Normand and first fitted in the British-built, Spanish Navy torpedo gunboat *Destructor*, permitted the steam produced in the engine's cylinder to be expanded into further, progressively larger cylinders, thus enabling the very high steam pressures then available to engineers to be utilised more efficiently: the triple expansion engine, for example, involved three cylinders and by the turn of the century was commonly applied to all the major navies, the first British capital ship installation being in *Victoria*.

By the late 1890s the water-tube boiler had made its appearance, in place of the customary fire-tube types: in a sense, the earlier process was reversed, steam being produced from water tubes heated by the boiler gases instead of from a water 'jacket' enclosing pipes through which the hot gases moved. The French Belleville type was one of the most widely used, and permitted steam to be raised more quickly and to higher working pressures.

Top: The Japanese battleship *Fuji* was British-built and closely similar to the *Royal Sovereign*, although the guns were of smaller calibre and the barbettes hooded.

Above: *Nevada* (BB-1) was the first tangible piece of evidence that the US 'New Navy' would be a potent force. Note the heavy 8in (203mm) turret-mounted secondary battery.

Left: The coast defence battleship continued to be developed through the 1890s, although the stark *Monitor* profile had been abandoned. This is the Russian *Admiral Seniavin* of the Admiral Ushakov class.

Right: By the 1890s the standard battleship propulsion unit was the vertical triple-expansion reciprocating engine. Steam from the ship's boilers was expanded successively into a series of three cylinders of increasing size, in order to utilise its potential to the maximum. Power output was governed principally by cylinder diameter and vertical height (stroke), and for any ship there was clearly a limit to the size of its powerplant if factors such as dimensions, armour and armament were to be considered. Thus the VTE represented a dead end, and was ultimately abandoned in favour of the turbine, introduced to capital ships from 1906 as part of the new Dreadnought era.

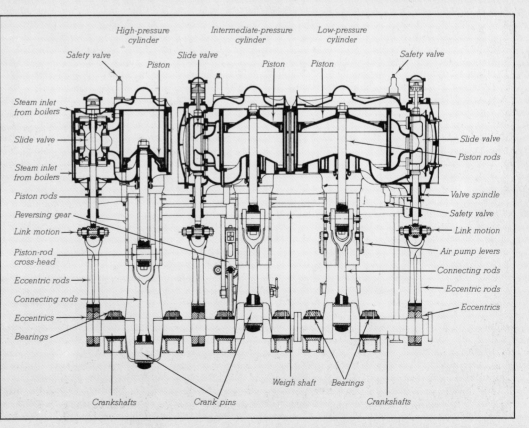

119

VICTORIA

1890 UK
Other ships in class: *Sans Pareil*

Laid down: 23 April 1885.
Launched: 9 April 1887.
Builder: Armstrong, Elswick.
Displacement: 10,470 tons (10,638 tonnes) load.
Dimensions: 363ft (110·64m) oa x 70ft (21·34m) x 29ft (8·84m) max.
Machinery: Two sets Humphreys 3-cylinder Triple Expansion engines; 8 boilers; 2 shafts; 8000 IHP natural draught, 14,244 IHP forced draught.
Armour: Compound 18in (457mm) belt; 16in (406mm) bulkheads; 17in (432mm) turret; 18in (475mm) redoubt; 6in-3in (152-76mm) battery screens; 14in (356mm) conning tower; 3in (76mm) deck.
Armament: 2 x 16·25in (413mm) BL; 1 x 10in (254mm) BL; 12 x 6in (152mm) BL; 12 x 6pdr QF; 9 x 3pdr QF; 4 x 14in (356mm) torpedo tubes; 2 x 14in (356mm) torpedo launching carriages.
Performance: 16kt (29·6km/h) natural draught, 17·3kt (32km/h) forced draught; coal 1,000 tons (1,016 tonnes) max; radius 7,000nm (12,950km) at 10kt (18·5km/h).
Crew: 550.

Victoria (until 1887 *Renown*) and *Sans Pareil* were designed by Barnaby—who probably followed the Board's detailed instructions somewhat unwillingly—to counter the French *Hoche* and Marceau class of 1881-83. The Admiral class barbette ships having been much criticised for supposed deficiencies in protection, the Victorias returned to the turret ship design. They also embodied the questionable doctrine of the value of the ram and of end-on (bow) fire at the expense of all-round firepower.

Because insufficient 13·5in (343mm) guns were available, a main armament of 2 x 16·25in (413mm) BL was specified. Even so, there was a 16-month delay when trials at the Elswick works of Armstrong—which, with *Victoria*, was building its first battleship as well as arming it—showed that the 110-ton (111·76 tonne) weapons needed strengthening.

Twin-mounting the big guns in one turret forward saved weight for added protection, but the heavy turret on the main deck reduced freeboard

to c12ft (3·66m). The big guns were thus only 15ft (4·57m) above water and their arc of fire (theoretically 300°) was restricted by the threat of blast damage to the deck when firing dead ahead and to the superstructure when firing much abaft the beam. The single-turret arrangement was not used again in a British battleship.

Turret and conning tower bases were further protected by a

Right: HMS *Victoria* in 1890 shortly after completion. The size of the single turret mounting the two 16·25in (413mm) main guns is very evident in this view.

pear-shaped redoubt which ran back to the forward end of the central citadel. Twelve 6in (152mm) BL were mounted in the superstructure in two batteries, divided by a 3in (76mm) bulkhead, with 6in (152mm) bulkheads guarding against raking fire fore and aft. Astern fire was provided by a lightly-shielded 10in (254mm) BL on the spar deck aft.

The first battleships with triple expansion engines, and the first

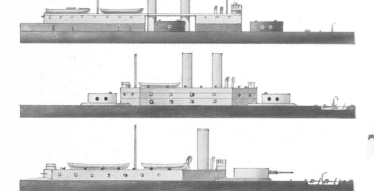

Above: Three of the six plans for ships to follow the Admiral class. The top vessel has one turret on either beam, each housing 1 x 63-ton (64 tonne) gun, with two similar weapons in the fore turret

and 22 x 6in (152mm) guns in the battery. Centre: An 11,700-ton (11,887 tonne) Admiral design of 1884 and (above) a further design with 2 x 63-ton (64 tonne) guns in a single turret forward.

British battleships to ship two funnels side by side, the Victorias were steady ships but were wet forward, which further impaired the efficiency of the main armament.

Victoria was flagship of the Mediterranean Fleet from the time of her commissioning. On 22 June 1893, during manoeuvres off Tripoli, a mistaken order by Vice-Admiral Sir George Tryon led to Victoria being rammed on the starboard bow, 12¼ft (3·66m) below water, by the Admiral class battleship Camperdown. Tryon and 358 officers and men were lost when Victoria filled and sank within 11 minutes. Survivors numbered 25 officers and 259 men.

Below: Victoria at Villefranche subsequent to the lengthening of her funnels in July-August 1890. As completed, they were 17ft (5·2m) shorter and draught was impaired.

Below: Victoria seen prior to her loss in 1893, showing the open armoured door in the battery bulkhead through which water poured when the foredeck became immersed. The gun ports were open to improve ventilation. The reason for Tryon's order leading to the collision, presumably based on a mistaken estimate of the distance between the columns, has never been satisfactorily explained.

Below: *Trafalgar* as seen after 1891, with raised funnels. It was thought at the time that the growing menace of torpedo boats might make these warships the last of their kind.

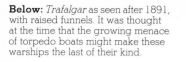

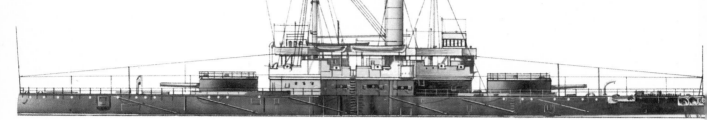

Below: *Sinope* in 1890. Hoods were later fitted over the big guns.

SINOPE

1890 *Russia*
Other ships in class: *Ekaterina II, Tchesma, Georgi Pobiedonosets*

Laid down: April 1883.
Launched: 20 June 1887.
Builder: Sevastopol.
Displacement: 11,230 tons (11,410 tonnes) full load.
Dimensions: 339ft 6in (103·48m) oa x 69ft (21·03m) x 28ft 9in (8·76m) max.
Machinery: Vertical Triple Expansion engines; 16 cylindrical boilers; 2 shafts; 13,000 IHP
Armour: Compound 16in-8in (406-203mm) belt; 12in (305mm) redoubt.
Armament: 6 x 12in (305mm); 7 x 6in (152mm); 12 smaller; 7 x 15in (381mm) TT; 100 mines.
Performance: 16·5kt (30·5km/h); coal 870 tons (884 tonnes) max.
Crew: 665.

The Ekaterina II class barbette ships, built for the Black Sea Fleet, were unique in the disposition of their main armament. Six 12in (305mm) guns were carried at the corners of a pear-shaped redoubt amidships, one twin mounting on either beam forward and one on the centre line aft.

By 1914, *Sinope* had a reduced armament of 4 x 8in (203mm) and 8 x 6in (152mm) and was a guardship at Odessa. Disarmed by White officers at Sevastopol in 1917, she was damaged by British interventionist forces in 1919 and was scrapped by the Soviet Navy in 1922.

PELAYO

1890 *Spain*

Laid down: April 1885.
Launched: 5 February 1887.
Builder: La Seyne.
Displacement: 9,745 tons (9,901 tonnes) load.
Dimensions: 334ft 8in (102·01m) pp x 66ft 3in (20·19m) x 24ft 9in (7·54m) max.
Machinery: Vertical Compound; 12 boilers; 2 shafts; 9600 IHP.
Armour: Creusot steel 17·75in-11·75in (451-298mm) belt; 15·75in-11·75in (400-298mm) barbettes; 3·125in (79mm) shields; 2·75in-2in (70-51mm) deck; 6·125in (156mm) conning tower.
Armament: 2 x 12·5in (317mm); 2 x 11in (279mm); 1 x 6·4in

(163mm); 12 x 4·7in (119mm); 5 x 6pdr QF; 14 MG; 7 torpedo tubes.
Performance: 16·7kt (30·9km/h) forced draught; coal 800 tons (813 tonnes).
Crew: 520.

Pelayo was French-built to a design based on the French *Marceau*, with slightly greater length and beam but draught reduced by some 3ft (0·91m) at full load to allow her to pass through the Suez Canal. She was originally rigged to carry 4,000ft² (372m²) of canvas, but military masts were shipped soon after her completion.

The complete belt of Creusot steel had a maximum thickness of 17·75in (451mm) amidships, where it extended some 5ft (1·52m) below the waterline and 2ft (0·61m) above. A 2·75in-2in (70-51mm) armour deck was flat below the belt and extensive compartmentation with 13 complete transverse bulkheads—such cellular protection being a feature of French designs—lay between this and the ship's double bottom.

Two 12·5in (317mm) Hontoria guns were carried fore and aft in centreline barbettes with all-round loading positions, the forward gun being some 31ft (9·4m) above water, and 2 x 11in (279mm) Hontorias in similar barbettes on either beam amidships. A single 6·4in (163mm) gun was mounted high in the bow and 12 x 4·7in (119mm) in an unarmoured battery amidships. Nine 5·5in (140mm) guns, four on each broadside and one as a bow chaser, later replaced the 6·4in (163mm) and 4·7in (119mm) weapons.

In reconstruction at La Seyne in 1897, *Pelayo* was reboilered and had 3in (76mm) Harvey armour fitted on the battery. In June 1898, after the Spanish Navy's crushing defeat in Manila Bay, she was ordered to the Philippines as flagship of Rear-Admiral Camara's squadron. Delayed at Suez when coaling facilities were denied them, the squadron was ordered back to protect the Spanish coast against possible attack by the US Navy. *Pelayo* was stricken in 1925.

TRAFALGAR

1890 *UK*
Other ships in class: *Nile*

Laid down: 18 January 1886.
Launched: 20 September 1887.
Builder: Portsmouth Dockyard.
Displacement: 12,590 tons
(12,791 tonnes) load.
Dimensions: 345ft (105·16m) pp
73ft (22·25m) x 28ft 6in (8·69m).
Machinery: Humphreys 3-cylinder
Triple Expansion; 6 cylindrical
boilers; 2 shafts; 7500 IHP natural
draught, 12,000 IHP forced draught.
Armour: Compound 20in-14in
(508-356mm) belt; 16in-14in
(406-356mm) bulkheads; 18in-16in
(457-406mm) citadel; 18in (457mm)
turrets; 3in (76mm) decks;
14in (356mm) conning tower.

Armament: 4 x 13·5in (343mm) BL;
6 x 4·7in (119mm) QF; 8 x 6pdr QF;
9 x 3pdr QF; 4 x 14in (356mm)
torpedo tubes.
Performance: 15·1kt (27·9km/h)
natural draught, 16·75kt (31km/h)
forced draught; coal 1,200 tons
(1,219 tonnes) max; radius 1,050nm
(1,943km) at 16·25kt (30km/h),
6,500nm (12,025km) at 10kt
(18·5km/h).
Crew: 577.

The design of the Trafalgar class
owed much to the insistence of the
First Sea Lord, Admiral Sir Arthur
Hood, on combining heavy main
armament with maximum protection.
Based on the *Dreadnought* of 1879,
these turret ships were the heaviest
British battleships then built and had
the extremely high percentage of

armour to displacement (exceeded
only in *Glatton*) of 33·5 per cent.

In order to permit heavier
protection amidships, the belt was
not full-length. It was 230ft (70·1m)
long and extended 5ft 6in (1·68m)
below water and 3ft (0·91m) above.
Maximum thickness was 20in
(508mm) amidships, tapering
through 16in (406mm) to 14in
(356mm) towards the ends and
terminating in a 16in (406mm)
bulkhead forward and a 14in
(356mm) bulkhead aft. Protection
before and abaft the belt was given
by a 3in (76mm) armour deck; this
extended over the octagonal citadel,
which had a maximum length of
193ft (58·83m) on the centreline.

Four 13·5in (343mm) BL were
carried in hydraulically-operated
twin turrets on the centre line, 14ft

(4·27m) above water with 260° arcs
of fire. In 1896-97, 6 x 6in (152mm)
QF replaced the 4·7in (119mm)
Armstrong QF. The secondary
battery in the superstructure was
protected by 5in-4in (127-102mm)
bulkheads; this accounted for most
of the increase in displacement over
the contemporary turret ship
Victoria.

Although their low freeboard of
11ft 9in (3·58m) made them wet ships
and forbade high speeds in any kind
of seaway, *Trafalgar* and *Nile* saw
most of their active service in the
Mediterranean, where this
disadvantage was less apparent.
Both were guardships in home
waters after 1897-98; *Trafalgar* was a
training ship for turret and TT crews
in 1907-09 and was sold for breaking
up in 1911.

Below: *Pelayo*, for many years the
Spanish Navy's most powerful unit,
with light rig, as completed.

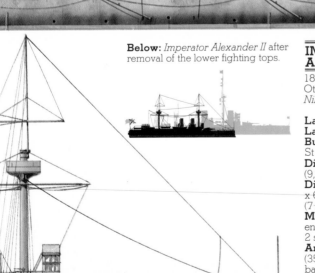

Below: *Imperator Alexander II* after
removal of the lower fighting tops.

IMPERATOR
ALEXANDER II

1891 *Russia*
Other ships in class: *Imperator
Nikolai I*

Laid down: November 1885.
Launched: 26 July 1887.
Builder: New Admiralty Yard,
St Petersburg.
Displacement: 9,500 tons
(9,652 tonnes) normal.
Dimensions: 333ft 6in (101·65m) wl
x 67ft (20·42m) x 25ft 10in
(7·87m) max.
Machinery: Vertical Compound
engines; 12 cylindrical boilers;
2 shafts; 8000 IHP.
Armour: Compound 14in-6in
(356-152mm) belt; 10in (254mm)
barbette; 6in-3in (152-76mm)
secondary armament; 10in (254mm)
conning tower; 2·5in (63mm) deck.
Armament: 2 x 12in (305mm);
4 x 9in (229mm); 8 x 6in
(152mm); 10 x 3pdr revolvers;
8 x 1pdr revolvers; 5 x 15in
(381mm) torpedo tubes.

Performance: 15·3kt (28·3km/h);
coal 1,200 tons (1,219 tonnes) max.
Crew: 611.

Alexander carried her 2 x 12in
(305mm) guns in a 10in (254mm)
armoured barbette protected by a 3in
(76mm) hood; her sister-ship had her
main armament in a turret. In both,
armament layout was designed to
maximise end-on fire power. The
secondary armament was at main
deck level—the 6in (152mm) guns
being unprotected—and a complete
belt, some 8ft (2·44m) wide,
supported a 2·5in (63mm) armoured
deck.

Nikolai was captured by Japan at
Tsushima, 1905, and renamed *Iki*.
Alexander was reconstructed in
1902-04: her torpedo tubes were
removed and a secondary
armament of 5 x 8in (203mm), 8 x 6in
(152mm) and 10 x 3pdr fitted.
Reboilered in 1905, she was taken
over by her crew during the October
Revolution and renamed *Sarıa
Svobodi* ('Freedom's Dawn') in 1917
and stricken in 1925.

HOCHE

1890 *France*

Laid down: June 1881.
Launched: September 1886.
Builder: Lorient Dockyard.
Displacement: 10,820 tons (10,993 tonnes).
Dimensions: 336ft 7in (102·59m) wl x 66ft 4in (20·22m) x 27ft 3in (8·31m) max.
Machinery: 4 Vertical Compound engines; 8 cylindrical boilers; 2 shafts; 12,000 IHP.
Armour: Compound 17·75in-10in (451-254mm) belt; 3·2in (81mm) steel upper belt; 16in (406mm) turrets and barbettes; 2·5in (63mm) conning tower; 9in (229mm) iron tubes.
Armament: 2 x 13·4in (340mm); 2 x 10·8in (274mm); 18 x 5·5in (140mm); 10 x 3pdr; 10 x 1pdr revolvers; 5 x 15in (381mm) torpedo tubes.
Performance: 16·5kt (30·5km/h); coal 740 tons (752 tonnes) max.
Crew: 611.

Unlike the Marceau class, which also had their main armament in a 'lozenge' layout, *Hoche* was built with both turrets and barbettes. Her 2 x 13·4in (340mm) were mounted in hydraulically-operated Canet turrets fore and aft on the centre line; the 2 x 10·8in (274mm) were in barbettes on either beam amidships, sponsoned out beyond the marked tumblehome of the sides to permit maximum fire on axial bearings.

In theory, the turret guns had arcs of fire of 260° and the barbette guns arcs of 180°; in fact, the problem of blast limited them to about 180° and 90° respectively. Seven 5·5in (140mm) were mounted on each broadside at the base of the large superstructure, with four more 5·5in (140mm), also unprotected, carried two decks above. A thick but narrow complete belt extended only 2ft (0·61m) above water, and even with a thin steel upper belt and a cellulose-filled cofferdam forward large areas were left unprotected.

Hoche shipped two heavy military masts and had twin funnels forward. In 1898-99 she was given new engines and boilers and her stability was improved by the reduction of the superstructure, main armament being unchanged. She was expended as a target in November 1913.

SIEGFRIED

1890 *Germany*
Other ships in class: *Beowulf, Frithjof, Heimdall, Hildebrand, Hagen, Odin, Ägir*

Laid down: 1888.
Launched: 10 August 1889.
Builder: Germaniawerft, Kiel.
Displacement: 3,691 tons (3,750 tonnes).
Dimensions: 259ft 2in (78·99m) oa x 49ft (14·9m) x 19ft (5·79m).
Machinery: Triple Expansion engines; 2 shafts; 5000 IHP.
Armour: 9·5in-7in (241-178mm) belt; 1·25in (32mm) deck; 8in (203mm) turrets.
Armament: 3 x 9·4in (240mm); 8 x 3·4in (88mm); 6 x 13·8in (350mm) torpedo tubes.
Performance: 14·5kt (26·8km/h).
Crew: 276.

These coast defence ships had their main armament in three shallow turrets, one aft and two forward; the latter set side by side in a structure extending across the full beam. A narrow (7·5ft; 2·29m) complete belt was fitted. All were disposed of in 1919.

Below: The small armoured coast-defence ship *Siegfried* in 1891.

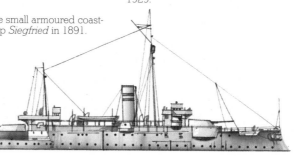

SPETSAI

1891 *Greece*
Other ships in class: *Psara, Hydra*

Laid down: 1887.
Launched: 26 October 1889.
Builder: Mediterranée, Granville.
Displacement: 4,808 tons (4,885 tonnes).
Dimensions: 334ft 8in (102m) pp x 51ft 10in (15·8m) x 18ft (5·49m) mean.
Machinery: 2 shafts; 6700 IHP.
Armour: Creusot/compound 12in-4in (305-102mm) belt; 14in-12in (356-305mm) battery; 12in (305mm) barbette.
Armament: 3 x 10·8in (274mm); 5 x 5·9in (150mm); 4 x 3·4in (86mm); 14 smaller; 3 x 14in (356mm) torpedo tubes.
Performance: 17kt (31·45km/h); coal 690 tons (701 tonnes) max.
Crew: 440.

Four 5·9in (150mm) were on the lower deck of a two-deck battery forward, with 2 x 10·8in (274mm), 34-cal, and 1 x 5·9in (150mm) above. One 10·8in (274mm), 28-cal, was in a barbette aft. *Spetsai* was discarded in 1929.

Below: *Spetsai* as completed. Her final rig was two military masts.

Below: *Marceau* as completed. The 'lozenge' disposition of the main armament gave good all-round fire.

Below: As completed, *Hoche* carried more than 3,600 tons (3,657 tonnes) of armour. The rig was later much reduced to improve stability.

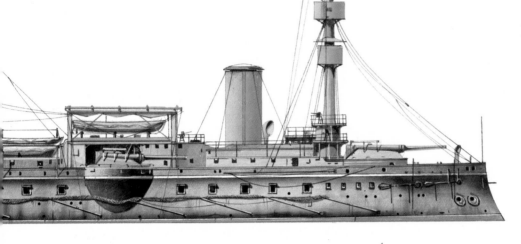

MARCEAU

1891 *France*
Other ships in class: *Magenta,
Neptune*

Laid down: 1881.
Launched: May 1887.
Builder: La Seyne.
Displacement: 10,558 tons
(10,727 tonnes).
Dimensions: 323ft 6in (98.6m) pp x
65ft 10in (20.07m) x 27ft 6in (8.38m).
Machinery: Vertical Compound
engines; 8 cylindrical boilers; 2 shafts;
11,000 IHP.

Armour: Compound 18in-9in
(457-229mm) belt; 16in (406mm)
barbettes; 9in-8in (229-203mm)
tubes; 2.5in (63mm) shields;
6in-4.7in (152-119mm) conning
tower.
Armament: 4 x 13.4in (340mm);
17 x 5.5in (140mm); 20 smaller;
3 x 15in (381mm) torpedo tubes.
Performance: 16kt (20.6km/h);
coal 740 tons (752 tonnes) max.
Crew: 643.

Marceau was a little smaller than
Magenta and *Neptune,* which had
much larger superstructures and
differed also in minor details of
protection and armament. Ten years
on the stocks, these barbette ships
were out-dated before entering
service.

Main armament was in 'lozenge'
layout: four hydraulically-trained
13.4in (340mm) were single-
mounted in barbettes forward and aft
on the centreline and on either beam
amidships, where they were
sponsoned out over the marked
tumblehome to the full beam. They
had arcs of fire of 250° at bow and
stern and 180° from the axial line
amidships. Of the 17 x 5.5in (140mm),
BL converted to QF, one fired
forward from the forecastle and eight
were on either broadside in unprotected positions at main deck level.

A complete belt extended from
c5.5ft (1.68m) below the waterline,
where it tapered to 14in (356mm)
thickness, to c2ft (0.61m) above,
where it attained maximum thickness
of 18in (457mm), reducing to
10in-9in (254-229mm) at the ends. A
compound armour deck of 3.6in
(91mm) maximum thickness lay
above the belt, with a cellulose-filled
cofferdam forward.

Ram-bowed and with high freeboard, *Marceau* shipped two military
masts. Reboilered during partial
rebuilding in 1901-03, she was taken
out of active service before World
War 1 and was scrapped in 1922.

Below: *Dvienadsat Apostolov* as
seen in 1897, with raised funnels,
reduced rig and hoods fitted over
her big guns fore and aft.

DVIENADSAT APOSTOLOV

1892 *Russia*

Laid down: February 1888.
Launched: September 1890.
Builder: Nicolaiev Dockyard.
Displacement: 8,709 tons
(8,848 tonnes).
Dimensions: 342ft (104.24m) oa x
60ft (18.29m) x 27ft 6in (8.38m) max.
Machinery: Vertical Triple
Expansion engines; 8 cylindrical
boilers; 2 shafts; 8750 IHP.
Armour: Compound 14in-6in
(356-152mm) belt; 12in-10in
(305-254mm) barbettes; 5in (127mm)
steel battery; 8in (203mm) steel
conning tower.
Armament: 4 x 12in (305mm);
4 x 6in (152mm); 26 smaller;
6 x 15in (381mm) torpedo tubes.
Performance: 15.7kt (29km/h);
coal 800 tons (813 tonnes) max.
Crew: 599.

Built for the Black Sea Fleet,
Dvienadsat Apostolov ('Twelve
Apostles') had twin-mounted
steam-trained 12in (305mm) in
barbettes fore and aft on the upper
deck; her 4 x 6in (152mm) were at
the corners of the main deck battery
amidships. An armour deck with
maximum 2.5in (63mm) thickness at
the ends lay flat on the 5.5ft (1.68m)
wide belt, which had an upper strake
220ft (67m) long and terminated in
12in-9in (305-229mm) bulkheads.
She was stricken in 1911.

ROYAL SOVEREIGN

1892 UK

Other ships in class: *Empress of India (ex-Renown), Ramillies, Repulse, Resolution, Revenge, Royal Oak, Hood*

Laid down: 30 September 1889.
Launched (undocked):
26 February 1891.
Builder: Portsmouth Dockyard.
Displacement: 14,150 tons (14,376 tonnes) load; 15,580 tons (15,829 tonnes) deep load.
Dimensions: 410ft 6in (125·12m) oa x 75ft (22·86m) x 27ft 6in (8·38m) mean.
Machinery: 3-cylinder Triple Expansion engines; 8 cylindrical boilers; 2 shafts; 9000 IHP natural draught, 11,000 IHP forced draught.
Armour: Compound and Harvey steel 18in-14in (457-356mm) belt; 16in-14in (406-356mm) bulkheads; 5in (127mm) upper belt; 17in-11in (432-279mm) barbettes; 6in (152mm) casemates; 3in-2·5in (76-63mm) decks; 14in (356mm) conning tower.
Armament: 4 x 13·5in (343mm) BL; 10 x 6in (152mm) QF; 16 x 6pdr QF; 12 x 3pdr QF; 7 x 18in (457mm) torpedo tubes.
Performance: 15·5kt (28·68km/h) natural draught, 16·5kt (30.5km/h)

forced draught; coal 1,490 tons (1,514 tonnes) max; radius 2,780nm (5,143km) at 14kt (25·9km/h), 4,720nm (8,732km) at 10kt (18·5km/h).
Crew: 712.

The Naval Defence Act of 1889 enshrined the doctrine that the strength of the Royal Navy should at least equal that of any two other nations. In providing for the seven first class battleships of the Royal Sovereign class—the first 'pre-dreadnoughts'—and their half-sister *Hood,* it also firmly established the principle that battleships should be built in large classes in order to form homogeneous squadrons.

Seeking to achieve both improved seakeeping qualities and increased fighting efficiency over the earlier Trafalgar and Admiral classes, Sir William White, Director of Naval Construction, determined that the Royal Sovereigns should be barbette ships with high freeboard. Improving the design of the Admirals, White achieved freeboard of 18ft (5·49m) by adding a complete deck, while giving the sides marked tumblehome to improve stability and reduce weight in the upper structure. It may also have reflected White's admiration for French hull design.

In deference to the strongly held

views of the First Sea Lord, Admiral Sir Arthur Hood, the eighth battleship provided under the Act, *Hood,* was built as a turret ship. Otherwise near-identical, *Hood* lacked the high freeboard of her half-sisters, because of the increased topweight imposed by her turrets, and was much inferior to them as a seaboat and fighting unit.

The main (compound armour) belt was 250ft (76·2m) long and had a maximum thickness of 18in (457mm), reducing through 16in (406mm) to 14in (346mm) at the ends. It extended 5ft (1·52m) below water and 3ft 6in (1·07m) above and was closed by transverse bulkheads of 16in (406mm) thickness forward and 14in (356mm) aft. Above the belt lay a 3in (76mm) armour deck, and fore and aft a 2·5in (63mm) armour deck curved down to the ends. Protection was extended to a height of *c*9ft 6in (2·9m) above water by an upper belt of 5in (127mm) Harvey steel (in *Royal Sovereign;* some units of the class had nickel-steel, here used by the Royal Navy for the first time) terminating in 3in (76mm) bulkheads which extended to the walls of the barbettes.

Only the upper parts of the pear-shaped barbettes, each housing 2 x 13·5in (343mm) BL, were visible above the weather deck,

where the big guns were carried 23 (7m) above water with arcs of fire o 240°. Walls of 17in (432mm) armou thinning to 11in (279mm) inboard the upper belt, ran down to the ma belt to guard against hits beneath th barbettes. Six 6in (152mm) QF we in shielded positions on the upper deck (they were given 5in, 127mm, casemates, as White had wished, ir 1902-04) and 4 x 6in (152mm) QF main deck casemates, too near the waterline to be worked efficiently in seaway.

Handsome ships, with twin funne amidships—and good seaboats afte the fitting of bilge keels corrected excessive roll—the Royal Sovereigr served in the Channel and Mediterranean Fleets until 1902 an thereafter in home waters. By Worl War I, all save *Revenge* had been so for breaking up (*Royal Sovereign* i October 1913) or otherwise expended.

Revenge, a gunnery training ship from 1906, was used to bombard German positions on the Belgian coast early in 1915 and, renamed *Redoubtable* in that year, was the fir warship to go into action fitted with external bulges as a protection against torpedoes. She was a tende to the *Victory* in 1918 and was sold November 1919 and scrapped at Appledore.

Left: *Royal Sovereign* in 1904, in standard grey finish with identification bands on her funnel. The high freeboard is particularly noteworthy. Only *Revenge* of this class remained in service into World War I.

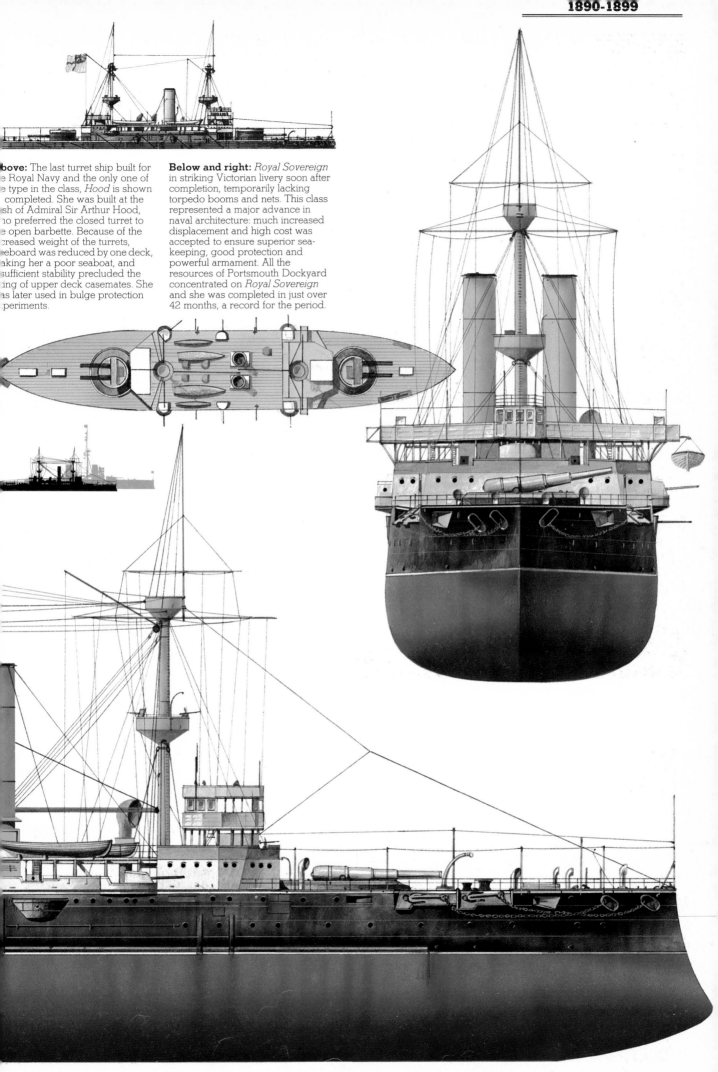

Above: The last turret ship built for the Royal Navy and the only one of the type in the class, *Hood* is shown completed. She was built at the wish of Admiral Sir Arthur Hood, who preferred the closed turret to the open barbette. Because of the increased weight of the turrets, freeboard was reduced by one deck, making her a poor seaboat, and insufficient stability precluded the fitting of upper deck casemates. She was later used in bulge protection experiments.

Below and right: *Royal Sovereign* in striking Victorian livery soon after completion, temporarily lacking torpedo booms and nets. This class represented a major advance in naval architecture: much increased displacement and high cost was accepted to ensure superior sea-keeping, good protection and powerful armament. All the resources of Portsmouth Dockyard concentrated on *Royal Sovereign* and she was completed in just over 42 months, a record for the period.

Below: *Hamidieh*, 1892; original rig.

HAMIDIEH

1892 *Turkey*

Laid down: 1874.
Launched: 1885.
Builder: Constantinople.
Displacement: 6,594 tons
(6,700 tonnes) normal.
Dimensions: 292ft (89m)
pp x 55ft 9in (16·99m) x 24ft 10in
(7·57m) max.
Machinery: Single Expansion
engines, 1 shaft; 6800 IHP.
Armour: Iron 9in (229mm) belt;
5in (127mm) ends; 7in (178mm)
battery and conning tower.
Armament: 4 x 9in (229mm) ML;
10 x 5·9in (150mm) BL; 6 x 37mm;
2 x 14in (356mm) torpedo tubes.
Performance: 13kt (24km/h);
coal 600 tons (610 tonnes) plus.
Crew: *c* 440.

Eighteen years building, *Hamidieh*
was completed with sub-standard
armour and machinery originally
intended for a wooden frigate of
1866. Her big guns were
single-mounted on the upper deck.
Judged unworthy of reconstruction
in 1903, she was stricken *c*1911.

Below: *Gangut* in 1897, just before
her loss.

GANGUT

1893 *Russia*

Laid down: 1889.
Launched: October 1890.
Builder: New Admiralty Yard,
St Petersburg.
Displacement: 6,590 tons
(6,695 tonnes).
Dimensions: 289ft 9in (88·72m) wl
x 62ft (18·9m) x 21ft (6·4m) max.
Machinery: Vertical Triple
Expansion engines, 8 cylindrical
boilers; 2 shafts; 6000 IHP.
Armour: Compound 16in-10in
(406-254mm) belt; 9in-7in
(229-178mm) barbette; 5in (127mm)
battery.
Armament: 1 x 12in (305mm);
4 x 9in (229mm); 4 x 6in (152mm);
20 smaller; 6 x 15in (381mm).
Performance: 14·7kt (27·2km/h);
coal 650 tons (660 tonnes) max.
Crew: 521.

A reduced *Imperator Alexander II*,
Gangut had a single 12in (305mm) in
an upper-deck barbette forward and
4 x 9in (229mm) in the battery and 4 x
6in (152mm) unprotected at main
deck level. She foundered in 1897.

CAPITAN PRAT

1893 *Chile*

Laid down: 1888.
Launched: 20 December 1890.
Builder: La Seyne.
Displacement: 6,901 tons
(7,011 tonnes).
Dimensions: 328ft (99·97m) pp x
60ft 8in (18·49m) x 22ft 10in (6·96m).
Machinery: Horizontal Triple
Expansion, 2 shafts; 12,000 IHP.
Armour: Creusot steel 11·8in-7·8in
(300-198mm) belt; 10·8in-8in
(274-203mm) barbettes.
Armament: 4 x 9·4in (239mm);
8 x 4·7in (119mm); 20 smaller;
4 x 18in (457mm) torpedo tubes.
Performance: 18·3kt (33·9km/h);
coal 1,100 tons (1,118 tonnes) max.
Crew: 480.

French-built, *Capitan Prat* had her
big guns single-mounted in 'lozenge'
layout and her 4·7in (119mm)
twin-mounted in 2in (51mm)
armoured turrets on the upper deck.
The Chilean Navy's most powerful
ship until after World War I, she was
stricken in the mid-1930s.

RE UMBERTO

1893 *Italy*
Other ships in class: *Sicilia,
Sardegna*

Laid down: 10 July 1884.
Launched: 17 October 1888.
Builder: Castellammare Navy Yard.
Displacement: 15,454 tons
(15,701 tonnes) full load.
Dimensions: 418ft 7½in (127·6m)
oa x 76ft 10½in (23·43m) x
30ft 6in (9·3m).
Machinery: 2-cylinder Vertical
Compound engines; 18 cylindrical
boilers; 2 shafts; 19,500 IHP.
Armour: Schneider steel 4in
(102mm) side; 3in (76mm) deck;
4in (102mm) turrets; 13·75in
(349mm) barbettes; 4in (102mm)
battery; 2in (51mm) secondary
armament shields; 11·8in (300mm)
conning tower.
Armament: 4 x 13·5in (343mm);
8 x 6in (152mm); 16 x 4·7in
(119mm); 16 x 6pdr/57mm;
10 x 37mm; 5 x 17·7in (450mm)
above-water torpedo tubes.
Performance: 18·5kt (34·23km/h);
endurance 4,000-6,000nm
(7,400-11,100km) at 10kt (18·5km/h).
Crew: 733.

These fast and powerful ships were
designed by Benedetto Brin. After
the authorization of *Re Umberto* and
Sicilia, Brin was reappointed Ministe

Below: Compact and powerful
Capitan Prat, 1893, with original
light rig.

Right: *Re Umberto*, 1894. Her
sisters had slightly different funnels

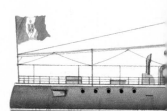

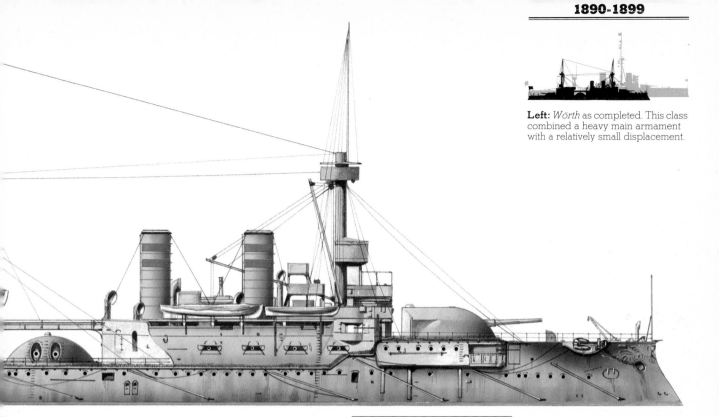

Left: *Wörth* as completed. This class combined a heavy main armament with a relatively small displacement.

Marine and was able to add to the class *Sardegna,* the first Italian warship to have 3-cylinder triple expansion machinery and the new Marconi W/T equipment.

Although he followed the pattern of protection established in *Italia,* Brin acknowledged the power of the newer QF guns and HE shells by fitting 4in (102mm) side armour in an amidships belt some 250ft (76·2m) long, extending from the level of the main (76mm) armour deck, c3ft (·91m) below the waterline, to the main deck. Deep coal bunkers lay behind the belt.

The big guns had Armstrong centre pivot mountings. From the magazine and ammunition room, a fixed trunk ran up to a ready ammunition store within the circular barbette, from which an all-round loading station in the barbette hood was supplied. This innovation, giving much improved rate of fire, was

taken up by the Royal Navy in 1898 in the *Caesar* and *Illustrious* of the Majestic class.

Re Umberto's 4 x 13·5in (343mm) guns were twin-mounted in 13·75in-4in (349-102mm) armoured barbette turrets on the centre line fore and aft. Eight 6in (152mm) guns were carried behind 2in (51mm) shields above the battery, which housed 12 x 4·7in (119mm), the remaining 4·7in (119mm) being mounted abreast the funnels on the superstructure.

Stricken in May 1914, *Re Umberto* was a depot ship until restored to the Navy list as a floating battery for harbour defence on 9 December 1915. In October 1918 she was armed with 8 x 3in (76mm) guns in order to spearhead an assault by torpedo boats on the Austro-Hungarian base at Pola. The war's end frustrated this plan and she was stricken once more in 1920.

WÖRTH

1893 Germany
Other ships in class: *Brandenburg, Kurfürst Friedrich Wilhelm, Weissenburg*

Laid down: 1890.
Launched: 6 August 1892.
Builder: Germaniawerft, Kiel.
Displacement: 10,501 tons (10,669 tonnes).
Dimensions: 379ft 7in (115·7m) oa x 64ft (19·5m) x 26ft (7·9m) max.
Machinery: Vertical Triple Expansion; 2 shafts; 10,200 IHP.
Armour: 16in-12in (406-305mm) belt; 12in (305mm) barbettes; 5in (127mm) turrets.
Armament: 6 x 11in (280mm); 6 x 4·1in (105mm); 8 x 3·4in (88mm); 12 MG; 6 x 17·7in (450mm) torpedo tubes.
Performance: 16·5kt (30·5km/h); coal 1,050 tons (1,067 tonnes) max; range 4,500nm (8,325km) at 10kt (18·5km/h).
Crew: 568.

Although their armament layout was not wholly satisfactory, the Brandenburg class, Germany's first large ocean-going battleships, represented a significant step towards the 'all big gun' dreadnought battleship of the early 20th century. The main armament of 6 x 11in (280mm) guns,

twin-mounted in three centre line barbettes, was the largest single-calibre main armament then mounted in any armoured ship.

The big guns were, however, of different lengths: those in the fore and aft mountings were 40-cal and those in the midships mounting were 35-cal, the shorter guns being intended to facilitate training on either beam. Although this arrangement permitted powerful all-round fire — the fore and aft mountings had arcs of fire of 250°; the midships guns arcs of c90° on either side — the guns in the midships barbette were carried so close to the deck that blast damage resulted from firing.

The armament layout also dictated an inadequate secondary armament of 3 x 4·1in (105mm) — later 4 x 4·1in (105mm) — in 5in (127mm) armoured casemates on either beam. A complete belt extended 3ft 9in (1·14m) below and 2ft 9in (0·84m) above the waterline.

The Brandenburgs were re-boilered and given increased bunker capacity in 1901-04. In 1910, *Kurfürst Friedrich Wilhelm* and *Weissenburg* were sold to Turkey and renamed *Heireddin Barbarossa* and *Torgud Reis* respectively. *Wörth* was relegated to coast defence by 1915, disarmed to become a barracks ship at Danzig in 1916-18, and stricken and subsequently broken up in 1919.

CENTURION

1894 *UK*
Other ships in class: *Barfleur*

Laid down: 30 March 1890.
Launched: 3 August 1892.
Builder: Portsmouth Dockyard.
Displacement: 10,500 tons
(10,668 tonnes) load.
Dimensions: 360ft (109·73m) pp
x 70ft (21·34m) x 25ft 6in
(7·77m) mean.
Machinery: Greenock Foundry
3-cylinder Triple Expansion engines;
8 cylindrical boilers; 2 shafts;
9000 IHP natural draught,
13,000 IHP forced draught.
Armour: 12in-9in (305-229mm)
compound main belt; 8in (203mm)
compound bulkheads; 4in (102mm)
Harvey nickel steel upper belt;
9in-5in (229-127mm) compound
barbettes; 6in (152mm) Harvey
nickel steel gun houses; 6in
(152mm) Harvey nickel steel
casemates; 2·5in-2in (63-51mm)
nickel steel decks; 12in (305mm)
compound conning tower.
Armament: 4 x 10in (254mm) BL;
10 x 4·7in (119mm) QF;
7 x 18in (457mm) torpedo tubes.
Performance: 17kt (31·45km/h)
natural draught, 18·5kt (34·2km/h)
forced draught; coal 1,125 tons

(1,143 tonnes) max; radius c6,000nm
(11,100km) at 10kt (18·5km/h).
Crew: 620.

The second class battleships
Centurion and *Barfleur* were fast,
handy, comparatively lightly armed
and armoured vessels intended
mainly to outweigh the large Russian
armoured cruisers likely to be
encountered in the Far East. Shallow
draught enabled them to navigate
Chinese rivers.

Armour accounted for less than 25
per cent of displacement. The main
belt, 200ft (60·96m) long, extended
2ft 6in (0·76m) above water and 5ft
(1·52m) below, terminating in 8in
(203mm) bulkheads. For the last time
in British battleships, the main
armour deck lay flat on the belt. The
Whitworth-designed circular
barbettes housing twin-mounted
10in (254mm) BL were given added
protection by 6in (152mm) hoods, or
gun houses, with open backs.

During refitting in 1901-04, 10 x
6in (152mm) guns in 5in (127mm)
armoured casemates replaced the
original secondary armament. To
make compensatory reduction in
weight elsewhere, the five
above-water torpedo tubes and other
fittings were removed and a reduced
foremast shipped. *Centurion*
completed her active service on the
China station in 1905 and was sold in
1910. Like *Centurion*, *Barfleur*
underwent reconstruction in 1902-04.
She was commissioned in reserve
in 1905 and sold in 1912.

Below: *Centurion* as completed, 1894.

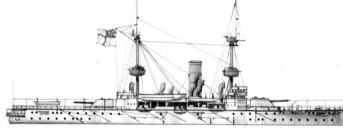

Below: *Admiral
Ushakov*, late 1890s.

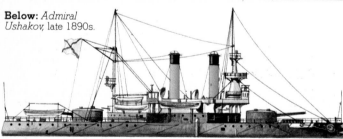

ADMIRAL USHAKOV

1895 *Russia*
Other ships in class: *Admiral
Seniavin, General Admiral Graf
Apraksin*

Laid down: June 1892.
Launched: November 1893.
Builder: New Admiralty Yard,
St Petersburg.
Displacement: 4,126 tons
(4,192 tonnes) designed.
Dimensions: 286ft 6in (87·33m) oa
x 52ft (15·85m) x 19ft 6in
(5·94m) max.
Machinery: Vertical Triple
Expansion engines; 4 cylindrical
boilers; 2 shafts; 5750 IHP.
Armour: Harvey 10in-4in

(254-102mm) belt; 8in (203mm)
turrets; 3in (76mm) deck;
8in (203mm) conning tower.
Armament: 4 x 10in (254mm);
4 x 4·7in (119mm); 22 smaller; 4 x 15in
(381mm) torpedo tubes.
Performance: 16kt (29·6km/h);
coal 450 tons (457 tonnes) max.
Crew: 404.

A Baltic coast defence ship, *Admiral
Ushakov* had her main armament
twin-mounted in fore and aft turrets,
with 4 x 4·7in (119mm) in an
unprotected battery amidships. A 3in
(76mm) armoured deck lay flat on
the 170ft (51·8m) long belt.

The Ushakovs formed part of
Vice-Admiral Rozhdestvensky's
squadron that sailed round the world
in October 1904-May 1905 to defeat
at Tsushima, where *Seniavin* and
Apraksin were taken. Out-ranged by
the 8in (203mm) guns of the IJN
cruisers *Iwate* and *Yakumo*, *Ushakov*
fought to the last; she was scuttled
on the evening of 28 May 1905.

JEMMAPES

1894 *France*
Other ships in class: *Valmy,
Amiral Tréhouart, Bouvines*

Laid down: 1890.
Launched: April 1892.
Builder: Société de la Loire.
Displacement: 6,476 tons
(6,580 tonnes).

Dimensions: 283ft 9in (86·49m) p
x 57ft 4in (17·47m) x 23ft 2in
(7·06m) max.
Machinery: Horizontal Triple
Expansion engines; 16 Lagrafel
d'Allest boilers; 2 shafts; 9000 IHP.
Armour: Nickel steel and steel
18in-10in (457-254mm) belt; 18in
(457mm) turrets; 16in (406mm)
bases; 4in (102mm) conning tower.
Armament: 2 x 13·4in (340mm);
4 x 3·9in (99mm) QF;
4 x 3pdr; 10 x 1pdr revolvers;
2 x 18in (457mm) torpedo tubes.
Performance: 16·7kt (30·9km/h);
radius 650nm (1,200km) at 16kt.
Crew: 313.

Above: The breastwork monitor
Tonnerre in 1880. The narrow
superstructure allowed the widely
spaced turret guns to fire aft.

Below: Fast and handy, the design
of *Jemmapes* closely approached
that of an ocean-going battleship.

Above: One of the early designs for
Texas. In another project, the turrets
were offset to the edge of the hull,
but still at either end of the ship. A
third design much resembled the
British *Victoria*.

Below: *Texas* as completed. The
small bridge structures were soon
removed.

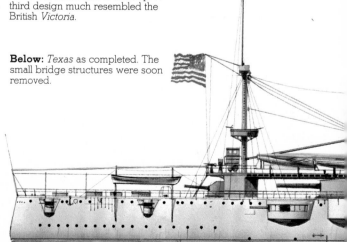

ench naval policy differed from that
Britain in that France favoured a
ery powerful coast defence force to
pport its ocean-going warships.
ench doctrine envisaged this
econd force' coming into action
ter both the French and enemy
ain battle fleets had sustained
sses in a major engagement.
In accordance with this policy,
rance laid down the armoured ram
ureau in 1863, the four Cerbère
ass rams in 1865, and the two much
rger monitors of the Tonnerre
ass and the two Tempête monitors
1873-75. These were followed by
e barbette ship Tonnant, laid down

in 1875, the higher-freeboard
Furieux of 1878, and the eight
armoured gunboats of the Fusée and
Achéron classes in 1882-89. In 1890
France laid down Jemmapes, her
sister-ship Valmy, and the similar
coast defence battleships Admiral
Tréhouart and Bouvines. At that time,
Britain's latest additions to her coast
defence force were the four Cyclops
class monitors, equivalent to the
Tonnerres and Tempêtes, laid down
in 1870.
De Bussy's design for the
Jemmapes group was based on that
of Furieux. The four ships differed
mainly in that Jemmapes and Valmy

were low-freeboard (c11ft, 3·35m)
ships while Admiral Tréhouart and
Bouvines had their hulls raised
forward, with forecastle decks
running as far as the mainmast. Since
this threatened an undesirable
increase in displacement, the main
armament of Tréhouart and Bouvines
was reduced to 2 x 12in (305mm)
and the belt was a little thinner aft as
compensating measures.
Jemmapes carried 2 x 13·4in
(340mm) BL single-mounted in fore
and aft turrets with c250° arcs of fire,
with 4 x 3·9in (99mm) QF behind 3in
(76mm) steel shields in the
superstructure. Four 3pdr guns

were carried in the lower top of the
military foremast. The full-length belt
was 7ft (2·13m) deep and 10in
(254mm) thick along the entire lower
edge. It had a maximum thickness of
18in (457mm) amidships, tapering to
17in (432mm) aft and 12in (305mm)
forward. A heavy, curved, 4in-2·8in
(102-71mm) armour deck was fitted,
but protection above this was hardly
adequate.
Jemmapes was hulked and Valmy
stricken in 1911. Tréhouart and
Bouvines both ended their service as
submarine depot ships and were
stricken in 1922 and 1920
respectively.

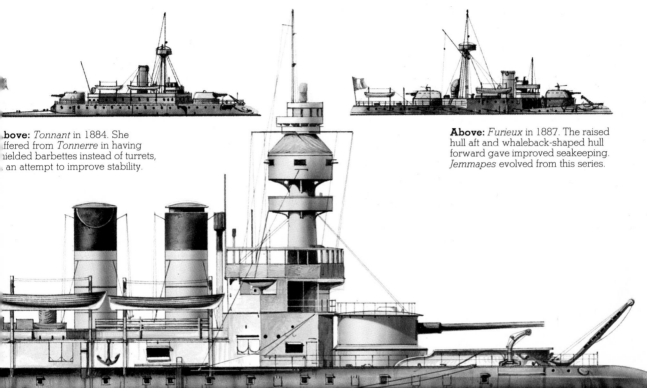

Above: Tonnant in 1884. She
ffered from Tonnerre in having
nielded barbettes instead of turrets,
an attempt to improve stability.

Above: Furieux in 1887. The raised
hull aft and whaleback-shaped hull
forward gave improved seakeeping.
Jemmapes evolved from this series.

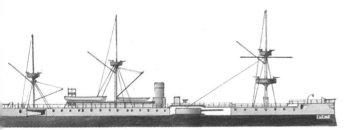

Above: Around 1887, when the US
Navy Department sought to make up
ground lost through Congressional
neglect and looked abroad for
designs, this interesting project was
put forward by Sir Edward Reed.

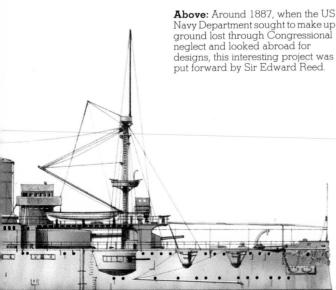

TEXAS

1895 USA

Laid down: 1 June 1889.
Launched: 28 June 1892.
Builder: Norfolk Navy Yard.
Displacement: 6,135 tons
(6,233 tonnes) normal; 6,665 tons
(6,722 tonnes) full load.
Dimensions: 308ft 10in (94·13m) oa
x 64ft 1in (19·53m) x 22ft 6in
(6·86m) mean.
Machinery: Vertical Triple
Expansion engines; 4 cylindrical
boilers; 2 shafts; 8,610 IHP.
Armour: Harvey and nickel steel
12in-6in (305-152mm) belt; 12in
(305mm) redoubt; 12in (305mm)
turrets; 6in (152mm) ammunition
hoists; 2in-3in (51mm-76mm) deck.
Armament: 2 x 12in (305mm);
6 x 6in (152mm); 12 x 6pdr;
6 x 1pdr; 4 x 14in (356mm)
torpedo tubes.
Performance: 17·8kt (32·9km/h);
coal 850 tons (864 tonnes) max.
Crew: 392 (1896); 508 (1910).

Construction of the second class
battleships Texas and Maine was
authorized in 1886. Designed by the
English naval architect William John,

Texas was not wholly satisfactory,
since John was required to combine
heavy armament, high speed and
good seakeeping qualities on a
limited displacement. After initial
trials, the ship's hull had to be
strengthened.
The Harvey armour belt was only
118ft (35·7m) long and 7ft (2·13m)
deep, extending 3ft (0·91m) above
water and terminating in 6in
(152mm) bulkheads. A 2in (51mm)
armour deck lay flat above the belt,
sloping down at the ends to a
maximum 3in (76mm). The 2 x 12in
(305mm) guns were single-mounted
in hydraulically operated turrets set
en échelon amidships on the upper
deck, atop a 12in (305mm) armoured
redoubt. The redoubt protected the
turret machinery, but the sides
between the redoubt and belt were
unprotected. Four 6in (152mm) guns
were in sponsoned casemates at
main deck level, two on either beam,
and two more fore and aft on the
upper deck.
In the Spanish-American War of
1898, Texas shared in the reduction
of shore installations in Cuba and in
the pursuit and destruction of
Admiral Cervera's squadron in the
Battle of Santiago, 3 July 1898. By
1904 her funnel had been raised, her
torpedo tubes removed, and armour
protection to the turret hoists
improved. Decommissioned in
February 1911, she was renamed
San Marcos and expended as a
target in 1911-1912.

MAINE

1895 USA

Laid down: 17 October 1888.
Launched: 18 November 1890.
Builder: New York Navy Yard.
Displacement: 6,682 tons
(6,789 tonnes) normal; 7,180 tons
(7,295 tonnes) full load.
Dimensions: 318ft (96·93m) wl
x 57ft (17·37m) x 21ft 6in
(6·55m) mean.
Machinery: Vertical Triple
Expansion engines; 8 single-ended
Scotch boilers; 2 shafts; 9,293 IHP.
Armour: Harvey and nickel steel
12in-7in (305-178mm) belt; 12in-10in
(305-254mm) barbettes; 8in
(203mm) turrets; 3in-2in (76-51mm)
deck; 10in (254mm) conning tower.
Armament: 4 x 10in (254mm);
6 x 6in (152mm); 7 x 6pdr;
8 x 1pdr; 4 Gatling; 4 x 18in (457mm)
torpedo tubes.
Performance: 16·45kt (30·4km/h);
coal 896 tons (910 tonnes) max.
Crew: 374.

In a series of Congressional debates
beginning in 1883 it was pointed out
that the United States stood as low as
20th in the list of the world's naval
powers and that new ships were
urgently needed to replace the
obsolete veterans of the Civil War
period. However, since it was not
then intended to attempt to raise the
USA to the status of a major naval
power, only two sea-going armoured

ships—*Texas* and *Maine*, originally
described as armoured cruisers but
redesignated second-class battleships
before they commissioned—were
among the vessels authorized under
the Act of 3 August 1886.

Both designs were influenced by
the need to counter such powerful
Latin American units as Brazil's
British-built battleships *Riachuelo*
and *Aquidaban*. The US Navy
Department's design for *Maine*, in
particular, strongly resembled an
enlarged *Riachuelo,* with a near
identical armament layout. Initial
plans to give her three masts and a
rig for two-thirds full sail power were
abandoned during building and she
was completed with two military
masts and no sails.

The main armament of 4 x 10in
(254mm), 30-cal BLR was
twin-mounted in 8in (203mm)
armoured, hydraulically-operated
turrets set en échelon on the main
deck amidships, the forward turret to
starboard and the after turret to port.
The individual barbettes protecting
the turrets were sponsoned out over
the ship's sides to facilitate direct fore
and aft fire, since end-on fire and the
ram were still considered to be the
most powerful weapons.

Although breaks in the centre line
superstructure theoretically allowed
both turrets to fire on either beam, in
practice the danger of blast damage
to the superstructure limited this
capability. Even end-on fire was in
some degree inhibited for the same

Above: *Maine* in 1896 at Bar Harbor
in the state of Maine. She is
seen here shortly after completion.
The way in which the barbette
protecting the port turret is
sponsoned out to facilitate fore
and aft fire is evident; as are
the two 6in (152mm) BLRs in the
stern casemates.

Below: *Maine* in 1898, shortly
before her loss. A major advance in
US naval development, she was
planned as an armoured cruiser similar
to the Brazilian turret ship *Riachuelo*
but was finally rated a 2nd class
battleship. The turret guns could fire
end-on past the narrow superstructure.

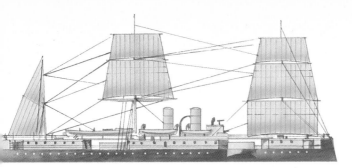

eason, and *Texas* and *Maine* were to
e the only US warships with this
rmament layout. Six 6in (152mm),
0-cal BLR were carried on the main
eck, two amidships and two each in
asemates at bow and stern.

The main belt, of 12in (305mm)
ickel steel tapering to 7in (178mm)
t the lower edge, was 180ft
54·86m) long and extended 3ft
0·91m) above the waterline and 4ft
1·22m) below, terminating in a 6in
152mm) bulkhead forward. The
rmour deck was of 2in (51mm)
nickness flat over the belt and
orward to the bow, where it
einforced the ram, and 3in-2in
76-51mm) aft, where it sloped down
o take the place of an after bulkhead
nd to protect the shafts and steering
ear.

On 25 January 1898, at a time of
onsiderable tension between the
JSA and Spain, *Maine* arrived in the
arbour of Havana, Cuba—then a
panish possession and a centre of

Above: It was originally intended to
provide the *Maine* with a large
spread of canvas, as seen here, to
give a good cruising range, but this
extensive rig was discarded during
her construction.

protest against Spanish rule—on a
goodwill visit. On the evening of 15
February, a massive explosion sank
the battleship with the loss of 260
men out of a 355-strong crew. Within
five weeks an American Court of
Inquiry announced that the
explosion of a mine beneath the ship
had detonated the forward
magazine. The implication was
obvious, and on 21 April America
declared war on Spain.

There is still controversy regarding
the sinking of *Maine*. It is now
thought likely that the magazine
explosion was caused internally,
possibly by a spontaneous fire in
bituminous coal stored in an adjacent
bunker.

Above: *Indiana* around 1910, after a refit in which a cage mast was added for gunnery spotting and to provide a searchlight platform. Modernization of these elderly units was, however, kept to a minimum.

Above: One of the preliminary designs for the US Navy's first major group of armoured warships for nearly 30 years — a development of the coast defence monitor *Monterey,* with mixed armament of 12in (305mm) guns in the fore turret and 10in (254mm) guns aft. No allowance is yet made for an 8in (203mm) intermediate battery.

Below: *Oregon,* 1896. The plan view particularly illustrates the Indianas' compact design, with a heavy weight of ordnance built into the relatively small displacement stipulated by Congress. Good all-round fire was achieved, although at certain angles the guns' blast effect on each other and on the superstructure was considerable.

INDIANA (BB-1)

1895 USA
Other ships in class:
Massachusetts (BB-2), *Oregon* ((BB-3)

Laid down: 7 May 1891.
Launched: 28 February 1893.
Builder: Cramp, Philadelphia, Pa.
Displacement: 10,288 tons (10,453 tonnes) normal; 11,528 tons (11,712 tonnes) full load.
Dimensions: 350ft 11in (106·96m) oa x 69ft 3in (21·1m) x 24ft (7·32m) mean.
Machinery: Vertical Triple Expansion engines; 4 double-ended Scotch boilers; 2 shafts; 9738 IHP.
Armour: Harvey and nickel steel 18in-8·5in (457-216mm) belt; 17in (432mm) barbettes; 15in (381mm) turrets; 8in-5in (203-127mm) secondary barbettes and turrets; 2·75in-3in (70-76mm) deck; 10in (254mm) conning tower.
Armament: 4 x 13in (330mm); 8 x 8in (203mm); 4 x 6in (152mm); 20 x 6pdr; 6 x 1pdr; 6 x 18in (457mm) torpedo tubes.
Performance: 15kt (27·75km/h); coal 1,597 tons (1,623 tonnes) max; radius 3,720nm (6,882km) at 10kt (18·5km/h).
Crew: 473 (later 636).

Above: *Oregon* photographed on the morning of 19 March 1898, before beginning her long voyage from the Pacific Station to Cuban waters for service in the Spanish-American War. With *Indiana*, she took part in the crushing defeat of the Spanish squadron commanded by Admiral Pascual Cervera at the Battle of Santiago de Cuba, 3 July 1898.

A US Navy special policy board of 1889 advocated construction of 192 warships over 15 years, including 10 first class and 25 coast defence battleships. Anti-militarist sentiment in Congress greatly curtailed these plans: the Act of 30 June 1890 authorized only three 'sea-going coast-line battleships'.

As that phrase suggests, the Indianas suffered from a design compromise: crowding heavy armour and armament onto a restricted displacement led to low freeboard, limited endurance and only moderate speed. The first US 'New Navy' battleships to approach foreign contemporaries in fighting capability—and the first with hull numbers—they were still no more than powerful coast defence ships.

Nickel-steel armour was specified, but Harvey steel became available during construction. The belt was 150ft (45·72m) long and 7ft 6in (2·29m) deep; it had a maximum thickness of 18in (457mm) amidships and tapered to 8·5in (216mm) at its lower edge, 4ft 6in (1·37m) below the waterline. Above it, 4in (102mm) side armour ran up to main deck level. The belt terminated in 14in (356mm) transverse bulkheads which connected it fore and aft to the main barbettes. A 2·75in (70mm) armour deck lay flat on the belt; its extension beyond the citadel increased to 3in (76mm) thickness and sloped down to protect the ends.

The écheloned turrets of *Texas* and *Maine* gave way in the Indianas to twin turrets fore and aft on the centre line, housing 4 x 13in (330mm) guns. These were only 17ft 9in (5·41m) above water and were hard to work in a seaway. Eight 8in (203mm) guns were mounted in twin turrets, two on either beam at upper deck level, 25ft (7·62m) above water. Four 6in (152mm) guns were in sponsoned casemates amidships at main deck level, where they, too, were hard to work in a seaway.

This heavy armament in a limited space posed other problems: the 13in (330mm) guns' crews were affected by blast from the 8in (203mm) guns and the 6in (152mm) guns. During alterations in 1905-08—which included reboilering and the addition of a cage mainmast—the 6in (152mm) guns and many of the 6pdr were replaced by 12 x 3in (76mm), and the main turrets, originally unbalanced and tending to cause heel when trained abeam, were partially balanced. Torpedo tubes were removed.

The Indianas served in the Spanish-American War but were obsolescent by World War I. *Indiana* was a gunnery school ship in 1917-19 and then was reclassified *Coast Battleship No 1*, *Massachusetts* being *No 2*. Both were expended as targets in 1920-21. *Oregon* was Flagship, Pacific Fleet, in 1917 and served in the Siberian intervention in 1918-19. Preserved at Portland, Oreg., until 1942, she was an ammunition hulk (*IX-22*) in the Pacific during World War II and remained at Guam until sold in 1956.

MAJESTIC

1895 *UK*

Other ships in class: *Caesar; Hannibal, Illustrious, Jupiter, Magnificent, Mars, Prince George, Victorious*

Laid down: 1894.

Launched (floated out): 31 January 1895.
Builder: Portsmouth Dockyard.
Displacement: 14,560 tons to 14,890 tons (14,793-15,128 tonnes) load; 15,750 tons to 16,060 tons (15,982-16,317 tonnes) deep load.
Dimensions: 421ft (128·32m) oa x 75ft (22·86m) x 27ft (8·23m) mean.
Machinery: 3-cylinder Triple Expansion engines; 8 cylindrical boilers; 2 shafts; 10,000 IHP natural draught, 12,000 IHP forced draught.
Armour: Harvey 9in (229mm) belt; 14in-12in (356-305mm) bulkheads; 14in (356mm) barbettes; 10in (254mm) gun houses; 6in (152mm) casemates; 4in-2·5in (102-63mm) decks; 14in (356mm) conning tower.
Armament: 4 x 12in (305mm) BL; 12 x 6in (152mm) QF; 16 x 12pdr QF; 12 x 3pdr QF; 5 x 18in (457mm) torpedo tubes.
Performance: 16·1kt (29·8km/h) natural draught; coal 1,900 tons (1,930 tonnes) max; endurance 4,700nm (8,695km) at 10kt (18·5km/h).
Crew: 672.

In the Majestics, the largest class of battleships ever built, Sir William White, Chief Constructor from 1886 to 1902, produced perhaps the best battleships of the period and set a standard that endured until the advent of *Dreadnought* in 1905-6. The Majestics were part of the Spencer Programme of 8 December 1893, which aimed to counter the growing naval strength of France and Russia by constructing 9 battleships, 28 cruisers and 122 other warships by 1898. It was adopted in somewhat reduced form

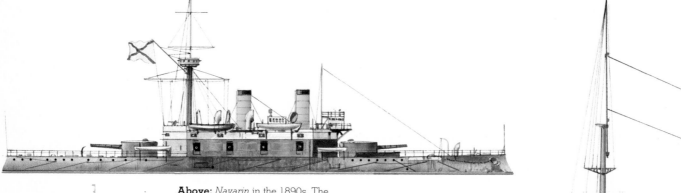

Above: *Navarin* in the 1890s. The foremast was later heightened.

Below: *Majestic* as completed. White made full use of the latest technical developments in these fine ships.

NAVARIN

1896 *Russia*

Laid down: 1889.
Launched: 20 October 1891.
Builder: Galernii Island Yard, St Petersburg.
Displacement: 10,206 tons (10,369 tonnes).
Dimensions: 357ft 8in (109m) oa x 67ft (20·42m) x 27ft 6in (8·38m).
Machinery: Vertical Triple Expansion engines; 12 cylindrical boilers; 2 shafts; 9140 IHP.
Armour: Compound 16in-8in (406-203mm) belt; 12in (305mm) nickel steel turrets; 5in (127mm) battery; 10in (254mm) nickel steel conning tower.
Armament: 4 x 12in (305mm); 8 x 6in (152mm); 8 x 3pdr; 15 x 1pdr; 6 x 15in (381mm) torpedo tubes.
Performance: 15·5kt (28·7km/h); coal 700 tons (711 tonnes) max.
Crew: 622.

Navarin, based on Britain's larger Trafalgar class turret ships, had a 220ft (67m) belt fitted in two strakes. The lower strake, with a maximum thickness of 16in (406mm) amidships, extended from 5ft (1·52m) below water to 2ft (0·6m) above; the upper strake was 8ft (2·44m) deep and 12in (305mm) thick throughout. A 2in-3in (51-76mm) armour deck lay flat on the belt.

Her 4 x 12in (305mm) were twin-mounted in centre line turrets before and abaft the superstructure, with arcs of fire of 270°. Secondary armament was in a 5in (127mm) armoured battery in the super-structure, above which rose twin pairs of funnels.

At Tsushima, 1905, the worth of *Navarin*'s protection was proved by her resistance to shell and torpedo hits sustained on 27 May. But as she ran for Vladivostok early next morning she was sunk with great loss of life by further torpedo hits.

Above: In 1907-10, all the Kaisers save *Karl der Grosse* underwent major modification to improve sea-keeping qualities. The original towering superstructure was drastically cut down and a light connecting bridge was fitted at a lower level. The secondary battery was reduced and thinner funnels were shipped.

Below: Although completed in 189[?] *Kaiser Friedrich III* is shown here so that her comparatively light main armament may be compared w[ith] that of *Navarin* and *Brennus*.

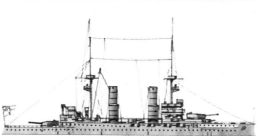

only after much political opposition, culminating in the retirement of W. E. Gladstone.

As in *Renown*, described below, the use of Harvey armour allowed adequate protection at less cost in weight by the provision of a lighter, deeper belt than in earlier battleships. *Majestic's* belt was 220ft (67·06m) long, 16ft (4·88m) deep, and of 9in (229mm) thickness throughout, rising to the height of the gun deck and terminating in a 14in (356mm) bulkhead forward and 12in (305mm) bulkhead aft. The

bulkheads were joined to the fronts of the barbettes to form an enclosed armoured citadel rising 9ft 6in (2·9m) above water. The armour deck curved down at an angle of c40° to meet the lower edges of the belt.

More weight was saved by fitting a main armament of 4 x 12in (305mm), 46-ton (46.74 tonne), wire-wound guns, equal to the earlier 13·5in (343mm) weapons in all but shell weight. This permitted secondary armament to be increased to 12 x 6in (152mm) QF. The big guns had pear-shaped barbettes (circular

barbettes, fitted in *Caesar* and *Illustrious*, became the norm thereafter) with 10in (254mm) gun houses, or hoods.

In 1905-06 *Mars* was the first battleship fitted for oil burning, carrying 400 tons (406 tonnes) of oil for the loss of 200 tons (203 tonnes) of coal. The remainder of the class was similarly fitted over the next two years. *Majestic* was Flagship, Channel Fleet, in 1895-1903 and, along with her sisters, four of which were converted to armed troop transports, was still active during

World War I.

In March 1915, *Prince George* and *Majestic* were sent to the Dardanelles, where the latter was Admiral Nicholson's flagship. On 27 May 1915, off Gaba Tepe, *Majestic* sank within 7 minutes, with the loss of 40 men ,after being struck by two torpedoes from the submarine *U.21*. *Prince George* survived the war despite being hit by a torpedo which failed to explode during the evacuation of Helles on 9 January 1916. She and her sisters were sold between 1920 and 1923.

Above: *Brennus* as completed. The superstructure was later reduced.

BRENNUS

1896 *France*

Laid down: January 1889.
Launched: October 1891.
Builder: Lorient Dockyard.
Displacement: 11,190 tons (11,369 tonnes).
Dimensions: 361ft 10in (110·29m) pp x 66ft 11in (20·4m) x 27ft 2in (8·28m) max.
Machinery: Vertical Triple Expansion engines; 32 Belleville boilers; 2 shafts; 13,900 IHP.
Armour: Steel and compound 18in-10in (457-254mm) belt; 4in (102mm) upper belt and battery; 18in (457mm) turrets; 4in (102mm) secondary turrets; 6in (152mm) conning tower.
Armament: 3 x 13·4in (340mm); 10 x 6·4in (163mm) QF; 4 x 9pdr; 14 x 3 pdr; 8 x 1pdr; 6 x 1pdr revolvers; 4 x 18in (457mm) torpedo tubes.
Performance: 18kt (33·3km/h); coal 980 tons (996 tonnes) max.
Crew: 673.

Brennus suffered from her designer's attempt to achieve too much in too small a compass: her construction was prolonged while steps were taken to improve inadequate stability due largely to lack of beam. She was one of the first battleships to have no ram, and the first to have Belleville boilers of simple type.

The 'lozenge' armament of *Hoche* and *Marceau* gave way to a main armament of 3 x 13·4in (340mm) guns, powerful but slow-firing, mounted in a twin turret forward and a single turret aft. A battery at main deck level amidships housed 6 x 6·4in (163mm) QF, with four more single-mounted in turrets above it. The full-length main belt extended c5ft 3in (1·6m) below water and c2ft (0·61m) above, with a 2·4in-2in (61-51mm) armour deck above it.

Although she was not scrapped until 1922, *Brennus* took no active part in World War I.

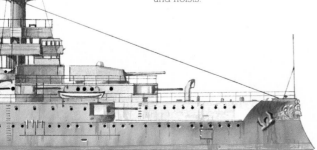

KAISER FRIEDRICH III

1898 *Germany*
Other ships in class: *Kaiser Wilhelm II, Kaiser Wilhelm der Grosse, Kaiser Barbarossa, Kaiser Karl der Grosse*

Laid down: May 1895.
Launched: 31 July 1896.
Builder: Wilhelmshaven Dockyard.
Displacement: 11,599 tons (11,785 tonnes).
Dimensions: 411ft (125·27m) oa x 67ft (20·42m) x 27ft (8·23m).
Machinery: 3-cylinder Triple Expansion engines; 12 boilers; 3 shafts; 14,000 IHP.
Armour: Krupp 12in-4in (305-102mm) belt; 10in (254mm) turrets and barbettes; 2·5in (63mm) deck; 10in (254mm) conning tower and hoists.

Armament: 4 x 9·4in (240mm); 18 x 5·9in (150mm); 12 x 3·4in (88mm); 12 MG; 6 x 17·7in (450mm) torpedo tubes.
Performance: 17kt (31·45km/h); coal 1,050 tons (1067 tonnes) max.
Crew: 651.

With the five battleships of the Kaiser class, the German Navy set a general pattern for its capital ships until the construction of the Westfalens, its first dreadnoughts, in 1907-10. Compared with most battleships of other powers, German pre-dreadnoughts had a lighter main and heavier secondary armament.

In the Kaisers, 4 x 9·4in (240mm) guns were in twin turrets in barbettes fore and aft, with 6 x 5·9in (150mm) in small 6in (152mm) armoured single turrets and 12 x 5·9in (150mm) in 6in (152mm) armoured casemates.

With the exception of *Karl der Grosse*, the Kaisers were reconstructed in 1907-10. Four 5·9in (150mm) guns and the above-water torpedo tube at the stern were removed; 2 x 3·4in (88mm) were added to the re-arranged tertiary armament. The superstructure was cut down and the funnels heightened. None took an active part in World War I: *Kaiser Friedrich III* was hulked as an accommodation ship in c1916; she and her sister-ships were scrapped in 1920-21.

CHARLES MARTEL

1897 *France*

(457-254mm) belt; 4in (102mm) upper belt; 15in (381mm) turrets; 6in (152mm) bases; 4in (102mm) secondary turrets; 9in (229mm) conning tower.
Armament: 2 x 12in (305mm); 2 x 10·8in (274mm); 8 x 5·5in (140mm) QF; 4 x 9pdr; 12 x 3pdr; 8 x 1pdr revolvers; 2 x 18in (457mm) submerged torpedo tubes.
Performance: 18kt (33·3km/h); coal 980 tons (996 tonnes) max; radius *c*1,200nm (2,220km) at *c*17kt (31·45km/h).
Crew: 644.

Charles Martel was authorized under the 1891 programme, which aimed at the replacement of all the French Navy's wooden-hulled ironclads by 1900. Although it is incorrect to describe them as sister-ships, the four

TRI SVITITELIA

1898 *Russia*

Laid down: 14 August 1891.
Launched: 12 November 1893.
Builder: Nicolaiev Dockyard.
Displacement: 13,318 tons (13,531 tonnes) full load.
Dimensions: 377ft 9in (115·14m) oa x 73ft (22·25m) x 28ft 5in (8·66m) max.
Machinery: Vertical Triple Expansion engines, 14 cylindrical boilers; 2 shafts; 11,300 IHP.
Armour: Harvey and nickel steel 18in-9in (457-229mm) belt; 16in (406mm) turrets; 5in (127mm) secondary armament; 12in (305mm) conning tower.
Armament: 4 x 12in (305mm); 8 x 6in (152mm); 4 x 4·7in (119mm); 50 smaller; 6 x 18in (457mm) TT.

Performance: 17kt (31·45km/h); coal 1,000 tons (1,016 tonnes) max.
Crew: 753.

Modernized in 1912, this low-freeboard turret ship served widely with the Black Sea Fleet in World War I. Hulked by interventionist forces in 1919, she was scrapped by the Soviet Navy in 1922.

Laid down: April 1891.
Launched: August 1893.
Builder: Brest Dockyard.
Displacement: 11,693 tons (11,880 tonnes).
Dimensions: 378ft 11in (115·49m) pp x 71ft (21·64m) x 27ft 6in (8·38m) max.
Machinery: Vertical Triple Expansion engines; 24 Lagrafel d'Allest boilers; 2 shafts; 14,900 IHP.
Armour: Nickel steel 18in-10in

Below: The impressive profile of *Charles Martel* in the 1890s; note the heavy military masts.

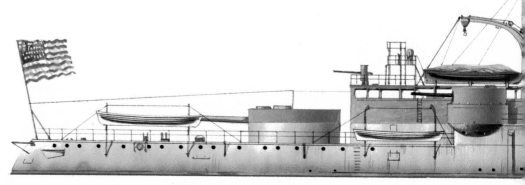

IOWA (BB-4)

1897 *USA*

Laid down: 5 August 1893.
Launched: 28 March 1896.
Builder: Cramp, Philadelphia.
Displacement: 12,510 tons (12,710 tonnes) full load.
Dimensions: 362ft 5in (110·46m) oa x72ft 3in (22·02m) x 24ft (7·32m) mean.
Machinery: Vertical Triple Expansion engines; 5 cylindrical boilers; 2 shafts; 11,834 IHP.
Armour: Harvey 14in-4in (356-102mm) belt; 15in-12·5in (381-317mm) barbettes; 17in-15in (432-381mm) main turrets; 8in-4in (203-102mm) secondary turrets; 10in (254mm) conning tower; 3in-2·75in (76-70mm) deck.
Armament: 4 x 12in (305mm); 8 x 8in (203mm); 6 x 4in (102mm); 20 x 6pdr; 4 x 1pdr; 4 x 14·2in (361mm) above-water torpedo tubes.
Performance: 16kt (29·6km/h); coal 1,795 tons (1,824 tonnes) max; radius 4,500nm (8,325km) at 10kt (18·5km/h).
Crew: 505 (1897); 654 (1908).

With lighter armament and armour on a larger displacement than the Indiana class, *Iowa* (BB-4) was a successful design. Provision of a forecastle deck gave her better speed

and seakeeping qualities, and improved fire-power by raising the forward twin 12in (305mm) centre line turret and the four twin 8in (203mm) wing turrets to 25ft 6in (7·77m) above water.

The 186ft (56·69m) long main belt was 7ft 6in (2·29m) deep, with 12in (305mm) transverse bulkheads fore and aft. Amidships, a shorter 4in (102mm) belt ran from the main belt to main deck level. The central citadel was covered by an armour deck of maximum 3in (76mm) thickness at its downward-curving ends.

Iowa served in the Cuban

blockade and at Santiago in the Spanish-American War, 1898. In 1908, 4 x 4in (102mm) were added to replace most of the smaller guns and a cage main mast was fitted. Used for gunnery training and coastguard duty in World War I, she was redesignated *Coast Battleship No 4*, then *IX-6*, in 1919-20, converted to a radio-controlled target ship, and sunk in that role on 23 March 1923. As she sank, the national anthem was played and a twenty-one gun salute fired at Secretary of the Navy Denby's behest, in recognition of *Iowa*'s service in 1898.

Below: The powerful battleship *Iowa* immediately after trials in 1897. The tumblehome allowed the 8in (203mm) guns near-axial fire.

attleships that followed in 397-98—*Carnot, Jauréguiberry, asséna* and *Bouvet*—all had much common with *Charles Martel*. Her complete belt was 7ft 7in ·31m) wide, extending 5ft 11in ·8m) below water, where its lower dge tapered to 10in (254mm) ickness amidships and forward d 6·75in (171mm) aft, and having a aximum thickness of 18in (457mm) nidships. The 4in (102mm) thick pper belt, also complete, was 4ft 22m) wide amidships, 10ft (3·05m) rward and 6ft 6in (1·98m) aft. An mour deck of c2·75in (70mm) ickness lay flat on the belt, with xtensive compartmentation etween it and a 1in (25mm) moured splinter deck below. The main armament was in ozenge' layout: 2 x 12in (305mm)

elow: *Carnot* in 1898—a further xample of the 'lozenge' armament yout favoured by French designers.

were carried in single centre-pivot turrets fore and aft and 2 x 10·8in (274mm) in similar turrets amidships on either beam. Eight 5·5in (140mm) QF were single-mounted in electrically worked turrets at main and upper deck level.

Charles Martel shipped two military masts with a flying deck running between them. Weight saved in the improved design of her turrets was used to fit a forecastle deck: this raised the forward 12in (305mm) gun to a height of c28ft (8·53m) above water and, by giving high freeboard forward, permitted high speed to be maintained in a seaway. Although boiler alterations delayed her completion, she emerged as an excellent steamer. She took no active part in World War I and was stricken in 1922.

CARNOT
1897 *France*

Laid down: July 1891.
Launched: July 1894.
Builder: Toulon Dockyard.
Displacement: 11,954 tons (12,145 tonnes).
Dimensions: 374ft (113·99m) pp x 70ft 6in (21·49m) x 27ft 5in (8·36m) max
Machinery: Vertical Triple Expansion engines; 24 Lagrafel d'Allest boilers; 2 shafts; 16,300 IHP.
Armour: Nickel steel 18in-10in (457-254mm) belt; 4in (102mm) upper belt; 15in (381mm) turrets; 6in (152mm) bases; 4in (102mm) secondary turrets; 9in (229mm) conning tower.
Armament: 2 x 12in (305mm); 2 x 10·8in (274mm); 8 x 5·5in (140mm) QF; 4 x 9pdr; 12 x 3 pdr; 8 x 1pdr revolvers; 2 x 18in (457mm) submerged torpedo tubes.
Performance: 17·8kt (32·9km/h); coal 980 tons (996 tonnes) max; radius c1,200nm (2,200km) at 17·5kt (32·4km/h).
Crew: 647.

Laid down soon after *Charles Martel* at a time when French designers aimed at achieving a great degree of homogeneity within the fleet, *Carnot* resembled her contemporary in most essentials. She differed in having no flying deck or military mainmast, reduced bridges, and funnels set farther apart, the aft funnel being noticeably thinner than the forward funnel.

The total weight of *Carnot*'s armour was c3,800 tons (3,861 tonnes), or some 32 per cent of her displacement. She had a complete main belt extending some 5ft 9in (1·75m) below and 1ft 9in (0·53m) above water, with a maximum thickness of 18in (457mm) amidships.

Her 2 x 12in (305mm) guns were single-mounted in centre-pivot turrets on the centre line at forecastle level forward, 27ft 6in (8·38m) above water and at upper deck level aft, 21ft 6in (6·55m) above water. The 10·8in (274mm) guns were in identical turrets extending over the tumblehome on either beam. Single 4in (102mm) armoured, electrically turned turrets housed 8 x 5·5in (140mm) QF in positions below and on either side of the main turrets.

Although still on the effective list in 1914, *Carnot* was laid up at Brest throughout World War I and took no part in hostilities. She was stricken in 1922.

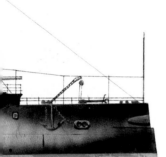

Below: *Renown* in 1905, when she carried a Royal party to India.

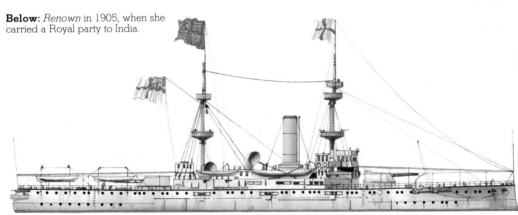

RENOWN
1897 *UK*

Laid down: February 1893.
Launched: 8 May 1895.
Builder: Pembroke Dockyard.
Displacement: 12,350 tons (12,548 tonnes) load.

Dimensions: 408ft (124·36m) oa x 72ft (21·95m) x 26ft 9in (8·15m) max.
Machinery: Maudslay 3-cylinder Triple Expansion engines; 8 cylindrical boilers; 2 shafts; 10,000 IHP natural draught, 12,000 IHP forced draught.
Armour: Harvey nickel steel 8in-6in (203-152mm) belt; 10in-6in (254-152mm) bulkheads; 6in (152mm) upper belt; 10in (254mm) barbettes; 6in (152mm) gun houses; 6in-4in (152-102mm) casemates; 3in-2in (76-51mm) decks; 9in (229mm) conning tower.

Armament: 4 x 10in (254mm) BL; 10 x 6in (152mm) QF; 12 x 12pdr QF; 12 x 3pdr QF; 5 x 18in (457mm) torpedo tubes.
Performance: 17·5kt (32·4km/h) natural draught, 18kt (33·3km/h) forced draught; coal 1,760 tons (1,788 tonnes) max; radius 8,500nm (15,725km) at 15kt (27·75km/h).
Crew: 674.

The Royal Navy's last second-class battleship, *Renown* was a much enlarged version of the Centurion class. The use of Harvey nickel steel permitted a lighter main belt, 210ft (64m) long with a maximum thickness of 8in (203mm) amidships, and better protection at lower deck level in the form of a 6in (152mm) thick upper belt. Instead of lying flat on the belt, the armour deck sloped down to meet the belt's lower edges.

Four 10in (254mm) BL were set in twin turrets fore and aft, with 6 x 6in (152mm) in casemates on the main deck and 4 x 6in (152mm) in upper deck casemates with a battery of 8 x 12pdr between them. This was the first time that upper deck casemates were fitted on a battleship.

Renown served as Vice-Admiral Sir John Fisher's flagship in the Mediterranean. By 1905 all *Renown*'s 6in (152mm) guns had been removed to facilitate her employment on Royal cruises. She was sold in 1914.

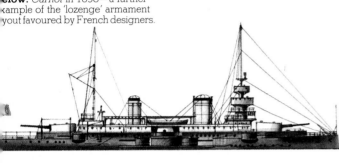

JAURÉGUIBERRY

1897 France

Laid down: 8 April 1891.
Launched: 27 October 1893.
Builder: La Seyne.
Displacement: 11,637 tons
(11,823 tonnes).
Dimensions: 356ft (108·51m) pp
x 72ft 8in (22·15m) x 27ft 8in
(8·43m) max.
Machinery: Vertical Triple
Expansion engines, 24 Lagrafel
d'Allest boilers; 2 shafts; 14,400 IHP.
Armour: Nickel steel 18in-10in
(457-254mm) belt; 4in (102mm)
upper belt; 15in (381mm) turrets;
6in (152mm) bases; 4in (102mm)
secondary turrets; 9in (229mm)
conning tower.
Armament: 2 x 12in (305mm);
2 x 10·8in (274mm); 8 x 5·5in
(140mm) QF; 4 x 9pdr;
12 x 3pdr; 8 x 1pdr revolvers;
6 x 18in (457m) torpedo tubes.
Performance: 17·7kt (32·7km/h);
coal 980 tons (996 tonnes) max;
endurance 3,820nm (7,252km)
at 10kt (18·5km/h).
Crew: 631.

Although, as noted above,
Jauréguiberry had much in common
with *Charles Martel*, she was
designed by Lagane as an enlarged
version of his Chilean battleship
Capitan Prat, launched in December
1890, which was also built at La

Seyne. Shorter than *Charles Martel*,
Jauréguiberry displayed the same
pronounced tumblehome but had
somewhat less lofty superstructure,
lacked a flying deck, and was not cut
down to main deck level astern.
Jauréguiberry was six years in
building and her commissioning was
delayed when, during a 24-hour sea
trial on 10 June 1896, one of the tubes
of her Lagrafel d'Allest multi-tubular
boilers burst, scalding to death six
men. An inquiry found that the
rupture had taken place along the
weld of the tube and it was
recommended that only weldless
tubes should henceforth be fitted in
positions directly exposed to flame.
Jauréguiberry subsequently had the
reputation of being a good steamer
and seaboat.

The complete main belt was 7ft 9in
(2·36m) deep and extended c6ft
(1·83m) below the waterline.
Maximum thickness was 18in
(457mm) amidships, thinning to 10in
(254mm) at the ends. A complete
upper belt of 4in (102mm) armour
extended 4ft (1·22m) above the main
belt amidships, 10ft (3·05m) forward
and 6ft 6in (1·98m) aft. Flat on the
main belt was an armour deck of
c2·75in (70mm) thickness and 2ft 8in
(0·81m) below it was a 1in (25mm)
splinter deck, the space between
being extensively compartmented.

The main armament was in
'lozenge' layout. Two 12in (305mm)
45-cal guns were single-mounted in
electrically and manually worked,
balanced turrets forward, at
forecastle deck level, and aft, at
upper deck level, on the centre line.
The reduction in length from *Charles
Martel* meant that these turrets were
set nearer the ship's ends, with arcs
of fire of 250°. Two 10·8in (274mm)
45-cal guns were single-mounted at
upper deck level in similar turrets,
sponsoned out over the tumblehome
on either beam amidships.

The saving in weight as compared
to *Charles Martel*, achieved by the
adoption of twin turrets for the
secondary armament of 8 x 5·in
(140mm), 45-cal QF, allowed a
greater height of gun axis: the four

win turrets were at forecastle deck
vel, two flanking the foremast and
o the mainmast, with 160° arcs.
nti-torpedo-boat defence was
rovided by 4 x 9pdr and 12 (later
3) x 3pdr, situated in the
uperstructure and in the two tops of
ich of the two heavy, tubular military
asts. Six 18in (457mm) torpedo
bes were fitted; by 1914 the
oove-water tubes at bow and stern
id been removed and she had only
o submerged beam tubes.
  Although in a poor state, with her
elt submerged, badly corroded
okehold bulkheads and
iprotected magazines with
efective flooding arrangements,
uréguiberry was active during
Vorld War I. In 1914-15 she escorted
onvoys to the Middle East and in
larch 1915 was sent to the
ardanelles, after Bouvet had been
ink there and Suffren crippled. As
dmiral Guépratte's flagship, she
ave good service on bombardment
issions, twice sustaining slight
amage from Turkish shore batteries.
  By early 1916 Jauréguiberry was a
uardship at Suez and, after further
onvoy and transport duty, she was
aced in reserve at Port Said in
918. She returned to France the
llowing year and was disarmed,
ecoming an engineering school ship
Toulon. She was stricken in 1920
id used as a barracks hulk until
932; she was finally sold for
reaking up in July 1934.

Above: An excellent photographic record of *Jauréguiberry* at speed, with a large bow wave surging along her tumblehome side.

Below: *Jauréguiberry* in 1897. A 'lozenge' armament layout permitted good all-round fire for the big guns, and the secondary armament, in turrets at either end of the superstructure, also had good arcs of fire. Note the marked tumblehome.

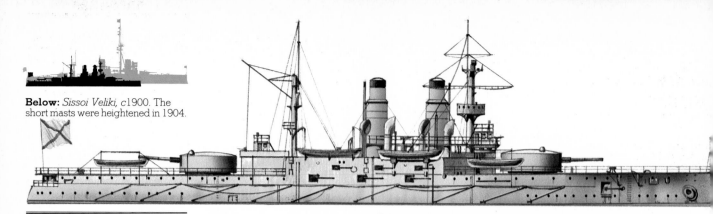

Below: *Sissoi Veliki, c*1900. The short masts were heightened in 1904.

SISSOI VELIKI

1897 *Russia*

Laid down: May 1892.
Launched: June 1894.
Builder: New Admiralty Yard,
St Petersburg.
Displacement: 10,400 tons
(10,566 tonnes).
Dimensions: 351ft 10in (107·24m)
oa x 68ft (20·73m) x 25ft 6in (7·77m).
Machinery: Vertical Triple
Expansion engines; 12 Belleville
boilers; 2 shafts; 8500 IHP.
Armour: Nickel steel 16in-4in
(406-102mm) belt; 12in (305mm)
turrets; 5in (127mm) secondary
armament; 8in (203mm) conning
tower.
Armament: 4 x 12in (305mm);
6 x 6in (152mm); 12 x 3pdr;
18 x 1pdr; 6 x 18in (457mm)
torpedo tubes.
Performance: 15·7kt (29km/h);
coal 800 tons (813 tonnes) max.
Crew: 586.

Sissoi Veliki much resembled a
reduced Royal Sovereign, with the
main armament in turrets rather than
barbettes. Her 4 x 12in (305mm)
were twin-mounted in hydraulically
operated centre-pivot turrets fore
and aft, with 270° arcs of fire. The 6 x
6in (152mm) were housed in a 5in
(127mm) armoured casemate at
main deck level.
The belt was 274ft (83·52m) long
and extended *c*5ft (1·52m) below
water, where it tapered to 4in
(102mm) thickness, and *c*2ft (0·61m)
above, terminating in 9in (229mm)
bulkheads. A 1·75in (44mm) armour
deck, thickening to 3in (76mm) at its
downward-curving ends, lay flat on
the belt.
This protection was proved
adequate at Tsushima, where *Sissoi
Veliki* remained afloat after some 12
hits from large-calibre shells and a
torpedo aft. But she was too badly
damaged to reach Vladivostok, and
on the morning of 28 May 1905 she
was scuttled to avoid capture by
Japanese armed merchant cruisers.

FUJI

1897 *Japan*
Other ships in class: *Yashima*

Laid down: 1 August 1894.
Launched: 31 March 1896.
Builder: Thames Iron Works
Poplar, London.
Displacement: 12,533 tons
(12,734 tonnes) normal.
Dimensions: 412ft (125·58m) oa
x 73ft (22·25m) x 26ft (8·1m).
Machinery: 3-cylinder
Reciprocating Vertical Triple
Expansion engines; 10 cylindrical
boilers; 2 shafts; 14,000 IHP.
Armour: Harvey nickel steel
18in-14in (457-356mm) main belt;
4in (102mm) upper belt; 14in-9in
(356-229mm) barbettes; 6in-2in
(152-51mm) casemates; 2·5in
(63mm) deck; 14in (356mm)

conning tower.
Armament: 4 x 12in (305mm);
10 x 6in (152mm) QF; 20 x 3pdr;
4 x 2½pdr; 5 x 18in (457mm)
torpedo tubes (4 above, 1 below
water).
Performance: 18kt (33·3km/h);
coal 1,200 tons (1,219 tonnes) max;
radius 4,000nm (7,400km) at 10kt
(18·5km/h).
Crew: 637.

In the early 1890s, anticipating war
with China and anxious to out-match
the German-built turret ships *Ting
Yuen* and *Chen Yuan*, Japan ordered
her first battleships from British
yards, although they were not
completed in time for the
Sino-Japanese War, 1894-95.
Fuji and *Yashima* were built to an
improved Royal Sovereign design by
G.C. Macrow of Thames Iron Works.
Weight saved by the fitting of
equally-powerful 12in (305mm) guns
rather than a 13·5in (343mm) main
armament was used to give added
protection in the form of turrets to the
barbettes. *Yashima* was given added
manoeuvrability by cutting away the
keel towards the rudder, but the
smaller turning circle thus attained
resulted in excessive strain on the
ship's hull.
The main belt was 230ft (70·1m)
long and 7·5ft (2·29m) deep. It had a
maximum thickness of 18in (457mm)
over the machinery amidships,
thinning through 16in (406mm) to
14in (356mm) at the ends and
terminating in a 14in (356mm)
bulkhead forward and a 12in
(305mm) bulkhead aft. A 2·5in
(63mm) armour deck with
down-curving ends lay flat above the
belt and a 4in (102mm) upper belt
extended to upper deck level.
The 4 x 12in (305mm)
Armstrongs—replaced by Japanese
models in 1910—were twin-mounted
in 14in (356mm) armoured
centre line barbettes with the added
protection of 6in (152mm) turrets.
They had arcs of fire of 240° and a
firing rate with end-on loading of one
shell in 80 seconds, loading in other
positions being much slower. Four
6in (152mm) guns were set in 6in
(152mm) armoured casemates
amidships and 6 x 6in (152mm)
behind shields on the upper deck,
good arcs of fire compensating for
their lack of protection. In 1900-01 all
the 3pdr save the four in the fighting
tops (themselves removed in 1905)
were removed and 16 x 12pdr
added.
Yashima was lost during the
Russo-Japanese War, striking a mine
off Port Arthur on 15 May 1904. *Fuji*
took part in the Battle of the Yellow
Sea, 10 August 1904, and fired the
final salvo at Tsushima, 25 May 1905,
sinking the Russian battleship
Borodino with a hit in a magazine.
Reboilered and rated a coast defence
vessel in 1910, *Fuji* became a training
ship, took no active part in World War
I, and was disarmed, immobilised
and stricken in 1922-23.

Below: *Poltava,* 1904, with raised funnels.

POLTAVA

1898 *Russia*
Other ships in class:
Petropavlovsk, Sevastopol

Laid down: May 1892.
Launched: 6 November 1894.
Builder: New Admiralty Yard,
St Petersburg.
Displacement: 11,354 tons
(11,536 tonnes) full load.
Dimensions: 369ft (112·47m) wl
x 70ft (21·34m) x 25ft 6in (7·77m).
Machinery: Vertical Triple
Expansion engines; 2 shafts;
11,250 IHP.
Armour: Harvey nickel steel
16in-5in (406-127mm) belt; 14in-10in
(356mm-254mm) turrets; 5in
(127mm) secondary turrets.
Armament: 4 x 12in (305mm);
12 x 6in (152mm); 40 smaller;
6 x 18in (457mm) torpedo tubes;
60 mines.
Performance: 16·5kt (30·53km/h);
coal 10,050 tons (10,211 tonnes).
Crew: 632.

Sunk at Port Arthur on 5 December
1904, *Poltava* was raised by the
Japanese, rearmed and reboilered at
Maizuru, and served as the coast
defence and training ship *Tango* until
returned to Russia in 1916.
Renamed *Tchesma* for service in the
White Sea, she was hulked by
interventionist forces at Murmansk
and scrapped by the Soviets in 1923.

OUVET
898 France

aid down: 16 January 1893.
aunched: 27 April 1896.
uilder: Lorient Dockyard.
isplacement: 12,007 tons
2,199 tonnes).
imensions: 386ft 6in (117·81m)
o x 70ft 2in (21·39m) x 27ft 6in
·38m) max.
achinery: Vertical Triple
xpansion engines; 32 Belleville
oilers; 3 shafts; 15,000 IHP.
rmour: Special steel 16in-8in
06-203mm) belt; 4in (102mm)
pper belt; 15in (381mm) turrets;
n (203mm) bases; 4.7in (119mm)
econdary turrets; 12in (305mm)
nning tower.
rmament: 2 x 12in (305mm);
x 10·8in (274mm); 8 x 5·5in

elow: The sleek lines of *Masséna*
the 1890s. Note the projecting
m bow and tumblehome sides.

(140mm) QF; 8 x 3·9in (99mm);
12 x 3pdr; 5 x 1pdr; 2 x 1pdr
pompom; 2 x 18in (457mm)
torpedo tubes (2 above water, 2 below
water).
Performance: 18kt (33·3km/h);
coal 980 tons (996 tonnes) max;
radius c3,500nm (6,475km) at 10kt
(18·5km/h).
Crew: 666 (c710 in World War I).

The last and best Charles Martel
variant, *Bouvet* lacked the huge
superstructure of the earlier ship and
had a built-up stern. Like *Masséna*,
she had triple screws; this was

henceforth standard in French
battleships. A fine steamer, she kept
station on trials at 17kt (31·45km/h)
for 24 hours, at c11 tons (11·18
tonnes) of coal per hour.
The complete main belt was 7ft
(2·13m) deep and extended 5ft
(1·52m) below water; the upper belt,
also complete, was 8ft (2·44m) deep
forward, 4ft (1·44m) amidships and
6ft (1·83m) aft. Armour decks were
fitted above (1·75in, 44mm) and below
(1in, 25mm) the belt. Two 12in
(305mm) guns were in single turrets
fore and aft on the centre line, and 2 x
10·8in (274mm) in single turrets one

deck lower, amidships on either beam.
Eight 4in (102mm) armoured turrets
sponsored out over the pronounced
tumblehome housed 4 x 5·5in
(140mm) guns on either beam.
Bouvet was one of three Allied
pre-dreadnoughts sunk while trying
to force the Dardanelles on 18 March
1915. After taking some eight hits
above the waterline from Turkish
forts which put her fore turret out of
action, she ran on a mine armed with
176lb (80kg) of TNT and, her
bulkheads being corroded, capsized
and sank within two minutes with the
loss of some 660 men.

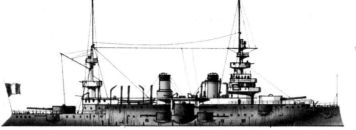

Above: *Bouvet* as completed, 1898;
a well-balanced design. She led an
active and eventful service life.

MASSÉNA
1898 France

Laid down: September 1892.
Launched: July 1895.
Builder: Chantiers de la Loire,
St Nazaire.
Displacement: 11,735 tons
(11,923 tonnes).
Dimensions: 369ft 7in (112·65m)
pp x 66ft 6in (20·27in) x c29ft
(8·84m) max.
Machinery: Vertical Triple
Expansion engines; 3 shafts;
14,200 IHP.
Armour: Nickel steel 18in-10in
(457-254mm) belt; 4in (102mm)
upper belt; 14in (356mm) turrets.
Armament: 2 x 12in (305mm);
2 x 10·8in (274mm); 8 x 5·5in
(140mm); 8 x 3·9in (99mm); 20
smaller; 4 x 18in (457mm) TT.
Performance: 17kt (31·45km/h);
coal 980 tons (996 tonnes) max.
Crew: 667.

An unsatisfactory Charles Martel
variant, distinguished by her very
pronounced snout bow, *Masséna*
was the first French warship to have
triple screws. Hulked in 1915, she
was expended as a breakwater at the
Gallipoli evacuation in 1916.

Left: *Fuji*, 1897. She and *Yashima*
were the IJN's first modern
battleships, representing the best
in naval architecture in the 1890s.

ROSTISLAV

1898 Russia

Laid down: 1895.
Launched: September 1896.
Builder: Nicolaiev Dockyard.
Displacement: 8,880 tons
(9,022 tonnes) designed.
Dimensions: 351ft 10in
(107·24m) oa x 68ft (20·73m)
x 22ft (6·71m) max.
Machinery: Vertical Triple
Expansion; 2 shafts; 8700 IHP.
Armour: Harvey 14in-5in
(356-127mm) belt; 10in-5in
(254-127mm) turrets; 6in (152mm)
conning tower.
Armament: 4 x 10in (254mm);
8 x 6in (152mm); 36 smaller; 6 TT.
Performance: 15·6kt (28·9km/h).
Crew: 650.

This Black Sea Fleet battleship was
notable in having her 8 x 6in
(152mm) secondary armament in
four 5in (127mm) armoured twin
turrets, two on either beam
amidships. She took an active part in
World War 1, and passed through
German and interventionist hands
before being run aground in 1920.

Below: *Rostislav* as seen in *c*189⁰

Below: *Wien*, 1898, with striking
black and white finish. She was a major
step in Austrian warship
development.

WIEN

1898 Austria-Hungary
Other ships in class: *Monarch,
Budapest*

Laid down: 16 February 1893.
Launched: 6 July 1895.
Builder: Stabilimento Tecnico
Triestino.
Displacement: 5,547 tons
(5,636 tonnes) normal.
Dimensions: 325ft 6in (99·21m) oa

x 55ft 9in (17m) x 21ft (6·4m).
Machinery: 3-cylinder Vertical
Triple Expansion engines; 2 shafts;
8500 IHP.
Armour: Harvey 10·6in-8·7in
(270-220mm) belt; 9·8in (250mm)
turrets; 3·1in (80mm) casemates;
1·6in (40mm) deck.
Armament: 4 x 9·4in (240mm);
6 x 5·9in (150mm); 14 x 47mm QF;
3 smaller; 2 x 17·7in (450mm) TT.
Performance: 17·5kt (32·4km/h);
coal 500 tons (508 tonnes) max.
Crew: 426.

The Monarch class coast defence
ships were obsolete by 1914. *Wien*,
serving as a gunnery school tender,
was sunk off Trieste by an Italian
MTB's torpedo on 10 December
1917.

Below: *Canopus* as seen around the
turn of the century. Her second funnel
was wider athwartships, but when
viewed abeam both funnels
appeared to be of the same size.

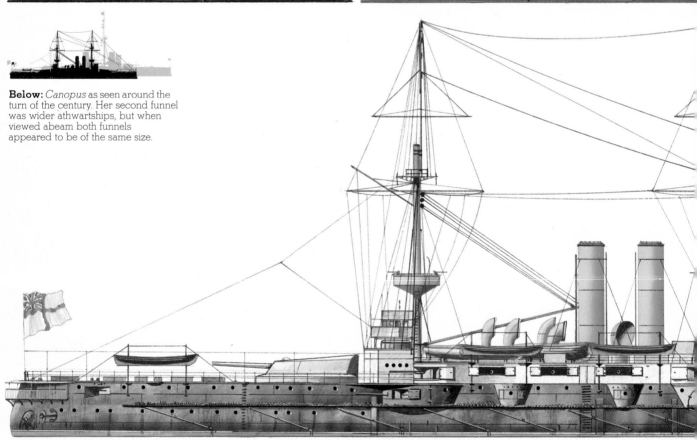

CHARLEMAGNE

1899 *France*
Other ships in class: *St Louis, Gaulois*

Laid down: 14 July 1894.
Launched: 17 October 1895.
Builder: Brest Dockyard.
Displacement: 11,100 tons
(11,278 tonnes) normal.
Dimensions: 374ft (114m) pp x
66ft 5in (20·24m) x 27ft 6in
(8·38m) max.
Machinery: Vertical Triple
Expansion engines; 20 Belleville
boilers; 3 shafts; 15,000 IHP.
Armour: Harvey nickel 14·5in-8in
(368-203mm) belt; 4in (102mm)
upper belt; 3in (76mm) battery;
15in (381mm) turrets; 8in (203mm)
bases; 13in (330mm) conning tower.
Armament: 4 x 12in (305mm);
10 x 5·5in (140mm) QF;
8 x 3·9in (99mm); 20 x 3pdr;
4 x 1pdr; 4 x 18in (457mm)
submerged torpedo tubes.
Performance: 18kt (33·3km/h);
coal 1,080 tons (1,097 tonnes) max;
endurance 4,000nm (7,400km)
at 10kt (18·5km/h).
Crew: 694.

Below: In *Charlemagne,* seen as
completed, France returned to fore
and aft positioning for big guns.

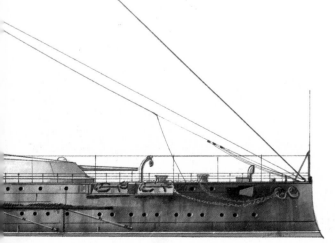

With the three Charlemagne class
battleships, France followed the lead
given by other powers and adopted
twin mountings for the main
armament. The Royal Navy was at
this time building the large Majestic
class and the French, unusually for a
period in which they favoured 'one
off' designs, laid down three
Charlemagnes. In comparison with
the Majestics, they suffered by trying
to achieve too much on too limited a
displacement and too small a beam.

A full-length main belt extended 5ft
(1·52m) below water, where it
tapered to 8in (203mm) thickness at
the lower edge, and 1ft 6in (0·46m)
above, with a maximum upper-edge
thickness of 14·5in (368mm)
amidships. A 1·5in-0·8in (38-20mm)
splinter deck lay flat below the belt;
between this and the 3·3in (84mm)
armour deck flat above the belt was a
cellular layer (*tranche cellulaire*),
some 7ft (2·13m) deep. The
upper belt extended to main deck
level forward but elsewhere was only
3ft 4in (1·02m) deep, leaving the
sides between the cofferdam,
inboard of the upper belt, and the
upper deck casemate unprotected.

Four 12in (305mm) guns were
twin-mounted in centre-pivot turrets
on the forecastle and upper decks,
with arcs of fire of 250°. Two 5·5in
(140mm) QF firing from shielded
positions on the forecastle deck had
arcs of 180°; the remaining 8 x 5·5in
(140mm), mounted in the 3in (76mm)
armoured upper deck battery, had
arcs of 110°.

The Charlemagnes were reputed
to be good seaboats and economical
steamers, consumption averaging
9·75 tons (9·9 tonnes) of coal per
hour at 18kt (33·3km/h). All took an
active part in World War I, *Gaulois*
being torpedoed and sunk by the
German submarine *UB.47* on 27
December 1916. Like her sisters,
Charlemagne served in the
Dardanelles campaign in 1914-15.
Paid off and disarmed at Toulon in
1917, she was stricken in 1920.

CANOPUS

1899 *UK*
Other ships in class: *Albion,
Glory, Goliath, Ocean, Vengeance*

Laid down: 4 January 1897.
Launched: 12 October 1897.
Builder: Portsmouth Dockyard.
Displacement: 13,150 tons
(13,360 tonnes) load.
Dimensions: 421ft 6in (128·47m) oa
x 74ft (22·56m) x 26ft 2in
(7·98m) mean.
Machinery: Greenock Foundry
3-cylinder Triple Expansion engines,
20 Belleville boilers; 2 shafts;
13,500 IHP.
Armour: Krupp cemented, Harvey
and Harvey nickel 6in (152mm) belt;
10in-6in (254-152mm) bulkheads;
12in (305mm) barbettes; 8in (203mm)
gun houses; 6in (152mm) casemates;
12in (305mm) conning tower; 2in-1in
(51-25mm) decks.
Armament: 4 x 12in (305mm) BL;
12 x 6in (152mm) QF;
10 x 12pdr QF; 6 x 3pdr;
2 x Maxims; 4 x 18in (457mm)
torpedo tubes.
Performance: 18·3kt (33·9km/h);
coal 1,800 tons (1,829 tonnes) max.
Crew: 682.

Somewhat smaller in beam and
draught than the Majestics on which
they were based, the Canopus class
ships were designed to be suitable
for sevice in the Far East, where
growing Japanese strength was
causing concern. A displacement
some 2,000 tons (2,032 tonnes) less
than the Majestics was achieved
largely through the use of Krupp
armour for belt and barbettes.

The belt was of 6in (152mm)
Krupp, reckoned equivalent to 8in
(203mm) Harvey nickel, and ran for
195ft (59·44m) amidships, extending
5ft (1·52m) below water and 9ft
(2·74m) above. An extension of 2in
(51mm) Krupp plating, effective only
against light guns and splinters, ran
to the bow, where it reinforced the
pronounced ram. It was believed,
wrongly, that the French were to
mount howitzers for high-angle fire
against decks, so a 1in (25mm)
armour deck was fitted over the belt,
the main armour deck reducing to
2in (51mm) throughout.

Four 12in (305mm) BL were
twin-mounted fore and aft, their flat
sided 8in (203mm) Krupp gun
positions protected by circular
barbettes of 12in (305mm) Krupp,
reducing to 6in (152mm) inboard of
the belt. Eight 6in (152mm) QF
were carried at main deck level, the
end casemates being sponsoned out
to permit end-on fire.

The Canopus class were the first
British battleships to have water-tube
boilers, giving faster steam raising,
higher power and better economy at
no cost in weight. With an increase in
speed of some 2kt (3·7km/h) over the
Majestics, they consumed 10· tons
(10·67 tonnes) of coal per hour at full
speed.

Unlike her sisters, *Canopus* did
not serve on the China station. In
World War I, lack of speed kept her
out of the Battle of Coronel, 1
November 1914, but as guardship at
Port Stanley she fired the opening
salvoes in the Battle of the Falkland
Islands, 8 December 1914. After
action in the Dardanelles in 1915 she
became a barracks ship at Chatham
and was sold in 1920. *Goliath* and
Ocean were war losses.

1900s Pre-Dreadnoughts

By 1900 the configuration of the capital ship was more or less settled throughout the world: four heavy twin-mounted guns of about 12in (305mm) calibre, disposed in hooded barbettes, with a battery of smaller, quick-firing weapons for anti-torpedo-boat defence; a waterline belt of between 7in (178mm) and 10in (254mm), topped by a horizontal armoured deck of 2-3in (51-76mm); a ram bow; triple expansion engines producing cruising speeds of around 12-13kt (22-24km/h) and maximum speeds (rarely practised) of some 18kt (33-34km/h); and displacements of 12,000-14,000 tons (12,200-14,220 tonnes) with ship lengths of about 400ft (135m). The evolution of French capital ships, hitherto characterised by a succession of heterogeneous individual designs, at last entered a period of relative stability, while the rise of Germany continued apace, the products of the 1898 First Naval Law seen through by Secretary of State Tirpitz—bolstered by the supplementary Bill of 1900—emerging as a powerful group of similar classes.

The early years of the twentieth century saw dramatic improvements in gunnery—it has often been remarked that naval gunnery changed sharply from a somewhat chancy, casual pursuit into an intense science during this period. The armoured cruising ship evolved into a reckonable battle-line unit as both guns and protection began to approach battleship proportions, while on the political front France and Great Britain drew more closely together as the threat of a powerful Germany was perceived. In the Far East, Japanese ascendancy was established with the virtual elimination of the Russian Fleet at Tsushima.

GUNS

The barbette principle—a revolving gun platform below and around which machinery and ammunition arrangements were protected by an armoured column—had by 1900 moved on a stage further: effective against shells with flat trajectories but vulnerable to dipping projectiles (an inevitable consequence of increasing ranges), the exposed breeches and gun crews were now enclosed by armoured gun houses (barbette 'hoods' or, more generally if somewhat inaccurately, 'turrets'), a scheme that was to carry through to the dying days of the battleship.

Two other trends of time should be noted. An 'intermediate' battery of heavy, turreted guns, generally barbette-mounted, made its appearance on capital ships of the major navies. British ships carried 9·2in (234mm) single (King Edward VII, Lord Nelson classes) and twin (Lord Nelson class) mountings; the French favoured 7·6in (193mm) weapons (*Liberté*); the United States, the innovator of this type of armament, settled on 8in (203mm) turrets, which appeared aboard the Indianas and subsequent classes; and Italy adopted a similar calibre in her Regina Elena vessels.

The second development was the location of this armament. The increasing space taken up by machinery, and the need to protect the latter efficiently, demanding as compact as possible an arrangement, had already driven the main armament to either end of the ship. There were only two options: wing turrets, disposed on either beam, not only (as is generally supposed) to provide some degree of ahead and astern fire, but also because this was the only available space for armoured barbettes and their associated loading arrangements, given the location of the boilers and engine rooms; or superfiring, which was not seriously contemplated owing to problems of topweight on small hulls and of blast damage brought about by axial fire. The US

Above: The final German pre-dreadnoughts were the Deutschlands (the name-ship of the class is shown). The secondary 6·7in (170mm) guns were casemate-mounted, which made the weapons difficult to work in heavy seas.

Below: A unique solution to the problem of providing effective secondary-battery fire over wide arcs was explored in the US Navy with the 'double-turret'. This photograph shows the after mounting of *Virginia* (BB-13).

Navy thought differently: in a unique concept (*Kearsarge*/*Virginia*), 8in (203mm) turrets were installed directly on the main turret crowns, rotating with them in a 'double-decked' system, which alleviated the need to extend hull dimensions but caused problems in ammunition supply and fire control and was consequently abandoned.

GUNNERY

MORE revolutionary were the moves made at the turn of the century towards improving gunnery, in other words towards achieving a greater percentage of hits against targets. The years of relative peace through the latter decades of the nineteenth century had both deprived the major navies of the opportunity of a realistic assessment of their fleets' capabilities and encouraged a mood of *laissez-faire*. There were, to be sure, drills and practices, but leisurely shoots at moored targets, in calm waters and on clear days, tended to be the norm; the smartness of the crew and the condition of a ship's paintwork was considered by many officers to be of more importance than proven battle efficiency. In this respect, the Royal Navy was among the worst culprits, and so it was in a sense ironic that the principal driving force behind the stark improvements that were about to become apparent was one Captain Percy Scott, a British officer.

Scott was quick to perceive that the shooting prowess of the Royal Navy—an average of around 25-30 per cent hits upon a target which conveniently lay stationary and did not fire back, was located at a known range and was of a size so small that near-misses were really hits, weren't they?—would prove little short of abysmal under battle conditions. He took steps to put matters right. He was, for example, responsible for encouraging the system of 'continous aim', wherein a target could be kept on sight by means of rapid gun elevation and depression to compensate for a ship's roll in a seaway; time-honoured practice had been for the guns to fire only when the sights came 'on' at some position during the roll. The 'dotter' was an extemporary machine devised by Scott to develop individual gunners' skills in this regard. He also introduced a 'deflection teacher', allowing crews to

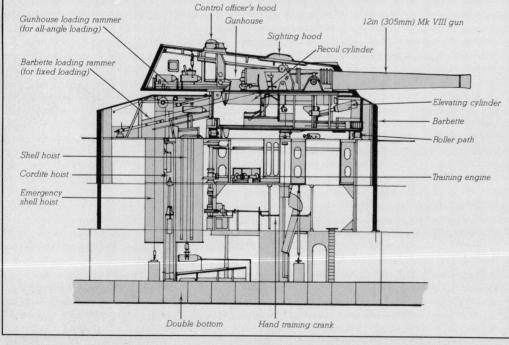

Above: A typical pre-dreadnought barbette mounting, the 12in (305mm) BII as carried by the 1895 Majestic class, showing the two separate shell rammers, one inside the barbette hood ('turret') which permitted up to eight ready-use rounds to be loaded at

any position and another within the barbette, via which loading could be achieved only with the guns trained fore and aft. Note that the barbette armour extends deep into the hull of the battleship—at its thickest it measured 14in (356mm).

Right: *Kearsarge* (BB-5) glides past two British Majestics, 1903. Despite the turret arrangement of the US ship, similarities in general appearance are quite marked. Note the tall funnels, lofty masts and prominent ventilator cowls.

Labels on diagram:
Gunhouse loading rammer (for all-angle loading)
Control officer's hood
Gunhouse
Sighting hood
12in (305mm) Mk VIII gun
Recoil cylinder
Barbette loading rammer (for fixed loading)
Elevating cylinder
Barbette
Roller path
Shell hoist
Cordite hoist
Training engine
Emergency shell hoist
Double bottom
Hand training crank

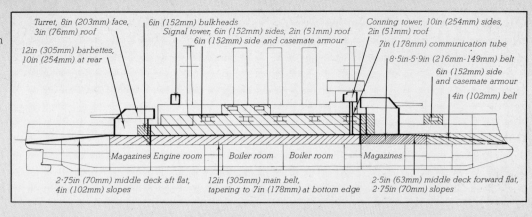

Right: The US battleship *Maine* shows a typical armour system of an American pre-dreadnought. The main belt protected the ship's vitals at the waterline; the casemate armour would stop light shells but not heavy ones, which, however, would be caused to burst and thus be unable to penetrate the horizontal armour covering the magazines and machinery. Weapon protection was the other area of concern (a ship that cannot fight is about as valuable as no ship at all), together with the positions from which the ship was fought, i.e. the control towers. Steering gear was protected only by the armour deck.

Turret, 8in (203mm) face, 3in (76mm) roof

12in (305mm) barbettes, 10in (254mm) at rear

6in (152mm) bulkheads

Signal tower, 6in (152mm) sides, 2in (51mm) roof
6in (152mm) side and casemate armour

Conning tower, 10in (254mm) sides, 2in (51mm) roof

7in (178mm) communication tube

8·5in-5·9in (216mm-149mm) belt

6in (152mm) side and casemate armour

4in (102mm) belt

Magazines | Engine room | Boiler room | Boiler room | Magazines

2·75in (70mm) middle deck aft flat, 4in (102mm) slopes

12in (305mm) main belt, tapering to 7in (178mm) at bottom edge

2·5in (63mm) middle deck forward flat, 2·75in (70mm) slopes

practise accurate gun training on a moving target, and a 'loader' for improved rates of fire. Most importantly, he engendered in gun crews a spirit of vehement competition among their ships, a spirit which caught the imagination of the Press and hence the public. Within a short space of time, hit percentages were regularly around the 80 mark.

Across the Atlantic, Rear Admiral Bradley Fiske had managed to overcome service apathy and pushed through the introduction of the telescopic sight, which narrowed a gunlayer's field of view and thus improved firing accuracy; Lieutenant W.S. Sims, fresh from meetings with Scott while both men were serving in the Pacific, overcame opposition with Presidential backing and forced Scott's methods on a reluctant US Navy.

OTHER DEVELOPMENTS

Fiske and Scott made further contributions. The former, for example, had introduced range-finders to the US Fleet by 1900, and had personally pioneered the 'aloft spotting' technique (at Manila Bay, 1899) whereby a range indicator was taken up the mast to allow a more accurate picture of a developing action to be compiled. Scott introduced the telescopic sight into the Royal Navy and had, like Fiske, appreciated the advantages of controlling fire from high platforms: by 1905 he had prepared plans for 'director

firing', another revolutionary development which would take the responsibility for firing guns out of the hands of individual gunlayers and move it to an officer in a ship's spotting top.

The drive and enthusiasm of 'Jackie' Fisher, CinC Mediterranean Fleet in 1900, were also beginning to make themselves felt; he was an advocate of long-range gunnery in particular, and products of his forceful character included the adoption of a number of fire control instruments to make his doctrine viable. The first was the Dumaresq calculator, which enabled the rate of change in a moving target's bearing and range to be read off, thus enabling the position of an enemy ship at the time shells would land to be predicted with some accuracy. Other contributions to efficiency were adopted apace. The coincidence range-finder, developed by Barr & Stroud, was in general use by the turn of the century, and in 1901 Arthur Pollen began work on a combined range-finder and plotting table which could define the relative movement of a target, taking both enemy- and own-ship courses into account and presenting the information continuously on a moving paper; it was based on the Dumaresq calculator. Communications throughout battleships also improved, as electric telegraphy replaced bugle calls and voicepipes. Further dramatic innovations were in prospect, innovations that would change the entire pattern of battleship construction . . .

SHIKISHIMA

1900 *Japan*
Other ships in class: *Hatsuse, Asahi*

Laid down: 29 March 1897.
Launched: 1 November 1898.
Builder: Thames Iron Works.
Displacement: 14,850 tons (15,086 tonnes) normal; 15,453 tons (15,700 tonnes) full load.
Dimensions: 438 ft (133·5m) oa x 75ft 6in (23m) x 27ft 6in (8·38m).
Machinery: Reciprocating Vertical Triple Expansion engines; 25 Belleville boilers; 2 shafts; 14,500 IHP.
Armour: Harvey nickel steel 9in-4in 229-102mm) main belt; 6in (152mm) upper belt: 4in-2·5in (102-63·5mm) deck; 14in-8in (356-203mm) barbettes; 6in-2in (152-51mm) casemates; 14in-3in (356-76mm) conning tower.
Armament: 4 x 12in (305mm); 14 x 6in (152mm); 20 x 12pdr QF; 6 x 3pdr; 6 x 2½pdr; 5 x 18in (457mm) torpedo tubes.
Performance: 18kt (33·4km/h); radius 5,000nm (9,260km) at 10kt (18·5km/h); coal 1,722 tons (1,750 tonnes).
Crew: 836.

International humiliations forced on Japan after her success in the Sino-Japanese War (1894-5) persuaded an aggressive Japanese government to implement during 1896 an ambitious Ten-Year Naval Expansion Programme, designed to provide the Imperial Navy with a number of powerful but balanced capital ships complementing its useful cruiser and torpedo boat forces. Japan's yards and ordnance factories were as yet not up to the efforts involved, so the four ships (two Shikishima class, *Asahi* and *Mikasa)* were ordered from British yards.

Drawn up by G.C. Macrow, the basic design for the four ships was based on that of the Royal Navy's *Majestic,* though the armament and machinery were identical and closely related, respectively, to those of the earlier Fuji class battleships *(Fuji* and *Yashima).* The provision of 261 watertight compartments and a double bottom amidships ensured a high degree of 'floatability', and extra protection was added by the type of curved armour deck pioneered in the *Renown:* instead of a standard arrangement (flat deck laid over the upper edges of the belt), the curved deck originated at the lower edges of the belt, with the result that a type of spaced protection was afforded against plunging fire, which would have to penetrate the belt and the deck before reaching the machinery and magazines. This in turn meant that armour thicknesses could be reduced, the weight-saving being used to lengthen the main belt and to provide a secondary belt above it.

Shikishima took part in the bombardment and blockade of Port Arthur in 1904, and was a notable participant in the Battles of the Yellow Sea and of Tsushima. In 1921 she was reclassified as a coast defence vessel, and in 1923 disarmed and stripped of her machinery; from that date to 1947, when she was broken up, she served as a training ship.

Hatsuse was built by Armstrong Whitworth at Elswick, being completed in 1901. She sank off Port Arthur on 15 May 1904.

Below: *Shikishima,* 1903; British designed and built, like many of Japan's earlier capital ships.

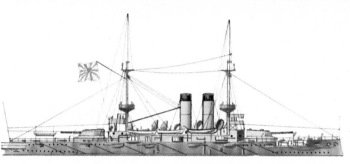

ALABAMA (BB-8)

1900 *USA*
Other ships in class: *Illinois* (BB-7), *Wisconsin* (BB-9).

Laid down: 2 December 1896.
Launched: 18 May 1898.
Builder: Cramp, Philadelphia.
Displacement: 11,565 tons (11,750 tonnes).
Dimensions: 374ft (114m) oa x 72ft 3in (22·03m) x 23ft 6in (7·16m).
Machinery: Vertical Triple Expansion engines; 8 cylindrical boilers; 2 shafts; 10,000 IHP.
Armour: Harvey nickel steel 16·5in-4in (419-102mm) belt; 15in-10in (381-254mm) barbettes; 14in (356mm) turrets; 6in-5·5in (152-140mm) secondary armament; 10in (254mm) conning tower.
Armament: 4 x 13in (330mm); 14 x 6in (152mm); 16 x 6pdr; 6 x 1pdr; 4 x 18in (457mm) torpedo tubes.
Performance: 16kt (29·6km/h); coal 1,355 tons (1,377 tonnes).
Crew: 536.

Authorized in 1896, the three battleships of the Illinois class recognized the experimental nature of the Kearsarges' armament disposition: the 13in (330mm) main battery was placed in barbetted turrets of British type, while the secondary battery consisted of 6in (152mm) weapons in casemates. Appearance was changed radically in comparison with the dimensionally similar Kearsarge class: there was a forecastle deck, and the two funnels were placed abreast of each other.

By 1911 both masts had been replaced by cage masts, and later alterations reduced the 6in (152mm) and 6pdr guns for several AA weapons. *Alabama* was sunk as a target in 1921, while *Illinois* (built by Newport News) was used as an armoury and accommodation ship from 1924 to 1956; *Wisconsin* (built by Union Iron Works) was sold for breaking up in 1922.

Above: Apart from carrying only two funnels, *Asahi,* seen here on completion in 1900, resembled the Shikishimas in almost every way and is generally considered as one of the Shikishima-class battleships.

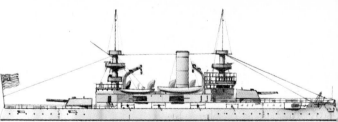

Above: *Alabama* (BB-8) as completed, 1900. Note the considerable visible changes form the Kearsarge class (above right): secondary armament has been rationalised; a forecastle deck is fitted; the two funnels are carried side-by-side. The original design specified two pairs of boat cranes, which *Alabama* carried. Her sisters, however, were fitted with one pair of cranes amidships.

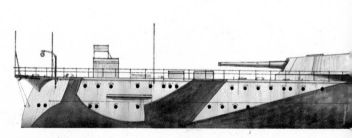

KEARSARGE (BB-5)

1900 USA

Other ships in class: Kentucky (BB-6)

Laid down: 30 June 1896.
Launched: 24 March 1898.
Builder: Newport News.
Displacement: 11,540 tons (11,725 tonnes); 12,850 tons (13,056 tonnes) full load.
Dimensions: 375ft 4in (114·4m) oa x 72ft 3in (22·03m) x 23ft 6in (7·16m) mean.
Machinery: Vertical Triple Expansion engines; 5 cylindrical boilers; 2 shafts; 10,000 IHP.
Armour: Harvey nickel steel 16·5in-4in (419-102mm) belt; 15in-12·5in (381-318mm) barbettes; 17in-15in (432-381mm) turrets; 11in-6in (279-152mm) secondary turrets; 10in (254mm) conning tower.
Armament: 4 x 13in (330mm); 4 x 8in (203mm); 4 x 5in (127mm); 20 x 6pdr; 8 x 1pdr; 4 x 18in (457mm) torpedo tubes.
Performance: 16kt (29·6km/h); coal 1,500 tons (1,524 tonnes) max.
Crew: 553.

The importance of Kearsarge lies in her armament, which formed a useful evolutionary step between the eras of the 'big and small gun' and 'all big gun' battleships. For whereas earlier types had standardised on a main battery of perhaps four 12in (305mm) guns and a secondary battery of some twelve 6in (152mm)

Below: Kearsarge (BB-5) on completion, 1900, in the white and buff livery that characterised US warships for many years. The US Navy was alone at this time in employing superimposed turrets.

guns, the Kearsarge epitomized the advent of the powerful secondary battery. Also notable in the Kearsarge was the disposition of the main and secondary battery turrets in an experimental superfiring arrangement. The advantages claimed for this layout were that the secondary battery enjoyed an improvement of 90° in broadside bearing, freedom from main-battery blast interference, good base protection and ammunition feed thanks to the use of a common barbette, high command, and control of all four guns by a single officer. On the debit side, it was soon appreciated, were the following factors: no independent fire facility for the secondary battery, the real possibility of four guns being disabled by one hit, a great concentration of weight on the main turret bearings, increase in top weight, the need for greater structural strength to accept heavier local weights, and great difficulty in dismounting the main armament.

Protection must be judged good, the belt being long and deep, and closed by substantial bulkheads. But as gun platforms both vessels were poor, and during World War I most of the 6pdr guns were removed, extra 6in (152mm) weapons and two 3in (76mm) AA guns being added. Kentucky was scrapped in 1923, while Kearsarge, stripped of her armour, ordnance and machinery, became a crane ship in 1920, serving as such until she was scrapped in 1955.

FORMIDABLE

1901 UK

Other ships in class: Implacable, Irresistible, Bulwark, London, Venerable, Queen, Prince of Wales.

Laid down: 21 March 1898.
Launched: 17 November 1898.
Builder: Portsmouth Dockyard.
Displacement: 14,500 tons (14,732 tonnes) load; 15,800 tons (16,053 tonnes) deep load.
Dimensions: 431ft 9in (131·6m) oa x 75ft (22·86m) x 25ft 11in (7·9m).
Machinery: 3-cylinder Triple Expansion engines; 20 Belleville boilers; 2 shafts; 15,000 IHP.
Armour: Krupp cemented 9in (229mm) belt; 12in-9in (305-229mm) bulkheads; 3in-1in (76-25mm) deck; 12in (305mm) barbettes; 10in-8in (254-203mm) turrets; 6in (152mm) casemates; 14in (356mm) conning tower.
Armament: 4 x 12in (305mm) BL; 12 x 6in (152mm) QF; 16 x 12pdr QF; 6 x 3pdr QF; 4 x 18in (457mm) torpedo tubes.
Performance: 18kt (33·4km/h).
Crew: 780.

The three units of the Formidable class were designed by Sir William White as an improvement of the Majestic class, though the ships could also be regarded as larger versions of the Canopus with extra protection afforded by the latest Krupp armour. Although the number and calibre of the guns remained unaltered in comparison with the fit on the Canopus (though White had proposed an increase of two guns in the secondary battery), offensive capability was improved by the fact that both main and secondary batteries had guns of five calibres greater length, and that the guns could be loaded at any elevation on any bearing. The main belt was 218ft (66·45m) long and 15ft (4·57m) deep, with extensions to the stem (3in, 76mm, thick and 12ft, 3.66m, deep) and to the stern (1·5in, 38mm, thick and 8ft, 2·44m, deep).

All three ships served in the Mediterranean from 1901 to 1908, and proved popular for their low fuel consumption, good speed and general handiness except at low speed. Formidable was torpedoed and sunk on 1 January 1915; Implacable, built by Devonport Dockyard, survived World War I and was sold for breaking up in 1921; and Irresistible, built by Chatham Dockyard, was mined in the Dardanelles on 18 March 1915.

Construction of the Formidables was immediately followed by that of five further battleships—Bulwark, London, Venerable, Queen and Prince of Wales—which resembled them in all respects save for improvements in protection. On 26 November 1914, Bulwark sank with the loss of almost all her crew at Sheerness, after ammunition exploded.

Below: The battleship London, a repeat of the Formidable design, is shown in striking dazzle paintwork late in World War I. By 1918 she had been converted to a minelayer, with the after turret removed and guns removed from the forward turret.

PERESVIET

1901 *Russia*
Other ships in class: *Osliabia, Pobieda*

Laid down: 21 November 1895.
Launched: May 1898.
Builder: New Admiralty Yard, St Petersburg.
Displacement: 12,683 tons (12,885 tonnes).
Dimensions: 434ft 6in (132·43m) oa x 71ft 6in (21·79m) x 26ft (8m) max.
Machinery: Vertical Triple Expansion engines; 32 Belleville boilers; 3 shafts; 15,000 IHP.
Armour: Krupp cemented and Harvey nickel steel 9in-5in (230-125mm) belt; 3in-2in (75-50mm) deck; 4in (100mm) bulkheads; 9in-5in (230-125mm) turrets; 5in (125mm) casemates; 6in (150mm) conning tower.
Armament: 4 x 10in (254mm); 11 x 6in (152mm); 20 x 11pdr; 20 x 3pdr; 8 x 1pdr; 5 x 15in (381mm) torpedo tubes; mines.
Performance: 19·12kt (35·4km/h); coal 2,100 tons (2,135 tonnes).
Crew: 752.

The three units of the Peresviet class were totally misconceived 'fast battleships', which were in fact notably deficient in speed, armament and protection, but whose importance perhaps lay in their pre-building reputation, sufficient to spur the Royal Navy into production of the six Duncan class battleships.

Below: *Emanuele Filiberto* on completion, 1902; her sister-ship, *Ammiraglio di Saint Bon,* had slightly shorter funnels. The heavy guns were on raised barbettes to allow easier working in a seaway.

To a certain extent based on French practice, the *Peresviet* had a high forecastle deck stretching as far aft as the mainmast, a fair amount of tumblehome, and main armament turrets of French pattern. These last were located fore and aft, while the guns of the secondary and tertiary batteries were disposed mainly in casemates on the main and upper decks, though there was an unprotected 6in (152mm) gun right in the bows.

The main belt was 312ft (95m) long and 7ft 10in (2·4m) deep, with a secondary belt, only 188ft (57·3m) long, protecting the centre of the

Below: *Peresviet* in 1903. The protection in these vessels was modelled on the French system. The 10in (254mm) guns fired 488lb (221kg) projectiles.

ship between the main belt and the main deck. This latter was quite thin, and the ends of the belts were boxed off by inadequate bulkheads.

Peresviet enjoyed a chequered career: in August 1904 she was damaged heavily by the Japanese in the Battle of the Yellow Sea; she regained Port Arthur only to be hit by a minimum of twenty-three 11in (280mm) howitzer shells and scuttled on 7 December 1904; she was raised by the Japanese, repaired and placed in service as the *Sagami;* in 1916 she was sold back to Russia, but went aground off Vladivostok; and her career finally ended on 4

January 1917, when she was sunk by a German mine off Port Said.

Osliabia was also built in the New Admiralty Yard, and was sunk by Japanese gunfire in the Battle of Tsushima. *Pobieda* was built by the Baltic Works, and differed slightly from her sisters in terms of armour and machinery. Not as heavily damaged in the Battle of the Yellow Sea as the *Peresviet,* she too retired to Port Arthur, where she sank on 7 December 1904 after being hit by twenty-one 11in (280mm) howitzer shells. She was raised by the Japanese and served as the *Suwo* until reduced to scrap in 1922.

Below: *Schwaben,* sister-ship of *Wettin,* soon after completion in 1904. In this class, a comparatively light main armament of 4 x 9·45in (240mm) guns was reinforced by a powerful secondary battery.

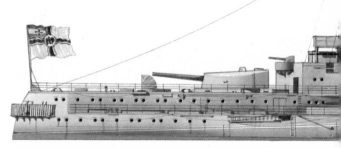

EMANUELE FILIBERTO

1902 *Italy*
Other ships in class: *Ammiraglio di Saint Bon*

Laid down: 5 October 1893.
Launched: 29 September 1897.
Builder: Castellammare Navy Yard.
Displacement: 9,645 tons (9,800 tonnes) normal; 9,940 tons (10,100 tonnes) full load.
Dimensions: 366ft 9½in (111·8m) oa x 69ft 3½in (21·12m) x 23ft 10in (7·27m).
Machinery: Triple Expansion engines; 12 cylindrical boilers; 2 shafts; 13,500 IHP.
Armour: Harvey nickel steel 9·8in (250mm) sides; 2·75in (70mm) deck; 9·8in (250mm) turrets; 5·9in (150mm) battery; 9·8in (250mm) conning tower.
Armament: 4 x 10in (254mm); 8 x 6in (152mm); 8 x 4·7in (120mm); 6 x 3in (76mm); 8 x 47mm; 4 x 17·7in

(450mm) torpedo tubes.
Performance: 18·1kt (33·5km/h) radius 5,500nm (10,200km) at 10kt (18·5km/h).
Crew: 565.

The two ships of the Ammiraglio di Saint Bon class were designed by Giacinto Pullino to the dictates of Admiral di Saint Bon, the Italian naval minister, who saw that huge ships were too expensive for the Italian Navy, took so long to build that they were obsolescent by the time they were commissioned, and were moreover not really suited to Italian tactical needs. Saint Bon's concept was continued after his death by Benedetto Brin and Admiral Racchia, and the two ships were laid down in 1893. In service they proved to be disappointing: though the armour protection was good, fire-power was little better than that of a cruiser, while speed was lacking. Freeboard was also low, at 9ft 10in (3m), making the use of the main armament difficult in any sort of sea. However, both ships survived into the first half of 1920.

Ammiraglio di Saint Bon was built at Venice Navy Yard and displaced slightly more than her sister.

Below: Short-lived *Iéna* lost 1907.

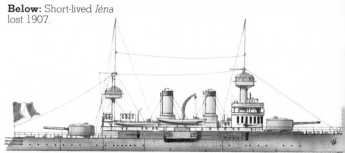

152

Below: Maine (BB-8) as completed in 1902. Cage masts were fitted in 1911.

MAINE (BB-10)

1902 USA
Other ships in class: *Missouri* (BB-11), *Ohio* (BB-12).

Laid down: 15 February 1899.
Launched: 27 July 1901.
Builder: Cramp, Philadelphia.
Displacement: 12,846 tons (13,050 tonnes); 13,700 tons (13,920 tonnes) full load.
Dimensions: 393ft 11in (120·06m) oa x 72 ft 3in (22·03m) x 24ft 4in (7·42m) mean.
Machinery: Vertical Triple

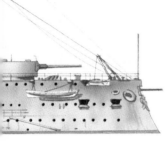

Expansion engines; 24 Niclausse boilers; 2 shafts; 16,000 IHP.
Armour: Krupp cemented and Harvey nickel steel 11in-4in (279-102mm) belt; 12in-8in (305-203mm) barbettes; 12in-11 in (305-279mm) turrets; 6in-5·5in (152-140mm) secondary guns; 10in (254mm) conning tower.
Armament: 4 x 12in (305mm); 16 x 6in (152mm); 6 x 3in (76mm); 8 x 3pdr; 6 x 1pdr; 2 x 18in (457mm) torpedo tubes.
Performance: 18kt (33·4km/h); coal 1,867 tons (1,897 tonnes).
Crew: 561.

This class was essentially an improved version of the Illinois class, and had the first submerged torpedo tubes carried by American battleships. They were not very successful, being very wet in heavy weather and having suspect ammunition handling safety. All three units had their military masts replaced by cage masts in 1911. *Maine* and *Missouri* were scrapped in 1922 in accordance with the Washington Treaty, *Ohio* following in 1923.

WETTIN

1902 Germany
Other ships in class: *Wittelsbach, Zähringen, Schwaben, Mecklenburg*

Launched: 6 June 1901.
Builder: Schichau.
Displacement: 12,598 tons (12,800 tonnes).
Dimensions: 416ft (126·8m) oa x 74ft 9in (22·8m) x 26ft 4in (8·04m).
Machinery: Triple Expansion engines; 3 shafts; 15,000 IHP.
Armour: Krupp 15·75in-11·8in (400-300mm) belt; 5·9in (150mm) bulkheads.
Armament: 4 x 9·45in (240mm); 18 x 5·9in (150mm); 12 x 3·5in (88mm); 12 smaller; 6 x 17·7in (450mm) torpedo tubes.
Performance: 17·5kt (32·4km/h).
Crew: 683.

Built under the provisions of the Navy Law of 1898 instigated by Admiral Alfred von Tirpitz, the *Wettin* was the first of the five-strong Wittelsbach class to be completed. Designed to make a major contribution to Germany's expansionist programme at the turn of the century, the ships in fact marked little real improvement over the preceding Kaiser class ships, of which four units were eventually built.

The feature that most marked German battleships of this interim period was a relatively light main battery and a comparatively heavy secondary battery; contemporary British ships, for example, had a 12in (305mm) main gun calibre (2·55in, 65mm, greater than the Germans' 9·45in, 240mm, guns) while the secondary battery, with guns of almost identical calibre, were some six fewer in number. Interestingly enough, the Germans pioneered the location of secondary armament in turrets rather than casemates, eight of the *Wettin's* 5·9in (150mm) guns being in four twin turrets.

By 1916 the ships of the Wittelsbach class were considered inadequate for combat and disarmed. All but the *Zähringen* were broken up in 1921. *Zähringen* had been used as a target from 1917, but was hulked after World War I; in 1926 she became a radio-controlled target, and was sunk by bombs in Gdynia harbour in 1944.

IÉNA

1902 France.

Laid down: 15 January 1898.
Launched: 1 September 1898.
Builder: Brest Dockyard.

Displacement: 11,860 tons (12,050 tonnes).
Dimensions: 400ft 9in (122·15m) wl x 68ft 3in (20·8m) x 27ft 6in (8·38m).
Machinery: Vertical Triple Expansion engines: 20 Belleville boilers; 3 shafts; 16,500 IHP.
Armour: Harvey nickel steel 12·8in-4·7in (325-120mm) belt; 4·7in-3·2in (120-80mm) upper belt; 2·5in (65mm) deck; 11·5in (290mm) turrets; 8in-3·5in (200-90mm) secondary turrets; 12in (305mm) CT.
Armament: 4 x 12in (305mm); 8 x

6·3in (160mm) QF; 8 x 3·9in (100mm); 20 x 3pdr; 4 x 1pdr; 2 x 18in (457mm) torpedo tubes.
Performance: 18kt (33·4km/h); coal 1,080 tons (1,100 tonnes).
Crew: 682.

In the last 20 years of the 19th century, the French failed to standardise: some ships had single large guns fore and aft with slightly smaller beam guns, while others had twin main-calibre guns fore and aft complemented by smaller secondary

batteries. The *Iéna* fell into this latter category, and may be regarded as an enlarged version of the *Charlemagne*. Protection was excellent, the full-length main belt extending 4ft 11in (1·5m) below the waterline and 3ft (0·9m) above it, the full-thickness central portion being 275ft (83·8m) long, tapering to 9in (230mm) at the ends. *Iéna* was largely destroyed by an internal explosion while in dry dock on 12 March 1907, but was later repaired sufficiently to serve as a target.

Above: *Mikasa* soon after completion by her British builder—Armstrong, Elswick—in 1902. Note the main-deck box battery housing five 6in (152mm) guns on either beam.

Below: *Mikasa* as completed in 1902. Open gun ports show the shields fitted on some of the smaller guns; note the light QF weapons mounted on the boat deck and in the fighting tops.

MIKASA

1902 *Japan*

Laid down: 24 January 1899.
Launched: 8 November 1900.
Builder: Armstrong, Elswick.
Displacement: 15,140 tons (15,383 tonnes) normal; 15,179 tons (15,422 tonnes) full load.
Dimensions: 432ft (131·7m) oa x 76ft (23·23m) x 27ft (8·28m).
Machinery: 3-cylinder Reciprocating Vertical Triple Expansion engines; 25 Belleville boilers; 2 shafts; 15,000 IHP.
Armour: Krupp cemented 9in-4in (229-102mm) belt; 6in (152mm) upper belt; 12in (305mm) bulkheads 3in-2in (76-51mm) deck; 14in-8in (356-203mm) barbettes; 6in-2in (152-51mm) casemates.
Armament: 4 x 12in (305mm); 14 x 6in (152mm); 20 x 12pdr QF; 8 x 3pdr QF; 4 x 2½pdr QF; 4 x 18in (457mm) torpedo tubes.
Performance: 18kt (33·4km/h); radius 4,600nm (8,530km) at 10kt (18·5km/h), 1,900nm (3,520km) at 16kt; coal 1,521 tons (1,545 tonnes).
Crew: 830.

The *Mikasa* was the last of the four Japanese battleships laid down under the terms of the 1896 Ten-Year Naval Expansion Programme: the two units of the Shikishima class had been followed by the *Asahi*, completed at the John Brown yard on Clydebank in July 1900 (with only rearranged machinery spaces and two rather than three funnels to differentiate her from *Shikishima* and *Hatsuse*). The *Mikasa* was very similar to the *Asahi*, but was a considerably more combat-worthy ship thanks to the use of Krupp cemented rather than Harvey nickel steel armour; thicknesses were not reduced, so protection was considerably improved compared with that of her three half-sisters.

The lessons learned with the earlier vessels were put to good use in a number of detail improvements, notably to the armament. The main and secondary batteries were by Armstrong at Elswick: the main armament could be worked by electric, hydraulic or manual power, and could be loaded at any angle of elevation or bearing; rate of fire was three rounds per gun every two minutes, and total 12in (305mm) ammunition stowage was 240 rounds. The secondary battery was unaltered in fire-power compared with the preceding ships, but was better protected; moreover, 10 of these 6in (152mm) guns were placed in a main-deck box battery (rather than in upper-deck casemates), which offered greater protection against fire from the rear, incoming shells now having to pierce the 6in (152mm) armour on the far side of the battery rather than just the 2in (51mm) plate backing the casemates. The battery was also protected from end-on fire by an extension of the bulkhead armour upwards to the upper deck. Ammunition stowage for the secondary battery was 2,800 rounds.

Despite a greater hull weight than her predecessors, and machinery heavier than all but that of *Asahi*, *Mikasa* turned out lighter than the preceding three vessels thanks largely to her lighter armour (a total of 4,097 tons, 4,163 tonnes, compared with an average of 4,526 tons, 4,598 tonnes) and armament (1,550 tons, 1,575 tonnes compared with an average of 1,605 tons, 1,631 tonnes).

At the outbreak of the Russo-Japanese War in 1904, *Mikasa* flew the flag of Vice-Admiral Togo, commanding the Imperial Japanese Navy's Combined Fleet in the climactic Battle of Tsushima. In her capacity as fleet flagship she attracted much of the Russian fire, but came through it exceptionally well thanks to her armour and sturdy construction. On 12 September 1905 *Mikasa* sank as a result of a magazine explosion whilst at anchor at Sasebo, but was refloated in August 1906 and recommissioned with new main and secondary batteries in 1907. In 1921 she was reclassified as a coast defence ship. After running aground and sustaining damage off Vladivostok, she was finally retired in 1923, being maintained as a national monument at Yokosuka. Her condition deteriorated considerably during World War II, but restoration put in hand in the late 1950s halted the decline and she is now on permanent display, the last surviving battleship of her period.

TSESSAREVITCH

1903 *Russia*

Laid down: June 1899.
Launched: 23 February 1901.
Builder: La Seyne.
Displacement: 12,915 tons (13,122 tonnes).
Dimensions: 388ft 9in (118·5m) oa x 76ft 1in (23·2m) x 26ft (7·92m) max.
Machinery: Vertical Triple Expansion engines; 20 Belleville boilers; 2 shafts; 16,500 IHP.
Armour: Krupp cemented 10in-7in (255-180mm) belt; 6·75in-4·75in (170-120mm) belt ends; 2·5in (65mm) main deck; 1·5in (40mm) lower deck; 10in (255mm) turrets; 6in (150mm) secondary turrets; 10in (255mm) conning tower.
Armament: 4 x 12in (305mm); 12 x 6in (152mm); 20 x 11pdr; 20 x 3pdr; 4 x 15in (381mm) torpedo tubes; 45 mines.
Performance: 18·5kt (34·3km/h); coal 1,350 tons (1,372 tonnes).
Crew: 782.

Along with the American-built battleship *Retvisan* (Japanese *Hizen* from 1908) and several powerful cruisers and destroyers, the

Below: *Tsessarevitch* was designed by Lagane and completed in 1903. The marked tumblehome is indicative of her French origin. Note heavy fighting tops and the torpedo tube set above the pronounced ram bow.

Above: The veteran *Tsessarevitch* in service with the Baltic Fleet during World War I. The large fighting tops originally carried have been replaced by light searchlight platforms; otherwise, few changes have been made, although the number of light guns is reduced.

...sessarevitch was constructed under £9 million expansion programme dditional to the Russian Naval stimates of 1898. Since Russia was nxious to obtain examples of p-to-date naval architecture—and so because Russian yards were nable to cope with the additional ork—the contracts were awarded foreign builders.

Tsessarevitch, built in a French ard, was of typically French design ith her blocky superstructure and ry distinct tumblehome. Another rench feature was the high bow, e forecastle deck being extended t as far as the mainmast.

The main armament of four 12in 305mm) guns was carried in a pair f turrets, again typically French, cated fore and aft. The secondary rmament was unusually modern, owever, for the twelve 6in (152mm) uns were carried in six twin turrets, ree on each beam: the forward and fter turrets were located on the high recastle deck, while the two centre urrets were sponsored out from the ward sloping sides of the vessel at e level of the upper deck.

The armour protection scheme as particularly interesting, specially with regard to its anti-torpedo provisions. The main belt ran the full length of the ship, stretching from 5ft (1·5m) below the waterline to 7ft (2·1m) above it. This belt had two strakes: the lower was 10in (255mm) thick amidships, and tapered to 7in (180mm) at its lower edge; the upper was 8in (200mm) thick. Towards the bows the upper strake thinned to 5·75in (145mm) and the lower to 5·9in (150mm), and towards the stern the thicknesses were 4·75in (120mm) and 6·75in (170mm) respectively.

The increasing threat posed to capital ships during the 1890s by craft armed with gyroscopically controlled torpedoes is evidenced by a number of measures to appear in about 1900, principally in French *(Henri IV)* and Russian *(Tsessarevitch)* ships. Though the only battleships sunk by such a weapon had been the *Blanco Encalada* and *Aquidaban*, it was realised that a later generation of torpedo represented a very real threat to even the latest battleships unless a means could be found to reduce the damage caused by the detonation of some 220lb (100kg) of high explosive just below the waterline. It was appreciated that longitudinal bulkheads, containing coal between themselves and the ship's outer hull, could help contain the force of the explosion, but that something better was needed. The expedient adopted in the *Tsessarevitch* was the use of an armoured bulkhead along each side of the ship. This was formed by a down curve of the lower armoured deck, which from a point some 6ft 7in (2m) inboard of the waterline was turned vertically downward to meet the ship's double bottom in the region of the bilge keel on each side. The system had been tested with good results at Toulon as far back as 1890, but it was later realised that the gap between the outer hull and the armour bulkhead was too small to be truly effective. As it was, this primary anti-torpedo measure stretched from just forward of 'A' turret to just aft of 'Y' turret, and when the *Tsessarevitch* was in fact torpedoed on 9 February 1904 in Port Arthur, the hit was aft of the special belt, whose efficiency could not therefore be assessed.

In the Battle of the Yellow Sea, on 10 August 1904, the *Tsessarevitch* was the flagship of Rear-Admiral Vilgelm Vitgeft. The battle was lost to the Russians when one 12in (305mm) shell hit the fore mast, killing Vitgeft and leaving the Russian forces without effective leadership. Later during the action, another 12in (305mm) shell hit the *Tsessarevitch*, this time on the conning tower to jam the helm. Interned in China, where she had made port, the *Tsessarevitch* was quickly repaired, it being discovered that 13 main-calibre hits had done very little real damage.

During World War I the *Tsessarevitch* was part of the Baltic Fleet, which played only a very small part in operations. Her one major moment came during an action with the German dreadnoughts *Kronprinz* and *König* off Moon Island in the Baltic on 17 October 1917. Hit by two 12in (305mm) shells from *Kronprinz*, the ship managed to escape without further damage, although her companion, the battleship *Slava*, was not so fortunate, being badly damaged and put out of action by *König*.

The *Tsessarevitch* was renamed *Grashdanin* during 1917, but received little attention once part of the Red fleet. She was broken up in 1922.

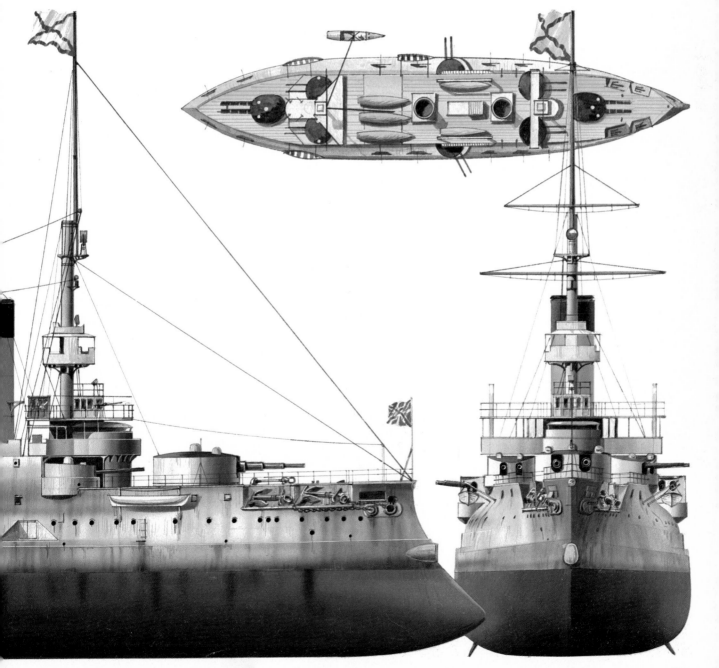

Below: American-built *Retvisan* is seen soon after completion in 1901.

RETVISAN

1901 Russia

Laid down: May 1898.
Launched: October 1900.
Builder: Cramp, Philadelphia.
Displacement: 12,900 tons (13,106 tonnes).
Dimensions: 386ft 8in (117·85m) oa x 72ft 2in (22m) x 26ft (7·92m) max.
Machinery: Vertical Triple Expansion engines; 24 Niclausse boilers; 2 shafts; 17,000 IHP.
Armour: Krüpp cemented 9in-5in (229-127mm) belt; 2in (51mm) belt ends; 9in-8in (229-203mm) turrets; 5in (127mm) casemates and battery; 10in (255mm) conning tower.
Armament: 4 x 12in (305mm); 12 x 6in (152mm); 20 x 11pdr; 24 x 2pdr; 8 x 1pdr; 6 x 15in (381mm) torpedo tubes; 45 mines.
Performance: 18·8kt (34·8km/h) coal 2,000 tons (2,032 tonnes).
Crew: 738.

Completed just under two years before the *Tsessarevitch*, the Russian capital ship *Retvisan* represented a midway approach to design, combining features of French and American vessels; the flush-deck hull reflected the American influence, and the turrets were typical of French practice. And in marked contrast with the *Tsessarevitch*, *Retvisan* relied for protection against torpedoes on nets boomed out from the hull sides.

Armour protection was not much different from that in preceding classes. The main belt ran the full length of the hull, and was formed by two strakes. The lower strake stretched from 4ft (1·2m) below the waterline to 3ft 6in (1·05m) above it, and maintained a constant thickness of 9in (229mm) for 256ft (78m); the upper strake connected the top edge of the lower strake with the main deck, and had a thickness of 6in (152mm) between the turrets. The main thickness of the belt was

closed off by 7in (178mm) bulkheads, and beyond these the belt tapered to 2in (51mm) ends. The deck armour was 2in (51mm) thick, with 3in (76mm) slopes. The main guns were located in two twin turrets before and abaft the superstructure, while eight of the 6in (152mm) guns were placed in a main-deck secondary battery, the remaining four 6in (152mm) guns being in upper-deck casemates.

At the time of the Russo-Japanese War, the *Retvisan* was deployed to the Far East and gave ample proof of her sturdiness: on 9 February 1904 she was torpedoed in Port Arthur and took in some 2,100 tons (2,135 tonnes) of water, but was soon repaired; on 10 August 1904 she was involved in the Battle of the Yellow Sea, where she took 18 hits from shells of 12in (305mm) and 8in (203mm) calibre; and during the seige of Port Arthur she took 13 strikes from 11in (280mm) howitzer shells, sinking after three very damaging rounds on 6 December 1904.

Retvisan was raised by the Japanese in 1905 and repaired at Sasebo between 1906 and 1908, when she entered service with the Japanese Navy as the *Hizen*. She became a coast defence ship in 1921, was removed from the effective list in 1923 and was sunk as a target in 1924.

Below: Diminutive *Habsburg* in 1902.

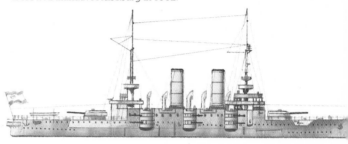

HABSBURG

1902 Austria-Hungary
Other ships in class: *Arpád*, *Babenburg*

Laid down: 13 March 1899.
Launched: 9 September 1900.
Builder: Stabilimento Tecnico Triestino.
Displacement: 8,823 tons (8,965 tonnes) full load.
Dimensions: 375ft 10in (114·57m) oa x 65ft (19·86m) x 24ft 6in (7·46m).
Machinery: 4-cylinder Vertical Triple Expansion engines; 16 boilers; 2 shafts; 15,063 IHP.
Armour: Skoda 8·66in-7·1in (220-180mm) belt; 11in-8·27in (280-210mm) turrets and casemates.
Armament: 3 x 9·45in (240mm); 1 x 5·9in (150mm); 16 smaller; 2 x 17·7in (450mm) torpedo tubes.
Performance: 19·6kt (36·3km/h).
Crew: 638.

The world's smallest capital ships, with a main armament disposed in twin turret forward and a single turret aft. As the ships proved to be top heavy, in 1910 *Habsburg* and *Arpád* had their superstructure trimmed by one deck. During World War I they were reclassified as harbour guard ships. Handed over to the UK in 1920, they were scrapped in Italy during 1921.

SUFFREN

1903 France

Laid down: 5 January 1899.
Launched: 25 July 1899.
Builder: Brest Dockyard.
Displacement: 12,527 tons (12,727 tonnes).
Dimensions: 411ft 9in (125·5m) wl x 70ft 2in (21·39m) x 27ft 6in (8·38m) max.
Machinery: Vertical Triple Expansion engines; 24 Niclausse boilers; 3 shafts; 16,700 IHP.

Below: Suffren as completed, 1903.

Armour: Harvey nickel steel 12in-4in (305-100mm) belt; 12·8in (325mm) turrets; 12in-10in (305-255mm) conning tower.
Armament: 4 x 12in (305mm); 10 x 6·3in (160mm) QF; 8 x 3·9in (100mm); 24 smaller; 4 x 18in (457mm) torpedo tubes.
Performance: 17·9kt (33·2km/h).
Crew: 714.

Suffren was a useful design notable for the revival of turreted secondary armament (six single units at upper-deck level), complemented by the remainder in casemates.

Severely damaged by shore fire on 18 March 1915 while supporting the Dardanelles operations, she blew up after being torpedoed off Portugal on 26 November 1916.

HENRI IV

1903 France

Laid down: 15 July 1897.
Launched: 23 August 1899.
Builder: Cherbourg Dockyard.
Displacement: 8,807 tons (8,948 tonnes).
Dimensions: 354ft 4in (108m) wl x 72ft 10in (22·2m) x 22ft 11in (6·98m) max.
Machinery: Vertical Triple Expansion engines; 12 boilers; 3 shafts; 11,000 IHP.

Below: Henri IV, completed in 1903.

Armour: Harvey nickel steel 11in-3in (280-75mm) belt; 12in (305mm) turrets; 9·5in (240mm) conning tower.
Armament: 2 x 10·8in (275mm); 7 x 5·5in (140mm); 14 smaller; 2 x 18in (457mm) torpedo tubes.
Performance: 17kt (31·5km/h).
Crew: 464.

Ranked as a coast defence battleship, *Henri IV* had several novel features, including an exceptionally low freeboard aft and a single 5·5in (140mm) gun above and slightly before the aft 10·8in (275mm) gun to provide wide arcs of bearing. She was a successful design, though hampered by financial restrictions. She was stricken in 1921.

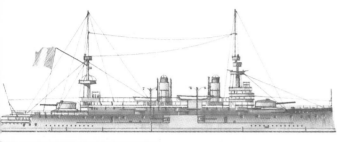

KNIAZ POTEMKIN TAVRITCHESKI

1903 Russia

Laid down: February 1898.
Launched: October 1900.
Builder: Nikolaiev Dockyard.
Displacement: 12,582 tons (12,783 tonnes).
Dimensions: 378ft 6in (115·36m) oa x 73ft (22·25m) x 27ft (8·23m) max.
Machinery: Vertical Triple Expansion engines; 22 Belleville boilers; 2 shafts; 10,600 IHP.
Armour: Krupp cemented 9in-5in (229-127mm) belt; 6in (152mm) upper belt; 7in-5in (178-127mm) bulkheads; 2·5in-2in (64-51mm) decks; 10in-5in (254-127mm) turrets; 6in (152mm) casemates; 9in (229mm) conning tower.

Below: Kniaz Potemkin Tavritcheski, immortalised in Eisenstein's film Battleship Potemkin, as she appeared in mid-1904. The powerful secondary armament — 16 x 6in (152mm) guns — was somewhat cramped by its concentration in a main-deck battery.

Armament: 4 x 12in (305mm); 16 x 6in (152mm); 14 x 11pdr; 6 x 3pdr; 5 x 15in (381mm) torpedo tubes.
Performance: 16·6kt (30·8km/h); coal 870 tons (885 tonnes).
Crew: 750.

Built as part of the battleship strength of the Russians' Black Sea Fleet the *Kniaz Potemkin Tavritcheski* had an unfortunate career best remembered for the mutiny immortalised by Eisenstein in his film *Battleship Potemkin.* In general design she was similar to the preceding *Peresviet,* though with an upper deck rather than forecastle deck extending to a position aft of the mainmast.

The main armament was disposed fore and aft in twin turrets of clear French origins, while the secondary armament (much improved over that of the unsuccessful *Peresviet*) was largely concentrated in a main-deck battery.

The main belt was only 237ft (72·25m) long, and was 7ft 6in (2·3m) high. The upper belt, which had a constant thickness of 6in (165mm), covered the area from the top of the main belt to the main deck, but was only 156ft (47·5m) long, some 14ft (4·25m) less than the battery armour. Compared with the *Peresviet,* the *Kniaz Potemkin Tavritcheski* had much thicker bulkheads to close off the armour belts, while the deck armour was roughly comparable with that of her predecessor: a 2in (51mm) flat

section with 2·5in (64mm) slopes outside the battery area and 3in (76mm) at their ends.

After the mutiny the ship was renamed *Pantelimon;* however, in April 1917 she was again renamed, this time *Potemkin,* and she finally became the *Boretz za Svobodu* in May 1917. The ship took part in most Russian actions in the Black Sea during World War I, two 11pdr anti-aircraft guns being added, and was finally scrapped in 1922.

RUSSELL

1903 UK.
Other ships in class: *Albemarle, Cornwallis, Duncan, Exmouth, Montagu*

Laid down: 11 March 1899.
Launched: 19 February 1901.
Builder: Palmer, Jarrow.
Displacement: 13,270 tons (13,482 tonnes) load; 14,900 tons (15,138 tonnes) deep load.
Dimensions: 432ft (131·67m) oa x 75ft 6in (23·01m) x 25ft 9in (7·85m).
Machinery: 4-cylinder Triple Expansion engines; 24 Belleville boilers; 2 shafts; 18,000 IHP.

Below: Russell's sister Exmouth in 'Home Fleet grey' before World War I. The design was a modified Formidable.

Armour: Krupp cemented and Krupp non-cemented 7in (178mm) belt; 11in-7in (279-178mm) bulkheads; 2in-1in (51-25mm) decks; 11in-4in (279-102mm) barbettes; 10in-8in (254-203mm) turrets; 6in (152mm) casemates; 12in (305mm) conning tower.
Armament: 4 x 12in (305mm); 12 x 6in (152mm) QF; 10 x 12pdr QF; 6 x 3pdr QF; 4 x 18in (457mm) torpedo tubes.
Performance: 19kt (35·2km/h); coal 2,240 tons (2,276 tonnes).
Crew: 720.

The *Russell* was the first of six Duncan class ships to be completed for the Royal Navy. The spur for this class was the possible threat posed by the Russian Peresviet class of 'fast battleships': as it turned out, the Russian ships were not as powerfully armed, so the six Duncans were markedly better in terms of fire-power, speed and protection.

The design was basically that of the Formidable class but with greater power for high speed. The main belt was 238ft (72·5m) long and 15ft (4·57m) deep, and was extended to the bows with 5in (127mm), 4in (102mm) and 3in (76mm) plates.

Montagu was wrecked in 1906, *Russell* was mined off Malta on 27 April 1916, *Cornwallis* was torpedoed off Malta in January 1917, and the other three were sold for breaking up in 1919 and 1920.

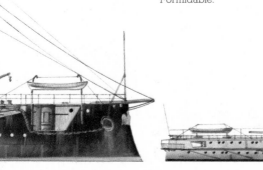

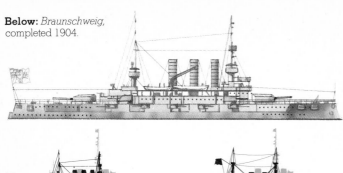

Below: *Braunschweig,* completed 1904.

Below: Swiftsure-class *Triumph,* 1905.

BRAUNSCHWEIG

1904 *Germany*
Other ships in class: *Elsass, Hessen, Preussen, Lothringen*

Laid down: 1901.
Launched: 20 December 1902.
Builder: Germaniawerft, Kiel.
Displacement: 14,167 tons (14,935 tonnes).
Dimensions: 419ft (127·7m) oa x 84ft (25·6m) x 26ft 7in (8·1m).
Machinery: Triple Expansion engines; 12 boilers; 3 shafts; 17,000 IHP.
Armour: Krupp 9in (230mm) belt; 11in (280mm) turrets.
Armament: 4 x 11in (280mm); 14 x 6·7in (170mm); 18 x 3·5in (88mm); 4 smaller; 6 x 17·7in (450mm) torpedo tubes.
Performance: 18·25kt (33·8km/h).
Crew: 743.

Larger and faster than the preceding Wittelsbach class, the five units of the Braunschweig class also had an armament of slightly increased calibre, though the main guns were smaller than the British equivalent.

In 1916 and 1917 all the ships were disarmed, though *Lothringen* kept 10 of her 6·7in (170mm) guns for another year. *Hessen* was converted to a radio-controlled target and survived to become the Russian *Tsel* in 1946, but the other four units had been discarded by the outbreak of World War II.

Below: Fast, lightly-protected *Regina Margherita* as completed, 1904.

REGINA MARGHERITA

1904 *Italy*
Other ships in class: *Benedetto Brin*

Laid down: 20 November 1898.
Launched: 30 May 1901.
Builder: La Spezia Navy Yard.
Displacement: 13,215 tons (13,426 tonnes) normal.
Dimensions: 454ft 10½in (138·65m) oa x 78ft 2½in (23·84m) x 28ft 11in (8·81m).
Machinery: Triple Expansion engines; 28 Niclausse boilers; 2 shafts; 21,790 IHP.
Armour: Terni Harvey nickel steel 6in (152mm) sides; 3·1in (80mm) decks; 8in (203mm) turrets; 6in (152mm) battery; 6in (152mm) conning tower.
Armament: 4 x 12in (305mm); 4 x 8in (203mm); 12 x 6in (152mm); 20 x 3in (76mm); 6 smaller; 4 x 17·7in (450mm) torpedo tubes.
Performance: 20·3kt (37·6km/h); radius 10,000nm (18,500km) at 10kt (18·5km/h).
Crew: 812.

Designed by Benedetto Brin, *Regina Margherita* was a compromise, with protection deliberately sacrificed to Brin's search for speed and firepower in an Italian battleship more capable of meeting other European capital units. As originally schemed by Brin, the ship was to have been armed with two 12in (305mm) and twelve 8in (203mm)

guns, but after Brin's death the design was re-cast to its definitive form, which may be regarded as a precursor of the battlecruiser type.

Despite the fact that the *Regina Margherita* had battleship armament with little more than cruiser protection, but without the cruiser's speed, the ship proved an effective unit with first-class seakeeping qualities. Her one major retrograde feature was her ability to burn only coal.

The *Regina Margherita* sank on 11 December 1916 after hitting two German mines. The *Benedetto Brin,* which was built at Castellammare Navy Yard, had a higher full-load displacement and was fitted with 28 Belleville boilers, was lost as a result of Austro-Hungarian sabotage at Brindisi on 27 September 1915, when she blew up.

SWIFTSURE

1904 *UK*
Other ships in class: *Triumph*

Laid down: 26 February 1902.
Launched: 12 January 1903.
Builder: Armstrong, Elswick.
Displacement: 11,800 tons (11,989 tonnes) load.
Dimensions: 479ft 9in (146·23m) oa x 71ft (21·64m) x 25ft 4in (7·72m).
Machinery: 3-cylinder Triple Expansion engines; 12 Yarrow boilers; 2 shafts; 12,500 IHP.
Armour: Krupp 7in-3in (178-76mm)

belt; 6in-2in (152-51mm) bulkheads; 3in-1in (76-25mm) decks; 10in-2in (254-51mm) barbettes; 10in-8in (254-203mm) turrets; 7in (178mm) battery and casemates; 11in (279mm) conning tower.
Armament: 4 x 10in (254mm); 14 x 7·5in (191mm); 14 x 14pdr QF; 2 x 12pdr QF; 4 x 6pdr QF; 2 x 18in (457mm) torpedo tubes.
Performance: 19kt (35·2km/h); coal 2,000 tons (2,032 tonnes) max.
Crew: 800.

Designed by Sir Edward Reed, the *Swiftsure* and *Triumph* were originally built for Chile as the *Constitucion* and *Libertad* to counter two armoured cruisers (*Rivadavia* and *Moreno*) building for Argentina in an Italian yard. The Chileans required 10in (254mm) and 7·5in (191mm) guns on a hull capabl of 19kt (35·2km/h) but small enough to fit into the country's relatively small graving dock.

In 1903 there was evidence that the Russians were interested in buying the two ships, which had both been launched in January of that year, so on 3 December 1903 both vessels were bought by the UK, not because the Royal Navy needed such second-class battleships, but merely to prevent them falling to the Russians. In fact the two ships did not conform at all with British practice: they were too lightly built, protected and armed to fight with British battleships, but they did have good speed and a powerful secondary battery, so might have proved useful ships against cruisers.

Both ships were able to achieve their designed speed on only 11,500 IHP, and on trials showed that they could top 20kt (37·1km/h). They

Below: King Edward VII-class *Dominion* on completion in 1905.

Below: *Borodino* in October 1904, on the eve of her voyage to Tsushima.

BORODINO

1904 *Russia*
Other ships in class: *Imperator Alexander III, Orel, Kniaz Suvarov, Slava*

Laid down: July 1899.
Launched: 8 September 1901.
Builder: New Admiralty Yard, St Petersburg.
Displacement: 13,516 tonnes (13,732 tonnes).

ere also very handy, the use of
[ba]lanced rudders and the reduction
[of] deadwood aft being the main
[fa]ctors in this latter asset.
[Both] ships played an important
[pa]rt in subsidiary operations during
[th]e early part of World War I, and
[*S*]*wiftsure* was placed in reserve
[in] 1916, being sold for breaking up
[in] 1920. *Triumph* was built by
[Vi]ckers at Barrow, and differed
[co]nsiderably in detail, being nearly
[2]00 tons (203 tonnes) heavier at full-
[lo]ad displacement. She was
[to]rpedoed and sunk by a German
[su]bmarine off the Dardanelles on 25
[M]ay 1915.

KING EDWARD VII

[1]905 *UK*
[O]ther ships in class: *Africa, Britannia,*
[C]ommonwealth, Dominion, Hibernia,
[H]industan, New Zealand

[L]aid down: 8 March 1902.
[L]aunched: 23 July 1903.
[B]uilder: Devonport Dockyard.
[D]isplacement: 15,630 tons (15,880
[to]nnes) load; 17,009 tons (17,281
[to]nnes) deep load.
[D]imensions: 453ft 9in (138·3m) oa
[x] 78ft (23·77m) x 25ft 8in (7·72m).
[M]achinery: 4-cylinder Vertical
[T]riple Expansion engines; 10
[B]abcock & Wilcox plus 6 cylindrical

boilers; 2 shafts; 18,000 IHP.
Armour: Krupp and nickel steel 9in-
8in (229-203mm) belt; 12in-8in (305-
203mm) bulkheads; 2·5in-1in (64-
25mm) decks; 12in (305mm)
barbettes; 12in-8in (305-203mm)
turrets; 9in-5in (229-127mm)
secondary turrets; 7in (178mm)
battery; 12in (305mm) conning
tower.
Armament: 4 x 12in (305mm); 4 x
9·2in (234mm); 10 x 6in (152mm)
QF; 14 x 12pdr QF; 14 x 3pdr QF;
4 x 18in (457mm) torpedo tubes.
Performance: 18·5kt (34·3km/h);
coal 2,200 tons (2,235 tonnes).
Crew: 777.

The latest British capital ships
designed by Sir William White, the
King Edward VII and her seven
sister-ships may be seen as the
culmination of the Victorian
battleship, with a direct relationship
to White's first battleships as Director
of Naval Construction, the Royal
Sovereign class of 1893.
    The design of *King Edward VII*
showed a marked change from
White's earlier battleships:
displacement was increased, an
intermediate armament of four 9·2in
(234mm) guns was provided, and
the tertiary armament of 6in (152mm)
guns was located in a central box
battery rather than in casemates.
Considerable criticism was levelled
at White for the provision of three
calibres of gun, but, as events
proved, the crews in the fire-control
tops (fitted for the first time on the
fore and main masts in place of the
previous fighting tops) were unable

Below: *Ehzherzog Karl,*
1906.

to distinguish between 9·2in
(234mm) and 12in (305mm) shell
splashes.
    Armour protection was based on
that of the London class (1902). The
main belt was 285ft (86·9m) long,
covering the sides between the main
turrets with a thickness of 9in
(229mm) at the waterline and 8in
(203mm) above it. At its rear this belt
was closed by a substantial 12in-8in
(305-203mm) bulkhead, while
towards the bows the belt was
continued with 7in (178mm), 5in
(127mm), 4in (102mm) and 3in
(76mm) up to the solid ram.
    The eight ships proved very
useful, being fast and handy despite
being built at different yards and
being fitted with several types of
boiler. They were the first British
battleships since the 1870s to have
balanced rudders, and were good
gun platforms. The *King Edward VII*
was mined and sunk off Cape Wrath
on 6 January 1916, the only other
casualty of World War I being
Britannia, lost to U-boat attack
in November 1918. The others (*New
Zealand* had been renamed
Zealandia in 1911) were sold for
breaking up in 1920 and 1921.

ERZHERZOG KARL

1906 *Austria-Hungary*
Other ships in class: *Erzherzog
Friedrich, Erzherzog Ferdinand Max*

Laid down: 24 July 1902.
Launched: 4 October 1903.
Builder: Stabilimento Tecnico
Triestino.
Displacement: 10,472 tons (10,640
tonnes).
Dimensions: 414ft 2in (126·24m)
oa x 71ft 5in (21·78m) x 24ft 7in
(7·51m).
Machinery: 4-cylinder Vertical
Triple Expansion engines; 12
Yarrow boilers; 2 shafts; 18,000 IHP.
Armour: Skoda 8·27in (210mm)
belt; 9·45in (240mm) turrets; 8·66in
(240mm) conning tower.
Armament: 4 x 9·45in (240mm); 12
x 7·5in (190mm); 12 x 2·75in
(70mm); 4 smaller; 2 x 17·7in
(450mm) torpedo tubes.
Performance: 20·5kt (38km/h).
Crew: 700.

The three units of the Erzherzog
Karl class were compact vessels of
useful performance, but in gun-
power inferior to their European
contemporaries. Secondary
armament was grouped in 12 single
turrets, all electrically powered.
Yugoslavia took over all three in
1919, but the first two were handed
over to France in 1920, while the last
went to the United Kingdom. All
were scrapped in 1920.

[D]imensions: 397ft (121m) oa x 76ft
[3]in (23·22m) x 26ft 2in (7·97m) max.
[M]achinery: Vertical Triple
[E]xpansion engines; 20 Belleville
[b]oilers; 2 shafts; 16,300 IHP.
[A]rmour: Krupp cemented 7·5in-6in
[(1]90-152mm) belt; 5·75in-4in (146-
[1]02mm) belt ends; 10in-4in (254-
[1]02mm) turrets; 6in (152mm)
[s]econdary turrets; 3in (76mm)
[b]attery; 8in (203mm) conning tower.
[A]rmament: 4 x 12in (305mm); 12 x
[6]in (152mm); 20 x 11pdr; 20 x 3pdr;
[4] x 15in (381mm) torpedo tubes.
[P]erformance: 17·5kt (32·4km/h);
[c]oal 1,520 tons (1,545 tonnes).
[C]rew: 835.

[N]ominally, the *Borodino* was an
[im]proved version of the

Tsessarevitch, but an extra 600 tons
(610 tonnes) of displacement,
coupled with a reduction in power,
meant that performance was
adversely affected. Moreover, the
alteration of the protection, intended
to provide more extensive coverage
than that of the *Tsessarevitch*, was
misconceived. The belt was thinned
by up to 2·5in (64mm) and reduced
in depth by 1ft (0·9m) to 11ft
(3·35m). The secondary battery,
consisting of six twin turrets (three
on each beam), was adequately
protected, while the tertiary battery
of 11pdr guns in casemates on the
main deck, had wholly insufficient
3in (76mm) armour between the
main and upper decks. Anti-torpedo
protection was also inferior to that of

the *Tsessarevitch:* the 1·25in (32mm)
bulkhead was not a continuation of
the 1·5in-1in (38-25mm) lower deck,
but a separate entity joined to the
deck by a slim flat. Upper and main
deck armour was minimal.
    The *Imperator Alexander III* was
built by the Baltic Works and
completed in November 1903; the
Orel was the work of Galernii Island
and completed in October 1904; and
the *Kniaz Suvarov* and *Slava* were
again products of the Baltic Works,
being completed in September 1904
and June 1905 respectively. All but
Slava were part of the Russian fleet
in the Battle of Tsushima against the
Japanese on 27 May 1905, Admiral
Zinovy P. Rozhdestvenski flying his
flag in the *Kniaz Suvarov.*

The result of the battle was a
disaster for Russia and for the
Borodino class: the *Borodino* was
destroyed by a magazine explosion
after Japanese shells had pierced her
inadequate armour; the *Imperator
Alexander III* sank after being hit
forward on the waterline by a large-
calibre shell; the *Orel* was badly
damaged and surrendered to the
Japanese, who repaired her and
placed her in service as the *Iwami*,
which was scrapped in 1922; and
the *Kniaz Suvarov* was damaged by
shellfire and then succumbed to
torpedo strikes. *Slava*, completed
too late for the Russo-Japanese War,
was badly damaged in action with the
German dreadnought *König* on
17 October 1917 and scuttled.

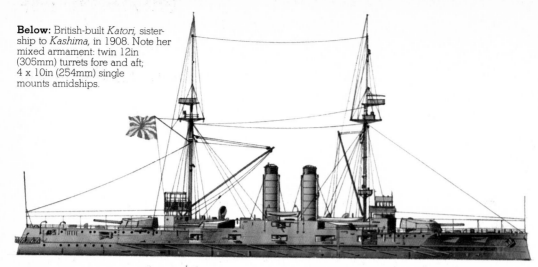

Below: British-built *Katori*, sister-ship to *Kashima,* in 1908. Note her mixed armament: twin 12in (305mm) turrets fore and aft; 4 x 10in (254mm) single mounts amidships.

Below: *Connecticut* (BB-18), sister to *Louisiana,* as completed in 1906.

KASHIMA

1906 *Japan*
Other ships in class: *Katori*

Laid down: 29 February 1904.
Launched: 22 March 1905.
Builder: Armstrong, Elswick.
Displacement: 15,950 tons (16,206 tonnes) normal.
Dimensions: 456ft 3in (139·08m) oa x 78ft (23·77m) x 27ft (8·23m).
Machinery: Vertical Triple Expansion engines; 20 Niclausse boilers; 2 shafts; 15,600 IHP.
Armour: Krupp cemented 9in-2·5in (229-64mm) belt; 9in (229mm) turrets; 9in (229mm) conning tower.
Armament: 4 x 12in (305mm); 4 x 10in (254mm); 12 x 6in (152mm); 21 smaller; 5 x 18in (457mm) torpedo tubes.
Performance: 18·5kt (34·3km/h); coal 2,150 tons (2,184 tonnes).
Crew: 980.

The two Kashima class battleships were amongst the world's most powerful warships, and roughly comparable to the Royal Navy's King Edward VII class, though the intermediate-calibre battery was more effective and two more tertiary-calibre guns were carried.

The armament was designed with long-range engagements in mind, and the main turrets could be operated by electric, hydraulic or even manual power. The armour weighed 4,439 tons (4,510 tonnes), and the belt covered the length of the hull from 5ft (1·52m) below the waterline to the upper deck, 7ft 6in (2·29m) of this being formed by the main belt.

The *Kashima* was stricken in 1922 and broken up in 1925. The *Katori* was built by Vickers at Barrow and had a displacement of 16,400 tons (16,663 tonnes); she too was stricken in 1922 and scrapped in 1925.

LOUISIANA (BB-19)

1906 *USA*
Other ships in class: *Connecticut* (BB-18), *Vermont* (BB-20), *Kansas* (BB-21), *Minnesota* (BB-22), *New Hampshire* (BB-25)

Laid down: 7 February 1903.
Launched: 27 August 1904.
Builder: Newport News.
Displacement: 16,000 tons (16,256 tonnes) normal; 17,666 tons (17,949 tonnes) full load.
Dimensions: 456ft 4in (139·09m) oa x 76ft 10in (23·42m) x 24ft 6in (7·47m) mean.
Machinery: Vertical Triple Expansion engines; 12 Babcock & Wilcox boilers; 2 shafts; 16,500 IHP.
Armour: Krupp cemented and Harvey nickel steel 11in-6in (279-152mm) belt; 6in (152mm) upper belt and bulkheads; 3in-1·5in (76-38mm) decks; 10in-6in (254-152mm) barbettes; 12in-8in (305-203mm) turrets; 9in (229mm) conning tower.
Armament: 4 x 12 in (305mm); 8 x 8in (203mm); 12 x 7in (178mm); 34 smaller; 4 x 21in (533mm) torpedo tubes.
Performance: 18kt (33·4km/h); coal 2,249 tons (2,285 tonnes).
Crew: 827.

With the two ships of the Connecticut class (followed by the four units of the Vermont class, which differed only in detail from the Connecticuts), the US Navy achieved a design in all ways comparable with the best European and Japanese battleships: protection was good, fire-power excellent and the performance more than adequate, especially in any sort of sea. The one weak point was the fitting of both 8in (203mm) and 7in (178mm) guns, whose shell splashes were almost indistinguishable for the purpose of fire control.

DEUTSCHLAND

1906 *Germany*
Other ships in class: *Hannover, Pommern, Schlesien, Schleswig-Holstein*

Laid down: 20 June 1903.
Launched: 19 November 1904.
Builder: Germaniawerft, Kiel.
Displacement: 13,993 tons (14,217 tonnes).
Dimensions: 418ft 8in (127·6m) oa x 73ft (22·2m) x 27ft (8·25m).
Machinery: Triple Expansion engines; 12 boilers; 3 shafts; 19,000 IHP.
Armour: Krupp 9·75in (250mm) belt; 11in (280mm) turrets; 12in (305mm) conning tower.
Armament: 4 x 11in (280mm); 14 x 6·7in (170mm); 20 x 3·5in (88mm); 4 machine-guns; 6 x 17·7in (450mm) torpedo tubes.
Performance: 18·5kt (34·3km/h); coal 1,800 tons (1,829 tonnes); oil 200 tons (203 tonnes).
Crew: 743.

Germany's last pre-dreadnought battleships differed only in minor respects from the Braunschweigs: the primary and secondary armaments remained unaltered, but the tertiary armament of 3·5in (88mm) guns was increased. Belt protection was improved, and main turret armour was also increased, but the ships' weak points remained the protection of the secondary armament and its magazines, which probably caused the loss of the *Pommern* to a single torpedo hit on 1 June 1916 at Jutland.

After World War I the *Deutschland* was scrapped in 1922; *Hannover* was rebuilt once and then scrapped in 1935; and *Schlesien* and *Schleswig-Holstein* were rebuilt twice before both were sunk during World War II.

RÉPUBLIQUE

1906 *France*
Other ships in class: *Patrie*

Laid down: December 1901.
Launched: 4 September 1902.
Builder: Brest Dockyard.
Displacement: 14,605 tons (14,83 tonnes).
Dimensions: 439ft (133·81m) pp x 79ft 7in (24·26m) x 27ft 7in (8·41m) max.
Machinery: Vertical Triple Expansion engines; 24 Niclausse boilers; 3 shafts; 18,000 IHP.
Armour: Krupp cemented 11in-3·2in (280-80mm) belt; 2·75in-2in (70-50mm) decks; 14in-11in (355-280mm) turrets; 5·9in-3·5in (150-90mm) secondary guns; 12in (305mm) conning tower.
Armament: 4 x 12in (305mm); 18 x 6·4in (160mm); 25 x 3pdr; 2 x 18in (457mm) torpedo tubes.
Performance: 19kt (35·2km/h); coal 1,800 tons (1,830 tonnes).
Crew: 766.

The two ships of the République class marked a determined effort by French designers to remedy the manifest faults in current French capital ships, which had inadequate armour (Harvey nickel steel instead of the more advanced Krupp cemented type), insufficiently powerful secondary armament, and only limited performance. The root cause of the failings was lack of displacement, forced upon the designers by financial restrictions. In the *République,* displacement rose by some 2,000 tons (2,032 tonnes) in comparison with the *Suffren,* allowing better armour, more armament and greater power, all in a hull of improved lines. The only problem now facing the French Navy was that the new ships took so long to build that they were obsolete by the time they entered service! *Patrie* was built at La Seyne; both ships were completed in December 1906.

The main belt ran almost the full length of the ship, with 4ft 11in (1·5m) of its 12ft 5in (3·8m) depth below the waterline. The bows as far aft as the foremast were also armoured to a thickness of 3·2in (80mm) from the belt up to a height of 16ft 5in (5m).

The forward and after main turrets were located on the forecastle and upper decks respectively, and 12 of the 6·3in (160mm) secondary guns were housed in six twin turrets, three on each beam on the forecastle deck; the other six secondary guns were to be found in two upper deck casemates forward, and in four main deck casemates just aft of amidships. The worst aspect of the armament was the hand loading of the 12in (305mm) guns.

Both ships served in the Mediterranean during World War I. The *République* was stricken in 1921, and the *Patrie* in 1928.

Below: Rebuilt *Schleswig-Holstein* of the Deutschland class as she appeared early in World War II.

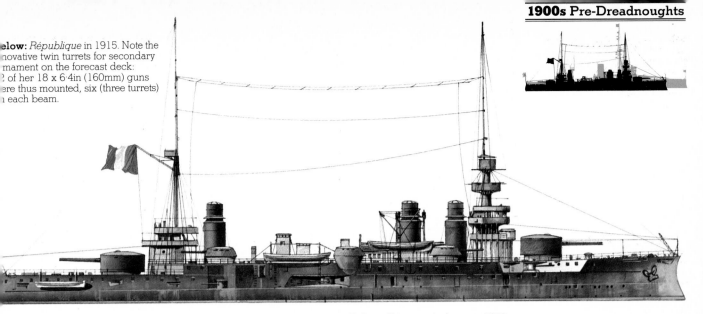

Below: République in 1915. Note the innovative twin turrets for secondary armament on the forecast deck: 12 of her 18 x 6·4in (160mm) guns were thus mounted, six (three turrets) on each beam.

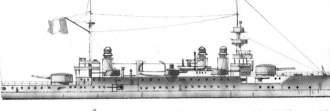

Below: Rhode Island (BB-17) in 1906.

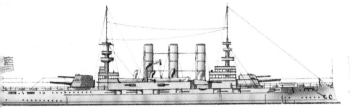

Below: *Démocratie* shown in 1909.

RHODE ISLAND (BB-17)

1906 USA
Other ships in class: *Virginia* (BB-13), *Nebraska* (BB-14), *Georgia* (BB-15), *New Jersey* (BB-16)

Laid down: 1 May 1902.
Launched: 17 May 1904.
Builder: Fore River Engine Co.
Displacement: 14,948 tons (15,187 tonnes) normal.
Dimensions: 441ft 3in (134·5m) oa x 76ft 3in (23·25m) x 23ft 9in (7·24m) mean.
Machinery: Vertical Triple Expansion engines; 12 Babcock & Wilcox boilers; 2 shafts; 19,000 IHP.
Armour: Krupp cemented and Harvey nickel steel 11in-6in (279-

152mm) belt; 12in-6in (305-152mm) turrets; 9in (229mm) conning tower.
Armament: 4 x 12in (305mm); 8 x 8in (203mm); 12 x 6in (152mm); 26 smaller; 4 x 21in (533mm) torpedo tubes.
Performance: 19kt (35·2km/h); coal 1,700 tons (1,727 tonnes).
Crew: 812.

Considerably larger than previous American battleships, the five units of the Virginia class were well armoured and fast flush-decked ships. Two of the four twin 8in (203mm) turrets were located in superfiring positions above the 12in (305mm) turrets (as in the Kearsarge class), suffering the same problems with lack of independent training capability and causing the vessels to be top heavy, much to the detriment of their roll characteristics.

The *Virginia* and *New Jersey* were expended as targets in 1923, and the remaining three were sold for scrapping in the same year.

DÉMOCRATIE

1908 France
Other ships in class: *Justice, Liberté, Verité*

Laid down: 1 May 1903.
Launched: 30 April 1904.
Builder: Brest Dockyard.
Displacement: 14,500 tons (14,732 tonnes).
Dimensions: 439ft (133·81m) pp x 79ft 7in (24·26m) x 27ft 6in (8·38m).
Machinery: Vertical Triple Expansion engines; 22 Belleville boilers; 3 shafts; 18,500 IHP.
Armour: Krupp cemented 11in-3·2in (280-80mm) belt; 14in-11in (350-280mm) turrets; 12in (305mm) conning tower.

Armament: 4 x 12in (305mm); 10 x 7·5in (190mm); 23 smaller; 2 x 18in (457mm) torpedo tubes.
Performance: 19kt (35·2km/h); coal 1,800 tons (1,830 tonnes).
Crew: 739.

The Liberté class comprised France's last four pre-dreadnought battleships, and the design was basically an improvement on the République class, particularly in the extremely powerful secondary armament. This was arranged in six forecastle deck beam turrets, two upper deck casemates below the forward turret, and two main deck casemates below the after turret. However, the class was obsolete by the time its units entered service.

Liberté blew up at Toulon on 25 September 1911, as a result of decomposition in 7·5in (190mm) ammunition propellant. The other three ships served in the Mediterranean during World War I and were stricken in 1921 and 1922.

Above: *Deutschland* as completed, 1906. These were Germany's last pre-dreadnought battleships.

Below: *Mississippi* (BB-23)—Greek *Lemnos* from 1914—as completed in 1908. Cage masts were fitted in 1909. Useful additions to the Greek Navy, they served many years.

Below: Precursor of the battle-cruiser: Regina Elena-class *Vittorio Emanuele* as completed in 1908. Additional light guns were soon added to her armament.

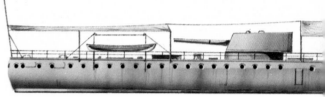

MISSISSIPPI (BB-23)

1908 *USA*
Other ships in class: *Idaho* (BB-24)

Laid down: 12 May 1904.
Launched: 30 September 1905.
Builder: Cramp, Philadelphia.
Displacement: 13,000 tons (13,208 tonnes) normal; 14,465 tons (14,696 tonnes) full load.
Dimensions: 382ft (116·43m) oa x 77ft (23·47m) x 24ft 8in (7·52m) mean.
Machinery: Vertical Triple Expansion engines; 8 Babcock & Wilcox boilers; 2 shafts; 10,000 IHP.
Armour: Krupp cemented and Harvey nickel steel 9in-7in (229-178mm) belt; 10in-6in (254-152mm) barbettes; 12in-8in (305-203mm) turrets; 9in (229mm) conning tower.
Armament: 4 x 12in (305mm); 8 x 8in (203mm); 8 x 7in (178mm); 12 x 3in (76mm); 6 x 3pdr; 2 x 1pdr; 2 x 21in (533mm) torpedo tubes.
Performance: 17kt (31·5km/h); coal 1,800 tons (1,828 tonnes).
Crew: 744.

Mississippi and *Idaho* were the two units of the US Navy's last pre-dreadnought battleship class, and were generally unsuccessful. The ships were an attempt to reproduce the capabilities of the excellent Vermont class on some 3,000 tons (3,048 tonnes) less displacement. Armour was as for the Vermonts, though the main belt had to be reduced to 244ft (74·4m) in length; and armament was also largely unchanged, though the tertiary battery had to be reduced in number. From 1909 the original pole foremast was replaced by a cage mast, while cage mainmasts were added. In July 1914 both vessels were sold to Greece, and the renamed *Lemnos* and *Kilkis* were sunk by German aircraft in Salamis on 10 April 1941. The United States used the money from their sale to buy a new dreadnought of the New Mexico class.

AGAMEMNON

1908 *UK*
Other ships in class: *Lord Nelson*

Laid down: 15 May 1905.
Launched: 23 June 1906.
Builder: Beardmore, Dalmuir.
Displacement: 15,925 tons (16,180 tonnes) load; 17,683 tons (17,966 tonnes) full load.
Dimensions: 443ft 6in (135·18m) oa x 79ft 6in (24·23m) x 26ft (7·92m)
Machinery: 4-cylinder Triple Expansion engines; 15 Yarrow boilers; 2 shafts; 16,750 IHP.
Armour: Krupp cemented 12in-8in (305-203mm) belt; 8in (203mm) bulkheads; 4in-1·5in (102-38mm) decks; 8in (203mm) citadel; 12in (305mm) barbettes; 12in (305mm) turrets; 8in-7in (203-178mm) secondary turrets; 12in (305mm) conning tower.
Armament: 4 x 12in (305mm); 10 x 9·2in (234mm); 24 x 12pdr QF; 2 x 3pdr QF; 5 x 18in (457mm) torpedo tubes.
Performance: 18kt (33·4km/h); coal 2,171 tons (2,206 tonnes); oil 1,090 tons (1,107 tonnes).
Crew: 800.

The two ships of the Lord Nelson class were the Royal Navy's last pre-dreadnought battleships, and they reflected a period of intense analytical thought about battleship design which came to the conclusion that subsequent battleships must

Below: *Lord Nelson,* shown in 1911, and her sister-ship *Agamemnon* were Britain's last pre-dreadnoughts.

have thicker and more extensive armour, and that a small-calibre secondary armament was useless.

The tendency already seen in the King Edward VII class was thus prosecuted with vigour, and in the two Lord Nelson class ships the combination of an intermediate-calibre secondary and small-calibre tertiary armament was eliminated in favour of a more substantial secondary battery of 9·2in (234mm) guns, located five on each beam in one single and two twin turrets. Some 24 single 12pdr guns provided for defence against torpedo boats.

The main belt covered the entire ship along the waterline, and was supplemented by an upper belt stretching as far aft as 'Y' turret barbette, and by a well-armoured citadel. Further protection was afforded by a number of solid bulkheads, the first used in any British battleship.

The two ships were excellent sea boats and very handy. *Lord Nelson* was built by Palmer at Jarrow and completed four months after *Agamemnon*; she was sold for breaking up in 1920. *Agamemnon* became a target ship in 1923, and was scrapped in 1926.

REGINA ELENA

1907 *Italy*
Other ships in class: *Vittorio Emanuele, Roma, Napoli*

Laid down: 27 March 1901.
Launched: 19 June 1904.
Builder: La Spezia Navy Yard.
Dimensions: 474ft 5in (144·6m) oa x 73ft 6in (22·4m) x 25ft 11½in (7·91m).
Machinery: 4-cylinder Vertical Triple Expansion engines; 28 Belleville boilers; 2 shafts; 19,299 IHP.
Armour: Terni Krupp cemented 9·8in (250mm) belt; 1·5in (38mm) decks; 8in (203mm) turrets; 6in (152mm) secondary turrets; 3·1in (80mm) battery; 10in (254mm) conning tower.
Armament: 2 x 12in (305mm); 12 x 8in (203mm); 16 x 3in (76mm); 2 x 17·7in (450mm) torpedo tubes.
Performance: 20·8kt (38·5km/h);

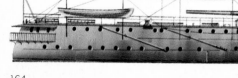

164

Above: Cuniberti's 1903 design for a 17,000-ton 'all-big-gun' ship which bore a close resemblance to his Regina Elena class.

adius 1,950 miles (3,140km) at 19kt 35.2km/h).
Crew: 742.

Designed by the justly celebrated Vittorio Cuniberti, the *Regina Elena* started life as a project for an 8,000-ton (8,128 tonne) ship armed with twelve 8in (203mm) guns, protected by 6in (152mm) armour and capable of 22kt (40.8km/h). With this concept there originated the notion of the 'one-calibre' ship with all its advantages of ammunition supply and simpler fire-control. This design was soon abandoned, but Cuniberti was able to use features of it in his next project, for a 13,000-ton (13,208 tonne) battleship faster than any British or French battleship, and with better protection and armament than any armoured cruiser serving in the navies of those countries. The resultant Regina Elena class was a rare breed: a hybrid design that was truly effective, and the real precursor of the battlecruiser design, which could outgun any cruiser and outrun any battleship. At this time, Cuniberti was also scheming a 17,000 ton 17,272 tonne) battleship with twelve 2in (305mm) guns, but the plan was judged too costly.

Below: *Ioann Zlatoust*, completed 1910.

The two main-calibre guns were disposed fore and aft in single centre line turrets, but the *Regina Elena*'s most important feature was her secondary armament, the 8in (203mm) guns occupying three twin turrets on each beam, where they enjoyed useful arcs of fire.

The *Regina Elena* and *Vittorio Emanuele* (built by Castellammare Navy Yard and completed some 11 months later, on 1 August 1908) were fruits of the 1901 naval programme. But it was clear that a homogeneous squadron of four would give the Italian navy some useful advantages, and a further pair were ordered under the 1902 programme: *Roma* was built at La Spezia and *Napoli* at Castellammare, being completed in December and September 1908 respectively. All four units differed in displacement, and the last pair had Babcock & Wilcox boilers as well as an extra eight 3in (76mm) guns. *Vittorio Emanuele* and *Roma* could each reach 21.4kt (39.7km/h), and *Napoli* was capable of 22.2kt (41.1km/h). The first pair were stricken in the first half of 1923, while the second pair survived to 1927 and 1926 respectively.

IOANN ZLATOUST

1910 *Russia*
Other ships in class: *Evstafi*

Laid down: November 1903.
Launched: 13 May 1906.
Builder: Sevastopol Dockyard.
Displacement: 12,840 tons (13,045 tonnes.
Dimensions: 387ft 3in (118.03m) oa x 74ft (22.55m) x 27ft (8.23m) max.
Machinery: Vertical Triple Expansion engines; 22 Belleville boilers; 2 shafts; 10,800 IHP.
Armour: Krupp cemented 9in-5in (230-125mm) belt; 10in-4in (255-100mm) turrets; 9in (230mm) conning tower.
Armament: 4 x 12in (305mm); 4 x 8in (203mm); 12 x 6in (152mm); 14 x 11pdr; 6 x 3pdr; 3 x 18in (457mm) torpedo tubes.
Performance: 16.5kt (30.6km/h); coal 800 tons (813 tonnes).
Crew: 879.

These two battleships were based on the *Kniaz Potemkin Tavritcheski*, but were modified while building to incorporate some of the lessons of the Russo-Japanese War: deck armour was thickened, the belt more extensive, and the earlier ship's four upper-deck 6in (152mm) casemated guns were replaced by 8in (203mm) weapons.

Both vessels were employed in the Black Sea during World War I and were scrapped in 1922.

IMPERATOR PAVEL

1910 *Russia*
Other ships in class: *Andrei Pervoswanni*

Laid down: April 1904.
Launched: 7 September 1907.
Builder: Baltic Works.
Displacement: 17,400 tons (17,678 tonnes).
Dimensions: 460ft (140.2m) oa x 80ft (24.38m) x 27ft (8.23m) mean.
Machinery: Vertical Triple Expansion engines; 22 Belleville boilers; 2 shafts; 18,000 IHP.
Armour: Krupp cemented 8.5in-5in (215-125mm) belt; 8in-4in (200-100mm) turrets; 8in (200mm) CT.
Armament: 4 x 12in (305mm); 14 x 8in (203mm); 12 x 4.7in (120mm); 4 x 3pdr; 3 x 18in (533mm) TT.
Performance: 17.5kt (32.4km/h).
Crew: 933.

Many lessons form the Russo-Japanese War were incorporated in these two ships, which emerged as powerful pre-dreadnoughts.

The main armament was conventional but capable of high elevation, while the hull was completely armoured and had no scuttles. Neither ship played an important part in World War I. *Imperator Pavel* became the *Respublika* in 1917 and was scrapped in 1923; and the *Andrei Pervoswanni* was sunk by British torpedo boat attack during August 1919 and scrapped in 1925.

Below: Russian pre-dreadnought *Andrei Pervoswanni* in 1912. Note absence of scuttles in hull; pole masts replaced cage masts by 1917.

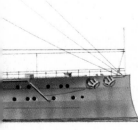

1900s Dreadnoughts

The first decade of the twentieth century a turning point in the history of battleship design. Developments unfolded at such a hectic pace that within a few years whole battle fleets were rendered obsolete: the comparative stability of the late nineteenth century was rudely shattered as ships were suddenly found to be too slow, undergunned and vulnerable. This was not, however, a time of revolution so much as a period of rapid evolution: given the drive of visionaries like Scott and Sims, it was inevitable that battle tactics and hence ships themselves would be reviewed—indeed, the seeds of change were already sown by 1900. Several factors coalesced to ensure that the evolutionary time scale became very compressed. The principal force was the enthusiasm and influence of Jackie Fisher, appointed First Sea Lord in the British Admiralty in October 1904—whose appetite for achievement at the greatest possible speed enabled an epoch-making design to be revealed to a startled world many months ahead of what would be regarded as a typical completion date. Another powerful factor was the continued build-up of the German Imperial Navy, which had by now overtaken France as the second largest in Europe and was seen as a latent, then imminent, threat to British interests. War clouds were perceptible on the horizon, if not yet actually gathering.

FIRE CONTROL

The decisive result of the Battle of Tsushima had apparently proven the validity of the 1900-style capital ship, or at least had not called it into doubt, but it had done nothing to advance the theories held by the proponents of long-range fire. Despite the close scrutiny by naval experts the world over of tactics, protective systems, gun dispositions, the efficiency or otherwise of torpedoes, and so on, the only practical lesson to be absorbed was the complete ineffectiveness of small-calibre guns in fleet actions, a result which was already imagined by long-range gunnery advocates. Nevertheless, the acceptance in US and British circles of the aloft spotter commanding an improved view of a battle in itself tended to open the range at which an action might be fought; however, a mixed battery of weapons, with shells arriving in the target area after differing flight times, following differing trajectories and causing splashes which at long range would be difficult to distinguish one from another, seemed only to cause confusion. The trend towards a larger number of heavier guns had already been initiated with the introduction of 'intermediate' batteries; now, the spotting problem could be overcome by the substitution of further main-calibre weapons for the smaller 9·2in (234mm) or 8in (203mm) mountings.

TURRET DISPOSITION

By 1905, with the acceptance of the idea of a new form of battleship carrying a large number of heavy guns of uniform calibre (an idea first mooted publicly in Cuniberti's 'Ideal Battleship for the British Navy', details of which appeared in the 1904 edition of *Jane's Fighting Ships*, but already under active consideration), the United States and Great Britain began serious design work on such a vessel. One problem, which was to be resolved in different ways, was how the turrets might be mounted. Fisher's influence came into play in respect of the British project: he was a champion of 'end-on fire', and forward fire at that, not merely because

Below: *Dreadnought,* the wonder of
the naval world and new symbol of
military might. The way in which
her existence was revealed was a
masterpiece of theatricals, but
the hectic pace of battleship
development led to her being
rapidly outclassed.

167

a ship approaching her target would be able to close the battle range to its own choosing, but also because in this way it would present a much smaller target itself. The problem was that, because of blast effects (sighting hoods were placed on turret tops), the number of guns that could be brought to bear would be severely limited. Broadside fire was still the major consideration, however, and so a compromise was achieved through the provision of wing turrets, which could fulfil both functions, at least to a large extent, although a superfiring arrangement was seriously contemplated in the sketch designs that led up to the ultimate layout.

The US disposition provided for superimposed turrets by the neat solution of moving the sights from the turret crowns to the sides, and the result was a more compact vessel, providing an identical broadside of eight heavy guns, double the astern fire, and a similar ahead-fire capability except along the precise fore-and-aft axis—all with one turret less.

MACHINERY

While the adoption of the 'all-big-gun' system for battleships was the product of an evolving trend, the other major influence of the time on capital ship design was truly innovative. In the late 1880s, Charles Parsons, the head of a Tyneside engineering company, had patented a new system of propulsion in which steam, instead of expanding into a series of cylinders and forcing pistons to move up and down at great speed, was directed on to a rotor comprising a large number of angled vanes. In order to apply the moment of the whirling blades to a propeller shaft, a system of progressively larger rotors was devised: installed in series, these reduced the ultimate revolutionary speed. The power-plant, known as a turbine, was first successfully used in a small craft dubbed, not unpredictably, *Turbinia*, which caused a stir when it was paraded along the lines of warships at the 1897 Fleet Review. It impressed the Admiralty sufficiently to order its introduction into Royal Navy service, first appearing in the destroyer *Viper*.

The advantages of turbine propulsion were many. First, it bestowed upon ships the capability of achieving much higher speeds than hitherto (*Viper* made over 36kt); second-

ly, it occupied less space, particularly vertical space, than reciprocating engine for a given output; thirdly, it provided smoother, cleaner and quieter machinery; and fourthly and most importantly, it enabled speed to be sustained—re ciprocating engines were prone to breakdown, especially i worked at their limits.

DREADNOUGHT

All these features were brought together in a single Britis vessel, *Dreadnought*, a warship that had so much impac

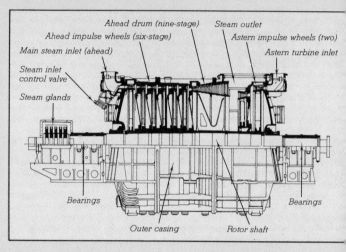

Ahead drum (nine-stage) Steam outlet
Ahead impulse wheels (six-stage) Astern impulse wheels (two)
Main steam inlet (ahead) Astern turbine inlet
Steam inlet control valve
Steam glands
Bearings Bearings
Outer casing Rotor shaft

Above: Cross-section of a Brown-Curtis steam turbine, as installed in *Kawachi*, one of Japan's early dreadnoughts. The particular problem with turbines was linkage: efficiency demands revolutionary speeds far in excess of those of the propeller—hence the need for 'stages'.

Below: The protective system of an early dreadnought, *Bellerophon*. The full-length waterline belt is retained, but note the innovative anti-torpedo splinter bulkheads, reflecting concerns about underwater magazine defence. Horizontal protection is still, however, relatively weak.

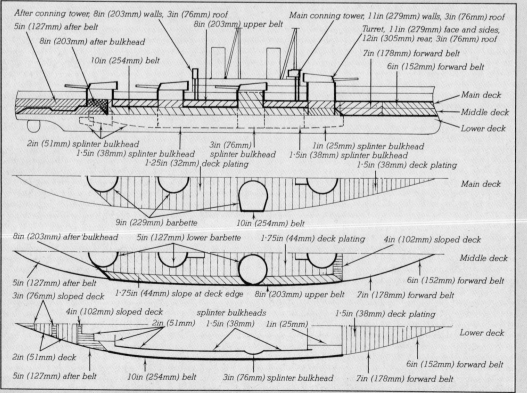

After conning tower, 8in (203mm) walls, 3in (76mm) roof
5in (127mm) after belt
8in (203mm) upper belt
Main conning tower, 11in (279mm) walls, 3in (76mm) roof
8in (203mm) after bulkhead
Turret, 11in (279mm) face and sides, 12in (305mm) rear, 3in (76mm) roof
10in (254mm) belt
7in (178mm) forward belt
6in (152mm) forward belt
Main deck
Middle deck
Lower deck
2in (51mm) splinter bulkhead
3in (76mm) splinter bulkhead
1in (25mm) splinter bulkhead
1·5in (38mm) splinter bulkhead
1·25in (32mm) deck plating
1·5in (38mm) splinter bulkhead
1·5in (38mm) deck plating
Main deck
9in (229mm) barbette
10in (254mm) belt
8in (203mm) after bulkhead
5in (127mm) lower barbette
1·75in (44mm) deck plating
4in (102mm) sloped deck
Middle deck
5in (127mm) after belt
6in (152mm) forward belt
3in (76mm) sloped deck
1·75in (44mm) slope at deck edge
8in (203mm) upper belt
7in (178mm) forward belt
4in (102mm) sloped deck
splinter bulkheads
1·5in (38mm) deck plating
2in (51mm)
1·5in (38mm)
1in (25mm)
Lower deck
2in (51mm) deck
6in (152mm) forward belt
5in (127mm) after belt
10in (254mm) belt
3in (76mm) splinter bulkhead
7in (178mm) forward belt

that all capital ships have since been classified as variants of her generic name. Built in the astonishing time of 366 days (materials from other shipbuilding projects were diverted to speed her completion), she rendered all existing capital ships obsolete at a stroke and gave Great Britain a three-year lead while other navies hastily reorganised themselves. The USS *South Carolina*, (see pages 180-1), was in fact designed before her, and the Japanese Satsumas, laid down some five months before her, were originally to have been fitted with a single-calibre main battery of twelve guns, but *Dreadnought* was the vessel to which all others were compared.

Above: A prewar photograph of *Bellerophon,* showing the 4in (102mm) anti-torpedo-boat guns atop turrets.

Below: *Nassau,* Germany's first dreadnought. All the main turrets are at forecastle deck level.

THE INTRODUCTION OF THE BATTLECRUISER

As early as 1896 the French constructor Émile Bertin had suggested the construction of an armoured cruiser with the latter's high relative speed but mounting battleship-calibre main weapons. The concept was also taken up by Fisher, who felt that cruisers, while retaining their traditional roles as scouts for the battle fleet and as ships to be employed in the protection of trade routes, would also be able to participate in fleet actions, given guns with sufficient range and sufficient destructive power.

His ideas were put into effect in 1906 with the laying down of a class of three 'armoured cruisers' (Invincibles), ostensibly no different in essential concept from earlier vessels but in fact, when revealed, shown to be armed with 12in (305mm) guns, possessing greater hull length than *Dreadnought*'s, and given a massive increase in power to drive them at even higher speeds. Their armour, however, remained thin, inadequately so for the fleet actions of World War I into which they would be thrust.

The years 1905-10 belonged to *Dreadnought* and her immediate successors. By 1909 competitors had begun to emerge, and the history of capital ship development for the next decade is really a catalogue of adjustments to the design, overshadowed by the break-neck building programme which culminated in the outbreak of a war that would engulf Europe.

DREADNOUGHT

1906 UK

Laid down: 21 October 1905.
Launched: 10 February 1906.
Builder: Portsmouth Dockyard.
Displacement: 17,900 tons (18,186 tonnes) normal; 21,845 tons (22,195 tonnes) full load.
Dimensions: 527ft (160·4m) oa x 82ft 1in (25m) x 26ft 6in (8·1m) mean.
Machinery: 4 Parsons turbines; 18 Babcock & Wilcox boilers; 4 shafts; 26,350 SHP.
Armour: Krupp cemented and Krupp non-cemented 11in-8in (270-203mm) belt; 6in-4in (152-103mm) belt ends; 11in (270mm) bulkheads; 4in-0·75in (152-19mm) decks; 11in-4in (270-102mm) barbettes; 11in-3in (270-76mm) turrets; 11in-8in (270-203mm) conning tower.
Armament: 10 x 12in (305mm); 27 x 12pdr; 5 x 18in (457mm) torpedo tubes.
Performance: 21·6kt (40km/h); radius 6,800nm (12,600km) at 10kt (18·5km/h); coal 2,900 tons (2,946 tonnes); oil 1,120 tons (1,138 tonnes).
Crew: 773.

The appearance of the battleship *Dreadnought* marked a major turning point in the evolution of warships: she was the first 'all big gun' ship in the world, and also the first capital ship to have an all-turbine powerplant. There was nothing basically radical about the armament: designers in Italy and the USA had already schemed such vessels, and practical moves in this direction had been made with the introduction of intermediate-calibre guns in several classes of the early 20th century. It was appreciated by all, however, that the installation of large- and intermediate-calibre guns on the same ship raised problems of gun disposition, of ammunition stowage and handling, and of fire control.

Right: Following completion of her sea and gunnery trials in the West Indies, *Dreadnought,* at this time the most powerful warship in the world, sails from Portsmouth as Flagship, Home Fleet, April 1907.

The chief proponent of the 'all big gun' battleship in the Royal Navy was Admiral 'Jackie' Fisher, whose first thoughts on the subject dated from 1900, when he was commanding the Mediterranean Fleet. Thereafter he worked with W.H. Gard on the evolution of the type through several designs nicknamed *Untakeable.* Fisher's thinking centred on the use of 10in (254mm) guns as the primary armament, as these offered so much better a rate of fire than contemporary 12in (305mm) guns. However, several of Fisher's captains preferred the 12in (305mm) weapon for its much greater destructive potential. Thus by the time Fisher became First Sea Lord in October 1904, the *Untakeable* had evolved into Design 'B' with eight 12in (305mm) guns, and interest engendered by this design was largely responsible for the formation of a Committee on Designs, appointed in December 1904 with Fisher as chairman. The committee was tasked with consideration of new battleship and battlecruiser designs, and the parameters for the former were a speed of 21kt (38·9km/h), adequate armour, and

an armament of 12in and anti-torpedo boat guns with nothing in the way of a conventional secondary battery. Various plans were taken into consideration, the main difficulties being Fisher's demands for end-on fire rather than a broadside capability and also his insistence on the need for speed even at the expense of protection. Among the projects taken under consideration were Battleships 'E' (reciprocating machinery and 12 x 12in, 305mm, guns in two groups of three superfiring twin turrets), 'D' (reciprocating machinery and 12 x 12in, 305mm, guns in two triangular groups of three twin turrets before and abaft the superstructure), 'G' (reciprocating machinery and 12 x 12in, 305mm, guns in six twin turrets located two on the centre line, fore and aft, and two on each beam) and 'H' (turbines and 10 x 12in, 305mm, guns in five twin turrets located three on the centre line and one on each beam).

It was the last which formed the basis for *Dreadnought,* which astounded the world not only with her power but with the speed at which she had been built (366 days), attributable in part to the skill and

Right: Plan views of basic designs for the revolutionary 'all big gun' battleship *Dreadnought.* The three upper studies are for ships of between 19,000 and 21,000 tons displacement, with reciprocating engines giving a maximum speed of 21kt (38·85km/h). The bottom study is for a turbine-powered warship of 18,500 tons.

efficiency of the yard, but also to the use of turrets already built for the Lord Nelson class, which was in consequence much delayed. A widely spaced armament disposition was chosen to mitigate the chances of a single hit disabling more than one turret, and so that a broadside of eight guns could be reconciled with Fisher's insistence on end-on fire by at least four guns in a ship without superfiring turrets. The light armament was later altered to 10 x 12pdr, 2 x 3pdr AA and 2 x 12pdr AA guns. Fire control was at first inadequate, but improved with the fitting of director firing in 1915.

Dreadnought had a quite peaceful career in World War I, never firing her guns in anger at a surface target. She was sold for scrap in 1921 and broken up in 1923.

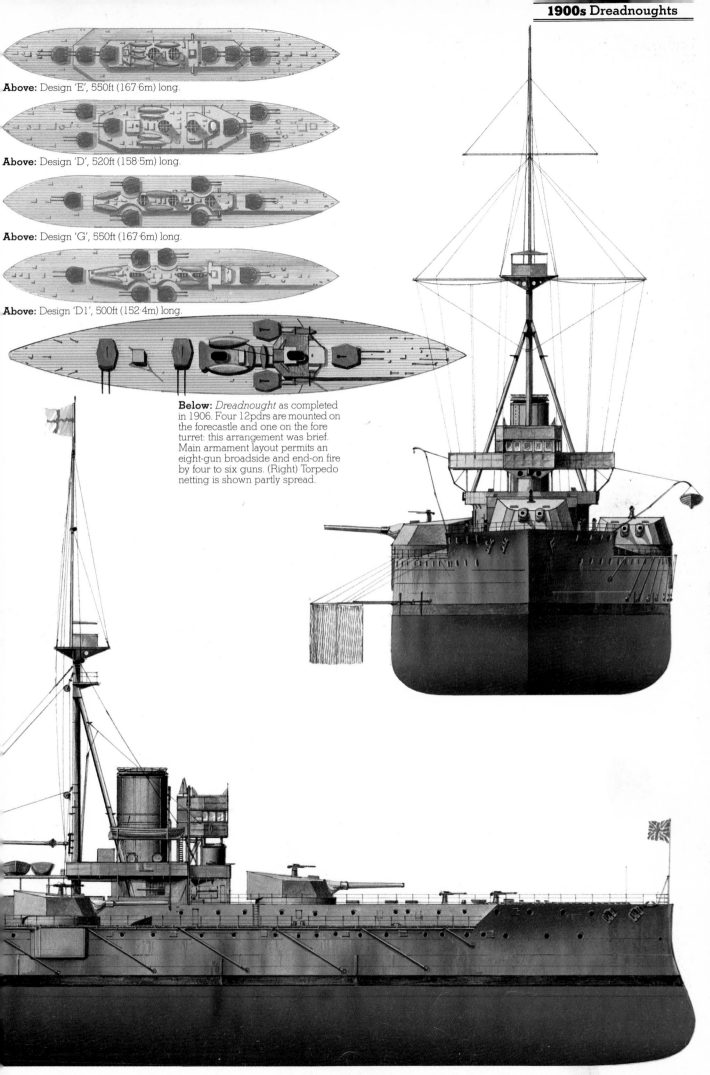

Above: Design 'E', 550ft (167·6m) long.

Above: Design 'D', 520ft (158·5m) long.

Above: Design 'G', 550ft (167·6m) long.

Above: Design 'D1', 500ft (152·4m) long.

Below: *Dreadnought* as completed in 1906. Four 12pdrs are mounted on the forecastle and one on the fore turret: this arrangement was brief. Main armament layout permits an eight-gun broadside and end-on fire by four to six guns. (Right) Torpedo netting is shown partly spread.

INVINCIBLE

1908 *UK*
Other ships in class: *Indomitable,
Inflexible*

Laid down: 2 April 1906.
Launched: 13 April 1907.
Builder: Armstrong, Elswick.
Displacement: 17,330 tons (17,607
tonnes) load; 19,940 tons (20,259
tonnes) deep load.
Dimensions: 567ft (172·82m) oa x
78ft 6in (23·93m) x 26ft 9½in
(8·17m) mean.
Machinery: 4 Parsons turbines; 31
Yarrow boilers; 4 shafts; 41,000
SHP.
Armour: Krupp cemented 6in-4in
(152-102mm) belt; 7in-6in (178-
152mm) bulkheads; 2·5in-0·75in
(64-19mm) decks; 7in-2in (178-
51mm) barbettes; 7in (178mm)
turrets; 10in-6in (254-152mm) conning
tower.
Armament: 8 x 12in (305mm); 16 x
4in (102mm); 5 smaller; 5 x 18in
(457mm) torpedo tubes.

Performance: 26·6kt (51·9km/h)
max; coal 3,000 tons (3,048 tonnes).
Crew: 784.

As noted in the *Dreadnought* entry,
the preoccupation of Fisher was with
speed and firepower, with protection
always subordinated to these two
offensive factors. With the
Dreadnought Fisher achieved a
battleship design close to his ideal;
but he also wanted an armoured
cruiser that would offer the same
degree of superiority over
contemporary types. As early as
1902 Fisher and W.H. Gard, the
Chief Constructor, had started work
on an ideal nicknamed
Unapproachable, with turbine
propulsion and an armament of
9·2in (234mm) and 7·5in (191mm)
guns. Further thought crystallized
the notion into an impressive vessel
with a mixed armament of four 9·2in
(234mm) guns in twin centreline
turrets fore and aft and no fewer than
12 x 7·5in (191mm) guns in six twin
turrets, three on each beam. Overall

displacement was seen as being in
the order of 14,000 tons (14,224
tonnes). The Admiralty could see the
virtues of Fisher's thinking, but met it
only halfway with the Shannon and
Minotaur classes, which were slower
than Fisher's ideal, and also less
powerfully armed.

However in 1904 the British
learned of the Japanese *Tsukuba* and
Ikoma, whose high speed and
powerful armament outmatched
anything the British had so far
considered: in theory they could
outfight anything fast enough to
catch them, and outrun anything
heavy enough to beat them. The
fears of the Admiralty were then
reinforced by information about the
Italian Regina Elena class, of which
four ships were about to be laid
down. The only possible British step
was a new type of cruiser,
combining the speed of the cruiser
with the firepower of a capital ship,
but in the process losing perhaps too
much protection. The nature of this
hybrid came into the purview of the

1904 Committee on Designs, which
considered five schemes for what
soon became labelled a battlecruiser.
The basic parameters were protection equal to that of the Minotaur
class, a speed of 25kt (46·3km/h),
and an armament of 12in (305mm)
guns and small weapons for
use against torpedo boats.

The three Invincible class ships
caused an enormous stir when their
details became known, though the
technical press was rightly worried
by the lack of protection, which
caused *Invincible*'s loss in the Battle
of Jutland on 31 May 1916.
Indomitable was built by Fairfield
and completed in June 1908, and
Inflexible came from Clydebank and
was completed in October 1908. All
three units were widely used in the
opening phases of World War I, but
the Battle of Jutland revealed their
shortcomings, and though armour
was increased and armament
modified, the two survivors were
thereafter less fully employed. Both
were sold for scrap in 1922.

Below: Battlecruiser *Indomitable* in
December 1914, the year in which
anti-torpedo netting and booms were
removed. Lack of protection was
the major fault of this class.

Below: *Satsuma*, first Japanese-built
battleship, soon after completion in
1909. When launched in 1906, she
was the world's biggest warship.

x 4in (102mm); 4 x 3pdr; 3 x 18in (457mm) torpedo tubes.
Performance: 22·1kt (41km/h); radius 5,000nm (9,260km) at 10kt (18km/h).
Crew: 733.

BELLEROPHON

1909 *UK*
Other ships in class: *Superb, Temeraire*

Laid down: 3 December 1906.
Launched: 27 July 1907.
Builder: Portsmouth Dockyard.
Displacement: 18,800 tons (19,101 tonnes) load.
Dimensions: 526ft (160·33m) oa x 82ft 6in (25·15m) x 27ft 3in (8·31m) mean.
Machinery: 4 Parsons turbines; 18 Babcock & Wilcox boilers; 4 shafts; 23,000 SHP.
Armour: Krupp cemented 10in-9in (254-229mm) belt; 11in (279mm) turrets; 11in-8in (279-203mm) conning tower.
Armament: 10 x 12in (305mm); 16

The Bellerophons were generally similar to the *Dreadnought,* but had improvements in armament and protection. A secondary battery of enhanced capability was introduced: of these 4in (102mm) guns, eight were located on turret roofs and eight on the superstructure. The major advance in protection was the installation of armoured anti-torpedo bulkheads, which covered the machinery spaces and magazines and reached down to the ships' double bottoms.

Superb and *Temeraire* were both completed in May 1909, and were built by Armstrong (Elswick) and Devonport Dockyard respectively. All three ships were at Jutland, and were sold for breaking up in 1921 and 1922.

Below: *Bellerophon* on completion in 1909. Class based on *Dreadnought,* with displacement increased to allow for improved secondary armament and anti-torpedo protection.

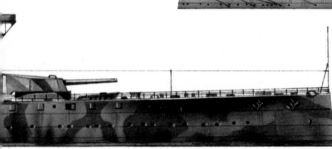

ST. VINCENT

1909 *UK*
Other ships in class: *Collingwood, Vanguard*

Laid down: 30 December 1907.
Launched: 10 September 1908.
Builder: Portsmouth Dockyard.
Displacement: 19,560 tons (19,873 tonnes) load; 23,030 tons (23,398 tonnes) full load.
Dimensions: 536ft (163·37m) oa x 84ft (25·6m) x 25ft 3in (7·7m) mean.
Machinery: 4 Parsons turbines; 18 Babcock & Wilcox boilers; 4 shafts; 24,500 SHP.
Armour: Krupp cemented 10in (254mm) belt; 11in (279mm) turrets; 11in-8in (279-203mm) conning tower.
Armament: 10 x 12in (305mm); 18

x 4in (102mm); 4 x 3pdr; 3 x 18in (457mm) torpedo tubes.
Performance: 21·7kt (40·2km/h); coal 2,800 tons (2,845 tonnes); oil 940 tons (955 tonnes).
Crew: 758.

Basically a repeat of the Bellerophon class, *St Vincent* and her two sister-ships differed only in detail. The chief alteration was the use of 50-cal rather than 45-cal 12in (305mm) guns, which raised muzzle velocity from 2,850ft (869m) to 3,010ft (917m) per second, with a consequent increase in range and armour penetration. The extent of protection was reduced, thinner plates being used at bows and stern.

Vanguard, built by Vickers and completed in February 1910, was lost to an internal explosion on 9 July 1917; *Collingwood* was commissioned in April 1910 after building at Devonport Dockyard. Both survivors were discarded under the Washington Treaty and sold for scrap in December 1922.

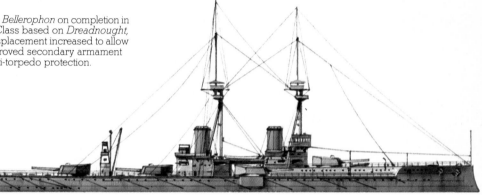

Below: *St. Vincent,* 1910; rig later reduced and upperworks modified.

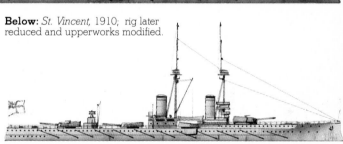

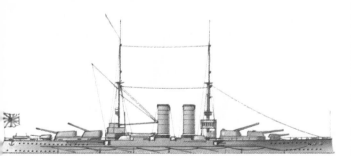

Above: Preliminary study for *Satsuma* shows a lightly-armoured ship of 17,000 tons, with 8 x 12in (305mm) and 16 x 6in (152mm) guns.

SATSUMA

1909 *Japan*

Laid down: 15 May 1905.
Launched: 15 November 1906.
Builder: Yokosuka Dockyard.
Displacement: 19,372 tons (19,683 tonnes) normal.
Dimensions: 482ft (146·9m) oa x 83ft 6in (25·5m) x 27ft 6in (8·38m) mean.

Machinery: Vertical Triple Expansion engines; 20 Miyabara boilers; 2 shafts; 17,300 IHP.
Armour: Krupp cemented and Krupp non-cemented 9in (229mm) belt; 7in (178mm) upper belt; 6in-4in (152-102mm) belt ends; 2in (51mm) deck; 9in-7in (229-178mm) turrets; 7in (178mm) secondary turrets; 5in (127mm) battery.
Armament: 4 x 12in (305mm); 12 x 10in (254mm); 12 x 4·7in (120mm); 8 x 3in (76mm); 5 x 18in (457mm) torpedo tubes.
Performance: 18·25kt (33·8km/h); coal 2,000 tons (2,032 tonnes); oil 300 tons (305 tonnes).
Crew: 1,100.

Satsuma has the distinction of being the first battleship built in Japan, and should also have had the honour of being the world's first 'dreadnought', for when she was laid down (five months before *Dreadnought*) she was schemed with an armament of 12 x 12in (305mm) guns. Apart from her guns, which were Armstrong weapons, she was of Japanese design and manufacture, and at the time of her launch the largest warship in the world. Performance was comparable with that of contemporary Japanese capital ships, while protection was very slightly less on the turrets.

The original armament pattern was for 12in (305mm) twin turrets on the centre line fore and aft, plus another four 12in (305mm) weapons on each beam in one twin and two single turrets. However, when it was appreciated that the chances of using both beam batteries at the same time were remote, it was decided to replace these very heavy turrets and guns with an intermediate battery, the pattern finally selected being three twin 10in (254mm) turrets on each beam. In this guise *Satsuma* may be regarded as a semi-dreadnought. Only later was it seen fully how ineffective was this arrangement in terms of ammunition stowage and fire control. One factor favouring the change to 10in (254mm) guns was cost: the money saved was used to buy turbines from the USA for *Aki,* which had a different arrangement of her machinery spaces and three rather than two funnels, and could reach 20kt (37·1km/h).

Satsuma saw only limited operational use in World War I, but was deployed to guard against the break-out by Von Spee's Squadron in 1914. She was disarmed in 1922 and became a target in 1923 for the new 24in (610mm) torpedo before being sunk as a bombing target in September 1924.

NASSAU

1909 Germany
Other ships in class: *Posen,
Rheinland, Westfalen*

Laid down: 22 July 1907.
Launched: 7 March 1908.
Builder: Wilhelmshaven Dockyard.
Displacement: 18,900 tons (19,200
tonnes) normal; 20,210 tons (20,533
tonnes) full load.
Dimensions: 479ft 4in (146·1m) oa
x 88ft 4in (26·9m) x 27ft 11in (8·5m).
Machinery: Vertical Triple
Expansion engines; 12 Marine
boilers; 3 shafts; 26,244 IHP.
Armour: Krupp cemented 11·5in-
3·9in (300-100mm) belt; 11in-3·5in
(280-90mm) turrets; 12in (305mm)
conning tower.
Armament: 12 x 11in (280mm); 12
x 5·9in (150mm); 16 x 3·5in (88mm);
6 x 17·7in (450mm) torpedo tubes.
Performance: 20kt (37·1km/h);
radius 8,150nm (15,125km) at 10kt
(18·5km/h); coal 2,700 tons (2,743
tonnes); oil 200 tons (203 tonnes).
Crew: 963.

Left: *Westfalen* leads a German
battle line, *c*1915. All four of the
Nassaus were present at Jutland.

Above: 14,000-ton design of 1904.

Above: 18,000-ton design of 1906.

Below: *Nassau* as completed, with
WT topmasts pointing obliquely aft.
Torpedo nets, seen in the process of
spreading in front view, were not
fitted throughout the class. Plan view
shows turret layout which was
dictated by positioning of engine
rooms.

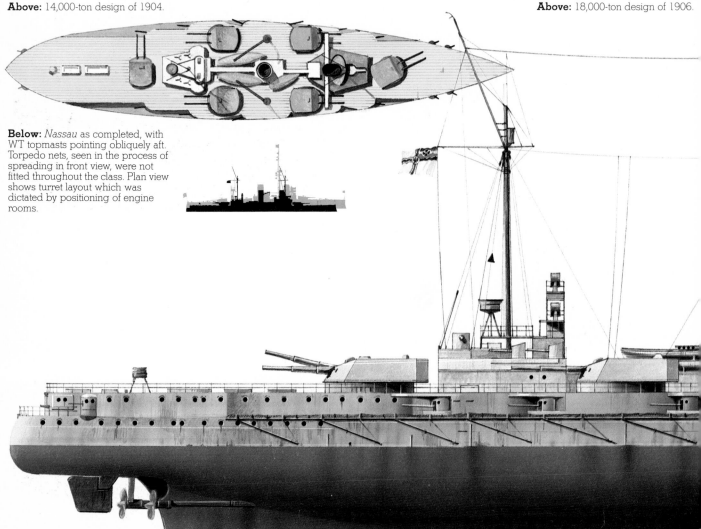

In building the revolutionary *Dreadnought,* Britain effectively began a new naval race in which all started equal, relying on her capability to outbuild any rivals. Germany, whose pre-dreadnought strength was far below that of Britain—24 pre-dreadnoughts built or projected, compared to Britain's 51—made a cautious start.

When details of the new class began to emerge, it was clear that Germany had opted for the course of least risk for her first dreadnoughts: the design was basically an enlargement of the pre-dreadnought Deutschland class, while the retention of the Deutschlands' reciprocating machinery (albeit in more powerful form) meant that the main armament had to be arranged in six twin turrets, two on the centre line fore and aft and the other four in 'wing' positions (two on each beam). The secondary armament was of a greater calibre than foreign estimates had first suggested, and was disposed in twelve casemate positions on the main deck.

The German choice of a smaller-calibre main armament was of great benefit for weight-saving, which

could be used for extra protection. This was markedly better than that of contemporary British dreadnoughts, and had as its basis a belt running from the bow to within a few feet of the stern: this was 11·5in (300mm) thick amidships, and tapered to 5·9in (150mm) forward and 3·9in (100mm) aft; the central part, between the centre-line turrets, was closed off by 7·9in (200mm) bulkheads, and above this was the battery armour some 6·3in (160mm) thick.

The type of 11in (280mm) gun used also made a contribution to weight-saving, for this 1904 version of the standard heavy gun had a high muzzle velocity, and hence a flat trajectory and considerable range with small angles of elevation: this permitted the turrets and gun mountings to be simpler and thus lighter and cheaper. A heavy secondary armament was retained in the erroneous belief that North Sea actions would be medium-range engagements in which such a secondary armament could play a decisive part.

Nassau served with the High Seas Fleet between 1910 and 1918, and took part in that force's operations in

World War I, notably the Battle of Jutland where she took two medium-calibre hits causing moderate damage. In 1915 the 2 x 3·5in (88mm) guns in the stern were removed, and in 1916 and 1917 the remaining twelve guns of the same calibre, all in poor positions, were removed; 4 x 3·5in (88mm) AA guns were added in 1917. *Nassau* was stricken early in 1919, and in 1920 allocated to Japan and sold for scrap. She was scrapped in 1924. *Posen*

was built by Germaniawerft in Kiel and completed in May 1910, had a career similar to that of *Nassau* and was scrapped in 1921. *Rheinland* was built by Vulkan in Stettin for completion in April 1910; she was slightly damaged at Jutland, and then damaged by running aground in April 1918; not repaired, *Rheinland* was scrapped in 1922. *Westfalen* was completed in November 1909 after building at the Bremen yard of Weser; she was scrapped in 1924.

Above: Final preliminary design.

1910-1919

The commissioning of *Dreadnought* had given Great Britain a decisive edge in capital ship design, but it also had, in a sense, brought about a measure of parity amongst the world's navies, and following a period of adjustment and planning, 'all-big-gun' battleships dominated naval construction. This was particularly the case in Germany, where *Nassau* was completed late in 1909. The United States continued to press on, following her South Carolinas with further, improved pairs in the Delawares, Floridas and Wyomings, while France (*Courbet*), Italy (*Dante Alighieri*) and Russia (*Gangut*) lagged behind, their first dreadnoughts not completing until 1913-14. In the Far East, Japan followed her 'semi-dreadnoughts' *Satsuma* and *Aki* with a pair of pure dreadnoughts (Kawachi class) early in 1912, and ordered a fast battlecruiser (*Kongo*) from a British yard. 'Dreadnought fever' struck in South America too, where traditional rivalries between Brazil, Argentina and Chile led to the purchase of such ships.

However, it was the rivalry between Britain and Germany which dominated the years immediately prior to World War I, a rivalry which took on a new impetus once it was learnt in Britain that her European challenger was stockpiling vast quantities of warship machinery and armour plate that could only have been required if a huge fleet were being planned.

Dominated by World War I, the decade 1910-20 saw the capital ship evolve into a fighting unit of unprecedented speed, size and power. By 1920 displacements had all but doubled, gun calibres had increased to the largest yet seen, triple-mounted weapons were much in favour in several navies, and vast improvements in fire control, protection (particularly in US and German designs) and propulsion systems had been made.

ARMAMENT

In 1909 the British *Orion* was laid down. She mounted ten guns of a new calibre—13·5in (343mm)—all on the centre-line, and was given 12in (305mm) side armour against the 10in (254mm) or 11in (279mm) of *Dreadnought* and her immediate successors. She represented a significant increase in firepower, and was immediately dubbed a 'super dreadnought'. Other navies were not slow to respond, and by mid-1914 the United States had commissioned the two New Yorks, with 14in (356mm) turrets and Japan the first two units of the Kongo class battlecruisers, also with 14in (356mm) guns. France's Bretagnes (13·4in, 340mm) were on the stocks, but meanwhile Britain had laid down the Queen Elizabeths and Revenges (15in, 381mm, guns). In a leap-frogging process reminiscent of the 1870s and 1880s, the calibre race seemed to be in full swing, culminating in the US- and Japanese-built 16in (406mm) gunned vessels completed towards the end of the decade and the 18in (457mm) gunned light battlecruiser *Furious* of the Royal Navy. Only Germany among the leading dreadnought powers clung initially to her 11in (280mm) and subsequently 12in (305mm) calibres, although two 15in (381mm) gunned Badens had been completed by the end of 1916.

Superfiring turrets were the norm by the outbreak of World War I, frequently with additional centre-line turrets amidships, considerations of blast effects on cross-deck and end-on fire, the adverse influence on ships' rolling characteristics and the desirability of effective anti-torpedo protection (hence space between barbettes and outer plating) leading to the final abandonment of wing turrets.

Below: *New Mexico* (BB-40) transits the Panama Canal in 1919 with six feet (1·8m) to spare either side: the locks would determine US warship beams for some time to come. Note the plated-over 5in (127mm) casemates forward and the typical 'basket' masts.

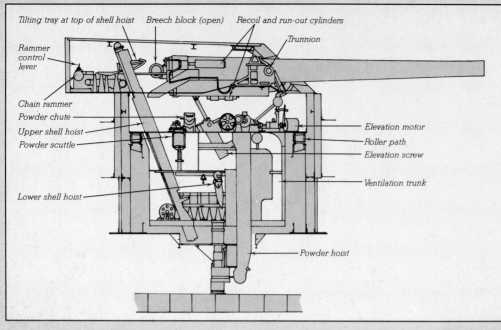

Tilting tray at top of shell hoist — Breech block (open) — Recoil and run-out cylinders

Trunnion

Rammer control lever

Chain rammer
Powder chute
Upper shell hoist
Powder scuttle

Elevation motor
Roller path
Elevation screw

Lower shell hoist

Ventilation trunk

Powder hoist

Left: The US 14in (356mm) 45-cal Mk 3 mounting, as installed aboard *Texas* (BB-35) and *New York* (BB-3... Weighing a total of 532 tons (540.5 tonnes), the mount reflected a growth in complexity brought abo... by, amongst other things, the introduction of the two-stage hoist (for greater safety) and any-elevation loading, both of which features are apparent in this drawing.

Below: One of the developments i... fire control during the 1910-20 decade was the practice of painting up turrets with training scales, helping nearby ships target an enemy. These are the after turrets of a Queen Elizabeth; note, too, the 'blimp', for spotting/reconnaissanc...

Bottom: In a further effort to enhance anti-torpedo protection, many capital ships were fitted with hull bulges, which had the added attraction of increasing stability in response to topweight, though generally with a speed penalty. This is *Pennsylvania*, during World War...

This was one factor that drove up ship length; another would be the increased centre-line space required by more powerful machinery.

Improvements in gunnery technique continued apace. A firing trial in 1912 between the British *Thunderer*, fitted with director gear, and *Orion*, lacking such equipment, led to the former firing 39 rounds and achieving 13 hits and 10 near-misses in 3½ minutes against the latter's 27 rounds, 2 hits and 2 near-misses—a 600 per cent improvement, taking into account ricochets. From 1913 all capital ships in the British fleet were fitted with director-firing equipment. Fire control continued to progress also, the Dumaresq calculator and Pollen plotter being developed by Lt Dreyer into a fire control table which combined calculated rates of change in enemy course and speed with actual rangefinder observations, cross-checking the two to cancel errors.

Rangefinding was developed too, particularly in Germany, where it was quickly appreciated that ever-increasing visual ranges demanded equipment with longer bases, if only to maintain accuracy. Rangefinders were the vital factor in the opening exchanges of a gun duel, before any observations could be made from shell splashes.

Meanwhile in Italy the problem of mounting the maximum number of guns on a hull that would not have to be of outrageous dimensions were partially solved by the introduction, in *Dante Alighieri,* of the triple turret, an idea that was received enthusiastically in Russia and the USA and would be developed in France into the quadruple turret of the abortive Normandies. The triple mounting was also pressed in Britain—indeed Vickers had given some assistance to Russia in this respect—but the concept was rejected because of the adverse effect it would have on controlled salvo (alternate guns per turret) firing doctrine, although it would be adopted in the 1920s. Austria-Hungary also pursued the idea, in a successful design, *Viribus Unitis.*

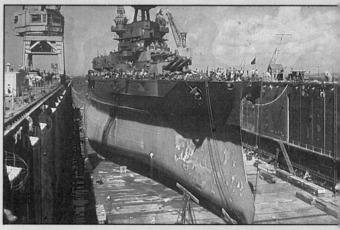

PROTECTION

The American *Nevada*, which introduced the triple turret to US Navy service, was an important design in another respect. Armour protection, as it had developed into the early 1900s, had to reconcile two approaches: the required thickness of plate over a given feature of the ship, and how best the scheme as a whole might be distributed. Clearly, if a ship was to carry a certain number of guns of a certain calibre at a certain speed, questions about the weights involved could be estimated. A hull could then be designed to transport this weight with the necessary efficiency, but if

it were to survive it would need to be protected, and th... weight of such protection would be more or less fixed unless changes were to be made to the elements of th... design already provided for. The principal areas of interes... were the main weapons, which would have to remain oper... able and would include not only the gun's crew and loadin... system but also the hoists and turret machinery; the maga... zines, where penetration by an incoming shell could, an... in all probability would, be catastrophic; the conning towe... from where an engagement would have to be directed; an... the machinery, since a motionless ship is more or less... dead one. A holed hull would not necessarily result in a los... ship, providing flooding could be controlled. To this wa... added the complication posed by increasing ranges an... the consequence that vitals might be penetrated by a projec... tile arriving through the decks, given the higher, arcin... trajectories that increased range brought about.

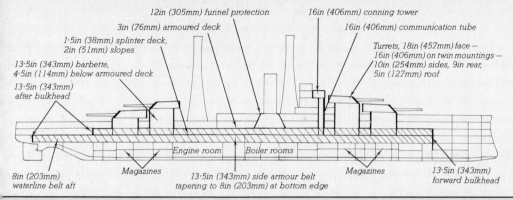

Above: HM battlecruisers *Tiger* (left) and *Renown* during heavy weather in the North Sea late in World War I. The photo clearly demonstrates the problems associated with working secondary-calibre guns mounted low down in casemates; they were abandoned in the early 1920s.

Left: The armour scheme of *Nevada* (BB-36) illustrates the radical 'all or nothing' system, with belt protection centralised across the ship's vitals and the ends entrusted to horizontal armour and extensive watertight subdivision: concentration made available greater thicknesses where they were most needed.

Hence the designers of *Nevada* abandoned the system wherein armour was spread out over as much of the ship as possible and replaced it with 'all or nothing': vital areas of the hull were screened by a maximum thickness of belt, which was kept narrow and capped by a thick armour deck which, while not stopping incoming shells, would cause them to detonate, the shrapnel being absorbed by a splinter deck closing the vertical belt along its bottom edge. The ends were left completely unarmoured, but they were no considered essential to the survival of the ship so long as flooding could be localised. So important was this scheme that every subsequent US capital ship—and ships of other navies—preserved its elements thereafter.

MACHINERY

The introduction, in *Dreadnought*, of the turbine was quickly adopted by other navies, although the United States lagged behind somewhat in this respect. By 1920 outputs as high as 144,000SHP were being achieved (*Hood*), compared to the *Dreadnought*'s 23,000, necessary not only to produce higher speeds, of course, but also to drive the considerably larger hulls through the water.

The most important innovation in the 1910-20 period in respect of propulsion, however, was the adoption of oil as the principal fuel for the capital ship. Its advantages over coal were compelling. It had a much greater inherent thermal output per ton, with the result that greater ranges, or higher speeds, could be obtained for the same weight of fuel. It could be led to the boilers from practically any location in the ship without the need for gangs of men transferring fuel by hand, perhaps under combat conditions when most might be needed and, more importantly, without the need

for stokers. It created no residue when burnt and hence reduced cleaning requirements. Furthermore, ship stability and buoyancy could be maintained at a constant level simply by filling used bunkers with seawater. Conversely, the raw material was not as accessible as coal (Germany rejected oil-firing for this reason), and the protective effect of coal as an absorbing barrier to enemy shells was considered lost—at least at first. Many navies hedged, adopting oil-sprayed coal as an interim measure, but by 1920 coal had given way. The Queen Elizabeth class set the pace.

The adoption of oil caused developments in anti-torpedo protection—a particularly worrying problem to naval chiefs at the time. However, it was soon shown that liquid, in the form of seawater and indeed oil fuel, could act as a shock-absorber against an incoming torpedo, transmitting the energy thrown out by the missile's explosion over a large area. This, in essence, was the basis of the anti-torpedo bulge, which was fitted or retrofitted to large numbers of capital ships during World War I.

The turbine, while not immediately adopted in the USA, did prompt a further development in that country. One problem with this form of propulsion was the need to introduce some more efficient means by which the velocity of the mechanism could be reduced before being imparted to the propeller shafts. Most navies evolved a system of gearing, but in the USA a novel approach was the coupling of the shafts to electric motors, which latter were driven by the turbine. Although there were advantages—the ability to control power output directly from the bridge being not the least—the sheer weight and complexity of turbo-electric drive brought its eventual demise. It was installed in the New Mexicos and subsequent vessels, but by the 1930s had been all but abandoned.

SOUTH CAROLINA (BB-26)

1910 USA
Other ships in class: *Michigan* (BB-27)

Laid down: 18 December 1906.
Launched: 11 July 1908.
Builder: Cramp, Philadelphia.
Displacement: 16,000 tons (16,256 tonnes) normal; 17,900 tons (18,186 tonnes) full load.
Dimensions: 452ft 9in (138·2m) oa x 80ft 3in (24·5m) x 24ft 6in (7·5m).
Machinery: Vertical Triple Expansion engines; 12 Babcock boilers; 2 shafts; 17,882 IHP.
Armour: Krupp cemented and non-cemented 12in-9in (305-229mm) belt; 12in-8in (305-203mm) turrets; 12in (305mm) conning tower.
Armament: 8 x 12in (305mm); 22 x 3in (76mm); 4 x 1pdr; 2 x 21in (533mm) torpedo tubes.
Performance: 18·9kt (35km/h); radius 4,340nm (8,045km) at 10kt (18·5km/h); coal 2,380 tons (2,418 tonnes).
Crew: 869.

The position occupied in naval history by the *Dreadnought* should perhaps more rightfully have belonged to the American battleship *South Carolina*, which, designed before *Dreadnought*, was the true precursor of the definitive battleship design ('all big gun' armament carried in centre-line turrets), but was built at a more leisurely pace and so appeared only after *Dreadnought* was in service.

Another reason for the *South Carolina*'s tardy appearance was the thought given to her design. For financial reasons the normal displacement was held at the 16,000 tons (16,256 tonnes) of the earlier Connecticut class, despite the proposed main armament of eight rather than four 12in (305mm) guns, carried in superfiring twin turrets after successful blast-effect trials with a monitor. It had originally been hoped to produce *South Carolina* as a flush-deck ship, but even the elimination of the earlier battleships' secondary (8in, 203mm) and tertiary

(7in, 178mm) batteries in favour of an anti-torpedo boat fit of light 3in (76mm) weapons could not provide the weight-saving to make this possible. Thus *South Carolina* had a forecastle deck extending as far aft as the main mast, with the two aftermost turrets carried one deck lower than the two foremost turrets. Most importantly, however, the turrets were all on the centreline, which meant that with two fewer 12in (305mm) guns *South Carolina* had the same effective weight of fire fore and aft (four guns) and on the broadside (eight guns) as *Dreadnought*.

Equally impressive was the arrangement of the armour. For weight and finance reasons this had been very carefully thought out, and was based on a substantial belt some 8ft (2·44m) deep, of which 6ft 9in (2·06m) was below the waterline. The main thickness of this belt stretched from forward of 'A' turret to just aft of 'Y' turret, and was boxed off by thick bulkheads. The redoubt above this belt was 300ft (91·44m) long, and also formidably thick. Military masts with fighting tops were at first considered, but *South Carolina* was the first US ship completed with the distinctive cage masts. These were at first somewhat light in structure, and after *Michigan* had lost her fore mast in a storm during January 1918 more substantial structures were introduced. The one retro-grade feature of the design was the use of reciprocating machinery, US turbines not yet being ready.

By 1918 the secondary battery had been cut back to 14 x 3in (76mm) casemated guns, though two 3in (76mm) AA guns had been fitted. *Michigan* was generally similar to *South Carolina*, but was built by the New York Shipbuilding Corp. and completed with Midvale armour in January 1910. Both ships were on the strength of the Atlantic Fleet from 1911 to 1916, and thereafter used for a number of secondary roles (training, escort, etc). Both were stricken in 1923 and scrapped in 1924.

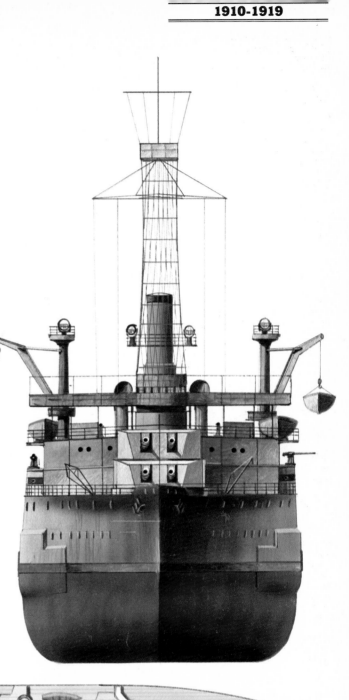

Above: USS *Michigan* at anchor with boats out. The importance of these vessels in dreadnought development has been underestimated. They combined a powerful armament on a limited displacement, but lengthy building times tended to diminish their impact on the naval scene.

Below: *South Carolina* upon completion. The lattice masts were only adopted after firing trials, but although light and strong, they were often badly affected by high winds. Superfiring guns were also fitted after extensive tests, and special screened sights were sited on the side walls of the turrets to minimise blast effects over the roofs of the lower turrets.

Below: *Von der Tann*, Germany's first battlecruiser, shown on completion in 1910. She had a lower freeboard than her British contemporaries, the Indefatigables, and was better protected.

Below: *São Paulo* as camouflaged in 1918, when Brazil intended to offer her for service in European waters with the British Grand Fleet.

MINAS GERAIS

1910 *Brazil*
Other ships in class: *São Paulo*

Laid down: 1907.
Launched: 10 September 1908.
Builder: Armstrong, Elswick.
Displacement: 19,280 tons (19,588 tonnes) normal; 21,200 tons (21,540 tonnes) full load.
Dimensions: 543ft (165·8m) oa x 83ft (25·3m) x 28ft (8·5m).
Machinery: Vertical Triple Expansion engines; 18 Babcock boilers; 2 shafts; 23,500 IHP.
Armour: Krupp cemented and non-cemented 9in-4in (229-102mm) belt; 12in-8in (305-203mm) turrets; 12in-9in (305-229mm) conning tower.
Armament: 12 x 12in (305mm); 22 x 4·7in (120mm); 8 x 3pdr.
Performance: 21kt (38·9km/h); radius 8,700nm (16,100km) at 10kt (18·5km/h); coal 2,360 tons (2,398 tonnes); oil 350 tons (356 tonnes).
Crew: 900.

Designed for Brazil by Armstrong Whitworth to counter two other Armstrong Whitworth ships (*Constitucion* and *Libertad*, later *Triumph* and *Swiftsure*) building for the Argentine Navy, *Minas Gerais* and *São Paulo* were initially planned as pre-dreadnoughts but then recast as the world's most powerful dreadnoughts, the first to be delivered to a minor power. The design was essentially an enlarged *Constitucion* with the 12in (305mm) guns in twin superfiring centre-line turrets fore and aft, plus a pair of wing turrets, en échelon, each with two guns. The freeboard was low, and the 4·7in (120mm) guns could not be worked in any sea. *São Paulo* was built by Vickers and completed in July 1910. Both ships were extensively modernized, in the USA in 1923, and in Brazil in 1934-37. *Minas Gerais* was scrapped in 1954, and *São Paulo* was lost at sea in bad weather while being towed to Italy for scrapping in 1951.

RADETZKY

1910 *Austria-Hungary*
Other ships in class: *Erzherzog Franz Ferdinand*, *Zrinyi*

Laid down: 26 November 1907.
Launched: 3 July 1909.
Builder: Stabilimento Tecnico Triestino.
Displacement: 14,722 tons (14,500 tonnes) normal; 15,851 tons (16,105 tonnes) full load.
Dimensions: 456ft (139m) x 80ft 4in (24·5m) x 26ft 7in (8·1m) mean.
Machinery: 4-cylinder Vertical Triple Expansion engines; 12 Yarrow boilers; 2 shafts; 20,600 IHP.
Armour: Krupp cemented 9·1in (230mm) belt; 9·8in (250mm) barbettes and turrets; 9·8in (250mm) conning tower.
Armament: 4 x 12in (305mm); 8 x 9·45in (240mm); 20 x 3·9in (100mm); 6 x 11pdr; 2 x 3pdr; 3 x 17·7in (450mm) torpedo tubes.
Performance: 20·5kt (38km/h); coal 1,580 tons (1,605 tonnes); oil 167 tons (170 tonnes).
Crew: 876.

Though launched well into the dreadnought era, the three units of the Radetzky class were conceived in 1905, and were caught in the intermediate period by the slow pace of Austro-Hungarian procurement. In overall design the Radetzky and her two sisterships represented that interim period when a primary armament of 4 x 12in (305mm) guns in twin centreline turrets fore and aft was complemented by an intermediate battery, in this case 8 x 9·45in (240mm) guns grouped in four twin turrets, located two to each beam. Thus though they were not far removed in concept from the preceding class (the three Erzherzog Karl units), in

practice they were, with a turreted main armament of 4 x 12in (305mm) guns in place of 4 x 9·45in (240mm) weapons, a secondary battery of 8 x 9·45in (240mm) turreted guns in place of 12 x 7·5in (190mm) turreted guns, and a tertiary battery of 20 x 3·9in (100mm) casemated guns in place of twelve exposed 11pdrs.

The main belt reached almost to the stern, and its thickest section, some 285ft 6in (87m) long and covering the area from forward of the front turret to aft of the rear

Below: Austro-Hungarian battleship *Radetzky* during World War I. Although not completed until 1910-11, the Radetzkys resembled the British King Edward VII pre-dreadnoughts, and were somewhat outclassed by their contemporaries.

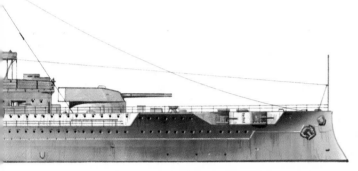

VON DER TANN

1910 Germany

Laid down: 25 March 1908.
Launched: 20 March 1909.
Builder: Blohm & Voss, Hamburg.
Displacement: 19,100 tons (19,406 tonnes) normal; 21,802 tons (22,150 tonnes) full load.
Dimensions: 563ft 4in (171·7m) oa x 87ft 3in (26·6m) x 26ft 7in (8·1m).
Machinery: 2 Parsons turbines; 18 Schulz-Thornycroft boilers; 4 shafts; 79,800 SHP.
Armour: Krupp cemented 9·8in (250mm) belt; 5·9in-3·9in (150-100mm) belt ends; 2in (50mm) decks; 9·1in (230mm) barbettes and turrets; 9·8in (250mm) conning tower.
Armament: 8 x 11in (280mm); 10 x 5·9in (150mm); 16 x 3·5in (88mm); 4 x 17·7in (450mm) torpedo tubes.
Performance: 27·75kt (51·4km/h); coal 2,756 tons, (2,800 tonnes); oil 197 tons (200 tonnes).
Crew: 923.

Von der Tann was Germany's first essay into battlecruiser design, and the first major German warship to have turbines and quadruple screws, an arrangement which proved highly effective in terms of speed and reliability. In contrast with British battlecruiser design, which tended towards high free-board and large superstructures, making the ships easily identified and ranged targets, *Von der Tann* set the German precedent of relatively low freeboard and a simple arrangement for the two widely-spaced funnels and the low superstructure.

The standard 11in (280mm) gun was again chosen for the main armament, and the turret disposition was similar to that of the Invincible class, with the four twin turrets disposed two on the centre line fore and aft, and the other two in wing positions. But in detail the German arrangement worked better because of the improved spacing of the wing turrets, which could each be brought to bear over relatively wide arcs across the beam, thus ensuring a true eight-gun broadside. The fitting of the secondary armament in midships casements allowed them to share the wing turrets' protection, which helped to save weight for better use elsewhere. Whereas the British battlecruisers' side armour comprised a shallow belt of little thickness which reached as far aft only as the rear centre-line turret, that of *Von der Tann* was altogether more practical; the thicker main belt was deeper than that of the British ships, and its main thickness covered the hull from before the forward turret to abaft the after turret, with useful protection being continued right to the bows and almost to the stern. Better magazine, barbette and turret armour, plus a more effective torpedo defence, was also provided.

Evidence of the comparative strengths and weaknesses of *Von der Tann* and the three Invincibles and Indefatigables is provided by the Battle of Jutland, in which *Indefatigable* and *Von der Tann* were pitted against each other: hit by two salvoes from *Von der Tann*, the *Indefatigable* suffered explosions in both her forward and after magazines, turned over and sank. *Von der Tann*, on the other hand, was hit by at least four heavy shells, which caused one major and one minor fire and also knocked out all her main guns, but the ship survived to return to port without major difficulty. Surrendered at the end of World War I, *Von der Tann* was scuttled in Scapa Flow during 1919.

Below: *Minas Gerais* in the late 1930s, with single funnel amidships. Her extensive modernization included conversion to oil-firing.

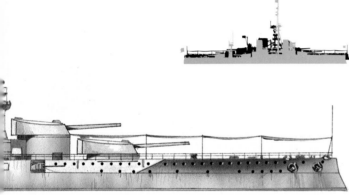

turret, was closed off by 5·9in (150mm) bulkheads; its depth of 7ft 6½in (2·3m) included 4ft 11in (1·5m) below the waterline. Some measure of protection against torpedoes was afforded by two longitudinal bulkheads stretching from the main deck to the bottom.

Erzherzog Franz Ferdinand and *Zrinyi* were also built by Stabilimento Tecnico Triestino, the former being completed in 1910 and the latter in 1911. All three were interned after World War I and scrapped in the early 1920s.

Below: *Delaware* (BB-28) shown as completed in 1910. The Delawares were the first US battleships to exceed 20,000 tons displacement.

DELAWARE (BB-28)

1910 USA
Other ships in class: *North Dakota* (BB-29)

Laid down: 11 November 1907.
Launched: 6 February 1909.
Builder: Newport News.
Displacement: 20,380 tons (20,706 tonnes) normal.
Dimensions: 518ft 9in (158·1m) oa x 85ft 3in (26m) x 27ft 3in (8·23m) mean.
Machinery: Vertical Triple Expansion engines; 14 Babcock boilers; 2 shafts; 24,578 IHP.
Armour: Krupp cemented, Krupp non-cemented and Midvale 11in-9in (279-229mm) belt; 12in-8in (305-203mm) turrets; 12in (305mm) conning tower.
Armament: 10 x 12in (305mm); 14 x 5in (127mm); 2 x 21in (533mm) torpedo tubes.
Performance: 21·6kt (40km/h); radius 5,650nm (10,470km) at 12kt (22·3km/h); coal 2,650 tons (2,692 tonnes); oil 380 tons (386 tonnes).
Crew: 946.

The first American battleships over 20,000 tons (20,320 tonnes), the two units of the Delaware class offered a broadside weight increased by a quarter, their extra length and displacement being used to accommodate another 12in (305mm) twin turret aft, for a total of five centreline turrets. At the same time a new calibre (5in, 127mm) of secondary armament was introduced. *North Dakota* was completed in April 1910 after building at Fore River's yard as the first US battleship with turbines (31,000 SHP). *Delaware* was scrapped in 1924, in which year *North Dakota* became a target ship. She was scrapped in 1931.

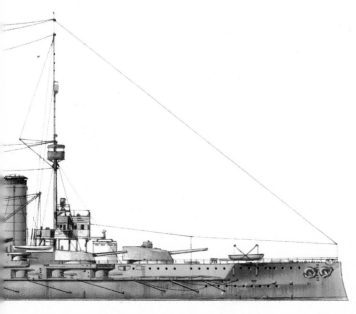

HELGOLAND

1911 Germany
Other ships in class: *Thüringen, Ostfriesland, Oldenburg*

Laid down: 24 November 1908.
Launched: 25 September 1909.
Builder: Howaldtswerke, Kiel.
Displacement: 22,800 tons (23,165 tonnes) normal; 24,312 tons (24,701 tonnes) full load.
Dimensions: 546ft (166·4m) wl x 93ft 6in (28·5m) x 27ft 6in (8·38m).
Machinery: Three 4-cylinder Vertical Triple Expansion engines; 15 Marine boilers; 3 shafts; 28,000 IHP.
Armour: Krupp steel 11·8in-4in (300-102mm) belt; 11in (280mm) turrets; 6·7in-3·15in (170-80mm) casemates; 3in (75mm) decks; 12in (305mm) conning tower.
Armament: 12 x 12in (305mm); 14 x 5·9in (150mm) QF; 14 x 3·5in (88mm) QF; 6 x 19·7in (500mm) torpedo tubes.
Performance: 20kt (37km/h); coal 3,150 tons (3,200 tonnes) max; radius 9,400nm (17,390km) at 10kt (18·5km/h), 3,600nm at 18kt (33·3km/h).
Crew: 1,113.

With the Helgoland class dreadnoughts, the German Navy adopted the 12in (305mm), 50-cal gun as main armament. This weapon, firing an 893lb (405kg) projectile to a maximum range of *c*21,000yds (19,200m), was reckoned the equal of the 13·5in (343mm) 45-cal gun mounted in the British Orion class. But the German dreadnoughts' apparent advantage in carrying 12 heavy guns to the Orions' 10 was negated because, due to lack of space for magazines, superfiring turrets were not fitted. The 'hexagon' arrangement of the Nassaus persisted, reducing the broadside to eight guns only.

The greater beam of the Helgolands allowed the side turrets to be set farther inboard, and both magazine and underwater protection were improved by fitting wide wing passages and 1·2in (30mm) torpedo bulkheads. Expansion machinery was fitted, rather than turbines, in an attempt to reduce construction time. Three comparatively short funnels, closely set amidships, made the class readily identifiable.

The two aftermost single-mounted 3·5in (88mm) QF were removed from beneath the quarterdeck, where they proved to be ineffective, in 1913-14. During World War I the remaining 3·5in (88mm) QF were landed and in *c*1917 4 x 3·5in (88mm) AA were added on the after superstructure.

All four Helgolands served with Battle Squadron I of the German High Seas Fleet during World War I and all saw action at Jutland, 31 May 1916. *Helgoland* and *Oldenburg* were both damaged there but were subsequently repaired. All were stricken on 5 November 1919 and, disarmed, were ceded to Allied powers. *Helgoland* went to Britain, where she was broken up in 1924; *Thüringen* to France, scrapped in 1923-33; and *Oldenburg* to Japan, sold for breaking up immediately.

Ostfriesland, ceded to the USA, was expended in gunfire and aerial bombing tests off Cape Henry, Virginia, on 20-21 July 1921. After withstanding hits and near-misses from some 24 shells and 80 bombs, she was sunk by 6 x 2,205lb (1,000kg) bombs from aircraft directed by Brig-Gen William ('Billy') Mitchell. She was the first battleship sunk by aerial bombing and, according to Mitchell's then strongly-opposed assertions, the proof that air power would soon make capital ships obsolete.

Below: Helgoland-class dreadnought *Oldenburg* soon after completion in 1912. Note short, close-set funnels.

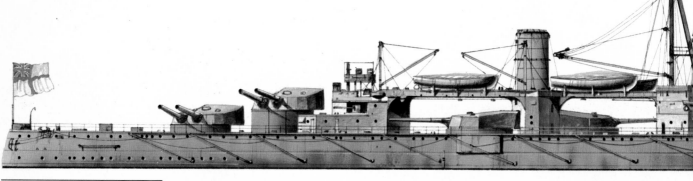

Below: *Hercules* as completed, 1911. The single tripod is badly sited just abaft the fore funnel, where exhaust affects the control top.

INDEFATIGABLE

1911 UK
Other ships in class: *Australia, New Zealand*

Laid down: 23 February 1909.
Launched: 28 October 1909.
Builder: Devonport Dockyard.
Displacement: 18,500 tons (18,796 tonnes) load; 22,080 tons (22,433 tonnes) full load.
Dimensions: 590ft (179·83m) oa x 80ft (24·38m) x 27ft (8·23m) max.
Machinery: 4 Parsons turbines;

HERCULES

1911 UK
Other ships in class: *Colossus*

Laid down: 30 July 1909.
Launched: 10 May 1910.
Builder: Palmers, Newcastle.
Displacement: 20,225 tons (20,549 tonnes) load; 23,050 tons (23,419 tonnes) full load.
Dimensions: 546ft (166·4m) oa x 85ft (25·91m) x 28ft 9in (8·76m) max.
Machinery: 4 Parsons turbines; 18 Yarrow boilers; 4 shafts; 25,000 SHP.
Armour: 11in-7in (279-178mm) belt; 10in-4in (254-102mm) bulkheads; 11in-4in (279-102mm) barbettes; 11in (279mm) turrets; 4in-1·5in (102-38mm) decks; 11in (279mm) conning tower.
Armament: 10 x 12in (305mm); 16 x 4in (102mm) QF; 4 x 3pdr; 3 x 21in (533mm) torpedo tubes.
Performance: 21kt (38·85km/h); coal 2,900 tons (2,946 tonnes) max; oil 800 tons (813 tonnes) full load; radius 6,680nm (12,358km) at 10kt (18·5km/h), 4,050nm (7,492km) at 18·5kt (34·2km/h).
Crew: 755.

Concern in British political and military circles over the growing belligerency of Germany and Austria-Hungary gave rise in 1908 to a vociferous campaign for a major increase in naval strength to match Germany's rumoured covert building programme. The 1909 Programme reflected the campaign's slogan, 'We want eight—and we won't wait!', in providing for a record construction of eight capital ships: the improved Neptunes *Colossus* and *Hercules*, four Orion class battleships, and the battlecruisers *Lion* and *Princess Royal*.

As compared to their half-sister *Neptune*, the ends of *Colossus* and *Hercules* were left unprotected, but side armour was strengthened. On the lower belt and exposed parts of the barbettes, armour increased to 11in (279mm) in thickness, the usual anti-torpedo bulkhead being replaced by 3in-1·25in (76-32mm) screens over the main magazine areas to compensate for the weight increase. Also to save weight, and because funnel exhaust had been found to hamper the efficiency of an after control top, an after tripod mast was omitted—although, unfortunately, the single tripod was positioned just *abaft* the forward funnel.

Secondary armament—changed in 1917 to 13 x 4in (102mm), 1 x 4in (102mm) AA and 1 x 3in (76mm) AA—was concentrated in the forward superstructure (with shields in *Hercules* only) for better anti-torpedo defence. For the first time, 21in (533mm) torpedo tubes were fitted; the single stern tube was removed in 1916.

Hercules served at Jutland—where *Colossus* was Flagship, 1st Battle Squadron, and the only main force battleship to sustain damage—and in 1919 carried the Allied Naval Commission to Wilhelmshaven. She was sold for breaking up in 1920.

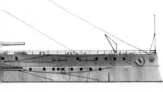

Below: *Aki* as completed, 1911. Note mixed armament: 12in (305mm) guns fore and aft; 10in (254mm) amidships.

31 Babcock and Wilcox boilers; 4 shafts; 44,000 SHP.
Armour: 6in-4in (152-102mm) belt; 4in (102mm) bulkheads; 7in (178mm) turrets; 7in-3in (178-76mm) barbettes; 2·5in-1in (63-25mm) decks; 10in (254mm) conning tower.
Armament: 8 x 12in (305mm); 16 x 4in (102mm) QF; 4 x 3pdr; 2 x 18in (457mm) torpedo tubes.
Performance: 25kt (46·25km/h); coal 3,170 tons (3,221 tonnes) max; oil 840 tons (853 tonnes); radius 6,330nm (11,710km) at 10kt (18·5km/h), 2,290nm (4,236km) at 23·5kt (43·5km/h).
Crew: 800.

Economic considerations, as well as Fisher's predilection for fast, lightly-protected capital ships,

dictated the construction of a second group of battlecruisers, the Indefatigables, the cheapest British capital ships of the 20th century. Incorporating the faults of the earlier Invincibles, they showed few improvements: the diagonally offset midships 12in (305mm) turrets were set a little wider apart to improve broadside fire.

Their faults were tragically demonstrated at Jutland, 31 May 1916. Engaging the German battlecruiser *Von der Tann,* with which she had been favourably compared by British pundits, *Indefatigable* blew up and sank, with only four survivors, when shells penetrated her upper deck and reached the magazines. Her sister ships both survived the war.

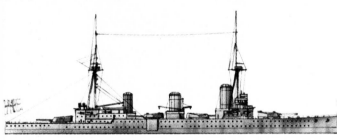

Above: The ill-fated battlecruiser *Indefatigable* as completed in 1911.

AKI

1911 Japan

Laid down: 15 March 1905.
Launched: 15 April 1907.
Builder: Kure Dockyard.
Displacement: 19,800 tons (20,117 tonnes) normal.
Dimensions: 492ft (149·96m) oa x 83ft 7in (25·48m) x 28ft 9in (8·76m) max.
Machinery: 2 Curtis turbines; 15 Miyabara boilers; 2 shafts; 24,000 SHP.
Armour: Krupp steel 9in-4in (229-102mm) belt; 9·75in-8in (248-203mm) main turrets; 8in-7in (203-178mm) secondary turrets; 6in (152mm) casemates; 3in-2in (76-51mm) deck; 10in (254mm) conning tower.
Armament: 4 x 12in (305mm); 12 x 10in (254mm); 8 x 6in (152mm) QF; 12 x 3in (76mm) QF; 3 MG; 5 x 18in (457mm) torpedo tubes.
Performance: 20kt (37km/h); coal 2,500 tons (2,540 tonnes) max; radius c9,100nm (16,835km) at 10kt (18·5km/h).
Crew: 931.

Laid down at the same time as *Satsuma, Aki* was also originally planned as an 'all big gun' ship. Two years longer in building, she differed considerably in appearance from her near-sister (compare her funnel arrangement with that of *Satsuma*, p.172) and incorporated significant improvements, notably the fitting of US-made turbines in place of triple expansion machinery and a revised tertiary battery. *Aki* was disarmed under the terms of the Washington Treaty in 1922 and expended as a target in 1923-24.

DANTON

1911 France
Other ships in class: *Condorcet, Diderot, Voltaire, Mirabeau, Vergniaud*

Laid down: 10 January 1908.
Launched: 4 July 1909.
Builder: Brest Dockyard.
Displacement: 18,400 tons (18,694 tonnes) normal; 19,450 tons (19,761 tonnes) full load.
Dimensions: 480ft 11in (146·58m) oa x 84ft 8in (25·8m) x 28ft 8in (8·74m) mean.
Machinery: 4 Parsons turbines; 26 Belleville boilers; 4 shafts; 22,500 SHP.
Armour: 10·5in-6in (267-152mm) belt; 11·8in (300mm) main turrets; 11in (280mm) barbettes; 8·7in (220mm) secondary turrets; 2·75in (70mm) deck; 11·8in (300mm) conning tower.
Armament: 4 x 12in (305mm); 12 x 9·4in (240mm); 16 x 2·9in (75mm) QF; 10 x 1·85in (47mm) QF; 2 x 18in (457mm) torpedo tubes.
Performance: 19·25kt (35·6km/h); coal 2,027 tons (2,059 tonnes) max; radius 3,370nm (6,234km) at 10kt (18·5km/h), 1,750nm (3,237km) at 18kt (33·3km/h).
Crew: 921.

France's last pre-dreadnoughts, the Dantons had 1·8in (45mm) armoured longitudinal anti-torpedo bulkheads. Struck by two torpedoes from the German submarine *U.64* on 19 March 1917, south of Sardinia, *Danton* remained afloat for c40 minutes and many of her crew were saved.

Below: *Danton*, name-ship of France's last, belated, pre-dreadnought class, soon after completion, 1911.

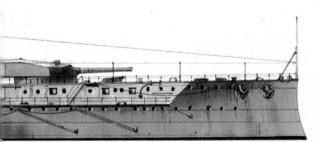

Below: *Neptune* in 1911. The fore funnel was later raised.

Below: *Goeben* (*Yavuz Sultan Selim*) under Turkish colours, World War I.

NEPTUNE

1911 *UK*

Laid down: 19 January 1909.
Launched: 30 September 1909.
Builder: Portsmouth Dockyard.
Displacement: 19,680 tons
(19,995 tonnes) load; 22,720 tons
(23,084 tonnes) full load.
Dimensions: 546ft (166·4m) oa x
85ft (25·9m) x 28ft 6in (8·69m) max.
Machinery: 4 Parsons turbines;
18 Yarrow boilers; 4 shafts; 25,000
SHP.
Armour: 10in-2·5in (254-63mm)
belt; 11in (279mm) turrets; 9in-5in
(229-127mm) barbettes; 8in-4in
(203-102mm) bulkheads; 3in-0·75in
(76-19mm) decks; 11in (279mm)
conning tower.
Armament: 10 x 12in (305mm);
16 x 4in (102mm) QF; 4 x 3pdr; 3
x 18in (457mm) torpedo tubes.
Performance: 21kt (38·85km/h);
coal 2,710 tons (2,753 tonnes) max;
oil 790 tons (803 tonnes); radius
6,330nm (11,710km) at 10kt
(18·5km/h), 3,820nm (7,067km) at
18·5kt (34·2km/h).
Crew: 759.

By the time that *Neptune* was
provided for by the Act of 1908, it
was obvious that the armament
layout of *Dreadnought*, with side
turrets firing on one broadside
only, was unsatisfactory. Rather
than adopt all-centre-line turrets, as
the US Navy had already done in
the South Carolinas, the side
turrets in *Neptune* were diagonally
offset to allow the guns wide arcs
of fire on both sides.
   Although the design of the
turrets, with sighting hoods at the
front ends, precluded one turret
from firing directly over another,
No 4 turret in *Neptune* had to be
superimposed to save excessive
hull length. Its training machinery
was 'stopped' to prevent dead
astern fire. Although all the big
guns could fire on either beam,
cross-deck firing imposed much
strain on the ship's fabric and led
to undesirable complexity in layout
both above and below decks.
   The secondary armament of 16
x 4in (102mm) QF was mounted in
unprotected positions in the ship's
three superstructures. By the end
of World War I, during which
Neptune survived Jutland
undamaged, it had been reduced
to 10 x 4in (102mm) QF, 1 x 4in
(102mm) AA and 1 x 3in (76mm)
AA. In reserve from 1919, *Neptune*
was discarded under the
Washington Treaty and was sold
for scrap on 1 September 1922.

FLORIDA (BB-30)

1911 *USA*
Other ships in class: *Utah* (BB-31)

Laid down: 9 March 1909.
Launched: 12 May 1910.
Builder: New York Navy Yard.
Displacement: 21,825 tons
(22,174 tonnes) normal; 23,400
tons (23,774 tonnes) full load.
Dimensions: 521ft 6in (158·95m)
oa x 88ft 3in (26·9m) x 30ft 1in
(9·17m) max.
Machinery: 4 Parsons turbines;
12 Babcock boilers; 4 shafts;
28,000 SHP.
Armour: 11in-6·5in (279-165mm)
belt; 12in-8in (305-203mm) turrets;
10in (254mm) barbettes; 3in
(76mm) deck; 12in (305mm)
conning tower.
Armament: 10 x 12in (305mm);
16 x 5in (127mm) QF; 2 x 21in
(533mm) torpedo tubes.
Performance: 21kt (38·85km/h);
coal 2,560 tons (2,601 tonnes) max;
oil 400 tons (406 tonnes); radius
6,720nm (12,432km) at 10kt
(18·5km/h), 4,600nm (8,510km) at
19kt (35·15km/h).
Crew: 1,001.

Improved Delawares, the Floridas
much resembled the preceding
class, the most noticeable difference
being the positioning of the after
cage mast abaft the second funnel.
The basic Delaware design was
adopted to cut construction time;
for the same reason, a plan to fit 8
x 14in (356mm) was abandoned in
favour of main armament and
layout identical to the Delawares.
Parsons turbines, introduced in the
Delaware class *North Dakota,* were

Below: *Utah* in 1937 when she was
used as a gunnery training ship.

fitted in both Floridas, the first
US warships to have four shafts.
   Florida served with the British
Grand Fleet in 1917-18, while *Utah*
was for a time Flagship, US
Atlantic Fleet. Two 3in (76mm) AA
mounted on platforms on the
derrick posts between the funnels
were added by 1918. Major reconstruction was carried out in 1924-26
(*Florida*) and 1926-28 (*Utah*), when
both were reboilered with four
oil-fired boilers and full load displacement became 27,726 tons
(28,170 tonnes).
   Horizontal protection in particular
was improved: a 3·5in (89mm)
armour deck was fitted over the
upper belt; 1·75in (44mm) armour
was added at the lower deck ends;
and 1·25in-1·75in (32-44mm)
Special Treatment Steel reinforced
existing protection over boilers and
on turrets and conning tower tops.
The torpedo tubes were removed
and torpedo bulges fitted, beam
rising to 106ft (32·3m). The layout
of the 12 x 5in (127mm) battery
guns was improved and 8 x 3in
(76mm) AA were now carried. The
second funnel and after cage mast
(replaced by a pole mast) were
removed to allow an aircraft catapult
to be fitted atop the midships turret.
   In 1931-32, to comply with the
London Naval Treaty, *Florida* was
scrapped and *Utah* (reclassified
AG-19) was disarmed as a radio-
controlled target ship. From 1935
she was an AA gunnery training
ship and in this role—with 8 x 5in
(127mm) AA, plus 20mm and
40mm—she was sunk by two
torpedo hits in the Japanese air
strike on Pearl Harbor, 7 December
1941. Only her guns were salvaged.

MOLTKE

1911 *Germany*
Other ships in class: *Goeben*

Laid down: 7 December 1908.
Launched: 7 April 1910.
Builder: Blohm & Voss,
Hamburg.
Displacement: 22,616 tons
(22,978 tonnes) normal; 24,999
tons (25,399 tonnes) full load.
Dimensions: 610ft 3in (186m) wl
x 96ft 9in (29·49m) x 27ft (8·23m).
Machinery: 2 Parsons turbines;
24 Schulz-Thornycroft boilers; 4
shafts; 52,000 SHP.
Armour: 10·6in-3·9in (270-100mm)
belt; 9·8in (250mm) turrets; 5in
(127mm) battery; 2·5in (63mm)
deck; 10in (254mm) conning tower.
Armament: 10 x 11in (280mm);
12 x 5·9in (150mm) QF; 12 x 3·5in
(88mm) QF; 4 x 19·7in (500mm)
torpedo tubes.
Performance: 25·5kt (47·2km/h);
coal 2,952 tons (2,999 tonnes) max;
radius 4,120nm (7,622km) at 14kt
(25·9km/h).
Crew: 1,053.

Enlarged versions of *Von der Tann,*
the battlecruisers *Moltke* and
Goeben mounted a fifth twin 11in
(280mm) superfiring turret aft. This
layout was identical with that
planned for the Kaiser class battleships, with wing turrets diagonally
offset to allow cross-deck fire
(limited by blast effect), and protection also approached battleship
standards.
   Low freeboard forward meant
that the forecastle was awash in any
kind of seaway, rendering the 3·5in
(88mm) QF mounted beneath it

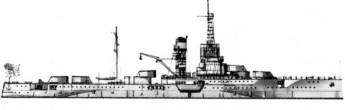

Below: *Utah* as she appeared while
serving with the Grand Fleet in 1918.
The top masts have been temporarily
stepped down. Note range bafflers
on masts.

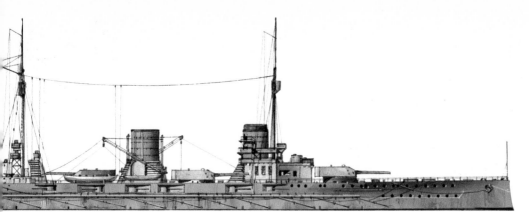

ORION

1912 *UK*
Other ships in class: *Conqueror,
Monarch, Thunderer*

Laid down: 29 November 1909.
Launched: 20 August 1910.
Builder: Portsmouth Dockyard.
Displacement: 22,200 tons
(22,555 tonnes) load; 25,870 tons
(26,284 tonnes) deep load.
Dimensions: 581ft (177·1m) oa x
88ft 6in (26·97m) x 28ft 9in (8·76m)
max.
Machinery: 4 Parsons turbines;
18 Babcock boilers; 4 shafts;
27,000 SHP.
Armour: 12in-8in (305-203mm)
belt; 10in-3in (254-76mm)
bulkheads; 10in-3in (254-76mm)
barbettes; 11in (279mm) turrets;
4in-1in (102-25mm) decks; 11in
(279mm) conning tower.
Armament: 10 x 13·5in (343mm);
16 x 4in (102mm) QF; 4 x 3pdr; 3
x 21in (533mm) torpedo tubes.
Performance: 21kt (38·85km/h);
coal 3,300 tons (3,353 tonnes) max;
oil 800 tons (813 tonnes); radius
6,730nm (12,450km) at 10kt
(18·5km/h), 4,110nm (7,603km) at
19kt (35·15km/h).
Crew: 752.

A 2,500-ton (2,540 tonne) increase
in displacement and provision, for
the first time since the Royal
Sovereigns of 1892-94, of 13·5in
(343mm) guns caused the Orions
to be regarded as 'super-
dreadnoughts'. With a lower muzzle
velocity than the 12in (305mm)
gun, the 13·5in (343mm) had
ample hitting power but was less
subject to barrel erosion and had
longer life and greater accuracy.
    The first dreadnoughts to carry
all their heavy guns in centre-line
turrets, the Orions had side armour
extending to upper deck level, 17ft
2in (5·23m) above water. All survived Jutland undamaged and in
1917 were fitted with take-off
platforms for scout aircraft atop 'B'
turret (and also 'X' turret in
Thunderer). Discarded under the
Washington Treaty, *Orion* was sold
for breaking up in December 1922.

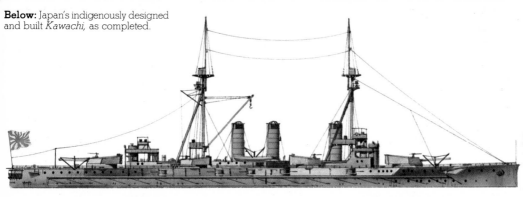

Below: Japan's indigenously designed
and built *Kawachi*, as completed.

unworkable. All were removed by
1916, to be replaced by 4 x 3·5in
(88mm) AA on the after superstructure. *Moltke* was scuttled at Scapa
Flow in June 1919.
    In the Mediterranean in August
1914, *Goeben* and the light cruiser
Breslau evaded British pursuit and
reached Constantinople, where
their 'sale' to Turkey was a major
factor in that country's becoming
Germany's ally. *Goeben*, renamed
Yavuz Sultan Selim (from 1936,
Yavuz) was often in action against
the Russian Black Sea Fleet and
against Allied ships in the Mediterranean, where, in January 1918,
she sank the British monitors
Raglan and *M.28*, went aground
after striking two mines, survived
heavy air attacks, and was at last
towed back to Constantinople and
repaired within two months. On 2
November 1918 she was genuinely
transferred to Turkey and,
modernized by Penhoët at Izmir in
1926-30, remained on the effective
list until c1960.

KAWACHI

1912 *Japan*
Other ships in class: *Settsu*

Laid down: 1 April 1909.
Launched: 15 October 1910.
Builder: Kure Dockyard.
Displacement: 20,823 tons
(21,156 tonnes) normal.
Dimensions: 526ft (160·32m) oa x
84ft 3in (25·68m) x 27ft (8·2m).
Machinery: 2 Curtis turbines; 16
Miyabara boilers; 2 shafts; 25,000
SHP.
Armour: Krupp steel 12in-5in
(305-127mm) belt; 11in (279mm)
turrets; 6in (152mm) casemates; 2in
(51mm) deck; 10in-6in
(254-152mm) conning tower.

Armament: 12 x 12in (305mm);
10 x 6in (152mm) QF; 8 x 4·7in
(119mm) QF; 12 x 3in (76mm) QF;
5 x 18in (457mm) torpedo tubes.
Performance: 21kt (38·85km/h);
coal 2,300 tons (2,337 tonnes) max;
oil 400 tons (406 tonnes); radius
2,700nm (4,995km) at 10kt
(18·5km/h).
Crew: 999.

Japan's first dreadnoughts, *Kawachi*
and *Settsu* were indigenous designs
much resembling the German
Helgolands. Their 12in (305mm)
Armstrong guns were in twin
turrets fore and aft (50-cal guns)
and two on either beam (shorter
45-cal guns). Battle experience in
the Russo-Japanese War dictated
extremely heavy secondary armament, although of mixed calibres.
    On 12 July 1918, an explosion of
defective cordite in the magazine
sank *Kawachi* in Tokuyama Bay
with the loss of some 700 men.
Settsu was used as a target ship
until sunk by air attack in 1945.

Below: 'Super-dreadnought' *Orion*,
with 13·5in (343mm) guns, in 1912.

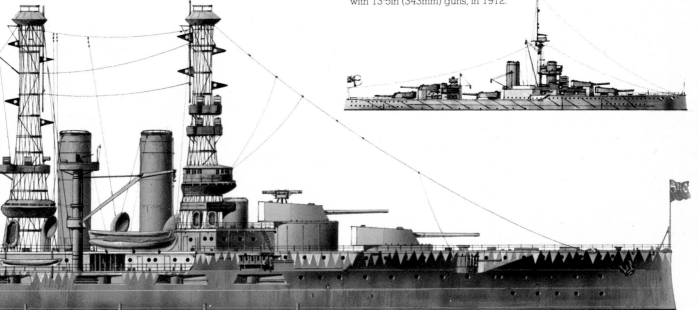

LION

1912 UK
Other ships in class: *Princess Royal, Queen Mary*

Laid down: 29 November 1909.
Launched: 6 August 1910.
Builder: Devonport Dockyard
Displacement: 26,270 tons (26,690 tonnes) load; 29,680 tons (30,155 tonnes) full load.
Dimensions: 700ft (213.36m) oa x 88ft 6in (26.97m) x 28ft 10in (8.79m) max.
Machinery: 4 Parsons turbines; 42 Yarrow boilers; 4 shafts; 73,800 SHP.
Armour: Krupp cemented 9in-5in (229-127mm) belt; 6in-4in (152-102mm) upper belt; 4in (102mm) bulkheads; 2.5in-1in (64-25mm) decks; 9in-8in (229-203mm) barbettes; 9in-4in (229-102mm) turrets; 10in (254mm) conning tower.
Armament: 8 x 13.5in (343mm); 16 x 4in (102mm); 2 x 21in (533mm) torpedo tubes.
Performance: 27kt (50km/h); radius 4,860nm (9,010km) at 10kt (18.5km/h); coal 3,500 tons (3,556 tonnes); oil 1,135 tons (1,153 tonnes).
Crew: 997.

Like earlier British battlecruisers, *Lion* was inspired by Admiral 'Jackie' Fisher, and was in essence the battlecruiser equivalent of the Orion class of 'super-dreadnoughts'. However, whereas earlier vessels had been a little longer but of somewhat lighter displacement than their battleship counterparts, the Lion class was considerably longer and had a displacement some 4,000 tons (4,064 tonnes) greater than the Orion. This was made inevitable by the volume needed for the armament and machinery in a hull of the right length:beam ratio to produce the required 27kt (50km/h).

The primary armament was eight of the excellent 13.5in (343mm) Mk V guns, which could fire a shell of 1,250lb (567kg) with a muzzle velocity of 2,700ft (823m) per second. These guns were located in four twin turrets, all on the centre line, but instead of superfiring turrets aft, as forward, the designers (W.T. Davis and E.L. Attwood) opted for a turret on the quarterdeck ('Y') and one on the forecastle deck amidships ('Q'): this reduced the bending moment to which the hull would have been subjected by turret locations fore and aft, and so made possible savings in hull weight, but at the same time it divided the boiler rooms into two groups. Additionally, 'Q' turret had only limited arcs of fire (120° on each beam). The 4in (102mm) guns were located in casemate positions, all but two at forecastle-deck level,

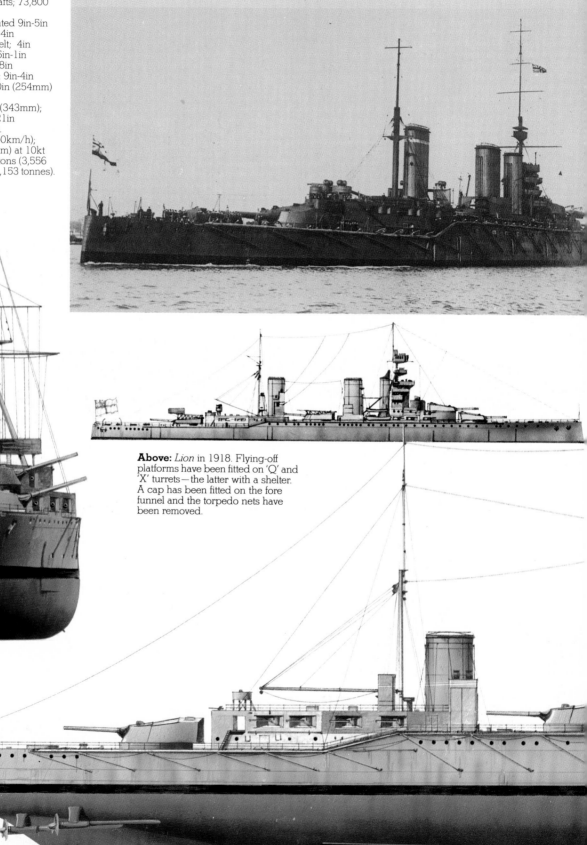

Above: *Lion* in 1918. Flying-off platforms have been fitted on 'Q' and 'X' turrets—the latter with a shelter. A cap has been fitted on the fore funnel and the torpedo nets have been removed.

four on each side of the two superstructure groupings.

The protection was much criticised but was in reality adequate for *Lion's* role (though thinner than that of German battlecruisers). For the first time on a British battlecruiser the side armour was extended vertically to the main deck, but the ship's ends were unprotected and, perhaps more importantly, so too were the sides of the ship between the upper and forecastle decks. This followed the practice established with earlier ships, which had been designed for engagements at a maximum range of 9,000 yards (8,230m), where horizontal rather than plunging fire might be expected. But *Lion* had been planned round the concept of longer-range engagements, where plunging fire was inevitable, so this design lapse was inexplicable as it exposed her magazines and machinery spaces.

Exaggerated accounts of the speeds attainable by *Lion* and her sisters were put about in the period leading up to World War I, and these added to the impressive appearance of the three ships to arouse the generic nickname 'the splendid cats'. They were good

Left: The Lion-class battlecruiser *Princess Royal* in 1912, soon after completion. These were the largest and most costly warships built for the Royal Navy up to that date.

Right: *Lion* on trials in 1912. It was quickly found that the control top on the heavy tripod mast just abaft the fore funnel was made unworkable by heat and smoke.

steamers and pleasant seaboats, though they tended to roll in a beam sea.

In 1914 *Lion* became the flagship of the 1st Battlecruiser Squadron, and as such took part in the Battles of Heligoland Bight and of Dogger Bank. In the latter she was hit by 18 heavy shells and disabled, having to be towed back to port by *Indomitable*. Following repairs, she became flagship of the Battlecruiser Force, and as such took part in the Battle of Jutland on 31 May 1916,

where she was hit by 12 heavy shells but continued to function despite 'Q' turret being burned out by a propellant fire. Repaired again, *Lion* continued in service but was deleted in December 1922 and scrapped in 1924. *Princess Royal* was built by Vickers at Barrow and completed in November 1912. Her career was very similar to that of *Lion,* and she too was damaged at Jutland, her fires proving difficult to extinguish as a result of power and water

failures. She was discarded in 1922 as a result of the Washington Treaty and then scrapped in 1926. The completion of *Queen Mary* (built by Palmers at Jarrow) was slowed by industrial action, and it was only late in 1913 that she entered service. At Jutland she was taken under fire by *Seydlitz* and *Derfflinger.* She was hit forward, and then 'Q' turret magazine exploded. *Queen Mary* then turned over and sank, with the loss of 67 officers and 1,209 men.

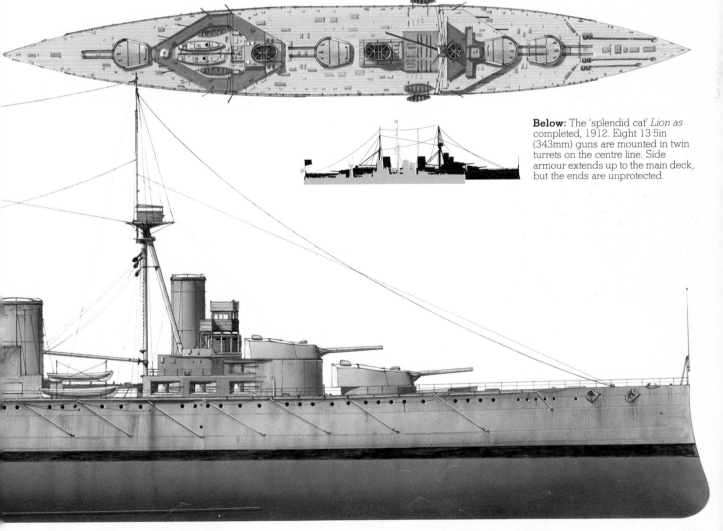

Below: The 'splendid cat' *Lion* as completed, 1912. Eight 13·5in (343mm) guns are mounted in twin turrets on the centre line. Side armour extends up to the main deck, but the ends are unprotected.

WYOMING (BB-32)

1912 USA
Other ships in class: *Arkansas*
(BB-33)

Laid down: 19 February 1910.
Launched: 25 May 1911.
Builder: Cramp, Philadelphia.
Displacement: 26,000 tons
(26,416 tonnes) normal; 27,700
tons (28,143 tonnes) full load.
Dimensions: 562ft (171·3m) oa x
93ft 3in (28·42m) x 29ft 7in (9m)
max.
Machinery: 4 Parsons turbines;
12 Babcock boilers; 4 shafts; 28,000
SHP.

Armour: 11in-5in (279-127mm)
belt; 12in (305mm) turrets; 11in
(279mm) barbettes; 6·5in (165mm)
battery; 3in-1in (76-25mm) decks;
12in (305mm) conning tower.
Armament: 12 x 12in (305mm);
21 x 5in (127mm) QF; 2 x 21in
(533mm) torpedo tubes.
Performance: 20·5kt (37·9km/h);
coal 2,660 tons (2,703 tonnes) max;
oil 400 tons (406 tonnes); radius
8,000nm (14,800km) at 10kt
(18·5km/h).
Crew: 1,063.

The basic design of the Delawares
and Floridas, albeit considerably
enlarged, was again used for

the Wyoming class. As in the
Floridas, plans for a 14in (356mm)
main armament were abandoned
because production of the new
guns was delayed. Fire-power was
improved, however, by fitting a
sixth twin turret superfiring aft: the
Wyomings were the first US
battleships to mount 12 heavy
guns—12 x 12in (305mm) of a new
50-cal pattern—and the last (save
for the Alaska class battlecruisers)
to have a 12in (305mm) main
armament.
   The Wyomings were flush-
decked; freeboard reduced from
25ft (7·62mm) forward to 16ft 3in
(4·95m) aft. Because US-manufac-

tured turbines were proving both
difficult and expensive to produce,
it was proposed to fit a combination
of turbines and reciprocating
machinery. Compromise with manufacturers on specifications and
price allowed all-turbine propulsion,
but in the next ships, *Texas* and
New York, the same problem was
solved by reverting to reciprocating
engines.
   Wyoming and *Arkansas* served
in the US 6th Battle Squadron with
the British Grand Fleet in 1918 and
were present at the surrender of
the German High Seas Fleet at
Scapa Flow, 21 November 1918.
War service showed that the 5in

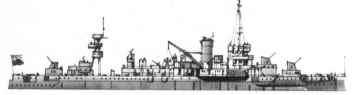

Above: *Wyoming* as an AA gunnery
training ship during World War II. Her
side armour has been removed and
5in (127mm) L51 guns are mounted
in twin turrets on the old barbettes.
Late in 1944, further 5in (127mm) guns
and 1·1in (28mm), 40mm and 20mm
mountings were added when she
joined an anti-*kamikaze* research unit.

Above: *Wyoming* passes through
the 8-mile (13km) long, 300ft (91m)
wide Gaillard Cut of the Panama
Canal, July 1919. Note the painted
deflection scale on 'X' turret (to
enable a ship following in the battle
line to train on the same target in
poor visibility) and the range clock
on the mainmast.

Above: A much modified *Wyoming*
is seen in Hampton Roads, Virginia,
in 1929. The after funnel has been
removed and a stump tripod replaces
the after cage mast. A launching
catapult, here seen bearing one of
the three light floatplanes now
carried, has been fitted on the top of
the third turret.

Below: *Wyoming* as completed,
1912. Her design incorporated an
increase in length of 44ft (13·4m) over
the preceding Florida class, in order
to accommodate a sixth turret for
twin 12in (305mm) guns.

127mm) gun casemate-mounted right aft at main deck level and the foremost pair on either side of the first turret were unworkable in bad weather. These were removed, along with the 2 x 5in (127mm) in unprotected positions on the bridge superstructure beside the second turret, and 2 x 3in (76mm) AA were added.

Major reconstruction came in 1925-27. Torpedo tubes were removed and torpedo bulges fitted: beam increased to 106ft (32.3m) and full load displacement to 30,610 tons (31,100 tonnes). Horizontal armour was improved as in *Florida*, and reboilering with four

White-Forster oil-fired boilers effectively increased underwater protection by reducing boiler space. The forward battery of 6 x 5in (127mm) guns was resited at upper deck level and a further 6 x 3in (76mm) AA were added. The after funnel was removed and the after cage mast replaced by a stump tripod. An aircraft catapult was fitted atop the third turret, with cranes abreast the funnel to handle three floatplanes.

Wyoming was demilitarized under the London Naval Treaty and became a training ship (AG-19) in 1931-32. Her side armour, torpedo bulges and conning tower

were removed; one boiler was disconnected, reducing her to 20,000 SHP at 18kt (33.3km/h); and the third, fourth and fifth 12in (305mm) turrets were removed. From 1935, she regularly embarked US Marines for training in amphibious assault landings, and in World War II she was an AA gunnery training ship. Rearmed in 1944 with 14 x 5in (127mm) DP, 7 x 3in (76mm) AA, 8 x 40mm AA, 4 x 20mm AA, 4 x 1.1in (28mm) AA and advanced fire control equipment and radars, she ended her war service as the major unit of Task Force 69, an anti-*kamikaze* research group. She was stricken

and scrapped in 1947-48.

Arkansas had her forward cage mast replaced by a low tripod and her remaining main deck 5in (127mm) guns removed in 1940-41, when 6 x 3in (76mm) AA were added. Retaining her 12 x 12in (305mm) she served in the bombardment force off Normandy, June 1944, and in the Pacific at Iwo Jima and Okinawa. Her final secondary/AA armament was 6 x 5in (127mm) QF, 10 x 3in (76mm) AA, 36 x 40mm AA and 28 x 20mm AA. She was expended as a target in the atomic bomb tests at Bikini Atoll in the Marshall Islands on 25 July 1946.

VIRIBUS UNITIS

1912 *Austria-Hungary*
Other ships in class: *Tegetthoff,
Prinz Eugen, Szent István*

Laid down: 24 July 1910.
Launched: 20 June 1911.
Builder: Stabilimento Tecnico
Triestino.
Displacement: 19,698 tons
(20,014 tonnes) normal; 21,255
tons (21,595 tonnes) full load.
Dimensions: 499ft 3in (152·18m)
oa x 89ft 8in (27·34m) x 27ft (8·23m)
mean.
Machinery: 4 Parsons turbines;
12 Yarrow boilers; 4 shafts; 25,000
SHP.
Armour: 11in-5·9in (280-150mm)
belt; 11in (280mm) turrets; 11in
(280mm) barbettes; 1·9in (48mm)
decks; 11in (280mm) conning
tower.
Armament: 12 x 12in (305mm);
12 x 5·9in (150mm) QF; 18 x
2·75in (70mm) QF; 4 x 21in
(533mm) torpedo tubes.
Performance: 20kt (37km/h); coal
2,000 tons (2,032 tonnes) max;
radius 4,200nm (7,770km) at 10kt
(18·5km/h).
Crew: 1,050.

Seeking to counter Italy's growing
naval superiority and to preserve
the capabilities of Stabilimento
Tecnico Triestino, Admiral Count
Montecuccoli, head of the Austrian
naval department, ordered his
country's first two dreadnoughts
from STT without parliamentary
sanction. However, in 1911 the
Austro-Hungarian legislature approved his action and, as part of an
ambitious programme, added two
ships to the class.
 To win Hungarian approval, the
fourth dreadnought, *Szent István*,
and other warships were ordered
from the Danubius shipyard, Fiume.
The yard was unprepared for an
order of such magnitude and *Szent
István* was three years building,
while *Viribus Unitis* was completed
in 26 months.
 The dreadnoughts were based
on the pre-dreadnought Radetzky
class, but with far superior armament and layout. Fire-power was
increased and length and displacement kept down by mounting a
single-calibre main armament of 12
x 12in (305mm) guns in four
Skoda-built triple turrets on the
centre line, with the inner turrets
superfiring. Thus six heavy guns
fired ahead, six astern, and all
twelve together in a broadside of
11,904lb (5,400kg) weight.
 Speed and radius were adequate
for the Mediterranean but, as
wartime experience would show,
underwater protection was poor: a
1·9in (50mm) anti-torpedo bulkhead
protected only the machinery, and
compartmentation was poor.
 During World War I the number
of 2·75in (70mm) QF singly
mounted on the main turrets was
reduced from 18 to 12, with 2 x 3in
(76mm) AA added. All save *Prinz
Eugen* were given funnel caps.
 On 10 June 1918 *Szent István*
was sunk in the southern Adriatic
by two torpedoes from the Italian
MTB *MAS 15*. On 1 November
1918, only hours after being taken
over by Yugoslavia after Austria-
Hungary's collapse, *Viribus Unitis*
was sunk in Pola harbour by the
375lb (170kg) detachable warhead
of an Italian manned-torpedo. *Prinz
Eugen,* ceded to France, was
expended as a target in 1922;
Tegetthoff, ceded to Italy, was
scrapped in 1924-25.

Below: *Viribus Unitis* immediately
before World War I. A compact design
was achieved by mounting the 12in
(305mm) main armament in triple
turrets on the centre line.

KING GEORGE V

1912 *UK*
Other ships in class: *Ajax,
Audacious, Centurion*

Laid down: 16 January 1911.
Launched: 9 October 1911.
Builder: Portsmouth Dockyard.
Displacement: 23,000 tons (23,368
tonnes) load; 25,700 tons (26,111
tonnes) full load.
Dimensions: 597ft 6in (182·1m)
oa x 89ft (27·13m) x 28ft 8in
(8·74m) max.
Machinery: 4 Parsons turbines;
18 Babcock boilers; 4 shafts;
27,000 SHP.
Armour: 12in-8in (305-203mm)
belt; 10in-4in (254-102mm) bulkheads; 11in (279mm) turrets;
10in-3in (254-76mm) barbettes; 3in
(76mm) battery; 4in-1in (102-25mm)
decks, 11in (279mm) conning tower
Armament: 10 x 13·5in (343mm);
16 x 4in (102mm); 4 x 3pdr; 3 x
21in (533mm) torpedo tubes.
Performance: 21kt (38·85km/h);
coal 2,870 tons (2,916 tonnes) max;
oil 800 tons (813 tonnes); radius
6,730nm (12,450km) at 10kt
(18·5km/h), 4,060nm (7,511km) at
18·15kt (33·58km/h).
Crew: 782.

Profiting from experience with the
Lions, the King George Vs
(improved Orions) were finally
given tripod masts *before* the fore
funnel; this became standard. They
were much criticised for their
comparatively weak secondary armament, wetness in a seaway and
poor internal protection, which
contributed to the loss of *Audacious*
when watertight bulkheads proved
ineffective after she struck a mine
on 27 October 1914.
 King George V and *Ajax* were
sold in 1926. *Centurion* survived as
a radio-controlled target ship and,
in World War II, a 'dummy'
battleship and AA battery, until
sunk as part of a Mulberry harbour,
9 June 1944.

Below: *King George V* in 1912; note
tripod mast *forward* of fore funnel.

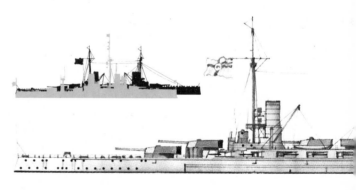

Below: *Dante Alighieri* soon after
completion in 1913, when she was
claimed to be the fastest
dreadnought afloat. The fore funnels
were raised and a tripod mast fitted
forward in 1923.

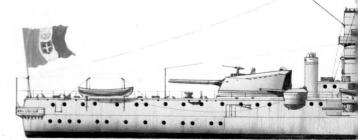

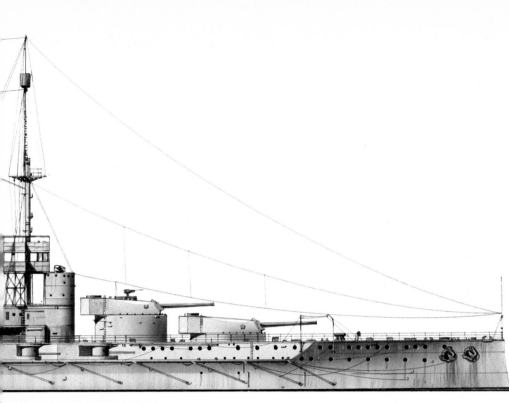

DANTE ALIGHIERI

1913 *Italy*

Laid down: 6 June 1909.
Launched: 20 August 1910.
Builder: Castellammare Navy Yard.
Displacement: 19,500 tons (19,812 tonnes) normal; 21,800 tons (22,149 tonnes) full load.
Dimensions: 551ft 6in (168·1m) oa x 87ft 3in (26·59m) x 31ft 10in (9·7m) max.
Machinery: 3 Parsons geared turbines; 23 Blechynden boilers (16 coal/supplementary oil burners, 7 oil); 4 shafts; 32,000 SHP.
Armour: 9·8in-5·9in (250-150mm) belt; 9·8in (250mm) turrets; 3·9in (100mm) secondary turrets and casemates; 1·2in-0·6in (30-16mm) decks; 11in (280mm) conning tower.
Armament: 12 x 12in (305mm); 20 x 4·7in (120mm) QF; 16 x 3in (76mm) QF; 3 x 17·7in (450mm) torpedo tubes.
Performance: 23kt (42·5km/h); coal 2,400 tons (2,438 tonnes) max; oil 600 tons (610 tonnes) max; radius 5,000nm (9,250km) at 10kt (18·5km/h).
Crew: 970.

KAISER

1912 *Germany*
Other ships in class: *Friedrich der Grosse, Kaiserin, Prinzregent Luitpold, König Albert*

Laid down: October 1909.
Launched: 22 March 1911.
Builder: Kiel Dockyard.
Displacement: 24,333 tons (24,722

Below: Kaiser in 1913; she made close on 23·5kt (43·5km/h) on trials.

tonnes) normal; 26,573 tons (26,998 tonnes) full load.
Dimensions: 565ft 8in (172·4m) oa x 95ft 3in (29m) x 27ft 3in (8·3m).
Machinery: 3 Parsons turbines; 16 Schulz-Thornycroft boilers; 3 shafts; 31,000 SHP.
Armour: 13·8in-7·1in (350-180mm) belt; 11·8in (300mm) turrets and barbettes; 6·7in-3·1in (170-80mm) casemates; 3in (76mm) decks; 13·8in (350mm) conning tower.
Armament: 10 x 12in (305mm); 14 x 5·9in (150mm) QF; 8 x 3·5in (88mm) QF; 4 x 3·5in (88mm) AA; 5 x 19·7in (500mm) torpedo tubes.
Performance: 21kt (38·85km/h); coal 2,953 tons (3,000 tonnes) max; oil 197 tons (200 tonnes); radius 7,900nm (14,615km) at 12kt (22·2km/h).
Crew: 1,084.

The Kaiser class battleships were direct contemporaries of the British Orions but, with 12in (305mm) guns as compared to the Orions'

13·5in (343mm), much inferior in weight of broadside: 8,600lb (3,901kg) in the Kaisers; 12,500lb (5,670kg) in the Orions. Armament layout was that of the British *Neptune* and Colossus class, with a superfiring turret forward of the after turret and diagonally offset wing turrets.

They were the first German battleships to have turbine machinery and supplementary oil burners. *Prinzregent Luitpold* was the first warship designed to combine steam and diesel propulsion, but the 6-cylinder, 2-stroke, 12,000 BHP Germania diesel, intended to give a cruising range of 2,000nm (3,700km) at 12kt (22·2km/h), was judged unready for service. Driven by the two outer shafts only, she was slower than her sisters.

Kaiser was twice hit at Jutland, but all the class survived World War I to be interned and scuttled at Scapa Flow. They were salvaged and broken up in 1929-37.

Designed by Eng-Gen Masdea and much influenced by Vittorio Cuniberti, a major figure in dreadnought design, *Dante Alighieri* was the first battleship planned to carry her main armament in triple turrets. These were on the centre line: one on the forecastle, two amidships between the two pairs of funnels, and one aft. In the absence of a superfiring arrangement, the size of the ship's superstructure was kept to a minimum to widen arcs of fire.

Another new and influential feature was the provision of 3·9in (100mm) armoured twin turrets abreast of the end main turrets for 8 of the 20 x 4·7in (120mm) secondary armament. However, the remaining 4·7in (120mm) guns were in armoured casemates at upper deck level and proved to be too low to be workable in any kind of seaway.

Dante Alighieri was a powerful unit for Mediterranean service, but her design sacrificed both freeboard and protection for fire-power and speed. Although she was sometimes referred to as the world's fastest battleship, some authorities deny that she ever made her designed speed of 23kt (42·5km/h): she certainly did not on her sea trials.

Her only action in World War I was the bombardment of Durazzo in October 1918. During reconstruction in 1923 a tripod mast was fitted forward of the fore funnel. She was stricken and scrapped in 1928.

KONGO

1913 *Japan*
Other ships in class: *Hiei, Haruna, Kirishima*

Laid down: 17 January 1911.
Launched: 18 May 1912.
Builder: Vickers, Barrow.
Displacement: 27,500 tons (27,940 tonnes) normal.
Dimensions: 704ft (214·58m) oa x 92ft (28·04m) x 27ft 6in (8·38m) max.
Machinery: 4 Parsons turbines; 36 Yarrow boilers; 4 shafts; 64,000 SHP.
Armour: 8in-3in (203-76mm) belt; 9in (229mm) turrets; 10in (254mm) barbettes; 6in (152mm) battery; 9in-5in (229-127mm) bulkheads; 2·75in (70mm) decks; 10in-6in (254-152mm) CT.
Armament: 8 x 14in (356mm); 16 x 6in (152mm) QF; 16 x 3in (76mm) QF; 8 x 21in (533mm) TT.
Performance: 27·5kt (50·88km/h); coal 4,200 tons (4,267 tonnes) max; oil 1,000 tons (1,016 tonnes); radius 8,000nm (14,800km) at 14kt (25·9km/h).
Crew: 1,221.

In order to profit from the study of British techniques, Japan ordered its first battlecruiser from the Vickers yard. Designed by Sir George Thurston as a modified version of his Turkish battleship *Reshadieh* (completed as HMS *Erin*), *Kongo* was the pattern for three Japanese-built ships, and so highly impressed British authorities that *Tiger,* the fourth Lion class battlecruiser, was modified along the lines of the Japanese unit.

Kongo excelled the earlier Lions in protection and armament layout. The 12ft 5in (3·78m) deep main belt, running from the forward turret's barbette to that of the after turret, and the 6in (152mm) thick upper belt, extending up to the forecastle deck and protecting the powerful secondary battery, were closed by armour bulkheads fore and aft to form a central citadel, and internal compartmentation was extensive. A superfiring turret was carried forward. Aft, the extension of the forecastle deck raised the third turret and allowed ample space between third and fourth turrets.

During World War I (when the Royal Navy's request for the loan of the Kongos in 1915 was refused by Japan) *Haruna* was damaged on a mine. All four vessels were twice extensively reconstructed and redesigned battleships in 1927-40. Length was increased by 26ft 3in (8m) aft; funnels were reduced from three to two; armour weight rose by c50 per cent; 'pagoda' foremasts were built up; torpedo tubes were removed; and new engines and boilers raised speed to c30kt (55·5km/h). Normal displacement rose to 31,720 tons (32,228 tonnes). Main armament was unchanged, but by late 1944 *Kongo* had 8 x 6in (152mm) in the battery, 12 x 5in (127mm) AA and 100 x 25mm AA, and three aircraft.

All four Kongos were lost in World War II. *Hiei* and *Kirishima* were sunk off Guadalcanal, November 1942, the former by aircraft and the latter in a surface action with two US battleships. *Kongo* was torpedoed and sunk by the US submarine *Sealion* off Formosa, 21 November 1944, and *Haruna* was sunk by carrier aircraft off Kure, 27 July 1945.

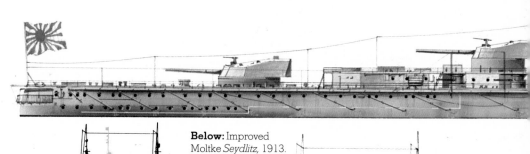

Above: *Kongo* in 1931, after a major refit that included the fitting of a typical 'pagoda' superstructure.

Below: *Kongo* as completed by Vickers in 1913, when she was the most powerful battlecruiser of the time.

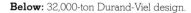

Below: Improved Moltke *Seydlitz*, 1913.

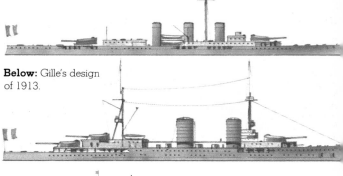

SEYDLITZ

1913 *Germany*

Laid down: 4 February 1911.
Launched: 30 March 1912.
Builder: Blohm & Voss, Hamburg.
Displacement: 24,610 tons (25,004 tonnes) normal; 28,550 tons (29,007 tonnes) full load.
Dimensions: 658ft 2in (200·6m) oa x 93ft 6in (28·5m) x 30ft 6in (9·3m).
Machinery: 2 Marine turbines; 27 Schulz-Thornycroft boilers; 4 shafts; 67,000 SHP.
Armour: 11·8in-3·9in (300-100mm) belt; 9·8in-2·8in (250-70mm) main turrets; 7·9in-3·9in (200-100mm) barbettes; 5·9in (150mm) casemates; 3·1in-1·2in (80-30mm) decks; 9·8in (250mm) conning tower.
Armament: 10 x 11in (280mm); 12 x 5·9in (150mm); 14 x 3·5in (88mm); 4 x 19·7in (500mm) torpedo tubes.
Performance: 26·5kt (49km/h) designed, 29·12kt (53·9km/h) trials at 89,738 SHP; coal 3,543 tons (3,600 tonnes) max; radius 4,200nm (7,770km) at 14kt (30km/h).
Crew: 1,068.

An improved Moltke, *Seydlitz* had the same armament and protection but, with a longer, slimmer hull, better speed. Seakeeping was much improved by raising the forecastle by one deck.

Seydlitz bombarded British east coast ports in late 1914 and on 24 January 1915 had both after turrets knocked out, with heavy casualties, at the Battle of Dogger Bank. At Jutland she survived more hits (21 heavy, 2 medium, 2 torpedoes) than any other ship, returning to port under her own power, although heavily flooded and with her forward freeboard reduced to 8ft 2in (2·5m). Scuttled at Scapa Flow, June 1919, she was raised and scrapped in 1928.

Below: 32,000-ton Durand-Viel design.

Below: Gille's design of 1913.

BATTLECRUISER DESIGNS

1913 *France*

Designers: (A) Gille; (B,C) Durand-Viel.
Displacement: (A) 28,100 tons (28,550 tonnes); (B,C) 27,065 tons (27,498 tonnes).
Dimensions: (A) 672ft 7in (205m) pp x 88ft 7in (27m) x 29ft 6in (9m); (B) 689ft (210m) wl x 88ft 7in (27m) x 28ft 7in (8·7m); (C) 682ft 5in (208m) wl x 88ft 7in (27m) x 28ft 7in (8·7m).
Machinery: (A) 4 turbines, 52 Belleville boilers, 4 shafts, 80,000 SHP; (B) 4 turbines, 21 Belleville boilers, 4 shafts, 74,000 SHP; (C) 4 turbines, 18 Belleville boilers, 4 shafts, 63,000 SHP, *or* 4 geared turbines, 18 Belleville boilers, 4 shafts, 80,000 SHP.

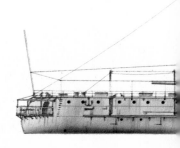

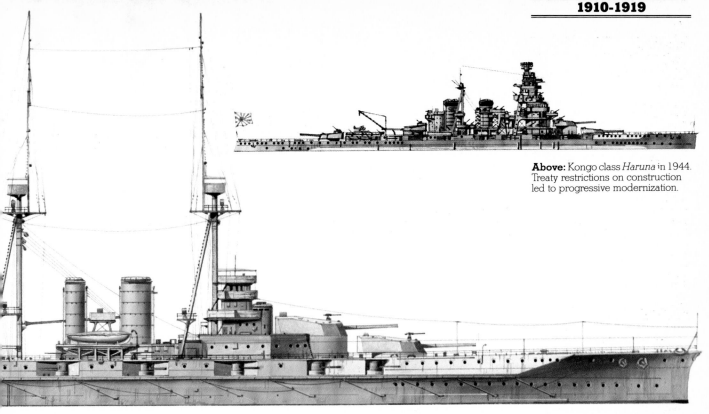

Above: Kongo class *Haruna* in 1944. Treaty restrictions on construction led to progressive modernization.

Armour: (A) max 10·6in (270mm) belt; (B,C) max 11in (280mm) belt.
Armament: (A) 12 x 13·4in (340mm), 24 x 5·5in (140mm) QF, 6 torpedo tubes; (B) 8 x 13·4in (340mm), 24 x 5·5in (140mm) QF, 4 x 17·7in (450mm) torpedo tubes; (C) 8 x 14·5in (368mm), 24 x 5·5in (140mm) QF, 4 x 17·7in (450mm) torpedo tubes.
Performance: (A) 28kt (51·8km/h), radius 6,300nm (11,655km) at 15kt (27·75km/h); (B,C) 27kt (50km/h), radius 3,500nm (6,475km) at 16kt (29·6km/h).
Crew: (A) 1,299.

Battlecruiser versions of the Normandie class battleships (*qv*) were projected from 1913 onward, but with no result. The designs detailed in the data table above all featured main armament in *quadruple* turrets. Design A, by Gille, provided for the endurance of a fast battleship; Durand-Viel put forward two battleship designs in addition to Designs B and C (illustrated left).

ESPAÑA

1913 *Spain*
Other ships in class: *Alfonso XIII*, *Jaime I*

Laid down: 5 February 1909.
Launched: 5 February 1912.
Builder: Ferrol Dockyard (SECN).
Displacement: 15,452 tons (15,699 tonnes) normal; 15,740 tons (15,992 tonnes) full load.
Dimensions: 459ft (139·9m) oa x 78ft 9in (24m) x 25ft 6in (7·8m) max.
Machinery: 4 Parsons turbines; 12 Yarrow boilers; 4 shafts; 15,500 SHP.
Armour: 8in-3in (203-76mm) belt; 8in (203mm) turrets; 10in (254mm) barbettes; 3in (76mm) battery; 1·5in

(38mm) deck; 10in (254mm) CT.
Armament: 8 x 12in (305mm); 20 x 4in (102mm) QF; 2 x 3pdr; 2 x MG.
Performance: 19·5kt (36km/h); coal 1,900 tons (1,930 tonnes) max; oil 20 tons (20·32 tonnes); radius 5,000nm (9,250km) at 10kt (18·5km/h), 3,100nm (5,735km) at 16·75kt (30·99km/h).
Crew: 854.

Spain's only dreadnoughts, the Españas were British-designed and -engined, with heavy guns from Vickers. *Jaime I* was *c*10 years in building because Britain could not supply materials during World War I. Plans for three 21,000-ton (21,336 tonne) ships of the Reina Victoria Eugenia class to be completed by 1920 were approved in 1913 but were soon abandoned.

Attempting to combine dreadnought armament with pre-dreadnought dimensions, the design of the Españas resulted in the smallest dreadnoughts ever built.

At some cost in speed, radius and protection, good all-round fire was achieved with a layout of twin turrets fore and aft and—since superfiring entailed increased displacement—diagonally offset turrets on either beam with cross-deck arcs of *c*80°. The main belt extended only 4ft 7in (1·4m) below water and 2ft (0·6m) above.

On 28 August 1923, *España* ran aground on the Moroccan coast and salvage attempts were abandoned after the recovery of her heavy guns. *Alfonso XIII*, renamed *España* in 1931, was taken by the Nationalists during the Spanish Civil War and was sunk on a mine during the blockade of Bilbao, 30 April 1937. *Jaime I* (damaged by a coastal battery in action against Riff insurgents in May 1924) fought on the Republican side in the Civil War and was badly damaged by air attack at Malaga, 13 August 1936. Wrecked by an internal explosion at Cartagena, 17 June 1937, she was scrapped in 1939.

Below: *Jaime I* of the España class in the early 1930s, before the Spanish Civil War, in which she served on the Republican side. This class underwent few external changes other than the removal of torpedo tubes and revision of foretops.

COURBET

1913 *France*
Other ships in class: *Jean Bart, Paris, France*

Laid down: 1 September 1910.
Launched: 23 September 1911.
Builder: Lorient Dockyard.
Displacement: 23,100 tons (23,470 tonnes) normal; 26,000 tons (26,416 tonnes) full load.
Dimensions: 551ft 2in (168m) oa x 91ft 6in (27·9m) x 29ft 6in (9m) max.
Machinery: 4 Parsons turbines; 24 Belleville boilers; 4 shafts; 28,000 SHP.
Armour: 10·6in-7·1in (270-180mm) belt; 7·1in (180mm) belt ends; 2·76in-1·2in (70-30mm) decks; 11in (280mm) barbettes; 11·4in-3·9in (290-100mm) turrets; 7·1in (180mm) casemates; 11·8in (300mm) conning tower.
Armament: 12 x 12in (305mm); 22 x 5·5in (139mm); 4 x 47mm; 4 x 18in (457mm) torpedo tubes.
Performance: 21kt (38·9km/h); radius 8,600nm (15,940km) at 10kt (18·5km/h); coal 2,707 tons (2,750 tonnes); oil 310 tons (315 tonnes).
Crew: 1,108.

The Courbet class represented France's first step into the dreadnought era. So slow was the pace of French naval construction

that all suitable slips were occupied until 1910 by the six units of the Danton class, pre-dreadnoughts which had not been laid down until after the *Dreadnought*'s completion. Many of the lessons and implications of the dreadnought era were absorbed by French designers between 1906 and 1910, but it was not until the advent of M. Delcassé as navy minister and Amiral de Lapeyrère as commander-in-chief that a revival of France's navy was begun.

The Courbets were interesting vessels, with some sensible features and some outmoded ideas. Among the former were the final abandonment of the last vestiges of the ram bow, which had lingered on among European and American battleships though the day of ramming was clearly long gone; the use of superfiring centre-line turrets to keep length to a minimum (because of limitations of French dry docks); and the provision of director fire control right from the beginning. Among the latter were the retention of 12in (305mm) calibre for the main armament at a time when the UK, USA and Germany were moving into the era of the 'super-dreadnought'; poorly located wing turrets when centre-line armament had become the norm; and poor disposition for

the otherwise powerful secondary armament. Protection was adequate, and was based on a belt running from the bows to within a few feet of the stern; the upper belt formed a substantial redoubt for the secondary armament.

The consensus was that the ships of the Corbet class were obsolescent by the time they were completed. On the other hand they brought France into the dreadnought age and the design by M. Lyasse was very sturdy, even if the heavy armour at the ends tended to make the ships pitch most uncomfortably in any sort of sea.

In 1914 and 1915 *Courbet* was flagship of the French Mediterranean Fleet, and on 16 August 1914 sank the Austro-Hungarian cruiser *Zenta*. From 1916 to the end of World War I she was allocated to the 1st Squadron. Like her two surviving sister-ships, *Courbet* was extensively refitted between 1921 and 1924, the fore funnel being altered and the pole fore mast being replaced by a tripod. Another refit in 1928 and 1929 saw the two foremost funnels trunked into a single uptake, the boilers replaced and the armament altered by the deletion of the torpedo tubes and the addition of four 2·95in (75mm) AA guns. From 1931 all the Courbets were used as training ships, and in

June 1940 *Courbet* escaped from Cherbourg to the UK, where she became an AA ship. She was expended as a breakwater for the 'Mulberry' artificial harbour on the Normandy coast on 10 June 1944, and was broken up after the war.

Jean Bart was also built at Brest but completed some five months earlier than *Courbet*, on 5 June 1913. She had a career similar to that of *Courbet*, but was demilitarised in 1936 and in 1937 was renamed *Océan* as a harbour-training ship. She was scuttled in Toulon on 27 November 1942, and was thereafter used by the Germans as a target. In 1944 she was raised, and in 1945 scrapped.

Paris was built by Forges et Chantiers de la Mediterranée at La Seyne, and completed in August 1914. In 1939 she was a harbour training ship, but escaped to the UK in June 1940, whereupon she became an accommodation ship. She was handed back to France in 1945 and scrapped in 1956.

France was built by Penhoët at St Nazaire, and completed in August 1914. She was flagship of the Mediterranean Fleet in 1916 and served at Corfu and Mudros. She was lost on 26 August 1922 when she foundered after hitting a rock in Quiberon Bay.

Above: *Courbet* in 1938, when she was serving as a training ship. She ended her career as a 'Mulberry' breakwater off the Normandy landing beaches after D-Day, 6 June 1944.

Below: *Courbet*, France's first dreadnought, on completion in 1913. The secondary armament, although powerful, was not well disposed; the battery amidships was carried 19ft (5·8m) above the waterline.

Left: An early photograph of the Courbet class dreadnought *Paris* at speed. By 1938, after modernization, she closely resembled *Courbet,* but with two closely-set fore funnels.

Above: The plan view shows that the main armament layout of the Courbet class resembled the 'lozenge' arrangement favoured by French designers in the 1880s and 1890s, giving good arcs of fire all round.

IRON DUKE

1914 UK

Other ships in class: *Marlborough, Benbow, Emperor of India.*

Laid down: 12 January 1912.
Launched: 12 October 1912.
Builder: Portsmouth Dockyard.
Displacement: 25,820 tons (26,233 tonnes) normal; 30,380 tons (30,886 tonnes) full load.
Dimensions: 622ft 9in (189·8m) oa x 90ft (27·43m) x 29ft 6in (9m) max.
Machinery: 4 Parsons turbines; 18 Babcock boilers; 4 shafts; 30,040 SHP.
Armour: Krupp cemented 12in-4in (305-102mm) belt; 9in (229mm) middle belt; 8in (203mm) upper belt; 8in-4in (203-102mm) bulkheads; 2·5in-1in (64-25mm) decks; 10in-7in (254-178mm) barbettes; 11in-4in (279-102mm) turrets; 6in-2in (152-51mm) battery; 11in (279mm) conning tower.
Armament: 10 x 13·5in (343mm); 12 x 6in (152mm); 4 x 3pdr; 4 x 21in (533mm) torpedo tubes.
Performance: 21·6kt (40km/h); radius 6,750nm (12,520km) at 10kt (18·5km/h); coal 3,250 tons (3,302 tonnes); oil 1,600 tons (1,626 tonnes).
Crew: 925.

The four units of the Iron Duke class were the third series of 'super-dreadnoughts' built for the Royal Navy. The design was based very closely on that of the King George V class from the same designers. The 13·5in (343mm) 45-cal gun that characterised the 'super dreadnoughts' was now well established, as was the centre-line disposition of the main armament in five twin turrets. Accurate and capable of throwing a heavy weight of metal, the 13·5in (343mm) gun in twin turrets was preferred to the higher-velocity 50-cal 12in (305mm) in twin turrets and equal-velocity 45-cal 12in (305mm) in triple turrets: the 50-cal 12in (305mm) gun suffered from excessive barrel wear and loss of accuracy at long ranges as a result of its 3,010ft (917m) per second muzzle velocity, while the triple turret with 45-cal 12in (305mm) was considered too complex for adequate reliability.

The secondary armament, which had consisted of 16 x 4in (102mm) guns in the King George V class, was completely revised in the light of the increasing threat posed by the size and armament of the latest generation of destroyers: after much debate it was decided to revert to a secondary battery of 6in (152mm) weapons in the Iron Duke class. Unfortunately, this battery was poorly designed, consisting as it did of six guns on each beam, five grouped closely together in the forecastle and the sixth abreast 'Y' turret on the upper deck, all in unarmoured casemates too close to the waterline to be worked in any sort of sea, and also so poorly sealed that water entered fairly constantly until a revised system had been implemented. Early in 1915 the 6in (152mm) guns abreast 'Q' turret were removed to new positions one deck above the other guns in the forward superstructure; and during World War I a pair of 3in (76mm) anti-aircraft guns was added on the after superstructure.

Armour protection was also very similar to that of the King George V class, though the rearward extension of the belt as 6in-4in (152-102mm) rather than 2·5in (64mm) thickness meant that adjustments had to be made to the after bulkheads, which were now 4in (102mm) and 6in (152mm) rather than 2·5in (64mm) and 10in (254mm). However, in common with all other British capital ships, anti-torpedo protection was deficient in comparison with contemporary German vessels.

The Iron Dukes tended to pitch in any sort of sea, and were thus quite wet. They were relatively manoeuvrable, however, and steadier gun platforms than the King George Vs, though somewhat slower. But their chief limitations in operational terms were the unfortunate results of the British predilection for superfiring turrets merely to reduce length, and of the retention of the 'Q' turret system to avoid the necessity for triple turrets: the former meant that blast interference was little considered, and was considerable in the superfiring 'A'/'B' and 'X'/'Y' turret pairs; and the latter ensured a high arithmetical broadside despite the fact that 'Q' turret could be brought into action only limited bearings.

Iron Duke was demilitarised in 1931 and became a training ship; in 1939 she was a depot ship at Scapa Flow, and was scrapped in 1946. *Marlborough, Benbow* and *Emperor of India* (built by Devonport Dockyard, Beardmore and Vickers respectively) like *Iron Duke* served in the Grand Fleet during World War I, and thereafter with the Mediterranean and Atlantic Fleets until scrapped in the early 1930s.

Below: Iron Duke class battleship *Marlborough* enters harbour at Malta, early 1920s. Note enlarged masthead control position and searchlight tower and wireless mast aft.

Above: *Iron Duke* as a depot ship at Scapa Flow on the eve of World War II, 1939. 'B' and 'Y' turrets, belt armour, conning tower and torpedo tubes have been removed.

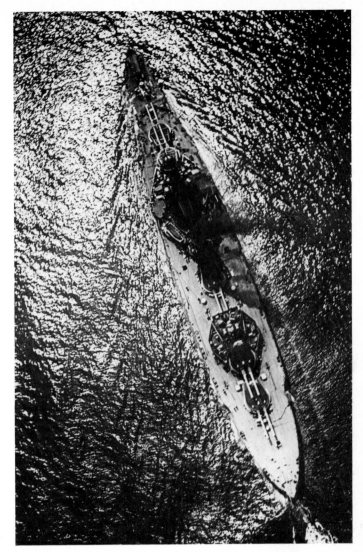

Below: *Iron Duke* at the beginning of World War I, August 1914. The secondary 6in (152mm) guns were mounted in poorly-sealed casemates and were too close to the waterline to be worked in any kind of sea.

Above: *Emperor of India* under way with main armament trained fore and aft. Aerial view shows restricted bearing of 'Q' turret amidships; blast interference in the superfiring pairs was considerable.

Below: The battlecruiser *Tiger* in 1924. Increased bridgework supports an enlarged control top and long rangefinder; the topmast has been moved aft to the derrick post.

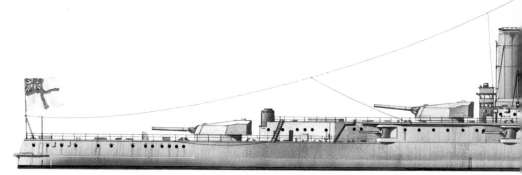

DERFFLINGER

1914 *Germany*
Other ships in class: *Lützow,*
Hindenburg

Laid down: 1 January 1912.
Launched: 12 July 1913.
Builder: Blohm & Voss, Hamburg.
Displacement: 26,181 tons
(26,600 tonnes) normal; 30,223
tons (30,707 tonnes) full load.
Dimensions: 689ft (210m) oa x
95ft 2in (29m) x 27ft 3in (8·3m).
Machinery: 2 Marine turbines; 18
Marine boilers; 4 shafts; 85,000
SHP.
Armour: 11·8in (300mm) belt;
3·1in (80mm) decks; 11in (280mm)
turrets.
Armament: 8 x 12in (305mm); 12
x 5·9in (150mm); 4 x 19·7in
(500mm) torpedo tubes.
Performance: 28kt (51·9km/h).
Crew: 1,112.

Lead-ship of Germany's last class
of battlecruiser before World War
I, *Derfflinger* was considerably
different from *Seydlitz,* being
flush-decked, carrying her main
armament of powerful 12in
(305mm) guns in two pairs of
superfiring twin turrets fore and
aft, and having her heavy secondary
battery in the superstructure.
 Derfflinger was seriously
damaged at Jutland, but survived
to be scuttled at Scapa Flow in
June 1919; *Lützow* was the only
German battlecruiser lost in the
war, being scuttled at Jutland after
heavy damage; and *Hindenburg,*
completed too late for Jutland, was
scuttled in 1919 with the High
Seas Fleet.

Below: Battlecruiser
Derfflinger, 1914.

Below: *Erin,* as completed in 1914,
resembled a compact Iron Duke.

Below: *König* on completion at the
outbreak of World War I; all five
turrets were on the centre line.

ERIN

1914 *UK*

Laid down: 1 August 1911.
Launched: 3 September 1913.
Builder: Vickers, Barrow.
Displacement: 22,780 tons
(23,144 tonnes) load; 25,250 tons
(25,654 tonnes) full load.
Dimensions: 559ft 6in (170·5m)
oa x 91ft 7in (27·9m) x 28ft 2in
(8·6m) max.
Machinery: 2 Parsons turbines;
15 Babcock & Wilcox boilers; 4
shafts; 26,500 SHP.
Armour: 12in-9in (305-229mm)
belt; 8in-4in (203-102mm) bulkheads; 3in-1in (76-25mm) decks;
11in-3in (279-76mm) turrets; 12in
(305mm) conning tower.
Armament: 10 x 13·5in (343mm);
16 x 6in (152mm); 6 x 6pdr.;
4 x 21in (533mm) torpedo tubes.
Performance: 21kt (38·9km/h);
radius 4,600nm (8,530km) at 10kt
(18·5km/h).
Crew: 1,070.

Designed by Sir G. Thurston and
built as the Turkish *Reshadieh,*
Erin was an exceptionally powerful
battleship produced without the
beam and draught limitations of
her Royal Navy contemporaries.
This permitted a very strong

secondary battery, although only
at the expense of shallower belt
armour. The chief difference in
comparison with British 13·5in
(343mm) gunned battleships was
the placing of 'Q' turret one deck
higher. *Erin* served with the
Grand Fleet throughout World War
I, was placed in reserve in 1919
and was scrapped in 1921.

KÖNIG

1914 *Germany*
Other ships in class: *Grosser
Kurfürst, Markgraf, Kronprinz*

Laid down: October 1911.
Launched: 1 March 1913.
Builder: Wilhelmshaven Dockyard.

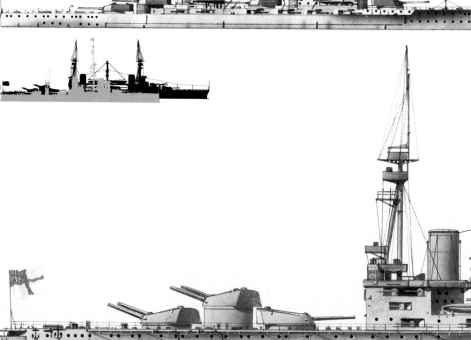

Below: The graceful lines of *Tiger* as completed, 1914. She was the last of the 13·5in (343mm) gunned battlecruisers and the Royal Navy's last coal-fired capital ship.

TIGER
1914 UK

Laid down: 20 June 1912.
Launched: 15 December 1913.
Builder: John Brown & Co, Clydebank.
Displacement: 28,430 tons (28,885 tonnes) normal; 35,160 tons (35,723 tonnes) full load.
Dimensions: 704ft (214·6m) oa x 90ft 6in (27·6m) x 28ft 5in (8·66m).
Machinery: 4 Brown-Curtis turbines; 39 Babcock & Wilcox boilers; 4 shafts; 108,000 SHP.
Armour: 9in-4in (229-102mm) belt; 6in (152mm) upper belt; 3in (76mm) under lower belt; 5in-4in (127-102mm) bulkheads; 3in-1in (76-25mm) decks; 9in-8in (229-203mm) barbettes; 9in-3·5in (229-89mm) turrets; 6in (152mm) battery; 5in-4in (127-102mm) battery bulkheads; 10in (254mm) conning tower.
Armament: 8 x 13·5in (343mm); 12 x 6in (152mm); 4 x 3pdr; 4 x 21in (533mm) torpedo tubes.
Performance: 30kt (55·6km/h); coal 3,320 tons (3,373 tonnes); oil 3,480 tons (3,536 tonnes).
Crew: 1,121.

Originally intended as the fourth unit of the Lion class, *Tiger* was completed as a considerably improved half-sister. The improvements, largely in speed and main armament efficiency, were made possible by a 2ft (0·61m) increase in beam and a 2,150-ton (2,184 tonne) gain in the nominal displacement, permitting the rearrangement and enlargement of the machinery spaces and boiler rooms to develop an additional 31,500 SHP for an extra 3kt (5·56km/h) nominal speed. Sir Eustace Tennyson D'Eyncourt, by now Director of Naval Construction, urged the adoption of small-tube boilers and geared turbines but the designer, E.L. Attwood, and most other British naval constructors preferred the heavier but more reliable large-tube boilers and direct-drive turbines, which were fitted. Had D'Eyncourt's advice been taken, *Tiger* might have reached 32kt (59·3km/h); but as it was the ship was the fastest as well as the largest capital ship of her day, and also the UK's last coal-burning capital ship.

The rearrangement of the motive power also allowed the exchange of 'Q' turret and the aftermost funnel, the Lions' layout having proved unsatisfactory. Moreover, as the two aftermost turrets were still separated by some 75ft (22·9m), one hit was unlikely to knock out both turrets, and both could fire dead astern without undue blast effects. *Tiger* was the only British battlecruiser to carry a secondary armament of 6in (152mm) guns, six to a side.

Armour was on the same scale as that in the Lions, but more extensive and with far better protection for the secondary armament. Testimony as to her strength is provided by the fact that *Tiger* took some 17 large-calibre hits at Jutland but was repaired in less than one month.

Tiger joined the Grand Fleet at Scapa Flow in November 1914, and saw action during the Battle of Dogger Bank in 1915 as well as at Jutland. In 1931 she was removed from the effective list, and then sold and scrapped in accordance with the life-duration clause of the Washington Treaty.

Displacement: 25,390 tons (25,796 tonnes) normal; 28,148 tons (28,598 tonnes) full load.
Dimensions: 576ft 5in (175·7m) oa x 96ft 9½in (29·5m) x 27ft 2½in (8·3m).
Machinery: 3 Parsons turbines; 15 Schulz-Thornycroft boilers; 3 shafts; 43,300 SHP.
Armour: 13·8in-5·9in (350-150mm) belt; 3·9in-1·2in (100-30mm) decks; 11·8in-3·2in (300-80mm) turrets.
Armament: 10 x 12in (305mm); 14 x 5·9in (150mm); 8 x 3·5in (88mm); 5 x 19·7in (500mm) torpedo tubes.
Performance: 22·5kt (41·7km/h); radius 8,700nm (16,100km) at 10kt (18·5km/h); coal 3,543 tons (3,600 tonnes); oil 689 tons (700 tonnes).
Crew: 1,150.

The four units of the König class were the last German battleships built before World War I, and the last with 12in (305mm) guns. They were also the first to feature a main armament located entirely along the centre line, and were remarkably well planned vessels with first-class protection. All four ships were at Jutland, and all were scuttled at Scapa Flow on 21 June 1919.

AGINCOURT
1914 UK

Laid down: 14 September 1911.
Launched: 22 January 1913.
Builder: Armstrong, Elswick.
Displacement: 27,500 tons (27,940 tonnes) normal; 30,250 tons (30,734 tonnes) full load.
Dimensions: 671ft 6in (204·7m) oa x 89ft (27·13m) x 27ft (8·23m) mean.
Machinery: 2 Parsons turbines; 22 Babcock & Wilcox boilers; 4 shafts; 40,270 SHP.
Armour: 9in-4in (229-102mm) belt; 6in (152mm) upper belt; 8in-4in (203-102mm) bulkheads; 2·5in-1in (64-25mm) decks; 9in-3in (229-76mm) barbettes; 12in-8in (305-203mm) turrets; 6in (152mm) battery; 12in-4in (305-102mm) conning tower; 9in (229mm) torpedo control tower.
Armament: 14 x 12in (305mm); 20 x 6in (152mm); 10 x 3in (76mm); 3 x 21in (533mm) torpedo tubes.
Performance: 22·4kt (41·5km/h); coal 3,200 tons (3,251 tonnes); oil 620 tons (630 tonnes).
Crew: 1,115 (increased to 1,267 in November 1918).

Below: *Agincourt*, 1914, had the largest number of main-calibre guns ever carried. After she was taken over by the Royal Navy her flying bridge was removed.

Undoubtedly the most impressive British-built battleship of the period up to World War I, *Agincourt* began her life as *Rio de Janeiro*, ordered by Brazil to provide her navy with the ultimate South American dreadnought in a period of intense rivalry with Argentina and Chile. She had been in the water for some 10 months and was over half way to completion when the Brazilian government changed its mind about the ship and put her up for sale. She was bought by Turkey and renamed *Sultan Osman I*, but her completion was slowed as the threat of war loomed over Europe, and in August 1914 she was taken over for the Royal Navy and named *Agincourt*.

With appearance as much as fighting ability featuring in the original design, the keynotes to the *Agincourt*'s plans were the greatest number of main-calibre guns and turrets ever carried, and a secondary battery then the most powerful afloat. But given this weight of artillery, and the machinery necessary to produce a relatively high speed, protection was quite modest.

Agincourt served with the Grand Fleet from September 1914 to the end of World War I, and fought at Jutland. She was placed in reserve in 1919, used for experimental purposes in 1921, began conversion to a depot ship in 1922 but was scrapped later that year.

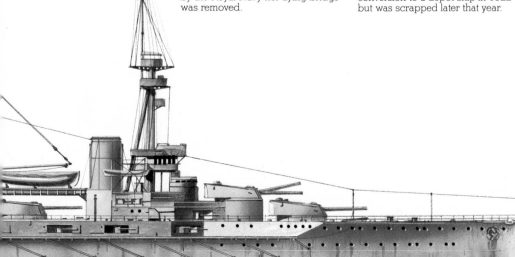

TEXAS (BB-35)

1914 *USA*
Other ships in class: *New York*
(BB-34)

Laid down: 17 April 1911.
Launched: 18 May 1912.
Builder: Newport News.
Displacement: 27,000 tons (27,432 tonnes) normal; 28,400 tons (28,854 tonnes) full load.
Dimensions: 573ft (174·65m) oa x 95ft 3in (29·03m) x 29ft 7in (9·02m) max.
Machinery: Two 4-cylinder Vertical Triple Expansion engines; 14 Babcock boilers; 2 shafts; 28,100 IHP.
Armour: 12in-6in (305-152mm) belt; 14in (356mm) turrets; 12in (305mm) barbettes; 7in (178mm) casemates; 3in (76mm) decks; 12in (305mm) conning tower.
Armament: 10 x 14in (356mm); 21 x 5in (127mm) QF; 4 x 21in (533mm) torpedo tubes.
Performance: 21kt (38·85km/h); coal 2,892 tons (2,938 tonnes) max; oil 400 tons (406 tonnes); radius 8,000nm (14,800km) at 10kt (18·5km/h).
Crew: 1,042.

Above: *Texas* (BB-35) photographed off the New York waterfront, *c*1916. Topmasts have been stepped down to allow passage beneath the bridge, and crewmen crowd the deck as two tugboats prepare to come alongside.

Below: *Texas* as completed, 1914. She and her sister-ship *New York* were the first US warships in which 14in (356mm) guns were fitted, replacing the 12in (305mm) main armament originally planned.

Below: Starboard elevation and (right) plan view of *Texas* in 1942. Extensive modernization has seen the cage masts replaced by tripods; one funnel has been removed, making way for increased AA armament, and a catapult is fitted atop the third turret. In spite of their age, both *Texas* and *New York* saw extensive service in World War II.

Right: *New York* in a two-tone colour scheme—haze grey above and navy blue on the lower part of the hull—almost certainly photographed during 'Operation Torch', the Allied landings in North Africa, around December 1942. The AA armament, already considerable, would soon be further augmented.

Basically similar in design to the Wyomings, with beamy, flush-decked hulls, *Texas* and *New York* were first designed to mount 15 x 12in (305mm) guns in triple turrets. However, the 14in (356mm), 45-cal weapons originally proposed for the Floridas at last became available, so 10 x 14in (356mm) were fitted in twin turrets, one central and two superfiring fore and aft.

Since US turbine manufacturers proved unwilling to meet the strict specifications laid down by the Navy Department's Bureau of Ships, and no compromise on standards and prices was reached after long argument, the Bureau reverted to reciprocating engines for *Texas* and *New York*. Although reciprocating machinery was said to give a 30 per cent improvement in economy at cruising speed and to be in no way inferior to turbines at full speed, this was a step that the European powers locked in naval rivalry could never have risked. But the threat succeeded in bringing turbine builders into line: apart from the Nevada class *Oklahoma*, turbine propulsion was fitted in US battleships from *Nevada* onwards.

Service in the US 6th Battle Squadron in World War I showed that, as in the Wyomings, the foremost 5in (127mm) guns and those mounted right aft were useless in bad weather; 5 x 5in (127mm) were therefore removed and 2 x 3in (76mm) added atop the stump masts of the cranes just forward of the second funnel. On 9 March 1919, *Texas* was the first US battleship to

fly off an aircraft—a British Sopwith Camel—from a temporary platform fitted atop the second turret.

Major reconstruction 1925-27 was along the lines described under *Florida* and *Wyoming*, the major differences being that *Texas* and *New York* had both cage masts replaced by tripods and were re-boilered with six Bureau-Express oil-fired units. They had always been wet ships with unsatisfactory sea-going qualities, and the addition of torpedo bulges—raising beam to 106ft 1in (32·33m) and full load displacement to 31,924 tons (32,435 tonnes)—made matters worse, degrading handling in rough weather and reducing maximum speed to 19·5kt (36km/h).

In 1940-41, the elevation of the 14in (356mm) guns was increased from 15° to 30° to give a maximum range of *c*25,000yds (22,860m). By the end of World War II—during which *Texas* and *New York* steamed more than 120,000nm (222,000km) each, supporting the North African landings in November 1942 and serving in the Pacific at Iwo Jima and Okinawa—secondary/AA armament was 6 x 5in (127mm), 10 x 3in (76mm) AA, 40 x 40mm AA and 36 x 20mm AA.

New York survived the atomic bomb tests at Bikini Atoll, July 1946, and was sunk as a target off Pearl Harbor on 8 July 1948. *Texas* was taken over by the State of Texas on 21 April 1948 and is preserved as a memorial in a specially-dredged canal in San Jacinto State Park.

Below: *Rivadavia* as completed, 1914. The cage mast forward points to her American origin: the Rivadavias were the only major warships built for a foreign power in US yards during this period.

BATTLESHIP DESIGNS

1913-14 Netherlands

Builders (designers): (A) Germaniawerft, Kiel; (B) Blohm & Voss, Hamburg; (C) Vickers, UK.
Displacement (full load): (A) 26,671 tons (27,098 tonnes); (B) 26,056 tons (26,473 tonnes); (C) 28,033 tons (28,482 tonnes).
Dimensions: (A) 603ft 8in (184m) wl x 91ft 10in (28m) x 27ft 7in (8·4m); (B) 566ft 11in (172·8m) wl x 95ft 2in (29m) x 28ft 7in (8·7m); (C) 587ft 4in (179m) wl x 90ft 11in (27·7m) x 31ft 2in (9·5m).
Machinery: (A) 3 turbines, 7 boilers, 3 shafts, 38,000 SHP; (B) 4 turbines, 6 double-ended boilers, 4 shafts, 38,000 SHP; (C) 4 turbines, 15 boilers, 4 shafts, 34,000 SHP.
Armour: (A) 10in-6in (254-152mm) belt, 12in-4·5in (305-114mm) barbettes, 2in-1in (51-25mm) deck, 12in (305mm) conning tower; (B) 10in-4in (254-102mm) belt, 12in-3in (305-76mm) barbettes, 1·2in (30mm) deck; (C) max 10in (254mm) belt, 12in-2in (305-51mm) barbettes, 1in (25mm) deck, 12in-6in (305-152mm) conning tower.
Armament: (A, B, C) 8 x 14in (356mm); 16 x 6in (152mm) QF; 12 x 3in (76mm) QF; 5 TT.
Performance: (A, B, C) 22kt (40·7km/h).

In 1913 the Netherlands announced a 35-year naval construction programme aimed at colonial protection and including 9 battleships. The specified standard displacement of 21,000 tons (21,336 tonnes) was exceeded by all three builders whose designs were under consideration when World War I put an end to the project. The German designs were possibly influenced by *Salamis* (qv), then building for Greece by AG Vulkan of Hamburg.

Below: Germaniawerft design of 1914.

Below: Blohm & Voss design of 1914.

Below: Design by Vickers, UK, 1914.

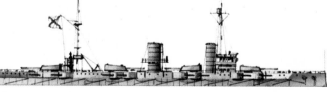

Below: *Gangut* as completed, 1914. More than 50 designs were submitted.

RIVADAVIA

1914 Argentina
Other ships in class: *Moreno*

Laid down: 25 May 1910.
Launched: 28 June 1911.
Builder: Fore River Company, Quincy, Massachusetts.
Displacement: 28,000 tons (28,448 tonnes) normal; 30,000 tons (30,480 tonnes) full load.
Dimensions: 585ft (178·3m) oa x 96ft 9in (29·49m) x 27ft 11in (8·5m).
Machinery: 3 Curtis turbines; 18 Babcock boilers; 3 shafts; 39,500 SHP.
Armour: 11in-4in (279-102mm) belt; 12in-9in (305-229mm) turrets and barbettes; 6in (152mm) battery; 3in-1·5in (76-38mm) decks; 12in (305mm) conning tower.
Armament: 12 x 12in (305mm); 12 x 6in (152mm) QF; 16 x 4in (102mm) QF; 2 x 21in (533mm) torpedo tubes.
Performance: 22·5kt (41·6km/h); coal 4,000 tons (4,064 tonnes) max; oil 660 tons (671 tonnes); radius 11,000nm (20,350km) at 11kt (20·35km/h); 7,000nm (12,950km) at 15kt (27·75km/h).
Crew: 1,050.

Below: *Gangut* (renamed *Oktyabrskaya Revolutsia*) in the late 1930s. The fore funnel has been raised and angled to clear the bridge of fumes; the cranes handle floatplanes or small motor torpedo boats.

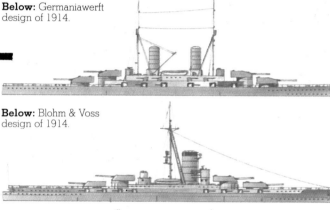

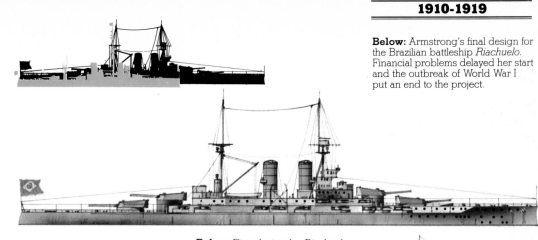

Below: Armstrong's final design for the Brazilian battleship *Riachuelo*. Financial problems delayed her start and the outbreak of World War I put an end to the project.

Below: First design for *Riachuelo*.

Below: Design with 10 x 15in guns.

South American rivalry was expressed in ambitious naval programmes which could not be fully implemented. Argentina aimed at three dreadnoughts to counter Brazil's British-built *Minas Gerais* and *São Paulo,* but for financial reasons only two were built, both in American yards.

Like the Brazilian ships, the Rivadavias mounted a main armament of 12 x 12in (305mm) in twin turrets, superfiring fore and aft and diagonally offset, with cross-deck arcs of *c*100°, on either beam. The large diagonally-arranged derrick posts amidships carried rangefinders on their tops. The 8ft (2·4m) deep main armour belt extended from 3ft 3in (1m) below the water line at normal draught to 4ft 9in (1·4m) above it.

Extensively modernized in the US in 1924-25, the Rivadavias were converted to oil burning. Their lattice masts forward were shortened and the pole masts aft replaced by tripods. Eight 4in (102mm) QF were removed and 4 x 3in (76mm) AA added. Full load displacement increased by *c*1,000 tons (1,016 tonnes). Both were stricken in 1956-57.

GANGUT

1914 *Russia*
Other ships in class: *Poltava, Sevastopol, Petropavlovsk*

Laid down: 13 July 1909.
Launched: 7 October 1911.
Builder: Admiralty Yard, St Petersburg.
Displacement: 23,000 tons (23,368 tonnes) normal; 25,850 tons (26,264 tonnes) full load.
Dimensions: 600ft (182·88m) oa x 88ft 3in (26·9m) x 27ft 3in (8·3m) mean.
Machinery: 4 Parsons turbines; 25 Yarrow boilers; 4 shafts; 42,000 SHP.
Armour: 8·9in-4in (225-102mm) belt; 8in-5in (203-127mm) turrets; 8in (203mm) barbettes; 4·9in (125mm) casemates; 1·5in-1in (38-25mm) deck; 10in (254mm) conning tower.
Armament: 12 x 12in (305mm); 16 x 4·7in (120mm) QF; 4 x 3pdr (47mm); 4 x 18in (457mm) torpedo tubes.
Performance: 23kt (42·55km/h); coal 3,000 tons (3,048 tonnes) max; oil 1,170 tons (1,189 tonnes) max; radius 4,000nm (7,400km) at 16kt

(29·6km/h), 900nm (1,665km) at 23kt (42·55km/h).
Crew: 1,125.

Russia's first dreadnoughts were authorized in 1909. The contract was won by Blohm & Voss, Hamburg, but the Duma refused funds unless the ships were Russianbuilt. Partly because high-tensile steel, which Russian industry could not produce in quantity, was used throughout, construction, to an indigenous design owing much to the Italian *Dante Alighieri,* was prolonged.

Protection and endurance were sacrificed for fire-power and speed. The armament layout, influenced by Vittorio Cuniberti, was 12 x 12in (305mm), 52-cal guns—the longest then at sea and of noted accuracy—in triple turrets on the centre line. In the absence of superfiring, bow and stern turrets were sited near the ends, so the flush-decked ships, with ice-breaking bows, were wet at any speed or in a seaway. Unlike *Dante Alighieri,* secondary turrets were not fitted: the 4·7in (120mm) QF were in casemates too low to be workable in bad weather.

On 18 August 1919, during Allied intervention, *Petropavlovsk* was torpedoed and sunk at Kronstadt by a British coastal motorboat. Salvaged and repaired, she was renamed *Marat* and, with *Gangut* (now *Oktyabrskaya Revolutsia)* and *Sevastopol* (now *Parizhskaya Kommuna),* extensively modernized before World War II. *Poltava* (renamed *Mikhail Frunze)* was partly destroyed by fire in 1922 and thereafter cannibalized.

Marat was crippled by German dive-bombers at Kronstadt, September 1941, but later served as a battery (named *Petropavlovsk* again) and gunnery ship (as *Volkhov)* until scrapped, 1952-53. Also reverting to her original name in World War II, *Sevastopol* carried out many bombardment missions; she was scrapped in 1956-57. *Oktyabrskaya Revolutsia,* damaged by shore batteries and air attack in 1941-42, survived to bombard German troops from the Neva River in early 1944. She was scrapped in 1956-59.

RIACHUELO

1914 (designs only) *Brazil*

Builder: Armstrong, Elswick.
Displacement: (A) 31,500 tons (32,004 tonnes); (B) 32,500 tons (33,020 tonnes); (C, D) 36,000 tons (36,576 tonnes).
Dimensions: (A) 685ft (208·8m) x 95ft 10in (29·2m) x 27ft 11in (8·5m); (B) 689ft (210m) x 95ft 10in (29·2m) x 28ft 6in (8·7m); (C, D) 740ft 2in (225·6m) x 98ft 1in (29·9m) x 28ft 10in (8·8m).
Machinery: (A, B) 4 Parsons turbines, 45,000 SHP; (C, D) not known.
Armour: (A) 12in (305mm) belt and turrets, 2in (51mm) deck; (B) 13in (330mm) belt, 12in (305mm) turrets; (C, D) not known.
Armament: (A) 12 x 14in (356mm), 16 x 6in (152mm) QF, 12 x 3in (76mm) QF, 4 x 3in (76mm) AA, 4-6 torpedo tubes; (B) 10 x 15in (381mm), 20 x 6in (152mm) QF, 10 x 3in (76mm) QF, 4 x 3in (76mm) AA, 6 torpedo tubes; (C) 10 x 16in (406mm), rest as (B); (D) 12 x 15in (381mm), rest as (B).
Performance: (A) Coal- and oil-fired 23kt (42·55km/h), oil-fired 24kt (44·4km/h); (B) coal- and oil-fired 24kt (44·4km/h), oil-fired 25·5kt (47·2km/h); (A, B) coal 4,000 tons (4,064 tonnes), oil 1,000 tons (1,016 tonnes), *or* oil 3,500 tons (3,556 tonnes), coal nil.

Largely because the Almirante Latorre class, with a main armament of 10 x 14in (356mm), was building for Chile, Brazil decided in 1913 to sell the partly completed *Rio de Janeiro* (see *Agincourt*) and order a more powerful unit from Armstrong, the British builder of the Latorres.

Four designs (A, B, C, D in the data table above) had been made by Armstrong by August 1914. Design A provided for a main armament of 12 x 14in (356mm) guns in three groups of superfiring twin turrets. In Design B, 10 x 15in (381mm) were to be mounted in five twin turrets, one central and two superfiring fore and aft. The outbreak of World War I, combined with the economic pressures that Brazil was suffering at this time, effectively ended the project.

QUEEN ELIZABETH

1915 *UK*
Other ships in class: *Warspite,
Valiant, Barham, Malaya*

Laid down: 21 October 1912.
Launched: 16 October 1913.
Builder: Portsmouth Dockyard.
Displacement: 27,500 tons
(27,940 tonnes) normal; 33,020
tons (33,548 tonnes) full load.
Dimensions: 646ft 1in (196·9m)
oa x 90ft 6in (27·6m) x 30ft (9·1m)
max.
Machinery: 4 Parsons geared
turbines, plus cruising turbines; 24
Babcock & Wilcox boilers: 4 shafts;
75,000 SHP.
Armour: 13in-4in (330-102mm)
belt; 6in-4in (152-102mm) upper
belt; 6in-4in (152-102mm) bulkheads; 3in-1in (76-25mm) decks:
10in-4in (254-102mm) barbettes;
13in-5in (330-127mm) turrets; 11in
(279mm) conning tower.
Armament: 8 x 15in (381mm); 16
x 6in (152mm); 2 x 3in (76mm)
AA; 4 x 21in (533mm) torpedo
tubes.
Performance: 23kt (46·3km/h);
radius 7,500nm (13,840km) at 12·5kt
(23·2km/h); oil 3,300 tons (3,353
tonnes); coal 100 tons (102 tonnes).
Crew: 925.

With the advent of 14in (356mm)
main armament in several foreign
capital ships, it was inevitable that
the British should try to restore a

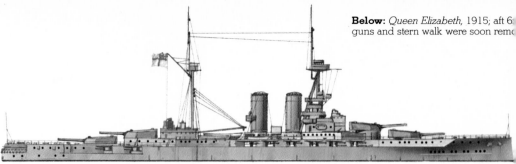

qualitative edge in the primary
armament of British battleships.
The result was the classic 15in
(381mm) Mk I gun, which with a
muzzle velocity of 2,655ft (809m)
per second could hurl its very
powerful 1,920lb (871kg) shell to a
range of 35,000 yards (32,005m)
with great accuracy and little barrel
wear. To mount the 15in (381mm)
gun a battleship larger than the
previous norm was needed. Under
the supervision of W.H. Gard, E.N.
Mooney designed a handsome
vessel developed from the *Iron
Duke* but with 20ft (6·1m) more
length and 6in (0·15m) more beam
for an extra 2,500 tons (2,540
tonnes) displacement.

For the first time in the world, a
capital ship was designed with
oil-burning boilers. The weight
saved could be used to increase
protection: the belt gained 1in
(25mm) in thickness and was

deepened to take in the main deck.
The five armoured decks were
thinner than the Iron Dukes' but
amidships totalled 3·75in (95mm)
compared to 3·5in (89mm). Underwater protection was also improved
by the use of two longitudinal
bulkheads covering the interior of
the hull between the torpedo flats
with a constant thickness of 2in
(51mm).

Four Queen Elizabeths were
planned as a homogeneous fast
battleship squadron. These were
the lead ship; *Valiant,* built by
Fairfield at Govan and completed
in February 1915; *Warspite,* built
by Devonport Dockyard and completed in March 1915; and *Barham,*
built by John Brown on Clydebank
and completed in October 1915.
However, a fifth unit, *Malaya,* was
contributed as a gift from the
Federated Malay States, built by
Armstrong Whitworth at High
Walker and completed in February
1916, and a sixth *(Agincourt)* was
cancelled in August 1914 before
being laid down at Devonport
Dockyard. The five ships built
formed the 5th Battle Squadron of
the Grand Fleet during a large part
of World War I, and all but
Queen Elizabeth were at Jutland;
Queen Elizabeth was the fleet

flagship in 1917 and 1918.

All five vessels were retained
after World War I, and were
extensively refitted during the late
1920s with long anti-torpedo
bulges, trunked funnels and anti-
aircraft guns. *Warspite* was completely rebuilt between 1934 and
1936 with new machinery, a
revised superstructure, and comprehensive aircraft facilities. *Queen
Elizabeth* and *Valiant* received
similar rebuilds (1937-39), but also
a revised secondary armament of
20 x 4·5in (114mm) dual-purpose
guns in twin turrets, fitted instead
of the original casemates. Horizontal
protection was also improved, with
4in (102mm) over the magazines
and machinery spaces, and
3in-1·5in (76-38mm) elsewhere.
Provision was also made for the
stowage of four aircraft, and a
catapult was fitted. The outbreak of
World War II prevented the reconstruction of the *Barham* and
Malaya along similar lines.

All five ships were very widely
used in the war, playing an
important part in British naval
affairs. *Barham* was lost to U-boat
attack on 25 November 1941, but
the other four ships survived
considerable punishment only to
be scrapped in 1947 and 1948.

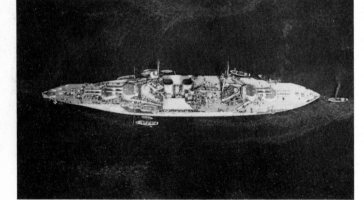

Above: Aerial photograph of *Queen
Elizabeth* in 1916, with awnings
spread amidships and several of her
numerous boats lowered. Eight 15in
(381mm) Mk I guns, among the best
naval ordnance ever built, are
mounted in twin turrets fore and aft.

Below: *Queen Elizabeth*, 1935, with trunked funnel and built-up bridge.

Below: *Warspite* in World War I; note range baffles on masts and funnels. The five Queen Elizabeths formed the 5th Battle Squadron, Grand Fleet, from early 1916 and all save *Queen Elizabeth* (then refitting; later Fleet Flagship, Grand Fleet) served at Jutland, where *Warspite, Barham* and *Malaya* were damaged.

Bottom: *Warspite* after her 1930s modernization. In service from 1915 to 1945, she took more damage than any other British battleship.

Below: *Queen Elizabeth* in 1943, with augmented AA armament and radar equipment after a refit in the United States. The aircraft and catapult were soon removed.

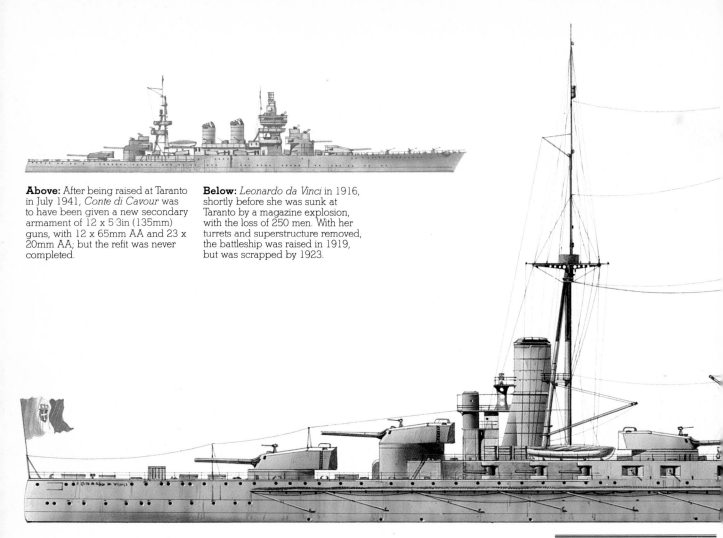

Above: After being raised at Taranto in July 1941, *Conte di Cavour* was to have been given a new secondary armament of 12 x 5·3in (135mm) guns, with 12 x 65mm AA and 23 x 20mm AA; but the refit was never completed.

Below: *Leonardo da Vinci* in 1916, shortly before she was sunk at Taranto by a magazine explosion, with the loss of 250 men. With her turrets and superstructure removed, the battleship was raised in 1919, but was scrapped by 1923.

CAIO DUILIO

1915 *Italy*
Other ships in class: *Andrea Doria*

Laid down: 24 February 1912.
Launched: 24 April 1914.
Builder: Castellammare Navy Yard.
Displacement: 22,694 tons (23,057 tonnes) normal; 25,200 tons (25,603 tonnes) full load.
Dimensions: 577ft 9in (176·1m) oa x 91ft 10in (28m) x 29ft 2in (8·9m) mean.
Machinery: 3 Parsons turbines; 20 Yarrow boilers; 4 shafts; 32,000 SHP.
Armour: 9·8in-5·1in (250-130mm)

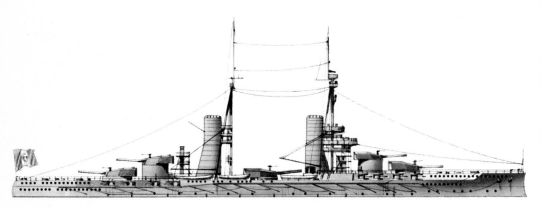

Above: *Andrea Doria* as completed. The Duilio class represented a logical step up from the Cavours, with the same main armament but a 6in (152mm) secondary battery; the central turret was carried one deck lower to counter the added weight of the secondary armament. The forward 6in (152mm) guns were difficult to work in a seaway.

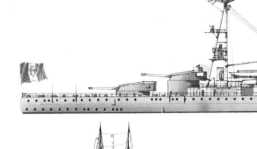

Above: *Giulio Cesare*, much altered after extensive modernization, in 1938. The hull has been lengthened and the central turret and amidships casemates suppressed. Main armament is now 10 x 12·6in (320mm), the original guns having been bored out.

CONTE DI CAVOUR

1915 *Italy*
Other ships in class: *Giulio Cesare, Leonardo da Vinci*

Laid down: 10 August 1910.
Launched: 10 August 1911.
Builder: Royal Dockyard, La Spezia.
Displacement: 23,088 tons (23,457 tonnes) normal; 25,086 tons (25,487 tonnes) full load.
Dimensions: 577ft 9in (176·1m) oa x 91ft 10in (28m) x 30ft 10in (9·4m) max.
Machinery: 3 Parsons turbines; 20 Blechhynden boilers; 4 shafts; 31,000 SHP.
Armour: 9·8in-5·1in (250-130mm) belt; 11in ((280mm) turrets; 9·4in (240mm) barbettes; 5·1in-4·3in (130-110mm) casemates; 1·7in (43mm) deck; 11in (280mm) CT.
Armament: 13 x 12in (305mm); 18 x 4·7in (120mm) QF; 13 x 3in (76mm) QF; 3 x 17·7in (450mm) torpedo tubes.
Performance: 21·5kt (39·8km/h); coal 1,450 tons (1,473 tonnes) max; oil 850 tons (864 tonnes) max; radius 4,800nm (8,880km) at 10kt (18·5km/h).
Crew: 1,197.

Designed in 1908 by Eng-Gen Masdea, the Cavours improved on the all round fire-power of *Dante Alighieri* by mounting 13 big guns in five centre-line turrets: triple turrets with superfiring twin turrets fore and aft, and one triple turret amidships. The secondary turrets of *Dante Alighieri* were not adopted, but the amidships battery was one deck higher.

The improved layout was, perhaps, outweighed by the fact that the Cavours were overlong in building and appeared when other navies had 13·5in-14in (343-356mm) guns at sea. Moreover, as in other Italian designs, protection took second place to fire-power and speed—although the designed speed of 22kt (40·7km/h) was only rarely achieved.

Leonardo da Vinci was sunk by a magazine explosion at Taranto, 2 August 1916, salvaged, and scrapped in 1919-23. The surviving Cavours, like the Dorias, were completely rebuilt in the 1930s and entered World War II with new machinery—2-shaft geared turbines providing 93,000 SHP at 28kt (51·8km/h)—and much improved protection. With the central triple turret and the secondary casemates suppressed, armament was 10 x 12·6in (320mm) guns (as in *Caio Duilio*), 12 x 4·7in (120mm) on the forecastle deck amidships, 8 x 3·9in (100mm) AA and c20 smaller AA.

Sunk by a British aerial torpedo at Taranto, 12 November 1940, *Conte di Cavour* was never again operational. *Giulio Cesare*, renamed *Z 11*, was handed to Russia as war reparation in 1948 and served in the Black Sea as *Novorossisk* until late 1955.

belt; 9·4in (240mm) turrets and barbettes; 5in (127mm) casemates; 1·6in (40mm) decks; 12·6in (320mm) conning tower.
Armament: 13 x 12in (305mm); 16 x 6in (152mm) QF; 18 x 3in (76mm) QF; 3 x 17·7in (450mm) torpedo tubes.
Performance: 21·5kt (39·8km/h); coal 1,488 tons (1,512 tonnes) max; oil 886 tons (900 tonnes) max; radius 4,800nm (8,880km) at 10kt (18·5km/h).
Crew: 1,233.

Caio Duilio and *Andrea Doria* were basically Cavours with a 6in (152mm) secondary armament. To maintain stability, the midships secondary battery of the Cavours was split into two groups fore and aft of amidships and the central 12in (305mm) triple turret was one deck lower. The forward tripod was before the fore funnel rather than abaft. A designed speed of 22kt (40·7km/h) could only be achieved with some 10,000 SHP in excess of designed output, and protection—particularly underwater, where only protective coal bunkers were fitted—was poor.

After extensive reconstruction in 1937-40 they were vitually new ships, with overall length up by 35ft 6in (10·8m), superstructures modelled on *Vittorio Veneto* (*qv*), and new machinery: 2-shaft geared turbines and 8 oil-fired boilers, providing 85,000 SHP at 27kt (50km/h). Protection over machinery and magazines was improved and 1·6in (40mm) anti-torpedo bulkheads fitted. Armament was now 10 x 12·6in (320mm)—the central triple turret being removed and the remaining big guns bored out—12 x 5·3in (135mm) in triple turrets and 10 x 3·6in (90mm) AA, plus c30 smaller AA.

Both were mainly deployed for convoy interception or escort in World War II, when *Caio Duilio* was out of action for six months in 1940 after a torpedo hit. They were finally scrapped in 1957-58.

Below: *Andrea Doria* in World War II, after extensive rebuilding.

Below: *Canada* as she appeared while serving with the Grand Fleet, 1916. Ordered for Chile, she was handed over after World War I and served the Chilean Navy as *Almirante Latorre* from 1920 until 1958.

SALAMIS

1915 (not completed) *Greece*

Laid down: 23 July 1913.
Launched: 11 November 1914.
Builder: Vulkan, Hamburg.
Displacement: 19,500 tons (19,812 tonnes) designed.
Dimensions: 569ft 11in (173·7m) wl x 81ft (24·7m) x 24ft 11in (7·6m).
Machinery: 3 AEG turbines; 18 Yarrow boilers; 3 shafts; 40,000 SHP.
Armour: 9·8in-3·1in (250-80mm) belt; 9·8in (250mm) turrets; 7in (180mm) casemates; 3in-1·6in (75-40mm) deck; 11·8in (300mm) conning tower.
Armament: 8 x 14in (356mm); 12 x 6in (152mm) QF; 12 x 3in (76mm) QF; 3 x 19·7in (500mm) torpedo tubes.
Performance: 23kt (42·5km/h).
Crew: Not known.

In July 1912, Greece ordered from Germany a 13,000-ton (13,208 tonne) armoured ship mounting 6 x 14in (356mm) guns, to be named *Vasilefs Georgios*. But the First Balkan War, beginning in October 1912, showed that greater power was needed to counter that of Turkey, and the contract was changed to provide for a battleship, named *Salamis*, mounting 8 x 14in (356mm) American-made (Bethlehem Steel) guns in twin turrets superfiring fore and aft.

Following the outbreak of World War I, work on *Salamis* at AG Vulkan, Hamburg, was suspended in December 1914. After the war, Greece, although considering a further modification of the design to a 28kt (51·8km/h) ship with 9 x 14in (356mm) guns, would not accept the *Salamis*, which was scrapped while still incomplete in 1932.

Below: If completed, German-built *Salamis* would have been a powerful unit of relatively small displacement.

Below: The original design for *Salamis:* a 13,000-ton armoured ship with 6 x 14in (356mm) guns.

PROVENCE

1915 *France*
Other ships in class: *Bretagne*, *Lorraine*

Laid down: 1 May 1912.
Launched: 20 April 1913.
Builder: Lorient Dockyard.
Displacement: 23,230 tons (23,602 tonnes) normal; 28,500 tons (28,956 tonnes) full load.
Dimensions: 544ft 8in (166m) oa x 88ft 3in (26·9m) x 32ft 2in (9·8m) max.
Machinery: 2 Parsons turbines; 18 Belleville boilers; 4 shafts; 29,000 SHP.
Armour: 10·6in-6·3in (270-160mm) belt; 15·7in (400mm) centre turret; 13·4in (340mm) end turrets; 9·8in (250mm) superfiring turrets; 9·8in (250mm) barbettes; 10·6in (270mm) superfiring barbettes; 7in (180mm) battery; 1·6in-1·2in (40-30mm) decks; 12·4in (314mm) conning tower.
Armament: 10 x 13·4in (340mm); 22 x 5·5in (139mm) QF; 4 x 2·9in (75mm) QF; 4 x 17·7in (450mm) torpedo tubes.
Performance: 20kt (37km/h); coal 2,680 tons (2,723 tonnes) max; oil 300 tons (305 tonnes); radius 4,700nm (8,695km) at 10kt (18·5km/h) 2,800nm (5,180km) at 13kt (24km/h).
Crew: 1,124.

Based on the hull of the Courbet class to cut construction time, the Bretagnes marked the French Navy's adoption of an all-centre-line main armament and of bigger guns. Ten 13·4in (340mm) guns were carried in twin turrets, one central and two superfiring fore and aft.

After serving in the Mediterranean in 1916-18, the Bretagnes underwent extensive modernization in 1921-23, 1927-30 and 1932-35.

Below: *Provence* as completed, 1915. An improvement on the preceding Courbet class, *Provence* and her sisters carried a heavier, all-centre-line main armament of 10 x 13·4in (340mm) guns. A tripod foremast was later shipped.

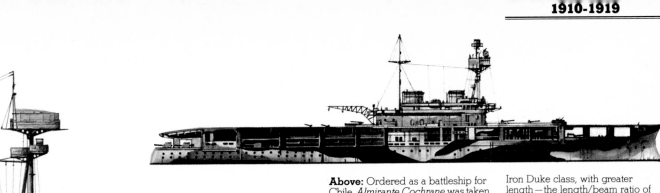

Above: Ordered as a battleship for Chile, *Almirante Cochrane* was taken over by Britain in 1917 and completed in 1920 as the aircraft carrier *Eagle*. She is shown here as she appeared in 1942.

They emerged with oil-burning machinery—4-shaft geared turbines and 6 Indret small-tube boilers providing 43,000 SHP at up to 21·4kt (39·6km/h), re-barrelled big guns with increased elevation, and improved internal protection.

Torpedo tubes were removed and, in *Lorraine*, the central turret was landed to make room for a catapult and a hangar for four aircraft. In 1939, the secondary armament in *Provence* was 14 x 5·5in (139mm) 8 x 2·9in (75mm) AA and 12 x 13·2mm AA MG. *Bretagne* was sunk and *Provence* badly damaged (later, raised and repaired at Toulon, she was used by the Germans as a coastal battery) by the fire of British battleships at Mers-el-Kebir, 3 July 1940. *Lorraine* served with the Free French Forces in the Mediterranean in 1943-45 and thereafter as a training ship and hulk until stricken in 1953.

CANADA

1915 UK
Other ships in class: *Eagle* (see text)

Laid down: 27 November 1911.
Launched: 27 November 1913.
Builder: Armstrong, Elswick.
Displacement: 28,600 tons (29,058 tonnes) load; 32,120 tons (32,634 tonnes) full load.
Dimensions: 661ft (201·47m) oa x 92ft (28m) x 29ft (8·84m) mean.
Machinery: 2 Brown-Curtis high-pressure turbines, 2 Parsons low-pressure turbines; 21 Yarrow boilers; 4 shafts; 37,000 SHP.
Armour: 9in-4in (229-102mm) belt; 10in (254mm) turrets; 10in-4in (254-102mm) barbettes; 6in (152mm) battery; 4·5in-3in (114-76mm) bulkheads; 4in-1in (102-25mm) decks; 11in-6in (279-152mm) conning tower.
Armament: 10 x 14in (356mm); 16 x 6in (152mm); 2 x 3in (76mm) AA; 4 x 3pdr; 4 x 21in (533mm) torpedo tubes.
Performance: 22·75kt (42km/h); coal 3,300 tons (3,353 tonnes) max; oil 520 tons (528 tonnes); radius 4,400nm (8,140km) at 10kt (18·5km/h).
Crew: 1,167.

The Chilean naval programme of 1909 provided for a battleship of 23,000 tons (23,368 tonnes) with 8 x 12in (305mm) guns. By 1911, however, Chile was faced with the challenge of Argentina's Rivadavia class and Brazil's projected *Rio de Janeiro* (see *Agincourt*); she therefore ordered two much more powerful units, *Almirante Latorre* (ex-*Valparaiso*, ex-*Libertad*) and *Almirante Cochrane* (ex-*Santiago*, ex-*Constitucion*) from the British yard of Armstrong, Elswick.

The design was based on the Iron Duke class, with greater length—the length/beam ratio of 6.8:1 was exceptionally high, making for good speed—and somewhat reduced protection. Work on the battleships ceased in August 1914, but quickly recommenced on *Almirante Latorre* when she was purchased for the Royal Navy and renamed *Canada*. Work on *Almirante Cochrane* was not resumed until 1917, when she too was purchased by Britain, to be modified and completed in 1920 as the aircraft carrier *Eagle*.

Although lacking the protection of the 'super-dreadnoughts' ordered for Britain, *Canada* was reckoned among the most effective units of the Grand Fleet, with which she served without damage at Jutland. Her 10 x 14in (356mm) guns were carried in five twin turrets, one central and two superfiring fore and aft; take-off platforms for aircraft were fitted atop 'B' and 'X' turrets in 1918. The two aftermost 6in (152mm) guns in the forward battery were suppressed in 1916 because of central turret blast effects.

Refitted and returned to Chile as *Almirante Latorre* in April 1920, the battleship was modernized at Devonport in 1929-31, receiving oil-burning machinery, anti-torpedo bulges of 5ft 3in (1·6m) maximum width and an AA armament of 4 x 4in (102mm) guns (finally 18 x 20mm AA). During World War II Chile refused an offer by the USA, made in the aftermath of the Pearl Harbor attack of December 1941, to purchase the veteran, and she remained the Chilean flagship until October 1958. She was sold for breaking up in 1959.

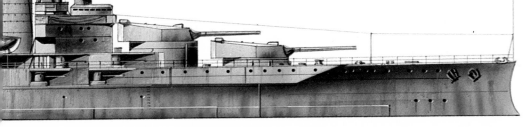

Above: *Fuso* on completion in 1915. Note that the third turret is at forecastle deck level between the funnels, with the fourth and fifth turrets carried one deck higher.

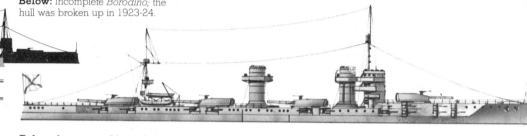

BORODINO

1915 (not completed) *Russia*
Other ships in class: *Navarin, Kinburn, Izmail*

Laid down: 19 December 1912.
Launched: 7 July 1915.
Builder: Galernii Island Yard, St Petersburg.
Displacement: 32,500 tons (33,020 tonnes) normal; 38,000 tons (38,608 tonnes) full load.
Dimensions: 750ft (228·6m) oa x 100ft 1in (30·5m) x 33ft 6in (10·2m) max.
Machinery: 4 turbines; 25 Yarrow boilers; 4 shafts; 68,000 SHP.
Armour: 12in-3·9in (305-100mm) belt; 12in (305mm) turrets and barbettes; 6in (152mm) casemates; 2·5in (63mm) deck; 12in (305mm) conning tower.
Armament: 12 x 14in (356mm); 24 x 5·1in (130mm) QF; 8 x 2·9in (75mm) QF; 4 x 2·5in (63mm) AA; 6 x 21in (533mm) torpedo tubes.
Performance: 26·6kt (49·2km/h); coal 1,950 tons (1,981 tons) max; oil 1,575 tons (1,600 tonnes) max; radius 3,830nm (7,085km) at 16kt (29·6km/h).
Crew: c1,250.

Designated battlecruisers, but with the speed, endurance and protection of fast battleships, the Borodinos were authorized for the Baltic Fleet in 1912. Layout was like that of the Ganguts, but with both central triple turrets training astern.
Construction proper began in 1914, but machinery ordered abroad was delayed by World War I and work ended in the pre-revolutionary uncertainty of 1917. Although more than half complete (all the ships had been launched), three were sold to Germany for breaking up in 1923. *Izmail* was scrapped incomplete at Leningrad in c1931.

Below: Incomplete *Borodino;* the hull was broken up in 1923-24.

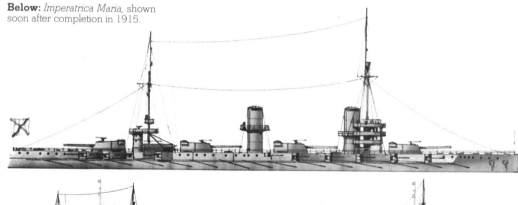

Below: *Imperatrica Maria,* shown soon after completion in 1915.

IMPERATRICA MARIA

1915 *Russia*
Other ships in class: *Imperatrica Ekaterin II, Imperator Alexander III*

Laid down: 30 November 1911.
Launched: 1 November 1913.
Builder: Russud Shipbuilding Co., Nikolaiev.
Displacement: 22,600 tons (22,962 tonnes) normal; c24,000 tons (24,384 tonnes) full load.
Dimensions: 550ft 7in (167·8m) pp x 89ft 7in (27·3m) x 27ft 3in (8·3m) mean.
Machinery: 4 Parsons turbines; 20 Yarrow boilers; 4 shafts; 26,500 SHP.
Armour: 10·4in (263mm) belt; 12in (305mm) turrets; 8in (203mm) barbettes; 5in (127mm) case-mates; 1·5in (38mm) decks; 12in

Below: If completed, *Lyon* would have been an improved Normandie, with 16 x 13·4in (340mm) guns mounted in four quadruple turrets.

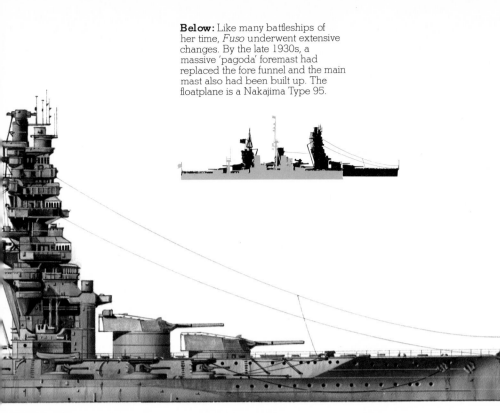

Below: Like many battleships of her time, *Fuso* underwent extensive changes. By the late 1930s, a massive 'pagoda' foremast had replaced the fore funnel and the main mast also had been built up. The floatplane is a Nakajima Type 95.

FUSO

1915 *Japan*
Other ships in class: *Yamashiro*

Laid down: 11 March 1912.
Launched: 28 March 1914.
Builder: Kure Dockyard.
Displacement: 30,600 tons (31,090 tonnes) normal; 35,900 tons (36,474 tonnes) full load.
Dimensions: 673ft (205·1m) oa x 94ft (28·65m) x 28ft 3in (8·61m).
Machinery: 4 Brown-Curtis turbines; 24 Miyabara boilers; 4 shafts; 40,000 SHP.
Armour: Krupp steel 12in-4in (305-102mm) belt and bulkheads; 12in-4·5in (305-114mm) turrets; 8in (203mm) barbettes; 6in (152mm) casemates; 2in-1·25in (51-32mm) deck; 13·75in-5·3in (349-135mm) conning tower.
Armament: 12 x 14in (356mm); 16 x 6in (152mm) QF; 4 x 3·1in (80mm) AA; 6 x 21in (533mm) torpedo tubes.
Performance: 23kt (42·55km/h); coal 5,022 tons (5,102 tonnes) max; oil 1,026 tons (1,042 tonnes); radius 8,000nm (14,800km) at 14kt (25·9km/h).
Crew: 1,193.

Laid down in home yards in 1912-13, with two further ships in the class—subsequently redesigned as *Hyuga* and *Ise*—planned, these battleships confirmed Japan's status as a major Pacific power. They out-gunned the US Navy's *Texas* and *Oklahoma* and matched the Pennsylvanias, although they were less heavily armoured and had their main armament in twin turrets throughout, entailing much greater length than the US ships. But this also made for greater speed—2kt (3·7km/h) better than the Pennsylvanias—and reduced vulnerability to battle damage.

Although based on the British 14in (356mm) mountings supplied for *Kongo*, the Fusos' heavy guns were, for the first time, of indigenous manufacture. In a unique arrangement, the third turret was carried at forecastle deck level between the funnels and the fourth turret one deck higher abaft the second funnel.

In a 1927-28 refit the Fusos were given built-up foremasts and 2 x 3·1in (80mm) AA guns were added. Both were extensively rebuilt in 1930-35, emerging with massive 'pagoda' fore masts replacing the fore funnel; built-up main masts; much improved deck and underwater protection—armour weight increasing from 8,588 tons (8,725 tonnes) to 12,199 tons (12,394 tonnes); and hulls lengthened aft to 698ft (212·75m) overall.

New machinery was fitted: 4-shaft Kampon geared turbines and 6 oil-fired boilers provided 75,000 SHP at 24·7kt (45·7km/h) and increased radius to 11,000nm (20,350km) at 16kt (29·6km/h). Secondary and AA armament was now 14 x 6in (152mm), 8 x 5in (127mm) twin-mounted DP, 16 x 25mm AA (increased to 37 x 25mm by mid-1944), and 3 aircraft.

A proposal in late 1942 to convert the Fusos to battleship-carriers like *Ise* and *Hyuga* was abandoned after the catastrophic losses of naval aircraft in the Battle of the Philippine Sea, June 1944. Both *Fuso* and *Yamashiro* were sunk by gunfire and torpedoes during the last action in which battleship fired on battleship—in Surigao Strait, Leyte Gulf, on 25 October 1944.

(305mm) conning tower.
Armament: 12 x 12in (305mm); 18 x 5·1in (130mm) QF; 4 x 2·9in (75mm) QF; 4 x 3in (76mm) AA; 4 x 18in (457mm) torpedo tubes.
Performance: 21kt (38·85km/h); coal 3,000 tons (3,048 tonnes) max; oil 720 tons (732 tonnes); radius 1,000nm (1,850km) at 21kt (38·85km/h).
Crew: 1,252.

Authorized in 1911 for the Black Sea Fleet, to counter Turkey's Reshadieh class (see *Erin*) these battleships had heavier protection and secondary armament but less speed and endurance than the Baltic Fleet's Ganguts. Main armament layout was similar, but with the second triple turret trained ahead. A partly complete fourth ship with improved protection and machinery, *Imperator Nikolai I*, was scrapped following war damage in 1922-23.

Imperatrica Maria was sunk by a magazine explosion in Sevastopol on 20 October 1916. *Ekaterina II*,

renamed *Svobodnaya Rossia* in April 1917, was torpedoed and sunk at Novorossisk by the Bolshevik destroyer *Kertch* to prevent her capture by the Germans, 16 June 1918. *Alexander III* passed through German (as *Wolga*), British and White Russian (as *General Alexeiev*) hands in 1918-20, was interned by the French, and in 1924 was handed over to the Soviet Union, where she was scrapped in 1926-36.

LYON

1915 (designs only) *France*
Other ships in class: *Lille, Duquesne, Tourville*

Builder: Loire/Penhoët, St Nazaire.
Displacement: 27,500 tons (27,940 tonnes) normal, 29,600 tons (30,074 tonnes) full load.
Dimensions: 638ft 2in (194·5m) oa x 95ft 2in (29m) x 30ft 2in (9·2m).
Machinery: 2 turbines/2 sets Triple Expansion engines; 4 shafts; 44,000 SHP.

Armour: Not known.
Armament: 16 x 13·4in (340mm); 24 x 5·5in (139mm) QF; ? 40/47mm AA; 6 x 17·7in (450mm) torpedo tubes.
Performance: 23kt (42·55km/h).
Crew: Not known.

Design work for the Lyon class battleships, based on an enlargement of the Normandie class, was begun in mid-1913. After examination of the relative merits of a 27,500-ton (27,940 tonne) ship mounting 14 x 13·4in (340mm) guns or 8 x 15in (380mm) guns, a 28,500-ton to 29,000-ton (28,448-29,464 tonne) ship mounting 16 x 13·4in (340mm) or 10 x 15in (380mm) guns, and even a ship mounting 20 x 12in (305mm) guns, the design specified in the data table above was agreed upon. Construction was to have begun in 1915, but the outbreak of World War I halted the project at the design stage.

As in the Normandies, the main armament was to be carried in quadruple turrets, one forward, one between the funnels and a superfiring pair aft, all on the centre line. The 5·5in (139mm) secondary armament was, like that of the Normandies, to be in casemates fore and aft, so closely grouped that the guns would have been subject to blast effect both from their neighbours and from the main turrets. Armour details were never finalised.

ERSATZ YORCK

1916 (not completed) *Germany*
Other ships in class: *Ersatz
Gneisenau, Ersatz Scharnhorst*

Laid down: 1916.
Builder: Vulkan, Hamburg.
Displacement: 32,972 tons
(33,500 tonnes) normal; 37,402
tons (38,000 tonnes) full load.
Dimensions: 748ft 1in (228m) oa
x 99ft 9in (30·4m) x 30ft 6in (9·3m).
Machinery: 4 Marine turbines;
16 double-ended Marine boilers (8
coal, 8 oil); 4 shafts; 90,000 SHP.
Armour: 11·8in-3·9in (300-100mm)
belt; 9·8in (250mm) turrets; 11·8in
(300mm) barbettes; 5·9in (150mm)
casemates; 3·5in-1·2in (90-30mm)
deck; 13·8in (350mm) conning tower.
Armament: 8 x 15in (380mm);
12 x 5·9in (150mm) QF; 8 x 3·5in
(88mm) AA; 3 x 23·6in (600mm)
torpedo tubes.
Performance: 27·3kt (50·5km/h);
coal 3,937 tons (4,000 tonnes)
max; oil 689 tons (700 tonnes).
Crew: 1,227.

These replacement (*Ersatz*) battlecruisers—improved Mackensens,
with 15in (380mm) guns and
single funnels—were to take the
places of the war losses of the
same names. *Ersatz Gneisenau*
was laid down at the Germaniawerft
yard and *Ersatz Scharnhorst* by
Blohm & Voss; work continued into
1918, but the hulls were scrapped
after the end of the war.

INCOMPARABLE

1915 (project only) *UK*

Displacement: 46,000 tons
(46,736 tonnes) normal; 51,000
tons (51,816 tonnes) full load.
Dimensions: 1,010ft 7in (308m)
oa x 88ft 7in (27m) x 32ft 10in (10m).
Machinery: 4 geared turbines; 4
shafts; 180,000 SHP.
Armour: 11in (279mm) belt; 14in
(356mm) barbettes.
Armament: 6 x 20in (508mm);
15 x 4in (102mm) QF; 4 x 4in
(102mm) AA; 9 x 1·8in (46mm)
AA; 8 x 21in (533mm) torpedo tubes.
Performance: 35kt (64·75km/h);
oil 5,000 tons (5,080 tonnes).

An enthusiastic proponent of large,
fast but lightly-protected capital ships
with very heavy guns—a policy
leading at last to *Furious* (see
Courageous)— Admiral Lord Fisher
projected the battlecruiser
Incomparable in 1914. A design was
completed before his resignation as
First Sea Lord in May 1915.
  Incomparable was to mount 6
x 20in (508mm) guns (a type non-
existent in Britain) in twin turrets on
the centre line, two superfiring
forward and one aft, with a close-range
armament of 15 x 4in (102mm) in
triple turrets on the superstructure.
She might have proved an effective
shore bombardment unit but her
combat value was dubious: the fate of
powerful but poorly protected capital
ships at Jutland finally buried the
project.

Below: Projected *Ersatz Yorck*,
with eight 15in (381mm) guns.

Below: Fisher's planned *Incomparable*
was to have six 20in (508mm) guns.

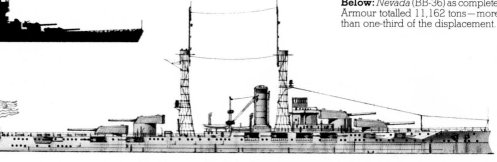

Below: *Nevada* (BB-36) as completed
Armour totalled 11,162 tons—more
than one-third of the displacement.

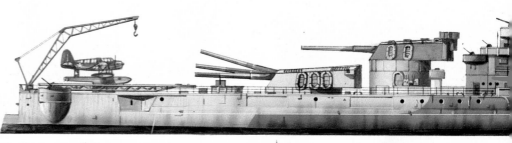

Below: Projected *Ersatz Monarch* was
to have had ten 14in (356mm) guns in
twin turrets superfiring over triples.

FRANCESCO CARRACIOLO

1915 (not completed) *Italy*
Other ships in class: *Cristoforo Colombo, Marcantonio Colanna, Francesco Morosini*

Laid down: 12 October 1914.
Launched: 12 May 1920.
Builder: Castellammare Navy Yard.
Displacement: 32,800 tons (33,325 tonnes) normal; 34,000 tons (34,544 tonnes) full load.
Dimensions: 695ft 11in (212.1m) oa x 97ft 1in (29.6m) x 31ft 2in (9.5m) max.
Machinery: 4 Parsons geared turbines; 20 Yarrow boilers; 4 shafts; 70,000 SHP normal draught, 105,000 SHP forced draught.
Armour: 11.8in-5.9in (300-150mm)

Below: *Francesco Carraciolo*, if completed, was to have carried eight 15in (381mm) guns. Note the unique wide spacing of the main armament, designed to overcome weight-spreading problems.

belt; 15.7in (400mm) turrets; 11.8in (300mm) barbettes; 5.9in (150mm) casemates; 1.4in-1.2in (35-30mm) deck; 13.4in (340mm) conning tower.
Armament: 8 x 15in (381mm); 12 x 6in (152mm); 12 x 40mm AA.
Performance: 25kt (46.25km/h) normal draught, 28kt (51.8km/h) forced draught; oil 3,500 tons (3,556 tonnes) max; radius 8,000nm (14,800km) at 10kt (18.5km/h).
Crew: Not known.

Eng-Gen Ferrati's design for a 'super-dreadnought' was chosen in 1913 by the Italian Admiralty over its original decision for a 29,000-ton (29,464 tonne) ship with 9 x 15in (381mm) and 20 x 6in (152mm) guns. Four Caracciolos were ordered in April 1914, when it was intended that they should have a secondary armament of 18 x 6in (152mm) QF, with 24 x 3in (76mm) QF.

In the final designed form, the Caracciolos basically resembled the British Queen Elizabeth class. Flush-decked, they carried 8 x 15in (381mm) Armstrong-designed guns (later allocated to monitors) in twin centre-line turrets, two fore and two aft, with a well-sited 6in (152mm) battery.

Work ceased early in 1916 and three of the class were dismantled. Work on *Francesco Caracciolo* began again late in 1919, but when plans to complete her as an aircraft carrier were shelved she was sold to a commercial line for completion as a high-speed passenger-cargo ship. Financial considerations killed this plan and the hull was scrapped in 1921.

NEVADA (BB-36)

1916 *USA*
Other ships in class: *Oklahoma* (BB-37)

Laid down: 4 November 1912.
Launched: 11 July 1914.
Builder: Fore River Company, Quincy, Massachusetts.
Displacement: 27,500 tons (27,940 tonnes) normal; 28,900 tons (29,362 tonnes) full load.
Dimensions: 583ft (177.7m) oa x 95ft 3in (29.03m) x 31ft (9.45m) max.
Machinery: 2 Curtis geared turbines, plus cruising turbines; 12 Yarrow boilers; 2 shafts; 26,500 SHP.
Armour: 13.5in-8in (343-203mm) belt; 18in-9in (457-229mm) triple turrets; 16in-9in (406-229mm) twin turrets; 13.5in (343mm) barbettes; 3in-2in (76-51mm) decks; 16in (406mm) conning tower.
Armament: 10 x 14in (356mm); 21 x 5in (127mm) QF; 2 x 21in (533mm) torpedo tubes.
Performance: 20.5kt (37.9km/h); oil 2,037 tons (2,070 tonnes) max; radius 10,000nm (18,500km) at 10kt (18.5km/h).
Crew: 1,049.

Firing trials against the *San Marcos* (ex-battleship *Texas*, 1895) in 1911-12 showed that medium and light armour was of no value against large-calibre armour-piercing shells. The Nevadas were designed accordingly as the first battleships armoured on the 'all-or-nothing' system — adopted by other navies after World War I — in which the thickest possible armour was applied to vital areas of the vessel's hull and the remainder left unprotected.

A 13.5in (343mm) belt in a single strake ran for c400ft (121.9m) amidships and extended 9ft (2.74m) above and 8ft 6in (2.59m) below the waterline. It was closed off fore and aft by 13.5in (343mm) transverse bulkheads to form a citadel over magazines and machinery. Heavy armour also protected turrets, barbettes and funnel base, but, apart from an 8in (203mm) strake over the steering machinery aft, only the armoured decks protected the ends. The secondary armament was unprotected.

Ten 14in (356mm) guns were in triple turrets (the first in US battleships) with superfiring twin turrets, fore and aft. These were the first oil-burning US battleships (reciprocating machinery was fitted in *Oklahoma*) and had single funnels. During extensive modernization in 1927-29, both were reboilered with six Bureau-Express units and *Nevada* was given 31,300 SHP geared turbines taken from the stricken *North Dakota* (BB-29). Horizontal protection was improved, AA armament augmented and aircraft catapults fitted atop the third turrets.

Oklahoma was sunk (415 killed) by Japanese aerial torpedoes at Pearl Harbor, 7 December 1941; she was later raised but never repaired. *Nevada*, badly damaged in the attack, was reconstructed and returned to action, serving off Normandy and at Iwo Jima and Okinawa, where her final secondary/ AA armament was 16 x 5in (127mm) DP, 40 x 40mm AA and 36 x 20mm AA. Surviving the Bikini Atoll atom bomb tests, July 1946, she was finally sunk as a target off the island of Hawaii on 31 July 1948.

Below: Modernised *Nevada*, 1944
The guns in triple turrets were in a single sleeve and fired as one unit. The guns in the 'Y' turret are shown at different elevations to display the care that was taken over the camouflage scheme. The floatplane is a Vought OS2U Kingfisher.

ERSATZ MONARCH

1916 (designs only) *Austria-Hungary*
Other ships in class: *Ersatz Wien, Ersatz Budapest, Ersatz Habsburg*

Builder: Stabilmento Tecnico Triestino (for *Ersatz Monarch*; builders for other ships in class were not announced).
Displacement: 24,605 tons (24,999 tonnes) normal.
Dimensions: 574ft 10in (175.2m) oa x 93ft 6in (28.5m) x 27ft 7in (8.4m).

Machinery: 2 turbines; 15 boilers (9 coal, 6 oil); 4 shafts; 31,000 SHP.
Armour: 12.2in-5.5in (310-140mm) belt; 9.8in (250mm) turrets; 12.6in (320mm) barbettes; 5.9in (150mm) casemates; 1.4in (36mm) decks; 12.6in (320mm) conning tower.
Armament: 10 x 14in (355mm); 18 x 5.9in (150mm) QF; 20 x 3.6in (90mm) QF; 6 x 21in (533mm) torpedo tubes.
Performance: 21kt (38.85km/h); coal 1,425 tons (1,448 tonnes) max; oil 1,425 tons (1,448 tonnes) max;

radius c5,000nm (9,250km) at 10kt (18.5km/h).
Crew: Not known.

Needed to preserve the capabilities of Austro-Hungarian shipyards as well as to counter Italy's 12in (305mm) gunned Cavours and Dorias, the Ersatz Monarchs were designed along the lines of the Viribus Unitis class, but with a raised forecastle deck. Ten specially designed 14in (355mm) guns (some of which were later used as artillery

ashore) were to be carried in centre-line turrets, twin turrets super-firing over triple turrets forward and aft. The secondary armament was to have been concentrated around the bridge and funnels.

Contracts were delayed by the unwieldy bureaucracy of the Austro-Hungarian Empire and work on the first ship, due to begin at Trieste on 8 August 1914, was postponed on the outbreak of World War I. All plans for the class were subsequently abandoned.

BAYERN

1916 *Germany*
Other ships in class: *Baden, Württemberg, Sachsen*

Laid down: 20 September 1913.
Launched: 18 February 1915.
Builder: Howaldtswerke, Kiel.
Displacement: 28,050 tons
(28,500 tonnes) normal; 31,691
tons (32,200 tonnes) full load.
Dimensions: 598ft 5in (182·4m)
oa x 99ft 1in (30·2m) x 27ft
10½in (8·5m) max.
Machinery: 3 Schichau turbines;
14 Marine boilers; 3 shafts; 52,000
SHP.
Armour: 13·8in-1·2in (350-30mm)
belt; 9·8in-6·7in (250-170mm)
upper belt; 4·7in-1·2in (120-30mm)
decks; 13·8in (350mm) barbettes;
13·8in-4·7in (350-120mm) turrets;
17·5in (445mm) conning tower.

Armament: 8 x 15in (380mm); 16
x 5·9in (150mm); 8 x 3·5in
(88mm); 5 x 23·6in (600mm)
torpedo tubes.
Performance: 22·25kt (41·2km/h);
radius 7,800nm (14,500km) at
10kt (18·5km/h); coal 3,346 tons
(3,400 tonnes); oil 610 tons (620
tonnes).
Crew: 1,171.

The four ships of the Bayern class
were the last German battleships
laid down before World War I,
and marked an overall shift in
German capital ship design
philosophy: for the first time the
Germans opted for gun-power
on a par with that of British ships
(Queen Elizabeth and Revenge
classes) together with an equality
of armour, rather than inferior-calibre
main armament and superior
protection. The key to this altera-

tion was the new Krupp 15in
(380mm) gun, of which trials
began in 1914. This weapon fired a
1,653lb (750kg) shell with a
muzzle velocity of 2,297ft (700m)
per second to a range of 22,200
yards (20,300m) at the maximum
16° elevation possible with
German turrets; even so, comparison with the performance of the
British gun (range 23,400 yards,
21,397m; muzzle velocity 2,450ft,
747m, per second) reveals the
overall inferiority of the German
weapon, which also fired a much
lighter shell.
    The hull design of *Bayern* was
based on that of the König class,
with increases in length and
beam to allow greater displacement.
Greater power was introduced,
and the main armament was
carried in only four centre-line
turrets, the 'Q' position being

Left: View of the aft 15in (380mm)
guns and structure of *Baden*. The
davits carried on the searchlight
platforms were used to lower the
lights before going into action.

Below: *Sachsen* had 78ft 9in (24m)
tall, fully-jacketed funnels as
compared to the 65ft 7in (20m) tall
funnels fitted on her sister-ships.

Right: This remarkable photograph,
taken at Scapa Flow at 1400 hours
on 21 June 1919, shows the interned
Bayern sinking by the stern after
being scuttled by her crew. She was
raised from 125ft (38m) of water in
1934 and subsequently scrapped.

deleted and the eight guns being
located in twin superfiring turrets
before and abaft the superstructure. Another departure for a
German capital ship was the use
of a heavy tripod rather than a pole
foremast to support the fire-control
position. *Bayern's* useful secondary
armament was in the standard
casemate positions, eight on each
beam at upper-deck level but well
spaced out in four pairs for better
fire control and immunity from a
single disabling hit.
    After World War I, the British
were able to compare *Baden* (built
by Schichau at Danzig and
completed in October 1916) with
Revenge, a contemporary vessel
with much the same armament,
protection and performance. The
decision came down decidedly in
favour of the British battleship.
The main points found were the
following: *Baden* was a very stiff
vessel in short seas, and thus a
good gun platform, but she

Below: *Bayern* (now without torpedo
nets) while serving in the Baltic in
1917. Note the heavy tripod mast,
innovatory in a German capital ship,
and the well-spaced casemates at
upper-deck level for secondary
armament.

would have an alarming roll in the longer seas found in open waters; underwater protection was good, thanks to extensive compartmentation resulting from the use of four longitudinal bulkheads, but the piercing of transverse bulkheads by doors, pipes, tubes, wires and ventilation trunks reduced much of this advantage, and made vital the

Germans' extensive counterflooding provisions; the Germans had concentrated protection against underwater damage and flat-trajectory shellfire, while British experience had shown that even in the North Sea ranges tended to be sufficiently great for *Revenge*'s superior horizontal armour to become decisive; the German ship burned a mixture of coal and oil (11 aftermost) and oil only (3 foremost); and, perhaps most important of all, the scantlings of the German ship were decidedly inferior to those of the British battleship, to the extent that her basic structural strength must have been seriously in doubt.

Bayern joined the High Seas Fleet just after Jutland, and surrendered in November 1918, being scuttled at Scapa Flow in June 1919. *Baden* differed from her sister in having a larger bridge, and was flagship of the High Seas Fleet from March 1917. She was beached before sinking at Scapa Flow, but salved for comparative evaluation and then used as a gunnery target until being sunk on 6 August 1921. Two other units, *Sachsen* and *Württemberg*, were launched in November 1916 and June 1917, but neither was completed.

PENNSYLVANIA (BB-38)

1915 *USA*
Other ships in class: *Arizona* (BB-39)

Laid down: 27 October 1913.
Launched: 16 March 1915.
Builder: Newport News.
Displacement: 31,400 tons (31,902 tonnes) normal; 33,000 tons (33,528 tonnes) full load.
Dimensions: 608ft (185.3m) oa x 97ft (29.57m) x 28ft 9in (8.76m) mean.
Machinery: 4 Curtis turbines, plus cruising turbines; 12 Babcock & Wilcox boilers; 4 shafts; 31,500 SHP.
Armour: 14in-8in (356-203mm) belt; 14in (356mm) bulkheads; 4in-1.5in (102-38mm) decks; 14in (356mm) barbettes; 18in-5in (457-127mm) turrets; 16in (406mm) conning tower.
Armament: 12 x 14in (356mm); 22 x 5in (127mm); 2 x 21in (533mm) torpedo tubes.
Performance: 21kt (38.9km/h); oil 2,322 tons (2,359 tonnes).
Crew: 915.

Whereas the preceding Nevada class ships had featured a primary armament of 10 x 14in (356mm) guns in two triple and two twin turrets, the two units of the Pennsylvania class went one better to carry a complete set of four triple turrets. This makes an interesting comparison with the contemporary Japanese Fuso class, which carried the same primary armament in six twin turrets, but was consequently some 65ft (19.8m) longer and needed an extra 15,000 SHP for 2kt (3.7km/h) more speed on the same displacement.
The two ships were rebuilt between 1928 and 1931: the secondary armament was changed to 12 x 5in (127mm) guns, while the AA battery became 8 x 5in (127mm) guns; bulges were added, increasing beam to 106ft 3in (32.4m), and normal displacement rose to 32,100 tons (32,614 tonnes). In 1940 further modernisaton removed two secondary battery 5in (127mm) guns, and added four 5in (127mm) AA guns. *Arizona*, built by New York Navy Yard and engined with Parsons turbines, was lost at Pearl Harbor on 7 December 1941; *Pennsylvania* was severely damaged, but was repaired with a dual-purpose secondary battery of 16 x 5in (127mm) guns in twin turrets and 82 smaller AA. She was used for A-bomb tests at Bikini in 1946 before being scuttled in 1948.

RENOWN

1916 *UK*
Other ships in class: *Repulse*

Laid down: 25 January 1915.
Launched: 4 March 1916.
Builder: Fairfield, Glasgow.
Displacement: 27,947 tons (28,394 tonnes) normal; 32,727 tons (33,250 tonnes) full load.
Dimensions: 794ft (242m) oa x 90ft (27.4m) x 25ft 8½in (7.82m) mean.
Machinery: 2 Brown-Curtis turbines; 42 Babcock & Wilcox boilers; 4 shafts; 126,300 SHP.
Armour: 6in-3in (152-76mm) belt; 1.5in (38mm) upper belt; 4in-3in (102-76mm) bulkheads; 3.5in-0.75in (89-19mm) decks; 7in-4in (178-102mm) barbettes; 11in-7in (279-178mm) turrets; 10in (254mm) conning tower.
Armament: 6 x 15in (381mm); 17 x 4in (102mm); 2 x 3in (76mm)

Above: *Pennsylvania* (BB-38) as a fire support ship in World War II. By now the cage masts have been replaced by a forward tripod mast and after pole mast; the funnel has been raised; the bridge superstructure altered, and better gunnery control fitted.

AA; 4 x 3pdr; 2 x 21in (533mm) torpedo tubes.
Performance: 32.7kt (60.6km/h); oil 4,243 tons (4,311 tonnes).
Crew: 967.

The success of the first-generation battlecruisers *Inflexible* and *Invincible* in the Battle of the Falkland Islands (December 1914) prompted Admiral Fisher to order two very fast battlecruisers armed with 15in (381mm) guns. The design was already under way for a pair of improved Revenge class battleships, and this was hurriedly recast in the form of Fisher's favourite fast battlecruiser concept: very high speed, crushing fire-power, and modest protection.
The construction of both ships (*Repulse* being built by John Brown & Co., and completed in August 1916) moved ahead with remarkable speed. The secondary armament was unusual in its return to 4in (102mm) calibre at the insistence of Fisher, and in its arrangement in triple units. This latter was a far-sighted but unfortunate move, for the five triple units (one on each of the bridge wings, and three on the after super-structure) offered strong tactical advantages in theory, but were a hindrance in actuality because of their individual breeches, 32-man crews and low rate of fire. The armour was quite inadequate, and on the ships' arrival with the Grand Fleet efforts were made to strengthen at least the horizontal protection in the light of experience at Jutland three months earlier. The one good feature, however, was the inclusion of integral bulges as protection against torpedoes.
Both ships were extensively modernized between the World Wars, especially in armour (an extra 4in, 102mm, or 3in, 76mm, being added over the magazines, boilers, engine rooms, etc) and armament (a secondary battery of 10 twin 4.5in, 114mm, dual-purpose guns in *Renown*'s more extensive reconstruction. *Repulse* was lost to Japanese air attack on 10 December 1941 while en route to attack an enemy force off Kota Bharu with the battleship *Prince of Wales*, but *Renown* survived arduous duties in many theatres to be scrapped in 1948.

NORMANDIE

1916 (not completed) *France*
Other ships in class: *Béarn, Flandre, Gascogne, Languedoc*

Laid down: 18 April 1913.
Launched: 19 October 1914.

Below: *Renown* in July 1942. AA armament was much augmented during the 1930s; additional armour was fitted over the magazine and machinery, and torpedo protection improved.

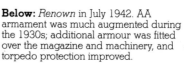

Builder: Ateliers et Chantiers de la Loire, St Nazaire.
Displacement: 24,833 tons (25,230 tonnes) normal.
Dimensions: 577ft 8½in (176.4m) oa x 88ft 5in (27m) x 28ft 6in (8.7m)
Machinery: 2 Parsons turbines plus 2 Vertical Triple Expansion engines; 21 Guyot du Temple boilers; 4 shafts; 40,000 SHP.
Armour: 11.8in-5.1in (300-130mm) belt; 2.75in-2in (70-50mm) decks; 11.2in (285mm) barbettes; 13.4in-9.8in (340-250mm) turrets.
Armament: 12 x 13.4in (340mm); 24 x 5.5in (139mm); 4 x 47mm; 6 x 17.7in (450mm) torpedo tubes.
Performance: 21kt (38.9km/h).
Crew: Not known.

In response to increased gun calibres in other countries, France in 1912 started work on four successors to the Bretagne class which would carry 12 x 13.4in (340mm) guns. To keep length down it was decided to fit these in three quadruple turrets, which were designed in the UK: each turret contained what was in effect two twin mounts on a single barbette. To provide cruising economy, and as a safeguard against the somewhat disappointing performance of French-built turbines, reciprocating machinery was coupled to the outer shafts.
Work on all five vessels was halted in 1915: *Béarn* was eventually completed as an aircraft carrier, and the other four were scrapped incomplete in 1924 and 1925.

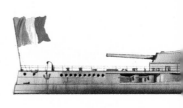

Below: *Normandie* as she would have appeared if completed. Work stopped in 1915, when materiel was diverted to meet the needs of the French Army.

Below: *Royal Sovereign* in 1942. The Revenge class battleships, less extensively modernized that the earlier Queen Elizabeths, were used mainly as escorts in World War II.

Below: *Pennsylvania* (BB-38) in 1915. Note the four triple turrets, with gun barrels set close together. Eight 5in (127mm) guns at bow and stern were removed in 1917-18.

REVENGE

1916 UK
Other ships in class: *Royal Oak, Royal Sovereign, Resolution, Ramillies*

Laid down: 22 December 1913.
Launched: 29 May 1915.
Builder: Vickers, Barrow.
Displacement: 28,000 tons (28,448 tonnes) normal; 31,200 tons (31,699 tonnes) deep load.
Dimensions: 624ft 3in (190·27m) oa x 88ft 6in (26·97m) x 28ft 7in (8·71m) mean.
Machinery: 4 Parsons turbines, plus cruising turbines; 18 Babcock & Wilcox boilers; 4 shafts; 42,650 SHP.
Armour: 13in-4in (330-102mm) belt; 6in (152mm) upper belt; 6in-4in (152-102mm) bulkheads; 4in-1in (102-25mm) decks; 10in-4in (254-102mm) barbettes; 13in-4·5in (330-114mm) turrets; 6in (152mm) battery; 11in (279mm) conning tower.
Armament: 8 x 15in (381mm); 14 x 6in (152mm); 2 x 3in (76mm) AA; 4 x 3pdr; 4 x 21in (533mm) torpedo tubes.
Performance: 22kt (40·8km/h); oil 3,400 tons (3,454 tonnes); coal 140 tons (142 tonnes).
Crew: 997.

The ultimate British battleships before World War I, the Revenge class was a version of the Iron Duke class with 15in (381mm)

guns and considerably lower meta-centric height to improve steadiness, and hence gunnery in any sort of sea. The concomitant reduction in stability was taken into account by raising the height of the protected freeboard (the armour deck being elevated to main-deck level) so that the ship would not lose too much protection in the event of flooding after damage along the waterline.

Particular emphasis was placed on underwater protection: between the 1·5in (38mm) bulkheads forward of 'A' turret and aft of 'Y' turret there was a pair of 1·5in-1in (38-25mm) longitudinal bulkheads running vertically downwards from the middle deck to the double bottom. Across the angle formed by the middle deck and the bulkhead, and connecting the 2in (51mm) main deck with the lower edge of the 13in (330mm) main belt, was the 2in (51mm) downward slope of the main deck to channel waterline blast upwards rather than inwards. Protection against torpedoes was taken a step further in another of the Revenge class, for *Ramillies* introduced the anti-torpedo bulge, which increased beam to 101ft 5in (30·91m) and reduced speed by only 0·33kt (0·61km/h). During the 1920s a less shallow bulge was developed, this increasing beam by another 1ft 1in (0·33m), and such bulges were retrofitted to some ships.

Though the Queen Elizabeth class had been designed exclusively for oil-burning, fears that war would result in shortages led to the Revenges' initial planning with coal-fired boilers. But when Admiral Fisher was reappointed First Sea Lord in 1914 he immediately ordered the completion of the ships as oil-burners, which permitted a 2kt (3·7km/h) increase in speed as well as much easier bunkering.

The Revenges were regarded as inferior to the similarly armed Queen Elizabeth class units by virtue of their considerably slower speed. Nevertheless, the 'R's were more robust ships, and their secondary armament was better disposed, being moved farther aft along the main deck to keep them out of the speed wave that had affected the Queen Elizabeth's guns. They were not greatly modernized after World War I, though some AA guns were provided, and were used mainly for escort duties in World War II. *Revenge* was scrapped in 1948; *Royal Oak*, built by Devonport Dockyard and completed in May 1916, was sunk by U-boat attack on 14 October 1939; *Royal Sovereign* was built by Portsmouth Dockyard and completed in May 1916, and became the Russian *Archangelsk* between 1944 and 1949, when she was scrapped; *Resolution* was completed in December 1916 after building at Palmers, and was scrapped in 1948; and *Ramillies* was built by Beardmore for completion in 1917, and was scrapped in 1948.

Above: *Béarn* in 1945. She was completed as an aircraft carrier in 1926—the only Normandie not to have been scrapped.

COURAGEOUS

1917 *UK*
Other ships in class: *Glorious,
Furious*

Laid down: May 1915.
Launched: 5 February 1916.
Builder: Armstrong, Elswick.
Displacement: 19,320 tons
(19,629 tonnes) load; 22,960 tons
(23,327 tonnes) full load.
Dimensions: 786ft (239·57m) oa x
81ft (24·7m) x 22ft 3in (6·78m)
mean.
Machinery: 4 Parsons geared
turbines; 18 Yarrow boilers; 4
shafts; 93,780 SHP.
Armour: 3in-2in (76-51mm) belt;
3in-1in (76-25mm) bulkheads;
3in-1in (76-25mm) decks; 13in-4·5in
(330-114mm) turrets; 10in
(254mm) conning tower.
Armament: 4 x 15in (381mm);
18 x 4in (102mm); 2 x 3in (76mm)
AA; 2 x 21in (533mm) torpedo
tubes.

Performance: 32kt (59·3km/h);
oil 3,160 tons (3,211 tonnes).
Crew: 842.

Perhaps the most remarkable
'capital' ships ever built, *Courageous* and *Glorious*, together with
their half-sister *Furious*, represented the ultimate physical
expression of Fisher's obsession
with fire-power and speed. The
particular context for these three
unique vessels was the admiral's
plan, formulated as far back as
1909, for landings in the Baltic, in
co-operation with Russian forces,
in the event of war with Germany:
for such operations ships with large
guns but very shallow draught
would be needed, so armour
protection was to be vestigial at
best. Thus though these vessels
have since been designated
battlecruisers, it is more accurate to
use Fisher's own description of large
light cruisers. Designed by S.V.
Goodall, the Courageous class was

based on armament and machinery:
the armament was already in hand, in
the form of the 15in (381mm) guns
and turrets intended for three
cancelled ships of the Revenge class.
The plan for machinery was scaled up
from light cruiser practice, with two
set of the geared turbines produced
for the Cambrian class of light
cruiser, but with 18 rather than eight
boilers. These were a small-tube
variety, and they proved very
successful in these large vessels.

The main armament was
disposed in twin turrets fore and aft,
while the secondary guns were
disposed in six triple mountings
pioneered unsuccessfully in the
Renown class. Armour was on light
cruiser lines, and hopelessly
inadequate for such large and
expensive vessels, which could
not be used to any real purpose by
the Grand Fleet. *Glorious* was
built by Harland and Wolff, and
was completed in January 1917.
Both ships were attached to

gunnery schools, at Portsmouth
and Devonport, after World War I,
and were converted into aircraft
carriers in the late 1920s.
Courageous was lost to U-boat
attack on 17 September 1939, and
Glorious to gunfire from the
German battlecruisers *Scharnhorst*
and *Gneisenau* on 8 June 1940.

Furious, built by Armstrong
Whitworth at Elswick and
completed in July 1917, was even
odder than her half-sisters.
Designed to have slightly greater
beam (88ft, 26·9m, instead of 81ft,
24·7m), she was to conform with
Fisher's ideal of speed and
fire-power while also testing in
operational service two new types
of gun. These were the 18in/40
(457mm/40) Mk I and the
5·5in/50 (140mm/50) Mk I
weapons, of which two and eleven
were to be mounted. The 18in
(457mm) gun was then the world's
largest piece of naval armament,
and weighed a prodigious 150
tons (152·4 tonnes). The difference
in the capabilities of this weapon
and the 15in (381mm) Mk I,
which weighed just under half as
much, is exemplified by the shell
weights of the two pieces: 1,920lb
(871kg) for the 15in (381mm) and
3,600lb (1,633kg) for the 18in
(457mm) gun, one of which was
to be mounted in each of the two
turrets carried by the *Furious*.
These turrets were to be mounted

Left: Battlecruiser-carrier hybrid
Furious while fitting out, July 1917.
Note single 18in (457mm) gun in
turret aft; hangar and flying-off
platform forward.

Right: *Furious* as a flush-deck
aircraft carrier after rebuilding in
1921-25. In 1927, palisades were
added to reduce the risk of losing
aircraft during landing operations
and by the outbreak of World War II
a small island has been fitted.

Below: Starboard elevation of
Courageous as she appeared towards
the end of World War I, with flying-off
platforms atop both main turrets.
Note Sopwith 1½-Strutter aircraft
forward, atop 'A' turret.

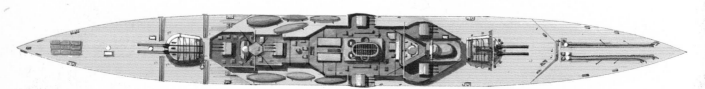

on barbettes of the same diameter as those for the 15in (381mm) turret, so that in the event of the failure of the 18in (457mm) gun, smaller turrets could be substituted.

Furious was designed with 6 x 21in (533mm) torpedo tubes (two submerged and four above water) but was completed with an above-water fit of four triple sets aft and one twin set forward on each beam. (The other two ships had been completed with extra deck tubes: six twin sets, two on each side of the after turret, and one on each side abreast the mainmast).

Before completion Furious was converted into a hybrid aircraft carrier, with a flight deck forward in place of the fore turret. She later had a landing-on deck fitted in place of the after turret, and finally was rebuilt as a flush-deck aircraft carrier with a small island to starboard. She was scrapped in 1948.

Below: Original plan for *Furious.*

Below: *Furious* in 1918.

Below: *Furious* in August 1942.

Above: The changing shape of *Furious,* 1918-42. (Top) As she would have appeared if completed to the original design, with two single 18in (457mm) turrets. (Middle) As an aircraft carrier in 1918, with flight decks before and abaft the funnel and bridgework. (Bottom) The veteran carrier in August 1942 while serving in the Mediterranean.

Above: *Courageous* in 1938. She was converted to an aircraft carrier in 1924-28, with an original complement of 48 aircraft. Both her and *Glorious'* 15in (381mm) were later used aboard *Vanguard.*

221

MACKENSEN

1917 (not completed) *Germany*
Other ships in class: *Graf Spee,
Ersatz Freya (Prinz Eitel Friedrich),
Ersatz Friedrich Carl (Fürst
Bismarck)*

Laid down: 30 January 1915.
Launched: 21 April 1917.
Builder: Blohm & Voss, Hamburg.
Displacement: 30,510 tons
(30,998 tonnes) normal; 34,742
tons (35,298 tonnes) full load.
Dimensions: 734ft 11in (224m) oa
x 99ft 9in (30·4m) x 30ft 6in
(9·3m) max.
Machinery: 4 Marine turbines;
24 single-ended coal-fired Marine
boilers, 8 double-ended oil-fired
Marine boilers; 4 shafts; 90,000
SHP.

Armour: 11·8in-3·9in (300-100mm)
belt; 12·6in (320mm) turrets;
11·4in (290mm) barbettes; 4·7in-
0·8in (120-20mm) decks; 13·8in
(350mm) conning tower.
Armament: 8 x 13·75in (350mm);
14 x 5·9in (150mm); 8 x 3·5in
(88mm) AA; 5 x 23·6in (600mm)
torpedo tubes.
Performance: 27kt (49·95km/h);
coal 3,937 tons (4,000 tonnes)
max; oil 1,968 tons (2,000 tonnes)
max; radius 5,500nm (10,175km)
at 14kt (25·9km/h).
Crew: 1,186.

Although potentially Germany's
most successful designs of the
period, these battlecruisers were
laid down at a time when increasing
matériel shortage made the likelihood of their completion for war

service remote. They were basically
improved Derfflingers, with the
same main armament layout, and
were to have mounted specially
designed 13·75in (350mm), 50-cal
guns.
Since construction material and
resources were then more
urgently required for U-boats, work
on the class ended in 1917 after
the launching of *Mackensen* and
Graf Spee. Post-war plans to
convert the first three ships to
diesel-powered 10kt (18·5km/h)
tankers of 18,500 tons (18,796
tonnes) dead weight were abandoned for lack of funds and all
were scrapped in 1920-24. The
Mackensen/Ersatz Yorck designs,
however, strongly influenced that
of the *Scharnhorst* and *Gneisenau*
of World War II.

Below: Laid down in 1915, but not
completed because of wartime
materiel shortages, the Mackensens
were basically improved Derfflingers
and were to have carried eight
13.75in (350mm) guns.

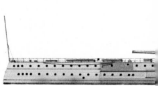

Above: *New Mexico* (BB-40) early in
her career, with typical cage masts.

ISE

1917 *Japan*
Other ships in class: *Hyuga*

Laid down: 10 May 1915.
Launched: 12 November 1916.
Builder: Kawasaki, Kobe.
Displacement: 29,980 tons (30,460
tonnes) normal; 32,063 tons (32,576
tonnes) full load.
Dimensions: 683ft (208·2m) oa x
94ft (28·65m) x 29ft 1in (8·86m) max.
Machinery: 4 Brown-Curtis turbines;
24 Kansai mixed-firing boilers; 4
shafts; 45,000 SHP.
Armour: 12in-3in (305-76mm) belt;
12in-8in (305-203mm) turrets; 12in
(305mm) barbettes; 6in (152mm)
casemates; 2in-1·25in (51-32mm)
deck; 12in-6in (305-152mm) conning
tower.
Armament: 12 x 14in (356mm); 20
x 5·5in (140mm) QF; 4 x 3·1in
(80mm) AA; 6 x 21in (533mm)
torpedo tubes.
Performance: 23kt (42·55km/h);
coal 4,607 tons (4,681 tonnes) max;
oil 1,411 tons (1,434 tonnes) max;
radius 9,680nm (17,908km) at 14kt
(25·9km/h).
Crew: 1,360.

Projected as modified Fusos, the
Hyugas had so many improvements
as to constitute a separate class. The
major change was in main armament
layout: the two central turrets were in
superfiring configuration amidships,
abaft the second and shorter of the
two funnels. A new 5·5in (140mm)
gun of indigenous design was fitted,
the casemates being farther forward
than in the Fusos and generally
well-sited—although the two foremost
guns, beneath the forecastle, could
not be worked in bad weather.
Armour and speed were equal to the

Fusos but, as in most Japanese
warships, habitability was not good.
Between the World Wars the
Hyugas were extensively modernized.
A 'pagoda' foremast (increased in
size during major reconstruction in
1934-37) was fitted in 1926-28, when
2 x 5·5in (140mm) were removed and
two floatplanes with a handling
derrick were shipped.
By 1937 the ships had been
lengthened aft by 25ft 1in (7·64m).
Ise's full load displacement was now
40,169 tons (40,812 tonnes). New
machinery was fitted: 4-shaft Kampon
geared turbines and 8 Kampon
oil-fired boilers provided 80,825
SHP at 25·3kt (46·8km/h) and gave a
radius of *c*12,500nm (23,125km) at
16kt (29·6km/h). Armour over
machinery and magazines was
increased to a maximum 4·7in
(120mm) and torpedo bulges were
fitted. Torpedo tubes and 2 x 5·5in
(140mm) QF were removed and 8 x
5in (127mm) DP and 20 x 25mm AA
were added.
After Japan's loss of aircraft
carriers at Midway, June 1942, *Ise*
and *Hyuga* were converted to hybrid
battleship-carriers. The two after
turrets gave way to a large hangar
intended to house 22 seaplane-
bombers or conventional dive-
bombers which would be catapult-
launched from the hangar's top.
Armament was finally 8 x 14in
(356mm), 16 x 5in (127mm) DP, 104
x 25mm AA and 6 x 4·7in (120mm)
30-barrelled AA rocket guns.
Although used as 'decoy' carriers
at Leyte Gulf, October 1944, the
Hyugas never operated aircraft in
action, since neither planes nor pilots
were available. Confined to Kure
from early 1945, both were sunk by
US carrier aircraft in July and raised
and scrapped after 1946.

Below: *Ise* as completed, 1917. Note
superfiring arrangement of 14in
(356mm) turrets amidships, a major
change from the preceding Fuso class.

Below: *Ise* in late 1943, after her
conversion to a battleship-carrier
'hybrid'. A hangar for 22 aircraft
replaces the after turrets.

NEW MEXICO (BB-40)

1918 USA
Other ships in class: *Mississippi*
(BB-41), *Idaho* (BB-42)

Laid down: 14 October 1915.
Launched: 23 April 1917.
Builder: New York Navy Yard.
Displacement: 32,000 tons
(32,512 tonnes) normal; 33,500
tons (34,036 tonnes) full load.
Dimensions: 624ft (190·2m) oa x
97ft 5in (29·69m) x 34ft (10·36m)
max.
Machinery: 2 General Electric
turbines/electric motors; 9
Babcock boilers; 4 shafts; 27,500
SHP.
Armour: 14in-8in (356-203mm)
belt; 18in-9in (457-229mm) turrets;
13·5in (343mm) barbettes; 6in-3in
(152-76mm) decks; 16in (406mm)
conning tower.
Armament: 12 x 14in (356mm);
14 x 5in (127mm) QF; 4 x 3in
(76mm) AA; 2 x 21in (533mm)
torpedo tubes.
Performance: 21kt (38·85km/h);
oil 3,277 tons (3,329 tonnes) max;
radius 10,000nm (18,500km) at
10kt (18·5km/h).
Crew: 1,084.

Although based on the Pennsylvanias, the New Mexicos featured a
hull form new to the US Navy, with
clipper bow, bulbous forefoot and
increased internal compartmentation.
The secondary batteries were raised
by one deck—the vulnerable hull
embrasures originally provided
being plated over—and the
12 x 14in (356mm), 50-cal guns in
triple turrets fore and aft were mounted in separate sleeves that, for the
first time in US battleships, allowed
individual elevation of heavy guns.

New Mexico (ex-*California*) was
the first battleship to have turbo-
electric drive: two steam turbines
were directly coupled to two gener-
ators which drove electric motors
directly coupled to the four shafts.
Although turbo-electric drive was
bulky, heavy and potentially
dangerous in wet conditions, it
proved economical at all speeds and
gave better manoeuvrability by
simplifying the changeover from
ahead to astern. Nevertheless, during
extensive reconstruction in 1931-33,
New Mexico, like her sisters, was
refitted with 40,000 SHP Westinghouse geared turbines for an increase
in speed of *c*0·75kt (1·4km/h).

During reconstruction, torpedo
tubes were removed and anti-
torpedo bulges fitted; 2in (51mm)
armour was added on the upper
protective deck; the elevation of the
big guns was increased from 15°
to 30° and AA armament augmented;
and tower bridges, with a pole mast
aft, replaced the cage masts. Beam
was increased to 106ft 3in (32·38m)
and full load displacement to 36,157
tons (36,736 tonnes).

Completed too late for World
War I, the New Mexicos saw extensive service in 1942-45. Their secondary and AA armament was much
modified, details varying from ship
to ship. All 5in (127mm) QF had
been removed from *Mississippi* and
Idaho by 1943, but in 1945 *New
Mexico* retained 6 x 5in (127mm)
QF, with 8 x 5in (127mm) AA,
40 x 40mm AA and 46 x 20mm AA.

New Mexico and *Idaho* were
stricken and scrapped in 1947-48.
Mississippi was converted to a
gunnery training and trials ship
(reclassified AG-128) in 1946-47,
and in 1952 received two twin
launchers for Terrier SAMs. She
was sold for breaking up in 1956.

Below: Much modified *Mississippi*
(BB-41) as she appeared off Luzon,
Philippines, early in January 1945.
The floatplane is a Vought OS2U
Kingfisher.

1920-1929

World War I had resulted in the collapse of Germany but it threw up new political problems. In the United States, the idea grew that the country should possess a navy 'second to none': the US should preserve the freedoms of democracy worldwide, and, more blatantly, the greatest industrial nation of the world required the greatest navy in the world in order to protect its interests. More immediately, the vast expansion of the US Navy brought about by the 1914-18 conflict was by 1920 still in progress. Meanwhile Japan, left somewhat to herself while war raged in Europe, was quietly building up her influence in the Pacific: her merchant fleet had expanded dramatically to fill the vacuum left by the more immediate concerns of the Western Powers, and her adventures on the Asian mainland and across former German-held island territories had produced aspirations similar to those held in the USA. An '8-8' programme of construction, to provide the Japanese Navy with eight modern battleships and eight modern battlecruisers by the end of the 1920s was set in train, in order to protect more 'national interests': Great Britain, in 1920 still by far the strongest naval power (in terms of numbers of ships at least), would not wish to relinquish her position, so recently preserved at immense cost, both material and human. And so, despite the waves of postwar pacifism on the one hand, the prospect of a further, economically damaging naval race was very real on the other, and it was against this background that the Washington Conference—the single most far-reaching determinant of battleship evolution since the *Dreadnought*—was convened; from it resulted the Naval Armament Limitation Treaty, signed on 6 February 1922.

WASHINGTON

The importance of the Washington Conference of 1921-22 and of the Treaty that resulted from it cannot be over-emphasised. In terms of warship design, it placed, for the first time, artificial limits on what could be achieved: the classical compromises among displacement, hull form, speed, protection and fire-power—and cost—were harshly concentrated as two of the elements, displacement (maximum 35,000 tons, 35,560 tonnes) and main armament (maximum calibre 16in, 406mm), were now dictated. In theory, the designer's task was eased in that he had to work within certain inviolable parameters; in effect, the imposition of such limitations made his problems much more acute, as the ideal capital ship could no longer be built.

The Treaty had quantitative, as well as qualitative, clauses, and these are referred to in more detail in the General Introduction, but in terms of actual capital ship construction the direct result was the immediate scrapping of a large number of US, British and Japanese battleships and battlecruisers then building, or well advanced in the design stage. The principal victims were the bulk of Japan's '8-8' programme, four large Amagi class battlecruisers of 40,000 tons (40,640 tonnes) and mounting 10 x 16in (406mm) guns and two Tosa class battleships, 39,930 tons (40,569 tonnes) and with 10 x 16in (406mm) guns; the US South Dakotas, battleships displacing 43,200 tons (43,891 tonnes) and mounting 12 x 16in (406mm) guns, and Lexingtons, battlecruisers with (final design) 8 x 16in (406mm) guns and displacing 43,500 tons (44,196 tonnes); and the super-lative British 'G3' battlecruisers, 48,400 tons (49,174 tonnes) and 9 x 16in (406mm) guns, and 'N3' battleships, 48,500 tons (49,276 tonnes) with 9 x 18in (457mm) guns.

THE LESSONS OF WORLD WAR I

While capital ship building programmes were curtailed by Washington, design and processes were not, and during the 1920s the full impact of the naval engagements of World War I, in particular of course Jutland, were absorbed and acted upon. With the aid of director firing, hits were being achieved at ranges improbable ten years earlier. Jutland proved that ships could be destroyed at 8 or 9 miles (13-14km), but by the early 1920s ranges double that were shown to be entirely practicable, accomplished partly by increased muzzle velocities and heavier calibres but mainly by the raising the angles of elevation of the barrels, 30° being typical.

Longer ranges required longer-base range-finders, and higher-sited ones too, and so evolved the armoured director placed in the spotting top—armoured because with the increased reliance on director fire one hit could seriously damage a ship's ability to fight. The Royal Navy adopted 'ladder' firing, already practised by the German Navy during World War I, in which salvoes were fired together according to a group of ranges based around that calculated by the range-finder equipment, instead of time-dispersed salvoes wherein follow-up shooting did not take place until the effects of the first shells could be observed. The battle line was still the standard fleet tactic, and to improve communication down the ships, range clocks were fitted and turrets painted up in scales to indicate angles of train which could be read off by other vessels operating within visual contact in the battle line.

Further problems were posed and solved. Increased angles of gun elevation caused loading systems to be reviewed: the options were all-angle loading, with the complications that implied, or enhanced machinery for elevation itself so that ranges could be resumed rapidly and efficiently. The difficulties were eased by the US adoption of the 'stable element', a device which could compute a ship's angle of roll and by means of gyroscope ensure that ranges were precisely maintained by keeping the guns at a fixed angle relative to the horizon rather than to the moving platform of the firing ship itself. Fire control tables for calculating enemy range, speed and the rates at which these factors changed with respect to the guns were improved, culminating in the mid-1920s in the German-developed *Ortungsgerat*, a compact system which was gyro-stabilised and thus compensated for the movement of the ship on board which it was carried.

Director firing for secondary armament appeared, the guns themselves rising from casemate-mounted single weapons, often too close to the water to be of use in anything other than a flat calm in the case of a speeding ship, to enclosed turrets that would at once provide dry, protected positions and also permit increased elevation to cope with longer ranges.

AIR POWER AND THE BATTLESHIP

Perhaps more than any other threat, the development of the aeroplane had a profound effect on the design of the post-World War I battleship. The impact, first localised, began with the placing of anti-Zeppelin fighters on turret-top flying-off platforms in the Grand Fleet during World War I and progressed through the installation of a few high-angle heavy anti-aircraft guns. By the early 1920s the efficiency of the strike aircraft was established, and it led to a rash of experiments with bomb- and torpedo-carrying planes, some organised by proponents bent on proving that the days of the battleship were over. The celebrated demonstration off the US East Coast in 1921 when the ex-German battleship *Ostfriesland*, in brilliant weather, stationary, and unable to fight back, was sunk by two near-misses after sixteen bomb hits had failed, was the rather flimsy evidence, and more prudent advocates of air power saw that the battleship's days were perhaps ending but by no means over, pointing to the fact that the US battleship test-hulk *Washington*, in 1924, survived every bomb that was unleashed against it. In truth, and with hindsight, it was the tactics that were faulty: level bombing was inherently inaccurate given the airborne director technology of the day (i.e. eyesight), and it would be the dive-bomber and airborne torpedo that would doom the capital ship.

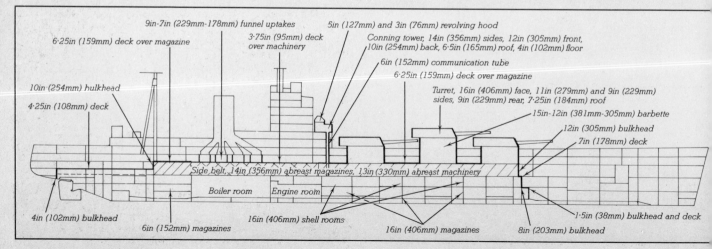

9in-7in (229mm-178mm) funnel uptakes

3·75in (95mm) deck over machinery

5in (127mm) and 3in (76mm) revolving hood

Conning tower, 14in (356mm) sides, 12in (305mm) front, 10in (254mm) back, 6·5in (165mm) roof, 4in (102mm) floor

6·25in (159mm) deck over magazine

6in (152mm) communication tube

6·25in (159mm) deck over magazine

Turret, 16in (406mm) face, 11in (279mm) and 9in (229mm) sides, 9in (229mm) rear, 7·25in (184mm) roof

10in (254mm) hulkhead

4·25in (108mm) deck

15in-12in (381mm-305mm) barbette

12in (305mm) bulkhead

7in (178mm) deck

Side belt, 14in (356mm) abreast magazines, 13in (330mm) abreast machinery

Boiler room

Engine room

4in (102mm) bulkhead

6in (152mm) magazines

16in (406mm) shell rooms

16in (406mm) magazines

8in (203mm) bulkhead

1·5in (38mm) bulkhead and deck

The diagram at top right shows a detailed cutaway of an anti-aircraft gun with the following labelled parts:

Deflection dial
Range dial
Range dial handwheel
Run-out cylinders
Cocking lever
Breech
Firing gear
Layer's telescopic sight
Cradle
Elevating arc
Firing lever
Layer's seat
Elevating handwheel
Carriage
Layer's footrest
Base clips
Baseplate

Above: The US battleship *California* (BB-44) with range clock on mainmast and scoutplanes on catapults.

Below: Converted battlecruiser hull: the aircraft carrier *Lexington* (CV-2) emerges from a smokescreen in 1929.

Above: The British 3in (76mm) Mk I anti-aircraft gun typified Royal Navy battleship AA defence through to the mid-1920s. Note that the weapon was essentially a surface-action gun married to a high-angle mounting (in this case HA Mk II).

Ineffective against a manoeuvring target as the aeroplane was in the early 1920s, it was still a threat and one that had to be met. Thus anti-aircraft batteries first sprung and then proliferated, while horizontal armour protection, as well as coping with plunging fire, was organised so as to defeat bombs as well. A comparison between the data tables given in this book for the dreadnoughts of World War I and for the Nelsons, the first battleships to incorporate the thinking of the early 1920s (and the first to be designed within the Washington limitations) is revealing.

One other effect of the Washington Treaty must be mentioned. The cancellation of battleship construction programmes and the direction that existing fleets be pruned led to the conversion of several US, Japanese and British hulls into aircraft carriers. Although the opportunities offered by sea-going platforms such as these were appreciated, in general the ships were seen principally as adjuncts to the main battle fleet, their aircraft functioning as scouting, spotting and reconnaissance machines subordinate to the heavy gun which would still determine the outcome of any action. Whether the aircraft carrier would have developed in quite the same way had it not been for the Treaty is an absorbing question, but as things worked out the agreement not only restricted the design of battleships and the sizes of fleets—it also, ultimately and unwittingly, contributed to their extinction.

Below: Protection scheme of the Nelson class, showing the innovative internal armour belt and 'internal bulge'. Note how the concentration of the main armament enabled magazine protection to be optimized.

Below right: *California* fires her 5in (127mm) anti-destroyer guns, 1933. These secondary battery weapons were mounted at forecastle-deck level and so could be worked effectively in a seaway.

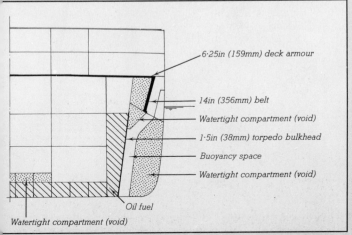

6·25in (159mm) deck armour
14in (356mm) belt
Watertight compartment (void)
1·5in (38mm) torpedo bulkhead
Buoyancy space
Watertight compartment (void)
Oil fuel
Watertight compartment (void)

HOOD

1920 *UK*
Other ships in class: *Anson, Howe, Rodney*

Laid down: 1 September 1916.
Launched: 22 August 1918.
Builder: John Brown & Co, Clydebank.
Displacement: 41,200 tons (41,859 tonnes) standard; 44,600 tons (45,314 tonnes) full load.
Dimensions: 860ft 7in (262·8m) oa x 105ft 2½in (34·5m) x 31ft 6in (9·6m) max.
Machinery: 4 Brown-Curtis geared turbines; 24 Yarrow boilers; 4 shafts; 151,280 SHP.
Armour: 12in-5in (305-127mm) belt; 5in-4in (127-102mm) bulkheads; 3in-1in (76-25mm) decks; 12in-5in (305-127mm) barbettes;

Left: A fine study of *Hood* taken in 1937. The ageing vessel still embodied power and grace, but her 20-year-old design no longer provided sufficient protection to guarantee her safety in the actions of World War II.

Left: *Hood* as she appeared at the time of her action with *Bismarck*. During her 1941 refit she received a gunnery radar set mounted on the foretop gun director. Note the 4in (102mm) dual-purpose guns along the shelter deck and low freeboard. *Hood* finally displaced over 48,000 tons (48,768 tonnes).

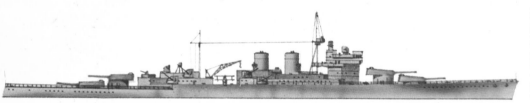

Left: *Hood* as she may have looked if the proposed major refit had been carried out in 1939. This envisaged new machinery, improved protection, replacing the control tower and forward superstructure with a tower bridge, and replacing the 5·5in (140mm) and 4in (102mm) with 8 twin 5·25in (133mm) mounts.

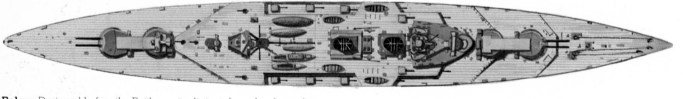

Below: Designed before the Battle of Jutland, and modified as a result of lessons learned there, *Hood*, seen here in 1923, remained the largest warship afloat for some 20 years. Note the spacious quarterdeck with its distinct sheer, the clipper bow — the first to be carried by a major British warship — and flared hull coupled with bulges running abreast the machinery and magazine spaces, and Fairey Flycatcher on 'X' turret.

15in-5in (381-127mm) turrets; 11in-3in (279-76mm) conning and control towers.
Armament: 8 x 15in (381mm); 12 x 5.5in (140mm); 4 x 4in (102mm) AA; 6 x 21in (533mm) torpedo tubes.
Performance: 32.1kt (59.5km/h); radius 5,200nm (9,600km) at 18kt (33.4km/h); oil 4,000 tons (4,064 tonnes).
Crew: 1,169.

With the revelation in 1915 that the Germans were preparing battle-cruisers with 15in (380mm) guns, the British Admiralty decided to respond with a new class of battlecruiser featuring the latest ideas in speed, armament and protection. In this respect the designers were aided by the wartime relaxation of rules tying capital ship dimensions to those of existing drydocks. Much care went into the design of *Hood* by E.L. Attwood and S.V. Goodall, for it was not until 1916 that suitable slips would become available and this gave ample time for the design to be finalised for a ship with superior gun-power to the Renowns and with superior protection to *Tiger*. What emerged, therefore, was a ship with the same armament as the Queen Elizabeths, but considerably greater speed thanks to the provision of greater power but less protection. Orders were placed in April 1916 for four ships: *Hood* from John Brown, *Anson* from Armstrong, *Howe* from Cammell Laird and *Rodney* from Fairfield. Three of the ships had been ordered before the Battle of Jutland was fought, and even the preliminary assessments of damage caused a radical review of the design: the battlecruiser concept was abandoned, and the class were re-armoured as very fast battleships with a slight reduction in speed. When it was learned that the Germans had ceased work on their 15in (381mm) gunned battlecruisers, all but *Hood* were cancelled in October 1918.

The *Hood* finally appeared as an impressive ship of classical beauty, and one that was immediately taken to the hearts of the British public. As a fighting ship she was a mixture of old and new: *Hood* was the last British capital ship with an open secondary battery and mast-head tops for

control, but on the other hand she had an inclined armour belt, high-elevation main battery, small-tube boilers (permitting the development of some 30 per cent more power than the Renowns for the same weight) and the new 5.5in (140mm) gun in the secondary armament.

The main armament, carried in four centre-line twin turrets (two forward and two aft in superfiring pairs), originally had an elevation of 20°, but this was increased to 30° when Jutland revealed how much battle ranges were increasing. Open sighting hoods were replaced by rangefinders, each turret having its own 30ft (9.14m) unit. The 5.5in (140mm) secondary armament was typical of that being fitted at the time; however, the disposition of the battery, in five open positions on each forecastle deck beam and two on the shelter deck, was anachronistic. None of the mountings could be trained aft of the beam, the four 5.5in (140mm) guns originally being intended for defence in this quarter having been deleted to save weight.

Above: *Hood* in the early 1930s, showing the aircraft catapult which was fitted on the quarterdeck in 1931. The catapult is folded to save space; the aircraft is a Fairey IIIF; note petrol tank at stern.

So far as armour was concerned, the system used in the *Hood* was typical of the period, with its main weight concentrated against low-angle fire but slightly modified with extra horizontal protection against high-angle fire and bombs. The belt was angled outward to worsen the impact angle of any incoming shell. Anti-torpedo bulges were fitted, and the bilges were filled with tubes to help absorb shock in the event of a torpedo strike.

Little was done in the way of modifications before World War II, when *Hood* had her AA armament increased. She would have undergone a major modernisation starting in 1939, but this was never begun, and she blew up after being hit by a salvo from *Bismarck* on 24 May 1941, only three of her crew surviving.

NAGATO

1920 *Japan*
Other ships in class: *Mutsu*

Laid down: 28 August 1917.
Launched: 9 November 1919.
Builder: Kure Dockyard.
Displacement: 32,720 tons
(33,245 tonnes) standard; 33,800
tons (34,340 tonnes) normal;
38,500 tons (39,116 tonnes) full
load.
Dimensions: 708ft (215·8m) oa x
95ft (29m) x 29ft 9in (9·1m).
Machinery: 4 Kampon turbines;
21 Kampon boilers; 4 shafts;
80,000 SHP.
Armour: 12in-4in (305-102mm)
belt; 3in-1in (76-25mm) decks; 12in
(305mm) barbettes; 14in (356mm)
turrets; 1in (25mm) casemates; 12in
(305mm) conning tower.
Armament: 8 x 16in (406mm); 20
x 5·5in (140mm); 4 x 3in (76mm)
AA; 8 x 21in (533mm) torpedo
tubes.
Performance: 26·75kt (49·6km/h);
radius 5,700nm (10,550km) at
15kt (27·8km/h); oil 3,400 tons
(3,454 tonnes); coal 1,600 tons
(1,625 tonnes).
Crew: 1,333.

The two units of the Nagato class
opened a new era in battleship
design: they introduced the 16in
(406mm) gun, were well protected,
and were exceptionally fast for ships
of their fire-power and protection. In
short, they were excellent examples of
the fast battleship concept. The hull
design was modelled on that of the
Hyuga class, but the use of the new
16in (406mm) gun meant that the
main armament could be reduced
from twelve to eight in number: the

Hyugas' 12 x 14in (356mm) guns
offered a broadside of 17,857lb
(8,100kg), while the equivalent weight
for the Nagatos' 8 x 16in (406mm)
guns was 17,513lb (7,944kg) fired to
a greater range with more destructive
power. Thus for a more effective
broadside, the Japanese were able to
do away with two turrets. The powerful secondary battery was made up
of 10 single 5·5in (140mm) guns on
each beam, seven mounted on the
upper deck and the other three one
deck higher. A control top was sited
in the pagoda foremast, the first of
these distinctive units fitted to a
Japanese capital ship.
   Protection was excellent, with a
notable increase in amount and
quality compared with the preceding
Hyuga class. The one retrograde

feature was perhaps the machinery, in
which a mixture of oil- and
coal/oil-fired boilers (15 and 6
respectively) was used.
   Mutsu was built at Yokosuka
Dockyard and completed in October
1921, and the two ships were
undoubtedly the most powerful
battleships available in the early
1920s, offering the Imperial Japanese
Navy an unbeatable mix of fire-power,
protection, speed and seaworthiness.
   During the 1920s the fore funnel
was swept aft at the top to remove
smoke from the area of the foremast,
which acquired its true pagoda style
from 1924 onwards with the fitting of
extra control and command positions.
From 1934 to 1936 both ships were
rebuilt: the stern was extended
(increasing length to 738ft, 224·9m);

Above: *Nagato* at Tsingtao, China,
in the late 1930s after the refit
which dramatically altered her
profile. The distinctive raked funnel
has gone, and the bridge has been
raised to house the new fire control
system.

bulges were added (raising beam to
113ft 6in, 34·6m); a triple bottom was
provided; the machinery was
replaced to provide each ship with 10
oil-fired boilers, whose space-saving
was augmented by the removal of the
fore funnel to permit an enlargement
of the pagoda mast; and the
armament was revised. The ships
were regunned, the main armament
now being able to elevate to 43°,
raising range to 40,480 yards
(30,015m) from the 30,800 yards

Below: *Nagato* as first completed in
1920. She retained torpedo nets at
this time, although other navies had
discarded them.

Below: *Nagato* in 1944 with raised
platforms around the funnel which
carried searchlights and some of the
many additional AA guns.

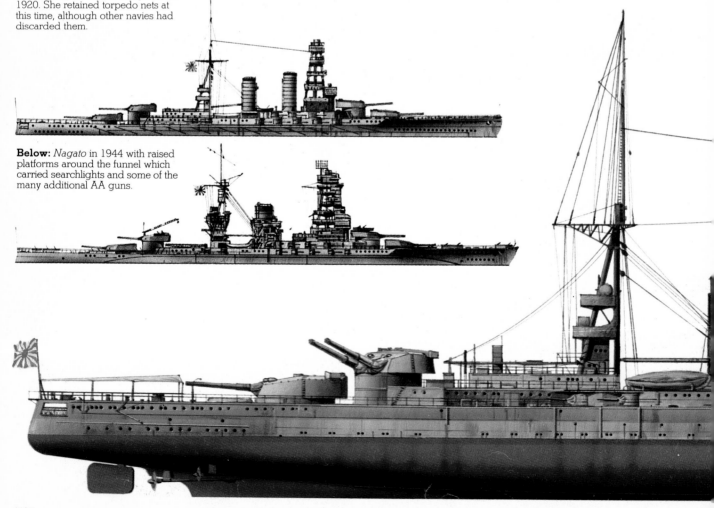

(28,165m) attainable with the previous 30° elevation. Two of the 5·5in (140mm) guns were removed, the others having their elevation increased from 25° to 35°. The 3in (76mm) AA guns were removed, four twin turrets with 5in (127mm) AA guns being shipped in their place; at the same time 10 twin 25mm mounts were added. The ships were also given 'eyes' in the form of three seaplanes launched from a catapult. Protection was augmented: the decks were now 7in (178mm) thick over the vitals, and the barbettes were increased to 22in (559mm) maximum. Tonnage rose by some 6,500 tons (6,604 tonnes), but the extra power meant that speed dropped only marginally. Oil-fired boilers also increased range very considerably.

Above: A dramatic study of *Nagato* in 1921 shortly after completion, with hexapod foremast and powerful 16in (406mm) main armament. In 1924 the forefunnel top was trunked back and the foremast built up in 'pagoda' fashion.

Both ships were heavily involved in World War II: *Mutsu* was lost as the result of a magazine explosion on 8 June 1943, but *Nagato* survived the war, being used as a floating AA battery from January 1945; her final AA armament was made up of the 5in (127mm) guns mentioned earlier, plus no fewer than 98 x 25mm cannon, aimed with the aid of radar. *Nagato* was expended as a target ship in the Bikini atom-bomb tests on 29 July 1946.

Below: *Nagato* in 1926 with fore-funnel raked back to clear smoke from the bridge which is still fairly open. The catapult fitted to the top of 'B' turret was a temporary measure and carried a Heinkel HD 25 or HD 26 float

biplane. Both catapult and aircraft were developed by Ernst Heinkel specifically for *Nagato* as a result of a 1925 contract. Note how the shape of the bow has also been altered, and the distinctive shape of the pagoda foremast.

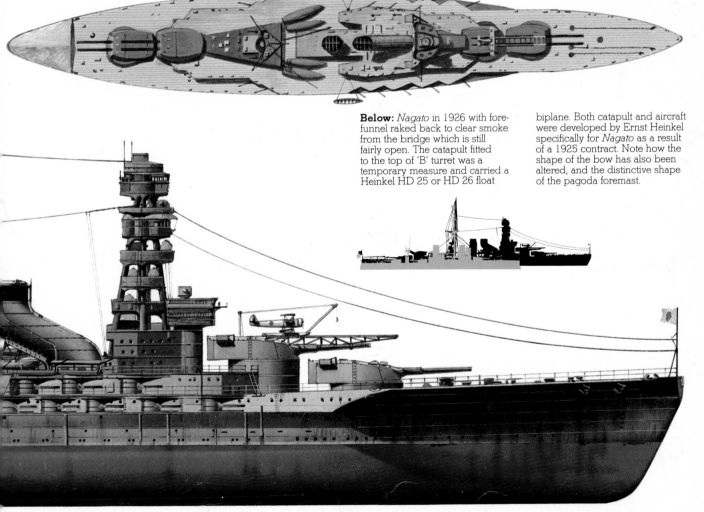

SOUTH DAKOTA (BB-49)

1920 (not completed) *USA*
Other ships in class: *Indiana* (BB-50), *Montana* (BB-51), *North Carolina* (BB-52), *Iowa* (BB-53), *Massachusetts* (BB-54)

Laid down: 15 March 1920.
Builder: New York Navy Yard.
Displacement: 43,200 tons (43,891 tonnes) standard.
Dimensions: 684ft (208·5m) oa x 106ft (32·3m) x 33ft (10·1m).
Machinery: 2 Westinghouse turbines/2 electric motors; 16 Babcock & Wilcox boilers; 4 shafts; 60,000 SHP.
Armour: 13·5in (343mm) belt; 13·5in-9in (343-229mm) bulkheads; 6in-1·25in (152-32mm) decks; 13·5in-4·5in (343-114mm) bar-

bettes; 18in-5in (457-127mm) turrets; 16in-8in (406-203mm) conning tower.
Armament: 12 x 16in (406mm); 16 x 6in (152mm); 4 x 3in (76mm) AA; 2 x 21in (533mm) torpedo tubes.
Performance: 23kt (42·6km/h).
Crew: 1,616.

Planned as 'ultimate dreadnoughts' with 'all-or-nothing' protection, the *South Dakota* and her five sisters were authorised in 1916 as the world's most powerful battleships, with a main armament of 12 x 16in (406mm) guns in two pairs of

superfiring triple turrets, and turbo-electric propulsion. The six ships were held back until after World War I to allow all the lessons of the latter to be digested.

The main armament would have had the prodigious broadside weight of 25,200lb (11,431kg), and the guns would have ranged to 33,000 yards (30,175m) with an elevation of 30°. Protection for the vital areas was to be first class, and bulges were to be abandoned in favour of internal compartmentation.

All the ships were cancelled under the Washington Treaty.

Below: *South Dakota* as she would have appeared if completed. The class was the first US design for 20 years to feature a 6in (152mm) secondary battery.

AMAGI

1920 (not completed) *Japan*
Other ships in class: *Akagi*, *Atago*, *Takao*

Laid down: 16 December 1920.
Builder: Yokosuka Dockyard.
Displacement: 41,217 tons (41,878 tonnes) normal; 47,000 tons (47,754 tonnes) full load.
Dimensions: 826ft 9in (251·8m) oa x 101ft (30·8m) x 31ft (9·5m).
Machinery: 4 Gijutsu turbines; 19 Kampon boilers; 4 shafts; 131,000 SHP.

Below: *Amagi*'s sister vessel, *Akagi*, upon completion as an aircraft carrier in 1927. The large, downward curving funnel can be seen projecting to starboard amidships; the three flight decks are also visible. *Akagi* was the Japanese flagship during the attack on Pearl Harbor; she was sunk at the Battle of Midway, 5 June 1942.

Below right: *Amagi* as she would have looked on completion, with her main armament on the centre-line.

TENNESSEE (BB-43)

1920 *USA*
Other ships in class: *California* (BB-44)

Laid down: 14 May 1917.
Launched: 30 April 1919.
Builder: New York Navy Yard.
Displacement: 32,300 tons (32,817 tonnes) normal; 34,000 tons (34,544 tonnes) full load.
Dimensions: 624ft 6in (190·7m) oa x 92ft 3in (29·7m) x 30ft 3in (9·2m).
Machinery: 2 Westinghouse turbines/3 electric motors, 8 Babcock & Wilcox boilers; 4 shafts; 30,908 SHP.
Armour: 14in-8in (356-203mm) belt; 5in-2·5in (127-64mm) decks; 13in (330mm) barbettes; 18in-9in (457-229mm) turrets; 16in (406mm) conning tower.
Armament: 12 x 14in (356mm); 14 x 5in (127mm); 4 x 3in (76mm) AA; 4 x 6pdr; 2 x 1pdr; 2 x 21in (533mm) torpedo tubes.
Performance: 21kt (38·9km/h); radius 8,700nm (16,100km) at 10kt (18·5km/h); oil 3,328 tons (3,381 tonnes).
Crew: 1,083.

Though very similar to the preceding New Mexico class battleships, the two units of the Tennessee class had a number of important differences, notably the first use of turbo-electric drive in a complete class and the removal of the secondary battery to a

higher level than in earlier American battleships. These were the last US battleships with 14in (356mm) guns, but this armament was very economically disposed in four triple centre-line turrets, in two superfiring pairs fore and aft. The turrets could maintain a rate of fire of three salvoes per minute, with a broadside weight of 16,800lb (7,620kg). Though the New Mexico class had a numerical advantage in the secondary armament (22 compared with 14 x 5in, 127mm guns), it was qualitatively inferior, being placed in the hull where it could not be worked in any sort of sea.

The use of turbo-electric propulsion was a bold step: the machinery took up more space, was heavier and needed careful insulation; on the other hand, it obviated the need for separate reversing turbines, and allowed rapid change from ahead to astern drive. But it could not be denied that the ships were slow by contemporary standards.

In 1928 the AA armament was augmented, but few other changes were effected before World War II. Both ships were damaged at Pearl Harbor, and reconstructed with a revised dual-purpose secondary armament, which by 1945 was made up of 16 x 5in/38 (127mm/38) guns, with an AA battery comprising 40 x 40mm and 50 x 20mm guns. Both vessels served extensively in the Pacific until the end of World War II, both surviving kamikaze attacks in early 1945. They were mothballed and were sold for scrap in 1959.

Below: *California* in the mid-1920s with twin funnels and cage masts. Additional aircraft were shipped in the 1930s. The aircraft shown here is a Curtiss TS-1.

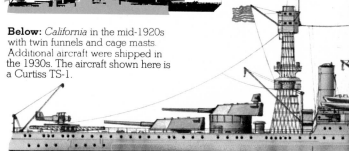

Below: *California* in dazzle scheme in June 1944. Damaged at Pearl Harbor, she emerged from the refit with a single funnel and compact superstructure. The floatplane is a Vought OS2U Kingfisher.

Armour: 10in (254mm) belt;
11in-9in (280-230mm) bulkheads;
3·9in-0·8in (100-20mm) decks;
11in-9in (280-230mm) barbettes;
11in-9in (280-230mm) turrets;
(356-254mm) conning tower.
Armament: 10 x 16in (406mm);
16 x 5·5in (140mm); 4 x 4·7in
(120mm) AA; 8 x 24in (609mm)
torpedo tubes.
Performance: 30kt (55·6km/h); oil
4,000 tons (4,064 tonnes); coal
2,000 tons (2,032 tonnes).
Crew: 1,600.

Designed as the first half of the fast
battlecruiser force called for in the
'8-8 Programme' of eight battleships
and eight battlecruisers to counter
the US Navy's 1916 programme, the
Amagi class was designed by
Y. Hiraga. The first two units were
laid down in 1920, and the other
two in 1921, and the class was
intended as a direct answer to the
US Lexington class. The Amagis
were the battlecruiser counterparts
to the two Tosa class battleships,

the second pair of battleships in
the '8-8 Programme' (Nagato and
Mutsu being the first pair). Amagi
was to be some 60ft (18·3m) longer
than Tosa and only 1ft (0·3m)
greater in beam; an additional
40,000 SHP would propel this
more streamlined hull and
additional 1,500 tons (1,524 tonnes)
of displacement at 4kt (7·4km/h)
greater speed.

The design was based on that of
Nagato, with an extra centre-line
turret. Compared with the Tosa
class, the Amagi class were flush-
decked and carried 'Q' turret one
deck higher. Both classes had
mixed coal- and oil/coal-fired
boilers.

The Washington Treaty led to the
cancellation of the class on 5
February 1922, though it was
decided to convert Amagi into an
aircraft carrier. However, the hull
was so severely strained in an
earthquake in September 1923 that
it was scrapped. Akagi was
completed as an aircraft carrier.

TOSA

1921 (not completed) Japan
Other ships in class: Kaga

Laid down: 16 February 1920.
Launched: 18 December 1921.
Builder: Mitsubishi, Nagasaki.
Displacement: 39,930 tons
(40,569 tonnes) normal.
Dimensions: 768ft (234·1m) oa x
100ft (30·5m) x 30ft 9in (11·4m).
Machinery: 4 Brown-Curtis
impulse-reaction turbines; 12 Kampon
boilers; 4 shafts; 91,000 SHP.
Armour: 11in (280mm) belt;
11in-9in (280-230mm) bulkheads;
6·3in-3·9in (160-100mm) decks;
11in-9in (280-230mm) barbettes;
14in-10in (356-254mm) conning
tower.
Armament: 10 x 16in (406mm);
20 x 5·5in (140mm); 4 x 3·1in (80mm)
AA; 8 x 24in (609mm) torpedo tubes.
Performance: 26·5kt (49·1km/h);
range 5,000nm (9,250km) at 16kt
(29·6km/h).
Crew: Not known.

Intended to be the second pair of
high-speed battleships required
under the Japanese '8-8 Programme', the two ships of the Tosa
class were advanced designs,
based on the preceding Nagatos
but with greater power for increased speed and an extra main
armament turret to raise gun-power
from eight 1918-pattern 16in
(406mm) to ten 1921-pattern 16in
(406mm) weapons. The secondary
armament comprised 10 x 5·5in
(140mm) guns on each beam,
located in casemates on the upper
and forecastle decks.

Armour protection was improved
in quality as well as thickness, and
for the first time in a Japanese
design inclined plates were used,
the belt being sloped at 15° to
worsen the impact angle for incoming rounds. Kaga and Tosa
were cancelled by the 1922
Washington Treaty: Kaga was finally
converted into an aircraft carrier,
while Tosa was expended as a
target on 9 February 1925.

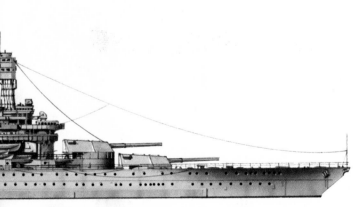

Below: Tosa as she would have
looked on completion with 16in
(406mm) main armament.

Below: Tosa's sister-ship, Kaga,
was completed as an aircraft carrier
similar to Akagi (opposite).

Below: Battlecruiser design of 1921;
note main armament disposition.

BATTLECRUISER DESIGN 'G3'

1921 UK

Displacement: 48,400 tons
(49,174 tonnes).
Dimensions: 856ft (260·9m) oa
x 106ft (32·3m) x 32ft 6in (9·9m)
mean.
Machinery: 4 Parsons geared
turbines; 20 small-tube boilers; 4
shafts; 160,000 SHP.
Armour: 14in-12in (356-305mm)
belt; 12in-4in (305-102mm) bulkheads; 8in-1in (203-25mm) decks;
14in (356mm) barbettes; 17in-8in
(432-203mm) turrets; 12in-6in
(305-152mm) conning tower.
Armament: 9 x 16in (406mm);
16 x 6in (152mm); 6 x 4·7in
(119mm) AA; 32 x 2pdr; 2 x
24·5in (622mm) torpedo tubes;
Performance: 32kt (59·3km/h).
Crew: 1,716.

With the 1921 Battlecruiser class,
whose units were numbered 1 to 4
(and were ordered from Swan Hunter,
Beardmore, Fairfields and John
Brown on 21 October 1921), E.L.
Attwood and S.V. Goodall designed
the most powerful British capital ships
of all time. The need for concentrating
armour and keeping length to a minimum resulted in a departure from
accepted main armament disposition:
the new 16in (406mm) gun was
adopted, and the nine weapons were
arranged in triple turrets located as a
superfiring pair forward of the
superstructure with the third turret
just to its rear.

The secondary armament was
turret-mounted in eight twin turrets,
four grouped round the tower bridge
and the other four near the stern. The
protection was limited in scope but
effective. These forward-looking
vessels were cancelled in 1922 as a
result of the Washington Treaty.

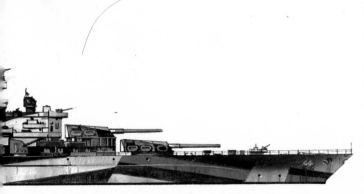

LEXINGTON (CC-1)

1921 USA

Other ships in class: *Constellation* (CC-2), *Saratoga* (CC-3), *Ranger* (CC-4), *Constitution* (CC-5), *United States* (CC-6)

Laid down: 8 January 1921.
Builder: Fore River Company.
Displacement: 43,500 tons (44,187 tonnes) standard.
Dimensions: 874ft (266·4m) x 105ft 5in (32·1m) x 31ft (9·45m).
Machinery: 4 General Electric turbines/4 electric motors; 16 Yarrow boilers; 4 shafts; 180,000 SHP.
Armour: 7·75in (197mm) belt; 11in-5in (279-127mm) turrets; 2in-1·25in (51-32mm) deck; 12in (305mm) conning tower.
Armament: 8 x 16in (406mm); 16 x 6in (152mm); 6 x 3in (76mm) AA; 4 x 21in (533mm) torpedo tubes.

Performance: 33·25kt (61·1km/h).
Crew: 1,430.

The United States did not at first share Britain's and Germany's enthusiasm for battlecruisers, preferring to develop the battleship which, although slower, was better protected. Not until 1913 were two such ships requested, along with four battleships, but this procurement was refused as it might have affected the battleship programme.

In 1916 the need for battlecruisers resurfaced, and six vessels of 35,000 tons (35,553 tonnes), armed with 10 x 14in (355mm), 20 x 5in (127mm) and 4 x 3in (76mm) AA guns, were ordered, with a speed of 35kt (64·9km/h) on 180,000 SHP, a speed made possible only by sacrificing protection. This weakness was exacerbated by placing half of the 24 boilers above the waterline. Dimensions were 874ft x 90ft x 31ft (226·4m

x 27·4m x 9·45m). To keep the ships dry at high speed, maximum freeboard was continued down 75 per cent of the hull; another innovation was the design's bulbous bow, developed in 1910 by Rear Admiral Taylor, which reduced hull resistance and helped support the weight forward. The whole concept met with little enthusiasm, however, and in 1917 a second plan emerged with slightly improved protection but now carrying 8 x 14in (355mm) and 14 x 6in (152mm) guns. Original contract price was $30 million per ship.

The lessons of Jutland now made themselves felt, and as a consequence a third design appeared which paid closer attention to protection, at the price of an increase of 8,000 tons (8,126 tonnes) in displacement and a reduction in speed to 33·25kt (61·6km/h). Beam was increased by 15ft (4·6m) which would have created problems in the 110ft (33·5m) wide

locks of the Panama Canal. The number of boilers was reduced to 16, all below the waterline. These led up to two large funnels, which gave the vessels a more balanced appearance. Armour was now 7in (178mm) on belt and bulkheads, with side armour inclined 12° to improve defence, and main armament comprised 16in (406mm) guns.

All six units were laid down in 1920-21 and when completed would have been impressive vessels. *Lexington* and *Constellation* would have been fleet flagships, but their careers were about to undergo a violent change. During World War I both the United States and Japan had drawn up large building programmes, and in 1919 America commenced with six South Dakota class battleships and the six Lexingtons. These were to be unrivalled anywhere in the world, but already Japan had started her own ambitious plans that would result in spectacular 45,000-ton (45,710 tonne) vessels armed with 18in (457mm).

Now realizing that their huge creations were soon to be outclassed, the US authorities were only too eager to end this race before it became a nightmare. Public opinion was against the spending, and there was a real fear that such rivalry could lead to war. There could be no question of these ships being replaced with bigger ones, and so the United States decided to call a conference on naval disarmament, to be held in Washington in 1921-22. Secretary of State Hughes later admitted that, in any case, it would not have been possible to complete the Lexington programme. The outcome of the conference was the Washington Treaty, which dictated the wholesale scrapping of a large number of capital ships. However, of the six Lexingtons it was agreed that two could be converted into aircraft carriers.

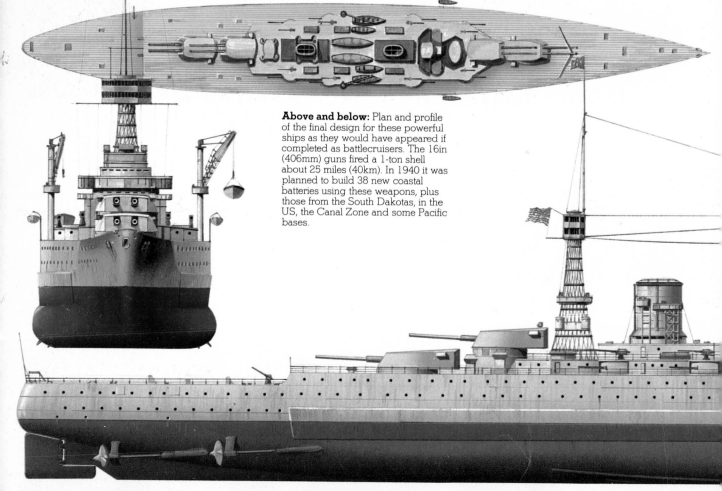

Above: The top picture shows the seven-funnelled design of 1916 in which the 35kt speed was achieved at the expense of armour. The 24 boilers were on two levels. The second illustration shows the 1917 design which still carried eight of its 20 boilers high up. The 1916 version had 10 x 14in (355mm) guns later used on railway mounts in France. The 1917 design sported 8 x 16in (406mm) guns.

Above and below: Plan and profile of the final design for these powerful ships as they would have appeared if completed as battlecruisers. The 16in (406mm) guns fired a 1-ton shell about 25 miles (40km). In 1940 it was planned to build 38 new coastal batteries using these weapons, plus those from the South Dakotas, in the US, the Canal Zone and some Pacific bases.

Above: The impressive outline of *Saratoga* in September 1944 with her new 'dazzle' camouflage scheme. These vessels were the largest and fastest aircraft carriers in the world until the end of World War II when the Midway class entered service. As they were not originally designed as carriers, fewer aircraft were embarked than their size suggested, but they played a major role in the growth of US naval aviation.

In 1927 *Lexington* finally emerged as the world's largest carrier. Displacement was 38,725 tons (39,364 tonnes) full load, and by World War II it had crept up to over 50,000 tons (50,790 tonnes) with the addition of extra AA armament etc. Turbo-electric drive had been specified mainly because of the difficulties in producing reduction gearing of adequate size and strength, and with 202,973 SHP *Lexington* made 34·59kt (64·1km/h) on trial.

Lexington served in the Pacific from 1927 to 1942. In action at Coral Sea, May 1942, her aircraft helped sink the Japanese carrier *Shoho*. She was herself sunk after suffering extensive damage after being hit by torpedoes and bombs from Japanese aircraft on 8 May 1942. Her sister, *Saratoga*, survived the war and was expended as a target at the atom-bomb tests in July 1946.

Above right: *Lexington* at anchor at Lahaina, Maui, in the Hawaiian Islands, February 1932. Her aircraft are ranged on the flight deck.

Right: A fine study of *Lexington* launching Martin T4M torpedo-bomber biplanes. The twin 8in (203mm) turrets were removed in 1941.

BATTLESHIP DESIGN 'N3'

1921 UK

Displacement: *c*48,500 tons (49,276 tonnes).
Dimensions: 820ft (249·94m) oa x 106ft (32·31m) x 32ft (9·75m) mean.
Machinery: Geared turbines; 2 shafts; 56,000 SHP.
Armour: 15in-13·5in (381-343mm) belt; 14in-6in (356-152mm) bulk-heads; 8in-6in (203-152mm) armour deck; 18in-8in (457-203mm) turrets; 15in (381mm) barbettes; 15in-6in (381-152mm) conning tower.
Armament: 9 x 18in (457mm); 16 x 6in (152mm); 6 x 4·7in (119mm) AA; 32 x 2pdr AA; 2 x 24·5in (622mm) torpedo tubes.
Performance: 23·5kt (43·5km/h).
Crew: Not known.

The Hood class was intended to make full use of the lessons learned at the Battle of Jutland, particularly with regard to the nature, location and inclination of the armour. But the demands of World War I meant that *Hood*'s design had to be speeded up, and only some of the revisions could be worked in. However, the four units to the 'N3' design were planned with very good protection. These ships were to be the battleship complement to the 1921 battlecruisers, giving the Royal Navy a qualitative edge over the latest US and Japanese plans (South Dakota and Lexington classes, and the ships of the '8-8 Programme'). Main armament disposition was similar to that of the 'G3s'. Among the numerous designs considered were the four illustrated, much thought being given to the optimum disposition of the main armament on hulls of such large displacement, similar to that of the 'G3s'.

The 'N3s' were never laid down, and the entire programme was brought to a close under the terms of the Washington Treaty.

BATTLESHIP DESIGN

1921 Japan

Displacement: 47,500 tons (48,260 tonnes) normal; *c*53,000 tons (53,848 tonnes) full load.
Dimensions: 915ft 4in (279m) oa x 101ft (30·8m) x 32ft (9·75m) max.
Machinery: 4 Gijutsu Honbu turbines; 22 Kampon boilers; 4 shafts; 150,000 SHP.
Armour: 13in (330mm) belt; 5in (127mm) deck; 11in-9in (280-230mm) barbettes; 14in-10in (356-254mm) conning tower.
Armament: 8 x 18in (457mm); 16 x 5·5in (140mm); 4 x 4·7in (120mm) AA; 8 x 24in (609mm) torpedo tubes.
Performance: 30kt (55·6km/h).
Crew: Not known.

Designed by Y. Hiraga, the battle-ships numbered 13, 14, 15 and 16 (to be built by Yokosuka Dockyard, Kure Dockyard, Mitsubishi and Kawasaki, but never ordered or named) were to have been the last four of the eight battleships in the ambitious '8-8 Programme'. The design had strong similarities with

Below: Design 'L^{III}', 9 x 18in (457mm).

Below: Design 'L2'; 8 x 18in (457mm).

Below: Design 'M2'; main armament concentrated amidships

Below: Design 'N3' bore a superficial resemblance to *Nelson*

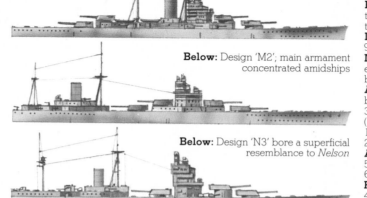

Below: Hiraga's battleship design of 1921; if completed these would have been among the most powerful warships in the world, combining high speed with potent armament.

that of the Tosa class, also designed by Admiral Hiraga, and the four units were to have been built on the slips used for *Nagato, Mutsu, Tosa* and *Kaga*, with all four scheduled for completion in 1927. Central to the design was the great 1922-pattern 18in (457mm) gun, of which eight were to be shipped in two twin pairs of superfiring turrets. One obsolescent feature was the placing of the secondary armament in eight casemates along each side of the superstructure just above the forecastle deck.

These four ships, which were can-celled in the aftermath of the Washington Treaty, would, on com-pletion, have been the world's most powerful capital ships, combining great speed and firepower.

NELSON

1927 UK
Other ships in class: *Rodney*

Laid down: 28 December 1922.
Launched: 3 September 1925.
Builder: Vickers-Armstrong, Newcastle.
Displacement: 33,950 tons (34,493 tonnes) standard; 38,000 tons (38,608 tonnes) full load.
Dimensions: 710ft (216·8m) oa x 106ft (32·4m) x 31ft 6in (9·6m) max.
Machinery: 2 Brown-Curtis tur-bines; eight 3-drum Admiralty boilers; 2 shafts; 45,000 SHP.
Armour: 14in-13in (356-330mm) belt; 14in-12in (356-305mm) bulk-heads; 6·25in-3in (159-76mm)

MARYLAND (BB-46)

1921 USA
Other ships in class: *Colorado* (BB-45), *Washington* (BB-47), *West Virginia* (BB-48)

Laid down: 24 April 1917.
Launched: 20 March 1920.
Builder: Newport News.
Displacement: 31,500 tons (32,004 tonnes) normal; 33,590 tons (34,127 tonnes) full load.
Dimensions: 624ft (190·2m) oa x 97ft 6in (29·7m) x 29ft 9in (9·1m) mean.
Machinery: 2 Curtis turbines/2 electric motors; 8 Babcock & Wilcox boilers; 4 shafts; 27,200 SHP.
Armour: 16in-8in (406-203mm) belt; 14in (356mm) bulkheads; 3·5in-1·5in (89-38mm) decks; 14in (356mm) barbettes; 18in-5in (457-127mm) turrets; 18in-8in (457-203mm) conning tower.
Armament: 8 x 16in (406mm); 14 x 5in (127mm); 4 x 3in (76mm) AA; 4 x 6pdr; 2 x 21in (533mm) torpedo tubes.
Performance: 21kt (38·9km/h); oil 4,570 tons (4,643 tonnes).
Crew: 1,119.

decks; 15in-14in (380-356mm) barbettes; 16in-7in (406-178mm) turrets; 1·5in-1in (38-25mm) secon-dary turrets; 16in (406mm) conning tower.
Armament: 9 x 16in (406mm); 12 x 6in (152mm); 6 x 4·7in (119mm) AA; 2 x 24·5in (622mm) torpedo tubes.
Performance: 23·5kt (43·5km/h); radius 14,300nm (26,500km) at 12kt (22·2km/h); oil 4,000 tons (4,064 tonnes).
Crew: 1,314.

Nelson and her sister-ship *Rodney* (built in Birkenhead by Cammell Laird and completed in August 1927), were the first battleships completed in accordance with the dictates of the Washington Treaty, which fixed

The Maryland class was a virtual repeat of the Tennessee class, but with each of the four turrets fitted with two 16in (406mm) guns instead of three 14in (356mm) weapons. *Colorado* was built by New York Shipbuilding and launched on 22 March 1921, while *West Virginia* was launched from Newport News on 19 November 1921. These two units were completed quite rapidly, but the fourth unit of the class, *Washington*, launched by New York Shipbuilding on 1 September 1921, was overtaken by the Washington Treaty and cancelled in February 1922. She nevertheless played an important part in American naval developments, being used for research into explosions and blast, and finally

succumbing to fourteen 14in (356mm) shell hits on 25 November 1924.

The three survivors were modernized in 1928-29, the major alterations being the removal of the underwater torpedo tubes, the installation of extra AA guns, and the addition of handling equipment and catapults for aircraft. Further modernization was undertaken between 1939 and 1941: two 5in (127mm) guns were removed, and extra light AA guns were shipped. However, the modifications carried out in World War II altered the ships radically. Those affecting *Maryland* and *Colorado* were similar: bulges increased beam to 108ft (32·9m), the cage main masts were shortened and replaced by control towers, and the AA armament was radically aug-

mented. By 1945 *Maryland* had a new dual-purpose secondary battery of 16 x 5in/38 (127mm/38) guns in eight twin turrets instead of her original secondary and tertiary batteries; and an AA armament of 48 x 40mm and 44 x 20mm. *Colorado* had her secondary battery reduced to 8 x 5in/51 (127mm/51) guns, but the AA armament comprised 8 x 5in/38 (127mm/38) dual-purpose guns, plus 40 x 40mm and 37 x 20mm. Both vessels had extra horizontal armour, and two HA/LA director control towers were added. These alterations raised full-load displacement to 39,000 tons (39,624 tonnes) in *Maryland* and to 40,396 tons (41,042 tonnes) in *Colorado*.

West Virginia was sunk at Pearl Harbor, but raised and by 1944 rebuilt along the lines of the Tennessee class, large bulges increasing beam to 114ft (34·75m) and 16 x 5in/38 (127mm/38) DP, 64 x 40mm and 82 x 20mm guns being added. *Maryland* and *Colorado* were scrapped in 1959, and *West Virginia* in 1961; all were broken up by Todd Shipyard.

Below: *Maryland* in 1921.

Below: *Maryland* in August 1944 with increased superstructure aft, control towers fitted, and greatly improved AA armament. By 1945, *West Virginia* resembled *California*.

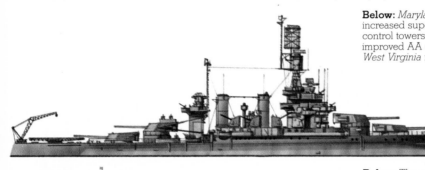

Below: *Nelson*'s sister-ship, *Rodney*, in 1942. The main armament was concentrated forward to make the most of the armour protection sanctioned by the Washington Treaty.

Below: The compact outline of the 1928-29 Italian battleship project.

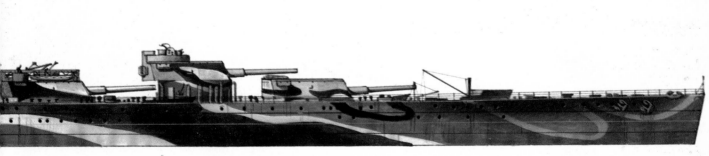

BATTLESHIP DESIGN

1928-29 Italy

Displacement: c27,000 tons (27,432 tonnes) full load.
Dimensions: 623ft 4½in (190m) oa x 91ft 10in (26m) x 26ft 3in (8m).
Machinery: 4 turbines; 4 shafts.
Armour: 9·45in (240mm) belt; 5·5in (140mm) deck; 13in-5·9in (330-150mm) turrets; 10·6in (270mm) conning tower.
Armament: 6 x 15in (381mm); 8 x 6in (152mm) or 4·7in (120mm); 12 x 3·9in (100mm) AA; 6 x 40mm AA; 2 x 17·7in (450mm) torpedo tubes.
Performance: 29kt (53·7km/h).
Crew: Not known.

Designed to see how best Italy could use the 70,000 tons (71,120 tonnes) of battleship displacement allowed to her within the terms of the Washington Treaty, the 1928-29 Project was an attempt to provide a viable capital ship of which three could be built. The result was a small ship bearing a strong resemblance to the Pola class heavy cruisers, with a centre-line main armament in three turrets (two forward and one aft) and the secondary armament in two twin turrets on each beam abreast the superstructure. There was provision for four aircraft. Armour details given above indicate the probable approximate disposition.
Neat though the design was, the Italians realised how impractical the ships would be. Some of the development work, however, bore fruit in the Vittorio Veneto class.

displacement at a maximum of 35,000 tons (35,560 tonnes) and gun calibre at a maximum of 16in (406mm).

E.L. Attwood and S.V. Goodall thus had a difficult task in designing the pair of ships permitted to the UK to balance the Japanese Nagato and US Maryland classes, whose ships had 16in (406mm) guns. What finally emerged was a cut-down version of the 1921 'G3' battlecruiser design with the same armament and level of protection, though the weight limitations had to be met by a reduction in the volume covered by the armour, and by fitting much less powerful machinery. The need to economise on the area of armour also dictated the arrangement of all three turrets forward of the tower bridge, instead of two forward and one aft as

in the battlecruiser design. Other special features of the Nelsons' design were that they were the only British capital ships with 16in (406mm) guns; were the first to have triple turrets, the main-deck secondary battery replaced by turrets, and tower bridges; and had their engines rooms forward of the boiler rooms. The Nelsons were also the last capital ships with separate conning towers, capped by armoured and revolving director control positions. The usual positions of the engine and boiler rooms were reversed in an unsuccessful attempt to keep the bridges clear of smoke.

The main turret disposition did achieve its object of reducing the quantity of armour needed, but also made fire aft of the beam impossible because of the guns' enormous blast

pattern. 'A', 'B' and 'C' turrets each mounted a trio of 16in (406mm) guns: each of these weighed 103·5 tons (105 tonnes) and fired a 2,461lb (1,116kg) shell with a muzzle velocity of 2,953ft (900m) per second to a range of 35,000 yards (32,005m) with an elevation of 40°, which also made it possible for the main armament to be used against distant aircraft. The secondary armament, grouped in six twin turrets (power-operated, for the first time in a Royal Navy ship) was located towards the stern. The AA armament was located abreast and aft of the tower bridge, and was later considerably augmented: by the end of the war it amounted, in *Nelson*, to 6 x 4·7in (120mm), 48 x 2pdrs, 16 x 40mm and 61 x 20mm.

Armour was on the 'all-or-nothing'

principle, with only the vital areas (waterline, turrets, magazines, barbettes, machinery spaces and conning tower) receiving protection. This was excellent in both the vertical and horizontal planes, and formed part of each ship's basic structure. However, by the beginning of World War II it was clear that the horizontal armour could be pierced by bombs.

To reduce weight to within the limitations of the Washington Treaty something had to be sacrificed, and in the case of the Nelson class it was power: speed was thus low, and both ships were poor seaboats which rolled badly and were slow in response to the helm. However, both performed nobly in World War II before being scrapped in 1948 and 1949.

1930-1939

As in the 1920s, battleship development in the 1930s was dominated by the restrictive measures imposed by international treaty, the spirit of Washington being continued in form if not in detail by the two London Naval Conferences, and the agreements which they spawned, of 1930 and 1935-36. However, with the countries involved limited to the three major maritime powers, Great Britain, the United States and Japan, in the first and to Great Britain, the USA and France in the second, and with the abandonment of quantitative limits and the insertion of various clauses covering action permissible should any of the signatories abrogate, the fragility of the new treaties was plain to see.

The decade was characterised also by the revival of capital ship construction—indeed, all naval construction—in Germany and by wide-ranging programmes of battleship modernization in all leading navies. From the mid-1930s, as the building 'holiday' imposed by Washington and extended under the First London Conference agreement lapsed, plans for new construction were put in hand. The resultant ships would be the last all-big-gun vessels to be built in the world's naval construction yards.

MODERNIZATION PROGRAMMES

The prohibition under Washington of new battleship construction—continued among the signatories of the First London Conference agreement—did not exclude the refitting of existing ships to improve their defensive qualities; indeed, an additional 3,000 tons (3,048 tonnes) per unit could be worked in, in the form of anti-aircraft (weapons, armour) and anti-torpedo (typically bulges) measures. Far more was in fact done. Oil-fired boilers were installed in place of coal-burning units where appropriate, complete sets of new machinery were installed, and aircraft catapults were fitted. In extreme cases, ships were gutted and completely rebuilt, emerging for all practical purposes as entirely new ships, quite unrecognisable from their original states. The Japanese Kongos, for example, had their hulls lengthened considerably in order to provide optimum lines for high speed, while the Italian Cavours and Duilios were totally reconfigured, having extended and reshaped bows, a heavier main armament (achieved by reboring the original barrels), a completely new secondary armament and a rebuilt superstructure. Three British Queen Elizabeths, plus *Renown*, were reconstructed with a new superstructure and other important changes, while their main armament elevation was increased from 20° to 30° in order to extend the range of their guns. Plans for further dramatic refits for existing ships were terminated only by the outbreak of World War II, when neither extensive periods out of service in dockyard hands nor the requisite appropriations (more effectively directed elsewhere) could really be justified for capital ships other than in the United States, where circumstances forced hands and thus offered special opportunities.

NEW CONSTRUCTION

Great Britain had been permitted to build two new 16in (406mm) gunned battleships (to emerge as the Nelsons) under the terms of the Washington Treaty, but the seeds of a new round of capital ship rivalry were not sown until early 1929 when Germany, prohibited from constructing warships displacing over 10,000 tons (10,160 tonnes), laid down the first of her unique class of *Panzerschiffe*, essentially

Below: Germany's solution to the 10,000-ton (10,160 tonne) limits imposed on her by the Washington Treaty was the unique *Panzerschiff* or so-called 'pocket battleship'. This is *Admiral Graf Spee*, astern of *Deutschland*, 1939. Diesel propulsion conferred great range.

cruisers but with a main armament of 11in (280mm) guns. France, whose allocation of 70,000 tons (71,120 tonnes) of battleship construction under Washington had not been used up, who was permitted to build one new vessel in 1927, but who in any case was not bound by its successor treaty from 1931, responded with *Dunkerque* and then a sister-ship *Strasbourg*, and Italy countered the French move with the Vittorio Veneto class. The European race was enlivened by the public denunciation by Hitler of the 1919 Versailles Treaty and the establishment of a building programme of enlarged, fast *Panzerschiffe, Scharnhorst* and *Gneisenau* (see pages 246 and 247).

The last vestiges of international concord died when it became clear that Japan would refuse to be bound by the clauses of the 1935-36 agreement, in which unlimited numbers of capital ships could be constructed provided their displacement did not exceed 35,000 tons (35,560 tonnes) nor their main armament 14in (356mm) in calibre. The escalator provisions allowed a reversion to 16in (406mm), the maximum agreed in 1922, in the event of Japan's non-ratification, but efforts to encompass comparable individual ship displacements, with a desirable ceiling of 40,000 tons (40,640 tonnes) expressed by Great Britain but one of 45,000 tons (45,720 tonnes) insisted upon

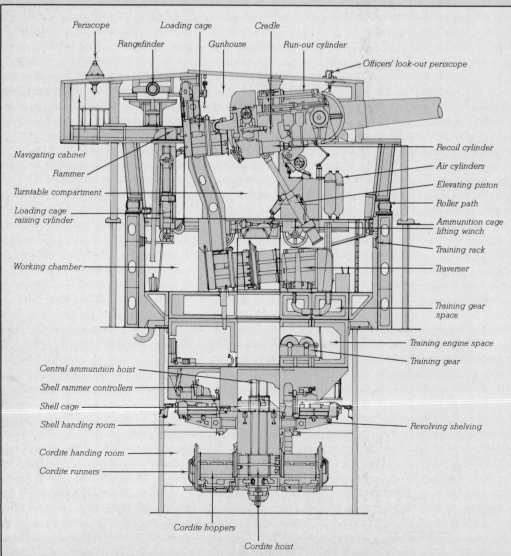

Above left: The direct response to the German Deutschlands was the French *Dunkerque* (shown, 1938) and *Strasbourg*. They were influenced by the Nelsons not only in the main armament layout but also in the adoption of an internal, inclined armour belt.

Above right: By the late 1930s the battleship building 'leap-frog' process was in full swing once more: the Germans countered the French Dunkerques with *Scharnhorst* (shown) and *Gneisenau*, much enhanced *Panzerschiffe*. Note the retrofitted 'Alantic' bow.

Right: As the air threat grew, ships responded by carrying ever-increasing numbers of light AA weapons in multiple mountings. This is the famous German 20mm 'vierling', developed during the late 1930s for installation aboard capital ships, cruisers and destroyers from 1941.

Left: The British 14in (356mm) Mk VII gun on the quadruple Mk III mounting, as fitted in 'A' and 'Y' positions aboard King George V class battleships. Designed in the late 1930s, the turret was a natural development of the 15in (381mm) systems of World War I, though any-elevation loading was abandoned owing to complexity. Rate of fire was about one round every 25 seconds and total weight *c*1,500 tons.

Right: The Second London Naval Treaty envisaged battleships limited to a main armament of 14in (356mm) guns, and although *North Carolina*'s battery was upgraded to 16in (406mm) the design was too far advanced by the late 1930s for her armour scheme, intended to defeat 14in (356mm) shells, to be changed. The main belt was sloped, but still external; otherwise the *Nevada* scheme was essentially retained.

Periscope · Rangefinder · Loading cage · Gunhouse · Cradle · Run-out cylinder · Officers' look-out periscope · Recoil cylinder · Air cylinders · Elevating piston · Roller path · Ammunition cage lifting winch · Training rack · Traverser · Training gear space · Training engine space · Training gear · Revolving shelving

Navigating cabinet · Rammer · Turntable compartment · Loading cage raising cylinder · Working chamber · Central ammunition hoist · Shell rammer controllers · Shell cage · Shell handing room · Cordite handing room · Cordite runners · Cordite hoppers · Cordite hoist

by the United States, failed. The provisions were invoked just prior to the outbreak of war, which later finally swept away all treaty constraints.

The Anglo-German Navy Treaty of 1935 was an attempt to contain Hitler's ambitions but its most important effect was the implicit recognition of Germany as a major European naval power once more; it also signalled the laying down of that country's large battleships *Bismarck* and *Tirpitz*. The British counter to German battleship rearmament was the King George V class, with ten 14in (356mm) guns on 35,000 tons (35,560 tonnes), their main calibre limited principally in hopes of encouraging other nations to abide by the 1935-36 agreement but also on grounds of economics and because a design revision to accommodate a large gun would cause too much delay; the Lions, mounting nine 16in (406mm) guns, were subsequently approved but never completed.

The United States meanwhile had already decided to press ahead with the 16in (406mm) calibre and laid down two classes totalling six ships, followed by a further six 45,000 ton (45,720 tonne) units, the Iowas, with plans for the even large Montanas. Japan's attitude became apparent when details emerged of the new Yamatos—the largest and most heavily armed capital ships ever built, with nine 18·1in (460mm) guns on around 70,000 tons (71,120 tonnes) displacement.

TECHNICAL DEVELOPMENTS

By the mid-1930s the importance of aircraft, both as an aid to fleet actions in the role of spotting and reconnaissance and as a threat in the form of hostile torpedo- and dive-bombing, was the single most important influence on battleship design; together with increased speed, requiring large hulls, it was the principal factor in driving up battleship size to unprecedented levels. By the mid-1930s battleships were typically fitted with catapults for floatplanes and amphibians, sometimes on turret tops (for example the US *Texas*, British *Ramillies* and Japanese *Fuso*), sometimes on quarterdecks (e.g. *Valiant*, *Yamashiro*) or both (e.g. *Mississippi*)—or occasionally on the forecastle (as in Italian capital ships). Rebuilds took into account the need not only for catapult sites but also for hangar facilities, British reconstructions for example incorporating the characteristic athwartships launching capability amidships. The growing potency of the dive-bomber in particular caused horizontal armour to be increased in thickness, the consequent effect of this additional topweight being compensated for by increased beams (anti-torpedo bulges had some purpose in this respect for reconstructed ships).

The threat of the aircraft was also responsible for the installation of enhanced anti-aircraft batteries aboard capital ships, and the dual-purpose gun—the US 5in/38 (127mm/38), the British 4·5in (114mm) and 5·25in (133mm) and various Japanese 5in (127mm) weapons—evolved, which eased the competition for weight and space on board ship not only because it cut the number of individual mountings required but also because it reduced the number of directors needed, although of course there would never be enough. Short-range, single-purpose light AA guns with high rates of fire were developed during the 1930s—US 1·1in (28mm), British 2pdr 'pom-pom', Japanese 25mm—in multiple mountings. The clutter of topside space that would distinguish battleship appearance during World War II—indicative of the desperate measures required to maintain the viability of the type—was set in train.

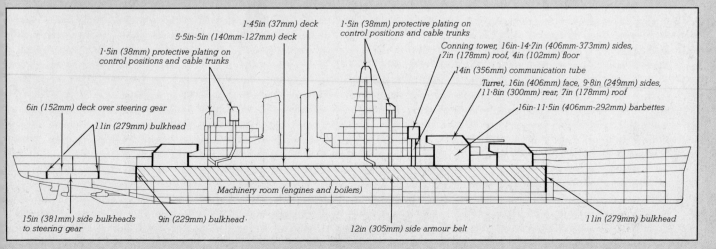

1·45in (37mm) deck

5·5in-5in (140mm-127mm) deck

1·5in (38mm) protective plating on control positions and cable trunks

1·5in (38mm) protective plating on control positions and cable trunks

Conning tower, 16in-14·7in (406mm-373mm) sides, 7in (178mm) roof, 4in (102mm) floor

14in (356mm) communication tube

Turret, 16in (406mm) face, 9·8in (249mm) sides, 11·8in (300mm) rear, 7in (178mm) roof

16in-11·5in (406mm-292mm) barbettes

6in (152mm) deck over steering gear

11in (279mm) bulkhead

15in (381mm) side bulkheads to steering gear

9in (229mm) bulkhead

Machinery room (engines and boilers)

12in (305mm) side armour belt

11in (279mm) bulkhead

DEUTSCHLAND

1933 *Germany*
Other ships in class: *Admiral Scheer, Admiral Graf Spee*

Laid down: 5 February 1929.
Launched: 19 May 1931.
Builder: Deutschewerke, Kiel.
Displacement: 11,750 tons (11,938 tonnes) standard; 15,900 tons (16,154 tonnes) full load.
Dimensions: 610ft 3in (186m) oa x 67ft 6in (20·6m) x 23ft 7½in (7·2m) max.
Machinery: Four 9-cylinder double-acting MAN diesels; 2 shafts; 50,000 BHP.
Armour: 3·1in-2·4in (80-60mm) belt; 1·8in-1·6in (45-40mm) bulkheads; 1·6in (40mm) deck; 5·5in-3·3in (140-85mm) turrets; 3·9in (100mm) barbettes; 5·9in-2in (150-50mm) conning tower.
Armament: 6 x 11in (280mm); 8 x 5·9in (150mm); 3 x 3·5in (88mm); 8 x 19·7in (500mm) torpedo tubes.
Performance: 28kt (51·9km/h); oil 2,755 tons (2,800 tonnes); radius 8,700nm (16,120km) at 19kt (35·2km/h).
Crew: 619.

Limited by the 1919 Versailles Treaty to a maximum displacement of 10,000 tons (10,160 tonnes) and a maximum gun calibre of 11in (280mm) for any ships that she might possess, Germany produced an ingenious solution in her celebrated 'pocket-battleships'. The object of the relevant Treaty clauses was to ensure that the German Navy could not operate blue-water capital

ships, and the partial effectiveness of the restrictions is evidenced by the fact that these three vessels were in reality no more than heavily gunned cruisers.

The Deutschlands were required principally for commerce raiding, and so the salient features of the design were a powerful main armament and long endurance. Diesel engines, economical and less complex than steam turbines, were fitted, and weight-saving measures included cruiser-type protection, the grouping of the main armament in two triple turrets, one forward and one aft, and hull construction of welded light alloy. Contemporary German claims for exceptionally high speeds for these vessels proved to be misleading.

Deutschland was fitted with a catapult and carried two aircraft from 1935 (her sister-ships were so equipped upon completion), and in that year received twin 3·5in (88mm) mountings in place of her original singles; four twin 37mm AA were also added and her torpedo tubes were replaced with 21in (533mm) mountings, as carried by the rest of the class. In 1940 the 3·5in (88mm) weapons were removed and standard 4·1in (105mm) AA fitted, by which time the ship had been renamed *Lützow* to avoid the possibility of a ship bearing the name of the Father-land being lost.

Admiral Scheer (launched 1 April 1933 at Wilhelmshaven Dockyard) and *Admiral Graf Spee* (launched 30 June 1934, also at Wilhelmshaven) showed important differences in appearance. Both had a tower-type

bridge instead of the tubular 'pole' fitted to *Deutschland* (*Scheer*'s was remodelled to a tubular design in 1940), and *Spee* was beamier (69ft 10in, 21·3m) than her sisters and also had a more substantial armour belt.

During the war both *Lützow* and *Scheer* had their bows modified to improve seakeeping, and both were fitted with a distinctive funnel cap. Close-range armament was strengthened considerably late in World War II: by 1945 *Scheer* was carrying 6 x 40mm AA and 24 x 20mm AA, and *Lützow* 6 x 40mm and 26 x 20mm.

All three vessels conducted successful anti-commerce operations

during the war. *Spee* was scuttled off Montevideo after the famous River Plate action: damaged by gunfire from the British cruisers *Exeter*, *Achilles* and *Ajax*, she ran for harbour, but her commander was duped into believing that heavy British units were awaiting her departure. She went down on 17 December 1939. *Lützow* was disabled in an air attack at Swinemünde and scuttled, 4 May 1945; she was broken up piecemeal in the post-war years. *Scheer* was sunk by RAF bombs in April 1945 at Kiel; after partial scrapping, the remains were covered during dockyard extension work at Kiel.

Below: The German 'pocket-battleship' *Admiral Graf Spee* as she appeared while raiding in the South Atlantic, shortly before she was scuttled off Montevideo on 17 December 1939.

Above: *Lützow* (formerly *Deutschland*) anchored behind anti-torpedo net and boom defences in a Norwegian fjord, World War II. Note the distinctive funnel cap, fitted also on *Scheer*.

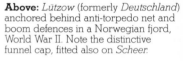

Above: *Admiral Graf Spee* before the outbreak of World War II. The biplane floatplane seen aft was later replaced by an Arado Ar 196 (see profile below).

Below: This ambitious German design of the inter-war years was for a compact battleship of 26,000 tons, driven by four Junkers diesel units and mounting 12 x 12in (305mm) guns.

Below: *Lützow* is shown in the 'splinter' camouflage scheme carried in Norwegian waters during the summer of 1942. Note that her bridge structure was lighter than that of her sister-ships, and her catapult was sited between bridge and funnel, rather than abaft the funnel.

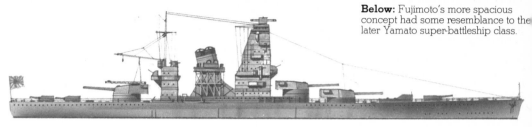

BATTLESHIP DESIGNS

1930 *Japan*

Designers: (A) Hiraga; (B) Fujimoto.
Displacement: (A) 35,000 tons (35,560 tonnes) standard, 39,200 tons (39,827 tonnes) load; (B) 35,000 tons (35,560 tonnes) standard, 39,250 tons (39,878 tonnes) load.
Dimensions: (A) 761ft 2in (232m) wl x 105ft 8in (32·2m) x 29ft 6in (9m); (B) 777ft 6in (237m) wl x 105ft (32m) x 28ft 6in (8·7m).
Machinery: (A) 4 Kampon turbines, 10 boilers, 4 shafts, 80,000 SHP; (B) 4 Kampon turbines, 4 shafts, 73,000 SHP.
Armour: Not known.
Armament: (A) 10 x 16in (406mm), 16 x 6in (152mm), 8 x 4·7in (120mm) AA, 2 x 24in (609mm) torpedo tubes; (B) 9 x 16in (406mm), 12 x 6in (152mm), 8 x 4·7in AA.
Performance: (A) 26·3kt (48·7km/h); (B) 25·9kt (48km/h).
Crew: Not known.

These two studies, had they been followed through, would undoubtedly have resulted in the ugliest capital ships ever. Hiraga's design, a *Kongo* replacement, showed a compact superstructure (a feature of the later Yamatos), with provision for aircraft catapults on 'B' and 'X' turrets and a casemated secondary armament. The unconventional disposition of the 6in (152mm) guns in Fujimoto's design *(Fuso* replacement), was presumably a product of cramped accommodation amidships.

Below: Hiraga's compact battleship design featured a large funnel trunked away from the bridge.

Below: Fujimoto's more spacious concept had some resemblance to the later Yamato super-battleship class.

BATTLESHIP DESIGN 'UP 41'

1936 *Russia*

Designer: Ansaldo.
Displacement: 42,000 tons (42,672 tonnes) standard; 50,000 tons (50,800 tonnes) full load.
Dimensions: 816ft 7in (248·9m) oa x 116ft 6in (35·5m) x 29ft 6in (9m).
Machinery: 4 turbines; 8 boilers; 4 shafts; 177,500 SHP.
Armour: 13·2in-5·7in (335-145mm) belt; 13·8in-5·7in (350-145mm) bulkheads; 2·2in (55mm) upper deck; 2·6in (65mm) main deck; 15·75in-5·7in (400-145mm) turrets; 13·8in (350mm) barbettes; 7·1in-3·5in (180-90mm) secondary turrets; 13·2in-7·9in (335-200mm) conning tower.
Armament: 9 x 16in (406mm); 12 x 7·1in (180mm); 24 x 3·9in (100mm) AA; 48 x 45mm AA; 24 x 13·2mm AA.
Performance: 32kt (59·3km/h).
Crew: Not known.

Worried by the German naval rearmament programmes under way in the 1930s, Stalin decided upon an ambitious Soviet response, to be spearheaded by the construction of 16 capital ships. Lacking design experience, the naval authorities made a number of approaches to foreign concerns, the first being to Ansaldo of Genoa. The Italian design bore a marked similarity to the *Littorio* then under construction by that company, both in general configuration and in protection arrangements. The outbreak of World War II prevented any further progress with the design.

BATTLESHIP DESIGNS

1937-39 *Russia*

Displacement: (A) 66,074 tons (67,131 tonnes) standard; (B) 71,850 tons (73,000 tonnes) standard, 74,000 tons (75,184 tonnes) full load; (C) 44,200 tons (44,907 tonnes) standard, 55,200 tons (56,083 tonnes) full load; (D) 45,000 tons (45,720 tonnes) standard, 53,680 tons (54,539 tonnes) full load.
Dimensions: (A) 1,000ft (304·8m) x 126 (38·4m) x 34ft 6in (10·5m); (B) 1005ft (306·3m) x 128ft (39m) x 34ft 6in (10·5m); (C) 844ft 10in (257·5m) x 129ft 6in (39·5m) x 33ft 6in (10·2m); (D) 903ft 10in (275·5m) x 113ft 6in (34·6m) x 33ft 6in (10·2m).
Machinery: Turbines, (A, B) 300,000 SHP; (C, D) 200,000 SHP.
Armour: Not known.
Armament: (A) 8 x 18in (457mm), 28 x 5in (127mm), 24 x 1·1in (28mm); (B) 12 x16in (406mm), 28 x 5in (127mm), 32 x 1·1in (28mm); (C) 10 x 16in (406mm), 20 x 5in (127mm); (D) 10 x 16in (406mm), 20 x 5in (127mm), 16 x 1·1in (28mm).
Performance: (A) 34kt (63km/h); (B, C) 31·9kt (59·1km/h); (D) 31kt (57·4km/h).
Crew: Not known.

Three hybrid battleship-carrier designs were drawn up by the US firm of Gibbs & Cox in response to Soviet requests. Somewhat optimistically, c30 aircraft were to have been operated via catapults and a landing deck amidships. A fourth design, for a more conventional battleship, was also studied. None was built.

PANZERSCHIFF DESIGN

1938 *Germany*

Displacement: 31,000 tons (31,496 tonnes).
Dimensions: 771ft (235m) oa x 88ft 7in (27m).
Machinery: 3/4 diesels; 3/4 shafts.
Armour: 5·7in (145mm) belt; 3in-2·4in (75-60mm) deck; 5·5in-3·3in (140-85mm) turrets.
Armament: 6 x 11in (280mm); 4 x 5·9in (150mm); 8 x 4·1in (105mm) AA; 12 x 37mm AA; 6 x 20mm AA; 8 x 21in (533mm) torpedo tubes.
Performance: c34kt.
Crew: Not known.

Work began in 1937 on a project designated *Kreuzer P,* intended to provide the German Navy with twelve improved Deutschlands as part of Hitler's 'Z-Plan'. The conceptual features of the original 'pocket-battleships' were retained, but more powerful machinery was to be installed in order to give the desired 20 per cent increase in speed, in turn necessitating a much larger hull. Protection was substantially improved, but armament was not drastically altered. In appearance the ships would have differed considerably, with twin funnels before and abaft the aircraft catapult, and hangarage abreast the second funnel. The hull featured an 'Atlantic'-type bow and, for the first time in a German capital ship, a transom stern. The project had all but died by the outbreak of war, resources and energies being diverted to more immediate problems facing the administrators of German Navy.

GASCOGNE

1938 (design only) *France*

Builder: St Nazaire-Penhoët.
Displacement: 35,000 tons (35,560 tonnes) standard; 40,900 tons (41,554 tonnes) normal.
Dimensions: 813ft (247·8m) oa x 108ft 1in (33·1m) x 35ft 1in (10·7m) max.
Machinery: 4 Parsons geared turbines; 6 Indret boilers; 4 shafts; 150,000 SHP.
Armour: 13·6in-9·8in (345-250mm) belt; 6·7in-5·1in (170-130mm) main deck; 1·6in (40mm) lower deck; 16·9in-6·7in (430-170mm) turrets; 5·1in-2·8in (130-70mm) secondary turrets; 13·4in (340mm) conning tower.
Armament: 8 x 15in (380mm); 9 x 6in (152mm); 16 x 3·9in (100mm) AA; 20 x 37mm AA; 36 x 13·2mm AA.
Performance: 30kt (55·6km/h); radius c8,000nm (14,285km) at 15kt (27·8km/h).
Crew: c1750.

Although of the same general dimensions and characteristics as the Richelieus, *Gascogne* would have had a revised main armament layout, with one quadruple 15in (380mm) turret forward and one aft, to give astern fire; to accommodate this, the entire superstructure would have been moved some 60ft (17·5m) further forward. An aircraft hangar was to have been sited below the quarterdeck, and the secondary armament was to be relocated in centre-line superfiring positions. The outbreak of war delayed, and the fall of France in June 1940 finally killed off, the project.

DUNKERQUE

1937 France
Other ships in class: *Strasbourg*

Laid down: 24 December 1932.
Launched: 2 October 1935.
Builder: Brest Dockyard.
Displacement: 26,500 tons (26,924 tonnes) standard; 35,500 tons (36,068 tonnes) deep load.
Dimensions: 703ft 9in (214·5m) oa x 102ft 3in (31·16m) x 28ft 6in (8·69m).
Machinery: 4 Parsons geared turbines; 6 Indret small-tube boilers; 4 shafts; 112,500 SHP.
Armour: 9·5in-7·7in (240-195mm) belt; 9in-3·9in (228-98mm) bulkheads; 5·1in-4·5in (130-115mm) main deck; 2in-1·6in (50-40mm) lower deck; 1·6in-1·2in (40-30mm) torpedo bulkheads; 13in-5·9in (330-150mm) turrets; 13·6in (345mm) barbettes; 3·5in-3·1in (90-80mm) secondary turrets; 10·6in (270mm) conning tower.
Armament: 8 x 13in (330mm); 16 x 5·1in (130mm) DP; 8 x 37mm AA; 32 x 13·2mm AA.
Performance: 29·5kt (54·67km/h); oil 6,500 tons (6,604 tonnes); radius 7,500nm (13,900km) at 15kt (27·8km/h).
Crew: 1,431.

The first French ships to be laid down after the 'battleship holiday' imposed by the Washington Treaty, the Dunkerques were the culmination of a series of design studies undertaken during the 1920s and were ultimately produced as a counter to the German Deutschlands. As such, they were armoured against 11in (280mm) shell-fire, and their consequent relatively light protection, combined with their high speed, led to their frequently being termed battlecruisers.

The design was interesting for the fact that the main armament—consisting of a new 13in (330mm) gun, a calibre considerably smaller than the maximum permitted under Washington—was mounted in two quadruple turrets forward. Although this arrangement enabled magazine protection to be concentrated (thereby saving weight), it had the disadvantage of restricting arcs of fire and entailed the risk of a single hit disabling half the battery. The secondary armament, in three quadruple turrets aft and two twins amidships, consisted of a new calibre, dual-purpose weapon which proved somewhat less than successful in service. An aircraft catapult and hangar were provided right aft, with facilities for four machines.

The main belt was sloped rather than vertical, and although not of battleship proportions the total weight of armour carried accounted for over 35 per cent of the standard displacement. Underwater protection was particularly comprehensive, and included layers of rubber compound designed to be impervious to water.

Strasbourg was launched on 12 December 1936 at the St Nazaire-Penhoët yard and differed from her sister only in bridge detail. Neither vessel received significant modification during its career. *Dunkerque*, twice attacked by the British to prevent her use by the Germans during World War II, was scuttled in 1942 at Toulon; *Strasbourg* met a similar fate, although she was salved in 1945 and used for experiments until being finally broken up in 1958.

Below: *Dunkerque,* seen as completed in 1937, and *Strasbourg* were the first battleships with purpose-designed hangars for the Lioré 130 aircraft carried aft. Main armament was concentrated forward to save weight.

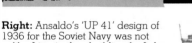

Right: Ansaldo's 'UP 41' design of 1936 for the Soviet Navy was not unlike *Littorio,* then building for Italy.

Right: Gibbs & Cox projected this 71,850-ton battleship-carrier hybrid for the Soviet Navy in 1937-39.

Right: Germany's projected *Kreuzer P* class of 1938 was intended to combine the wide cruising radius of the Deutschland class with higher speed and improved protection.

Right: France's projected *Gascogne* of 1938—based on the Richelieus but with a revised main armament layout: quadruple turrets fore and aft.

GNEISENAU

1938 *Germany*
Other ships in class: *Scharnhorst*

Laid down: 3 March 1935.
Launched: 8 December 1936.
Builder: Deutschewerke, Kiel.
Displacement: 34,840 tons (35,397 tonnes) standard; 38,900 tons (39,522 tonnes) deep load.
Dimensions: 753ft 11in (229·8m) oa x 98ft 5in (30m) x 27ft (8·23m).
Machinery: 3 Germania geared turbines; 12 Wagner boilers; 3 shafts; 160,000 SHP.
Armour: 13·8in-7·9in (350-200mm) belt; 0·8in (20mm) belt ends; 7·9in-5·9in (200-150mm) bulkheads; 2in-0·8in (50-20mm) armoured deck; 2in (50mm) upper deck; 1·8in (45mm) torpedo bulkheads; 14·2in-5·9in (360-150mm) turrets; 13·8in-7·9in (350-200mm) barbettes; 5·5in-2in (140-50mm) secondary turrets; 5·9in (150mm) secondary barbettes; 13·8in-3·9in (350-100mm) conning tower.
Armament: 9 x 11in (280mm); 12 x 5·9in (150mm); 14 x 4·1in (105mm) AA; 16 x 37mm AA; 8 x 20mm AA.
Performance: 31kt (57·45km/h); oil 6,000 tons (6,096 tonnes) max; radius 8,500nm (15,570km) at 17kt (31·5km/h).
Crew: 1,669.

Gneisenau and her sister-ship *Scharnhorst* were the subject of considerable political controversy before work on them was begun, and in fact they started life as the fourth and fifth units of the Deutschland class. Hitler had for some time been advocating the construction of larger and better-protected versions of the Deutschlands, but the news that the French were building their Dunkerques prompted the German Navy to urge a more appropriate response. A gun of heavier calibre than the 11in (280mm) then in service was what was really needed, but such a weapon was only in the design stage; however, the Navy argued, three triple 11in (280mm) rather than the two Hitler deemed sufficient would be the absolute minimum required if the ships were not to be seriously inferior. The Navy got its way, and even managed to head off a fresh demand from Hitler that the ships be equipped with 15in (380mm) guns by allowing for subsequent installation of this weapon in the design.

Although diesel engines were originally envisaged, it was quickly appreciated that only steam turbines would drive a ship of this size satisfactorily, albeit at the

Above: *Gneisenau* in 1938; a Heinkel He 114 seaplane on the midships catapult, with an Arado Ar 95 aft.

Below: *Gneisenau* as seen before alteration in 1939, with a straight stem and flat-topped funnel.

Right: *Gneisenau* is followed by *Admiral Graf Spee, Admiral Scheer* and *Deutschland,* August 1938.

price of range; however, the machinery proved notoriously unreliable in service.

The overall design harked back to the ill-fated Mackensens and Ersatz Yorcks of World War I, which were the most recent warships of comparable dimensions that Germany had laid down. Both ships were originally built with straight stems but problems of wetness forward led to their being given lengthened 'Atlantic' bows soon after completion; the flat-topped funnels were fitted with raked caps, and at the same time *Scharnhorst* had her main mast separated from the funnel,

redesigned as a tripod, and moved aft. Both vessels were equipped with aircraft catapults, on the hangar amidships and atop 'Y' turret, though the turret catapult was taken out soon after commissioning.

Appearance differences, other than the positioning of the main mast, were minimal, being confined chiefly to the hangar dimensions, bridge detail and handling cranes. AA armament was improved in service with the addition of 20mm guns, and the ships were fitted with 6 x 21in (533mm) torpedo tubes in 1941.

Gneisenau, which conducted

some successful commerce raids in company with her sister early in the war, was the subject of constant attention from British forces during World War II, culminating in a heavy air raid whilst she was at Kiel in November 1942 which left her bows badly damaged. Her reconstruction to take 15in (380mm) guns was seriously contemplated—and indeed begun—but in the event she languished where she was docked until towed to Gotenhafen and sunk as a blockship in March 1945. *Scharnhorst* enjoyed a rather longer and somewhat more successful career: among her victims were the

AMC *Rawalpindi* (November 1939) and, in company with *Gneisenau,* the aircraft carrier *Glorious* (June 1940). A break-out into the Atlantic with *Gneisenau* in early 1941 resulted in the loss of 22 Allied merchant ships. However, after being damaged by mines whilst engaged, with her sister and the cruiser *Prinz Eugen,* in the 'Channel Dash' in February 1942, she kept to home waters and was much less of a threat to the British. She was sunk on 26 December 1943 off the North Cape by gunfire and torpedoes from British forces led by the battleship *Duke of York* whilst on an anti-shipping sortie.

Above: *Scharnhorst* (foreground) and *Gneisenau* leave a northern base for a raiding cruise into the Atlantic.

Below: *Scharnhorst* as she appeared during 'Operation Cerberus'—the 'Channel Dash' from Brest to Kiel, with *Gneisenau* and *Prinz Eugen,* on 11-12 February 1942. Grey paint has been hastily applied on her upperworks; the turret tops are blue.

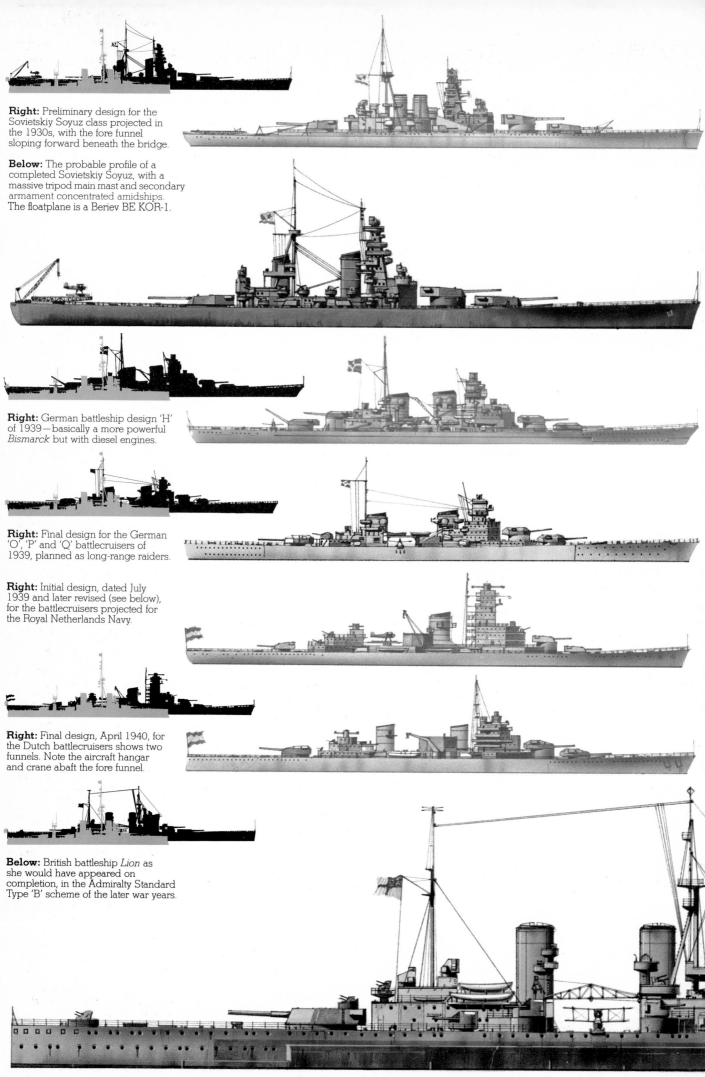

Right: Preliminary design for the Sovietskiy Soyuz class projected in the 1930s, with the fore funnel sloping forward beneath the bridge.

Below: The probable profile of a completed Sovietskiy Soyuz, with a massive tripod main mast and secondary armament concentrated amidships. The floatplane is a Beriev BE KOR-1.

Right: German battleship design 'H' of 1939—basically a more powerful *Bismarck* but with diesel engines.

Right: Final design for the German 'O', 'P' and 'Q' battlecruisers of 1939, planned as long-range raiders.

Right: Initial design, dated July 1939 and later revised (see below), for the battlecruisers projected for the Royal Netherlands Navy.

Right: Final design, April 1940, for the Dutch battlecruisers shows two funnels. Note the aircraft hangar and crane abaft the fore funnel.

Below: British battleship *Lion* as she would have appeared on completion, in the Admiralty Standard Type 'B' scheme of the later war years.

SOVIETSKIY SOYUZ

1939 (not completed) *Russia*
Other ships in class: *Sovietskaya Ukraina, Sovietskaya Byelorossia, Sovietskaya Rossia*

Laid down: 28 August 1938.
Builder: Ordzhonikidze Yard, Leningrad.
Displacement: 59,150 tons (60,096 tonnes) standard; 65,150 tons (66,192 tonnes) full load.
Dimensions: 889ft 1in (271m) oa x 127ft 8in (38·9m) x 33ft 6in (10·2m).
Machinery: 4 Stalin turbines/electric motors; 8 boilers; 4 shafts; 231,000 SHP.
Armour: 16·75in-14·75in (425-375mm) belt; 8·7in (220mm) deck; 2·95in (75mm) torpedo bulkheads; 19·7in (500mm) turret faces; 3·9in (100mm) secondary turrets; 16·75in (425mm) conning tower.
Armament: 9 x 16in (406mm); 12 x 6in (152mm); 8 x 3·9in (100mm) AA; 32 x 37mm AA; 8 x 0·5in (12·7mm) AA.
Performance: 28kt (51·9km/h); radius 7,200nm (13,343km) at 14·5kt (26·9km/h).
Crew: Not known.

In view of the failure of the Soviets to obtain substantial foreign assistance in the production of new battleships (see 'UP 41' and other designs), it was decided to proceed with the laying down of indigenous vessels, sketch designs leading to which had been the subject of studies during the late 1930s. These appear to have been modified in the light of 'UP 41', since the general arrangements of both show some marked similarities, but the Sovietskiy Soyuz class ('Project 23') were to be considerably larger: it may well be that overseas aid was sought merely to compare ideas. In any event, since the design and construction of heavy guns and armour plate are more complex and time-consuming than the building of hulls and machinery, and bearing in mind that the Russians were virtually starting from scratch in these fields, it is difficult to believe that the project would have met with total success.

Almost nothing is known about the ships other than their basic specifications and general overall appearance, and the class has been the subject of a good deal of conjecture. Only the first three units were ever laid down (1938-39), none were launched, and the incomplete hulls were dismantled in the late 1940s.

BATTLESHIP DESIGN 'H'

1939 (not completed) *Germany*
Other ships in class: 'J', 'K', 'L', 'M', 'N'

Laid down: 15 July 1939.
Builder: Blohm & Voss, Hamburg.
Displacement: 55,453 tons (56,340 tonnes) standard; 62,497 tons (63,497 tonnes) deep load.
Dimensions: 911ft 6in (277·8m) oa x 122ft (37·2m) x 33ft 6in (10·2m).
Machinery: Twelve 9-cylinder double-acting MAN diesels; 3 shafts; 165,000 BHP.
Armour: 11·75in-7·1in (300-180mm) belt; 8·7in (220mm) bulkheads; 4·7in-3·9in (120-100mm) armoured deck; 3·1in-1·2in (80-30mm) upper deck; 1·75in (45mm) torpedo bulkheads; 15·2in-5·1in (385-130mm) turrets; 14·4in-9·4in (365-240mm) barbettes; 3·9in-1·4in (100-35mm) secondary turrets; 15·2in-5·9in (385-150mm) conning tower.
Armament: 8 x 16in (406mm); 12 x 5·9in (150mm); 16 x 4·1in (105mm) AA; 16 x 37mm AA; 24 x 20mm AA; 6 x 21in (533mm) torpedo tubes.
Performance: 30kt (55·6km/h); oil 10,000 tons (10,160 tonnes); radius 14,000nm (25,950km) at 19kt (35·2km/h).
Crew: 2,600.

Intended to be the lynch-pins of the German 'Z-Plan', these huge vessels may be summarised as more powerful, diesel-driven Bismarcks. Only 'H' and 'J' were laid down (the latter on 15 August 1939 at Weser's yard at Bremen), and work ceased a few weeks later owing to the outbreak of war and consequent new priorities.

BATTLECRUISER DESIGNS

1939 *Germany*

Displacement: 30,500 tons (30,988 tonnes) standard; 35,720 tons (36,292 tonnes) deep load.
Dimensions: 841ft 6in (256·5m) oa x 98ft 5in (30m) x 36ft 9in (11·2m) deep load.
Machinery: Eight 24-cylinder double-acting MAN diesels, 1 Brown-Boveri geared turbine; 3 shafts; 176,000 HP.
Armour: 7·1in-3·9in (180-100mm) belt; 3·9in-1in (100-25mm) bulkheads; 3·1in (80mm) armoured deck; 2in (50mm) upper deck; 1·8in (45mm) torpedo bulkheads; 8·25in-2in (210-50mm) turrets; 7·1in-5·7in (180-145mm) barbettes; 0·5in (14mm) secondary turrets; 11in-2in (280-50mm) conning tower.
Armament: 6 x 15in (380mm); 6 x 5·9in (150mm); 8 x 4·1in (105mm) AA; 8 x 37mm AA; 20 x 20mm AA; 6 x 21in (533mm) torpedo tubes.
Performance: 33·4kt (61·9km/h); oil 5,100 tons (5,182 tonnes); radius 12,150nm (22,520km) at 19kt (35·2km/h).
Crew: 1,950.

The battlecruisers 'O', 'P' and 'Q' were envisaged as long-range commerce raiders and were designed as an important element of the 'Z-Plan'. Mixed propulsion was adopted to give both the necessary radius of action and the high dash speed required to evade enemy units. Side armour was light, although the decks would have withstood air attack quite well. None was proceeded with, and in fact only 'Q' was ordered.

BATTLECRUISER DESIGNS

1939-40 *Netherlands*

Displacement: (A) 27,500 tons (27,940 tonnes) standard, 30,890 tonnes (31,384 tonnes) full load; (B) 27,950 tons (28,397 tonnes) standard; 31,500 tons (32,004 tonnes) full load.
Dimensions: (A) 771ft (235m) x 95ft 2in (29m) x 24ft 7in (7·5m); (B) 777ft 11in (237·1m) x 98ft 5in (30m) x 25ft 7in (7·8m).
Machinery: (A) 4 turbines, 8 Werkspoor boilers, 4 shafts, 155,000 SHP; (B) 4 turbines, 8 Werk-spoor boilers, 4 shafts, 180,000 SHP.
Armour: (A) 8·7in (225mm) belt; 3·9in-1·2in (100-30mm) armoured deck, 1·6in (40mm) torpedo bulkheads; (B) 8·7in-3·9in (225-100mm) belt, 11·8in (300mm) bulkheads, 3·9in-1·2in (100-30mm) armoured deck, 1·6in (40mm) torpedo bulkheads, 9·8in-3·9in (250-100mm) turrets.
Armament: (A) 9 x 11in (280mm), 8 x 4·7in (120mm), 14 x 40mm AA, 8 x 20mm AA; (B) 9 x 11in (280mm), 12 x 4·7in (120mm), 14 x 40mm AA, 8 x 20mm AA.
Performance: (A) 33kt (61·2km/h); (B) 34kt (63km/h).
Crew: (A) c1,000; (B) 1,050.

Showing strong German influence—and featuring standard German 11in (280mm) guns—a class of three units were designed to counter the latent Japanese threat to Dutch possessions in the East Indies. The original plans were drawn up in 1939 and a larger revision projected later, but the German invasion of the Netherlands halted all work.

Below: Conversion of the Lion class to battleship-carrier hybrids would have resulted in a main armament concentrated forward; secondary guns mounted in sponsons along the sides; and a raised flight deck aft.

LION

1939 (not completed) *UK*
Other ships in class: *Temeraire, Conqueror, Thunderer*

Laid down: 4 July 1939.
Builder: Vickers-Armstrong, Newcastle.
Displacement: 40,550 tons (41,199 tonnes) standard; 46,300 tons (47,041 tonnes) deep load.
Dimensions: 785ft (239·27m) oa x 104ft (31·7m) x 33ft 6in (10·21m) deep load.
Machinery: 4 Parsons geared turbines; eight 3-drum Admiralty boilers; 4 shafts; 130,000 SHP.
Armour: 15in-5·5in (381-140mm) belt; 12in-4in (305-102mm) bulkheads; 6in-5in (152-127mm) main deck; 5in-2·5in (127-63mm) lower deck; 15in-6in (381-152mm) turrets; 15in-12in (381-305mm) barbettes; 2in-1in (51-25mm) secondary turrets; 4·5in-2in (114-51mm) conning tower.
Armament: 9 x 16in (406mm); 16 x 5·25in (133mm); 48 x 2pdr AA.
Performance: 30kt (55·6km/h); oil 3,720 tons (3,780 tonnes); radius 12,150nm (22,530km) at 10kt (18·53km/h).
Crew: 1,680.

The London Naval Treaty of 1936, in accordance with the terms of which the five King George Vs had been laid down, contained a clause which permitted capital ship main armament to revert to a maximum 16in (406mm) in calibre should Japan, a non-signatory, not abide by the limits. When it became apparent that the Japanese had no intention of doing so, the clause was invoked and designs for a 35,000-ton (35,560 tonne) vessel carrying 9 x 16in (406mm) guns were prepared.

There were considerable difficulties in accommodating these two features, at least without a dangerous compromise either on machinery (hence speed) or on protection, and it was realised that a satisfactorily balanced ship could only be achieved by raising displacement, first to 38,000 tons (38,608 tonnes) and finally to 40,000 tons (40,640 tonnes). Agreement was reached with the other major naval powers (save Japan) to raise battleship limits to 45,000 tons (45,720 tonnes), but problems with docking and the additional cost of producing such vessels kept the Lions to the lower figure.

In essence, the class were enlarged King George Vs with transom sterns and an armour belt intended to defeat a 16in (406mm) shell. The main armament was of a new design, and two aircraft were to be carried. *Temeraire* was the first unit to be laid down, on 1 June 1939 by Cammell Laird at Birkenhead; *Conqueror* and *Thunderer* were to have been built by John Brown and Fairfield respectively, but neither had their keels laid. A fifth and a sixth member of the class were projected but not ordered. Work on *Lion* and *Temeraire* was halted in the autumn of 1939, in order to concentrate resources on more immediate construction.

The designs were revived in later years, considerably enlarged to take account of additions deemed essential in the light of wartime experience, and the class was still under active consideration up to 1946, but post-war economies and the appreciation that the battleship concept itself was outdated put an end to the last vestiges of the programme.

1940 onwards

With the outbreak of war the classical battleship concept faced its ultimate test. The events of the first two years were not auspicious: within six weeks of war being declared in Europe a major British unit had been lost to a daring torpedo attack; the Italian Fleet was crippled by air attack; and in 1941 the battleship *Bismarck* had been sunk, air power again sealing its fate. In December 1941 not only was the US Fleet devastated by carrier-borne aircraft at Pearl Harbor but two British ships, *Repulse* and *Prince of Wales*, were sunk while actually under way, the first time such a feat had been achieved via aerial attack and an event which proved beyond all reasonable doubt that the era of the big gun as the dominant factor in naval power was finally closing.

There were some 'traditional' surface actions on the high sea, but all were conducted without major interference from aircraft, and none was staged between opposing battle fleets in the World War I sense (principally because the ships were not available in the required numbers)—and all were influenced by the single most important wartime innovation: the fitting of onboard radar systems.

ABORTIVE PROGRAMMES

As in World War I, battleship construction programmes did not quite realise the plans originally envisaged, since more pressing needs revealed themselves as hostilities developed. Perhaps the most ambitious scheme was that set out in the late 1930s by Germany—the so-called 'Z-Plan'—wherein a ten-year schedule would result in a fleet that would be headed by eight battleships (two Bismarcks, six 'H' class), five battlecruisers (two Scharnhorsts, 'O', 'P' and 'Q'), four aircraft carriers and twelve improved Deutschlands (*Kreuzer P* project). Reference has been already made already to the British Lion class and the US Montana class battleships, none of which was completed, but Japan's Yamato class was also curtailed after the first two ships, one hull being adapted for use as an aircraft carrier (*Shinano*) and material for the fourth unit being transferred to escort carrier building programmes, and enlarged follow-ups remained paper projects only. Russian ambitions were similarly thwarted by the realities of wartime priorities.

Only two big-gun battleships were commissioned post-war, both of whose completion had been delayed owing to wartime pressures: the British *Vanguard*, seen primarily as a means of getting spare 15in mountings to sea with relative ease, and the French *Jean Bart,* which commissioned as late as 1955 (though she was 75 per cent finished when France fell in the early summer of 1940), mainly under pressure from public opinion. Big-gun battleships continued in service through the 1950s, but most of the remaining ships were scrapped from that time on.

THE ADVENT OF RADAR

Probably the single most significant technical development of the 1939-45 war, affecting not only battleships but indeed the whole field of mechanised combat, was that of radar. Its potential for naval use was quickly forseen, at least in the United States and Great Britain, and from its early, primitive applications to warships in the late 1930s it developed with astonishing rapidity during the course of the war. In simple terms, radar, or radio direction-finding as it was at first (and more descriptively) termed, involves the despatch by transmitter of short-wavelength radio pulses, their reception

Below: The battleship *Washington* (BB-56), in company with the carrier *Lexington* (CV-16), is overflown by a Douglas SBD dive-bomber, symbolic of the instrument that swept away the last remnants of the world's battlefleets during the encounters of World War II. *Sic transit . . .*

back again on reflection from a distant object, and their translation into meaningful information by operators at the receiver. The time that elapses between transmission and reception of a pulse is convertible into linear distance, while the bearing of the detected object is determined by the direction at which the transmitter is pointed. Hence the system can be employed both to warn of the proximity hostile objects (the US designation was, more aggressively, 'search') be they ships, aircraft or even periscopes, and to provide range and bearing data on a target, be it airborne or on the surface. The importance of radar is most obvious in bad weather or at night, but the range and accuracy achievable as improved sets were developed quickly proved that no warship could afford not to be so equipped—with dramatic effects on warship silhouettes.

ANTI-AIRCRAFT BATTERIES

By 1939 the anti-aircraft armament installed on board battleships was generally held to be effective to meet the potential threat: older vessels would have a few single heavy guns and modernized or newer ships perhaps half a dozen or more dual-purpose twin mountings, in both cases backed up by a few multiple mountings of light AA and machine guns. It was quickly appreciated, however, that more needed to be done. Allied ships adopted first the

20mm Oerlikon, which had the great virtue of total independence for the parent ship's power supply and hence could be set up in any available space, and then the more complex (and very much more effective) 40mm Bofors gun, which continues in service, in modified form, aboard warships today. Semi-automatic and, later, fully automatic 37mm weapons were developed by Germany, while the Japanese proceeded with the development of their 25mm AA batteries.

In all battleships, the numbers of light AA proliferated, with mountings installed around the superstructure, on turret tops, on funnel platforms, on the quarterdeck, on the forecastle—in fact any place where reasonable sky arcs could be commanded. At the end, indeed, some US vessels, notably *New York* and *Texas*, were employed principally as anti-aircraft defence platforms, as a response to the Japanese kamikaze menace in the latter stages of the Pacific war.

FIRE SUPPORT—AND A NEW LEASE OF LIFE

The battleship, since the early 1900s, has been written off many times, but the decisive air-sea battles of World War II spelt the end of the all-big-gun warship—almost. The potency of the heavy naval gun as a land bombardment weapon had been appreciated from very early days, and

Above left: The French *Richelieu* was one of the few battleships to remain in commission after World War II. She is shown here, in pristine condition, in 1947, just prior to a Presidential cruise.

Above: *Bismarck*, foundation of Admiral Raeder's ill-fated 'Z-Plan'. Her modern lines belie her World War I design origins, but she and *Tirpitz* represented a major threat to Great Britain in 1941-44.

Left: The development and installation of radar systems aboard capital ships brought a new dimension both to the detection of hostile forces at sea and to their engagement. This diagram shows the main elements of radar-controlled surface gunnery. The aerial, mounted atop the director, transmitted electrical pulses and received their reflection back from the target and enabled range to be accurately determined since the time lapse between each function was measurable and, the speed of the pulses being known, convertible to distance; bearing was identified by the angle of train of the director. Data were fed to the fire control table and transmitted to the guns. Radar-controlled gunnery was instrumental in the sinking of the German *Scharnhorst* and the Japanese *Kirishima* in particular, both in night actions.

Gunnery radar aerial
Director
Captain's sight
Captain
Control officer
Spotting officer
Rate officer
Cross-levelling officer
Director trainer
Director layer
Phone man
Range-taker
Director training
Director elevation
Rangefinder range
Surface warning radar aerial
Plot office
Gunnery radar office
Transmitting station
Officer of quarters
Loader
Breech worker
Gunlayer
Phone man
Trainer
Sight-setter
Telephone exchange operator
Gun elevation
Gun training
Deflection officer
Officer in charge
Clock operator
Range operator
Spotting plot operator
Radar operators
Surface warning radar office
Radar and electrical transmission cables
Telephone lines

specialised vessels like the slow, oddly configured monitors of World War I had been effectively used in different theatres. The battleship was also allocated this role, and showed itself to be a continuing asset as such in World War II, provided there was no determined opposition from the air; ships such as *Warspite* and *Texas* were for example employed as fire support ships during the Allied landing in Normandy in mid-1944, and in the late 1960s the 'mothballed' USS *New Jersey* was reactivated for service in the same role off Vietnam. With the end of the US involvement in that conflict and the 'final' retirement of *New Jersey* and her three decommissioned sister-ships, the battleship era, everybody said, was finally laid to rest.

It was not. The emergence of the Soviet missile ship *Kirov* in 1980 showed the battleship in a new guise: a capital ship that did not possess the armour system inherent in the traditional battleship concept but certainly reintroduced a fixed battery of immense power and range, though of missiles, not guns. The United States' response has been the recommissioning yet again of the much written-off Iowas, their 16in (406mm) guns still serviceable but their potency enhanced by the installation of Tomahawk and Harpoon surface-to-surface missile launchers.

The big-gun battleship, its role albeit modified and its heavy weapons subordinated to other requirements, is still with us—and is destined to remain so for years to come.

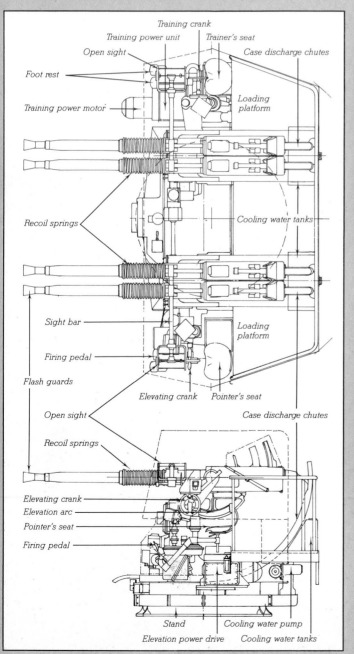

Left: The dedicated US late-war AA mounting was the quadruple 40mm Bofors; it was fitted in large numbers to virtually every major US vessel. It was a water-cooled, power-driven mounting, the standard configuration being a twin; quads comprised pairs of twins in a comon tub. Shell weight was about 2lb (0·9kg) and rate of fire has been measured at a figure of 150-175 rounds per minute for each barrel of the mounting.

Above: Battleship reborn: the Soviet *Kirov*, at sea in 1980. There are no heavy guns, but the foredeck hatches conceal launcher tubes for long-range surface-to-surface and surface-to-air missiles.

Below: US response: a reactivated *New Jersey* now deploys Tomahawk and Harpoon missiles. Note the two radar domes of the CIWS (Phalanx) 20mm guns and the proliferation of radar aerials.

BISMARCK

1940 *Germany*
Other ships in class: *Tirpitz*

Laid down: 1 July 1936.
Launched: 14 February 1939.
Builder: Blohm & Voss, Hamburg.
Displacement: 41,676 tons (42,344 tonnes) standard; 45,226 tons (45,951 tonnes) normal; 50,153 tons (50,996 tonnes) full load.
Dimensions: 823ft 6in (251m) oa x 118ft 1in (36m) x 29ft 6in (9m).
Machinery: 3 Blohm & Voss turbines; 12 Wagner boilers; 3 shafts; 150,170 SHP.
Armour: Wotan 12·6in-5·7in (320-145mm) belt; 8·7in-1·75in (220-45mm) bulkheads; 4·7in-1·2in (120-30mm) decks; 8·7in (220mm) barbettes; 14·1in-5·1in (360-130mm) turrets; 3·9in-0·5in (100-20mm) secondary turrets; 13·8in-1·2in (350-30mm) conning tower.
Armament: 8 x 15in (380mm); 12 x 5·9in (150mm); 16 x 4·1in (105mm) AA; 16 x 37mm AA; 12 x 20mm AA.

Left: *Bismarck* about to undergo trials upon completion at the Blohm & Voss shipyard in 1940. The top of the armour belt can be clearly seen; the crane amidships handled both boats and floatplanes. She has not yet been fitted with fire control positions.

Below: The first 1936-37 design for *Bismarck* featured a light main mast and straight stem (cf *Gneisenau*).

Below: *Bismarck* as she appeared in May 1941 during her ill-fated sortie into the Atlantic. The distinctive stripes carried while in the Baltic have now been eliminated.

Below: *Tirpitz* as she was in March 1944 during her stay in Norwegian waters. Apart from adopting the camouflage scheme illustrated, her crew further tried to evade observation from the air by laying newly-cut trees across her decks. When at sea, the major German units closely resembled one another; this reflected a deliberate policy designed to confuse hostile vessels. Apart from the aft turret layout, the similarity between *Tirpitz* and *Gneisenau* can be remarked upon.

Performance: 30·1kt (55·8km/h); radius 8,900nm (16,500km) at 17kt (31·5km/h); oil 7,344 tons (7,462 tonnes).
Crew: 2,092.

The gap in the design and construction of major warships forced upon Germany by the Treaty of Versailles in 1919 meant that while the other major naval powers (the UK, USA and Japan) could experiment with older or redundant ships to assess the efficacy of shells and armour, Germany could not. At the same time, the process of uninterrupted capital ship evolution was denied to Germany. Nevertheless, theoretical work continued in secret, and when the Anglo-German Naval Treaty of 1935 came into force, the Germans were well placed to proceed rapidly with the design of two of the three 35,000-ton (35,560 tonne) battleships permitted by the treaty.

Germany's enforced 'battleship holiday' meant that the basic design of the World War I Baden class was re-used for the hull: but to cater for the 6kt (11·1km/h) greater speed, radically improved underwater protection and much enhanced AA armament now needed, the design was revised in terms of overall size and of length:beam ratio, the latter altering from 6·04:1 to 6·71:1.

Unfortunately, the retention of a basic design from World War I meant the retention also of several vital flaws:

the rudders and steering gear were poorly protected, and the location of the main armoured deck towards the lower edge of the belt (at a time when other major powers had shifted it towards the upper edge of the belt) left most of the ship's communications and data-transmission systems exposed. Both these factors played a crucial role in *Bismarck's* loss. Another poor feature of the design stemmed from Germany's lack of research into dual-purpose secondary batteries. This meant that extra displacement had to be provided for

separate low-angle (anti-ship) and high-angle (anti-aircraft) batteries. A further fault was the poor quality of the armour in comparison with that of countries which had been able to test World War I ships to destruction: *Bismarck's* control tower was in theory armoured against 15in (381mm) shell-fire, but was in the event pierced by British 8in (203mm) rounds. Finally, the quality of the German 15in (380mm) shells was poor, a high proportion failing to detonate properly.

But for all her faults, *Bismarck* was a fine ship with a number of good points: she was very sturdily built, which made her very difficult to sink; her fire-control systems were first class (especially those for the HA armament); she was fitted with gunnery radar; and for her main role of commerce-raiding she was well planned and constructed. For the main armament and the LA secondary armament there were three separate directors each in the forward and after command positions, while

Left: February 1941: *Bismarck* at speed; like most German World War II heavy units, *Bismarck* was a poor seaboat for her size, but she was well suited to her main role of commerce raider.

Above: *Bismarck* at anchor in a Norwegian fjord in May 1941, as seen from the heavy cruiser *Prinz Eugen.* A few days later she broke out into the Atlantic, sank *Hood,* and was then herself destroyed.

the foretop command post had four directors to control both batteries at the same time. Six reconnaissance aircraft could be carried.

After working up in the Baltic, *Bismarck* was dispatched in May 1941 for a commerce-raiding foray into the Atlantic with *Prinz Eugen.* After destroying *Hood, Bismarck* was crippled by air-launched torpedoes as she made for Brest, and was brought to action by the battleships *King George V* and *Rodney.* Overwhelmed by British gunfire, *Bismarck* finally sank on 27 May 1941 after her crew had fired scuttling charges and the cruiser *Dorsetshire* had put three torpedoes into her.

Tirpitz was built at Wilhelmshaven Dockyard and completed in February 1941. She differed principally in greater power and range, and was later fitted with eight triple 21in (533mm) torpedo tubes and a light AA armament of 58 x 20mm guns. Damaged by midget submarine attack, *Tirpitz* was finally sunk by bombing on 12 November 1944.

KING GEORGE V

1940 *UK*
Other ships in class: *Prince of Wales, Duke of York, Anson, Howe*

Laid down: 1 January 1937.
Launched: 21 February 1939.
Builder: Vickers-Armstrong, Newcastle.
Displacement: 38,000 tons (38,608 tonnes) standard; 44,460 tons (45,171 tonnes) full load.
Dimensions: 745ft (227·1m) oa x 103ft (31·4m) x 34ft 6in (10·5m) max.
Machinery: 4 Parsons turbines; eight 3-drum Admiralty boilers; 4 shafts; 110,000 SHP.
Armour: 15in-4·5in (381-114mm) belt; 15in (381mm) bulkheads; 6in-5in (152-127mm) decks; 13in-11in (330-280mm) barbettes; 13in-6in (330-152mm) turrets; 1·5in-1in (38-25mm) secondary turrets.
Armament: 10 x 14in (356mm); 16 x 5·25in (133mm); 48 x 2pdr AA.
Performance: 29·25kt (54·2km/h); radius 13,000nm (24,000km) at 10kt (18·5km/h); oil 3,842 tons (3,903 tonnes).
Crew: 1,640.

The period in which battleship design was restricted to 35,000 tons (35,560 tonnes) standard displacement and 16in (406mm) main-armament calibre had witnessed a number of British design exercises to test the practical limitations of the Washington Treaty of 1922.

In 1934 the British began to plan a new class of battleships for the 1936 programme of construction. These ships were designed within the constraints of the Washington Treaty, and were originally planned with a main armament of 9 x 15in (381mm) guns and a secondary battery of 6in (152mm) weapons, plus a modest speed. Further evolution of the design in 1934 replaced the 6in (152mm) guns with 4·7in (120mm) mounts, but these in turn gave way to the excellent 5·25in (133mm) dual-purpose mount introduced in the Dido class light cruisers. In 1936 the London Naval Treaty ordained a maximum calibre of 14in (356mm) unless a signatory of the Washington Treaty objected, and the design was recast for this weapon.

Though there appeared every likelihood that the treaty would not be ratified, by Japan at least, the British were faced with a problem, for the mountings had to be ordered by mid-1936 if the first two ships were to be ready by 1940, when the UK could well be at war with Germany. So though there was a great clamour for a primary armament of 16in (406mm) guns, the Admiralty decided to stay with the 14in (356mm) already ordered, which would give the ships a good balance of fire-power and protection, combined with a good turn of speed. As an insurance against the return of the 16in (406mm) gun, the protection was designed with this calibre of adversary in mind.

The class were originally to have had three triple 14in (356mm) mountings, giving a broadside weight of 19,080lb (8,655kg) over a maximum range of 36,000 yards (32,920m). But tests against 16in (406mm) rounds showed that additional horizontal protection was necessary, so two of the guns in 'B' turret were sacrificed to permit the weight of extra armour. The final disposition was thus two quadruple turrets, forward and aft, plus a superfiring twin turret forward.

Protection was on the 'all-or-nothing' principle as in the preceding Nelson class capital ships, but whereas the Nelsons had featured an internal sloping belt, the King George Vs had a vertical external belt, second thoughts having shown that repairs to an internal belt were very difficult. Compared with that of the Nelsons, the belt was 1in (25mm) thicker over the magazines. Sir Arthur Johns, the designer, also deepened the belt well below the waterline, where tests with the surrendered *Baden* had shown many capital ships to be very vulnerable to plunging shell-fire. Johns also raised the main horizontal armour by one deck in keeping with contemporary US and Japanese practice, but in contrast did away with the external bulge, instead

Below: *Howe* in 1942, shortly after her completion. Particularly notable is the low freeboard forward, dictated by the Naval Staff's insistence on no-elevation fire directly ahead.

Below: A weatherbeaten *Prince of Wales* as she looked on arrival at Singapore in December 1941. She is wearing the distinctive First Admiralty Disruptive type of camouflage introduced that year. The aircraft being swung out is a Supermarine Walrus I spotter.

relying on the double bottom, an internal 2in (51mm) longitudinal bulkhead with two watertight compartments sandwiching an oil-filled compartment occupying the space between the longitudinal bulkhead and the hull on each side.

King George V was a good gun platform, and her roll was less accentuated than that of the Nelsons, but she took a lot of water over the bows in any sort of sea, and this affected speed in these conditions. Some trouble was experienced initially with the 14in (356mm) mountings, and with some of the auxiliary systems (power for the AA guns and pumps), but nevertheless it was a good design that W.G. Sanders and H.S. Pengelly evolved under Sir Arthur Johns' overall control.

Early in their service lives the ships received 16 x 20mm AA guns, later supplemented by 2pdrs and 40mm cannon. *King George V* served in

home waters, the Atlantic, the Mediterranean and the Pacific, and was scrapped in 1957. *Prince of Wales* was built by Cammell Laird and commissioned in March 1941; she was sunk by Japanese air attack on 10 December 1941. *Duke of York* was completed in November 1941 after building at the John Brown yard, served in the Home Fleet throughout World War II, and was scrapped in 1958. *Anson* was built at Swan Hunter and was commissioned in June 1942; she served at home and in the Pacific and was scrapped in 1957. *Howe* was built by Fairfield and completed in August 1942; she was scrapped in 1958.

Right: *King George V* steams up Chesapeake Bay in January 1941 on her way to deliver Lord Halifax, ambassador to the USA, to his new appointment. The novel arrangement of the forward turrets is well shown.

RICHELIEU

1940 *France*
Other ships in class: *Jean Bart,
Clemenceau*

Laid down: 22 October 1935.
Launched: 17 January 1939.
Builder: Brest Dockyard.
Displacement: 38,500 tons (39,116 tonnes) standard; 47,500 tons (48,260 tonnes) full load.
Dimensions: 813ft 3in (247·85m) oa x 108ft 9in (33m) x 31ft 9in (9·63m).
Machinery: 4 Parsons geared turbines; 6 Indret boilers; 4 shafts; 155,000 SHP.
Armour: 13·6in-9·8in (345-250mm) belt; 6·7in-5·1in (170-130mm) main deck; 1·6in (40mm) lower deck; 16·9in-6·7in (430-170mm) turrets; 5·1in-2·8in (130-70mm) secondary turrets; 13·4in (340mm) conning tower.
Armament: 8 x 15in (380mm); 9 x 6in (152mm); 12 x 3·9in (100mm) AA; 16 x 37mm AA; 8 x 13·2mm AA.
Performance: 32kt (59·3km/h); radius c8,000nm (14,285km) at 15kt (27·8km/h); oil 6,791 tons (6,900 tonnes).
Crew: 1,670.

Fine ships though the two units of the Dunkerque class undoubtedly were, it was clear to the French naval authorities by the early 1930s that new German and Italian construction would have to be countered with heavy battleships if France were to maintain her position. So the French designed the Richelieu class, with high speed, true battleship armament, and protection to match. The basic pattern was that of the Dunkerque class, scaled up to provide·the necessary displacement. Among the features retained were the location of the main armament in a pair of superfiring quadruple turrets·forward of the superstructure,

Right: *Richelieu* enters New York harbour early in 1943 en route to a total refit. The two paired 15in (380mm) guns in each main turret are notable, as is the absence of one of these guns from its normal position in 'B' turret.

and the grouping of the secondary armament in turrets abreast and abaft the superstructure.

The main armament was the excellent new 15in (380mm) gun, which could fire a 1,940lb (880kg) shell at the rate of two rounds per minute to 49,210 yards (45,000m) at an elevation of 35°. Each of the quadruple mountings was in fact two twin mountings in a common gunhouse. The secondary armament comprised five triple 6in (152mm) turrets, three aft and two amidships in the fashion of the Dunkerques. While *Richelieu* was building, her original arrangement of funnel amidships and control tower/mainmast aft was altered to a combined unit amidships, the top of the funnel being angled back rakishly to keep smoke away from the tower bridge farther forward. Protection was more extensive and better arranged than that in the Dunkerques, and included an inclined internal belt.

Richelieu was nearly complete in June 1940 (when France capitulated) and escaped to Dakar in Senegal. She joined the Allied cause in 1942, and sailed to the USA for completion in 1943. The final disposition was much as the original design had intended, though the quarterdeck catapults and aircraft were deleted, radar was added, the secondary battery was restricted to the three aftermost triple turrets, and the AA armament was augmented to 14 quadruple 40mm and 48 single 20mm mounts. Displacement increased by some 3,000 tons (3,048 tonnes) as a result of these alterations and the provision of increased bunkerage.

In 1943 *Richelieu* was attached to the British Home Fleet, and in 1944 and 1945 to the British Pacific Fleet. She returned to France in 1946 after a spell of duty off Indo-China. In 1956 she was put into reserve, and in 1968 scrapped.

Jean Bart was built by Penhoët at

St Nazaire, and was just beginning to fit out when France fell. She nonetheless managed to escape, reaching Casablanca on 22 June 1940. Work proceeded slowly, and in November 1942 she fired on American forces landing in North-West Africa. But she was badly damaged, and was completed only after World War II, with a secondary battery of 9 x 6in (152mm) guns, and an AA armament of 12 twin 3·9in (100mm) and seven quadruple 57mm guns. She was also given bulges, increasing maximum beam to 116ft 3in (35·454m). She was scrapped in 1969.

As part of the 1938 programme, another pair of Richelieu class battleships was authorised. These were *Clemenceau,* to be built at Brest Dockyard, and *Gascogne* (*qv*). *Clemenceau*'s incomplete hull was sunk in 1944; she would have had a secondary battery of 12 x 6in (152mm) guns in two superfiring turrets aft and two turrets amidships, but no aircraft.

Below: The initial design for *Richelieu,* drawn up in 1934; the basic pattern was derived from the Dunkerque class.

Below: One result of the Washington Treaty of 1922, which limited the total tonnage of a nation's warship types, was a proposal for an aircraft carrier/battleship hybrid which would mount 16in (406mm) guns on a displacement of about 29,000 tons (29,464 tonnes). Nothing came of this at the time, but during World War II plans were outlined for completing *Jean Bart* as such a vessel (see below). The scheme was not carried out, but Japan pursued the idea by building a flight deck aft on *Ise* and *Hyuga* to handle up to 22 floatplanes.

Below: Based at Toulon after World War II, *Richelieu* was used mostly as a training ship. Note the triple 6in (152mm) turrets, the centre-line unit located one deck higher and farther forward than the two beam units. Well illustrated also is the raked funnel, intended to keep the bridge clear of smoke.

Below: *Richelieu* as she looked in late 1942 with Lioré 130-handling equipment still in position. This was soon replaced by additional AA armament. Note the concentration of heavy armament forward, and the angling applied to the funnel in order to keep the bridges clear of obscuring smoke.

MONTANA (BB-67)

1940 (design only) *USA*
Other ships in class: *Ohio* (BB-68),
Maine (BB-69), *New Hampshire*
(BB-70), *Louisiana* (BB-71)

Builder: Philadelphia Navy Yard.
Displacement: 60,500 tons (61,468
tonnes) standard; 70,500 tons
(71,628 tonnes) full load.
Dimensions: 921ft 3in (280·8m) oa
x 121ft (36·88m) x 36ft 8in (11·18m)
max.
Machinery: 4 Westinghouse geared
turbines; 8 Babcock & Wilcox
boilers; 4 shafts; 172,000 SHP.
Armour: 16·1in-10·2in (409-259mm)
on 1in (25mm) main belt; 7·2in-1in
(183-25mm) internal belt;
21·3in-18in (541-457mm) barbettes;
22·5in-9·15in (572-232mm) turrets;
6in-7·35in (152-187mm) armour
deck; 18in (457mm) conning tower.
Armament: 12 x 16in (406mm); 20
x 5in (127mm) DP; 32-40 x 40mm
AA; 20-48 x 20mm AA.
Performance: 28kt (51·8km/h); oil
7,300 tons (7,417 tonnes); radius
15,000nm (27,750km) at 15kt
(27·75km/h).
Crew: 2,149.

Influenced by reports of Japanese
'super-battleship' projects, the US
Navy originally considered an 18in
(457mm) main armament for the
Montanas, for which construction
orders were placed in September
1940. Although 16in (406mm)
weapons were soon adopted, the
high speed of the Iowas was
sacrificed in favour of an additional
16in (406mm) triple turret and much
increased protection. It was
anticipated that the 16in (406mm)
guns would fire a projectile
over 42,000yds (38·5km), i.e. over
the horizon.

Armour weight amounted to some
21,000 tons (21,336 tonnes), with an
outer belt extending from the armour
deck to the bulged hull and an
internal belt descending from the
middle deck to the bottom and
constituting an anti-torpedo
bulkhead. The Montanas' great
beam would have prevented them
from traversing the Panama Canal, a
requirement that had hitherto acted
as a limit on the dimensions and
displacement of US battleships.

As was the case with most of the
Japanese monsters they were
intended to contain, orders for the
Montana class were cancelled, in July
1943, to make way for the
construction of aircraft carriers.

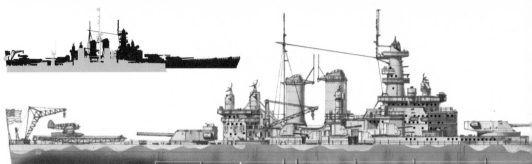

NORTH CAROLINA (BB-55)

1941 *USA*
Other ships in class: *Washington*
(BB-56)

Laid down: 27 October 1937.
Launched: 13 June 1940.
Builder: New York Navy Yard.
Displacement: 38,000 tons (38,608
tonnes) standard; 46,770 tons
(47,518 tonnes) full load.
Dimensions: 728ft 9in (222·12m)
oa x 108ft 4in (33·02m) x 32ft 11½in
(10·04m) max.
Machinery: 4 General Electric
geared turbines; 8 Babcock and
Wilcox boilers; 4 shafts; 121,000
SHP.
Armour: 12in-6·6in (305mm-168mm)
on 0·75in (19mm) belt; 14·7in-
16in (373-406mm) barbettes; 16in-
7in (406-178mm) turrets; 5·5in-5in
(140-127mm) armour deck; 11in
(279mm) bulkheads; 16in-14·7in
(406-373mm) conning tower.
Armament: 9 x 16in (406mm); 20 x
5in (127mm) DP; 16 x 1·1in (28mm)
AA; 12 x 0·5in (12·7mm) AA.
Performance: 28kt (51·8km/h); oil
6,260 tons (6,360 tonnes); radius
17,450nm (32,282km) at 15kt
(27·75km/h).
Crew: 1,880.

The North Carolinas were the first
American battleships built after the
lifting of the Washington Treaty
limitations; the original design,
however, observed the London Treaty
(1936) limitation of main armament to
a maximum 14in (356mm) calibre.
When Japan refused to ratify this
agreement, triple 16in (406mm)
turrets replaced the planned
quadruple 14in (356mm) turrets in the
North Carolinas and were fitted on all
subsequent US battleships. The
heavier armament entailed a 2kt
(3·7km/h) reduction in speed, but
protection, although planned only to
counter 14in (356mm) fire, proved
adequate in service.

The armoured main deck ran into
the upper edge of the 16ft (4·88m)
deep, outward-angled main belt,
which extended to the forward and
after barbettes with a narrow strake
running to the stern. Particularly
strong protection was given to the
steering gear, which had 11·75in
(298mm) side armour, 11in (279mm)
bulkheads and a 6in (152mm) deck.
Anti-torpedo protection was also
comprehensive, with an externally
bulged hull and three longitudinal
bulkheads reaching up to the lower
deck.

Nine 16in (406mm), 45-cal guns —
firing a 2,700lb (1,225kg) shell to
36,900yds (33,741m) at maximum
elevation of 45° — were mounted in
three triple turrets, two forward and
one aft. Twenty 5in (127mm) DP guns
in twin turrets were concentrated
amidships, and a crane and two
catapults for three aircraft were on the
quarterdeck right aft. By 1945, *North
Carolina*'s original tertiary armament
had been replaced by *c*96 x 40mm
and 36 x 20mm.

During World War II both ships saw
extensive service in the Pacific where,
on 15 November 1942, *Washington*
shared with *South Dakota* in sinking
by gunfire the Japanese battlecruiser
Kirishima, off Savo Island,
Guadalcanal. *Washington* was sold
and broken up in 1960-61, but *North
Carolina*, stricken in June 1960, is preserved as a memorial at Wilmington,
North Carolina.

Below: *North Carolina* in June 1942 carrying a Vought OS2U Kingfisher. Note the closely spaced slender funnels, and long bridge structure. AA armament was later increased.

Below: The German 'H-41' design, forerunner of the 90,000-ton (91,440 tonne) 'H-42'. With the exception of the second funnel, the design echoes that of *Bismarck*.

SOUTH DAKOTA (BB-57)

1942 USA
Other ships in class: *Indiana* (BB-58), *Massachusetts* (BB-59), *Alabama* (BB-60)

Laid down: 5 July 1939.
Launched: 7 June 1941.
Builder: New York Shipbuilding.
Displacement: 37,970 tons (38,578 tonnes) standard; 44,519 tons (45,231 tonnes) full load.
Dimensions: 680ft (207·26m) oa x 108ft 2in (32·97m) x 35ft 1in (10·69m) max.
Machinery: 4 General Electric geared turbines; 8 Babcock & Wilcox boilers; 4 shafts; 130,000 SHP.
Armour: 12·2in (310mm) on 0·875in (22mm) main belt; 17·3in-11·3in (439-287mm) barbettes; 18in-7·25in (457-184mm) turrets; 6in-5·75in (152-146mm) armour deck; 11in (279mm) bulkheads; 16in-7·25in (406-184mm) conning tower.
Armament: 9 x 16in (406mm); 16 x 5in (127mm) DP; 20 x 1·1in (28mm) AA; 12 x 0·5in AA.
Performance: 27·5kt (50·9km/h); oil 6,959 tons (7,070 tonnes); radius

15,000nm (27,750km) at 15kt (27·75km/h).
Crew: 1,793.

In the South Dakotas certain design limitations—notably reduced habitability and some degree of blast interference between the 5in (127mm) DP turrets and the lighter AA mountings—were accepted in order that the speed and striking power of the North Carolinas might be maintained on a hull shortened by some 50ft (15·2m) to allow for improved horizontal and underwater protection. The most apparent differences from the North Carolinas were the provision of a single funnel, faired into the after part of the bridge, and the extension of the 1·5in (38mm) weather deck almost to the hull sides, resulting in the 5in (127mm) DP battery being carried one deck higher. Three aircraft were carried.

The internal side armour sloped down at an angle of 19° from the heavy armour deck, extending to the double bottom as a longitudinal anti-torpedo bulkhead. Outboard of the belt was a large, deep bulge,

subdivided on either side by three longitudinal bulkheads. A 0·625in (16mm) splinter deck of mild steel lay only 2ft 7in (0·8m) below the main armour deck. A 'tunnel' stern, in which the large skegs of the outboard propellers were intended to give added anti-torpedo protection, was fitted.

The main armament layout was the same as that of the North Carolinas. *South Dakota* was fitted as a Force Flagship with an elevated conning tower and, to save topweight, had only eight twin 5in (127mm) turrets. The others of the class had 10 x 5in (127mm) turrets, but were originally intended to mount only 12 x 1·1in (28mm) AA—although all the ships were eventually fitted with 48-72 x 40mm and 56-72 x 20mm AA.

All four South Dakotas saw wide service in World War II and were decommissioned in 1946-47. In the early 1960s, various schemes for their updating or conversion proving abortive, *South Dakota* and *Indiana* were sold and scrapped *Massachusetts* and *Alabama* however, are preserved as memorials in their name states.

BATTLESHIP DESIGNS H-41/42/43/44

1941-44 Germany

Displacement: (H-42) 90,000 tons (91,440 tonnes) standard; 98,000 tons (99,568 tonnes) full load.
Dimensions: (H-42) 1,001ft 4in (305·2m) wl x 140ft 5in (42·8m) x 42ft 8in (13m) max.
Machinery: (H-42) Eight 9-cylinder double-acting MAN diesels, 2 geared turbines; 6 extra-high-pressure oil-fired boilers; 3 (H-41) or 4 shafts; 120,000 BHP (diesel), 160,000 SHP max (turbines).
Armour: (H-42) 11·8in (300mm) belt; 5·7in (145mm) citadel; 5·9in-5·1in (150-130mm) armour deck.
Armament: (H-41, H-42) 8 x 16in (406mm); 12 x 5·9in (150mm); 32 x 4·1in (105mm) AA; 32 (H-41) to 56 x 37mm AA; 96 (H-41) to 160 x 20mm AA; 6 x 21in (533mm) torpedo tubes.
Performance: (H-41) 22kt (40·7km/h) diesel, 30kt (55·5km/h) with turbines; (H-42) 24kt (44·4km/h) diesel, 32·2kt (59·6km/h) with turbines; radius (H-42) 20,000nm (37,000km) at 19kt (35·15km/h).

The battleship design designated 'H-41'—a 1941 study for a vessel with better horizontal and anti-mine protection than the Bismarcks, and with heavier armament and slightly greater maximum speed—would have resulted in a ship about the size of the Japanese Yamatos. Provision was made for a triple bottom and for mixed propulsion, with diesels driving the two outer shafts for cruising and a turbine on the central shaft for maximum speeds above 30kt (55·5km/h). Four aircraft were to be carried.

The displacement and dimensions planned for 'H-41' were increased in the more heavily armoured 'H-42'—and soared into the realms of fantasy with the Hitler-inspired studies of 1943 for 'H-43' (111,000 tons, 112,776 tonnes, standard; 1,083ft 5in, 330·2m, wl; 15in, 380mm, belt) and of 1944 for 'H-44' (131,000 tons, 133,096 tonnes standard; 1,132ft 3in, 345·1m, wl) both of which were to mount 8 x 20in (508mm) guns.

Below: *Indiana* in April 1942 in a camouflage scheme appropriate to operations among the Pacific Islands. Note the compact super-structure and Vought OS2U aft.

YAMATO

1941 *Japan*
Other ships in class: *Musashi, Shinano,* No 111

Laid down: 4 November 1937.
Launched: 8 August 1940.
Builder: Kure Dockyard.
Displacement: 68,010 tons (69,098 tonnes) trial; 71,659 tons (72,806 tonnes) full load.
Dimensions: 862ft 9in (263m) oa x 121ft 1in (36·9m) x 34ft 1in (10·39m).
Machinery: 4 Kampon geared turbines; 12 Kampon boilers; 4 shafts; 150,000 SHP.
Armour: 16·1in (410mm) belt; 9·1in-7·9in (230-200mm) deck; 21·5in-2in (546-50mm) barbettes; 25·6in-7·6in (650-193mm) turrets; 19·7in-11·8in (500-300mm) conning tower; 11·8in-3in (300-75mm) torpedo bulkhead.
Armament: 9 x 18·1in (460mm); 12 x 6·1in (155mm); 12 x 5in (127mm) DP; 24 x 25mm AA; 4 x 13·2mm AA.
Performance: 27kt (49·95km/h); oil 6,300 tons (6,401 tonnes); radius 7,200nm (13,320km) at 16kt (29·6km/h).
Crew: 2,500.

No fewer than 23 designs were prepared between 1934, when plans for the Japanese 'super-battleships' were first made, and 1937, when two Yamato class ships—the largest and most heavily armed and protected battleships ever built—were ordered. Construction was attended by great secrecy: advance measures at Kure, for *Yamato,* and Mitsubishi,

Above: *Yamato* in September 1941 during her final stages of fitting out. Her decks are still littered with constructors' workshops.

Below: *Yamato,* late 1944; she is now carrying increased AA armament. The secondary beam turrets gave way to further AA guns in 1943.

Left: *Shinano,* the third vessel of the class, as completed as an aircraft carrier. She was fitted with an armoured flight deck, and was to have carried some 45 aircraft of her own, as well as being capable of supplying and maintaining aircraft for other carriers. She was sunk by USS *Archerfish* in November 1944, her loss attributable to ineffective damage control.

Nagasaki, for *Musashi*, included the erection of high fences, protective roofing and camouflage netting. The Kure building dock was specially enlarged, while *Musashi* was launched from a 13ft (3·96m) wide slipway at a weight (surpassed only by the liner *Queen Mary*) of 35,737 tons (36,309 tonnes).

Two further Yamatos were ordered in 1939: *Shinano*, converted to an aircraft carrier while building and sunk by a US submarine on her maiden voyage, 29 November 1944; and hull No 111, scrapped at Kure when 30 per cent complete, 1941-42. Plans in 1942 for the Yamato class No 797 and for Nos 798-799, which were to mount 6 x 20in (508mm) guns apiece, were soon abandoned.

Yamato had a bulbous bow, a massive beam, and a relatively shallow draught suitable for Japanese coastal waters. To maximise protection, her vital machinery was crammed into a length representing only some 54 per cent of her waterline. The main armour deck could withstand anything up to a 2,200lb (998kg) AP bomb dropped from 10,000ft (3,048m). Below it, 16·1in (409mm) side armour sloping outward at 20° and able to withstand an 18in (457mm) shell at 23,000-32,000yds (21,000-29,300m) ran down for some 63ft (19·2m) to a 7·9in-3in (201-76mm) anti-torpedo bulkhead. This in turn sloped down at 14° to the outer plates of the double bottom and extended fore and aft as a 3in-2in (76-51mm) screen beneath the magazines.

Each of the three triple 18·1in (460mm) turrets weighed 2,774 tons (2,818 tonnes), and each gun fired up to two 3,240lb (1,470kg) shells per minute to a range of 45,290yds (41,400m) at a maximum elevation of 45°. Triple 50ft (15·24m) range finders (and later radars) for the main armament were positioned atop the streamlined cylindrical tower that replaced the clumsy 'pagoda'

Above: *Yamato* running trials in late October 1941. Note the large bow wave, and the sweep of the sea along her hull.

foremasts of other Japanese capital ships. The two triple 6·1in (155mm) turrets on either side of the single funnel amidships were replaced by an additional 12 x 5in (127mm) DP in *Yamato* in 1943. Her final light AA armament, in 1945, was 150 x 25mm.

Although fine seaboats (and extremely handsome ships) of great potential power, *Yamato* and *Musashi* had undistinguished combat careers, largely because of reluctance to hazard them without the air cover that Japan increasingly lacked. When thus exposed, both were sunk by air attack. *Musashi* absorbed 11-19 torpedo strikes and at least 17 direct bomb hits before sinking in the Sibuyan Sea, Leyte Gulf, 24 October 1944. *Yamato*, heading a task force on a one-way 'suicide mission' to Okinawa, was intercepted in the East China Sea by US carrier planes and was sunk by 11-15 torpedo strikes and at least 7 direct bomb hits, 7 April 1945.

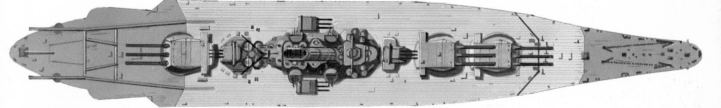

Below: *Yamato* in December 1941, one week after the Japanese attack on Pearl Harbor. She has not yet received the Type 21 radar; the structure abaft the funnels is the fire control system for the secondary battery. The 6·1in (155mm) guns were sited in turrets, while the 5in (127mm) guns had screens to protect the crew from blast.

VITTORIO VENETO

1940 *Italy*
Other ships in class: *Littorio, Impero, Roma*

Laid down: 28 October 1934.
Launched: 25 July 1937.
Builder: Cantieri Riuniti dell'Adriatico, Trieste.
Displacement: 41,377 tons (42,040 tonnes) standard; 45,752 tons (46,485 tonnes) full load.
Dimensions: 778ft 8½in (237·8m) oa x 107ft 9½in (32·9m) x 31ft 5in (9·6m).
Machinery: 4 Belluzzo geared turbines; 8 Yarrow boilers; 4 shafts; 134,616 SHP.
Armour: 13·8in-2·4in (350-60mm) belt; 8·1-1·4in (205-35mm) decks; 13·8in (350mm) barbettes; 13·8in-3·9in (350-100mm) turrets; 5·9-1·4in (150-35mm) secondary turrets.
Armament: 9 x 15in (381mm); 12 x 6in (152mm); 4 x 4·7in (120mm); 12 x 3·5in (90mm) AA; 20 x 37mm AA; 32 x 20mm AA.
Performance: 31·4kt (58·2km/h); radius 4,000nm (7,400km) at 16kt (29·65km/h); oil 3,937 tons (4,000 tonnes).
Crew: 1,861

France's refusal to ratify the London Naval Agreement and the building of the Dunkerque class fast battleships left Italian security and nationalist pride with little alternative but to counter the French threat. Hence orders were placed for two examples of a design originally drawn up in 1928. This first pair were *Vittorio Veneto* and *Littorio*, the latter to be built by Ansaldo in Genoa. The original design displacement had been 35,000 tons (35,560 tonnes), but when the ships were launched this had grown to a standard displacement some 6,400 tons (6,502 tonnes) above this figure.

Left: *Roma* is seen while still completing in early 1942. Unlike her sisters she was built with the revised bow which added 6ft (1·83m) to the freeboard at the stem, and had only one starboard bow anchor.

The two ships were particularly impressive in the water, combining an aggressive appearance with considerable elegance of line in the manner common to most Italian warships designed after World War I. The one odd feature of the design was the high position of the aftermost 15in (381mm) turret, which was dictated by the Italians' desire to locate unhangared aircraft on the quarter-deck, where they would have been vulnerable to blast damage from 15in (381mm) fire in a lower position.

The three triple 15in (381mm) turrets were located in the definitive centre-line arrangement with a superfiring pair forward and a single unit aft. The secondary battery comprised 12 x 6in (152mm) guns in four triple turrets, a pair abreast 'B' and 'X' turrets. The tertiary AA battery comprised 12 x 3·5in (90mm) guns, located in single mountings six to a side; the four single 4·7in (120mm) guns were mounted on the forecastle deck, two on each beam abreast the fore funnel; and the AA cannon were dotted about the superstructure and upper works wherever space was available.

Armour was on the parsimonious side in comparison with that of contemporaries, the Italians preferring to rely on the ships' speed and agility to evade serious damage. The main belt was both thin and shallow, and covered only the area from just forward of 'A' turret to aft of 'X' turret. Thinner armour extended to the bows and stern, and also covered the sides between the turrets as far up as the forecastle deck. Perhaps the weakest point of the design was the horizontal armour, which proved wholly inadequate to withstand the weight of bomb used in World War II.

Vittorio Veneto and *Littorio* were built with slightly curved stems, but after their initial sea trials were fitted with straight stems that allowed greater flare, thus making for drier forecastles. Overall length was increased by 5ft 11in (1·8m) as a result of the alteration.

Vittorio Veneto was twice damaged by torpedoes in 1941, and by bombs in 1943 before the Italian surrender;

Below: *Vittorio Veneto* in early 1942 carrying an effective example of a dazzle camouflage scheme. The identification stripes evident in the top view were for the benefit of Italian aircrew, who might otherwise confuse the unit with enemy vessels. Most major Italian warships carried a similar scheme until the end of the war. The aircraft shipped is a Reggiane Re 2000 fighter.

she spent the rest of the war in the Bitter Lakes (Suez Canal) before being allocated to the UK as part of Italy's war reparations in 1946, and was scrapped between 1948 and 1950. The *Littorio* was completed one week later than *Vittorio Veneto*, on 6 May 1940; she suffered very extensive damage during the British air raid on Taranto on 11 November 1940, and it was mid-1941 before she rejoined the fleet. She was then hit on two occasions by bombs, and on a third by a torpedo before being renamed *Italia* in June 1943; she was badly damaged by a German glider bomb while steaming to surrender in Malta during September 1943. She was scrapped between 1948 and 1950. Two other units were ordered from the same yards in 1938: *Impero* was never completed after launching on 15 November 1939, and *Roma* was completed in June 1942 only to be sunk by a German glider bomb on 9 September 1943.

Right: The camouflaged *Roma* seen in August 1943. Particularly striking is the high position of 'X' turret to keep the quarterdeck clear of blast for the two Reggiane Re.2000 fighters carried as an emergency measure.

Above: *Vittorio Veneto* under way, showing the revised stem and increased bow flare to keep the forecastle drier. An impressive ship, she wasted displacement by having separate LA and HA batteries, though the latter could throw up a formidable AA fire.

IOWA (BB-61)

1943 USA

Other ships in class: *New Jersey* (BB-62), *Missouri* (BB-63), *Wisconsin* (BB-64), *Illinois* (BB-65), *Kentucky* (BB-66)

Laid down: 27 June 1940.
Launched: 27 August 1942.
Builder: New York Navy Yard.
Displacement: 44,560 tons (45,273 tonnes) standard; 55,710 tons (56,601 tonnes) full load.
Dimensions: 887ft 2½in (270·4m) oa x 108ft 2½in (33m) x 38ft (11·6m).
Machinery: 4 General Electric geared turbines; 8 Babcock & Wilcox boilers; 4 shafts; 212,000 SHP.
Armour: 12·25in (311mm) belt; 11in-8·5in (279-216mm) bulkheads; 6in-0·5in (152-13mm) decks; 17·3in-1·5in (439-38mm) barbettes; 19·7in-7·25in (495-184mm) turrets; 1in-0·75in (25-19mm) secondary turrets; 17·5in-16in (445-406mm) conning tower.
Armament: 9 x 16in (406mm); 20 x 5in (127mm); 60 x 40mm AA; 60 x 20mm AA.
Performance: 33kt (61·2km/h); radius 18,000nm (33,350km) at 12kt (22·2km/h); oil 7,073 tons (7,186 tonnes).
Crew: 1,921.

With every indication suggesting that Japan would fail to ratify the London Naval Treaty of 1936, the US Navy put in hand during late 1936 the

Left: *Iowa* bombards positions on the east coast of Korea on 15 December 1952. The Iowas were reactivated specifically to carry out fire support in this war.

design of a new class of fast battleship to succeed the South Dakota class currently building. Battleship displacement was increased to a limit of 45,000 tons (45,720 tonnes) by the failure of the London Naval Treaty, and the Americans decided to use the tonnage for extra power and protection rather than for additional or more powerful armament, which the US Navy considered to have reached an acceptable plateau. Beam was limited by the maximum that could pass through the Panama Canal, but length was increased greatly. With an extra 70,000 SHP available from the more extensive machinery, the Iowa class easily made 33kt (61·2km/h) to be the fastest battleships ever built.

Although the armament was not increased in terms of calibre or number, it was improved in quality,

Right: *New Jersey* (BB-62) as she appears in 1983 after the reactivation programme that was carried out at Long Beach, California. The vertical domed structures on the superstructure are the 20mm Phalanx guns that are designed to provide close-in, radar-directed protection for the ship against hostile sea-skimming missiles and aircraft.

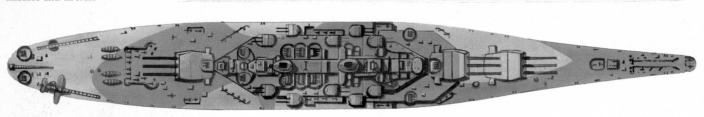

Below: *Missouri* as she appeared in July 1944. This class presented a relatively clean and uncluttered profile, ensuring a wide field of fire for the secondary battery amidships. The floatplane aft is a Vought OS2U Kingfisher. The front view clearly shows the flat hull form of these vessels.

the new 50-cal 16in (406mm) gun replacing the 45-cal weapon used in the South Dakotas; at the same time a new turret had been designed, and this saved almost 850 tons (864 tonnes) in total. The secondary battery remained unaltered at 20 x 5in/38 (127mm/38) dual-purpose weapons in twin turrets located five on each beam. However, a tertiary battery of 30 x 3in (76mm) AA guns (carried in 15 twin turrets) was at first envisaged, but replaced by a massive battery of heavy and light AA cannon when operations in Europe revealed the general superiority of this type of volume fire for the defence of point targets.

Protection was on the same scale as the South Dakotas, but was carefully designed along more conventional lines: from the lower edge of the main belt a layer of 1·5in (38mm) armour ran to the turn of the

bilge, and instead of bulges the class was given very solid internal protection. This consisted of four substantial longitudinal bulkheads, alternate bulkheads reaching up to the armoured main deck to provide wing compartments; and solid armour decks running into the top and bottom edges of the main belt. For an increase of 200ft (61m) in length and 10,000 tons (10,160 tonnes) in displacement, therefore, the US Navy acquired a design that was exceptionally fast and well protected, and thus admirably suited to the changed role of the battleship in the World War II, with surface combat subordinate to aircraft carrier

Below: *New Jersey* escorts the aircraft carrier USS *Hancock* through a typhoon off the Philippines in 1944. The Iowa class are fair seaboats and steady gun platforms.

escort and shore bombardment.

The first pair (*Iowa* and *New Jersey*) were ordered in 1938, the second pair (*Missouri* and *Wisconsin*) in 1939, and a final pair (*Illinois* and *Kentucky*—never completed) in 1940. *New Jersey* was very similar to *Iowa* apart from her turbines, which were by Westinghouse, and her complement of 40mm guns, which numbered 64 rather than 60; *New Jersey* was also 3in (7·6cm) longer than *Iowa* and 3in (7·6cm) greater in beam. *New Jersey* was completed in May 1943 after building at Philadelphia Navy Yard. The next pair were also built in the same yards, *Missouri* at New York

Below: USS *New Jersey* in 1982 having undergone alterations at the Long Beach yard. Four radar-controlled Phalanx anti-missile gun systems are sited amidships.

for completion in June 1944, and *Wisconsin* at Philadelphia for completion in April 1944. The two ships had General Electric and Westinghouse turbines respectively, and had a slightly smaller full-load displacement. These two ships also had a revised AA armament, with 80 x 40mm guns in 20 quadruple mountings, and 49 single 20mm guns. By the end of the war, each ship had individual radar-fitted directors for its 40mm mounts, making the ships formidable AA escorts.

Placed in reserve during the late 1940s, the ships were reactivated for the Korean War, while *New Jersey* was also used off Vietnam. The ships are currently being recommissioned as hybrid gun/helicopter/V/STOL aircraft/missile platforms (Tomahawk and Harpoon) to counter the Soviet Kirovs.

Above: The second phase of the Iowa modernisation plan will involve removing the aft turret, adding a ski jump flight deck for AV-8B V/STOL aircraft, and vertical launchers for Tomahawk cruise missiles. This is scheduled for 1988.

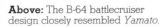

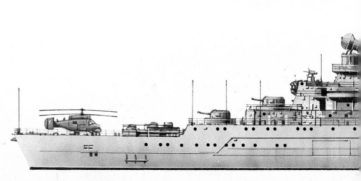

Above: The B-64 battlecruiser design closely resembled *Yamato*.

BATTLESHIP DESIGNS
B-64/65

1942 Japan

Displacement: 31,495 tons (31,999 tonnes) standard; 34,800 tons (35,357 tonnes) trial.
Dimensions: 802ft 6in (244·6m) oa x 89ft 3in (27·2m) x 28ft 10in (8·79m).
Machinery: 4 Kampon geared turbines; 8 Kampon boilers; 4 shafts; 160,000 SHP.
Armour: 7·5in-0·8in (190-20mm) belt; 4·7in (120mm) deck.
Armament: (B-64) 9 x 12·2in (310mm), 16 x 3·9in (100mm) AA, 8-12 x 25mm AA, 4-8 x 13·2mm AA, 8 x 24in (610mm) torpedo tubes; (B-65) 9 x 14·2in (360mm), then as B-64 but no torpedo tubes.
Performance: 33kt (61km/h); oil 4,545 tons (4,618 tonnes); radius 8,000nm (14,800km) at 18kt (33·3km/h).

Although planned from 1939 onward as 'Super Type A (heavy) cruisers', the B-64 class ships, to which the hull numbers 795 and 796 were given under the 1942 programme, were in fact battlecruisers which would have resembled smaller *Yamato* class battleships—flush-decked, with an identical armament layout and funnel and bridge arrangement.

The design was redesignated B-65 in 1941-42, when the original main armament of 9 x 12·2in (310mm) guns was altered to 9 x 14·2in (360mm) to counter the USN's *Alaska* class battlecruisers—themselves designed as an answer to non-existent Japanese 'pocket battleships'! Early wartime experience showed that aircraft carriers must be accorded greater construction priority, and the B-64/65 orders were never placed.

Also part of the aborted 1942 programme were two 'Super Yamato' class battleships, allocated hull numbers 798 and 799. These monsters were to displace some 70,000 tons (71,120 tonnes), with a main armament of 6 x 20in (508mm) guns, and resembled the 64/65 design.

ALASKA (CB-1)

1944 USA
Other ships in class: *Guam* (CB-2), *Hawaii* (CB-3), *Philippines* (CB-4), *Puerto Rico* (CB-5), *Samoa* (CB-6)

Laid down: 17 December 1941.
Launched: 15 August 1943.
Builder: New York Shipbuilding.
Displacement: 29,779 tons (30,255 tonnes) standard; 34,253 tons (34,801 tonnes) full load.
Dimensions: 808ft 6in (246·43m) oa x 91ft 1in (27·76m) x 31ft 10in (9·7m) full load.
Machinery: 4 General Electric geared turbines; 8 Babcock & Wilcox boilers; 4 shafts; 150,000 SHP.
Armour: 9in-5in (229-127mm) belt; 12·8in (325mm) turrets; 13in-11in (330-279mm) barbettes; 4in-3·8in (102-97mm) main deck; 10·6in (269mm) conning tower.

Armament: 9 x 12in (305mm); 12 x 5in (127mm) DP; 56 x 40mm AA; 34 x 20mm AA.
Performance: 33kt (61·05km/h); oil 3,619 tons (3,677 tonnes); radius 12,000nm (22,200km) at 15kt (27·75km/h).
Crew: 1,517.

Although often called battlecruisers, the *Alaskas* were officially designated large cruisers (CB). They were not designed to engage battleships, but to counter the fast raiders of the *Scharnhorst* type believed to be under development by the Japanese Navy in the late 1930s. Orders for the last three of the class were cancelled prior to laying down in June 1943, when the Japanese ships proved chimerical.

The *Alaskas* were basically enlarged *Baltimores* with three triple turrets for specially designed 12in (305mm), 50-cal guns replacing the three 8in (203mm) triple turrets of the heavy cruisers and armour scaled up in proportion. They were flush-decked, and a single heavy funnel was flanked amidships by cranes for the two catapults (four aircraft carried) just abaft the large battleship-type tower bridge. Machinery was identical to that of the *Essex* class carriers.

Fast, and fine seaboats, *Alaska* and *Guam* served in the Pacific in 1945 as escorts to the USN's fast carrier task forces. Both were in reserve from 1947 and were scrapped in 1960-61. Work on *Hawaii* was suspended in August 1945 when she was about 82 per cent complete. Plans to convert her to a guided missile ship or a tactical command ship were abandoned because it was cheaper to build new ships, and she was sold for breaking up in 1959.

VANGUARD

1946 UK

Laid down: 2 October 1941.
Launched: 30 November 1944.
Builder: John Brown & Co, Clydebank.
Displacement: 44,500 tons (45,212 tonnes) standard; 51,420 tons (52,243 tonnes) full load.
Dimensions: 814ft 4in (248·2m) oa x 108ft (32·92m) x 36ft (10·97m) max.
Machinery: 4 Parsons geared turbines; eight 3-drum Admiralty boilers; 4 shafts; 130,000 SHP.
Armour: 14in-4·5in (356-114mm) belt; 13in-6in (330-152mm) turrets; 13in-11in (330-279mm) barbettes; 6in-5in (152-127mm) main deck; 3in-1in (76-25mm) conning tower.
Armament: 8 x 15in (381mm); 16 x 5·25in (133mm) DP; 73 x 40mm; 4 x 3pdr.

Performance: 30kt (55·5km/h); oil 4,423 tons (4,494 tonnes); radius 6,950nm (12,857km) at 20kt (37km/h).
Crew: 1,893.

Following cancellation of the *Lion* class battleships, it was decided to adopt a suggestion made in 1939 by Sir Stanley Goodall, Director of Naval Construction, and to construct a single battleship in which building time would be cut by using the four 15in (381mm) twin turrets removed from *Courageous* and *Glorious* on their conversion to aircraft carriers in 1924-25. The order was placed on 14 March 1941; completion was originally expected in 1943.

Vanguard was basically an improved *King George V*, with a hull lengthened to accommodate four centre-line turrets and thus a longer main belt, reduced by 1in (25mm) in

Below: HMS *Vanguard* in 1946: she bears a resemblance to the King George V class but mounts an additional turret aft. Note the transom stern and sheer forward.

Below: The distinctive profile of *Guam* in 1944; the upper deck carries a profusion of light guns. The aircraft is a Vought OS2U.

Although probably classified by the Soviets as an RKR (rocket cruiser), *Kirov* represents in size—more than twice the displacement of any Western cruiser in service—and speed the continuation of the battlecruiser concept. Her functions, however, are probably closer to those of a World War II battleship: she may form the centre of a Surface Action Group, screening aircraft carriers, or she may act independently against NATO surface forces. It is thought that the Soviets intend to build at least four ships of this class.

The first Soviet surface warship with nuclear propulsion, *Kirov* is believed to have a combined nuclear and steam (CONAS) plant. Two reactors are probably supplemented by a completely independent geared turbine system or by oil-fired superheaters, to give a maximum speed in excess of 30kt (55·5km/h); cruising speed, using the nuclear powerplant alone, is probably 24kt (44·4km/h).

The main armament of 20 x SS-N-19 anti-ship missiles, with a range of *c*250nm (460km), is housed in a large box magazine forward and launched vertically from independent silos. Forward of these are 12 hatches for vertically launched SA-N-6 surface-to-air missiles (total probably about 72 rounds), believed to have a range of some 27nm (50km) and a speed of up to Mach 6.

Close-range protection against air attack comes from 2 x SA-N-4 launchers forward (*c*36 missiles), 2 x 3·9in (100mm) guns and four twin-mounted 'Gatlings'. A twin-tube launcher for SS-N-14 anti-submarine missiles (*c*16 in number) is carried in the forecastle. It is probable that three 'Hormone-A' helicopters for AS patrol and missile targeting are housed with two 'Hormone-B' SSM mid-course guidance helicopters in a hangar beneath the quarterdeck. The helicopter lift is forward of the landing pad between the after 'Gatlings'.

The electronics fit is comprehensive, with 'Top Pair' and 'Top Steer' surveillance radar and two 'Pop Group', two 'Top Globe', two 'Eye Bowl', one 'Kite Screech' and four 'Bass Tilt' fire control sets. Sonars comprise an LF bow-mounted set and a variable-depth sonar (VDS) system at the stern.

Kirov's vertical-launch capability enables her to carry out saturation missile attacks against such targets as carrier battle groups. She is, however, a high-value target herself—such a major investment of Soviet power, in fact, that her deployment in the event of hostilities might be limited.

maximum thickness to save weight. More weight was saved by fitting a transom stern, unique in British battleships: this, together with a marked sheer forward—where freeboard was 37ft (11·28m) as compared to 27ft 9in (8·46m) in *King George V*—made her a splendid seaboat, steady and dry under the most severe conditions. The increase in freeboard, however, did mean that 'A' turret was not capable of being fired directly ahead at low angles of elevation.

The 15in (381mm) turrets were given heavier armour and had their faces raised, with armoured hoods above the ports, to permit elevation to 30°. The 16 x 5·25in (133mm) DP were twin-mounted in gun houses flanking the funnels amidships. No aircraft were carried. Transverse bulkheads divided the ship into 27 main compartments, with 1,059

watertight compartments below the main deck. To improve sub-division, the longitudinal bulkheads outboard of the 1·75in-1·5in (44-38mm) protective bulkhead were taken up to the middle deck. As in *King George V*, engine and boiler rooms constituted four separate units and each could operate independently. General standards of habitability were good, as systems of heating and air-conditioning were designed to allow the ship to serve in both Arctic and tropical waters.

By 1944, the completion of *Vanguard* was no longer a wartime priority. Accepted in August 1946, she carried the British royal party on a South African tour in February-May 1947 and thereafter served mainly as a training ship. From 1955 she was Flagship, Reserve Fleet, and NATO HQ ship at Portsmouth until sold for breaking up in 1960.

KIROV

1980 *Russia*
Other ships in class: 1 + ? building

Laid down: *c*1974.
Launched: December 1977.
Builder: Baltic Yard, Leningrad.
Displacement: *c*25,000 tons (25,400 tonnes).
Dimensions: 814ft (248·1m) oa x 91ft 10in (28m) x 32ft 10in (10m).
Machinery: CONAS (2 nuclear reactors, plus oil-fired boilers for steam turbines); *c*150,000 SHP.
Armament: 20 x SS-N-19 SSM; 12 x SA-N-6 SAM; 2 x SA-N-4 SAM; 2 x SS-N-14 ASW weapons; 2 x 3·9in (100mm) AA; 8 x 30mm 'Gatling' AA; 1 x RBU 6000 ASW mortar; 2 x RBU 1000 ASW mortars; 10 x 21in (533mm) torpedo tubes.
Performance: 30kt (55·5km/h).
Crew: 900.

Below: The Soviet rocket cruiser *Kirov* in late 1980. The control position for the Kamov Ka-25 helicopters forms part of the aft structure. The bare forecastle houses the vertical launch systems.

181

Index

Page numbers in **bold** type indicate main entries. Where more than one ship carries a particular name, individual vessels are identified by their completion date or, for uncompleted units, the date of keel-laying ('LD') or projection ('P').

A

Abdul Aziz (Turkey), **49**
Abyssinia (UK), **74**
Achilles (UK), **43**, 59
Acton, Ferdinando, 112
Admiral class (*UK*), 75, **110-11**, **114-15**, 120
Admiral Graf Spee (Germany), 22, 239, **242**
Admiral Scheer (Germany), **242**
Admiral Seniavin (Russia), 119, **130**
Admiral Ushakov (Russia), **130**
Admiral Ushakov class (*Russia*), **130**
Adzuma (Japan), see *Stonewall*
Affondatore (Italy), 14, **54-5**
Africa (UK), **161**
Agamemnon (1855, *UK*), 12
Agamemnon (1883, *UK*), **105**
Agamemnon (1908, *UK*), **164**
Agamemnon class (1883, *UK*), **105**, 109
Agamenticus (USA), **42**
Agincourt (1867, *UK*), **59**
Agincourt (1913P, *UK*), 206
Agincourt (1914, *UK*), **201**, 205, 211
Agir (Germany), **124**
Ajax (1883, *UK*), **105**
Ajax (1913, *UK*), **192**
Akagi (Japan), **232-3**
Aki (Japan), 173, 176, **185**
Alabama (1900, *USA*), **150**
Alabama (1942, *USA*), **261**
Alaska (*USA*), **268**
Alaska class (*USA*), 190, **268**
Albemarle (UK), **159**
Albion (UK), **145**
Alexandra (UK), 16, **89**, 90
Alfonso XIII (Spain), **195**
Alma (France), **50**
Almirante Brown (Argentina), **104**
Almirante Cochrane (1875, *Chile*), 16, 49, **90-1**
Almirante Cochrane (1913LD, *Chile*), 211
Almirante Cochrane class (1875-76, *Chile*), **90-1**
Almirante Latorre (Chile), see *Canada*
Almirante Latorre class (*Chile*), 205, 211
Amagi (Japan), **232-3**
Amagi class *(Japan)*, 224, **232-3**
Amiral Baudin (France), **115**
Amiral Baudin (Formidable) class, 114, **115**
Amiral Duperré (France), 101, **104**, 115
Amiral Tréhouart (France), **130-1**
Ammiraglio di Saint Bon (Italy), **152**
Ammiraglio di Saint Bon class (*Italy*), **152**
Ancona (Italy), **38**
Andrea Doria (1891, *Italy*), **112-13**
Andrea Doria (1916, *Italy*), **208-9**
Andrei Pervoswanni (Russia), **165**
Andrei Pervoswanni class (*Russia*), **165**
Anson (1889, *UK*), **114-15**
Anson (1916P, *UK*), **228-9**
Anson (1942, *UK*), **256-7**
Aquidaban (Brazil), **112**, 132, 157
Arabi, Colonel, 16
Arapiles (Spain), **50**
Archangelsk (Russia), see *Royal Sovereign* (1916)
Arizona (USA), **218**
Arkansas (USA), **190-1**
Armide (France), **50**
Arminius (Germany), **46**
Arpád (Austria-Hungary), **158**
Asahi (Japan), **150**, 155
Assari Shevket (Turkey), **62**
Assari Shevket class *(Turkey)*, **62**, 75
Assari Tewfik (Turkey), **75**
Atago (Japan), **232-3**
Atalante (France), **50**
Attwood, E.L., 188, 201, 229, 233, 237
Aube, Admiral, 99
Audacious (1870, *UK*), **74-5**
Audacious (1913, *UK*), **192**
Audacious class (1870-71, *UK*), 70, **74-5**
Australia (UK), **184-5**
Avni Illah (Turkey), **62**
Avni Illah class (*Turkey*), **62**

B

B-64/65 (Japan), **268**
Babenburg (Austria-Hungary), **158**
Baden (1883, *Germany*), **92**
Baden (1916, *Germany*), **216-17**
Baden class (1916, *Germany*), see Bayern class
Barba, J., 96
Barfleur (UK), **130**
Barham (UK), 22, **206**
Barnaby, Nathaniel, 61, 80, 89, 102, 109, 110, 120
Barrozo (Brazil), **44**
Bartol, B., 34
Basileos Georgios (Greece), **61**, 76
Basilissa Olga (Greece), **76**
Batsch, Rear-Admiral von, 64
Battles
Alexandria (1882), bombardment of, 16-17, 103
Alicante (1873), attack on, 51
Bilbao (1937), blockade of, 195
Callao (1866), attack on, 51
'Channel Dash' (1942), the, 247
Charleston (1863), attack on, 24, 34
Comisa (1866), bombardment of, 46
Coral Sea (1942), battle of the, 235
Coronel (1914), battle of, 145
Dardanelles campaign (1915), the, 137 et seq, 151, 159, 161
Dogger Bank (1914), battle of the, 20, 189, 194, 201
Durazzo (1918), bombardment of, 193
Falkland Islands (1914), battle of the, 20, 145, 218
Fort Fisher (1864-65), attack on, 42
Fort George (1866), attack on, 54
Guadalcanal (1942), battle for, 22-3, 194
Hampton Roads (1862), battle of, 13-14, 36, 39
Heligoland Bight, (1916), battle of the, 19-20, 189
Iqueque (1879), blockade of, 49
Jutland (1916), battle of, 20-1, 162, 172 et seq, 183 et seq, 226, 234, 237
Kagoshima (1863), attack on, 26
Kinburn (1855), bombardment of, 13, 29
Kolberg (1870), attack on, 59
Lissa (1866), battle of, 14, 16, 33 et seq, 81, 83, 100, 101, 106, 108
Manila Bay (1898), battle of, 18, 122, 149
Matapan (1941), battle of, 22
Mers-el-Kebir (1940), attack on, 211
Min River (1884), battle of the, 15
North Cape (1943), battle of the, 23, 247
'Operation Torch' (1942), 203
Pearl Harbor (1941), attack on, 22, 186, 211, 215, 218, 232, 237, 250
Philippine Sea (1944), battle of the, 213
Port Arthur (1904), attack on, 18, 150, 152, 158
Richmond (1865), attack on, 42
River Plate (1939), battle of the, 242
Saintes (1782), battle of the, 11
Santiago di Cuba (1898), battle of, 18, 99, 131, 135, 138
Sinope (1853), battle of, 13, 14
Surigao Strait (1944), battle of, 23, 213
Taranto (1940), attack on, 209, 265
Trafalgar (1805), battle of, 10, 11
Tsushima (1905), battle of, 19, 123 et seq, 146, 150 et seq, 166
Valparaiso (1866), bombardment of, 51
Yalu River (1894), battle of, 17, 91, 105
Yellow Sea (1904), battle of the, 142, 150, 152, 157, 158
Bayard (France), **104**
Bayard class *(France)*, **104**, 108
Bayern (1882, *Germany*), **92**
Bayern (1916, *Germany*), **216-17**
Bayern (Baden) class (*Germany*), 176, 195, **216-17**, 255
Béarn (France), **218**
Beatty, Admiral Sir David, 20-1
Belleisle (UK), **92**
Belleisle class (*UK*), **92**
Bellerophon (1866, *UK*), 53, **57**, 61
Bellerophon (1909, *UK*), 168, 169, **173**
Bellerophon class (1909, *UK*), **173**
Belliqueuse (France), **50**
Belliqueuse class *(France)*, **50**
Benbow (1888, *UK*), 98, 99, **114-15**
Benbow (1914, *UK*), **198**
Benedetto Brin (Italy), **160**
Beowulf (Germany), 19, **124**
Bertin, Emile, 169
Bismarck (Germany), 22, 228, 229, 241, 250, 252, **254-5**
Bismarck class (*Germany*), 249, 250, **254-5**, 261
Black Prince (UK), **30-1**, 32
Blanco Encalada (Chile), 16, 49, 71, **90-1**, 157
Boordhi-Zaffer (Turkey), see *Orion* (1882)
Boretz za Svobodu (Russia), see *Kniaz Potemkin Tavritcheski*
Borodino (1904, *Russia*), 19, 142, **160-1**
Borodino (1912LD, *Russia*), **212**
Borodino class (1903-05, *Russia*), **160-1**
Borodino class (1912LD, *Russia*), **212**
Bouvet (France), 139, 141, **143**
Bouvines (France), **130-1**
Brandenburg (Germany), **129**
Brandenburg class (*Germany*), **129**
Brasil (Brazil), **37**
Braunschweig (Germany), **160**
Braunschweig class (*Germany*), **160**, 162
Brennus (France), 118, **137**
Bretagne (France), **210-11**
Bretagne class (*France*), 176, **210-11**, 218
Brin, Benedetto, 100, 106, 128-9, 152, 160
Britannia (UK), **161**
Brown, Commander, 12
Browne, Captain Orde, 96
Budapest (Austria-Hungary), **144**
Bulwark (UK), **151**
Bushnell, David, 16
Bussy, L. de, 93, 101

C

Caesar (UK), 129, **136-7**
Caïman (France), **109**
Caio Duilio (Italy), **208-9**
Caio Duilio (Doria/Duilio) class (Italy), **208-9**, 215, 238
Caledonia (UK), **39**
California (1915LD, *USA*), see *New Mexico*
California (1921, *USA*), 227, **232**, 237
Camperdown (UK), 17, **114-15**, 121
Canada (UK), **211**
Canonicus class (*USA*), 42
Canopus (UK), **145**, 151
Canopus class (*UK*), **145**
Capellini, Captain, 53
Capitan Prat (Chile), **128**, 140
Captain (UK), 15, 63, **72-3**, 78
Carnot (France), **139**
Castelfidardo (Italy), **38**
Catskill (USA), 27
Cavalli, 35
Cavour, Count Camillo di, 35
Cavour class (*Italy*), see Conte di Cavour class
Centurion (1894, *UK*), **130**
Centurion (1913, *UK*), **192**
Centurion class (1894, *UK*), **130**, 139
Cerbère class (*France*), 131
Cerberus (UK), **75**
Cerberus class (UK), **75**
Cervera, Admiral Pascual, 135
Charlemagne (France), **145**, 153
Charlemagne class *(France)*, **145**
Charles Martel (France), **138-9**, 140
Chen Yuan (China), 17, **105**, 142
Cheops (CSA), **44**
Clarke, Major, 99
Clemenceau (France), **258**
Colbert (France), **90**
Colbert class *(France)*, **90**
Coles, Captain Cowper, 38, 52, 72-3
Collingwood (1887, *UK*), 98, **110-11**, 114
Collingwood (1910, *UK*), **173**
Colomb, Sir John, 17
Colorado (USA), **236-7**
Colossus (1886, *UK*), **109**
Colossus (1911, *UK*), **184**
Colossus (USA), see *Kalamazoo*
Colossus class (1886-87, *UK*), 105, **109**
Colossus class (1911, *UK*), **184**, 193
Commonwealth (UK), **161**
Condorcet (France), **185**
Connecticut (USA), **162**
Connecticut class (*USA*), **162**
Conqueror (1886, *UK*), **108**
Conqueror (1913, *UK*), **187**
Conqueror (1939P, *UK*), **249**
Conqueror class (1886-88, *UK*), **108**
Constellation (USA), **234-5**
Constellation class (*USA*), see Lexington class
Constitucion (1902LD, *Chile*), see *Swiftsure*
Constitucion (1913LD, *Chile*), see *Almirante Cochrane* (1913LD)
Constitution (USA), **234-5**
Conte di Cavour (Italy), **209**
Conte di Cavour class (*Italy*), 208, **209**, 215, 238
Conte Verde (Italy), **46**
Cornwallis (UK), **159**
Courageous (UK), **220-1**, 268
Courageous class (*UK*), **220-1**
Courbet (1886, *France*), **101**
Courbet (1913, *France*), 176, **196**
Courbet, Admiral, 15
Courbet class (1882-86, *France*), **101**
Courbet class (1913-14, *France*), **196**, 210
Couronne (France), **33**
Cramp, Charles, 34
Cristoforo Colombo (Italy), **215**
Cuniberti, Vittorio, 165, 166, 193, 205
Cushing, Lieutenant, 15
Custoza (Austria-Hungary), 83, **84**, 89

D

Dandolo (Italy), 16, 71, 98, **100-1**, 102, 106
Danmark (Denmark), **43**
Dannebrog (Denmark), **37**
Dante Alighieri (Italy), 176, 178, **193**, 205, 209
Danton (France), **185**
Danton class *(France)*, **185**, 196
Davis, W.T., 188
Defence (UK), **32**, 37, 75
Defence class (*UK*), **32**
Delano, 62
Delaware (USA), **183**
Delaware class (*USA*), 176, **183**, 186, 190
Delcasse, M., 196
De Luca, Insp Eng Giuseppe, 46, 53, 83
De Luppis, Captain Giovanni, 15, 71
Democratie (France), **163**
Derfflinger (Germany), 21, 189, **200**
Derfflinger class *(Germany)*, **200**, 222
Designs
1913 Battlecruiser *(France)*, **194-5**
1913-14 Battleship *(Netherlands)*, **204**
1921 Battleship *(Japan)*, **236**
1928-29 Battleship *(Germany)*, **237**
1930 Battleship *(Japan)*, **244**
1937-39 Battleship *(Russia)*, **244**
1939 Battlecruiser (*Germany*), **249**
1939-40 Battlecruiser *(Netherlands)*, **249**
Deutschland (1875, *Germany*), **85**
Deutschland (1906, *Germany*), 148, **162**
Deutschland (1933, *Germany*), 239, **242**
Deutschland class (1906-08, *Germany*), 162, **175**
Deutschland class (1933-36, *Germany*), **242**, 244, 245, 250
Dévastation (France), **101**
Devastation (UK), 71, **80**, 85
Devastation class (*UK*), **80**, 94, 110, 113
Dewey, Admiral, 18, 85
D'Eyncourt, Sir Eustace Tennyson, 201
Dictator (USA), 24, **42**, 45
Diderot (France), **185**
Diome, Lebelin de, 108
Dominion (UK), **161**
Don Juan d'Austria (Austria-Hungary), **88**
Doria class (*Italy*), see Caio Duilio class
Drache (Austria-Hungary), **32-3**
Drake, Sir Francis, 12
Dreadnought (1879, *UK*), 71, **94**, 123
Dreadnought (1906, *UK*), 13, 18, 106, 110, 136, 167, 168-9, **170**, 172, 173, 175, 176, 179, 180, 186, 196, 224
Dreyer, Lieutenant, 178
Duguesclin (France), **108**
Duilio (Italy), 71, **100-1**, 102, 106
Duilio class (1880-82, *Italy*), **100-1**, 112
Duilio class (1915-16, *Italy*), see Caio Duilio class
Duke of York (UK), 23, **256-7**
Duncan (UK), **159**
Duncan class (*UK*), 152, **159**
Dunderberg (USA), 27, 45, **59**, 62
Dunkerque (France), 240, **245**
Dunkerque class (*France*), **245**, 258, 264
Du Pont, Rear-Admiral, 34
Duquesne (France), **213**
Durand-Viel, 194-5
Divienadsat Apostolov (Russia), **125**

E

Edinburgh (UK), **109**
Ekaterina II (Russia), **122**
Ekaterina II class *(Russia)*, **122**
Ellis, J.D., 70
Elsass (Germany), **160**
Emanuele Filiberto (Italy), **152**
Emperor of India (UK), **198**
Empress of India (UK), **126**
English, Captain, 99
Enterprise (UK), **40-1**
Ericsson, Captain John, 12, 13, 42, 45
Erin (UK), 194, **200**, 213
Ersatz Budapest (Austria-Hungary), **215**
Ersatz Freya (Germany), **222**
Ersatz Friedrich Carl, (Germany), **222**
Ersatz Gneisenau (Germany), **214**
Ersatz Habsburg (Austria-Hungary), **215**
Ersatz Monarch (Austria-Hungary), **215**
Ersatz Monarch class *(Austria-Hungary)*, **215**
Ersatz Scharnhorst (Germany), **214**
Ersatz Wien (Austria-Hungary), **215**
Ersatz Yorck (Germany), **214**
Ersatz Yorck class (*Germany*), **214**, 222, 247
Erzherzog Albrecht (Austria-Hungary), **83**, 84
Erzherzog Ferdinand Max (1866, *Austria-Hungary*), 14, **51**, 83
Erzherzog Ferdinand Max (1907, *Austria-Hungary*), **161**
Erzherzog Ferdinand Max class (1866-67, *Austria-Hungary*), **51**
Erzherzog Franz Ferdinand (Austria-Hungary), **182-3**
Erzherzog Friedrich (Austria-Hungary), **161**
Erzherzog Karl (Austria-Hungary), **161**
Erzherzog Karl class *(Austria-Hungary)*, **161**, 182
España (1913, *Spain*), **195**
España (1915, *Spain*), see *Alfonso XIII*
España class (*Spain*), **195**
Evstafi (Russia), **165**
Evstafi class (*Russia*), **165**
Exmouth (UK), **159**

F

Farragut, Admiral, 15
Fatikh (Turkey), see *König Wilhelm*
Faure, 99
Favorite (UK), **53**
Ferdinand Max (Austria-Hungary), see *Erherzog Ferdinand Max* (1866)
Ferrati, Eng Gen, 215
Fethi Bulend (Turkey), **77**
Fethi Bulend class (*Turkey*), **77**
Fisher, Admiral Sir John ('Jackie'), 139, 149, 166 et seq, 185 et seq, 228, 229
Fiske, Rear-Admiral Bradley, 149
Flandre (1865, *France*), **46**
Flandre (1913LD, *France*), **218**
Florida (USA), **186**, 191, 203
Florida class (*USA*), 176, **186**, 190, 203
Formidabile (Italy), **35**, 54
Formidabile class *(Italy)*, **35**
Formidable (France), 114, **115**
Formidable (UK), **151**
Formidable class (*France*), see Amiral Baudin class
Formidable class (*UK*), **151**, 159
France (France), **196**
Francesco Carraciolo (Italy), **215**
Francesco Carraciolo class *(Italy)*, **215**
Francesco Morosini (1889, *Italy*), **112-13**
Francesco Morosini (1915LD, *Italy*), **215**
Friedland (France), **88**
Friedrich Carl (Germany), **58**
Friedrich der Grosse (1877, *Germany*), **87**
Friedrich der Grosse (1912, *Germany*), **193**
Frithjof (Germany), **124**
Fuji (Japan), 119, **142**, 150
Fuji class *(Japan)*, **142**, 150
Fujimoto, Captain, 244
Fulton, Robert, 11, 16
Furieux (France), 131
Furious (UK), 176, 214, **220-1**
Fürst Bismarck (Germany), see *Ersatz Friedrich Carl*
Fury (UK), see *Dreadnought* (1879)
Fusée class (*France*), 131
Fuso (1878, *Japan*), **91**
Fuso (1915, *Japan*), 23, **213**, 241, 244
Fuso class (1915-17, *Japan*), **213**, 218, 222

G

'G3' (UK), 224, **233**, 237
Gangut (1894, *Russia*), **128**
Gangut (1914, *Russia*), 176, **205**
Gangut class (1914, *Russia*), **205**, 212, 213
Gard, W.H., 170, 172, 206
Gascogne (1913LD, *France*), **218**
Gascogne (1938P, *France*), **244**, 258
Gauloise (1867, *France*), **46**
Gauloise (1899, *France*), **145**
General Admiral Graf Apraskin (Russia), 19, **130**
General Alexeiev (Russia), see *Imperator Alexander III* (1917)
Georgia (USA), **163**
Georgi Pobiedonosets (Russia), **122**
Gille, 194-5
Giulio Cesare (Italy), 22, **209**
Glatton (UK), **79**, 83, 123
Gloire (France), 13, **28-9**, 30, 32, 37, 46, 51, 106
Gloire class (France), **28-9**
Glorious (UK), **220-1**, 268
Glory (UK), **145**
Gneisenau (Germany), 22, 220, 222, 240, **246-7**
Goeben (Germany), **186-7**
Goliath (UK), **145**
Goodall, Sir Stanley, 220, 229, 233, 237, 268

Gorm (Denmark), **76**
Graf Spee (1915LD, *Germany*), **222**
Graf Spee (1936, *Germany*), see *Admiral Graf Spee*
Grashdanin (Russia), see *Tsessarevitch*
Grasse, Admiral Comte de, 11
Grosser Kurfürst (1878, *Germany*), 64, 65, **87**
Grosser Kürfurst (1914, *Germany*), **200-1**
Grosser Kurfürst class (1876-78, *Germany*), 86, **87**
Guam (USA), **268**
Guépratte, Admiral, 141
Guyenne (France), **46**

H

'H' (*Germany*), **249**
H-41 (*Germany*), **261**
H-42 (*Germany*), **261**
H-43 (*Germany*), **261**
H-44 (*Germany*), **261**
'H' class (*Germany*), **249**, 250
Habsburg (1867, *Austria-Hungary*), **51**
Habsburg (1902, *Austria-Hungary*), **158**
Habsburg class (1902-04, *Austria-Hungary*), **158**
Hagen (Germany), **124**
Hamidieh (1873LD, *Turkey*), see *Superb* (1880)
Hamidieh (1892, *Turkey*), **128**
Hannibal (UK), **136-7**
Hannover (Germany), **162**
Hansa (Germany), **86**
Haruna (Japan), **194**
Harvey, H.A., 116
Hatsuse (Japan), **150**, 155
Hawaii (USA), **268**
Hecla (USA), see *Shackamaxon*
Hector (UK), **37**
Hector class (*UK*), **37**
Heimdall (Germany), **124**
Heireddin Barbarossa (Turkey), see *Kurfürst Friedrich Wilhelm*
Helgoland (Denmark), **92**
Helgoland (Germany), **184**
Helgoland class (*Germany*), **184**, 187
Henri IV (France), 157, **159**
Hercules (1868, *UK*), **60-1**, 76, 78, 100
Hercules (1911, *UK*), **184**
Hercules (USA), see *Quinsigamond*
Hero (UK), **108**
Héroïne (France), **46**
Hessen (Germany), **160**
Hibernia (UK), **161**
Hiei (Japan), **194**
Hifzi Rahman (Turkey), **62-3**
Hildebrand (Germany), **124**
Hindenburg (Germany), **200**
Hindustan (UK), **161**
Hipper, Admiral Franz von, 20-1
Hiraga, Admiral Y., 233, 236, 244
Hizen (Japan), see *Retvisan*
Hoche (France), 120, 124, 137
Holtzer, 118
Hood (1893, *UK*), 118, **126**
Hood (1920, *UK*), 22, 179 **228-9**, 236. 255
Hood class (1916P, *UK*), **228-9**, 236
Hood, Admiral Sir Arthur, 123, 126
Hotspur (UK), **79**, 83
Housatonic (USA), 16
Howe (1889, *UK*), **114-15**
Howe (1916P, *UK*), **228-9**
Howe (1942, *UK*), **256-7**
Huascar (Peru), 16, **49**, 91
Hunley, H.L., 16
Hydra (Greece), **124**
Hyuga (Japan), 213, **222**
Hyuga class (Japan), **222**, 230

I

Idaho (1908, *USA*), **164**
Idaho (1919, *USA*), **223**
Idjalieh (Turkey), **75**
Iéna (France), **153**
Ihosho Maru (Japan), see *Ryujo*
Iki (Japan), see *Imperator Nikolai I* (1891)
Illinois (1901, *USA*), **150**
Illinois (1945LD, *USA*), **266-7**
Illinois class (1900-01, *USA*), 150, 153
Illustrious (UK), 117, 129, **136-7**
Imperator Alexander II (Russia), **123**, 128
Imperator Alexander II class (*Russia*), **123**
Imperator Alexander III (1903, *Russia*), 19, **160-1**
Imperator Alexander III (1917, *Russia*), **212-13**
Imperator Nikolai I (1891, *Russia*), **123**
Imperator Nikolai I (1915LD, *Russia*), **213**
Imperator Pavel (Russia), **165**
Imperatrica Ekaterin II (Russia), **212-13**
Imperatrica Maria (Russia), **212-13**
Imperatrica Maria class (*Russia*), **212-13**
Impero (Italy), **264-5**
Implacable (UK), **151**
Incomparable (UK), **214**
Indefatigable (UK), 21, 183, **184-5**
Indefatigable class (*UK*), 182, 183, **184-5**
Independencia (Argentina), 86
Independencia (Brazil), see *Neptune* (1881)
Independencia (Peru), **48-9**
Indiana (1895, *USA*), 119, **135**
Indiana (1920LD, *USA*), **232**
Indiana (1942, *USA*), 261
Indiana class (1895-96, *USA*), **135**, 138, 146
Indienne (France), see *Montcalm*
Indomitable (UK), **172**, 189
Indomptable (France), 97, **109**
Inflexible (1881, *UK*), 16, 96, 99, **102-3**, 105
Inflexible (1908, *UK*), 19, 20, **172**, 218
Invincible (France), **28-9**
Invincible (1870, *UK*), **74-5**
Invincible (1908, *UK*), 19, 20, 21, **172**, 218
Invincible class (1908, *UK*), 20, 169, **172**, 183, 185
Ioann Zlatoust (Russia), **165**
Ioann Zlatoust class (*Russia*), **165**
Iowa (1897, *USA*), 18, **138**
Iowa (1920LD, *USA*), **232**
Iowa (1943, *USA*), **266-7**
Iowa class (1943-44, *USA*), 23, 241, 260, **266-7**
Iron Duke (1871, *UK*), **74-5**
Iron Duke (1914, *UK*), **198**, 206
Iron Duke class (1914, *UK*), **198**, 206, 211, 219
Irresistible (UK), 147, **151**
Ise (Japan), 213, **222**
Isherwood, Benjamin F., 42
Italia (Italy), 96, **106**, 129
Italia class (*Italy*), **106**, 112
Iver Hvitfeldt (Denmark), **112-13**
Izmail (Russia), **212**

J

'J' (*Germany*), **249**
Jaime I (Spain), **195**
Jauréguiberry (France), 139, **140-1**
Javary (Brazil), **82**
Javary class (*Brazil*), **82**
Jean Bart (1913, *France*), **196**
Jean Bart (1955, *France*), 250, **258**
Jellicoe, Admiral Sir John, 19, 20-1
Jemmapes (France), **130-1**
Jemmapes class (*France*), **130-1**
John, William, 131
Johns, Sir Arthur, 256-7
Juan de Austria (Austria-Hungary), **36**, 55
Jupiter (UK), **136-7**
Justice (France), **163**

K

'K' (*Germany*), **249**
Kaga (Japan), **233**, 236
Kaga class (*Japan*), see Tosa class
Kaiser (Austria-Hungary), 39, 54, **81**
Kaiser (1875, *Germany*), **85**
Kaiser (1912, *Germany*), **193**
Kaiser class (1875, *Germany*), **85**
Kaiser class (1898-1902, *Germany*), **137**, 153
Kaiser class (1912-13, *Germany*), 186, **193**
Kaiser Barbarossa (Germany), **137**
Kaiser Friedrich III (Germany), **137**
Kaiserin (Germany), **193**
Kaiser Karl der Grosse (Germany), **137**
Kaiser Max (1863, *Austria-Hungary*), **36**
Kaiser Max (1876, *Austria-Hungary*), **88**
Kaiser Max class (1863, *Austria-Hungary*), **36**
Kaiser Max class (1876-78, *Austria-Hungary*), **88**
Kaiser Wilhelm II (Germany), **137**
Kaiser Wilhelm der Grosse (Germany), **137**
Kalamazoo (USA), **62**
Kalamazoo class (*USA*), 24, 45, **62**
Kansas (USA), **162**
Kashima (Japan), **162**
Kashima class (*Japan*), **162**
Katori (Japan), **162**
Kawachi (Japan), 168, **187**
Kawachi class (*Japan*), 176, **187**
Kearsarge (1862, *USA*), 27
Kearsarge (1900, *USA*), 148, **151**
Kearsarge class (1900, *USA*), 150, **151**, 163
Kentucky (1900, *USA*), **151**
Kentucky (1944LD, *USA*), **266-7**
Key, Captain Cooper, 52, 61
Kilkis (Greece), see *Idaho* (1908)
Kinburn (Russia), **212**
King Edward VII (UK), **161**
King Edward VII class (*UK*), 146, **161**, 162, 164, 182
King George V (1912, *UK*), **192**
King George V (1940, *UK*), 22, 255, **256-7**, 269
King George V class (1912-13, *UK*), **192**, 198
King George V class (1940-42, *UK*), 240, 241, 249, **256-7**, 268-9
Kirishima (Japan), 22, **194**, 252, 260
Kirov (Russia), 253, **269**
Kirov class (*Russia*), **269**
Kniaz Pojarski (Russia), **77**
Kniaz Potemkin Tavritcheski (Russia), **159**, 165
Kniaz Suvarov (Russia), 19, **160-1**
Koketsu (Japan), see *Stonewall*
Kongo (Japan), 176, **194**, 213, 244
Kongo class (*Japan*), 176, **194**, 238
König (Germany), 157, 161, **200-1**
König class (*Germany*), **200-1**, 216
König Albert (Germany), **193**
König Wilhelm (Germany), **64-5**
Koning der Nederlanden (Netherlands), 82
Konstantin (Russia), 35
Kreiser (Russia), see *Petr Veliki*
Kreml (Russia), **56**
Kronprinz (1867, *Germany*), **58**
Kronprinz (1914, *Germany*), 157, **200-1**
Kronprinz Erzherzog Rudolf (Austria-Hungary), **115**
Kronprinzessin Erzherzogin Stefani (Austria-Hungary), **115**
Kuchina, Josef, 115
Kumbor (Yugoslavia), see *Kronprinz Erzherzog Rudolf*
Kurfürst Friedrich Wilhelm (Germany), **129**

L

'L' (*Germany*), **249**
La Galissonnière (France), **81**
La Galissonnière class (*France*), **81**
Lagane, 140
Languedoc (France), **218**
Lapeyrère, Admiral de, 196
La Plata (Argentina), **86**
La Plata class (*Argentina*), **86**
Lemnos (Greece), see *Mississippi* (1908)
Lenthall, John, 42, 59
Leonardo da Vinci (Italy), **209**
Lepanto (Italy), 96, **106**
Lexington (USA), 227, **234-5**
Lexington (Constellation) class (*USA*), 224, 233, **234-5**, 236
Libertad (1902LD, *Chile*), see *Triumph*
Libertad (1911LD, *Chile*), see *Canada*
Liberté (France), 146, **163**
Liberté class (*France*), **163**
Lille (France), **213**
Lindormen (Denmark), **61**, 76
Lion (1912, *UK*), 20, 21, 184, **188-9**
Lion (1939LD, *UK*), **249**
Lion class (1912-13, *UK*), **188-9**, 192, 194, 201
Lion class (1939P, *UK*), 241, **249**, 250, 268
Lissa (Austria-Hungary), **78**
Littorio (Italy), 244, 245, **264-5**
Lôme, Dupuy de, 16, 28-9, 32, 46, 76
London (1860, *UK*), 13
London (1899, *UK*), 147, **151**
London class (1898-1902, *UK*), **151**, 161
Lord Clyde (UK), 25, **53**
Lord Clyde class (*UK*), **53**
Lord Nelson (UK), **164**
Lord Nelson class (*UK*), 146, **164**, 170
Lord Warden (UK), 25, **53**
Lorraine (France), **210-11**
Los Andes (Argentina), **86**
Lothringen (Germany), **160**
Louisiana (1906, *USA*), **162**
Louisiana (1940P, *USA*), **260**
Lufti Djelil (Turkey), **62-3**
Lufti Djelil class (*Turkey*), **62-3**
Lützow (1915, *Germany*), 20, 21, **200**
Lützow (1933, *Germany*), see *Deutschland* (1933)
Lyasse, M., 196
Lyon (France), **213**
Lyon class (*France*), **213**

M

'M' (*Germany*), **249**
Mackensen (Germany), **222**
Mackensen class (*Germany*), 214, **222**, 247
Mackrow, George C., 34, 61, 142, 150
Magdala (UK), **75**
Magenta (1862, *France*), **32**
Magenta (1893, *France*), **125**
Magenta class (1862, *France*), **32**
Magnanime (France), **46**
Magnificent (UK), **136-7**
Mahan, Alfred, 17
Mahmudieh (Turkey), **49**
Maine (1895, *USA*), 131, **132-3**, 135
Maine (1902, *USA*), 149, **153**
Maine (1940P, *USA*), **260**
Maine class (1902-04, *USA*), **153**
Majestic (1887, *UK*), see *Edinburgh*
Majestic (1895, *UK*), **136-7**, 150
Majestic class (1895-98, *UK*), 129, **136-7**, 145, 148, 151
Makarov, Admiral, 18
Malaya (UK), **206**
Marat (Russia), see *Petropavlovsk* (1914)
Marcantonio Colanna (Italy), **215**
Marceau (France), 122, **125**, 137
Marceau class (*France*), 120, 124, **125**
Marengo (France), **76-7**
Markgraf (Germany), **200-1**
Marlborough (UK), **198**
Mars (UK), **136-7**
Maryland (USA), **236-7**
Maryland class (*USA*), 21, **236-7**
Masdea, Eng Gen Eduardo, 193, 209
Massachusetts (1863LD, *USA*), see *Passaconaway*
Massachusetts (1921LD, *USA*), **232**
Massachusetts (1942, *USA*), **261**
Masséna (France), 139, **143**
Mattei, Insp Eng, 46
Mecklenburg (Germany), **153**
Mello, Rear-Admiral de, 82
Memdouhied (Turkey), see *Superb* (1880)
Mendez Nunez (Spain), **67**
Merrimack (CSA), 13-14, 36
Messina (Italy), **46**
Messudieh (Turkey), **87**
Miantonomoh (USA), **42**
Micheli, Giuseppe, 112
Michigan (USA), **180**
Mikasa (Japan), 19, 150, **155**
Mikhail Frunze (Russia), see *Poltava* (1914)
Minas Gerais (Brazil), **182**, 205
Minas Gerais class (*Brazil*), **182**
Minin (Russia), **63**
Minnesota (USA), **162**
Minotaur (UK), **59**
Minotaur class (*UK*), **59**
Mirabeau (France), **185**
Mississippi (CSA), see Scorpion class
Mississippi (1908, *USA*), **164**
Mississippi (1917, *USA*), 23, **223**, 241
Mississippi class (1908, *USA*), **164**
Missouri (1903, *USA*), **153**
Missouri (1944, *USA*), **266-7**
Mitchell, Brigadier-General William, 184
Moltke (Germany), **186-7**
Moltke class (*Germany*), **186-7**, 194
Monadnock (USA), **42**
Monadnock class (*USA*), **42**, 62
Monarch (Austria-Hungary), **144**
Monarch (1869, *UK*), 16, **66**, 70, 73, 76, 78, 87, 100
Monarch (1912, *UK*), **187**
Monarch class (*Austria-Hungary*), **144**
Monitor (USA), 13-14, 15, 39, 42
Montagu (UK), **159**
Montana (1920LD, *USA*), **232**
Montana (1940P, *USA*), **260**
Montana class (1940P, *USA*), 241, 250, **260**
Montcalm (France), **50**
Montecuccoli, Admiral Count, 192
Monterey (USA), 134
Mooney, E. N., 206
Moras, de, 32
Moreno (Argentina), **204-5**
Muin-i-Zaffer (Turkey), **62**
Mukaddami Khair (Turkey), **77**
Musashi (Japan), 22, **262-3**
Mutsu (Japan), 21, **230-1**, 233, 236

N

'N' (*Germany*), **249**
Nagato (Japan), **230-1**, 233, 236
Nagato class (*Japan*), **230-1**, 233, 237
Napoléon (France), 12, 29
Napoli (Italy), **164-5**
Nassau (Germany), 169, **174-5**, 176
Nassau (Westfalen) class (*Germany*), 137, **174-5**, 184
Navarin (1896, *Russia*), 118, **136**
Navarin (1914LD, *Russia*), **212**
Nebraska (1863LD, *USA*), see *Shackamaxon*
Nebraska (1907, *USA*), **163**
Nelson (UK), 225, 227, **236-7**
Nelson class (*UK*), **236-7**, 238, 256, 257
Neptune (France), **125**
Neptune (1881, *UK*), **100**, 113
Neptune (1911, *UK*), 184, **186**, 193
Netron Menya (Russia), **34-5**
Nevada (USA), 21, 178-9, 203, **215**
Nevada class (*USA*), 203, **215**, 218
New Fury (UK), see *Inflexible* (1881)
New Hampshire (1906, *USA*), **162**
New Hampshire (1940P, *USA*), **260**
New Ironsides (USA), **34**, 39
New Jersey (1906, *USA*), **163**
New Jersey (1943, *USA*), 23, 253, **266-7**
New Mexico (USA), 177, **223**
New Mexico class (*USA*), 164, 179, **223**, 232
New York (USA), 178, 190, **202-3**, 252
New York class (*USA*), 176, **202-3**
New Zealand (1905, *UK*), **161**
New Zealand (1912, *UK*), **184-5**
Nicholson, Admiral, 137
Nijmi Shevket (Turkey), **62**
Nile (UK), **123**
Nishimura, Vice-Admiral, 23
Normand, Benjamin, 119
Normandie (1862, *France*), **28-9**
Normandie (1913LD, *France*), **218**
Normandie class (1913P, *France*), 178, 195, 213, **218**
North, Lieutenant, 43
North Carolina (CSA), see Scorpion class
North Carolina (1920LD, *USA*), **232**
North Carolina (1941, *USA*), 240, **260**
North Carolina class (1941, *USA*), **260**, 261
North Dakota (USA), **183**, 186, 215
Northumberland (UK), **59**
Novorossisk (Russia) see *Giulio Cesare*
Numancia (Spain), 51
No 111 (*Japan*), see Yamato class

O

'O' (*Germany*), **249**
Océan (1870, *France*), **76-7**
Océan (1913, *France*), see *Jean Bart* (1913)
Ocean (1865, *UK*), **39**
Ocean (1900, *UK*), **145**
Océan class (1870-75, *France*), **76-7**, 88
Odin (Denmark), **80**
Odin (Germany), **124**
Ohio (1904, *USA*), **153**
Ohio (1940P, *USA*), **260**
Oklahoma (USA), 203, 213, **215**
Oktyabrskaya Revolutsia (Russia), see *Gangut* (1914)
Oldenburg (1886, *Germany*), **108**
Oldenburg (1912, *Germany*), **184**
Oldendorf, Rear-Admiral, 23
Onodaga (USA), 42
Oregon (1864LD, *USA*), see *Quinsigamond*
Oregon (1896, *USA*), **135**
Orel (Russia), **160-1**
Orion (1882, *UK*), **92**
Orion (1912, *UK*), 176, 178, **187**
Orion class (1912-13, *UK*), 184, **187**, 188, 192, 193
Orkanieh (Turkey), **49**
Osliabia (Russia), 19, **152**
Osmanieh (Turkey), **49**
Osmanieh class (*Turkey*), **49**
Ostfriesland (Germany), **184**, 226

P

'P' (*Germany*), **249**
Paixhans, Colonel, 12
Palestro (1866, *Italy*), 14, 51, **53**, 54
Palestro (1875, *Italy*), **83**
Palestro class (1866, *Italy*), **53**
Pallas (UK), **53**, 94
Palliser, Sir William, 99
Pantelimon (Russia), see *Kniaz Potemkin Tavritcheski*
Panzerschiff (1938P, *Germany*), **244**
Paris (France), **196**
Parizhskaya Kommuna (Russia), see *Sevastopol* (1914)
Parsons, Charles, 168
Passaconaway (USA), **62**
Passaic class (*USA*), **42**
Patrie (France), **162**
Peder Skram (Denmark), **43**
Peki-Shereef (Turkey), see *Belleisle*
Pelayo (Spain), 44, **122**
Penelope (UK), **61**
Pengelly, H. S., 257
Pennsylvania (USA), 178, **218**
Pennsylvania class (*USA*), 213, **218**, 223
Peresviet (Russia), **152**, 159
Peresviet class (*Russia*), **152**, 159
Persano, Admiral Count Carlo di, 14, 54
Pervenetz (Russia), **34-5**, 56
Pervenetz class (*Russia*), **34-5**
Petropavlovsk (1865, *Russia*), **50**
Petropavlovsk (1899, *Russia*), 18, **142**
Petropavlovsk (1914, *Russia*), **205**
Petropavlovsk class (1899, *Russia*), **142**
Petr Veliki (Russia), 70, **84-5**
Pettit-Smith, Francis, 12
Petz, Commodore Anton von, 81
Philippines (USA), **268**
Pobieda (Russia), **152**
Pollen, Arthur, 149
Poltava (1899, *Russia*), **142**
Poltava (1914, *Russia*), **205**
Pommern (Germany), **162**
Popov, Vice-Admiral A. A., 85
Posen (Germany), **174-5**
Potemkin (Russia), see *Kniaz Potemkin Tavritcheski*
Preussen (1876, *Germany*), **87**
Preussen (1905, *Germany*), **160**
Prince Albert (UK), 39, **52**, 72
Prince Consort (UK), **39**, 57

Index

Prince Consort class (UK), **39**, 57
Prince George (UK), **136-7**
Prince of Wales (1904, UK), **151**
Prince of Wales (1941, UK), 22, 218, 250, **256-7**
Princess Royal (UK), 184, **188-9**
Principe Amedeo (Italy), **83**
Principe Amedeo class (Italy), **83**
Principe di Carignano (Italy), **46**
Principe di Carignano class (Italy), **46**
Prins Hendrik der Nederlanden (Netherlands), **56**
Prinz Adalbert (Prussia), 44
Prinz Eitel Friedrich (Germany), see Ersatz Freya
Prinz Eugen (1863, (Austria-Hungary), **36**
Prinz Eugen (1878, Austria-Hungary), **88**
Prinz Eugen (1914, Austria-Hungary), **192**
Prinzregent Luitpold (Germany), 20, **193**
'Project 23' (Russia), see Sovietskiy Soyuz class
Provence (1865, France), **124**
Provence (1915, France), **210-11**
Provence class (1865-67, France), **46**
Psara (Greece), **124**
Puerto Rico (USA), **268**
Pullino, Giacinto, 152
Puritan (USA), 42, **45**

Q
'Q' (Germany), **249**
Queen (UK), **151**
Queen Elizabeth (UK), **206**
Queen Elizabeth class (UK), 20, 176, 178, 179, **206**, 215, 216, 219, 229, 238
Queen Mary (UK), 21, **188-9**
Quinsigamond (USA), **62**
Quintard, 42

R
'R' class (UK), see Revenge class
Racchia, Admiral, 152
Radetzky (Austria-Hungary), **182-3**
Radetzky class (Austria-Hungary), **182-3**, 192
Ramillies (1893, UK), **126**
Ramillies (1917, UK), **219**, 241
Ranger (USA), **234-5**
Re di Portogallo (Italy), **39**, 81
Re d'Italia (Italy), 14, **39**, 51, 53, 54, 83
Re d'Italia class (Italy), **39**
Redoutable (France), 69, **92-3**, 101
Reed, Sir Edward J., 40, 53, 61, 64, 66, 75 et seq, 100, 131, 160
Regina Elena (Italy), **164-5**
Regina Elena class (Italy), 146, **164-5**, 172
Regina Margherita (Italy), **160**
Regina Margherita class (Italy), **160**
Regina Maria Pia (Italy), **38**
Regina Maria Pia class (Italy), **38**
Reine Blanche (France), **50**
Reine Victoria Eugenia class (Spain), 195
Renown (1885LD, UK), see Victoria
Renown (1889LD, UK), see Empress of India
Renown (1897, UK), 137, **139**, 150
Renown (1916, UK), 179, **218**, 238
Renown class (1916, UK), **218**, 220, 229
République (France), **162**
République class (France), **162**, 163
Repulse (1870, UK), **74**
Repulse (1894, UK), **126**
Repulse (1916, UK), 22, **218**, 250
Requin (France), **109**
Research (UK), **40-1**
Research class (UK), **40-1**
Reshadieh (Turkey), see Erin

Reshadieh class (Turkey), see Erin
Resistance (UK), **32**
Resolucion (Spain), see Mendez Nunez
Resolution (1893,.UK), **126**
Resolution (1916, UK), **219**
Respublika (Russia), see Imperator Pavel
Retvisan (Russia), 156, **158**
Re Umberto (Italy), **128-9**
Re Umberto class (Italy), **128-9**
Revanche (France), **46**
Revenge (1894, UK), **126**
Revenge (1916, UK), 216-17, **219**
Revenge class (1916-17, UK), 176, 216, 218, **219**
Rheinland (Germany), **174-5**
Rhode Island (USA), **163**
Riachuelo (1883, Brazil), 112, **113**, 132
Riachuelo (1914P, Brazil), **205**
Riboty, Rear-Admiral Augusto, 100, 106
Richelieu (1876, France), **88**
Richelieu (1940, France), 244, 252, **258**
Richelieu (1940-55, France), 244, **258**
Rio de Janeiro (Brazil), see Agincourt (1914)
Rivadavia (Argentina), **204-5**
Rivadavia class (Argentina), **204-5**, 211
Roanoke (USA), **36**
Rochambeau (France), see Dunderberg
Rodney (1888, UK), **114-15**
Rodney (1916P, UK), **228-9**
Rodney (1927, UK), 22, **236-7**, 255
Rodney, Admiral, 11
Rolf Krake (Denmark), **36**
Roma (1869, Italy), **66**
Roma (1908, Italy), **164-5**
Roma (1942, Italy), 22, **204-5**
Roma class (1869-73, Italy), **66**
Romako, Josef von, 33, 51, 83, 84, 89
Rostislav (Russia), **144**
Royal Alfred (UK), **57**
Royal Oak (1863, UK), 31, **35**, 39
Royal Oak (1894, UK), **126**
Royal Oak (1916, UK), 21, **219**
Royal Oak class (1863, UK), 57
Royal Sovereign (1864, UK), **38-9**, 72
Royal Sovereign (1892, UK), 118, **126**
Royal Sovereign (1916, UK), **219**
Royal Sovereign class (1892-94, UK), **126**, 142, 161, 187
Rozhdestvensky, Vice-Admiral Zinovy P., 19, 130, 161
Ruggiero di Lauria (Italy), **112-13**
Ruggiero di Lauria class (Italy), **112-13**
Rupert (UK), **83**, 108
Russell (UK), **159**
Ryujo (Japan), **63**

S
Sachsen (1878, Germany), 70, **92**
Sachsen (1914LD, Germany), **216-17**
Sachsen class (1878-83, Germany), **92**, 108
Sagami (Japan), see Peresviet
Sagunto (Spain), **67**
Saint Bon, Admiral di, 100, 106, 152
St Louis (France), **145**
St Vincent (UK), **173**
St Vincent class (UK), **173**
Salamander (Austria-Hungary), **32-3**
Salamander class (Austria-Hungary), **32-3**, 36
Salamis (Greece), 204, **210**
Samoa (USA), **268**
Sanders, W. G., 257
San Martino (Italy), 15, **38**, 53
Sans Pareil (UK), 98, **120-1**
Santiago (Chile), see Almirante Cochrane (1913LD)
São Paulo (Brazil), **182**, 205
Saratoga (USA), **234-5**

Sardegna (Italy), **128-9**

Sara Svobodi (Russia), see Imperator Alexander II
Satsuma (Japan), **173**, 176, 185
Satsuma class (Japan), 169; see also Aki, Satsuma
Savoie (France), **46**
Scharnhorst (Germany), 22, 23, 220, 222, 240, **246-7**, 252, 268
Scharnhorst class (Germany), **246-7**, 250
Scheer, Admiral Reinhardt von, 20-1
Schlesien (Germany), **162**
Schleswig-Holstein (Germany), **162**
Schley, Commodore, 18
Schwaben (Germany), **153**
Scorpion (UK), **48-9**
Scorpion class (UK), **48-9**
Scott, Captain Percy, 19, 148-9, 166
Settsu (Japan), **187**
Sevastopol (1865, Russia), **50**
Sevastopol (1899, Russia), **142**
Sevastopol (1914, Russia), **205**
Sevastopol class (1865, Russia), **50**
Seydlitz (Germany), 20, 21, 189, **194**, 200
Shackamaxon (USA), **62**
Shannon (UK), 90
Shikishima (Japan), **150**, 155
Shikishima class (Japan), **150**, 155
Shinano (Japan), 250, **262-3**
Sicilia (Italy), **128-9**
Siegfried (Germany), **124**
Siegfried class (Germany), **124**
Sims, Lieutenant W. S., 19, 149, 166
Sinope (Russia), **122**
Sissoi Veliki (Russia), **142**
Slava (Russia), 157, **160-1**
Smerch (Russia), 36
Solferino (France), **32**
Solimoes (Brazil), **82**
South Carolina (USA), 169, **180**
South Carolina class (USA), 176, **180**, 184
South Dakota (1920LD, USA), **232**
South Dakota (1942, USA), 22, **261**
South Dakota class (1920-21LD, USA), 224, **232**, 234, 236
South Dakota class (1942, USA), 260, **261**, 266, 267
Sovietskaya Byelorossia (Russia), **249**
Sovietskaya Rossia (Russia), **249**
Sovietskaya Ukraina (Russia), **249**
Sovietskiy Soyuz (Russia), **249**
Sovietskiy Soyuz class (Russia), **249**
Spetsai (Greece), **124**
Spetsai class (Greece), **124**
Sphinx (CSA), see Stonewall
Stonewall (CSA), 42, **44**
Stonewall class (CSA), **44**
Strasbourg (France), 240, **245**
Suffren (1875, France), **76-7**
Suffren (1903, France), 141, **159**, 162
Sultan (UK), 16, **78-9**
Sultan Osman I (Turkey), see Agincourt (1914)
Superb (1880, UK), 16, 87, **100**
Superb (1909, UK), **173**
'Super Yamato' class (Japan), 268
Surveillante (France), **46**
Suwo (Japan), see Pobieda
Svobodnaya Rossia (Russia), see Imperatrica Ekaterin II
Swiftsure (1872, UK), **74-5**
Swiftsure (1904, UK), **160-1**, 182
Swiftsure class (1904, UK), **160-1**
Symington, William, 11
Szent István (Austria-Hungary), 191, **192**

T
Takao (Japan), **232-3**
Tango (Japan), see Poltava (1899)
Taureau (France), 131
Taylor, Rear-Admiral, 234
Tchesma (1889, Russia), 122
Tchesma (1899, Russia), see Poltava (1899)
Tecumseh (USA), 15

Tegetthoff (1881, Austria-Hungary), 101
Tegetthoff (1913, Austria-Hungary), **192**
Tegetthoff, Admiral, 14, 51
Temeraire (1877, UK), 16, **89**, 90
Temeraire (1909, UK), **173**
Temeraire (1939LD, UK), **249**
Tempête (France), 69
Tempête class (France), 131
Tennessee (USA), **232**
Tennessee class (USA), **232**, 237
Terrible (Italy), **35**
Terrible (France), **109**
Terrible class (France), **109**, 110, 115
Tetuan (Spain), 44
Texas (1895, USA), **131**, 132, 133, 135, 215
Texas (1914, USA), 178, 190, **202-3**, 213, 241, 252, 253
Thetis (France), **50**
Thunderer (1877, UK), 71, **80**
Thunderer (1912, UK), 178, **187**
Thunderer (1939P, UK), **249**
Thunderer (USA), see Passaconaway
Thüringen (Germany), **184**
Thurston, Sir George, 194, 200
Tiger (UK), 179, 194, **201**, 229
Ting Yuen (China), 17, **105**, 142
Ting Yuen class (China), **105**
Tirpitz (Germany), 241, 252, **254-5**
Tirpitz, Admiral Alfred von, 18, 153
Togo, Vice-Admiral Heihachiro, 18-19, 155
Tonawanda (USA), **42**
Tonnant (France), 99, 130
Tonnerre (France), 99, 130
Tonnerre class (France), 131
Torgud Reis (Turkey), see Weissenburg
Tosa (Japan), **233**, 236
Tosa (Kaga) class (Japan), 224, **233**, 236
Tourville (France), **213**
Trafalgar (UK), **123**
Trafalgar class (UK), **123**, 136
Trident (France), **90**
Triomphante (France), **81**
Tri Svititelia (Russia), 118, **138**
Triumph (1873, UK), **74-5**
Triumph (1904, UK), **160-1**, 182
Tryon, Vice-Admiral Sir George, 17, 121
Tsel (Russia), see Hessen
Tsessarevitch (Russia), 19, **156-7**, 158, 161
Turenne (France), 104

U
United States (USA), **234-5**
'UP 41' (Russia), **244**, 247
Utah (USA), **186**

V
Valeureuse (France), **46**
Valiant (1868, UK), **37**
Valiant (1916, UK), 22, **206**, 241
Valmy (France), **130-1**
Valparaiso (1876, Chile), see Blanco Encalada
Valparaiso (1911LD, Chile), see Canada
Vanguard (1870, UK), **74-5**
Vanguard (1910, UK), **173**
Vanguard (1946, UK), 221, 250, **268-9**
Varese (Italy), **53**
Vasco da Gama (Portugal), **93**
Vasilefs Georgios (Greece), 210
Vauban (France), **108**
Vauban class (France), **108**
Venerable (UK), **151**
Venezia (Italy), **66**
Vengeance (UK), **145**
Vergniaud (France), **185**
Vérité (France), **163**

Vermont (USA), **162**
Vermont class (USA), 162, 164
Victoria (UK), 17, 98, 119, **120-1**, 123
Victoria class (UK), **120-1**
Victorieuse (France), **81**
Victorious (UK), **136-7**
Virginia (CSA), see Merrimack
Virginia (USA), 148, **163**
Virginia class (USA), **163**
Viribus Unitis (Austria-Hungary), 178, **192**
Viribus Unitis class (Austria-Hungary), **192**, 215
Vitgeft, Rear-Admiral Vilgelm, 18-19, 157
Vitoria (Spain), 44, **60**
Vittorio Emanuele (Italy), **164-5**
Vittorio Veneto (Italy), 209, **264-5**
Vittorio Veneto class (Italy), 237, 240, **264-5**
Voltaire (France), **185**
Von der Tann (Germany), 21, **183**, 185, 186

W
Walker, Sir Baldwin, 32
Warrior (France), 162, 164
Warrior (UK), 13, 23, 24, 26, **30-1**, 32, 35, 37, 39, 43
Warrior class (UK), **30-1**
Warspite (UK), 22, **206**, 207, 253
Washington (1919LD, USA), 226, **236-7**
Washington (1941, USA), 22, 251, 260
Watts, Isaac, 31, 43, 59
Weissenburg (Germany), **129**
Westfalen (Germany), **174-5**
Westfalen class (Germany), see Nassau class
West Virginia (USA), 22, 23, **236-7**
Wettin (Germany), **153**
White, Sir William, 115, 126, 136, 151, 161
Whitehead, Robert, 15-16, 71
Wien (Austria-Hungary), **144**
Wilhelm I (Germany), see König Wilhelm
Wilson, A., 70
Wisconsin (1901, USA), **150**
Wisconsin (1944, USA), **266-7**
Wittelsbach (Germany), **153**
Wittelsbach class (Germany), **153**, 160
Wivern (UK), **48-9**
Wolga (Germany), see Imperator Alexander III (1917)
Worth (Germany), **129**
Wurttemberg (1881, Germany), **92**
Wurttemberg (1915LD, Germany), **216-17**
Wyoming (USA), **190-1**
Wyoming class (USA), 176, **190-1**, 203

Y
Yamashiro (Japan), 23, **213**, 241
Yamato (Japan), 22, 23, **262-3**
Yamato class (Japan), 241, 244, 250, 261, **262-3**, 268
Yashima (Japan), **142**, 150
Yavuz (Turkey), see Goeben
Yavuz Sultan Selim (Turkey), see Goeben

Z
Zähringen (Germany), **153**
Zalinsky, Lieutenant, 98-9
Zaragosa (Spain), **58**
Zealandia (UK), see New Zealand (1905)
Zealous (UK), **57**
Zédé, Gustave, 16
Zrinyi (Austria-Hungary), **182-3**

Picture Credits

Unless otherwise credited, all photographs in this book were supplied from the author's own collection

Marius Bar:
240, 252 (left)

Foto Druppel:
168-9, 240-1, 243, 247, 252 (right), 255 (lower).

Imperial War Museum, London:
Endpapers, 12 (lower), 15, 19, 22, 23 (upper), 30, 95, 103, 110 180-1, 199, 206, 207 (upper), 216, 220, 224-5, 238-9, 241, 254, 263.

Italian Ufficio Storico:
265 (lower).

MARS:
10 (National Maritime Museum), 132 (US Navy), 141 (W.P. Trotter collection), 240 (Foto Druppel), 242 (US Navy), 262.

Ministry of Defence, London:
253 (upper).

Musée de la Marine, Paris:
28.

National Gallery, London:
8-9.

National Maritime Museum, London:
10, 10-11.

Roger-Viollet:
259.

W.P. Trotter collection:
141.

US Navy:
1, 2-3, 6-7, 13, 14-15, 16, 18, 20, 20-1, 22-3, 26-7, 41, 70, 98, 118, 118-9, 121, 132, 148, 148-9, 149, 154, 176-7, 178 (lower), 189, 190, 191, 202, 203, 217, 226-7, 227, 229, 230, 231, 235, 242, 246, 246-7, 250-1, 253 (lower), 255 (upper), 257, 258, 264, 265 (upper), 266, 266-7, 267.